Instructor's Edition

Marketing Dynamics

Third Edition

Brenda Clark, EdD
CTE Director
Jenison High School
Jenison, Michigan

Cynthia Gendall Basteri, EdD
Grants Coordinator
Marketing Coordinator Emeritus
Tewksbury Public Schools
Tewksbury, Massachusetts

Chris Gassen, MBA, CFA
Faircourt Valuation Investments
Grosse Pointe Woods, Michigan

Michelle Walker, PhD
Director of Education
DECA Inc.
Reston, VA

Publisher
The Goodheart-Willcox Company, Inc.
Tinley Park, Illinois
www.g-w.com

Instructional Package

Instructional Strategies

Instructional Package

Introduction

Marketing Dynamics introduces the concepts of marketing including the four Ps of product, place, price, and promotion. By studying this comprehensive text, students will explore the framework needed to become a marketing professional.

One of the major goals of the text is to guide students in creating a marketing plan. To accomplish this goal, each unit has a project-based activity designed to lead students through this process. A template is available on the companion website to assist in writing a customized marketing plan.

The DECA® Emerging Leaders feature provides a first-hand opportunity for students to explore learning activities, which will help prepare them for college and careers. In addition, coverage of the marketing standards as identified by the MBA Research and Curriculum Center are indicated on each unit opener where appropriate.

The information that follows will help you use the textbook and the other components of the teaching package. In addition to the student text, the teaching package includes the Instructor's Annotated Edition, G-W Online Textbook, Student Workbook, Instructor's Annotated Workbook, Instructor's Resources, Instructor's Presentations for PowerPoint®, **EXAM**VIEW® Assessment Suite, the G-W Learning companion website, and the G-W Learning mobile site.

Student Textbook

Marketing Dynamics is written to introduce marketing concepts as they apply to our current economy. The text is divided into 10 units with a total of 33 chapters. Although the textbook was written to be studied in its entirety, individual chapters and sections are complete enough to be studied independently. Numerous illustrations and photos elaborate on the concepts for clear understanding. Opportunities to evaluate what students have learned, as well as apply the concepts, help to assure students grasp the topics that have been presented. The Math Skills Handbook at the end of the text serves as a reference to help students understand math concepts presented in content examples.

The preliminary pages of the student textbook include a walkthrough of the features and benefits of the text. Reviewing this information will help you to understand and incorporate this material into your teaching strategy. Suggestions for using these features are also included in the margins of the Instructor's Annotated Edition as well as in the lesson plans provided in the Instructor's Resources.

G-W Online Textbooks

G-W Online Textbooks will give your students access anytime, anywhere to popular Goodheart-Willcox titles. Students can instantly access the *Marketing Dynamics* Online Textbook with browser-based devices, including iPads®, netbooks, PCs, and Mac computers. With G-W Online Textbooks, students can easily navigate the *Marketing Dynamics* linked table of contents, search specific topics, quickly jump to specific pages, enlarge for full screen reading mode, and print selected pages for offline reading. Go to www.g-wonlinetextbooks.com to access the content you need, when you need it.

Instructor's Annotated Edition of Student Textbook

The Instructor's Annotated Edition of the student text provides teaching materials for convenience of the presenter. Each chapter begins with a list of materials that are available to help organize each day's presentation. Instructor notes in the margin offer suggestions on how to present the lesson. Answers are noted in the margin for those exercises that require students to provide a solution. Vocabulary definitions are not provided at the end of the Checkpoint sections, but can be found in the glossary.

Student Workbook and Instructor's Annotated Workbook

The Student Workbook is designed for use with *Marketing Dynamics*. Using the workbook will reinforce the concepts students learn in the textbook as well as provide enrichment activities to improve students' understanding of how to become financially responsible.

After reading the corresponding chapter in the text, students are directed to complete as many exercises as they are able without referring to the text. For ease in using the workbook in the classroom, the Instructor's Annotated Workbook provides the answers as they appear on the student's page. The Instructor's Annotated Workbook is also provided in the Instructor's Resources.

Instructor's Resources

G-W's Instructor's Resources include everything you need to utilize *Marketing Dynamics* in your classroom. A variety of materials are provided to help you make the most of every aspect of the instructional package needed to teach each chapter.

Resource Materials

Here you will find everything you need to customize the format for your own teaching style. Included is the Instructor's Annotated Edition of the textbook in an electronic format, a suggested curriculum schedule, and various assessment rubrics.

College and Career Readiness

National Standards

National Standards include product correlations. *Marketing Dynamics* is correlated to the Common Core State Standards for reading, writing, speaking, and listening anchor standards in technical subjects as well as the Career Ready Practices of the Common Career Technical Core. The College and Career Readiness logo is used so you can easily identify these activities.

The text is also correlated to marketing standards as identified by the MBA Research and Curriculum Center.

Chapter Resources

For your convenience, all materials needed to teach each chapter are grouped together. Answer keys, electronic version of the Instructor's Annotated Workbook, annotated editions of the textbook and workbook, and lesson plans are provided.

Answer Keys

Answer keys for the Checkpoint questions and end-of-chapter review and assessment activities for each chapter are provided.

Instructor's Annotated Workbook

The Instructor's Annotated Workbook is provided in an electronic format. It includes the answers to all workbook activities as they appear on the student's page.

Lesson Plans

Lesson plans are included to assist in planning the daily presentations. The lesson plans are intended to provide an outline for presentation. They may be modified based on your classroom needs and teaching style. You are encouraged to use these lesson plans as a starting point and customize them to meet your curriculum needs.

Because each chapter is presented in several sections to improve student comprehension, lesson plans are organized by section as well as chapter. For each section of the chapter, a lesson plan is organized by the Five Es:

1. Engage—get the student involved
2. Explore—provide hands-on opportunities
3. Explain—present the concepts
4. Elaborate/Extend—expand on what students have learned
5. Evaluate—assess student learning

For each lesson plan, there are multiple opportunities to use special features and assessment activities. The suggestions in these lesson plans are only guidelines, and you may choose how you prefer to use them.

Instructor's Presentations for PowerPoint®

The Instructor's Presentations for PowerPoint® provide a useful teaching tool when presenting the lessons. These slides help you teach and visually reinforce the key concepts from each chapter.

EXAMVIEW®
Assessment Suite

The **EXAM**VIEW® Assessment Suite allows you to quickly and easily create and print tests from a test bank of hundreds of questions. The components include the **EXAM**VIEW® Test Generator, **EXAM**VIEW® Test Manager, and **EXAM**VIEW® Test Player. You can choose to have the software generate a test for you with randomly selected questions. You can also opt to choose specific questions from the question banks and, if you wish, add your own questions to create customized tests to meet your classroom needs. You may want to make multiple versions of the same test to use during different class periods. Automatically generated answer keys simplify grading. Additionally, you can manage your class roster, administer and score online tests, and automatically score paper tests.

Tests you create may be published for LAN-based testing, or be packaged for online testing using WebCT, Blackboard, or ANGEL. The **EXAM**VIEW® software products are compatible with interactive whiteboard technology.

G-W Learning Companion Website and Mobile Site

The G-W Learning companion website provides additional study materials in an interactive electronic format. Vocabulary activities reinforce important terms and definitions. Pretests and posttests for each chapter help students self-assess their understanding. Checkpoint solutions and other additional resources are also available on the companion website.

The G-W Learning mobile site is a study reference for students to use when they are on the go. The mobile site is easy to read, easy to use, and fine-tuned for quick access.

For *Marketing Dynamics,* the G-W Learning mobile site contains the chapter pretests and posttests and e-flash card vocabulary practices. If students do not have a smartphone, these same features can be accessed using an Internet browser to visit the G-W Learning companion website.

G-W Learning mobile site: www.m.g-wlearning.com

G-W Learning companion website: www.g-wlearning.com

Instructional Strategies

Learning and Working in a Changing World

Your students will be entering a rapidly changing workplace—not only in the area of technology, but also in the diverse nature of the workforce. Today's workforce is made up of people who represent many different views, experiences, and backgrounds. The workforce is aging, too, as the ranks of mature workers swell. Because of these trends, young workers must learn how to interact with a variety of people who are considerably unlike them.

Helping Students Develop Critical-Thinking Skills

As today's students leave their classrooms behind, they will face a world of complexity and change. They are likely to work in several career areas and hold many different jobs. Young people must develop a base of knowledge and be prepared to solve complex problems, make difficult decisions, and assess ethical implications. In other words, students must be able to use critical-thinking skills. These skills are often referred to as the higher-order thinking skills. Benjamin Bloom listed these as:

- analysis—breaking down material into its component parts so its organizational structure may be understood;
- synthesis—putting parts together to form a new whole; and
- evaluation—judging the value of material for a given purpose.

In a broader perspective, students must be able to use reflective thinking in order to decide what to believe and do. According to Robert Ennis, students should be able to:

- define and clarify problems, issues, conclusions, reasons, and assumptions;
- judge the credibility, relevance, and consistency of information; and
- infer or solve problems and draw reasonable conclusions.

Critical thinking goes beyond memorizing or recalling information. Critical thinking cannot occur in a vacuum; it requires individuals to apply what they know about the subject matter. It requires students to use their common sense and experience. It may involve controversy, too.

Critical thinking also requires *creative thinking* to construct all the reasonable alternatives, consequences, influencing factors, and supporting arguments. Unusual ideas are valued and perspectives outside the obvious are sought.

Finally, the teaching of critical thinking does not require exotic and highly unusual classroom approaches. Complex thought processes can be incorporated in ordinary, basic activities, such as reading, writing, and listening, if the activities are carefully planned and skillfully executed.

Help your students develop their analytical and judgment skills and go beyond what they see on the surface. Rather than allowing students to blindly accept what they read or hear, encourage them to examine ideas in ways that show respect for different perspectives and the opinions of others. Encourage students to think about points raised during discussion. Ask them to evaluate how new ideas relate to their attitudes about various subjects.

Debate is an excellent way to explore opposite sides of an issue. You may want to divide the class into two groups, each to take an opposing side of the issue. You can also ask students to work in smaller groups and explore opposing sides of different issues. Each group can select students from the group to present the points for their side.

Helping Students Develop Problem-Solving and Decision-Making Skills

An important aspect in the development of critical thinking skills is learning how to solve problems and make decisions. Some very important decisions lie ahead for your students, particularly those related to their future education and career choices.

Simulation games and role-play allow students to practice solving problems and making decisions under nonthreatening circumstances. Role-playing allows students to examine others' feelings, as well as their own. It can help them learn effective ways to react or cope when confronted with similar situations in real life.

Helping Students Recognize and Value Diversity

Appreciating and understanding diversity is an ongoing process. The earlier and more frequently young people are exposed to diversity, the better able they will be to bridge cultural differences. If your students are exposed to different cultures within your classroom, the process of understanding cultural differences can begin. This is the best preparation for success in a diverse society. In addition, instructors have found the following strategies for teaching diversity helpful.

- Actively promote a spirit of openness, consideration, respect, and tolerance in the classroom.
- Use a variety of teaching styles and assessment strategies.
- Use cooperative learning activities whenever possible and make sure group roles are rotated so everyone has leadership opportunities.
- When grouping students, make sure the composition of each group is as diverse as possible with regard to gender, race, and nationality.
- Make sure one group's opinions do not dominate class discussions.
- If a student makes a sexist, racist, or other offensive comment, ask the student to rephrase the comment in a manner that will not offend other class members. Remind students that offensive statements and behavior are inappropriate.
- If a difficult classroom situation arises involving a diversity issue, ask for a time-out and have everyone write down thoughts and opinions about the incident. This allows students a chance to carefully consider ideas and allows you to plan a response.
- Arrange for guest speakers who represent diversity in gender, age, and ethnicity.
- Have students change seats occasionally throughout the course and introduce themselves to their new "neighbors" so they become acquainted with all of their classmates.
- Several times during the course, ask students to make anonymous, written evaluations of the class. Have them report any problems that may not be obvious.

Meeting the Needs of Each Learner

In addition to having specific learning needs related to their abilities, students come to you with various backgrounds, interests, and learning styles. Differentiating instruction can help all students attain learning goals. The strategies you use to differentiate instruction in your classroom will depend on the specific learning needs of the students.

The following pages provide descriptions of students with varying learning abilities you may find in your classes, as well as strategies and techniques to keep in mind as you work with these students. You will be asked to meet the needs of all of your students in the same classroom setting. It is a challenge to modify daily lessons with varying accommodations to meet the demands of all your students.

Learning Disabled

Students with learning disabilities (LD) have neurological disorders that interfere with their ability to store, process, or produce information, creating a "gap" between ability and performance. These students are generally of average or above average intelligence. Examples of learning disabilities are distractibility, spatial problems, and reading comprehension problems.

- Assist students in getting organized.
- Give short oral directions.
- Use drill exercises.
- Provide computers with specialized software (that checks spelling and grammar and/or recognizes speech) to students with poor writing and reading skills.
- Break assignments into small segments and assign only one segment at a time.
- Demonstrate skills and have students model them.
- Give prompt feedback.
- Use continuous assessment to mark students' daily progress.
- Prepare materials at varying levels of ability.
- Shorten the number of items on exercises, tests, and quizzes.
- Provide more hands-on activities.

Cognitively Disabled

Students with cognitive disabilities (also known as intellectual disabilities) have limitations in their intellectual functioning compared with others their age. They may have difficulty remembering, associating and classifying information, reasoning, problem solving, and making judgments. They may also have difficulties with such adaptive behavior as daily living activities and developing occupational skills.

- Use concrete examples to introduce concepts.
- Make learning activities consistent.
- Use repetition and drills spread over time.
- Provide work folders for daily assignments.
- Use behavior management techniques, such as behavior modification, in the area of adaptive behavior.
- Encourage students to function independently.
- Give students extra time to both ask and answer questions while giving hints to answers.
- Give simple directions and read them over with students.
- Use objective test items and hands-on activities because students generally have poor writing skills and difficulty with sentence structure and spelling.

Behaviorally and Emotionally Disabled

Students with these disabilities exhibit undesirable behaviors or emotions that may, over time, adversely affect educational performance. The inability to learn cannot be explained by intellectual, social, or health factors. Such students may be inattentive, withdrawn, timid, restless, defiant, impatient, unhappy, fearful, lack initiative, have negative feelings and actions, and blame others.

- Call students' names or ask them questions when you see their attention wandering.
- Call on students randomly rather than in a predictable sequence.
- Move around the room frequently.
- Improve students' self-esteem by giving them tasks they can perform well, increasing the number of successful achievement experiences.
- Decrease the length of time for each activity.
- Use hands-on activities instead of using words and abstract symbols.
- Decrease the size of the group, so each student can actively participate.
- Make verbal instructions clear, short, and to the point.

Academically Gifted

Students who are academically gifted are capable of high performance as a result of general intellectual ability, specific academic aptitude, and/or creative or productive thinking. Such students have a vast fund of general knowledge and high levels of vocabulary, memory, abstract word knowledge, and abstract reasoning.

- Provide ample opportunities for creative behavior.
- Make assignments that call for original work, independent learning, critical thinking, problem solving, and experimentation.
- Show appreciation for creative efforts.
- Respect unusual questions, ideas, and solutions these students provide.
- Encourage students to test their ideas.
- Provide opportunities and give credit for self-initiated learning.
- Avoid overly detailed supervision and too much reliance on prescribed curricula.
- Allow time for reflection.
- Resist immediate and constant evaluation. This causes students to be afraid to use their creativity.
- Avoid comparisons with other students, which imply subtle pressure to conform.

Limited English Proficiency (LEP)

You may have students in your classroom who have a limited proficiency in the English language. English is generally their second language. Such students may be quite capable academically, but they lack the language skills needed to reason and comprehend abstract concepts.

- Use a slow but natural rate of speech; speak clearly; use shorter sentences; repeat concepts in several ways.
- Act out questions using gestures with hands, arms, and the whole body. Use demonstrations and pantomime. Ask questions that can be answered by a physical movement, such as pointing, nodding, or manipulation of materials.
- When possible, use pictures, photos, and charts.
- Write key terms on the board. As they are used, point to them.
- Corrections should be limited and appropriate. Do not correct grammar or usage errors in front of the class, causing embarrassment.
- Give honest praise and positive feedback through your voice tones and visual articulation whenever possible.
- Encourage students to use language to communicate, allowing them to use their native language to ask and answer questions when they are unable to do so in English.
- Integrate students' cultural background into class discussions.
- Use cooperative learning during which students have opportunities to practice expressing ideas without risking language errors in front of the entire class.

Physically Disabled

These students have physical, mobility, visual, speech, hearing (deaf, hard-of-hearing), or health (diabetes, asthma, cystic fibrosis, epilepsy) impairments. Strategies will depend on the specific disability.

- Seat students with visual and hearing impairments near the front of the classroom. Speak clearly and say aloud what you are writing on the board.
- To reduce the risk of injury in lab settings, ask students about any conditions that could affect their ability to learn or perform.
- Rearrange lab equipment or the classroom and make necessary modifications to accommodate any disability.
- Investigate and utilize assistive technology devices that can improve students' functional capabilities.
- Discuss solutions or modifications with the student who has experience with overcoming his or her disability and may have suggestions you may not have considered.
- Provide an opportunity for the student to test classroom modifications before utilizing them in class.
- Ask advice from special education instructors, the school nurse, or physical therapist.
- Plan barrier-free field trips that include all students.

Learning Styles and Multiple Intelligences

Educators and researchers are continually analyzing the complex factors that affect learning and achievement. There is a continual desire and push to improve education.

One of the biggest concerns today is how to help *all* students learn effectively, not just most. There is better recognition that each student is an individual. While the majority of students function in regular classes, many fail to reach their real potential. When instructors better understand the differences in how students learn, they can more effectively teach in ways that maximize learning for more students. Information about learning styles and multiple intelligences are two helpful guides to gaining insight into such differences.

Learning Styles

Imagine that you just got a new game. How would you choose to learn how to play? Would you read the directions? Perhaps you would ask a friend to explain the rules of the game. Maybe you would learn best by jumping in and playing, learning the rules as you went.

People learn in different ways. *Learning styles* are the methods individuals prefer and find most effective to absorb and process information. Some people are *visual learners* who learn best by seeing. *Auditory learners* learn most easily by hearing or listening to information. Those who learn best by performing hands-on or physical activities are often called *kinesthetic-tactile learners.* Most people learn in all three ways, but one style is often dominant.

Learning styles is an important concept for instructors. When they realize that the ways students learn most effectively varies, they can plan their lessons to incorporate different modes of learning. Knowing how each student learns best allows instructors to help individual students. Also, when instructors know their own preferred learning style, they can make certain they do not emphasize only that style in teaching or favor students with a similar style. There is no one right way to learn. The characteristics of people with each of three learning styles and associated learning strategies are shown in Figure TE-1.

Learning Styles			
Learning Styles	**Visual**	**Auditory**	**Kinesthetic-Tactile**
Characteristics	• Prefers written and visual materials • Remembers details of how things look • Takes detailed notes • Often distracted by movement • Doodles • Prefers written directions	• Prefers to listen to information • Sounds and songs stimulate memory • Takes incomplete notes • Often distracted by sounds or talking • Prefers oral directions	• Prefers to learn by doing • Remembers how things were done • May not take notes • Often distracted by movement • Finds it difficult to sit still • Prefers directions with examples
Learning Strategies	• Reading • Photos, diagrams, charts • PowerPoint® presentations • Films, television • Flashcards	• Lectures, explanations • Discussions • Listening to recordings • Films, television • Reading aloud • Repeating information	• Demonstrations • Hands-on activities • Models • Projects • Field trips • Dramatizing • Labs, experiments • Singing, clapping • Games

Figure TE-1

Visual Learners

Visual learners learn best when they can see the information to be learned. When presented with a spoken math problem, a visual learner often responds by saying, "Wait a minute, let me write it down." Seeing the problem on paper is a key to comprehending and processing it.

Imagine that you are learning about the main battles of the Civil War. As a visual learner, you could learn the material visually in several ways. You might read about the battles (seeing written words) and take notes. You might draw a time line to be able to visualize the sequence of the battles. You could view pictures, watch a movie about the battles, or see someone act them out. When studying, you could highlight the main points in your notes, assigning a different color to each battle. Each of these techniques could help you visualize the information and help you recall it when assessed.

Auditory Learners

Can you sit in a class and, without taking notes or looking at the board or computer, learn by simply listening? Do you find it easy to remember spoken directions? Auditory learners learn best when they hear information. Although lecturing is generally considered the least effective teaching method, auditory learners get the most from lectures.

Auditory learners often say, "Can you explain that to me?" They find information presented orally easiest to understand and remember.

To learn about Civil War battles, as an auditory learner, you would prefer to listen to an instructor explain when and where important battles occurred. Discussing the significance of each battle would further reinforce learning. You might study by reciting the battle sequence aloud. During a test, mentally pretending to tell someone about the battles might help you as an auditory learner formulate answers.

Many auditory learners can easily recognize song tunes and rhythms. Young children who are auditory learners often find it easy to repeat lines from a movie or a television show. Young auditory learners are often praised for their ability to remember what they have been told to do.

Kinesthetic-Tactile Learners

You have just purchased an item that requires assembly. If you open the box and attempt to put the item together without instructions (the trial-and-error method), you are probably a kinesthetic-tactile learner. (*Kinesthetic* refers to using bodily movement. Tactile refers to touch.) Kinesthetic-tactile learners learn best by doing or through hands-on activity. They often say, "Let me play around with it for a while."

A kinesthetic-tactile learner would find it hard to sit still during a lecture. Reading a textbook chapter might be punctuated with breaks. To learn the sequence of Civil War battles, as a kinesthetic-tactile learner, you might physically place numbers on a map showing, in sequence, where the key battles occurred. Another technique would be to use an object to represent each battle and place them in order by date. Briefly dramatizing the battles could also serve as a memory aid. Studying with others, particularly other students with a similar learning style, might be helpful. During a test, you might visualize the memory of placing the numbers on the map or objects in order.

Young children are especially open to kinesthetic-tactile learning. Babies explore their world through touch. Dancing to the rhythm of a song can help a child learn the alphabet. A special clap may help a young child remember to quiet down. As with older kinesthetic-tactile learners, the physical actions reinforce the learning.

Multiple Intelligences

The term *intelligence* is often used to mean learning ability. In the 1980s, Howard Gardner of Harvard University published his theory of **multiple intelligences.** His research and observations led him to the idea that individuals have a broad range of types of intelligence, each to a different degree.

Gardner identified a variety of types of intelligences as shown in Figure TE-2. The list is still evolving. Gardner believes that each person possesses all of these types, but to different degrees.

Schools typically focus on just a few of these types of intelligence. If you have strong logical intelligence, you may get high grades in math. However, you are not graded directly on strong interpersonal skills or dramatic abilities.

Gardner's work has prompted many schools and instructors to take a broader view of intelligence. They have found that by using activities that draw on more types of intelligence, students learn more, all areas of intelligence improve, and behavior problems are reduced.

Gardner's Multiple Intelligences			
Type of Intelligence	**Strengths**	**Student Characteristics**	**Preferred Learning Activities**
Logical-mathematical	Good with logical problems and math	Performs well in math and science, abstract thinking, classifying	Strategy games, experiments, math problems, logic exercises, problem solving
Spatial	Good at visualizing	Has artistic skills, imagination, can think in three dimensions	Drawing, picturing, making models, seeing patterns, visual puzzles
Bodily-kinesthetic	Good with movement, hands-on activities	Coordinated, athletic, may like art, crafts, or building	Drama, dance, crafts, experiments
Linguistic	Good with words	Has good written or oral communication skills and large vocabulary, learns languages easily	Reading, storytelling, writing, note taking, summarizing, word puzzles
Musical	Good with rhythm and sound patterns	Understands rhythm, tone, sings or hums to self, emotionally sensitive	Music, auditory activities, those requiring emotional sensitivity
Intrapersonal	Good analyzer of self, own strengths and weaknesses	Reflective, goal-oriented, instinctive, makes good personal decisions	Journaling, reflection exercises, self-paced work, personal projects
Interpersonal	Good with communication	Communicates well, leadership, sensitive to others, understands others, resolves conflicts	Group activities, discussions, group projects
Naturalistic	In tune with and analyzes environment	Observes, classifies, visualizes.	Collections, observations, journaling, creating charts
Existentialist	Good at asking philosophical questions	Learns best through seeing the "big picture" of human existence	Interactive communication tools, such as e-mail, teleconferencing

Figure TE-2

Best Practices for Using Smartphones in the Classroom

If used appropriately, smartphones can be a valuable teaching tool. Instructors should reinforce appropriate smartphone usage with students before beginning to use them in class, including sharing information on smartphone safety and expectations for using phones in class. Following are some guidelines to help you with this discussion.

Safety

Explain that mobile activities (including all forms of communication such as pictures, texts, and online posts) are part of a student's digital footprint. Students should understand that their digital footprint has a long-term impact, and may even be part of a background check in the future when they apply to college or for a job. Remind students that communication on a smartphone is not private and is part of their permanent online identity.

Encourage students to know their mobile plan. Students may know all of the features of their smartphones, but may not know what they are being charged to use these features. You should encourage students to take time to know their plans and what they are being charged to access the Internet and use the features of their phone.

Appropriate Usage

If you are allowing students to use their smartphones in the classroom, you may want to outline guidelines for usage. Examples of some of these guidelines include the following.

- Students may only use the phones in the classroom for educational purposes with instructor permission under the guidance of the instructor.
- Smartphones should be turned off until students are told to turn them on.
- Smartphones must be on vibrate at all times.
- Smartphones should be left on the corner of students' desks or at the front of the classroom until they are ready to be used.

You may want to encourage students' involvement in creating classroom rules for smartphone use and have students sign a contract agreeing to these rules.

Access

Alternatives should exist for students who do not have access to smartphones, such as using cooperative learning, differentiating assignments based on smartphone functions, or using alternative methods to access the content. All information available through the G-W Learning mobile site can be accessed using an Internet browser on the G-W Learning companion website.
G-W Learning mobile site: www.m.g-wlearning.com
G-W Learning companion website: www.g-wlearning.com

Parents

Parents might also be included in the learning process. You can consider sending a letter home letting parents know what a powerful instructional tool smartphones can be and your plans to include them in the classroom.

Student Performance

The Common Core State Standards, The States' Career Clusters, Career and Technical Student Organizations (CTSOs), and various assessment techniques are incorporated throughout the *Marketing Dynamics* textbook to aid in student learning. Suggestions for using these features with the teaching package are provided as follows.

Assessment Types

Various assessment strategies are included throughout each chapter. Some can be used to measure student progress in understanding the concepts (formative assessment), while others can be used to measure student progress based on a given rubric (performance assessment), and still others can be used to measure the extent to which they have mastered the concepts (summative assessment).

Formative Assessment

Formative assessment takes place often and is ongoing throughout a course. The many comprehension strategies used throughout the textbook can be used as formative assessment techniques. They measure students' grasp of the concepts, as well as their abilities to internalize the skills and apply them to new situations. Many formative assessments can be completed as groups, because the main focus is on the learning that is taking place and student self-assessment. Formative assessment includes the following.
- Checkpoint activities at the end of each section
- Build Your Vocabulary at the end of each section
- End-of-chapter activities

Summative Assessment

The **EXAM**VIEW® Assessment Suite has traditionally been used for summative assessment. This method of evaluation is good to use when assigning grades. The textbook also contains end-of-chapter summative assessments.

Performance Assessment

When assigning students some of the projects from the textbook that you plan to use as either formative or summative assessment, a rubric can be helpful for measuring student achievement. A rubric consists of a set of criteria that includes specific descriptors or standards that can be used to arrive at performance scores for students. A point value is given for each set of descriptors, leading to a range of possible points to be assigned, usually from one to five. The criteria can also be weighted. This method of assessment reduces the guesswork involved in grading, leading to fair and consistent scoring. The standards clearly indicate to students the various levels of mastery of a task. Students are even able to assess their own achievement based on the criteria.

When using rubrics, students should see the criteria at the beginning of the assignment. They can then focus their efforts on what needs to be done to reach a certain level of performance or quality of project. Therefore, they have a clear understanding of your expectations of achievement.

Though you may want to design many of your own rubrics, a generic one is included in the Instructor's Resources within the Resource Materials. It is designed to assess:
- individual participation;
- individual reports; and
- group participation.

These rubrics allow you to assess a student's performance and arrive at a performance score. Students can see what levels they have surpassed and what levels they can still strive to reach.

College and Career Readiness Portfolio

A portfolio is a selection of related materials compiled as evidence of an individual's skills, talents, or experiences. Methods of collection, as well as selection and storage of materials, are addressed in the College and Career Readiness Portfolio activities that appear at the end of each chapter.

The completed portfolio can be used by the student to apply for a job, apply for a community volunteer program, or admission to a college program of study.

The process of collecting and evaluating items to be included in the portfolio is a course-long project-based activity. The Portfolio Rubric, found in the Instructor's Resources, can be used to evaluate the students' work. It is suggested to distribute copies of the rubric to students before they begin the portfolio activities. This will prepare them for the expectations of the project and how they will be evaluated.

Marketing Plan

One of the goals of a marketing text is to teach students how to complete a marketing plan. For those students who pursue a college marketing course of study, writing a marketing plan will be a requirement.

Building the Marketing Plan activities provide a project-based, hands-on learning experience. Starting at the end of Unit 1, students will begin creating a marketing plan for a business that the student, or the instructor, selects. By the end of the text, students will have completed their own marketing plan.

The Building the Marketing Plan project addresses 21st Century learning skills:
- creativity and innovation
- critical thinking and problem solving
- communication and collaboration

This project-based activity will be written based on a business plan. You may choose to have each student write their own marketing plan. Or, you may decide to use this as a class project. If you opt to assign this activity to your students, you will need to prepare in advance by locating a business plan for them to use. There are several options for locating a business plan.

1. Sample business plans are readily available on the Internet. The website www.bplan.com has a multitude of business plans from which to select. You may preselect a business or assign students to visit the site and select a business that is of interest to them.
2. You may choose to require students to either work with a local business or publicly traded company. Students would need to be able to obtain a copy of the company's business plan.

It will be necessary to impress upon students the importance of researching and selecting a company that works for them. It will be challenging if they select a company, start a marketing plan, then realize it doesn't work.

Common Core State Standards

The Common Core State Standards were developed by the Common Core State Standards Initiative, a state-led effort coordinated by the National Governors Association Center for Best Practices (NGA Center) and the Council of Chief State School Officers (CCSSO). Developed in collaboration with instructors, school administrators, and experts, the standards were created to provide a consistent framework to prepare students for college and the workforce.

The Common Core State Standards are a framework on which student achievement can be built. The standards are rigorous and reflect the skills needed to succeed in the global economy. To that end, the Common Core State Standards are benchmarked against those used by high-performing schools in the US and internationally.

The Common Core State Standards provide clear expectations for students' performance across all content areas and grade levels. They focus on the development of higher-order thinking skills, in addition to achieving proficiency in reading, writing, speaking, and listening. Research shows that the acquisition of these skills helps promote college and career readiness.

Each chapter features a Reading Prep activity geared toward meeting these standards, as well as two end-of-chapter reading, writing, speaking, or listening activities. A college and career readiness icon indicates these activities in the text. In addition, a correlation to the Common Core State Standards is provided in the National Standards section of the Instructor's Resources.

For up-to-date information about this program, go to www.corestandards.org.

The Career Ready Practices of the Common Career Technical Core (CCTC) is a state-led effort coordinated by the National Association of State Directors of Career Technical Education Consortium (NASDCTEc). This initiative represents the state and territory heads of secondary, postsecondary, and adult CTE. Forty-two states and the District of Columbia supported the development of these standards. The CCTC includes standards for each of the 16 career clusters and their pathways.

Each chapter features an end-of-chapter activity geared toward meeting these standards. A college and career readiness icon indicates these activities in the text. In addition, a correlation to the Career Ready Practices Standards is provided in the National Standards section of the Instructor's Resources.

For up-to-date information about this program, go to www.careertech.org.

Math Skills Handbook

Reinforcement of math skills is important for the marketing student. A Math Skills Handbook is provided at the conclusion of the text. This handbook presents a broad overview of math skills that every student should master. Each topic begins with an overview, followed by practical examples that are easy to follow. This information will assist students in understanding basic math concepts and their application in the real world.

Incorporating the Career Clusters

In the mid 1990s, a project called Building Linkages began development, led by the Office of Vocational and Adult Education (OVAE). Building Linkages was funded in partnership by the US Departments of Labor and Education. The goal of the project was to create a reliable set of standards for the integration of academics with workplace skills. Another goal was to show how higher levels of skills and knowledge lead to higher positions. Eventually, the organization of the project emerged as *career clusters,* and The States' Career Clusters Initiative was launched in 2001. The career clusters are now accessed through the Career Technical Education (CTE) website.

In total, there are 16 career clusters in the National Career Clusters Framework. Depending on the business and industry environment, many states adapt a career cluster to reflect their state's educational objectives, standards, and economic development practices. Within the 16 career clusters, there are 79 different career pathways. In each cluster, three levels of knowledge and skills exist, ranging from broad to specific. The *foundation* level applies to all levels of the careers. The *pathway* level lists the skills necessary for a career subgroup within a cluster. The *career/occupation* level is the highest level of skill and knowledge within a given cluster. All levels promote employability, academic, and technical skills.

Career Planning

Students should not be fooled into thinking the right job will simply "come along." In today's highly competitive workplace, that is most unlikely. People who make no career plans usually find themselves left with jobs no one else wants. Instead, investigate what resources are needed to achieve a goal and map out a plan. What can be done now, next semester, next year, and so on to improve the chances of successfully entering the career of choice?

Having a career means individuals will hold several occupations related by a common skill, purpose, or interest over a lifetime. A *career* is a series of related occupations that show progression in a field of work. The term *job* is commonly used to mean *occupation.* Strictly speaking, a *job* is a task, while an *occupation* is paid employment that involves handling one or more jobs.

An example of a career is the course followed by some construction workers over a span of several years. They may enter the field doing one job well, learn to do others, and eventually supervise parts or all of various construction projects. As workers move from one job to the next, they will gain new skills and knowledge.

Career clusters are groups of occupations or career specialties that are similar or related to one another. The occupations within a cluster require a set of common knowledge and skills for career success. These are called *essential knowledge and skills.*

The 16 clusters, as shown in Figure TE-3, were developed by state partnerships among educators, employers, and professional groups. The purpose of the clusters is to prepare students to transition from school to a rewarding career in an era of changing workplace demands.

The 16 Career Clusters

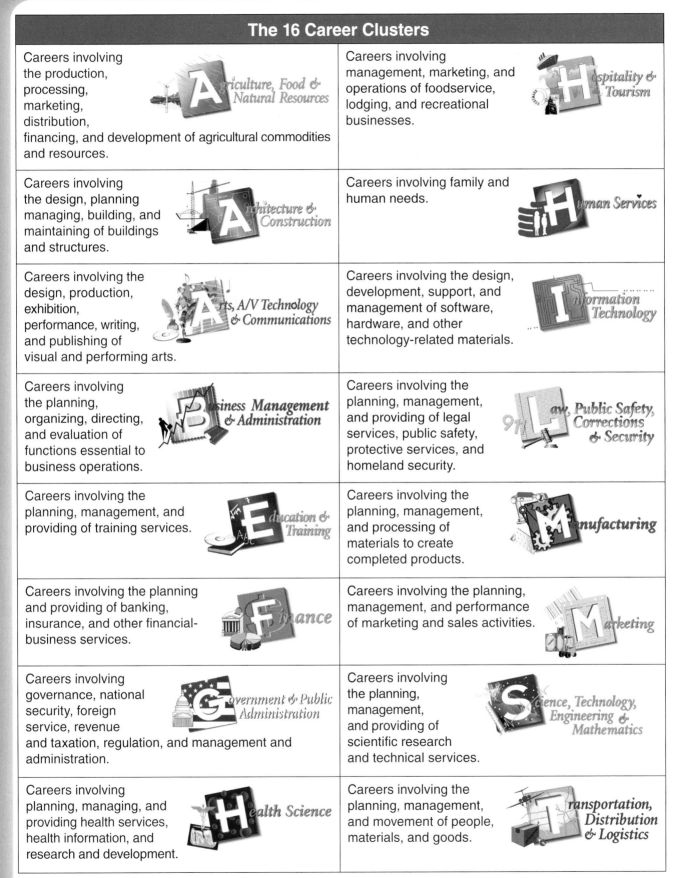

Careers involving the production, processing, marketing, distribution, financing, and development of agricultural commodities and resources.

Agriculture, Food & Natural Resources

Careers involving management, marketing, and operations of foodservice, lodging, and recreational businesses.

Hospitality & Tourism

Careers involving the design, planning managing, building, and maintaining of buildings and structures.

Architecture & Construction

Careers involving family and human needs.

Human Services

Careers involving the design, production, exhibition, performance, writing, and publishing of visual and performing arts.

Arts, A/V Technology & Communications

Careers involving the design, development, support, and management of software, hardware, and other technology-related materials.

Information Technology

Careers involving the planning, organizing, directing, and evaluation of functions essential to business operations.

Business Management & Administration

Careers involving the planning, management, and providing of legal services, public safety, protective services, and homeland security.

Law, Public Safety, Corrections & Security

Careers involving the planning, management, and providing of training services.

Education & Training

Careers involving the planning, management, and processing of materials to create completed products.

Manufacturing

Careers involving the planning and providing of banking, insurance, and other financial-business services.

Finance

Careers involving the planning, management, and performance of marketing and sales activities.

Marketing

Careers involving governance, national security, foreign service, revenue and taxation, regulation, and management and administration.

Government & Public Administration

Careers involving the planning, management, and providing of scientific research and technical services.

Science, Technology, Engineering & Mathematics

Careers involving planning, managing, and providing health services, health information, and research and development.

Health Science

Careers involving the planning, management, and movement of people, materials, and goods.

Transportation, Distribution & Logistics

States' Career Clusters Initiative 2008

Figure TE-3

Career Pathways

To help narrow down career options, each career cluster is further divided into *career pathways.* These subgroups often require additional and more specialized knowledge and skills.

Knowing the relationship between careers in a given pathway is helpful when researching information about careers. The skills required for different jobs in a similar field may overlap somewhat. Preparing for more than one career in a related field allows more flexibility when searching for employment. If an individual cannot find the exact position desired, skills will be needed by other occupations in the same pathway. The more students learn about related careers now, the more easily they will be able to adapt to changes in an occupation later.

Programs of Study

Since occupations in a career pathway require similar knowledge and skills, they also require similar programs of study. A *program of study* is the sequence of instruction used to prepare students for occupations in a given career pathway. The program includes classroom instruction, cocurricular activities such as student organizations, and other learning experiences including work site and service learning.

Customizing a program of study for an individual learner's needs and interests results in a *personal plan of study.* A plan of study will help prepare a student for the career direction chosen. The first step is taking the appropriate classes in high school and participating in related organizations.

Once the foundation has been laid, students should seek out programs that address their career interest. It is possible that some high school classes can count toward college credit. A plan of study does not expire with high school. Students should update their plans at least yearly, but more often if plans change.

Incorporating Career and Technical Student Organizations

The purpose of Career and Technical Student Organizations (CTSOs) is to help students acquire knowledge and skills in career and technical areas as well as leadership skills and experience. CTSOs achieve these goals by enlisting instructor-advisors to organize and lead local chapters in their schools. Support for instructor-advisors and their chapters is often coordinated through each state's education department. The chapters elect officers and establish a program of work. The program of work can include a variety of activities, including community service, cocurricular projects, and competition preparation. Student achievement in specified areas is recognized with certificates and/or public acknowledgment through awards ceremonies.

DECA® Emerging Leaders

At the beginning of each chapter in the textbook, there is a DECA Emerging Leaders activity. DECA is a national association for students of marketing. The learning activity begins with identification of the career cluster, instructional area, and performance indicators associated with the activity content. Performance indicators are specific work-based skills and knowledge that identify what an employee must know or be able to do in order to achieve a performance element in an instructional area. Performance indicators define performance elements.

DECA Emerging Leaders provides first-hand opportunity for students to explore learning activities to prepare for college and careers. Engagement in rigorous project-based learning activities will help develop creative solutions with practical outcomes. Completion of these learning activities provides realistic insight into industry. Students discover what it means to become an academically prepared, community oriented, professionally responsible, and experienced leader through DECA.

Competitive Events

Competitive events are a main feature of most CTSOs. The CTSO develops events that enable students to showcase how well they have mastered the learning of specific content and the use of decision-making, problem-solving, and leadership skills. Each CTSO has its own list of competitive events and activities. Members develop career and leadership skills even though they may not participate in or win competitions.

To prepare students for competitive events, do the following:

1. Contact the organization a year before the next competition to have time to review and decide which competitive events are correct for the student or his/her team.
2. Closely read all of the guidelines. These rules and regulations must be strictly adhered to or disqualification can occur.
3. Read about which communication skills are covered for the event the student selects. Communication plays a role in all the competitive events. Research and preparation are important keys to successful competition. Use this book as a guide to help prepare the communication aspects of all competitive events.
4. Go to the organization's website to locate specific information for the events. Visit the site often, as information can change.
5. Pick one or two events that are of interest to the student. Print the information for the events and discuss your interest with the student's instructor.

Advisor's Role

Preparing students for competitions takes much time and commitment, often beyond the traditional school day. Dedication to this process, however, does have its rewards. You see your students develop complex skills and grow in their roles as leaders and team members. Their ultimate goal is to become competent, successful members of the workforce.

Once you and your students commit to participating in one or more competitions, much responsibility is involved in your role as advisor. If this is a new experience for you or your school, there are some important first steps to take. They include, but are not limited to, the following.

- Obtain membership and competition requirements from organizations that sponsor the competitions.
- Meet with school administrators to gain permission to start a CTSO or gain support for an existing chapter. Contact advisory committee members to build support in the school and community.
- Identify competitions that best meet the needs of your students.
- Make sure local, state, and national membership requirements are met.
- Find out where state meetings and competitions are held and attend them.
- Research application or competition deadlines and plan accordingly.
- Build parent support for competitive events. Emphasize that through competition, students enhance their workplace skills and may also receive recognition awards and, in some cases, scholarships, if they win at state and national levels.

Career and Technical Student Organizations (CTSOs) offer a wide variety of activities that can be adapted to almost any school and classroom situation. If you would like more information, visit the websites of the individual CTSOs.

CTSOs Officially Recognized by the US Department of Education

BPA
Business Professionals of America
www.bpa.org

DECA
An Association of Marketing Students
www.deca.org

FBLA/PBL
Future Business Leaders of America—Phi Beta Lambda
www.fbla-pbl.org

FCCLA
Family, Career and Community Leaders of America
www.fcclainc.org

FEA
Future Educators Association
www.futureeducators.org

FFA
National Future Farmers of America
www.ffa.org

HOSA
Health Occupations Students of America
www.hosa.org

SkillsUSA
www.skillsusa.org

TSA
Technology Student Association
www.tsaweb.org

Goodheart-Willcox Welcomes Your Comments

We welcome your comments or suggestions regarding *Marketing Dynamics* and its supplements. Please send any comments you may have to the editor by visiting our website at www.g-w.com or writing to:

Managing Editor—BMC
Goodheart-Willcox Publisher
18604 West Creek Drive
Tinley Park, IL 60477-6243

Marketing Dynamics

Third Edition

Brenda Clark, EdD
CTE Director
Jenison High School
Jenison, Michigan

Cynthia Gendall Basteri, EdD
Grants Coordinator
Marketing Coordinator Emeritus
Tewksbury Public Schools
Tewksbury, Massachusetts

Chris Gassen, MBA, CFA
Faircourt Valuation Investments
Grosse Pointe Woods, Michigan

Michelle Walker, PhD
Director of Education
DECA Inc.
Reston, VA

Publisher
The Goodheart-Willcox Company, Inc.
Tinley Park, Illinois
www.g-w.com

ii

Library of Congress Catalog Card Number 2012048954

ISBN 978-1-61960-343-1

1 2 3 4 5 6 7 8 9 – 14 – 19 18 17 16 15 14 13

The Goodheart-Willcox Company, Inc. Brand Disclaimer: Brand names, company names, and illustrations for products and services included in this text are provided for educational purposes only and do not represent or imply endorsement or recommendation by the author or the publisher.

The Goodheart-Willcox Company, Inc. Safety Notice: The reader is expressly advised to carefully read, understand, and apply all safety precautions and warnings described in this book or that might also be indicated in undertaking the activities and exercises described herein to minimize risk of personal injury or injury to others. Common sense and good judgment should also be exercised and applied to help avoid all potential hazards. The reader should always refer to the appropriate manufacturer's technical information, directions, and recommendations; then proceed with care to follow specific equipment operating instructions. The reader should understand these notices and cautions are not exhaustive.

The publisher makes no warranty or representation whatsoever, either expressed or implied, including but not limited to equipment, procedures, and applications described or referred to herein, their quality, performance, merchantability, or fitness for a particular purpose. The publisher assumes no responsibility for any changes, errors, or omissions in this book. The publisher specifically disclaims any liability whatsoever, including any direct, indirect, incidental, consequential, special, or exemplary damages resulting, in whole or in part, from the reader's use or reliance upon the information, instructions, procedures, warnings, cautions, applications, or other matter contained in this book. The publisher assumes no responsibility for the activities of the reader.

Library of Congress Cataloging-in-Publication Data

Clark, Brenda, 1960-
  Marketing dynamics / Brenda Clark, Ed.D, Cynthia Gendall Basteri,
  Ed.D,
Chris Gassen, MBA, CFA, Michelle Walker, Ph.D. -- Third Edition.
    pages cm

  Includes index.
  ISBN 978-1-61960-343-1
  1. Marketing. I. Title.

  HF5415.C52785 2013
  658.8--dc23
                                    2012048954

Introduction

In today's competitive workspace, investigating multiple career options is more challenging than ever. *Marketing Dynamics* helps you meet that challenge. By studying this comprehensive text, you will explore the framework needed to become a marketing professional.

The workplace is changing quickly. It is important to understand how social media and ethics will influence your future career, as well as how DECA® Emerging Leaders features will expand your professional knowledge base. Step-by-step narrative will lead you through the application of the marketing standards as identified by the MBA Research and Curriculum Center.

One of the major goals of the text is to create your own marketing plan. To help you accomplish this, each unit has a project-based activity designed to lead you through this process. A template is available on the G-W companion website to assist you in writing your own customized marketing plan.

In addition, building a college and career portfolio will help you pull all the pieces together as you pursue volunteer, education and training, or career opportunities. A separate Math Skills Handbook is also provided as a quick reference for basic math functions.

A new learning tool has been included to help you study. QR codes are provided to use with your smartphone. They will take you directly to selected text activities. In addition, the G-W Learning mobile site makes it easy for you to study on the go!

About the Authors

Brenda Clark is CTE director, marketing instructor, SBE advisor, and DECA advisor for Jenison, Michigan, Public Schools. She was named Marketing Teacher of the Year at state and national levels. She also is a consultant for MBA Research and Curriculum Center and is the coauthor of *Entrepreneurship*. Clark's program was named Business of the Year by the Jenison Chamber of Commerce. Two of her marketing department's school-based enterprises were awarded Gold Certification in 2010 and 2013 respectively. She earned a bachelor degree in marketing education, a master degree in educational leadership, and an EdD in educational leadership with a concentration in career and technical education from Western Michigan University.

Cynthia Gendall Basteri, EdD, is a retired high school math and marketing teacher who served as a DECA competitive events coordinator at the district, state, and international level. Currently, Basteri is the grants coordinator for Tewksbury Public Schools and is the Director of Marketing for a family-owned business. She continues to volunteer as a series director for Massachusetts DECA competitive events.

Chris M. Gassen is the principal of an investment firm and formerly an equity mutual fund manager, financial analyst, accountant, and college instructor. Gassen writes educational materials and business valuations. He holds a master of business administration degree with a concentration in finance from Indiana University and a bachelor of science degree in management from Oakland University. He is a Chartered Financial Analyst (CFA) and served as a grader for the national CFA exam.

Michelle Walker is the director of education at DECA Inc. She provides leadership in education outreach, professional development for 5,900 advisors in the high school and collegiate divisions, professional division recognition programs, and advisor services. She is a former associate professor at the University of North Texas. Walker has a doctor of philosophy degree in applied technology, training and development from the University of North Texas. She also taught marketing education and was a DECA advisor in the Dallas Independent School District.

Reviewers

The authors and publisher are grateful to the following reviewers who provided valuable input to this edition.

Erica Marshall
Marketing and Business Teacher, DECA
  Advisor
Reagan High School
San Antonio, TX

Darren C. McCauley
Marketing Education Teacher
Fluvanna County High School
Palmyra, VA

Tarrie McDaniel
Academy Lead Teacher
Tri Cities High School
East Point, GA

Thomas W. Miller, G-W Advisory Council
Marketing Instructor and DECA Advisor
Kentucky Tech, Ohio County ATC
Hartford, KY

Lou Ellen Moore Blackmon
Career and Technology Instructor
Socastee High School
Myrtle Beach, SC

Paul Van Ness
Marketing Strategy Leader
University of Notre Dame
Notre Dame, IN

Jackie Phillips
Business/Marketing Teacher
El Dorado High School
El Dorado, AR

Christopher Power, G-W Advisory Council
Business and Technology Teacher
Francis Lewis High School
Queens, NY

Deborah Rogers, G-W Advisory Council
Marketing Teacher, Coordinator
Nottoway High School
Crewe, VA

Robyn Rogers, G-W Advisory Council
Marketing Education Teacher
North Side High School
Fort Worth, TX

Shenley Roundtree
Marketing Teacher
Lawier Charter Career Academy
Gainesville, GA

Sherry Silver
Marketing Instructor/DECA Advisor
Alma High School
Alma, AR

Joy Smith
Business, Marketing, and Finance Career
  Cluster Consultant
Tennessee Department of Education
Nashville, TN

Gayle C. Struthers
Business Technology Department Head
Countryside High School
Clearwater, FL

Emily Toothill
Career Academy Department Chair
Lambert High School
Suwanee, GA

Mary Susan Williamson
Business and Marketing Teacher, DECA
  Advisor
Brookland-Cayce High School
Cayce, SC

Linda Wilson
Marketing Teacher
Sandia High School
Albuquerque, NM

Contents in Brief

Expanded Table of Contents

Unit 4
Product Dynamics .. 278

Unit 5
Price Dynamics. 342

Unit 6
Place Dynamics 388

Unit 7
Promotion Dynamics. . 440

Student Focused

Marketing is all around us. Marketing influences how we think, what we buy, and even the careers we choose. *Marketing Dynamics* will help guide you to understanding how marketing will personally affect your decisions as a consumer, as well as a career that you might choose.

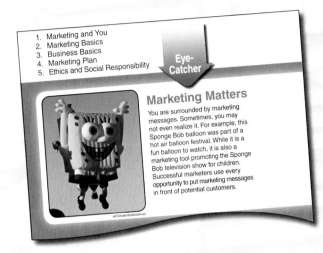

Marketing creates eye-catchers. Webster's defines *eye-catcher* as "something that arrests the eye." To illustrate how marketing *arrests* the eye of the consumer, each unit opens with an example of a business that used a clever eye-catcher to gain attention. These features will have you thinking about other eye-catchers that you see every day.

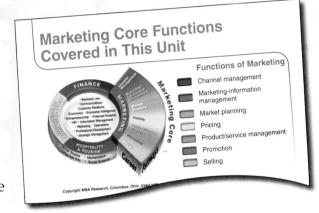

Marketing Standards are important to the presentation of content. In each unit opener, you will find which of the seven specific marketing core functions are presented in that unit. These are the marketing core functions as identified by the MBA Research and Curriculum Center.

One of the goals of a marketing course is to learn how to put a marketing plan together. Ongoing Building the Marketing Plan activities provide a project-based, hands-on learning experience. Starting at the end of Unit 1, you will begin the marketing plan for a business you select. By the end of the text, you will have completed your own plan. The Building the Marketing Plan project addresses 21st Century learning skills:

- creativity and innovation
- critical thinking and problem solving
- communication and collaboration

It is all about getting ready for college and career. College and Career Readiness activities address literacy skills to help prepare you for the real world. The Common Core State Standards for English Language Arts for reading, writing, speaking, and listening are incorporated in a Reading Prep activity as well as end-of-chapter Common Core activities. Common Career Technical Core Career Ready Practices are also addressed.

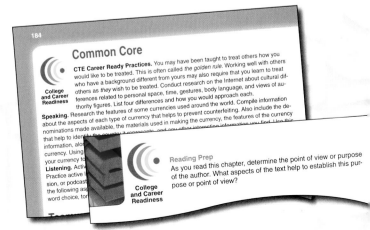

Content Connected

Ever wonder how the world of marketing connects with your life? Practical activities relate everyday learning to enable you to experience real life marketing.

- **Exploring Careers** presents information about the marketing career cluster. By studying these features, you can learn more about career possibilities for your future.
- **Case In Point** scenarios highlight real companies and how they apply marketing concepts to their businesses. These cases will help you understand the connection between marketing theory and real application.
- **College and Career Readiness Portfolio** activities enable you to create a personal portfolio for use when exploring volunteer, education and training, or career opportunities.
- **Math Skills Handbook** provides you with a quick reference for basic math functions. This helpful information will help clarify marketing math that is presented in the chapters.

It is important to assess what you learn as you progress through the text. Multiple opportunities are provided to confirm learning as you explore the content. **Formative assessment** includes the following.

- **Checkpoint** activities at the end of each major section of the chapter provide you with an opportunity to review what you have learned before moving on to the additional content.
- **Review Your Knowledge** covers basic concepts presented in the chapter so you can evaluate your understanding of the material.
- **Apply Your Knowledge** challenges you to begin the planning process for creating a marketing plan.
- **Teamwork** encourages a collaborative experience to help you learn to interact with other students in a productive manner.
- **College and Career Readiness** activities provide ways for you to demonstrate the literacy and career readiness skills you have mastered.
- **Building the Marketing Plan** is an ongoing project-based activity that guides you through preparing a complete marketing plan.

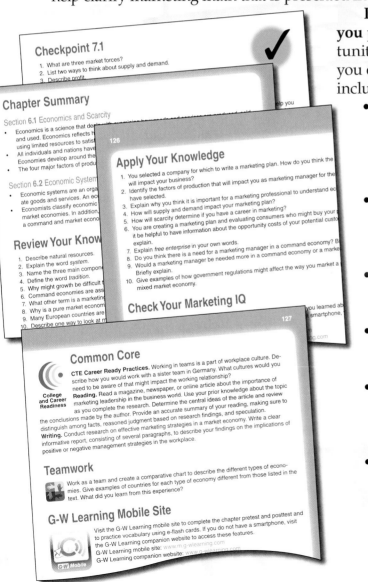

Features Spotlighted

DECA prepares emerging leaders and entrepreneurs in marketing, finance, hospitality and management in high schools and colleges around the globe. DECA Emerging Leaders provides first hand opportunity for you to explore learning activities that prepare you for college and careers. Engagement in rigorous project-based learning activities will help you develop creative solutions with practical outcomes. Completion of these learning activities provides realistic insight into industry. Discover what it means to become an academically prepared, community oriented, professionally responsible, and experienced leader through DECA.

◇DECA Emerging Leaders

Introduction
This learning activity, DECA Emerging Leaders, is designed for you to become familiar with DECA activities and connect them to chapter content. Where appropriate, the learning activity begins with identification of the career cluster, instructional area, and performance indicators associated with the activity content. Performance indicators are specific work-based skills and knowledge that identify what an employee must know or be able to do in order to achieve a performance element in an instructional area. Performance indicators define performance elements.

Career Cluster: Marketing
Instructional Area: Professional Development

Performance Indicators
- Explain marketing and its importance in a global economy.
- Explain career opportunities in marketing management.
- Assess the services of professional organizations in marketing.
- Employ career-advancement strategies in marketing.

Purpose
Designed for DECA members, this activity enables student members to better under...

- **Educational Conferences** provide targeted, highly focused learning experiences for members and advisors while connecting with corporate professionals.
- **Educational Partners** provide learning opportunities for members and professional development in industry content for DECA advisors.
- **Global Entrepreneurship Week (GEW)** engages millions of young people around the world each November to embrace innovation, imagination, and creativity.
- **School-Based Enterprises** reinforce and enhance career preparation.
- **Webcasts** provide short video segments filmed at DECA's conferences to further engage members.

Procedure
1. DECA members should become familiar with the organization and its diverse learning activities. Use the following activities to learn about DECA, identify membership benefits, and apply DECA's connection to college and career preparation.
2. The information will be presented to you through the navigation of the DECA website. Visit the DECA website at www.deca.org to become familiar with the activities and opportunities available to you as a student and DECA member. Select the tab that says *Chapter Resources*. Then select

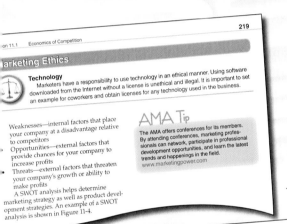

219

on 11.1   Economics of Competition

arketing Ethics

Technology
Marketers have a responsibility to use technology in an ethical manner. Using software downloaded from the Internet without a license is unethical and illegal. It is important to set an example for coworkers and obtain licenses for any technology used in the business.

Weaknesses—internal factors that place your company at a disadvantage relative to competitors
Opportunities—external factors that provide chances for your company to increase profits
Threats—external factors that threaten your company's growth or ability to make profits
A SWOT analysis helps determine marketing strategy as well as product development strategies. An example of a SWOT analysis is shown in Figure 11-4.

AMA Tip

The AMA offers conferences for its members. By attending conferences, marketing professionals can network, participate in professional development opportunities, and learn the latest trends and happenings in the field.
www.marketingpower.com

Social Media

Sharing Information
There are over 250 million active Twitter use counts. If you decide to use Twitter as a co will need to create a business account throu you have a Twitter account for the business learn how best to optimize your tweets. For ated a national Twitter account, @RedCross. However, it soon also needed to interact with their local community members. S local chapters to create their own accounts. Post useful informa community members will want to share that information with information is one of the most p

Green Marketing

Cause Marketing
Cause marketing is a type of marketing in which a work together for a common mutual benefit. An exampl employees a day off to pick up trash for the city to crea marketing is a great way to show the company's social

Practical information helps you prepare for your future. Special features add realism and interest to enhance learning.

- **Marketing Ethics** offers insight into ethical issues that arise for marketing professionals and tips on how to make ethical decisions.
- **Green Marketing** shares information for marketers on best business practices for the environment.
- **AMA Tips** from the American Marketing Association help you understand the value of professional organizations for the profession.
- **Social Media** features illustrates the use of social media practices in a professional setting.

Technology Applied

Technology is an important part of your world. So, it should be part of your everyday learning experiences. In this text, you will find:

- Pretests and posttests are available for each chapter on the G-W Learning companion website as well as the G-W Learning mobile site. Taking the pretest will help you activate your prior knowledge of the content. Taking the posttest will help you evaluate what you have learned about the chapter content.
- Research skills are critical for college and career. The Web Connect feature at the beginning of each section provides opportunity to put those skills to work.
- Creating a marketing plan takes work. To make your experience easier, data files are provided on the companion website to guide you through the marketing plan project.

G-W Learning Companion Website

The G-W Learning companion website for *Marketing Dynamics* is a study reference that contains e-flash cards, vocabulary exercises, and interactive quizzes. Also included are data files for the Building the Market Plan activity to assist you as you create your own marketing plan.

G-W Learning companion website: www.g-wlearning.com

G-W Learning Mobile Site

The G-W Learning mobile site* is a study reference to use when you are on the go. The mobile site is easy to read, easy to use, and fine-tuned for quick access.

For *Marketing Dynamics*, the G-W Learning mobile site contains chapter pretests and posttests as well as e-flash cards and vocabulary practice. These features can be accessed by a smartphone or other handheld device

Scan now!

with Internet access. These features can also be accessed using an Internet browser to visit the G-W Learning companion website.

G-W Learning mobile site: www.m.g-wlearning.com

Goodheart-Willcox QR Codes

This Goodheart-Willcox product contains QR codes, or quick response codes. These codes can be scanned with smartphone bar code reader to access information or online features.*

For more information on using QR codes and a recommended QR code reader, visit the G-W Learning companion website at www.m.g-wlearning.com.

Scan now!

An Internet connection is required to access the QR code destinations. Data-transfer rates may apply. Check with your Internet service provider for information on your data-transfer rates.

Unit 1

Marketing Dynamics

Chapters

1. Marketing and You
2. Marketing Basics
3. Business Basics
4. Marketing Plan
5. Ethics and Social Responsibility

Eye-Catcher

Jeff Schultes/Shutterstock.com

Marketing Matters

You are surrounded by marketing messages. Sometimes, you may not even realize it. For example, this Sponge Bob balloon was part of a hot air balloon festival. While it is a fun balloon to watch, it is also a marketing tool promoting the Sponge Bob television show for children. Successful marketers use every opportunity to put marketing messages in front of potential customers.

Marketing Core Functions Covered in This Unit

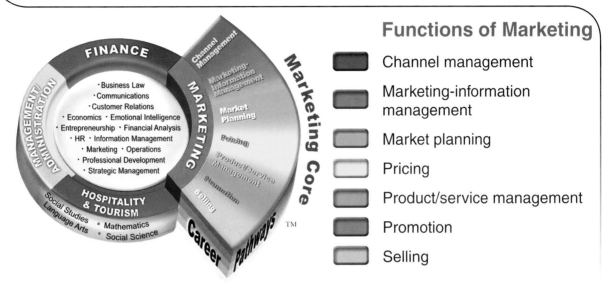

Functions of Marketing

- ▮ Channel management
- ▮ Marketing-information management
- ▮ Market planning
- ▯ Pricing
- ▮ Product/service management
- ▮ Promotion
- ▮ Selling

Copyright MBA Research, Columbus, Ohio. Used with permission.

Developing a Vision

Exploring career opportunities is an important step. The choices are endless. In this text, you will have an opportunity to investigate the career choice to become a marketing professional. Unit 1 introduces you to marketing and business basics. This will be the foundation for learning about the marketing profession.

One of the most important tasks a marketing person will perform is to create a marketing plan. In this unit, you will learn the basics that create a good marketing plan. You will also learn about the importance of ethics and social responsibility. Putting these pieces together will help you expand your knowledge of the business world.

CHAPTER

1

Marketing and You

| Section 1.1 | Marketing |
| Section 1.2 | Careers in Marketing |

"The things we fear most in organizations—fluctuations, disturbances, imbalances—are the primary sources of creativity."

—Margaret J. Wheatley, author, consultant, and speaker

College and Career Readiness

Reading Prep
Before you begin reading this chapter, try to find a quiet place with no distractions. Make sure your chair is comfortable and the lighting is adequate.

Check Your Marketing IQ

Before you begin the chapter, see what you already know about marketing by taking the chapter pretest. If you do not have a smartphone, visit the G-W Learning companion website.
G-W Learning mobile site: www.m.g-wlearning.com
G-W Learning companion website: www.g-wlearning.com

Explore

Assign the College and Career Readiness Reading Prep activity before students read the chapter. Reading Prep activities give students the opportunity to apply the Common Core State Standards.

Engage

Assign the Chapter 1 pretest.

◇DECA Emerging Leaders

Introduction

This learning activity, DECA Emerging Leaders, is designed for you to become familiar with DECA activities and connect them to chapter content. Where appropriate, the learning activity begins with identification of the career cluster, instructional area, and performance indicators associated with the activity content. Performance indicators are specific work-based skills and knowledge that identify what an employee must know or be able to do in order to achieve a performance element in an instructional area. Performance indicators define performance elements.

Career Cluster: Marketing
Instructional Area: Professional Development

Performance Indicators

- Explain marketing and its importance in a global economy.
- Explain career opportunities in marketing management.
- Assess the services of professional organizations in marketing.
- Employ career-advancement strategies in marketing.

Purpose

Designed for DECA members, this activity enables student members to better understand opportunities available through DECA in marketing, finance, hospitality, and management.

DECA's Comprehensive Learning Program consists of all DECA activities by category.

- **College and Business Partnerships** provide scholarships, classroom presentations and career guidance, internships, work experience and community service activities.
- **Competitive Events Program** provides authentic situations relating to current business practices.
- **DECA Direct Magazine** is a full-color international publication featuring articles on career development in leadership; community service; and professionalism.
- **Educational Conferences** provide targeted, highly focused learning experiences for members and advisors while connecting with corporate professionals.
- **Educational Partners** provide learning opportunities for members and professional development in industry content for DECA advisors.
- **Global Entrepreneurship Week (GEW)** engages millions of young people around the world each November to embrace innovation, imagination, and creativity.
- **School-Based Enterprises** reinforce and enhance career preparation.
- **Webcasts** provide short video segments filmed at DECA's conferences to further engage members.

Procedure

1. DECA members should become familiar with the organization and its diverse learning activities. Use the following activities to learn about DECA, identify membership benefits, and apply DECA's connection to college and career preparation.
2. The information will be presented to you through the navigation of the DECA website. Visit the DECA website at www.deca.org to become familiar with the activities and opportunities available to you as a student and DECA member. Select the tab that says *Chapter Resources.* Then select *High School Resources.*

Critical Thinking

1. Review the components of DECA's Comprehensive Learning Program.
2. Which activities enhance your career or personal goals? How do they help you achieve your career and personal goals?
3. Select two activities you wish to learn more about and discuss with your teacher.

Visit www.deca.org for more information.

Section 1.1 Marketing

Objectives

After completing this section, you will be able to
- **define** the function of marketing.
- **explain** the importance of marketing.
- **describe** why it is important to study marketing.

Key Terms

market
marketing
need
want
business

function
functions of
    business
consumer

Web Connect

Do an Internet search for a definition of marketing. After reading a number of definitions, write your own definition of marketing.

Critical Thinking

Do you know of any businesses that have been successful without marketing? Write five reasons a business might fail if it does not market its products or services.

What Is Marketing?

Marketing was around before the Internet, retail stores, cars, and computers existed. In fact, the word *market* is derived from the Latin word *mercaris,* which means "to trade." Sometime in 12th century Europe, *market* came to mean the meeting of buyers and sellers of livestock or other goods. Today, a **market** is anywhere a buyer and a seller convene to buy and sell goods.

How would you define marketing? Experts define marketing in many different ways, all with similar themes. Some examples of marketing definitions follow.
- Marketing is "to find out what your customers want and then give it to them," from Tim Cohn, marketing consultant.

- The purpose of marketing is "to reach customers and compel them to purchase, use, and repurchase your product," from Alexander Hiam, marketing consultant.
- The job of marketing is "to sell lots of stuff and make lots of money," from Sergio Zyman, former chief marketing officer of Coca-Cola.
- "Marketing is getting someone who has a need to know, like, and trust you," from John Jantsch, author of *Duct Tape Marketing.*

If marketing could be defined in one sentence, there would be no need for an entire textbook. **Marketing** consists of dynamic activities that identify, anticipate, and satisfy customer demand while making a profit. The function of marketing is to meet customer needs and wants with products they can and will buy.

A **need** is something necessary for survival, such as food, clothing, and shelter. A need can also be defined as something necessary to function in society. Your needs might include schoolbooks, transportation, and power. A **want** is something that a person desires, but could live without, such as a new cell phone or a vacation.

However, in order to understand marketing, it is necessary to understand the basic concepts of business. **Business** is the term for all of the activities involved in developing and exchanging products and services. Business is the engine that powers economies around the world. Businesses perform many activities or functions. **Function** is a general word for a category of activities. The **functions of business** are *production, finance, marketing,* and *management,* as shown in Figure 1-1.

Without customers, there would be no businesses. Marketing is the function of business that focuses on customers. Marketers help the entire business focus on the needs and wants of customers. The marketing function includes learning about customers. This helps the business to create and offer products customers want and are able to buy. The promotion and selling of the products also fall under marketing. Finally, marketing provides customer service to make sure customers are satisfied and will buy again.

The American Marketing Association (AMA) revises its definition of *marketing* as it deems necessary. In 2011, the definition was: "Marketing is the activity, set of institutions, and processes for creating, communicating, delivering, and exchanging offerings that have value for customers, clients, partners, and society at large." www.marketingpower.com

Importance of Marketing

It has been said that by building a better mousetrap, it will sell itself. That is not necessarily true. If customers do not know you have a better mousetrap, how would they know they can buy it? Marketing tells the product story so people will want to buy it.

Marketing Helps Businesses Grow and Increase Profits

In today's business world, it is often difficult to get the attention of customers. Marketing efforts can target the best customers, research how to improve a product, and find new ways to sell it. Without marketing, business profits would decline because there would be fewer sales. Workers would lose jobs, and many businesses might close.

Marketing efforts help businesses sell more products and increase profits. When customers are spending more, companies are willing to invest more. They can expand a current business or start new ones. Marketing helps to create a positive cycle of economic growth.

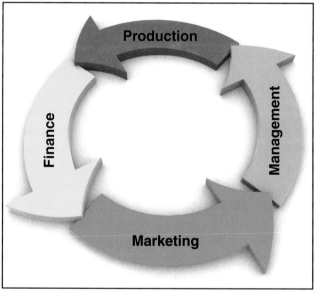

Goodheart-Willcox Publisher

Figure 1-1 The four functions of business work together to create customer satisfaction and business success.

Marketing Creates Jobs and Improves Community Standing

Marketing positions account for between 25 and 30 percent of all jobs in the United States. Jobs are vital to the success of any community. Businesses are aware of the importance of their standing in the community. When an economy grows, more people are employed. More purchases are made and businesses can help their communities more.

Marketing Builds Relationships

It would be hard for a company to have loyal customers if marketing did not exist. Personal selling and other marketing activities help customers learn to trust and depend on certain businesses to meet their needs. People are more likely to buy from companies they know and trust. Marketing can make a positive impact on business.

Why Study Marketing?

Learning about marketing will make you a better consumer. A consumer is a person who buys products or services and also uses them. You are, and will always be, a consumer. As a consumer, you need to make informed decisions about the products you buy. Knowing about marketing

helps you understand how businesses influence purchasing. Marketing includes the products they offer, the prices charged, and other information to help you make wise purchasing decisions.

In the competitive working environment in the United States, employers look for workers who will add something to the business. Learning about marketing will make you a better employee. Many people in a company often perform their job duties. But, they do not know the company's vision and what it wants to achieve. You will be a more valuable worker by understanding the marketing functions and how to work with the marketing team.

Learning about marketing also helps you learn how to market yourself. Marketing is not just about selling product, but selling your talents and abilities as well. Whether you are job hunting, applying for college, or being a volunteer, learning how to market helps you sell yourself.

Marketing is global. No matter where you go or what you do, marketing will impact the decisions you make about what to buy, where to travel on vacation, and even what you eat for lunch today.

FYI

Understanding the function of marketing in your business will help you become a well-rounded worker.

Social Media

Social Media as a Marketing Tool

Social media plays an important part of your life every day of the week. You use social media to build your personal brand, develop a community, and to communicate with others. Businesses have also learned the many advantages of using social media. Merriam-Webster Dictionary defines social media as, "forms of electronic communication (as websites for networking and microblogging) through which users create online communities to share information, ideas, personal messages, and other content (as videos). Social media is one tool that can complement a company's marketing strategies when used wisely. One of the things social media can add to the marketing plan is helping a business increase its visibility. Companies can keep their brands in front of customers through regular product updates, company events, or recognizing customer feedback.

Explain

Identify local or regional companies that influence the economy. Discuss with students how the marketing done by the companies influences the local community.

Explain

Discuss with students the importance of marketing when it comes to finding a job as a teen but even more importantly when they are seeking a career.

Customers rely on experienced people in a business to help them make the best purchase decisions, which is a form of marketing.

TylerOlson/Shutterstock.com

Checkpoint 1.1

1. Describe the marketing function.
2. Why is marketing dynamic?
3. Describe the difference between business and marketing.
4. List two reasons we need marketing.
5. Why is business vital to economic growth?

Build Your Vocabulary

As you progress through this course, develop a personal glossary of marketing terms and add it to your portfolio. This will help you build your vocabulary and prepare you for a career. Write a definition for each of the following terms, and add it to your personal marketing glossary.

market   business
marketing   function
need   functions of business
want   consumer

Extend

Discuss with students why marketing is global. Ask students to identify some companies that do business globally.

Evaluate

Assign Checkpoint questions at end of section. Assess student comprehension using the Checkpoint activity as a self-assessment tool.

Checkpoint Answers

1. The marketing function includes learning about customers so that the business can create and offer products customers want and are able and willing to buy.
2. The needs and wants of customers are constantly changing and business must change to meet those needs and wants.

3. Business is the term for all activities involved in the development and exchange of products and includes finance, production, marketing, and management. Marketing is one of the functions of business and is responsible for identifying, anticipating, and satisfying customer demand while remaining profitable.

4. Answers may vary but should include any of the following: helps drive the economy, provides jobs, and influences sales of products around the world.
5. Economic growth occurs when businesses grow and profits increase.

Build Your Vocabulary Answers

Definitions for these terms can be found in the glossary of this text.

Section 1.2 Careers in Marketing

Objectives

After completing this section, you will be able to
- **describe** a marketing professional.
- **discuss** the importance of planning for your career.
- **explore** whether a marketing career might be for you.

Key Terms

marketing professional
job
career
profession
career clusters
career pathways
goal
short-term goal
long-term goal
goal setting
SMART goals

Web Connect

There are community organizations that can help you in your quest to become a marketing professional. Before you begin reading, do an Internet search for marketing associations. Select one in your community. Read about this organization and how it can help you in your journey to become a marketing professional.

Critical Thinking

Think of your future. Write about where you see yourself in five, ten, or even twenty years. If you were to become a marketing professional, for which type of business would you want to work?

Marketing Professionals

You may have been talking all of your life about what you want to be when you grow up. Now the time is here, and you are making career plans. It is an exciting time in your life. There are many traditional careers you could pursue. Are you a person who is creative or is great talking with others? Are you always coming up with new ideas? Then being a marketing professional may be a career choice for you.

Many years ago, a *marketer* was defined as the person who promoted products in a market or to a market. Today, marketing is much more than just promoting a product in a market. To fully define someone involved in marketing today, a broader term and definition is needed. A marketing professional is the person who helps determine the marketing needs of a company, develops and implements marketing plans, and focuses on customer satisfaction.

Marketing is taking on both the risks and responsibilities of getting others to buy products. Activities involved in marketing include
- determining what type of research about customers is needed;
- deciding how to get products to the customers;
- pricing, promoting, and selling the products; and
- deciding how to manage data and information.

Explore

Provide an opportunity for students to explore by assigning a hands-on activity. Review the vocabulary terms at the beginning of the section. Where have students encountered these terms before? Help students make educated guesses about the meanings of the terms with which they are least familiar.

Explore Your Career Options

The average worker spends 36 percent of his or her day working, as shown in Figure 1-2. This means a choice of career is one of the most important decisions a person will make as an adult.

A job is the work a person does regularly in order to earn money. A career is a series of related jobs in the same profession. Profession is the term used for jobs in a business field requiring similar education, training, or skills. For example, a doctor has a career in the medical profession. The doctor would have started as an intern and then become a resident before becoming a doctor. With each new job, a worker usually acquires greater knowledge and expertise. The series of jobs often leads to more responsibility and higher income. Many career counselors recommend that you think in terms of developing a career.

The workplace is changing rapidly, and researching a career can seem overwhelming. Studying the career clusters is a good starting point to see where your interests lie. The career clusters, as shown in Figure 1-3, are 16 groups of occupational and career specialties that share common knowledge and skills.

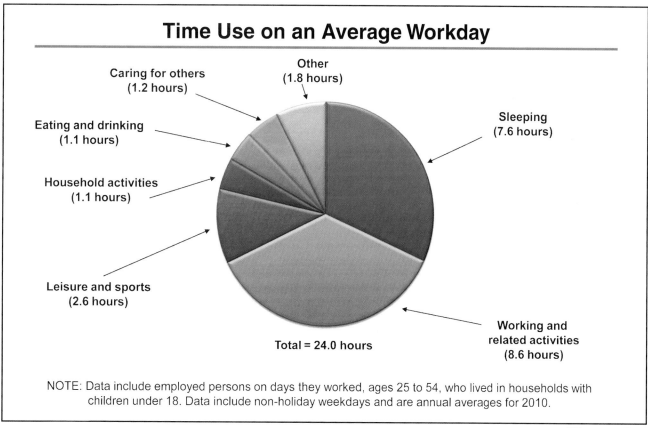

Time Use on an Average Workday

Caring for others (1.2 hours)
Other (1.8 hours)
Eating and drinking (1.1 hours)
Sleeping (7.6 hours)
Household activities (1.1 hours)
Leisure and sports (2.6 hours)
Working and related activities (8.6 hours)
Total = 24.0 hours

NOTE: Data include employed persons on days they worked, ages 25 to 54, who lived in households with children under 18. Data include non-holiday weekdays and are annual averages for 2010.

US Department of Labor

Figure 1-2 Average workday for working adults with children.

The 16 Career Clusters	
Careers involving the production, processing, marketing, distribution, financing, and development of agricultural commodities and resources. *Agriculture, Food & Natural Resources*	Careers involving management, marketing, and operations of foodservice, lodging, and recreational businesses. *Hospitality & Tourism*
Careers involving the design, planning managing, building, and maintaining of buildings and structures. *Architecture & Construction*	Careers involving family and human needs. *Human Services*
Careers involving the design, production, exhibition, performance, writing, and publishing of visual and performing arts. *Arts, A/V Technology & Communications*	Careers involving the design, development, support, and management of software, hardware, and other technology-related materials. *Information Technology*
Careers involving the planning, organizing, directing, and evaluation of functions essential to business operations. *Business Management & Administration*	Careers involving the planning, management, and providing of legal services, public safety, protective services, and homeland security. *Law, Public Safety, Corrections & Security*
Careers involving the planning, management, and providing of training services. *Education & Training*	Careers involving the planning, management, and processing of materials to create completed products. *Manufacturing*
Careers involving the planning and providing of banking, insurance, and other financial-business services. *Finance*	Careers involving the planning, management, and performance of marketing and sales activities. *Marketing*
Careers involving governance, national security, foreign service, revenue and taxation, regulation, and management and administration. *Government & Public Administration*	Careers involving the planning, management, and providing of scientific research and technical services. *Science, Technology, Engineering & Mathematics*
Careers involving planning, managing, and providing health services, health information, and research and development. *Health Science*	Careers involving the planning, management, and movement of people, materials, and goods. *Transportation, Distribution & Logistics*

States' Career Clusters Initiative 2008

Figure 1-3 There are 16 career clusters. Each cluster contains several career pathways.

Elaborate/Extend

Provide an opportunity for students to exhibit their understanding
of concepts in context of the material as it is presented. As time
permits, have students read and discuss the special features in
the chapter.

Each of the 16 career clusters includes several **career pathways.** Under these pathways, or career areas, you will find careers ranging from entry-level to those requiring advanced college degrees and years of experience. All of the careers within any given pathway share a foundation of common knowledge and skills. All of these pathways have marketing positions—marketing is everywhere.

The career pathways that fall specifically under the marketing cluster include: *Marketing Communications, Marketing Management, Marketing Research, Merchandising,* and *Professional Sales.*

Career exploration can be an exciting time in your life. No matter which direction you choose, education and training will be necessary to be successful. There are many foundation skills that are necessary for success in any career. Some of those skills include

- basic skills—reading, writing, listening, speaking, and math;
- thinking skills—decision making, creative thinking, problem solving, visualization, reasoning;
- personal qualities—self-management, integrity, honesty, sociability, responsibility;
- technology skills—social media knowledge, software skills, systems skills; and
- business skills—planning, organizing, negotiating, leadership, communication.

Exploring Careers

Marketing Professional

A company's marketing policies play a large role in the products or services it offers. People who work in marketing identify potential customers and develop strategies to market the company's products or services effectively to these customers. In addition, marketing professionals help keep the company on track by monitoring customer wants and needs and suggesting new products or services to satisfy those needs. Typical job titles for these positions include *marketing manager, marketing director, marketing coordinator, brand manager, commercial lines manager,* and *market development manager.*

Some examples of tasks marketing professionals perform include:
- coordinate marketing activities and policies to promote the company's products or services;
- develop marketing and pricing strategies;
- perform market research and analysis; and
- coordinate or participate in promotional activities and trade shows to showcase the company's products or services.

Marketing professionals need a strong background in sales and marketing strategy, as well as customer service and employee management. They need a solid knowledge of the English language, business and management principles, media production, and communication. Marketing professionals must also be able to think creatively and use critical-thinking skills to solve problems. A bachelor degree in marketing, advertising, communications, or a related field is required. Management positions generally require one to five years of work experience. For more information, access the *Occupational Outlook Handbook* online.

Strengthen the skills that you have and set a goal to improve those that need additional work. For example, if you need to improve your writing skills, then consider taking a writing course now or in the near future. If you are a strong leader, look for additional opportunities to lead. Consider running for president of a Career and Technical Student Organization (CTSO) or volunteer to chair a school or work event. DECA is the CTSO for marketing students.

The career opportunities in marketing are endless. Remember that careers are constantly changing. By the time you finish school, there will be new careers and job titles that do not exist today.

Five Levels of Careers

In each career area, there are multiple opportunities for employment. The positions are generally grouped by skill levels or education.

An *entry-level* position is usually a person's first or beginning job. It requires very little training. Entry-level positions in marketing include a retail salesperson, market research interviewers, assistant account director, junior sales associate, or event worker.

A *career-level* position requires employees to have the skills and knowledge for continued employment and advancement in a field. Career-level positions in marketing include sales promotion coordinators, marketing specialist, customer-insights specialist, buyer trainee, and account executive.

A *specialist-level* position requires specialized knowledge and skills in a specific field of study but does not supervise other employees. Specialist-level positions in marketing include public relations specialist, industrial sales agent, merchandiser, and assistant product analyst.

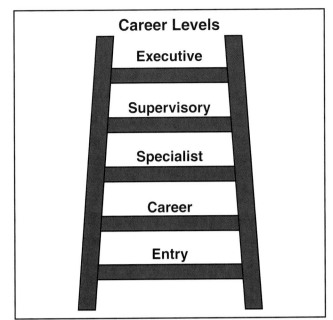

Goodheart-Willcox Publisher

Most careers have different position levels based on years of experience, education, and technical skills.

A *supervisory-level* position requires specialized knowledge and skills and has management responsibility over other employees. Supervisory-level positions in marketing include public relations manager, product manager, marketing research supervisor, merchandise manager, and national sales manager.

An *executive level* is the highest level position responsible for the planning, organizing, and management of a company. Executive-level positions in marketing include vice president of marketing, vice president of merchandising, and vice president of sales.

The American Marketing Association (AMA) is a professional marketing association. Its members range from professional businesspeople in the practice of marketing to entrepreneurs to marketing teachers. The association exists to offer members access to a vast range of resources and career development opportunities. www.marketingpower.com

Explain

Review the career clusters. Share your own career path to your present teaching position.

Explain

Ask students to explain the difference between specialist-level, supervisory-level, and executive level.

There are entry-level
positions in every career.

Career Planning

Success and happiness usually do not happen by accident. Success is a lifelong journey. When you read about a person's *overnight success,* you usually discover that the person has been working hard for many years. Successful people often have a long-term goal, for example, to become a professional actor or the president of a company. Successful people usually have a detailed plan for achieving that goal.

You may not have any goals or career plans at this point in your life. However, now is the perfect time to start thinking about and planning for your future. Planning now for your future career can help assure your career success.

Planning actually has two parts. The first part is setting a goal. The second part is developing activities that will lead you to achieve your goal.

Goals

A **goal** is something a person wants to achieve in a specified time period. You can have a wide variety of goals. Areas in which people have goals include personal growth, finances, possessions, education, career, relationships, family, and community. For example, a personal-growth goal might be to run a half marathon. An educational goal might be to get a college degree.

The advantage of having goals is that they can help you organize your activities to more efficiently achieve them. Once you know your goals, you can make decisions to help you reach them. Not having goals is like being in an airport and taking the first plane you see. You may or may not like your destination. However, if you know where you want to go before you get to the airport, you will buy the proper ticket, get there on time, and arrive at your chosen destination. You may have delays along the way, but you are more likely to reach the destination you chose.

Hyatt

Happy customers are generally repeat customers. Companies looking to provide superior customer service often go the extra mile for their customers. However, employees of any business are only human, and sometimes even the best employees can make mistakes. The most important thing for continued success is to acknowledge a mistake when it happens and attempt to correct it. One Hyatt hotel even took advantage of the social media site Twitter to raise customer service to a new level. A Hyatt guest had an unfortunate experience when entering the room that had been previously booked. When the guest opened the in-room refrigerator, the last guest's food was still there. The hotel's housekeeping department had forgotten to clean the refrigerator.

The customer took a picture of the food in a dirty refrigerator and tweeted it to @HyattConcierge. Within a matter of hours, the guest received a phone call from Hyatt management apologizing for the inconvenience. The situation was fixed immediately, and a handwritten note and gift were also sent to his room. The Hyatt staff turned a potentially damaging tweet into an opportunity for exemplary customer service.

There are two types of goals: short term and long term. A **short-term goal** is one that can be achieved in less than one year. For example, running two miles today is a short-term goal. A **long-term goal** is one that will take a longer time to achieve, usually longer than one year. For example, a long-term goal is to successfully run a half marathon in the next year. In terms of schooling, a short-term goal is to get an *A* on Friday's test. A long-term goal is to get a college degree. In terms of career, a short-term goal is to get a job as a cashier. A long-term goal is to become the vice-president of sales for a retail chain.

Goal setting is a process of deciding what a person wants to achieve. Your goals must be based on who you are, your strengths, your interests, and what you want in life. Suppose you think it would be exciting to be a surgeon like one of the characters in a TV show. However, you did not enjoy biology or chemistry even though you did well in the classes. Choosing the goal of becoming a surgeon may not be the best choice since those are the primary types of high-level classes that occupation requires. However, perhaps you are a very good writer and enjoy working with words.

You might like to become a writer in a hospital public relations department.

FYI

Marketing is more than a high school class or college major. It is a critical business function. A background in marketing can help to you to sell your idea to management, an opportunity to an investor, or yourself to a potential employer.

SMART Goals

Everyone has goals. You may have a goal to get a good grade on your next test. Your friend may have a goal to save enough money to take a trip over spring break. Well-defined goals follow the SMART goal process. **SMART goals** are specific, measurable, attainable, realistic, and timely as illustrated in Figure 1-4.

Specific

How will you know if you have reached your career goal? You must be specific about it. For example, "I want to be rich" is not a very specific goal. Instead, you might say, "I want to have $100,000 in a savings account."

SMART Goals

S — Are my short- and long-term goals **specific**? Exactly what do I want to achieve?

M — Are my goals **measurable**? How will I know when a goal is achieved?

A — Are my goals **attainable**? Am I setting goals that can be achieved?

R — Are my goals **realistic**? Have I set goals that are practical?

T — Are my goals **timely**? Are the dates for achieving my goals appropriate?

Goodheart-Willcox Publisher

Figure 1-4 Set SMART career goals.

Measurable

For a goal to be measurable, the progress should be able to be tracked. Many people say, "My goal is to…" but never figure out how or when they will reach their goal. Measuring goals is like keeping track of mileage on a trip. Following the map helps to know how much farther a destination is at any point in time.

Attainable

Is the goal actually attainable? For example, a student may want to be an electrical engineer. Engineers, however, need very strong math and science skills. The goal becomes more attainable with a plan to obtain the necessary aptitudes and skills.

Realistic

For a goal to be realistic, it must also be practical. High goals can be achieved if the person is highly motivated and has a plan to achieve them. Sometimes several shorter, more realistic goals are necessary to reach a final goal. For example, your final goal may be to own a clothing store. Your first goal might be to become a manager in the store where you currently work. After learning how to manage that store, perhaps the next goal could be to obtain a position in the marketing department at the store's corporate headquarters.

Timely

Setting a time for achieving a goal is the step most often overlooked. A goal needs an end date for progress to stay on track. For example, you may have a goal to find a summer job. If you do not set a firm date for starting the job search, summer might come without you applying for a job. However, if you decide to apply to three businesses every week—with the goal of having a job by May 15—you now have an end date. This helps you remain motivated to reach your goal on time.

Why a Career in Marketing?

The better question might be why not a career in marketing? There are many marketing careers that fit different interests, skills, and abilities. Good at math? Consider a career as a market researcher. Love art? Consider a career in advertising or graphic

Marketing Ethics

Business Ethics

Ethics is a set of rules that defines what is wrong and right. Ethics helps people make good decisions in both their personal and professional lives. *Business ethics* is a set of rules that help define appropriate behavior in the business setting. It is important for marketing professionals to set the example of ethical behavior for the business.

Engage

Assign the College and Career Readiness Common Core activities found at the end of the chapter.

Engage

Discuss the variety of marketing careers available. Ask students to identify a career that might match their interests.

design. Enjoy meeting and interacting with new people? A career as a professional sales person may be perfect for you. You could work for profit or nonprofits, small companies, large companies, in large cities and small towns. The opportunities are endless.

Later chapters will explore marketing careers in more depth. As you progress through the text, think about your personal connection with marketing. Will it be a career choice for you?

Franco Volpato/Shutterstock.com

Photography is one important part of marketing promotions, and there are many choices for a career in that field.

Checkpoint 1.2

1. How can the career clusters help you decide which career path to pursue?
2. What are five foundation skills necessary for success in any career?
3. What is the difference between long- and short-term goals?
4. What are the two parts of planning?
5. What are SMART goals?

Build Your Vocabulary

As you progress through this course, develop a personal glossary of marketing terms and add it to your portfolio. This will help you build your vocabulary and prepare you for a career. Write a definition for each of the following terms, and add it to your personal marketing glossary.

marketing professional	goal
job	short-term goal
career	long-term goal
profession	goal setting
career clusters	SMART goals
career pathways	

Chapter Summary

Section 1.1 Marketing

- Marketing consists of dynamic activities that are responsible for identifying, anticipating, and satisfying customer demand to remain profitable. The function of marketing is to meet customers' needs and wants with products they can and will buy.
- Marketing is responsible for a number of important business functions. Marketing helps businesses sell more products to customers to increase profits; creates a positive cycle of economic growth; provides between 25 and 30 percent of all US jobs; and enables a business to build trusting relationships with consumers.
- Learning about marketing will help you, as a consumer, to understand business strategies that influence the products available, the prices you will pay, and other relevant information. Understanding marketing helps you make more informed decisions about the products you purchase.

Section 1.2 Careers in Marketing

- A marketing professional helps determine the marketing needs of a company, develops and implements marketing plans, and focuses on customer satisfaction. He or she is responsible for customer research; deciding how to get products to the customers; pricing, promoting, and selling the products; and managing data and information.
- Planning for your career is important because by setting short- and long-term goals and taking actions to fulfill these goals, you can begin to lay the foundation for your future success.
- There are many marketing careers that fit different interests, skills, and abilities. Think about your personal connection with marketing to determine if it is a good career choice for you.

Review Your Knowledge

1. List three reasons why marketing is important.
2. Define and explain the importance of business.
3. What are the four functions of business?
4. Identify two reasons why it is important to study marketing.
5. Why explore the career clusters?
6. What are the two parts of planning?
7. Why is a career plan important for a high school student?
8. What is goal setting?
9. What are the five marketing career pathways?
10. Identify at least one career for each of the five marketing pathways.

Apply Your Knowledge

1. Identify three ways that marketing has influenced you.
2. What inspired you to take this marketing course?
3. Of the 16 career clusters identified, which one(s) do you think will fit you best for your future career? Why?
4. List three ways that marketing has influenced your local economy.
5. How can taking this course help you market yourself to a future employer or when applying to college?
6. Conduct research on marketing careers that are available in your city. What different opportunities did you find?
7. Select one or two marketing positions that interest you. What are the education requirements for these positions?
8. Outline your current career plan. Where do you see yourself in five years?
9. Do an Internet search for *hottest marketing careers.* What are the top five positions on the list?
10. Identify the job level to which you aspire in your career.

Check Your Marketing IQ

Now that you have finished the chapter, see what you learned about marketing by taking the chapter posttest. If you do not have a smartphone, visit the G-W Learning companion website.

G-W Learning mobile site: www.m.g-wlearning.com
G-W Learning companion website: www.g-wlearning.com

6. The first part is setting a goal and the second part is developing activities that will lead you to achieve your goal.
7. Answers may vary but may include helping to motivate a person, provides a direction, helps to set a plan, and provides a vision of where you want to go.
8. Goal setting is the process of deciding what you want to achieve.
9. Marketing Communications, Marketing Management, Marketing Research, Merchandising, and Professional Selling
10. Answers will vary. but should include at least one career from each marketing career pathway.

Apply Your Knowledge Answers
Student answers will vary for questions 1–10.

Evaluate

Evaluate the students' understanding and knowledge. Assign the Chapter 1 posttest. The test may be accessed by using the QR code or going to the companion website. What questions were students able to answer that they couldn't when they took the pretest?

Common Core

College and Career Readiness

CTE Career Ready Practices. Successful employees also are responsible citizens. Exceeding expectations is a way to be successful at school and in your career. Make a list of five things that you expect of yourself on a daily basis, such as being on time, completing tasks as assigned, or being courteous. For each of the things you expect from yourself, think about and then record what you could do to exceed those expectations. What effect do you think exceeding your expectations has on your success?

Reading. Active reading involves concentration. Go to an online job search site. Search for a marketing position. Choose two job postings and read each posting carefully. Create a Venn diagram that shows the unique qualifications for each job and the common qualifications.

Writing. Interview someone who has a job as a marketing professional. Ask that person what he or she likes best and least about the job as well as several other questions of your own. Write a one-page paper describing what you learned from the interview and whether it affected your desire to have a career in marketing.

Teamwork

Working with a teammate, access the 16 career clusters and make a list of marketing career opportunities. After creating the list, identify the three careers you would each be interested in learning more about. Discuss with your teammate why those careers might interest you.

G-W Learning Mobile Site

Visit the G-W Learning mobile site to complete the chapter pretest and posttest and to practice vocabulary using e-flash cards. If you do not have a smartphone, visit the G-W Learning companion website to access these features.

G-W Learning mobile site: www.m.g-wlearning.com
G-W Learning companion website: www.g-wlearning.com

G-W Mobile

Marketing Plan

In this text, students will have an opportunity to write a complete marketing plan. This is a project-based activity that appears at the end of each unit. The marketing plan will be written based on a business plan. If you opt to assign this activity to your students, you will need to prepare in advance and locate a business plan for them to use.

There are several options for locating a business plan.
1. Sample business plans are readily available on the Internet. The website www.bplan.com has a multitude of business plans

from which to select. You may preselect a business or assign students to visit the site and select a business that is of interest to them.
2. You may choose to require students to either work with a local business or publicly traded company. Students would need to be able to obtain a copy of the company's business plan.
It will be necessary to impress on students the importance of researching and selecting a company that works for them. It will be challenging if they select a company, start a marketing plan, then realize it doesn't work.

2 Marketing Basics

| Section 2.1 | Importance of Marketing |
| Section 2.2 | Marketing Concept |

"I wake up every morning and think to myself, 'how far can I push the company forward in the next 24 hours?'"

— Leah Busque, founder of TaskRabbit

College and Career Readiness

Reading Prep
Before reading this chapter, go to the end of the chapter and read the summary. The chapter summary highlights important information that was presented in the chapter. Did this help you prepare to understand the content?

Check Your Marketing IQ

Before you begin the chapter, see what you already know about marketing by taking the chapter pretest. If you do not have a smartphone, visit the G-W Learning companion website.
G-W Learning mobile site: www.m.g-wlearning.com
G-W Learning companion website: www.g-wlearning.com

G-W Mobile

Explore
Assign the College and Career Readiness Reading Prep activity before students read the chapter. Reading Prep activities give students opportunity to apply the Common Core State Standards.

Engage
Assign the Chapter 2 pretest.

◇DECA Emerging Leaders

Business Administration Core

Career Cluster: Marketing
Instructional Area: Emotional Intelligence

Performance Indicators

- Demonstrate responsible behavior.
- Demonstrate honesty and integrity.
- Demonstrate ethical work habits.
- Describe legal issues affecting businesses.

Purpose

Designed for DECA members, this activity helps individuals to understand opportunities available through DECA in marketing, finance, hospitality, and management.

DECA's Comprehensive Learning Program consists of all DECA activities by category.

- **College and Business Partnerships** provide scholarships, classroom presentations and career guidance, internships, work experience, and community service activities.
- **Competitive Events Program** provides authentic situations relating to current business practices.
- ***DECA Direct* Magazine** is a full-color international publication featuring articles on career development in leadership; community service; and professionalism.
- **Educational Conferences** provide targeted, highly focused learning experiences for members and advisors while connecting with corporate professionals.
- **Educational Partners** provide learning opportunities for members and professional development in industry content for DECA advisors.
- **Global Entrepreneurship Week (GEW)** engages millions of young people around the world each November to embrace innovation, imagination, and creativity.
- **School-Based Enterprises** reinforce and enhance career preparation.
- **Webcasts** provide short video segments filmed at DECA's conferences to further engage members.

Procedure

1. DECA members should become familiar with the organization and its diverse learning activities. Use the following activities to learn about DECA, identify membership benefits, and apply DECA's connection to college and career preparation. One way to learn about business culture is to become familiar with the company.
2. The information will be presented to you through the navigation of the DECA website. Visit the DECA website at www.deca.org to become familiar with the activities and opportunities available to you as a student and DECA member. Select the tab that says *Partners.* DECA has more than 60 business partners that support DECA's guiding principles. Business partners include corporations, foundations and associations that provide classroom presentations and career guidance, community service activities, internships and work experience, and scholarships.

Critical Thinking

1. Select three companies you wish to learn about based on your career goals.
2. For the companies you select, click on the website link and research the following: core values, corporate and social responsibilities, social policies, and history.
3. Record the information you discovered. Keep the information for use as you make college and career decisions.
4. What conclusions can you draw about the companies as it relates to their ethical behavior and social responsibility?
5. Find at least two classmates who researched the same DECA college and business partners. Compare your findings.

Visit www.deca.org for more information.

Section 2.1 Importance of Marketing

Objectives

After completing this section, you will be able to
- **explain** why marketing is dynamic.
- **state** how marketing is focused.
- **identify** and describe the four Ps of marketing.
- **list** the steps necessary for creating a successful marketing mix.

Key Terms

dynamic
customer
target market
purchase incentive
four Ps of marketing
product
good

service
idea
price
place
promotion
public relations
marketing mix

Web Connect

Do an Internet search on how marketing has changed since 2000. List three of the major shifts that have happened since the turn of this century. What was the largest influencer that changed the direction of marketing products?

Critical Thinking

Look for two of your favorite marketing messages in print. Bring them into class and discuss why you like them.

Marketing Is Dynamic

We live in a dynamic, fast-paced, ever-changing world. Products are being bought and sold around the world at a record pace. For example, a business in Dubai may be placing an order for lightbulbs from a company in Michigan. That company in Michigan may have had the lightbulbs produced in Tennessee and will have them drop shipped directly to Dubai. In the not-too-distant past, the Dubai company would have been more likely to buy the lightbulbs from a nearby supplier than one halfway around the world. With the advent of the Internet and other technologies, companies can now shop for best prices and companies around the world, regardless of their locations.

violetkaipa/Shutterstock.com

Technology has made marketing easier and able to fulfill needs faster than ever before.

Explore

Provide an opportunity for students to explore by assigning a hands-on activity. Review the vocabulary terms at the beginning of the section. Where have students encountered these terms before? Help students make educated guesses about the meanings of the terms with which they are least familiar.

Resource

Use the Chapter 2 presentation on the optional Instructor's Presentations for PowerPoint® CD as an outline for presenting the chapter.

Teens are a very important target market for many businesses.

MANDY GODBEHEAR/Shutterstock.com

How did the company in Dubai find the company in Michigan selling lightbulbs for a good price? Through the company's marketing efforts. Marketing is the *dynamic force* that helps drive business around the world.

What makes marketing dynamic? The word **dynamic** describes something that is constantly changing. The needs and wants of customers are *constantly changing*. The goal of marketing is to meet customers' needs and wants with products they will buy. Therefore, marketing must be *dynamic* to meet those needs and wants.

Marketing Is Focused

Marketing is focused on the customer. A **customer** is an individual or group who buys products. A customer can be an individual, a business, a nonprofit organization, or a governmental agency. Customers may purchase goods and services for their own use, which also makes them consumers. Customers, however, also purchase on behalf of others. For example, retail businesses generally sell to consumers. Other types of businesses, such as manufacturing and distribution companies, generally sell to other businesses known as their customers or clients.

Target the Customer

Marketing professionals must first know and understand their current and potential customers in order to meet the unique needs and wants of those people. In the past, when there were fewer products and limited services, most products were advertised to everyone. Times have changed dramatically, however, and the choices of products and services are often overwhelming. How can marketers find the people who want and need their particular products?

As the old saying goes, "If you try to sell to everyone, you end up selling to no one." If you think about it, that saying makes sense. You and your classmates are about the same age, attend the same school, live in the same area, and yet have very different interests and needs. Some enjoy sports, others music. Some may like to shop, while others prefer

Explain

Discuss the term *dynamic* with the class. Share some examples of how marketing constantly changes to meet people's needs and wants.

to save. One product no longer appeals to everyone. Only the smaller group of classmates with similar needs and wants will be interested in the same products.

The smaller group is a target market. A **target market** is the specific group of customers whose needs a company will focus on satisfying. There are many kinds of target markets. Think of the potential customers for clothing. There are many groups of customers with different clothing needs. For example, teens need different kinds of clothing from business people working in offices. Babies need different clothing from adults.

Build Relationships

Everyone lives in a world of *now*. Right now, customers have access to more information in one day than the generation before them had in one week. Instant information and the ability to shop the world means that companies must focus on building relationships to get and keep customers.

Marketing is based on the relationship between the buyer and the seller. A long-term relationship leads to customers who are more satisfied and loyal to the business. Research has shown that it is less costly to keep a current customer than to get a new one. Developing and maintaining relationships with customers is not only cost efficient, it is good business practice.

Some marketers use purchase incentives as a way to attract customers to the business. **Purchase incentives** are items that help persuade a customer to make a purchase, such as rewarding loyal customers with discounts or free products. Programs that offer such rewards include airlines' frequent flier programs. Many bookstores, coffee shops, and sandwich cafes also offer free products after a certain number are purchased. Companies might send birthday

greetings and notices of sales of items that are of special interest to each customer. For example, Amazon customers can sign up for personalized recommendations based on their interests and preferences. Through these programs, the marketers hope to establish long-term customer relationships and loyalty.

AMA Tips

The American Marketing Association was started in 1937 when the National Association of Marketing Teachers and the American Marketing Society merged. Currently, the AMA has both professional business chapters and college chapters throughout the United States.
www.marketingpower.com

Marketing Is the Four Ps

Many people think of marketing as merely advertising. Marketing is much more, however. It includes product, price, place, and promotion—also called the **four Ps of marketing,** as shown in Figure 2-1. When marketing meets the customers' needs and wants in these areas, businesses are generally more successful. Later chapters will focus on each of the four Ps in more detail.

Product

A **product** is anything that can be bought or sold. Product may be the most important of the four Ps because without it, there are no sales. Price, place, and promotion relate directly to the product.

Products include goods, services, and ideas. A **good** is a physical item that can be touched. Examples of goods include jeans, food items, and cell phones. A **service** is an action that is done for you, usually for a fee. Examples of services include a haircut,

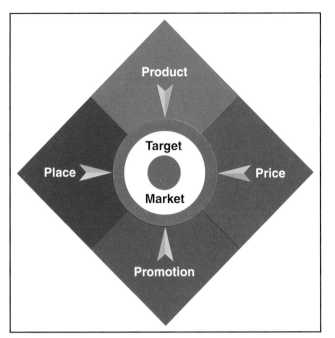

Figure 2-1 The four Ps of marketing should fulfill the needs and wants of target-market customers.

concert, and medical care. An **idea** is a concept, cause, issue, image, or philosophy that can be marketed. Examples of ideas include *contribute to this charity, buckle up for safety,* or *vote for this candidate.* Image has

become a very important product. Marketers sell the image of goods and services, the business itself, and people.

You already know what a person is, but do you know why people could be considered a product? Think about a movie star, a band, or a politician. Marketing professionals not only market the *ideas* and *images* of these people, but they may also need to market the person or the group in which he or she belongs. A politician might be marketed as family oriented or interested in the environment. A movie star might be marketed as interested in charities or as an advocate for the poor. Image has become a very important part of selling a product. Marketers sell the image of goods and services, the business, and people.

Price

Price is the amount of money requested or exchanged for a product. Marketers can set prices at any level. However, if the price is too high, customers might not buy the product. If the price is too low, the business might not take in enough money to cover expenses and make a profit. Setting the *best price* is important for both business success and customer satisfaction.

Case in Point

Trader Joe's

When was the last time a company wowed you? If your answer is never, what would it take to really impress you? For one Trader Joe's customer, it was customer service that went far above and beyond expectations. During one holiday season, an elderly man was snowbound in Pennsylvania for several days. Because he could not get to the store, his daughter was concerned that he would not have enough food. She called multiple local stores located near her father and received the same answer: "Sorry, we do not deliver." Then she called Trader Joe's. Trader Joe's does not deliver, either. However, after hearing her story, the employee who answered the phone took the order, made some additional suggestions for food items, and delivered the food—at no cost. Thirty minutes later, the food was at her father's home, and they were all able to enjoy the holidays without worry. By performing that one small customer service, Trader Joe's now has the entire family as customers for life. The company enhanced its brand and image and earned positive public relations coverage that money simply cannot buy.

Explain

Discuss companies that have developed loyalty programs such as airlines, banks, and restaurants. Explain why this may be an important part of the marketing plan for a company. Ask students if they think loyalty programs help to increase sales.

Explain

Write the four Ps on the board or project onto a screen. Ask students to provide examples of each P for a product they have recently purchased or one that is sold at the business where they work.

Think about the last time you were shopping. Were there things that you did not purchase because of the price? Were there items you did purchase because of the price?

Place

In marketing, **place** refers to the activities involved in getting a product or service to the end users, as illustrated in Figure 2-2. Place is also known as *distribution.* Physical distribution activities include shipping, order processing, inventory warehousing or storage, and stocking of goods.

Place decisions involve determining when, where, and how products get to customers. Place includes decisions about where to locate manufacturing plants, warehouses, and stores. It also involves making decisions about whether to have a physical location or an Internet location. Marketers try to make products available to customers at convenient times and places.

For example, originally, gas stations sold only gas. Then the marketers of milk

realized that it would be very convenient for customers needing milk to buy it when they buy gas. These marketers partnered with gas stations to also sell milk. The result was more convenience for customers and more sales of milk. Today most gas stations are also convenience stores.

The objective of place is to deliver exactly what the end user wants—at the right time, in the right place, and at the right price. Good decisions about place help a business run smoothly. When poor place decisions are made, major problems can result. Customers get upset because products are not available when they want them. Customers might express their dissatisfaction by shopping at a competitor's store. Continued customer loss might eventually lead to financial problems for the business. For example, suppose you went to a shoe store, but they were out of the specific pair of shoes that you wanted to buy. This is an example of a poor place decision because the store did not have the product when you wanted to buy it. As a result, you

Figure 2-2 The factors that influence place are also known as *distribution.*

might go to a competing shoe store. If your experience at the competitor's store is satisfying, you may never return to the first store.

Promotion

Promotion is the process of communicating with potential customers in an effort to influence their buying behavior. It includes telling people about the price and the place where it is offered. If customers do not know that a product exists, they cannot buy it. If customers do not know where to find a product, they will not be able to buy it.

Promotion is the most visible part of marketing. These activities include personal selling, advertising, sales promotions, and public relations. For example, a salesperson delivers promotional messages when he or she helps a customer. Advertising delivers paid promotional messages on TV, radio, mobile apps, the Internet, video games, and through many other formats. Sales promotion may include store displays, free samples, and contests.

Another type of promotion is public relations, or the activities that promote goodwill between the company and the public. Public relations is also called *PR* or *publicity.* It cannot be bought and usually happens when a media outlet covers an interesting story about something good a company is doing. For example, the marketer may send out a press release about the local breast-cancer walk or collecting items for earthquake victims the company sponsored.

astudio/Shutterstock.com

Promoting the fact that a product is natural or organic is a useful marketing message and a big selling point for many consumers.

Marketing Is the Marketing Mix

Marketers have hundreds of choices for the four Ps. For each product that a company markets, the marketers develop a plan called the marketing mix. The marketing mix is the strategy for using the elements of product, price, place, and promotion. It consists of the decisions made about each of the four Ps for that product. A marketing mix can also be developed for a group of products or an entire business. Figure 2-3 illustrates the marketing mix.

Decisions about each piece of the marketing mix affect each other. For example, the decision to sell a car for a low price to meet the needs of first-time car buyers also affects the product and place decisions. The car will have to be made and shipped as inexpensively as possible so that the price can remain low.

FYI

Goods are tangible. They physically exist and can be touched. Examples include food, clothes, and furniture. A service or idea is intangible. It is not physical and cannot be touched. Examples include car repair, dental services, hair styling, etc.

Figure 2-3 The marketing mix consists of all the decisions made about each of the four Ps.

One marketing mix usually does not meet the needs of all customers. The key to finding a successful marketing mix is
- choosing the right product;
- selling it at the right price;
- making it available at the right place; and
- promoting it in a way that will reach the target customers.

For example, perhaps you want a smartphone. You search the Internet for a sale on smartphones and an ad pops up for a $199 smartphone on sale. You have saved $225 to buy a phone, so this is good price for your budget. You click on the ad, which takes you to a website showing the phone at a store in the nearby mall. When you go to the store, a salesperson helps you find the right phone and buy it. Can you identify the four Ps in this marketing mix?

The phone is the *product*. The Internet ad and store salesperson are the *promotion*. The *price* is $199. The retail store is the *place*. Since, in this example, you bought the phone, that phone's marketers developed the right marketing mix for you. Notice that you, as the *customer*, are not part of the marketing mix. The customer is the target of the marketing mix. The marketing mix decisions are made to satisfy the customer.

Green Marketing

Cause Marketing

Cause marketing is a type of marketing in which a profit and nonprofit organization work together for a common mutual benefit. An example is a corporation that gives its employees a day off to pick up trash for the city to create a cleaner environment. Cause marketing is a great way to show the company's social responsibility.

Evaluate

Assign Checkpoint questions at end of section. Assess student comprehension using the Checkpoint activity as a self-assessment tool.

Elaborate/Extend

As time permits, have students read and discuss the chapter's special features.

College and Career Portfolio

Portfolio Overview

When you apply to a college, for a job, or for a community service position, you may need to tell others about why you are qualified for this position. A *portfolio* is a selection of related materials that you collect and organize. These materials show your qualifications, skills, and talents. For example, a certificate that shows you have completed lifeguard and first-aid training could help you get a lifeguard job at a local pool. An essay you wrote about protecting native plants could show that you are serious about ecofriendly efforts and help you get a volunteer position at a park. A transcript of your school grades could help show that you are qualified for college.

Two types of portfolios are commonly used: print portfolios and electronic portfolios. Electronic portfolios are also called e-portfolios or digital portfolios.

1. Use the Internet to search for *print portfolio* and *e-portfolio*. Read articles about each type of portfolio. In your own words, briefly describe each type.
2. You will be creating a portfolio in this class. Which portfolio type would you prefer to create? Write a paragraph describing the type of portfolio you would prefer to create.

Checkpoint 2.1

1. Why is marketing dynamic?
2. As a marketer, why is it important to know your customers?
3. List the four elements of promotion.
4. What are four product strategy decisions a marketer might make?
5. List the four Ps.

Build Your Vocabulary

As you progress through this course, develop a personal glossary of personal marketing terms and add it to your portfolio. This will help you build your vocabulary and prepare you for a career. Write a definition for each of the following terms, and add it to your personal marketing glossary.

dynamic	service
customer	idea
target market	price
purchase incentive	place
four Ps of marketing	promotion
product	public relations
good	marketing mix

Section 2.2 Marketing Concept

Objectives

After completing this section, you will be able to:
- **explain** the marketing concept in business.
- **describe** the seven functions of marketing and related activities.

Key Terms

marketing concept
customer satisfaction
profit
channel
channel management

marketing-information management (MIM)
market planning
product/service management
selling

Web Connect

Do an Internet search for the *best customer service in the United States*. Review the top-ten list of companies that appear in the search results. What do they do that makes them the best? Is there a common theme with the companies? Write a paragraph about what makes these companies recognized for their customer service.

Critical Thinking

Think about what is important to you when you make a large purchase. Make a list and prioritize your criteria. What is number one?

Marketing Concept

The **marketing concept** is an approach to business that focuses on satisfying customers as the means of achieving profit goals. The three elements of the marketing concept as shown in Figure 2-4 are customer satisfaction, total company approach, and profit.

Customer Satisfaction

Customer satisfaction is the degree to which customers are pleased with a company's goods or services. One of the ways it can be measured is by the number of repeat customers. The marketing concept benefits customers because the business is focused on meeting their needs. Think about a store you like and shop at often. Why do you like it? Would you consider yourself a satisfied

Goodheart-Willcox Publisher

Figure 2-4 The marketing concept focuses on every aspect of the business to keep the customer satisfied because that is the key to long-term profit.

Each person who inter-acts with a customer influences that customer's opinion of the company and its products.

customer? Customers are satisfied when the products and services meet or exceed their expectations.

Total Company Approach

The functions of business were defined in Chapter 1 as *production, finance, marketing,* and *management.* Businesses using the marketing concept integrate the total company in the goal of customer satisfaction. Employees in production, finance, and management must work together as a team to achieve that goal.

Marketing-oriented companies believe that every interaction with a customer should be viewed as a marketing opportunity. This means every person in the business, from the delivery people to the technical support staff, has a goal of satisfying their customers. By sharing information about customers with production, finance, and management departments, marketers help an entire business focus on customer satisfaction goals.

Profit

Profit is the money that a business has left after all the expenses and costs of running the business are paid. How does a business make a profit? Because sales are the basis of business, more sales tend to mean higher profits, as long as the costs of the running the business are reasonable. Businesses using the marketing concept understand that building a strong base of satisfied customers leads to healthy profits. Satisfied customers are repeat customers and repeat customers ensure higher sales. Satisfying customers successfully over the long term benefits businesses.

Functions of Marketing

If the role of marketing is to help a company focus on customers, how is that accomplished? Marketing consists of hundreds of activities. These marketing activities can be organized in many different ways. One way is to organize around the customers (also called the market) and the four Ps: product, price, place, and promotion. Another way is to organize them by the seven functions of marketing, as shown in Figure 2-5.

In a small company, all these functions might be performed by one or two people. In a large corporation, each function might have its own department. The seven functions of marketing are

- Channel management
- Marketing-information management
- Market planning
- Pricing
- Product/Service management
- Promotions
- Selling

Channel Management

The different routes a product takes from the producers to the customers are called channels. The channel management function handles activities involved in getting products through the different routes from the producers to the customers. These may include managing the methods used to transport and store goods, deciding where products are sold, finding sources for products, on-time delivery, and transferring product ownership.

Marketing-Information Management (MIM)

Marketing-information management (MIM) involves gathering and analyzing information about markets, customers,

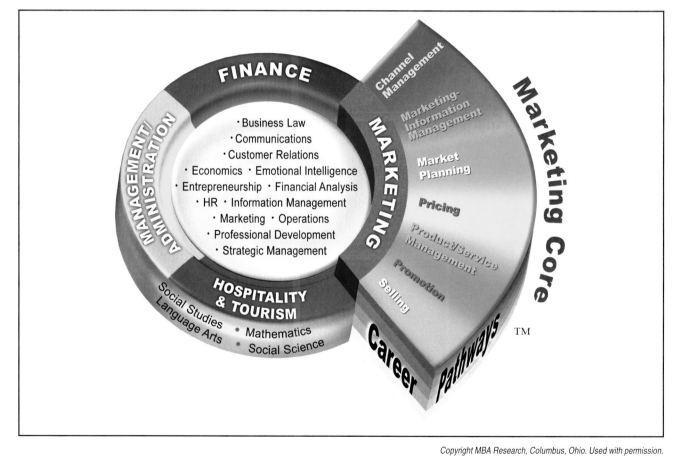

Figure 2-5 Seven Functions of Marketing

Explore

Review the seven functions of marketing. Have students create a graph, chart, or a poster of the functions with the customer in the middle.

Elaborate/Extend

Assign the College and Career Readiness Portfolio activity at the end of the chapter.

Stores always attempt to display merchandise in the most attractive ways to encourage sales.

Adisa/Shutterstock.com

industry trends, new technology, and the competing businesses. It also includes making sure the right people in an organization get the information needed to make good business decisions. MIM is also called *marketing research*. Activities might include developing surveys, analyzing survey results, preparing recommendations, and meeting with customers.

Market Planning

The market planning function is creating an actionable marketing plan designed to achieve business goals. Activities in market planning include identifying the target market, determining appropriate marketing strategies, setting a marketing budget, and using metrics to measure budget effectiveness.

Engage

Assign the College and Career Readiness Common Core activities found at the end of the chapter.

Elaborate/Extend

If students are using the optional *Marketing Dynamics* workbook, assign activities to engage active learning.

Pricing

Pricing directly affects the bottom line of any business. The pricing function handles all activities involved in setting acceptable prices for products. This includes researching and analyzing pricing of competitors. It also involves using financial information to set prices that cover costs and include a reasonable profit, as well as adjust prices when conditions change.

Product/Service Management

The **product/service management** function determines which products a business should offer to meet customer needs. Activities can include developing a new product or service or improving a current one. In retail, product/service management includes deciding which products to carry or services to offer in a store. Other decisions are about which brands, quantities, colors, sizes, features, or options to offer.

Promotions

Promotions refer to the nonpersonal communications with customers designed to influence purchasing. Activities for promotions include creating and running advertising, designing in-store displays and promotions, or monitoring sales incentives. It may also include public relations efforts, such as sending press releases or running a press conference.

Selling

The **selling** function includes all personal communications with customers. Selling activities include helping customers in a store, making sales presentations or product demonstrations, and providing any form of customer service.

Checkpoint 2.2

1. Explain the importance of customer satisfaction.
2. List the four functions of business.
3. List the seven functions of marketing.
4. What is another term for marketing-information management?
5. Give examples of selling activities.

Build Your Vocabulary

As you progress through this course, develop a personal glossary of personal marketing terms and add it to your portfolio. This will help you build your vocabulary and prepare you for a career. Write a definition for each of the following terms, and add it to your personal marketing glossary.

marketing concept
customer satisfaction
profit
channel
channel management

marketing-information management (MIM)
market planning
product/service management
selling

Chapter Summary

Section 2.1 Importance of Marketing

- Marketing is dynamic because the needs and wants of customers are constantly changing, and marketing helps businesses to meet those needs and wants.
- Marketing is focused on the customer. It is necessary for marketers to know and understand current and potential customers in order to meet their needs and wants.
- The four Ps of marketing are product (anything that is bought or sold), price (the amount of money requested in exchange for a product), place (the activities involved in getting a product to the end user), and promotion (the process of communicating with potential customers to influence their buying behavior).
- The steps necessary for creating a successful marketing mix are choosing the right product; selling the product at the right price; making the product available in the right place; and promoting the product in a way that will reach the target customers.

Section 2.2 Marketing Concept

- The marketing concept is an approach to business that focuses on satisfying customers to achieve profit goals. The three basic elements in this concept are: customer satisfaction, which is the degree to which a customer is pleased with products; total company approach, which is the idea that every person within the company has the goal of satisfying the customers; and profit, or the money a company has left after paying all expenses.
- The seven functions of marketing are: channel management; marketing-information management; market planning; pricing; product/service management; promotion; and selling.

Review Your Knowledge

1. Why is marketing dynamic?
2. Why is it important to target the market?
3. Describe the difference between a good and a service.
4. Why is it important to build relationships with customers?
5. How can the ideas or image of a person be marketed?
6. What is a total company approach?
7. What is the difference between how a large and a small company might handle the marketing functions?
8. What are two ways to organize marketing activities?
9. Give an example of each marketing function.
10. Name one way that channel management supports the marketing function.

Evaluate

Assign end-of-chapter activities.

Review Your Knowledge Answers

1. Marketing is dynamic because customer's needs and wants are constantly changing.

2. If you try to sell to everyone, you will sell to no one. It is important to know who your customer is.

3. A good is a tangible item that can be taken with you and a service is an intangible item, something that is done for you.

4. Long-term relationships lead to customers who are more satisfied and loyal. Customers who trust a business will be repeat customers.

5. A politician might be marketed as family oriented or interested in the environment. A movie star might be marketed as interested in charities or as an advocate for the poor. Image has become a very important part of selling a product. Marketers sell the image of goods and services, the business, and people.

6. A total company approach is having production, finance, management, and marketing work together as a team to focus on earning profit by satisfying customer needs and wants.

Apply Your Knowledge

1. Imagine yourself as a marketing manager for a sports equipment company. How would you define marketing for your business?
2. As a marketing manager, how would you explain to the company management team why you think marketing is dynamic?
3. What are some ways you would build relationships with customers?
4. Divide a piece of paper into three columns. In the first column, make a list of four or five of your friends. In the second column, write down where you and your friends most like to shop. In the third column, write down why you believe those are your favorite places. What makes the stores you listed different from other stores selling similar products?
5. Identify a nonprofit organization in your area or one with which you are familiar. For whom do you think the nonprofit targets to secure donations or volunteer work? Why do you think it targets that group of people?
6. Explain how "think global, act local" would apply to your job as a marketing manager.
7. Imagine yourself as a marketing manager. How would you make the customer the focus of your marketing plans?
8. How can you use the marketing concept to promote your school store or CTSO?
9. Choose a local company that you know well. Describe how the marketing functions of the company support the marketing concept.
10. Create a statement that reflects how you would focus on customer satisfaction.

Check Your Marketing IQ

Now that you have finished the chapter, see what you learned about marketing by taking the chapter posttest. If you do not have a smartphone, visit the G-W Learning companion website.

G-W Learning mobile site: www.m.g-wlearning.com
G-W Learning companion website: www.g-wlearning.com

7. In a small company, the owner might do all the functions. In a large company, there may be a different department for each function.

8. Organize around the customer and the four Ps or by the seven functions of marketing.

9. Examples of marketing functions may vary, but should include forms of the following: shipping products (channel management); conducting research (marketing-information management); identifying your target market (market planning); choosing the products to sell (product/service management); setting the price of a laptop computer at $499 (pricing); advertising for game apps (promotion); and having a salesperson available to sell cars (selling).

10. Answer: Channel management supports the marketing function by making products available at convenient locations.

Apply Your Knowledge Answers

Student answers will vary for questions 1–10.

Evaluate

Evaluate the students' understanding and knowledge. Assign the Chapter 2 posttest. The test may be accessed by using the QR code or going to the companion website. What questions were students able to answer that they couldn't when they took the pretest?

Common Core

College and Career Readiness

CTE Career Ready Practices. It is important for a marketing manager to apply both technical and academic skills in the workplace. Conduct an online search for *desirable workplace skills.* Then conduct another search for *top academic skills.* Create a Venn diagram showing the overlap between the two lists.

Listening. Active listening requires the listener to fully participate while processing what others are saying. Practice active listening skills while listening to a broadcast business report on the radio, on television, or podcast. Pick a single story about marketing for a business and create a report in which you analyze the following aspects of the business story: the speaker's audience, point of view, reasoning, stance, word choice, tone, points of emphasis, and organization.

Writing. Good writing skills require clear presentation of logical thoughts. Conduct a short research project to learn about the history of marketing. Use multiple authoritative print and digital sources. Where did the idea of marketing originate? Write several paragraphs about your findings to demonstrate your understanding of marketing.

Teamwork

Working with a teammate, select a business for which you would like to be employed as a marketing team member. Start a blog or write a one-page paper about your business. Describe the company, including the products. Explain how the company will utilize the marketing concept, the four Ps, and the seven marketing functions.

G-W Learning Mobile Site

Visit the G-W Learning mobile site to complete the chapter pretest and posttest and to practice vocabulary using e-flash cards. If you do not have a smartphone, visit the G-W Learning companion website to access these features.

G-W Learning mobile site: www.m.g-wlearning.com

G-W Learning companion website: www.g-wlearning.com

Marketing Plan

In this text, students will have an opportunity to write a complete marketing plan. This is a project-based activity that appears at the end of each unit and was described in the Chapter 1 teacher notes.

Writing a marketing plan is a valuable, real-world experience. Marketing professionals are expected to be able to write a marketing plan. For those students who pursue a college marketing course of study, writing a marketing plan will be a requirement. The writing experience in this text will provide first-hand experience.

Refer to the teaching notes in Chapter 1 to prepare for this end-of-unit activity. Begin the selection process for business plans so that you have time to review appropriate selections for your students. You may decide that this activity is an individual assignment. Or, you may prefer to divide the class into several teams and make it a team project.

CHAPTER

3

Business Basics

Section 3.1   Business Defined
Section 3.2   Importance of Business

"Someone's sitting in the shade today because someone planted a tree a long time ago."

—Warren Buffet, primary shareholder, chairman, and CEO of Berkshire Hathaway

Reading Prep
In preparation for reading the chapter, think about what makes a marketing professional successful. How would you measure success? As you read, consider how the information in this chapter supports or contradicts your answers to these questions.

College and Career Readiness

Check Your Marketing IQ

Before you begin the chapter, see what you already know about marketing by taking the chapter pretest. If you do not have a smartphone, visit the G-W Learning companion website.
G-W Learning mobile site: www.m.g-wlearning.com
G-W Learning companion website: www.g-wlearning.com

G-W Mobile

Explore

Assign the College and Career Readiness Reading Prep activity before students read the chapter. Reading Prep activities give students opportunity to apply the Common Core State Standards.

Engage

Assign the Chapter 3 pretest.

◇DECA Emerging Leaders

College and Career Connection

Career Cluster: Business Administration Core
Instructional Area: Financial Analysis

Performance Indicator

- Explain types of business ownership.

Purpose

Designed for DECA members, this activity enables student members to better understand opportunities available through DECA in marketing, finance, hospitality, and management.

DECA's Comprehensive Learning Program consists of all DECA activities by category.

- **College and Business Partnerships** provide scholarships, classroom presentations and career guidance, internships, work experience, and community service activities.
- **Competitive Events Program** provides authentic situations relating to current business practices.
- *DECA Direct* **Magazine** is a full-color international publication featuring articles on career development in leadership; community service; and professionalism.
- **Educational Conferences** provide targeted, highly focused learning experiences for members and advisors while connecting with corporate professionals.
- **Educational Partners** provide learning opportunities for members and professional development in industry content for DECA advisors.
- **Global Entrepreneurship Week (GEW)** engages millions of young people around the world each November to embrace innovation, imagination, and creativity.
- **School-Based Enterprises** reinforce and enhance career preparation.
- **Webcasts** provide short video segments filmed at DECA's conferences to further engage members.

Procedure

1. DECA members should become familiar with the organization and its diverse learning activities. Use the following activities to learn about DECA, identify membership benefits and apply DECA's connection to college and career preparation.
2. The information will be presented to you through the navigation of the DECA website. Visit the DECA website at www.deca.org to become familiar with the activities and opportunities available to you as a student and DECA member. Select the tab that says *Events.* Then select *Competitive Events, High School.*
3. Read the Purpose, Procedure, and Knowledge and Skills Assessed sections in the competitive event guidelines for the Business Management and Entrepreneurship Events.

Critical Thinking

1. List the type of business ownership that relates to each event. Explain why the type of business ownership is appropriate for the event.
2. Which events allow team participants? Which events are for an individual participant? What do team participants and individual participant mean?
3. Which functions of business appear to be addressed in each event?
4. Which of the Business Management and Entrepreneurship Events do you find interesting? How will the event support your career goals?
5. Share with your class how participating in a DECA competitive event enhances your college and career preparation.

Visit www.deca.org for more information.

Section 3.1 Business Defined

Objectives

After completing this section, you will be able to
- **describe** the purpose of business.
- **list** several functions of businesses.
- **compare and contrast** three types of business ownership.

Key Terms

wages	finance
barter	management
money	liability
medium of exchange	sole proprietorship
unit of value	partnership
store of value	corporation
time value of money	contract
production	nonprofit organization

Web Connect

Do an Internet search for *basic business concepts*. Make notes on the concepts that you believe are important to marketing.

Critical Thinking

How does business fulfill the marketing concept of satisfying the customer? List three ways in which you think this happens.

What Is Business?

In order to understand marketing, you first need to understand the basic concepts of business. You learned in Chapter 1 that *business* is the term for all of the activities involved in developing and exchanging products and services. Business includes manufacturing, construction, mining, wholesaling, retailing, and farming.

Business provides most of the goods and services that you use every day. Businesses also employ people in exchange for supplying wages. **Wages** are the money earned for working that people use to buy what they need.

Explore

Provide an opportunity for students to explore by assigning a hands-on activity. Review the vocabulary terms at the beginning of the section. Where have students encountered these terms before? Help students make educated guesses about the meanings of the terms with which they are least familiar.

Money

In ancient times, people exchanged goods for other goods. The exchange of one good or service for another good or service is called **barter.** Barter can be very difficult, time-consuming, and sometimes unsuccessful. To solve problems with bartering, money was created. **Money** is anything of value that is accepted in return for goods or services. Coin or paper money represents different values. Another word for money is *currency*.

Money makes it easier to do business and exchange goods and services. As you learned earlier, *function* is a general word for a category of activities. In our economy, money serves three functions: medium of exchange, unit of value, and store of value, as shown in Figure 3-1.

Explore

Distribute a variety of magazines and newspapers to students. Ask students to cut out advertisements and make a collage of different goods and services.

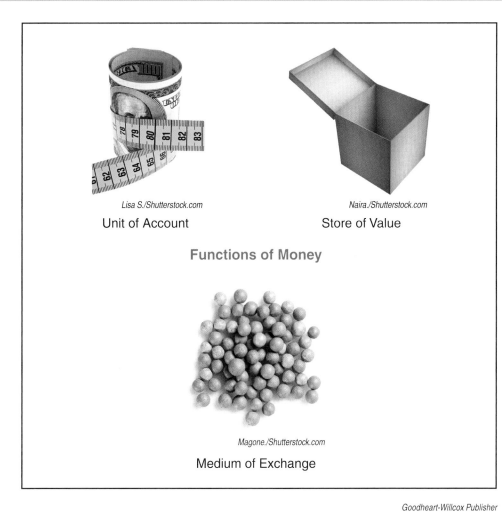

Lisa S./Shutterstock.com
Unit of Account

Naira./Shutterstock.com
Store of Value

Functions of Money

Magone./Shutterstock.com
Medium of Exchange

Goodheart-Willcox Publisher

Figure 3-1 Money serves three functions in our economy.

Medium of Exchange

Medium of exchange means that money is used in exchange for goods and services. Money is a convenient tool for trading. It is the basis of our economy.

Unit of Value

Unit of value means that money is a common measure of what something is worth or what something costs. Each country has its own unit of value, or currency. In the United States, everyone knows what a dollar is and how much it is worth. Using money as a unit of value is an easy way to place a price on an item or service.

Store of Value

Money is also a **store of value,** meaning in can be saved, or stored, and used at a later date. An item that holds its value over a period of time is said to have a good store of value. Currency is fairly stable. However, it can lose some of its purchasing power.

Time Value

The idea that money is worth more today than would be in the future is called the **time value of money.** Understanding the time value of money can help you manage your own money. You can decide if you want

Explore

Discuss with students the difference between *barter* and *money.*

Engage

Ask students to explain the difference between *unit of value* and *store of value.*

Resource

Use the Chapter 3 presentation on the optional Instructor's Presentations for PowerPoint® CD as an outline for presenting the chapter.

Exploring Careers

Product Management

Retail stores, such as department stores, boutiques, and electronics super-stores offer a large variety of products and usually several different brands of each product. Who decides which products the store will carry? A product manager investigates new products, analyzes buying trends, and for current products, reviews sales records to determine how profitable each product is likely to be. Based on this information, the product manager buys products for resale to the store's customers. Typical job titles for a product manager include *buyer, merchandiser, merchandise manager, purchasing manager,* and *procurement specialist.*

Some examples of tasks that product managers perform include:

- use spreadsheet software to organize, locate, and analyze sales figures on products in inventory;
- meet with sales personnel to get information about customers wants and needs;
- analyze sales records and trends to determine how much of each product to purchase;
- negotiate prices and discounts in order to purchase the selected products; and
- set markups and selling prices for the products.

Product managers must be able to analyze product performance based on financial figures. They also need good negotiation skills in order to get the best prices and terms for the products they buy. Most jobs in this field require an associate degree or equivalent training in a vocational school, but on-the-job training may be substituted for these. For more information, access the *Occupational Outlook Handbook* online.

---

to buy something now or save your money. There are trade-offs between spending and saving.

For example, suppose you want to go on a spring break vacation. The cost for the plane ticket and hotel is $1,000. You decide not to spend that money on a trip because you think it will be worth more in the future if you invest it instead. After a year, your investment increases to $1,055. During the same time, however, the cost of that same spring break vacation has risen to $1,100. You still want to take a spring break vacation, but now it costs more than it did a year ago. Did you make the right decision based on the time value of money and the value you placed on the trip?

Profit

The main goal of most businesses is to make a profit. In Chapter 2, you learned that the marketing concept is an approach to

business that says the way to make a profit is to focus on customer satisfaction. Satisfied customers buy more. Therefore, most businesses make a profit by satisfying the needs and wants of their customers. Research helps marketers learn what customers want or need and how much they are willing to pay. Businesses then develop, produce, distribute, advertise, and sell their products. Marketing is key in every aspect of business.

Functions of Business

Businesses carry out numerous functions. All business functions must work together if a business is to be successful. All the pieces must come together like a puzzle, as shown in Figure 3-2. These functions are production, finance, marketing, and management, as discussed in Chapter 2.

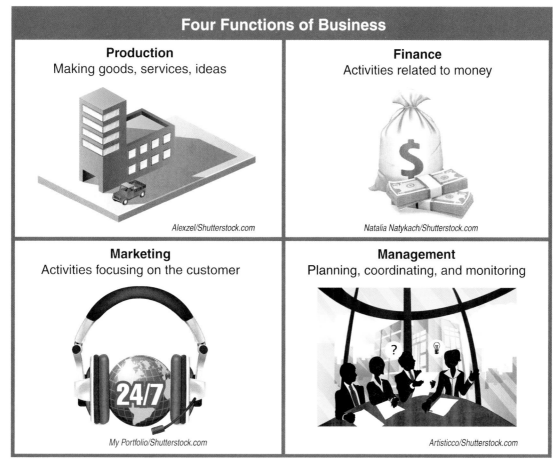

Goodheart-Willcox Publisher

Figure 3-2 The four functions of business work together to make a successful, profitable company.

Production

Production is any activity related to making a product (good, service, or idea). Have you ever seen production at a large manufacturing plant? When you think of production, you often think of long assembly lines with people putting together cars, washing machines, or TVs.

Production also includes farming, mining, and construction. The work done at a TV station to prepare a program for broadcast is called *broadcast production*. In service industries, production is often the service itself, for example, cutting and styling hair. In farming, production is growing the crops.

Finance

Businesses handle a large amount of money. The finance function of business includes all activities involving money. Businesses handle the money that customers pay them. Businesses pay for raw materials and business services. Businesses pay wages and send income taxes to the government. Sometimes businesses borrow money from financial institutions like banks.

An important task of the finance function is planning. The people who work in finance are often responsible for developing budgets. A *budget* is a spending plan for a fixed period of time. A budget helps the business make

All businesses must stay within their budgets when making purchases.

Morgan Lane Photography/Shutterstock.com

sure it has enough money to cover expenses. It also helps make sure that the business is handling its money wisely and making a profit. If a business decides to take a loan, the financing function plans for the repayment of the loan.

Accounting is one part of finance. Accounting keeps track of all money that enters or leaves the business. It pays bills and receives payments.

Marketing

Marketing is the part of a business that focuses on the customer. Marketers are responsible for helping the entire business focus on the needs and wants of customers. The marketing function includes learning about customers, developing products, and pricing them for sale. Marketing then promotes

and sells the products to those customers. Marketing also follows up to find out how satisfied customers are with their products.

Management

Management is the process of controlling and making decisions about a business. It includes all of the activities required to plan, coordinate, and monitor a business. The managers look at the big picture and lead workers to make changes to make the business better. A manager plans, implements plans, and controls. Managers also hire, train, and supervise employees.

FYI

In business, *control* means to monitor and evaluate results.

Forms of Business Ownership

In 2009, the US Census Bureau recorded 27.5 million businesses in the United States. Over six million of those businesses have employees. There are three main forms of business ownership: sole proprietorship, partnership, and corporation. As a marketing professional, you may find yourself working for one of these business types.

There are advantages and disadvantages to each form of ownership, as shown in Figure 3-3. One of the main differences among the ownership forms is the amount of liability the owners have. Liability means legal responsibility. In business, owners may or may not be held personally liable for the losses a business may have.

Sole Proprietorship

A sole proprietorship is a business owned by one person. That person makes all the decisions and gets all the profits from the business. It is the simplest form of business to start and own. According to the US Census Bureau, over 70 percent of all businesses in the United States are sole proprietorships. Sole proprietors have unlimited liability in the business. *Unlimited liability* means they alone are personally responsible for all business losses and other risks.

Partnership

A partnership is the relationship between two or more people who join to create a business. Each partner contributes to the business. They may contribute money, property, labor, or expertise to the business.

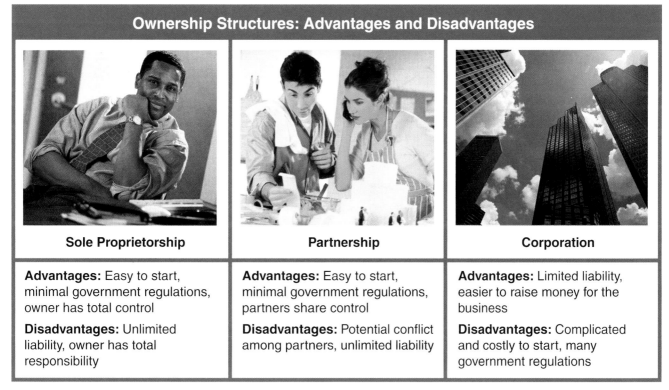

Ownership Structures: Advantages and Disadvantages

Sole Proprietorship	Partnership	Corporation
Advantages: Easy to start, minimal government regulations, owner has total control	**Advantages:** Easy to start, minimal government regulations, partners share control	**Advantages:** Limited liability, easier to raise money for the business
Disadvantages: Unlimited liability, owner has total responsibility	**Disadvantages:** Potential conflict among partners, unlimited liability	**Disadvantages:** Complicated and costly to start, many government regulations

Goodheart-Willcox Publisher

Figure 3-3 Each ownership structure has advantages and disadvantages.

Social Media

Social-Media Marketing (SMM)

Social-media marketing (SMM) is the use of social media as a part of the marketing plan to convince consumers to buy products or services. For SMM to be effective, consistent communication must take place. Traditional marketing efforts, such as print brochures, catalogs, and postcards require time, money, and commitment to create each piece. After the piece is mailed, it is hoped that customers will respond and want more information or to buy the product. There are lapses in time in the communication stream. However, with social-media marketing, regular communications must take place in order for it to be effective. SMM requires human resources to plan, execute, and monitor traffic.

Most partnerships also have unlimited liability. This means that all partners are responsible for any decision made by another partner. Depending on how the partnership agreement is written, the partners are also personally liable for business losses and risks.

Corporation

A corporation is defined by the US Supreme Court as "an artificial being, invisible, intangible, and existing only in contemplation of the law." A corporation is considered to be a legal entity and is, in the eyes of the law, a person. This means it can buy property, earn money, manufacture and distribute products, pay taxes, sue or be sued, and enter into contracts.

A contract is a legally binding agreement. In effect, the law views corporations as people, but with limited rights and privileges. Businesses organized as corporations are responsible for nearly 90 percent of all sales in the United States. A corporation's owners are *not* personally liable for the business risks—because the corporation is the legal entity. There are two categories of corporations: for-profit and nonprofit.

For-Profit

The goal of a for-profit corporation is to make a profit for the owners. Most corporations are for-profit businesses. When the term *corporation* is used alone, it refers to a for-profit corporation. Well-known corporations include companies like Microsoft, Exxon Mobil, and General Electric.

Nonprofit

A nonprofit organization is an entity that exists to serve some public purpose. Nonprofit corporations are also called *nonprofits* or *not-for-profit organizations*. Nonprofits receive special treatment under the law. A nonprofit corporation can make a profit. However, any profit it makes goes to support the nonprofit goal. The goals of a nonprofit corporation usually fall into one of five categories: charity, education, public benefit, mutual benefit, and religion. Examples of nonprofits include the United Way, American Heart Association, and any church or religious organization.

FYI

Partnerships are common in the law, accounting, and medical fields.

Some nonprofits, such as the American Red Cross, help with disaster relief around the world.

Checkpoint 3.1

1. Describe the term *business*.
2. List the three functions of money.
3. Explain the differences between a sole proprietorship, a partnership, and a corporation.
4. What are the guidelines for a nonprofit making a profit?
5. Is a corporation considered a person? Explain.

Build Your Vocabulary

As you progress through this course, develop a personal glossary of personal marketing terms and add it to your portfolio. This will help you build your vocabulary and prepare you for a career. Write a definition for each of the following terms, and add it to your personal marketing glossary.

wages
barter
money
medium of exchange
unit of value
store of value
time value of money
production

finance
management
liability
sole proprietorship
partnership
corporation
contract
nonprofit organization

Checkpoint Answers

1. Answer: Business is the term for all the activities involved in the development and exchange of products. Business is the engine that powers economies around the world.
2. Medium of exchange, unit of value, and store of value.
3. A sole proprietorship is owned by one person, a partnership is owned by two or more people, and a corporation is a legal entity that is considered a person.

4. A nonprofit can make a profit but the money has to go back into running the business.
5. A corporation is considered a legal entity, or person, and can buy property, earn money, manufacture and distribute products, pay taxes, sue or be sued, and enter into contracts.

Build Your Vocabulary Answers

Definitions for these terms can be found in the glossary of this text.

Section 3.2 Importance of Business

Objectives

After completing this section, you will be able to
- **describe** how businesses provide utility.
- **differentiate** between the two different markets for products.
- **explain** the difference between a consumer and a customer.

Key Terms

utility
adding value
form utility
place utility
time utility
information utility
possession utility
consumer market
business market
business-to-consumer (B2C)
business-to-business (B2B)
industry
commercial

Web Connect

On the Internet, research the term *economic utility.* Write a paragraph about utility and its importance in our society.

Critical Thinking

Some terms are often used interchangeably, even when it is not always correct. Before reading this section, write your definition of *consumer market* and *business market.* After you complete the chapter, compare your definitions with the ones in the text and see if they are correct.

Business Provides Utility

One of the major tasks of business is to provide utility. *Utility* means usefulness. In a business context, **utility** defines the characteristics of a product that satisfies human wants and needs. Marketers often refer to the process of adding utility as adding value. **Adding value** means enhancing a feature or service to inspire a customer to purchase. There are five types of utility, as shown in Figure 3-4.

Utility Examples	
Form	Any manufacturing process
Place	Convenience stores
Time	Daily newspaper delivery
Information	Product advertising
Possession	Credit cards

Goodheart-Willcox Publisher

Figure 3-4 In marketing, all five types of utility are needed to ensure customer satisfaction.

Form Utility

Form utility is added when a business changes the form of something to make it more useful. The main job of the production function of business is to add form utility. For example, an auto manufacturer turns steel, plastic, fabric, and glass into an automobile. In a service business, the production of the service itself provides the utility. Marketing influences the creation of product in a business.

Explore

Provide an opportunity for students to explore by assigning a hands-on activity. Review the vocabulary terms at the beginning of the section. Where have students encountered these terms before? Help students make educated guesses about the meanings of the terms with which they are least familiar.

Engage

Use the Teamwork exercise at the end of the chapter to engage students with each other to solve a problem or make a group presentation.

Case in Point

Eataly

Making your business stand out from the competition is important. It is also one of the main roles of marketing. If potential customers do not know why you are different and better, they may take their business elsewhere. Nicola Farinetti at the Eataly in New York City understands that education is important when creating loyal customers. Eataly is a unique business that has a fresh market and 16 Italian eateries and cafés under one roof. The fresh market displays signage informing customers about each product, including its Italian history.

Each of the to-go or eat-in restaurants uses ingredients sold in the fresh market. Customers enjoy sampling different items and learning about what they are eating. Being able to shop for the food that is served in the restaurant is a personal touch customers cannot resist. Eataly also offers cooking classes—in Italian cuisine, of course. And to continue the experience after customers leave, cooking hints and recipes are sent to anyone who signs up to receive them through Twitter, Facebook, e-mails, and newsletters. Eataly is targeting their customers with a message of unique products, services, and information—all in the same place.

Place Utility

Place utility is added when products are available at convenient places. For example, people often need to get cash when they are not near the bank. Financial institutions provide place utility through automated teller machines (ATMs) at convenient places, such as a supermarket or airport. Marketing guides business in adding place utilities.

Time Utility

Time utility is added when products are made available at the times that customers need and want them. For example, banks used to close at 4:00 p.m. and were never open on Saturdays. Many people who needed to do business at the bank were working during the time that banks were open. To provide time utility, most banks now stay open later, are open on Saturday mornings, or offer online banking 24 hours a day. Marketing research helps provide the data to make decisions about time utility.

Information Utility

Information utility is added when marketing provides information about a product to a customer. A major part of information utility is telling the customer about products and where to buy them. Websites provide information utility by describing products and giving purchase opportunities. Advertising and other promotions provide information utility as well. Product information also includes giving customers directions or instructions, such as through owner manuals.

Possession Utility

Possession utility is added when it becomes easier for a customer to acquire a product. Possession utility includes offering various kinds of credit. For example, you need a car to get to work, but you do not have enough money to pay for it. The auto dealer provides possession utility by helping you arrange for a loan. The loan enables you to take possession and use the car while you are still paying for it.

Engage

Ask students what their favorite food is and if having it adds utility for them. Ask them how it adds utility—identify each utility that is added. Discuss with students the concept of utility and how it enhances the marketing of a product. If possible, bring a couple of items into class and have students identify the types of utility for each product. If you have a school-based enterprise, bring in a few items from the business.

Managing finances is becoming more and more convenient thanks to technology innovations marketed to both consumers and businesses.

Buyers

As you learned in Chapter 2, people who buy products from a business are called *customers* or *clients*. People in a business' target market who might buy a product are its potential customers. There are two types of markets based on the type of buyers: the consumer market and the business market. The **consumer market** consists of customers who buy products for their own use. The **business market** consists of customers who buy products for use in a business.

Consumer Market

Many people use the terms *consumer* and *customer* interchangeably. They do not, however, mean exactly the same thing. The consumer market is the one with which you are most familiar. As described in Chapter 1, consumers buy products for their own personal use. Consumers are actually the *end users* of

products. The consumer market of businesses selling primarily to individual consumers is called **business-to-consumer (B2C).**

The consumer market consists of people like you, your family, and your friends. Customers in the consumer market buy groceries, clothes, home goods, cars, gifts, and much more. People in the consumer market do not use their purchases for any business reason. Most of the commercials you see on TV are aimed at customers in the consumer market.

When you buy a gift or things for your family to use at home, you are still part of the consumer market. However, as soon as you buy something to sell to someone else, that purchase is part of the business market. For example, if you buy beads to make jewelry to sell to your friends, that bead purchase is part of the business market. Suppose you mow lawns as a part-time job. If you buy a lawnmower to use, that lawnmower purchase is part of the business market.

Whenever you buy a service or product that you also use, you are a consumer.

AVAVA/Shutterstock.com

Business Market

Customers in the business market buy products for business purposes. In other words, a customer in the business market is a *business* that buys products from another business. The business market of businesses selling primarily to other businesses is called **business-to-business (B2B).**

Other terms for the business market include industrial market, organizational market, and commercial market. The term *industrial market* is used because many of the businesses that sell to each other are considered industries. An **industry** is a group of businesses that produce similar goods or

services. Examples of industries include the following: advertising, automobile, banking, broadcasting, construction, farming, steel, and petroleum.

Commercial market may be used because the term **commercial** refers to buying and selling on a large scale. Sometimes the term *commercial* implies a for-profit business, and the term *organizational* implies a nonprofit business.

FYI

The term *organizational market* is used because organization is another word for business.

Marketing Ethics

Code of Ethics

Most companies establish a set of ethics that employees must follow. The code of ethics outlines acceptable behaviors when interacting with coworkers, suppliers, and customers. Some businesses even post their codes of ethics on their websites. As a marketing professional, it is important to know the code of ethics for your company, so you can make correct decisions on behalf of the company.

Explore

Ask students to make a chart showing each type of customer in the business market and a product(s) they would purchase and/or resell.

Many businesses buy and sell products and services only to other businesses, such as to this architectural firm. Consumers cannot buy most B2B products.

kRie/Shutterstock.com

Consumer versus Customer

As you may have noticed, many terms used in marketing have more than one meaning. *Consumer* is one of these terms. Most of the time, *consumer* refers to the consumer market. When a newspaper or a marketing textbook says, "consumers do this" or "consumers think that," they are referring to individuals in the consumer market. In this context, the term *consumer* is used simply to distinguish the consumer market from the business market.

However, *consumer* also has a more specific meaning. It can refer to the person who actually uses a product that is purchased. In this context, the term *consumer* is used to distinguish the *user* of the product from the *buyer* of the product, who may or may not also be the end user. What is the difference?

First, think of a product that you buy for yourself, such as a jacket. You are the customer because you bought the jacket. You are also the consumer because you wear the jacket. When the marketers developed a marketing mix for that jacket, they most likely had people much like you in mind.

Explain

Have students explain the difference between a consumer and a customer. Which of the two would provide the best assistance to market research?

Now consider a product that you buy for someone else. For example, imagine that you are a parent buying food for your baby. The parent is the customer, or the person who buys the product. However, the parent does not eat the baby food, so he or she is not the consumer. The baby is the consumer, or the user of the product, by eating it. When marketers develop a marketing mix for baby food, they must consider the customer (parent) who buys the product and the consumer (baby) who actually eats the product. The baby food must meet the needs of the baby (the consumer), not the parent (the customer). However, the price, place, and promotion of the baby food must appeal to the parent, the customer who will actually buy the baby food.

The parent is part of the consumer market, even though he or she does not consume the baby food. The parent also did not buy the baby food to sell to someone else. Therefore, the parent is still part of the consumer market, not the business market.

In the business market, the customers are generally *not* the consumers. Many businesses have a special department called *purchasing* that buys all the products needed for doing business. For example, the buyer in a purchasing department will research and purchase computers for the finance department. That buyer is considered a B2B customer. The employees in the finance department are the consumers; that is, they are the ones who use the computers. When marketers develop a marketing mix for the computers, they will keep both the business buyer and the finance department employees in mind.

The AMA's *Journal of Marketing* is a leading publication of cutting-edge, thought-provoking articles that cover all aspects of the marketing industry. The journal is relevant for marketing professionals, academics, and students alike, and each issue includes original research. The journal is available to AMA members. www.marketingpower.com

Checkpoint 3.2

1. Why is utility important for marketing?
2. List the five types of utility.
3. Explain the difference between the consumer market and the business market.
4. What are the three ways that businesses use products?
5. What differentiates a consumer from a customer?

Build Your Vocabulary

As you progress through this course, develop a personal glossary of personal marketing terms and add it to your portfolio. This will help you build your vocabulary and prepare you for a career. Write a definition for each of the following terms, and add it to your personal marketing glossary.

utility
adding value
form utility
place utility
time utility
information utility
possession utility
consumer market
business market
business-to-consumer (B2C)
business-to-business (B2B)
industry
commercial

Checkpoint Answers

1. Utility adds usefulness.
2. Five types of utility are form, place, time, information, and possession.
3. The consumer market sells to individuals who use the products, while the business market sells to businesses to be used in the production of products, for resale to the consumer market, or for the operation of the business.

4. Businesses use products to make new products, to resell to customers, or to use within the business.
5. A consumer uses the product whereby a customer purchases the product but may not actually use it.

Build Your Vocabulary Answers

Definitions for these terms can be found in the glossary of this text.

Chapter Summary

Section 3.1 Business Defined

- Business is the term that involves developing and exchanging products and services. Business provides goods and services for consumers and provides wages for employees.
- The four functions of businesses are production, finance, marketing, and management. All pieces must work together if a business is successful.
- The three main forms of business ownership are sole proprietorship, partnership, and corporation. Each has distinct advantages and disadvantages.

Section 3.2 Importance of Business

- Businesses provide utility by making products more useful, more convenient, and available at opportune times. Providing appropriate information about products and making it easier for customers to acquire products are also utilities provided by businesses.
- The two types of markets for products are the consumer market, in which customers buy products for their own use, and the business market, in which customers buy products for business uses.
- A customer is the person who buys a product, while the consumer is the person who actually uses the product.

Review Your Knowledge

1. Why is money considered a medium of exchange?
2. What is the time value of money?
3. A majority of businesses in the United States are which type of business ownership?
4. The goals of a nonprofit corporation usually fall into what five categories?
5. Name one major task of business.
6. What is a major part of information utility?
7. Name the two types of markets based on the type of buyers.
8. List three synonyms for the business market.
9. Explain how a person can be a customer but not a consumer.
10. What is the acronym for business-to-consumer market?

Evaluate

Assign end-of-chapter activities.

Review Your Knowledge Answers

1. Money is a medium of exchange because it is exchange for a good or service.
2. Time value of money is the idea that a sum of money today has more value than in the future.
3. The majority of businesses in the United States are sole proprietorships.
4. The goals for a nonprofit corporation fall into the five categories of charity, education, public benefit, mutual benefit, and religion.
5. To provide utility or usefulness to product and services.
6. Telling the customer about products and where to buy them.
7. Two types of markets are the consumer market and the business market.
8. Three synonyms for business market are industrial market, organizational market, and commercial market.
9. A businessperson could be a customer buying for a company, but would not be a consumer who buys for his or her own personal use.
10. B2C market.

Apply Your Knowledge

1. At the end of this unit, you will begin writing a marketing plan. Consider a type of business that you might select for this project. Visit the website of a similar business that you have chosen. What type of product does this business sell? Describe how utility plays a role in the product for which you will write a marketing plan.
2. In your opinion, which utility do you think is most important for the type of business you selected in question 1?
3. Visit the website of the business you are considering as your selection for writing a marketing plan. How does the website describe its products and offerings?
4. For the business you selected, which type of business ownership does this company have?
5. For the business you selected, are the products or services sold to the consumer market or business market?
6. Is the business a producer, reseller, or provider of services?
7. Does the business describe the type of customer who buys the service or product? If so, what is the description?
8. Can a business sell the same products to both the consumer market and the business market? Explain your answer and give an example.
9. Visit the American Marketing Association (AMA) website. Find information about the consumer market that could help you as you write your marketing plan.
10. Visit the Small Business Administration (SBA) website. Find information about the consumer market that could help you as you write your marketing plan.

Check Your Marketing IQ

Now that you have finished the chapter, see what you learned about marketing by taking the chapter posttest. If you do not have a smartphone, visit the G-W Learning companion website.

G-W Learning mobile site: www.m.g-wlearning.com

G-W Learning companion website: www.g-wlearning.com

Common Core

College and Career Readiness

CTE Career Ready Practices. Successful employees model integrity. What role do you think ethics and integrity have in decision making? Think of a time when your ideals and principles helped you make a decision. What process did you use to make the decision? In retrospect, do you think you made the correct decision? Did your decision have any consequences?

Reading. When reading for specific information, combine skimming, scanning, and reading for detail. Research a marketing professional who you know personally or one who is well known. List the person's name, business title, and the business for which the person works. Cite specific evidence that supports the person's marketing spirit.

Writing. The prewriting process includes thinking about a topic, plan the content, and researching to gather information. Use the prewriting process to produce a clear and coherent writing about the importance of utility in marketing. The audience for your writing will be your classmates in your marketing class.

Teamwork

Working in teams, create a presentation about a company that sells to both the consumer and business markets. Identify which type(s) of business customer the business sells to and identify how the company markets the products to each market.

G-W Learning Mobile Site

Visit the G-W Learning mobile site to complete the chapter pretest and posttest and to practice vocabulary using e-flash cards. If you do not have a smartphone, visit the G-W Learning companion website to access these features.

G-W Learning mobile site: www.m.g-wlearning.com

G-W Learning companion website: www.g-wlearning.com

Marketing Plan

In this text, students will have an opportunity to write a complete marketing plan. This is a project-based activity that appears at the end of each unit and was described in the teacher notes in Chapter 1.

Refer to the notes in Chapter 1 to prepare for this end-of-unit activity. Begin the selection process for business plans so that

you have time to review appropriate selections for your students. You may decide that this activity is an individual assignment. Or, you may prefer to divide the class into several teams and assign as a team project. Writing a marketing plan will take many hours, so plan accordingly.

CHAPTER

4

Marketing Plan

Section 4.1   Describe the Marketing Plan
Section 4.2   Write the Marketing Plan

"I have found no greater satisfaction than achieving success through honest dealing and strict adherence to the view that, for you to gain, those you deal with should gain as well."

—Alan Greenspan, American economist and former Chairman of the Federal Reserve Board

Reading Prep
Before reading this chapter, look at the chapter title. What can you predict will be presented?

College and Career Readiness

Check Your Marketing IQ

Before you begin the chapter, see what you already know about marketing by taking the chapter pretest. If you do not have a smartphone, visit the G-W Learning companion website.
G-W Learning mobile site: www.m.g-wlearning.com
G-W Learning companion website: www.g-wlearning.com

Explore

Assign the College and Career Readiness Reading Prep activity before students read the chapter. Reading Prep activities give students opportunity to apply the Common Core State Standards.

Engage

Assign the Chapter 4 pretest.

◇DECA Emerging Leaders

Principles of Business Management and Administration Event

Career Cluster: Business Management and Administration
Instructional Area: Professional Development

Performance Indicators

- Explain the need for innovative skills.
- Describe techniques for obtaining work experience.
- Analyze employer expectations in the business environment.
- Explain employment opportunities in business.

Purpose

Designed for first-year DECA members who are enrolled in introductory-level principles of marketing/business courses, the event measures the individual's ability to explain core business concepts in the format of a content interview in a role-play. This event consists of a 100-question, multiple-choice, business administration core exam and a content interview. Participants are not informed in advance of the performance indicators to be evaluated.

Procedure

1. The event will be presented to you through your reading of these instructions, including the Performance Indicators and Interview Situation. You will have up to 10 minutes to review this information to determine how you will handle the role-play situation and demonstrate the performance indicators of this event. During the preparation period, you may make notes to use during the role-play situation.
2. You will have up to 10 minutes to role-play your situation with a judge. You may have more than one judge.
3. You will be evaluated on how well you meet the performance indicators of this event.
4. Turn in all your notes and event materials when you have completed the role-play.

Interview Situation

You are to assume the role of applicant for the career services specialist position at State Business College. The career services specialist assists students nearing graduation with their professional skills needed to secure employment in the field. You have submitted your résumé, completed an initial informal interview, and are now invited back for a more formal interview with the **director of career services (judge).** This interview will be used to measure your understanding of the steps and skills needed to begin a career in the business field.

In the first part of your interview, you will explain the common requirements and skills needed for securing employment in the business field, along with characteristics employers look for when hiring. The director of career services would also like you to suggest methods for finding career opportunities. Following your explanation, the director of career services will ask you to respond to additional questions.

The interview will take place in the director's office. The director of career services will begin the interview by greeting you and asking to hear your ideas regarding securing employment after college. After you have provided your explanation and have answered the director's questions, the director of career services will conclude the interview by thanking you for your presentation.

Critical Thinking

1. What role does a student's academic history play in securing employment?
2. Once a job is secured, why is ongoing education important?

Visit www.deca.org for more information.

Section 4.1 Describe the Marketing Plan

Objectives

After completing this section, you will be able to
- **explain** the importance of a marketing plan.
- **define** the marketing mix.
- **describe** the purpose of a marketing plan template.

Key Terms

marketing plan
product strategy
price strategy
place strategy
promotion strategy
promotional mix
template

Web Connect

Numerous marketing plan templates and sample plans are available at no charge on the Internet. Do a search for *marketing plan templates.* Compare your findings with the one you will use in this text. Compare and contrast the section names within the different documents.

Critical Thinking

Think about the purpose of the marketing plan. What are the parts you think are important for the marketing plan? Why?

What Is a Marketing Plan?

As you learned in Chapter 1, marketing consists of dynamic activities: identifying, anticipating, and satisfying customer demand. Marketing touches every part of business operations.

Successful marketing efforts take time, money, and advance planning. Just as you would not take a trip without a map, a successful marketer will not spend time or money on marketing activities without a plan. A marketing plan is a document describing business and marketing objectives and the strategies and tactics to achieve them. Marketing plans are usually written a year in advance of being implemented. They can, and should be, modified throughout the year to address market changes or take advantage of new opportunities.

The marketing plan should answer the five questions shown in Figure 4-1.

Every marketing plan is unique and will change over time. If working for a start-up company, you will probably not develop a full marketing plan until the second year of business. If working for an established company, you will develop a yearly marketing plan and review it often.

Larger companies generally have multiple marketing managers. They are responsible for individual product lines. Each marketing manager will complete a plan for his or her product line. In a smaller company, there may only be one marketing manager who creates the plan for the entire company.

Preparing a marketing plan takes time and research. Marketers spend many months gathering information about past performance of the company. They also analyze

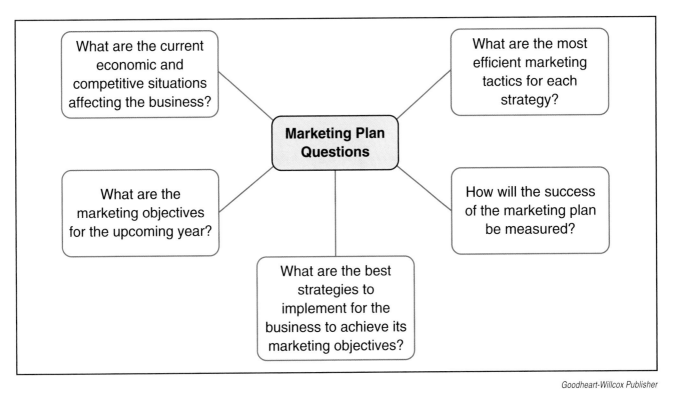

Goodheart-Willcox Publisher

Figure 4-1 These critical marketing questions should be addressed in a good marketing plan.

how marketing could influence future company performance. Marketing teams help drive sales, so the sales team is an important partner. Sales goals influence the direction that the marketing plan may take.

One way to understand a marketing plan is to view the document itself as a set of travel plans. The marketing objective is *where* you plan to travel, such as to Ireland, Asia, or the East Coast. The marketing strategies are *how* to get to the area such as flying, taking a train, or driving. The marketing tactics are the specific *paths* taken to reach the final destination, such as highways and roads.

FYI

The marketing manager may be the person who is in charge of creating the marketing plan. However, that could vary depending on the company structure.

Explain

Review the Marketing Plan questions. Discuss the importance of answering these questions as part of completing a successful marketing plan.

Marketing Mix

In Chapter 2, you learned about the four Ps—product, price, place, and promotion—that make up the marketing mix. Decisions about the marketing mix are the basis of a marketing plan. Those decisions provide the important framework for choosing specific marketing strategies and tactics to implement the plan.

Before developing a marketing mix, the target market should be determined first. Then the strategies for each of the four Ps are made to meet the needs and wants of those customers. Marketers help determine the best products to offer. They also help to set prices and make the products available at convenient locations. Marketers decide where, when, and how to promote the products so the target market will see the message.

Maps are useful, and often necessary, when travelling to find your destination. The marketing plan is your company's road map.

auremar/Shutterstock.com

Product Strategies

Product strategies are the decisions marketers help make about what products a business should sell. Product strategies can include decisions on quantities, sizes, packaging, warranties, brand names, image, and design. In an established company, these decisions may already be in place.

However, product lines are constantly reviewed to see whether actual sales are in line with the sales goals. Marketers influence the creation of new products appealing to the target market.

Price Strategies

Price strategies are the business decisions about pricing and how prices are set to make a profit. Pricing policies affect company image. The marketing plan will cover price points, percentage of annual sales, and expected profit by product. Part of a price strategy is how your prices compare to the competition.

Decisions about raising or lowering prices relate to very different business goals and require much thought. Higher prices may mean a higher-quality image to the customer. Or, lower prices might increase sales and generate the desired profit.

Place Strategies

Place strategies are the decisions about how and where the products are produced, acquired, shipped, and sold to customers. The sales team is a good source of information to help make some place decisions because they are in direct contact with the customers. Place strategies involve decisions about not only a physical location but how goods or services are distributed. Is the product offered on the Internet, internationally, locally, or through other stores?

Explore

Ask students to bring in ads for products and identify the product strategies used in the ads. Emphasize the importance of product decisions in influencing customers to purchase. Ask students to identify either a new product in the market or an "improved" product and how it has changed.

Explain

Using the Apple iPhone as an example, discuss with students why Apple can charge the high prices it does for the latest versions of its iPhone. Ask if a higher-priced phone is equal to greater quality.

Promotion Strategies

Promotion strategies are decisions about which selling, advertising, sales promotions, and public relations activities to use in the promotional mix. The **promotional mix** is a combination of the elements used in a promotional campaign. A promotional mix can include any or all of the promotional elements, as shown in Figure 4-2.

Promotion decisions also include who will handle specific promotions and public relations efforts. Large companies may have a communications team that works with the marketing team to help create the advertising and sales pieces. However, in many companies, the marketing manager may be responsible for the entire promotion strategies. For both current and new products, it is important to describe the benefits as they relate to how the product will make life better or easier.

Marketing Plan Templates

Marketing plans can appear in many different formats. There is no right or wrong way to write a plan. If you are creating a marketing plan for an established company, the company may already have a preferred plan format. If you need to create the marketing plan format, there are many professional and business organizations that provide free or low-cost templates. A **template** is a document that already has a basic format that can be used many times.

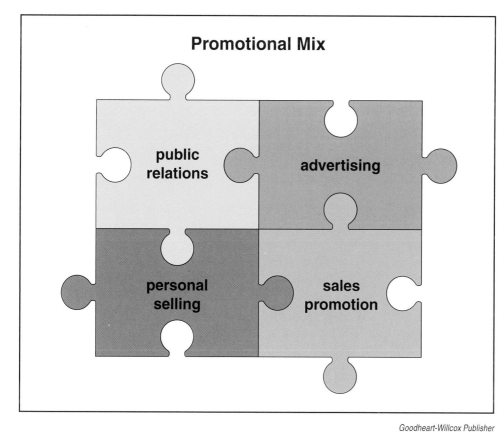

Promotional Mix

public relations

advertising

personal selling

sales promotion

Goodheart-Willcox Publisher

Figure 4-2 The pieces of the promotional mix fit together to form a promotional campaign.

Engage

Ask students what eBay, Amazon, Avon, Miche, Ford, and the local bakery all have in common. They all sell their products in a *place*, whether that is in someone's home, on the Internet, at a brick-and-mortar store, or anywhere else.

Explore

Ask students to make a list of all the promotions they can remember seeing in the last 24 hours. How did the promotions affect the student? Did they purchase a product, decided to purchase but plan on doing it later, or ignore the different promotions? Why?

Case in Point

Loudmouth®

Creating a marketing plan is important for any business. A marketing plan helps marketers to identify strategies, create a time line, and ensure the focus remains on promoting the company and its products. Scott "Woody" Woodworth knows the importance of the marketing plan. Woody owns a company called Loudmouth that sells very colorful athletic clothing with *loud* designs. Loudmouth has been strategic in its marketing efforts by using well-known sports figures to promote the brand. For example, Woody hired celebrity golfer, John Daly, to help the company promote its signature line of golf apparel. Loudmouth also entered the Olympics by outfitting the 2010 Norwegian curling team. In 2012, the company sponsored and outfitted the US men's Olympic beach volleyball team. At the same time, Loudmouth announced its expansion into beachwear—perfect timing. The current Loudmouth marketing plan includes licensing its designs to other manufacturers and adding a youth athletic line. A strong marketing plan + a solid vision + a unique product = success for Loudmouth.

As long as all of the important information is covered, a business chooses how to best present the information. Sources of marketing plan templates include
- Small Business Association (SBA);
- chambers of commerce;
- universities;
- American Marketing Association (AMA);
- Service Corps of Retired Executives (SCORE);
- state websites; and
- industry groups, such as marketing associations.

AMA Tip

The AMA offers its members access to a free Marketer's Toolkit. It contains a comprehensive collection of interactive tools, templates, and resources in a single location.
www.marketingpower.com

Checkpoint 4.1

1. Should marketing plans be changed or modified? Why?
2. What is the foundation for the marketing plan?
3. How does price influence image?
4. Name one place strategy.
5. Where can a marketing plan template be obtained?

Build Your Vocabulary

As you progress through this text, develop a personal glossary of marketing terms and add it to your portfolio. This will help you build your vocabulary and prepare for a career as a marketing professional. Write a definition for each of the following terms, and add it to your personal marketing glossary.

marketing plan
product strategy
price strategy
place strategy

promotion strategy
promotional mix
template

Section 4.2 Write the Marketing Plan

After completing this section, you will be able to
- **summarize** the sections of a marketing plan.
- **format** a marketing plan.

vision statement
mission statement
situation analysis
market segmentation
SWOT analysis
unique selling
  proposition (USP)
marketing objective
market share
marketing strategy
marketing tactic
action plan
metric
return on investment
  (ROI)

Use the Internet to research the steps involved in writing a marketing plan. Make a list of the recommendations that the research resources suggest.

Some people believe the only reason to write a marketing plan is to create ideas for advertising. However, a marketing plan does far more than just plan advertising. Write your thoughts about what you think a good marketing plan provides to a business.

Sections of the Marketing Plan

Every marketing plan will be different because every business and its goals are different. Companies create a marketing plan to fit the type of business. Your business may already have an established marketing-plan template in place.

As you progress through this text, you will be writing your own marketing plan. The template you will use has the following sections:
- Title Page
- Table of Contents
- Executive Summary
- Business Description
- Sales Analysis

- Situation Analysis
- Marketing Objectives
- Marketing Strategies
- Bibliography
- Appendices

Title Page

The title page makes the first impression about what will follow in the marketing plan. All formal reports include a title page with the following:
- company name;
- the product line or products being discussed;
- the marketing manager name;
- any team members that should be noted; and
- date the plan is presented.

Table of Contents

A table of contents is necessary so the reader knows what is included in the plan and where each section is located. Prepare the table of contents after the plan is complete.

Executive Summary

An *executive summary* provides the overview of the marketing plan by highlighting the critical points in the plan. The goal is to provide a snapshot that will entice the reader to review the entire document. Even though the executive summary is the beginning of the marketing plan, it should be written last. Keep the executive summary short and to the point, not over two pages.

Marketing plans are read by company executives and select members of the sales, marketing, and product development teams. If the company is seeking additional funding from outside sources, the marketing plan will accompany the request for funding. This is your opportunity to show how marketing can help drive future sales and profits for the company.

Business Description

The business description gives an overview of the business as outlined in the business plan. The business description will come directly from the yearly business plan or annual report. It is fine to condense this information. However, do not change anything created by the company executives.

Include the company goals, vision statement, mission statement, short business overview, and description of the products. Including this information shows how the marketing plan aligns with the overall direction of the business.

Company Goals

Company goals project where the company should be this year and up to five years in the future. These goals lay the foundation for revenue projections. They are written by the executive team and are found in the business plan or annual report.

Vision Statement

A **vision statement** is the overall goal for the future of the company. The vision statement is like looking into a crystal ball and seeing the future of the company. One example of a vision statement is, "To become the safest, most customer-focused manufacturer in the world." A good vision statement should inspire employees and help drive the business.

Green Marketing

Office Supplies

Businesses make many buying decisions. These decisions range from expensive purchases to low-dollar purchases, such as the type of lightbulbs used in the business. Compact fluorescent lamps (CFL) can save up to 80 percent of the energy used by a regular incandescent lightbulb. By using bulbs that last longer, the business will save money by saving energy. A CFL lasts up to 10 times longer than an incandescent bulb. However, CFLs contain mercury, so they must be disposed of properly. Consider recommending to your company that you switch to CFL if you are not using them all ready.

Elaborate/Extend

Provide an opportunity for students to exhibit their understanding of concepts in context of the material as it is presented. As time permits, have students read and discuss the special features in the chapter.

Explain

Discuss with students the importance of the executive summary. Explain that the summary will either create interest or possibly cause disinterest in the reader. It is like reading a good book—you have to *catch* the reader on the first page.

College and Career Portfolio

Objective

It is helpful to have a checklist of components that should be included in your portfolio. Your instructor may provide you with a checklist. If not, create a checklist that works best for you.

Before you begin collecting information for your portfolio, you should write an objective related to creating your portfolio. An *objective* is a complete sentence or two that states what you want to accomplish. The language should be clear and specific. The objective should contain enough details so you can easily judge when it is accomplished. Consider this objective: "I will try to get better grades." Such an objective is too general. A better, more detailed objective might read: "I will work with a tutor and spend at least three hours per week on math homework until my math grade has improved to a B." Creating a clear objective is a good starting point for beginning work on your portfolio.

1. Create a checklist to use as an ongoing reference as you create your portfolio throughout this class.
2. Decide on the purpose of the portfolio you are creating—temporary or short-term employment, career, and/or college application.
3. Do research on the Internet to find articles about writing objectives. Also, look for articles that contain sample objectives for creating a portfolio.
4. Write an objective for creating your portfolio that will be used in applying for a job or for college. Include statements for both a print portfolio and an e-portfolio.

Mission Statement

The **mission statement** is the company message to customers about why the business exists. It describes the business, identifies the customers, and shows how the business adds value. One example of a mission statement is, "Providing the most fuel-efficient cars to help you save money and the environment."

Business Overview

The business overview comes from the business plan or annual report. It identifies the company as a service, retail, wholesale, or manufacturing business. It will also describe if the business is online, brick-and-mortar store, or a combination.

Product Descriptions

The product descriptions section explains the products or services in more detail. Much of this information may come from the business plan. As a member of the marketing team, you may know more specific information about your product lines. Give details that the audience should know, such as exactly what the product is, how it works, its selling price, and other important information. Your description should be very specific so each person reading the plan understands the product being marketed.

Sales Analysis

The sales analysis section will typically help determine future sales goals. Before sales goals can be created, however, it is necessary to analyze sales history, make sales forecasts, and evaluate the best sales opportunities. The sales team and management set the sales goals.

Sales Goals

Sales goals identify where new and repeat sales can be generated and at what levels. Customer targets or geographic regions on which the company should focus are defined. Opportunities to take business away from competitors, new geographic areas, and other potential sales sources are identified.

Sales History and Projections

To create a marketing plan for a specific product or product line, you will discuss previous sales by year for up to five years. These numbers are analyzed and future sales projections are made. *Sales projections,* or forecasts, are the dollars and units of product the company wants to achieve. The sales and executive teams create these forecasts. Sales forecasts are typically made for a minimum of one year and from three to five years in the future.

Best Opportunities

What are the best opportunities for making new and repeat sales? This information will come from market research and sales team feedback. Some sales teams will identify the top-ten sales opportunities that will be pursued in the upcoming year. The marketing team will work with the sales team by assisting them to make the sales.

Situation Analysis

A business cannot determine where to go or how to get there without knowing where it has been. The **situation analysis** is a snapshot of the environment in which a business has been operating over a given time, usually the last 12 to 16 months.

The situation analysis begins with a statement of both the internal and external environments as related to marketing and sales. The *external environment* is the condition of the local and national economies. The economies may have had a positive

Some businesses, like this bridal store, have small, well-defined target markets, while others, such as shopping malls and supermarkets, have much broader target markets.

or negative impact on past sales. How the economy may affect sales for the coming year is discussed. The *internal environment* is the condition of the company including its staff and any internal issues that could affect marketing.

Target Market

The next step is to define the target market. By reviewing sales data, you can analyze the current customers and identify the target market. If one of the objectives for the coming year is to expand the customer base, additional research may be needed.

Detailed market research is often part of the target market section of a marketing plan. Marketers analyze all aspects of the target market as well as the competition. It is a necessary step to position a business for getting its share of sales. This section
- defines the target market.
- estimates the total size of the target market; it is important to be as accurate as possible.
- includes information from sales histories, marketing studies, reports, or test-mar-

keting activities completed that describe marketing trends.
- describes factors that may affect purchasing of the product, such as season, price, availability, emotions, services, or tax considerations.
- includes a profile of the targeted customers based on age, gender, education, income level, or lifestyle.

Knowing this information about current and potential customers helps determine the best strategies for reaching them effectively.

Market Segmentation

The process of dividing a large market into smaller groups is called **market segmentation.** A *market segment* is the smaller group of people, families, businesses, or organizations with common characteristics or needs. It is the market segments that eventually become target markets for various products or businesses.

Depending on the products your company offers, it may be wise to segment your target market. By breaking the market into separate groups, messages can be

How do direct competitors, such as those in this airport, distinguish themselves from each other? Planning helps.

Tupungato/Shutterstock.com

targeted just to those groups. How the message is delivered to each group may also change. You might segment your market by lifestyle factors, habits, demographics, or another set of factors unique to the business.

Competition

Competition is two or more businesses attempting to attract the same customers. One of the most important parts of the marketing plan is the section describing the other businesses also competing for your customers. In order for the company to achieve sales goals, it may need to take business away from the competition. The sales team will be helpful in providing information about competitors. Competition is the focus of Chapter 11.

In the marketing plan, competition information is usually presented in grids. The grids list and describe the competitors, their physical locations, their product lines, pricing, and market share. These grids analyze the strengths and weaknesses of the competition. Use this section as an opportunity to explain how your company will compete with others to gain your share of the sales.

It will also be necessary to provide a SWOT Analysis for your company. A **SWOT analysis** lists company strengths, weaknesses, opportunities, and threats the business faces. It helps to explain why your product is different or better than those offered by the competition. For example, does your business offer a wider variety, better prices, or better sizing than the competitors?

It is also important to discuss the unique selling proposition (USP) for your company as well as the value proposition for the business or the products. A **unique selling proposition (USP)** is a statement of how your company or products are different or better than the competition. It explains why customers should purchase goods and services from your company rather than another. The USP will be a strength in the SWOT analysis.

Marketing strategies will come from researching your target markets. They will cover the four Ps of marketing—product, pricing, place, and promotion strategies.

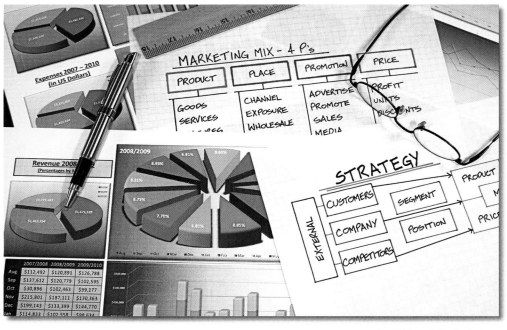

Chad McDermott/Shutterstock.com

Marketing Objectives

The business description has laid the groundwork for the marketing plan. Based on the gathered information, it is time to state the specific marketing objectives. **Marketing objectives** are the goals a business wants to achieve during a given time, usually one year, by implementing the marketing plan.

Most businesses have several marketing objectives that address both marketing and financial goals.

Just as a business has SMART company goals, the marketing team also sets SMART goals in the marketing plan. Marketing goals include defining market share and image. **Market share** is the percentage of total sales in a market that is held by one business. Examples of marketing objectives might be:

- increase sales by 15 percent in 20-- (a financial goal); and
- increase company brand awareness and market share by 10 percent in 20-- (a marketing goal).

The marketing objectives should be written as specific, measurable, attainable, realistic, and timely SMART goals. They may be short-term goals, which are achieved in less than one year. Or, they may be long-term goals that are achieved in a year or more.

Most marketing plans include two to four marketing objectives that will outline the goals for the next year.

All businesses have financial goals in the business plan. These financial goals serve as the guideline for sales and marketing to create their plans for the year. The marketing plan will help drive sales to meet the company financial goals. Describe the role that marketing will play in reaching those goals.

Marketing Strategies

Marketing strategies are the decisions made about product, price, place, and promotion.

Marketing strategies outline the *who, what, when, where,* and *how* of the marketing process.

The marketing strategies directly support the marketing objectives. For example, marketing strategies to achieve the marketing goal mentioned earlier might include:

- Offer one new product each year.
- Provide free delivery to customers within ten miles of the store.
- Price products at or below the competition.
- Increase sales in the critical teen demographic by 25 percent through targeted promotions.

Once the marketing strategies are in place, determine the marketing tactics to execute those strategies. **Marketing tactics** are the specific activities to carry out the marketing strategies. Every marketing strategy will have a set of tactics designed to accomplish it. For example, tactics for the *price products at or below the competition* strategy might include:

- Assign the intern to monitor online competition prices every Monday.
- Monitor sales, advertising, and coupons in the local weekend papers.
- Meet with the vice president every Tuesday to review competitive pricing information.
- Reset prices as needed.

Marketing tactics may be the longest section of the marketing plan because it lists very specific activities. Most plans include a one-year promotional plan that includes the promotional mix of personal selling, advertising, sales promotions, and public relations activities.

Once the marketing plan is written, the action is put into place for the marketing tactics. The **action plan** includes a detailed time line, the budget, and the metrics to evaluate the effectiveness of any campaigns. A strong marketing plan includes an action plan to ensure the marketing efforts remain on track and funds are spent wisely.

Engage

Conduct a brainstorming session with the class. Divide the class into teams. Ask students to identify as many tactics as possible. Combine each group's responses to create a comprehensive list. Examples might be hiring celebrities or creating marketing opportunities on social media.

Resource/Evaluate

Assign the optional Chapter 4 test for **EXAM**VIEW® Assessment Suite as a formal assessment tool.

Time Line

The time line lists when each activity starts, where it happens or runs, the end date, and the person responsible. A time line keeps the marketing team on track and moves the plan forward. A spreadsheet is a good tool to use to create a calendar, or time line, for the promotional plan.

Budget

Most businesses base the overall marketing budget on a percentage of sales for the company or other factors related to sales. The detailed budget shows the costs to implement the marketing tactics and promotional activities. Some tactics may have several sets of costs. Once again, a spreadsheet is helpful in creating the budget. List each marketing activity and the cost for each.

Metrics

Metrics are standards of measurement. An action plan also includes the methods and metrics that will be used to track and evaluate marketing activities. Marketing is an expensive part of operating a business. The company executives expect a system to measure marketing effectiveness and justify the expense.

Most companies look for a good return on investment (ROI) for the dollars spent on marketing. **Return on investment (ROI)** is a ratio that shows the efficiency of an investment by comparing the gains from the investment to its cost. You will not know if your marketing plan worked without measuring the success of each element. Describe the metrics that will be used for each marketing activity and indicate the acceptable results for each.

Depending on the marketing activity, the metrics used to measure success will differ. Sometimes it is easy to tie sales directly to marketing activities by using coupons or electronic product codes. Other times it may be harder to track direct sales. Regardless of the metrics used, it is important to track all campaigns to see if they are worth repeating.

Bibliography

The *bibliography* lists all of the resources used to develop the marketing plan, as shown in Figure 4-3. Resources might include interviews, books, periodicals, and websites cited; or other information you gathered while researching the plan. Set up the bibliography

Bibliography

Internet Retailer. "Sales." Trends & Data. Accessed May 9, 2012. http://www.internetretailer.com/trends/sales/.

eMarketer. "Social Media Key Influencer in Multi-Exposure Purchase Path." Last modified February 16, 2012. Accessed May 9, 2012. http://www.emarketer.com/Article.aspx?R=1008845.

US Bureau of Labor Statistics. "Employment Situation Summary." Economic News Release. Last modified May 4, 2012. Accessed May 9, 2012. http://www.bls.gov/news.release/empsit.nr0.htm.

Goodheart-Willcox Publisher

Figure 4-3 The bibliography is an important record of the sources used to write the marketing plan.

right away so that you can easily add each resource as it is used. This is easier than trying to remember the sources when you are finished with the plan.

Appendices

The appendices may include financial projections, data about the target market or competitors, and other documents that support your plan. Arrange these documents in a logical order and list them in the table of contents under the appendices section.

Binding

Marketing plans are usually bound to look more professional. Consider using the binding services of an office-supply store. Ask for suggestions on the most appropriate way to package your plan.

FYI

Both external and internal environment factors affect the creation of a marketing plan and its execution.

Format the Marketing Plan

It is important for the marketing plan to look professional and be organized. The marketing plan may be presented to a wide audience. Obviously, the company executives and shareholders will want to review the yearly marketing plans. The sales team and other internal teams will also be interested in the marketing plan because it directly affects them. If the business needs to obtain funding, it will be distributed to investors or lenders to show how revenue is created.

The plan should be:

- well written; sentences and paragraphs must make sense and describe the marketing plans;
- grammatically correct; words selected must be appropriate and the punctuation used should be accurate;
- exciting and enthusiastic; describe ideas and plans in the most inviting way possible;
- unique; marketing is the place to showcase creativity; and
- attractive; make the marketing plan a compatible part of the business plan.

Professional-looking marketing plans help the readers focus on the information.

Explain

Stress that a marketing plan that does not look professional will not be taken seriously.

Engage

Invite an English or business teacher to the class to review proper

writing and formatting skills.

Evaluate

Assess student comprehension using the Checkpoint activity as a self-assessment tool.

Checkpoint 4.2

1. What purpose does the table of contents serve in a marketing plan?
2. Describe the difference between a vision statement and a mission statement.
3. What is a sales forecast?
4. What is a market segment?
5. What purpose does a competitive grid serve?

Build Your Vocabulary

As you progress through this text, develop a personal glossary of marketing terms and add it to your portfolio. This will help you build your vocabulary and prepare for a career as a marketing professional. Write a definition for each of the following terms, and add it to your personal marketing glossary.

vision statement
mission statement
situation analysis
market segmentation
SWOT analysis
unique selling proposition (USP)
marketing objective
market share
marketing strategy
marketing tactic
action plan
metric
return on investment (ROI)

Checkpoint Answers

1. The table of contents identifies the elements in the marketing plan.
2. The vision statement is the overall goal for the future of the company, while the mission statement is the company message to customers about why the business exists.
3. Sales forecasts are the dollars and units of product the company will strive to accomplish.

4. The smaller group of people, families, businesses, or organizations with common characteristics or needs.
5. A competitive grid enables the marketer to see the strengths and weaknesses of each individual competitor.

Build Your Vocabulary Answers

Definitions for these terms can be found in the glossary of this text.

Chapter Summary

Section 4.1 Describe the Marketing Plan

- A marketing plan is important because it contains the marketing team objectives, strategies, and tactics for achieving both business and marketing goals.
- The marketing mix is a plan of action for marketing a product, and consists of the decisions made about that product, price, place, and promotion.
- The purpose of a marketing plan template is to provide a basic format that displays the essential information in an appropriate manner.

Section 4.2 Write the Marketing Plan

- The sections of a marketing plan are the title page, table of contents, executive summary, business description, sales analysis, situation analysis, marketing objectives, marketing strategies, marketing tactics, bibliography, and appendices.
- When formatting a marketing plan, make sure that it is professional, organized, and accurate. The plan should be well written, grammatically correct, exciting and enthusiastic, unique, and attractive.

Review Your Knowledge

1. List the sections of a marketing plan.
2. Why does a company need a marketing plan?
3. The marketing mix is the foundation of the marketing plan. What should be developed before the marketing mix is created?
4. What purpose does a title page serve in a marketing plan?
5. What does an executive summary provide?
6. Who will read the marketing plan?
7. What information should the product descriptions of the marketing plan include?
8. Why is a SWOT analysis important in a marketing plan?
9. When analyzing the selling situation, what two environments should be considered?
10. Why do companies set financial goals?

Evaluate

Assign end-of-chapter activities.

Review Your Knowledge Answers

1. The sections of a marketing plan are the title page, table of contents, executive summary, business description, situation analysis, marketing objectives, marketing strategies, marketing tactics, action plan, bibliography, and appendices.
2. A marketing plan is a document describing the marketing objectives and the strategies and tactics to achieve them.
3. The target market should be first determined.
4. The title page identifies the company, product lines or services being discussed, the name of the marketing manager, team members, and the date of the presentation.
5. The executive summary provides the overview of the marketing plan by highlighting critical points in the plan.
6. Executives in the company, selected members of the sales and marketing teams, as well as product development teams.
7. Details about what the product is, how it works, its selling price, and other important information.
8. SWOT analysis is important to explain why your product is different or better than the competitors.
9. External environment and internal environment.
10. Financial goals serve as a guideline when orchestrating sales and marketing plans for the year.

Apply Your Knowledge

1. List three topics you will need to research when writing your marketing plan.
2. Choose a local company. What is the marketing mix for that business?
3. Think about students at your school. What types of promotions affect students at your school the most?
4. Create a chart with two columns. In column one, list a local company. In column two, list a competitor. Identify what you believe are its unique selling position and value proposition as compared to its competitor.
5. Conduct a SWOT analysis for your school-based enterprise or for another local company.
6. Failure to do research is one of the reasons some marketing plans fail. List the ways you would research your idea for a marketing plan. How can you ensure that your plan will not fail?
7. As you progress through this text, you will be creating a marketing plan. The ideas that you explored in question one may be a starting place for your new marketing plan. Write a letter or e-mail to one or two businesses for which you would consider creating marketing plans and why you chose those businesses.
8. Create a title page description for a business for which you might like to write a marketing plan.
9. Using the Internet, select a business in an industry in which you are interested. Conduct a SWOT analysis for the business you select.
10. In the Situation Analysis section of the marketing plan, you will evaluate industry and economic conditions. Using the Internet, research the current conditions of the industry in which you would like to work. Write an example of how the marketing plan you create will fulfill market needs.

Check Your Marketing IQ

Now that you have finished the chapter, see what you learned about marketing by taking the chapter posttest. If you do not have a smartphone, visit the G-W Learning companion website.

G-W Learning mobile site: www.m.g-wlearning.com
G-W Learning companion website: www.g-wlearning.com

Apply Your Knowledge Answers
Student answers will vary for questions 1–10.

Evaluate
Evaluate the students' understanding and knowledge. Assign the Chapter 4 posttest. The test may be accessed by using the QR code or by going to the companion website. What questions were students able to answer that they could not answer when they took the pretest?

Common Core

College and Career Readiness

CTE Career Ready Practices. To become career ready, it is necessary to utilize critical-thinking skills in order to solve problems. Give an example of a problem that you needed to solve that was important to your success at work or school. How did you apply critical-thinking skills to arrive at a solution?

Listening. Engage in a conversation with someone you have not spoken with before. Ask the person how he or she makes decisions both informally and in more formal circumstances, such as at school or a job. Actively listen to what that person is sharing. Build on his or her ideas by sharing your own. Try this again with other people you have not spoken to before. How clearly were the different people able to articulate themselves? How do you think having a conversation with someone you do not normally speak to is different from a conversation you might have with a friend or family member you speak with every day?

Speaking. The way you communicate with other people will have a lot to do with the success of the relationships you build with them. There are formal and informal ways of communicating your message. Create a speech showing how you introduce yourself to a new acquaintance. Deliver the speech to your class. How did the words, phrases, and tone you used influence the way the audience responded to the speech?

Teamwork

Hold a brainstorming session. Working with a team, brainstorm ideas on creating an environmentally friendly product. Use the brainstorming process and record your ideas. Divide the workload by having one person record the ideas, another create a drawing that portrays the product idea, and a third person create the written narrative. Present your findings to the class.

G-W Learning Mobile Site

Visit the G-W Learning mobile site to complete the chapter pretest and posttest and to practice vocabulary using e-flash cards. If you do not have a smartphone, visit the G-W Learning companion website to access these features.

G-W Learning mobile site: www.m.g-wlearning.com
G-W Learning companion website: www.g-wlearning.com

Marketing Plan

In this chapter, students begin the marketing plan. This chapter is the foundation for the project-based activity. Students will refer to this chapter frequently as they create their own marketing plan. The marketing plan is an ongoing activity that will take many hours to complete, so plan accordingly.

Refer to the notes in Chapter 1 to prepare for this end-of-unit activity. If you have not already done so, begin the selection process for business plans so you have time to review appropriate selections for your students. You may decide that this activity is an individual assignment. Or, you may prefer to divide the class into several teams and assign as a team project.

CHAPTER

5 Ethics and Social Responsibility

Section 5.1 Ethics
Section 5.2 Social Responsibility

"We know that the profitable growth of our company depends on the economic, environmental, and social sustainability of our communities across the world. And we know it is in our best interests to contribute to the sustainability of those communities."

—Travis Engen, CEO, Alcan Inc.

Reading Prep
In preparation for reading the chapter, consider what the term *ethics* means to you. Have you ever been confronted with an ethical dilemma?

College and Career Readiness

Check Your Marketing IQ

Before you begin the chapter, see what you already know about marketing by taking the chapter pretest. If you do not have a smartphone, visit the G-W Learning companion website.
G-W Learning mobile site: www.m.g-wlearning.com
G-W Learning companion website: www.g-wlearning.com

G-W Mobile

Explore

Assign the College and Career Readiness Reading Prep activity before students read the chapter. Reading Prep activities give students opportunity to apply the Common Core State Standards.

Engage

Assign the Chapter 5 pretest.

◇DECA Emerging Leaders

Principles of Hospitality and Tourism Event

Career Cluster: Hospitality and Tourism
Instructional Area: Human Resources Management / Professional Development

Performance Indicators

* Discuss the nature of human resources management.
* Assess personal interests and skills needed for success in business.
* Orient new employees.
* Analyze employer expectations in the business environment.

Purpose

Designed for first-year DECA members who are enrolled in introductory-level principles of marketing/business courses, the event measures the individual's ability to explain core business concepts in the format of a content interview in a role-play. This event consists of a 100-question, multiple-choice, business administration core exam and a content interview. Participants are not informed in advance of the performance indicators to be evaluated.

Procedure

1. The event will be presented to you through your reading of these instructions, including the performance indicators and interview situation. You will have up to 10 minutes to review this information to determine how you will perform the task and demonstrate the performance indicators of this event. During the preparation period, you may make notes to use during the interview situation.
2. You will have up to 10 minutes with the judge, including five to seven minutes to accomplish the task and several minutes to respond to follow-up questions. (You may have more than one judge.)
3. You will be evaluated on how well you meet the performance indicators of this event.
4. Turn in all your notes and event materials when you have completed the interview.

Interview Situation

You are to assume the role of applicant for a full-time position in the human resources department at Majestic Hotel, a family-oriented hotel chain. You have already submitted your résumé and completed one interview. You have been invited back for a second interview with the **hotel manager (judge).** This second and final interview will be used to measure your knowledge and understanding of human resources management and professional development.

Majestic Hotel is currently experiencing an extremely high turnover of employees. This turnover is causing a significant decrease in hotel profits and employee morale. Before offering you the position, the manager wants to be sure that you understand staff growth and development to increase productivity and employee satisfaction.

In the first part of the interview, you will explain why human resources management and professional development are important to the success and profitability of a business. Your presentation should also address the additional performance indicators listed on the first page of this event. The second part of the interview will consist of answering questions the manager will ask you.

The interview will take place in the manager's office. The manager will begin the interview by greeting you and asking you to explain why human resources management and professional development are important to the success and profitability of a business. After you have given a complete explanation and have answered the manager's questions, the manager will conclude the interview by thanking you for the work.

Critical Thinking

1. What is the value of employee orientation?
2. What are several ways to reward employee loyalty?
3. What are several current employment trends in the hospitality and tourism industry?

Visit www.deca.org for more information.

Section 5.1 Ethics

Objectives

After studying this section, you will be able to
- **explain** the concept of ethics.
- **define** workplace ethics.
- **summarize** the rights of consumers.
- **describe** the impact of ethics on business organizations.
- **identify** some of the costs of unethical behavior on a business.

Key Terms

ethics
code of ethics
code of conduct
Federal Trade
  Commission (FTC)
copyright
software piracy
shareware
freeware
customer relationship
  management (CRM)
netiquette
phishing
cyber bullying
false advertising
spam
Sarbanes-Oxley Act

Web Connect

Do an Internet search for the term *business ethics.* Write your own definition of business ethics.

Critical Thinking

Why is it important to let your customers know that you, personally, are ethical and are an ethical marketing professional? Write a paragraph about the importance of ethics to the long-term success of a marketing professional.

Code of Ethics

You may have heard the phrase, "be ethical," but what does it really mean? **Ethics** are the rules of behavior based on ideas about what is right and wrong. *Business ethics* are the rules for professional conduct and integrity in all areas of business. For anyone in business, ethics are vital to their success.

A **code of ethics** is the general principles or values, often social or moral, that guide the organization. Your company may have a written code of ethics like the one in Figure 5-1 or one that is assumed. As a marketer, ethics play an important role. Ethical behavior is necessary when you are working with customers or clients, other businesses, and employees within your company.

Business ethics help marketers and businesses make fair decisions. From the Industrial Revolution in the 18th century until recently, business had a reputation for a lack of ethics. For example, some businesses did not have worker safety measures until laws were passed forcing them to do so. Even then, some did not comply until they were sued by the ill and injured.

Certain ethical behaviors, such as honesty, are expected in a business environment. They are assumed and may not always be in writing.

**Yours in Retro
CODE OF ETHICS**

Yours in Retro is committed to putting customers first and being responsible members of the community. Yours in Retro will create meaningful work, protect the environment, be socially responsible, produce a solid return for our owners and employees, and provide an important service to society.

Integrity

Integrity is at the core of everything we do at Yours in Retro. We are an honest, ethical, and trustworthy organization. Integrity is the foundation of our relationship with our clients, our communities, and each other. We will never record hours not worked or bill a client for hours that were not spent directly on

Respect

Respect is the foundation of any good relationship. Discrimination or harassment based on age, race, ethnicity, gender, or any other legally protected status is not tolerated.

Figure 5-1 This is an example of a partial code of ethics.

Goodheart-Willcox Publisher

Ethical behavior is essential to developing business relationships. Good business relationships are the key to success in the 21st century. In order for business to run smoothly, people must be able to trust each other.

For example, imagine you are in charge of maintaining equipment in a large factory. An important machine just broke. The company that usually repairs that machine promised to send a repairperson right away. However, the repairperson did not show up nor did the company call you. Most likely, you would find a different company to repair your equipment from then on, because you no longer trust the first one. Business is always lost when trust is lost.

In the late 20th century, changes in society pressured businesses to be more ethical. For example, customers wanted products that did not harm the environment. They also wanted products that were not made using child labor in foreign countries. When a business acted in an unethical way, the media covered it. The result was often a loss of sales or a drop in stock value.

About 70 percent of businesses in the United States have a formal ethics program.

Workplace Ethics

Ethics in the workplace is a significant issue in the business world and for marketers in particular. Over 90 percent of business schools now require ethics courses as part of their curriculum. Marketers and other employees develop a personal set of ethics based on what they were taught at home and through their personal experiences. Some may differ in their own personal ethics.

However, most employers agree on the type of ethical behavior they expect from employees. This includes honesty, integrity, responsibility, and confidentiality.

- *Honesty* includes telling the truth, not stealing, doing the work assigned to you, not wasting time, keeping accurate records, and respecting the property of others.
- *Integrity* is the quality of being honest and fair. Integrity includes treating people fairly, applying rules consistently, and being unbiased.
- *Responsibility* is the quality of being reliable, following through on promises, and performing tasks assigned to you.
- *Confidentiality* is the ability to keep confidential information private. Company

information that is private is called *confidential* or *proprietary information.* For example, plans for a new product are confidential. If anyone outside the business knew this information, the result could damage the company.

Companies differ in their approach to workplace behavior. Some assume that employees bring their own high standards to the job. Others develop a code of conduct that lists specific behaviors expected from employees representing the company in business situations. The American Marketing Association is a major professional organization for marketers. Figure 5-2 shows a portion of its statement of ethics.

Today, more and more businesses are adopting clearly formulated ethics programs to guide behavior and decisions in the workplace. In companies that take ethics seriously, top management will project the value system that drives behavior. A company may convey its expectations for ethics on the job in different

Figure 5-2 The AMA Statement of Ethics addresses expected behaviors of those in the marketing industry.

AMA Statement of Ethics

"The American Marketing Association commits itself to promoting the highest standard of professional ethical norms and values for its members (practitioners, academics, and students). Norms are established standards of conduct that are expected and maintained by society and/or professional organizations. Values represent the collective conception of what communities find desirable, important and morally proper. Values also serve as the criteria for evaluating our own personal actions and the actions of others. As marketers, we recognize that we not only serve our organizations but also act as stewards of society in creating, facilitating and executing the transactions that are part of the greater economy. In this role, marketers are expected to embrace the highest professional ethical norms and the ethical values implied by our responsibility toward multiple stakeholders (e.g., customers, employees, investors, peers, channel members, regulators, and the host community)."

Goodheart-Willcox Publisher

Social Media

Business Pages

To take advantage of social media to increase the visibility of your company, decide which platform or tool you are going to use first. It is not necessary to use every social media option at the same time. Research each one and see which vehicles make sense for your business. Work with the marketing team or management and select one or two to start. Most social media sites require businesses to create a business page through a current personal user with a verified e-mail. Each of your business social media accounts will include some kind of company profile. Profile fields may include a business bio, company website links, blogs, locations, and an image. Be sure to completely fill out your profile on any social media sites you use. Then read the rules as they apply to businesses. As a marketer, you are representing your company, not yourself. It is important to understand what is expected for professional accounts.

ways. These include employee handbooks, training sessions or seminars, or printed formal statements of company values and ethics.

The ethical standards only have meaning when the message comes from management and managers lead by example. Stated codes of ethics generally address relationships of the business with employees, customers, suppliers, investors, creditors, competitors, and community. Business codes of ethics frequently relate to such issues as fair treatment of employees, teamwork, competition, and conflicts of interest. Other issues include use of business resources and assets, confidentiality, working with suppliers, and environmental concerns.

When applying for jobs, inquire about the company policies regarding employee decisions and behavior on the job. If ever in doubt about what is and is not acceptable, ask before acting.

Consumer Rights

In 1962, President John F. Kennedy addressed the Congress and outlined four basic consumer rights. Since 1962, four more rights have been added. The marketing concept directs businesses to focus on customer satisfaction. One way to do this is

for businesses to respect the *Consumer Bill of Rights* and treat customers ethically. The eight rights of consumers are
- the right to safety;
- the right to be informed;
- the right to choose;
- the right to be heard;
- the right to satisfaction of basic needs;
- the right to redress;
- the right to education; and
- the right to a healthful environment.

Business Issues

If an action is legal, should you worry if it is unethical? Yes. The line between legal and ethical can be very thin. If a company or employee acts unethically, it can have long-lasting effects.

Respected companies self regulate and voluntarily adhere to ethical behavior. Many marketing professionals join the American Marketing Association (AMA). The AMA sets the standards for marketing behavior. Businesses join the Better Business Bureau (BBB). The BBB sets the standards for ethical business behavior. Ethical issues include legal, privacy, promotions, pricing, accounting, and selling practices.

Explore

As a class, have students create a code of ethics for either your class or your school-based enterprise.

Explain

Discuss the functions of the Better Business Bureau (BBB). Have students consider the advantages of having access to the BBB.

While recycling is not enforced by law, most businesses choose to recycle because it is ethically responsible behavior that helps the environment.

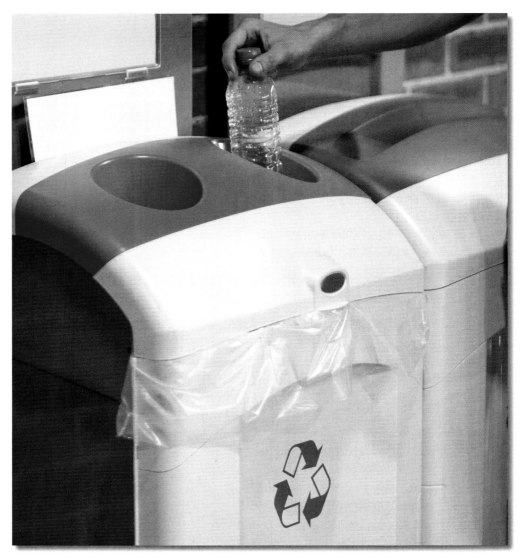

wavebreakmedia/Shutterstock.com

Legal

Businesses must comply with local, state, and federal laws. Part of the commitment a business makes to its customers is to operate within the legal system. Marketers who misrepresent their products or services risk losing customers, at the very least. Marketers must also be aware of the laws concerning the software they use. There are legal consequences when businesses break laws. These can include lawsuits, fines, jail time for the

owners and managers, or even having the business closed. Some of the laws that businesses must follow are in Figure 5-3.

Misrepresentation

The *Food and Drug Administration (FDA)* and *Consumer Product Safety Commission (CPSC)* regulate the safety of most consumer products. There are very strict rules and regulations for businesses that produce consumer products.

In addition, it is important to be aware of the guidelines of the Federal Trade Commission.

US Consumer Laws	
Federal Food, Drug, and Cosmetic Act (1938)	Gave the US Food and Drug Administration power to oversee the safety of all food, drugs, and cosmetics.
Fair Packaging and Labeling Act (1966)	Requires labels to list the product, the manufacturer's name and location, and the net amount of contents.
Child Safety Protection Act (1966)	Requires toy labels to list appropriate ages for toys and any potential safety hazards.
Truth in Lending Act (1968)	Requires disclosure of all finance charges on consumer credit agreements and in advertising for credit plans.
Child Protection and Toy Safety Act (1969)	Protects children from toys and other products that contain toxic materials or thermal, electrical, or mechanical hazards.
Fair Credit Reporting Act (1970)	Protects individuals from consumer reporting agencies sending inaccurate credit reports. Gives individuals the right to examine and correct their own credit histories.
Consumer Product Safety Act (1972) amended 1990	Created the Consumer Product Safety Commission. Protects the public against risks of injury or death from unsafe products. Monitors over 15,000 products.
Fair Credit Billing Act (1986)	Protects consumers from unfair billing practices. Consumers can dispute credit card billing errors.
Nutrition Labeling and Education Act (1990)	Requires food labels to list the calories and amounts of fat, cholesterol, sodium, and fiber per serving.
Children's Online Privacy Protection Act (2000)	Applies to the online collection of personal information from children under age 13. Requires website owners to seek parental consent for collecting the information. Sets rules for protecting children's online privacy and safety.
Country of Origin Labeling Law (2009)	Requires product labels to list the product's country of origin.

Goodheart-Willcox Publisher

Figure 5-3 Many laws have been created in the United States over the years that protect the rights of consumers.

The **Federal Trade Commission (FTC)** is the main federal agency that enforces advertising laws and regulations. Under the Federal Trade Commission Act:
- advertising must be truthful and nondeceptive;
- advertisers must have evidence to back up their claims; and
- advertisements cannot be unfair.

Software Use

All software is protected by a copyright, although some software may be released by its owner for free use. A **copyright** is the exclusive right to copy, license, sell, or distribute material. In the United States, an original work is copyrighted as soon as it is in tangible form. A copyright statement is *not* required. For example, if you write a story, as soon as the story is transferred from your mind to the paper or computer file, it is copyrighted. Almost everything found on the Internet is copyrighted, including images, music, videos, and textual information.

When you buy software, you are buying a license. A *license* is the legal permission to use a software program. All software has terms of use that outline for what purposes the license can be used.

Explore

Assign each student one of the laws to research further and give an oral report.

Marketing Ethics

Copyrights

It is unethical and illegal to use something created or written by another person without the permission to do so. Under copyright law, as soon as something is in tangible form, it is automatically copyrighted. Anything in print, including music, in TV or movies, or on the Internet is copyrighted. If any material is copied or used without permission by the owner, a theft has occurred. It is critical for a marketing professional to *not* use copyrighted material in promotions without permission from the owner.

The *fair-use doctrine* allows exceptions to copyright under certain limited situations. It allows for use of copyrighted material in teaching, news reporting, editorial commentary, and other similar situations. However, the copyrighted work may not be claimed as your own.

If you buy software, you have the license and you can use it on your computer. If a business buys software, it has the license for the software. A software license allows you to use the software, just like a driver's license allows you to drive a car. **Software piracy** is the illegal copying or downloading of software. This includes scanning or downloading images or music. Never engage in software piracy.

Some software may only be legally used if it is purchased. This is known as *for-purchase software.* **Shareware** is copyrighted software that is available free of charge on a trial basis, then must be purchased for continued use. Shareware usually has a notice screen, time-delayed startup, or reduced features. Purchasing the software removes these restrictions.

Freeware is fully functional software that can be used forever without purchasing it. To be considered freeware, the software cannot be a demo or restricted version of software meant for purchase. Figure 5-4 identifies the differences between the software types.

Public-domain software is similar to freeware in that it is free. However, freeware is copyrighted, while *public-domain software* either has no copyright, or the copyright has expired.

Privacy

Customers have the right to expect a company to keep their information confidential. Most businesses use a system to manage their customer relationships.

Figure 5-4 Each type of software has different payment structures and functionalities.

Characteristics	Software Type		
	For-Purchase	**Freeware**	**Shareware**
Cost	• Must be purchased to use • Demo may be available	Never have to pay for it	• Free to try • Pay to upgrade to full functionality
Features	Full functionality	Full functionality	Limited functionality without upgrade

Customer relationship management (CRM) is a system to track contact information and other information for current and potential customers. All CRM information should be considered private. CRM systems are typically electronic and used for marketing and sales purposes. Businesses that collect customer information may not sell it or abuse it by sending customers unwanted communications.

Internet Access

Internet access provided by the company should be used only for business purposes. Checking personal e-mail or shopping online is not acceptable. When communicating using the Internet, you are representing the company. Proper netiquette should be followed.

Netiquette is the accepted social and professional guidelines for communicating using the Internet. Never use texting language in a business environment. It is unprofessional to do so. Also, always proof-read and spell-check e-mails before clicking the send button. You may be responding to a customer e-mail, sending a marketing text, or blogging about a new product. In any communication, it is important to follow the same common courtesy you would in a face-to-face discussion.

Phishing, which is pronounced fishing, is a fun-sounding name for an activity that is not fun at all. **Phishing** is the use of fraudu-lent e-mails and copies of legitimate websites to trick people into providing personal, financial, and other data.

The most common form of phishing is done by sending an e-mail to the intended victim. The e-mail message pretends to be

If you create publications or blogs as a marketing task, you might think of using images, video, text, or sounds you find on the Internet. Remember, almost everything on the Internet is protected by copyright.

from a legitimate source, such as the person's bank. The e-mail asks the victim to send certain information, such as an account number and password, or it provides a link to a web page. If the person goes to the web page, the site looks real, but it collects the private information entered. That information can then be used to commit fraud.

Marketers protect customers from phishing e-mails by keeping customer information secure. They should also warn customers if information has been stolen. Legitimate businesses do not request confidential information through e-mail.

Cyber Bullying

Cyber bullying is using the Internet to harass or threaten an individual. Cyber bullying includes sending threatening messages or something as simple as intentionally flooding someone's e-mail account. Do not engage in any activity that could be seen as bullying another person or group of people.

Promotions

As you begin your marketing career, you will create marketing pieces to promote the company for which you are working. It is important to show the business in the best light. However, be honest in the messages. **False advertising** is overstating the features and benefits of products or services or making false claims about them. False advertising is both unethical and illegal.

It is unethical to send spam when promoting a business electronically. **Spam** is electronic messages sent in bulk to people who did not give a company permission to e-mail them. Sending spam can reflect poorly on a company and irritate current and potential customers. Marketing efforts should include sending e-mails only to customers who have given permission to do so.

Marketers should be aware that businesses sending spam are breaking antispam laws as well as hurting their companies' images.

Lim Yong Hiam/Shutterstock.com

Engage
Promote a discussion about cyber bullying and proper Internet use. Have students create a list of do's and don'ts for using the Internet.

Pricing

It is both unethical and illegal for businesses to engage in unfair pricing practices. There are many state and federal laws that prevent pricing tactics that harm consumers. In addition, the laws keep any one company from having total control of a market. If one company has all of the business, it could set unfair prices due to lack of competition. These laws are discussed in greater detail in Chapter 18.

Accounting

Businesses that do not accurately report the use of company funds commit an unethical and illegal act. In 2002, the US Congress passed the Sarbanes-Oxley Act, which requires open and honest business accounting and reporting practices. The act was passed due to a number of accounting frauds at major corporations. The accounting scandals, which included Enron and WorldCom, cost investors billions of dollars.

Selling

Ethical selling practices are important for the success of a company. As part of the marketing team, you will have some influence on your company's selling activities. Many businesses address the following issues in a code of conduct.

- It is illegal to accept or pay bribes for the purpose of closing a sale or obtain business licenses.
- High-pressure selling is not illegal, but many customers perceive it as unethical.
- It is unethical to accept gifts from suppliers in exchange for the promise to continue buying from them.
- Breaking business laws because you think you will not be caught is both illegal and unethical.

AMA Tip

The American Marketing Association promotes ethical norms and values for its members with its Statement of Ethics. Professional marketers who are members of the AMA commit themselves to the three following principles: do no harm, foster trust in the marketing system, and embrace ethical values. www.marketingpower.com

Cost of Unethical Behavior

Some say that image is everything, especially in the business world. Unethical behavior may not end in jail time, but companies can lose public trust. Losing trust hurts a business both in the short and long term. For example, British Petroleum's (BP) image was damaged when it caused the 2010 oil spill in the Gulf of Mexico. It was later revealed that warnings were given about possible problems yet were ignored by BP management. BP's sales dropped. The company spent many millions to both clean up the oil spilled in the Gulf and to reverse its negative image.

Businesses may lose customers who either no longer trust the company or approve of its business practices. When clients and customers cannot trust a business, they will buy elsewhere, which hurts profits. On the positive side, customers willingly go out of their way to purchase from companies they trust.

Ethics will always be a gray area. Marketers, however, should be ethical in all of their marketing efforts. While the payoff for it may not always be immediate, ethical behavior is noticed. The long-term effect on your success as a marketing professional will be positive.

Checkpoint 5.1

1. Describe the importance of a business code of ethics.
2. What ethical behavior is expected by most employers?
3. Name four consumer rights.
4. What precaution can be taken so that marketers do not send spam?
5. Explain the netiquette rules.

Build Your Vocabulary

As you progress through this text, develop a personal glossary of marketing terms and add it to your portfolio. This will help you build your vocabulary and prepare you for a career as a marketing professional. Write a definition for each of the following terms, and add it to your personal marketing glossary.

ethics
code of ethics
code of conduct
Federal Trade Commission (FTC)
copyright
software piracy
shareware
freeware
customer relationship management (CRM)
netiquette
phishing
cyber bullying
false advertising
spam
Sarbanes-Oxley Act

Checkpoint Answers

1. Ethical behavior is essential to developing business relationships. Good business relationships are the key to success in the 21st century. In order for business to run smoothly, people must be able to trust each other.
2. Most employers agree on the type of ethical behavior they expect from employees. This includes honesty, integrity, responsibility, and confidentiality.
3. List four of the following: the right to safety; right to be informed; right to choose; right to be heard; right to satisfaction of basic needs; right to redress; right to education; and right to a healthful environment.

4. Always obtain permission from customers to send any e-mail to them.
5. Never use texting language in a business environment. It is unprofessional to do so. Also, always proofread and spell-check e-mails before clicking the send button. In any communication, it is important to follow the same common courtesy you would in a face-to-face discussion.

Build Your Vocabulary Answers

Definitions for these terms can be found in the glossary of this text.

Section 5.2 Social Responsibility

After studying this section, you will be able to
- **explain** the role of business in society.
- **describe** corporate culture.

social responsibility
corporate social
 responsibility
goodwill
philanthropy
Environmental
 Protection Agency
 (EPA)
corporate culture

Consumers are often unaware of the ways in which their favorite businesses give back to society. Select a local business and visit its website. How is that business socially responsible?

Many businesses are socially responsible and give back to their communities. For example, a business may support a particular charity or give employees paid time off to perform volunteer activities of their choosing. Why would the company you identified above want to be involved in activities that are not obviously profitable?

Role of Business in Society

Social responsibility is behaving with sensitivity to social, environmental, and economic issues, as shown in Figure 5-5. It includes a duty to help others and to improve society in general. **Corporate social responsibility** is the actions a business takes to further social good. It goes beyond the profit interests and legal requirements of a business. Examples include donating to nonprofits, recycling, supporting local businesses, using nonanimal testing, or supporting a cause like cancer research.

Many businesses provide social benefits in addition to making a profit. For example, the very profitable corporation, Sony, has a company-wide volunteer program. Called

SOMEONE NEEDS YOU, each office tailors its volunteer activities to meet local community needs. In 2011, 180,000 Sony employees volunteered in many activities funded by the company.

Business also has the potential to do great harm. Some companies have caused great harm to society. For example, a chemical company produced fertilizer to help farmers grow crops. However, at the same time, the company put dangerous chemical waste into the nearby water supply. The dangerous waste contaminated drinking water and caused people to become ill with cancer and other diseases.

For-profit businesses have to make money to stay open. Customers are necessary to generate sales, and they can choose to buy from any business. Being a good corporate citizen promotes goodwill and may

Goodheart-Willcox Publisher

Figure 5-5 Think of the components of social responsibility as the pieces of a puzzle.

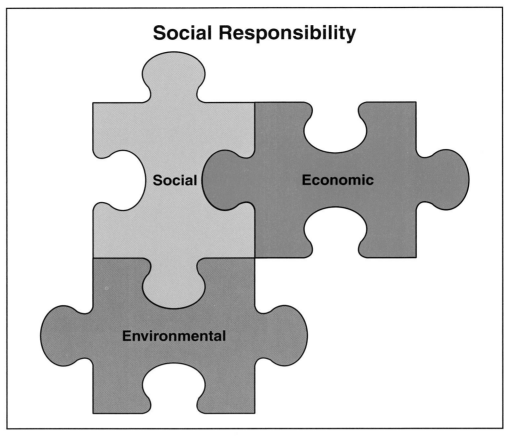

encourage customers to buy from a business. **Goodwill** is the advantage a business has due to its good reputation; it cannot be bought. Goodwill creates customer loyalty and is vitally important to success in business. Customer-oriented businesses know that people are more likely to buy from businesses that reflect their own values.

Social Issues

Businesses have a responsibility to help society achieve its basic goals. **Philanthropy** is promoting the welfare of others—usually through volunteering, protecting resources, or donating money or products. Giving back when you can is the basis of creating goodwill

for the marketing profession and the business for which you work.

There are many ways to give back. Many businesses support a charity or social cause on a regular basis. Social responsibility does not always mean giving money, though. You could volunteer your time. For example, some businesses allow employees paid time off work to volunteer at local schools. It could be reading to preschoolers, mentoring a high school student, or even speaking about marketing on career day. Companies can adopt a school and may help reward children for reading, getting good grades, or having good attendance.

Consider supporting a cause that fits well with your company's products or services.

Most employees consider volunteering through their businesses a work benefit. From a marketing standpoint, community assistance is good for business.

mangostock/Shutterstock.com

For example, if you work for an advertising agency, you could volunteer to help a nonprofit develop a marketing plan. Another option is to consider supporting those causes important to your customers. As another example, some businesses donate $1 to a local nonprofit for each purchase a customer makes.

Economic Issues

There is also an economic part of social responsibility that goes beyond volunteering or donating. What does social responsibility have to do with economics? All businesses operate within a community. It is important for any business to put money back into its community and support the local economy.

A socially responsible marketing professional will try to do business locally whenever possible. After all, the people in a community depend on each other for their livelihoods. Using local vendors whenever possible also supports the local economy.

For example, a market research company might hire people in the local community where the research is conducted. Hiring local helps the community. It also lowers the cost of doing business, which can increase profit. The new employees, in turn, spend their money locally. It is a system that benefits everyone.

Environmental Issues

Protecting the environment impacts society as a whole. There are many ways for socially responsible businesses to conserve natural resources and reduce pollution. Use environmentally friendly or *green* products—both in business operations and for product packaging. Provide customers with reusable shopping bags or those made from recycled materials. Recycle everything the business uses, such as paper, printer cartridges, or glass bottles.

Look for other ways your business might help to protect the environment. Become familiar with government resources helping

Exploring Careers

Sales Management

The sales force is often the first point of contact with potential customers. A sales manager hires, trains, and directs salespeople to achieve company sales goals. Sales managers establish sales territories and quotas for sales representatives, monitor sales potential and inventory requirements, and analyze sales statistics. In larger companies, the sales manager may report to a regional or national sales manager. In smaller companies, the sales manager reports directly to the company executives. Other typical job titles for a sales manager include *director of sales, sales supervisor, sales executive,* and *store manager.*

Some examples of tasks sales managers perform include:

* hire and train local sales representatives;
* monitor customer preferences to help focus the efforts of sales representatives;
* prepare sales budgets;
* complete performance evaluations of local sales representatives; and
* resolve customer complaints as needed.

Sales managers must be able to manage and motivate employees effectively to maximize each person's potential. They should understand the principles and methods of selling and marketing. In addition, they should be familiar with all of the products offered for sale by the company and those offered by the competition. Many jobs in this field require a bachelor degree as well as considerable experience or on-the-job training. For more information, access the *Occupational Outlook Handbook* online.

businesses use green practices. The **Environmental Protection Agency (EPA)** is the federal agency providing information about environmental-compliance rules and regulations. These laws vary by business sector.

The EPA at www.epa.gov also has a vast amount of information devoted to environmental law and sustainable business practices. As you progress through this text, notice the *Green Marketing* features. These features highlight different ways for marketers to use green practices.

FYI

Basic activities, such as recycling, using energy-efficient lightbulbs, and turning off lights save money and conserve resources.

Explain

To review, ask a student to explain the purpose of Environmental Protection Agency.

Corporate Culture

The term **corporate culture** describes how the owners and employees of a company think, feel, and act as a business. As a member of the marketing team, you will have an impact on the corporate culture. The level of social responsibility is part of corporate culture.

When creating the marketing plan, make social responsibility an important part of the plan. Look to management to see who they support. How will your marketing plan impact a particular cause or nonprofit? How will it recycle or reduce pollution? Explain how socially responsible choices will affect the community and the business as a whole.

Extend

Discuss corporate culture. Have students describe what the corporate culture might be like at Google compared to Bank of America.

All electronic marketing techniques are considered green because they greatly reduce use of paper.

Ivelin Radkov/Shutterstock.com

Many marketers increase visibility by using their company websites to discuss socially responsible activities. Social media is another great marketing tool for explaining the corporate culture of a company. Companies with positive corporate cultures attract great employees and loyal customers.

Case in Point

method®

Companies that are ethically and socially responsible can influence the success of their businesses. There are many examples of companies that are good corporate citizens and financially successful. One example is a company called method®. It makes nontoxic cleaning products that are free of harsh chemicals in 100 percent recycled plastic bottles. In addition, the company promotes using only one bottle and refilling it with the lower-cost method® product refills.

The company was started in 2001 by two young entrepreneurs who had been exposed to harmful toxins in standard cleaning products. They began producing several environmentally friendly cleaners that also smelled good. As method®, they first sold four cleaning-spray products to one local store in California. By 2002, Target test-marketed several products in 90 stores. Seven months later, method® was carried in all Target stores. By 2010, the company had gone global and is honored by many organizations for its commitment to social responsibility. Today method® is one of the fastest growing private American companies. Being a responsible business creates loyal customers who will continue to purchase your products, and more importantly, tell others about them.

Checkpoint 5.2

1. Give an example of corporate social responsibility.
2. What is the difference between corporate social responsibility and philanthropy?
3. Give an example of corporate environmental awareness.
4. Explain ways social responsibility influences the economy.
5. Why is goodwill important to a business?

Build Your Vocabulary

As you progress through this text, develop a personal glossary of Marketing terms and add it to your portfolio. This will help you build your vocabulary and prepare you for a career as a marketing professional. Write a definition for each of the following terms, and add it to your personal marketing glossary.

social responsibility
corporate social responsibility
goodwill
philanthropy
Environmental Protection Agency (EPA)
corporate culture

Checkpoint Answers

1. Examples include donating to nonprofits, recycling, supporting local businesses, using nonanimal testing, or supporting a cause like cancer research.
2. Corporate social responsibility is the actions of a business to further social good. Philanthropy is promoting the welfare of others—usually through volunteering, protecting resources, or donations.
3. Use environmentally friendly or *green* products—both in the business and when packaging products. Provide customers with reusable shopping bags or those made from recycled materials.

Recycle everything the business uses, such as paper, printer cartridges, or glass bottles.
4. Socially responsible businesses hire people in the local community. These people spend their wages in the community, in turn, helping the economy.
5. Goodwill creates customer loyalty and is vitally important to the success of any business.

Build Your Vocabulary Answers

Definitions for these terms can be found in the glossary of this text.

Chapter Summary

Section 5.1 Ethics

- Ethics is the rules of behavior based on ideas about what is right and wrong. Ethics plays an important role in business.
- Ethical behavior is important in the workplace. Most businesses have a code of ethics or code of conduct to guide appropriate behavior in the workplace.
- The *Consumer Bill of Rights* gives consumers the following eight rights: safety, to be informed, choice, to be heard, satisfaction of basic needs, redress, education, and a healthful environment.
- Businesses must comply with laws and conduct business in an ethical manner. They are obligated to maintain customer privacy; be truthful in promotions; and use fair pricing policies, accurate accounting procedures, and ethical selling practices.
- Unethical business behavior may result in loss of customers, public image, and profits.

Section 5.2 Social Responsibility

- In addition to making a profit, many businesses provide social benefits. Corporate social responsibility is the actions a business takes to further social good.
- *Corporate culture* is a term that describes how a company's owners and employees think, feel, and act as a business. As a member of the marketing team, you will have an impact on your company's corporate culture

Review Your Knowledge

1. List four behaviors that are expected from ethical employees.
2. Why is corporate ethics important to a marketing professional?
3. Explain the importance of respecting the private information of customers.
4. Which agencies regulate the safety of most consumer products?
5. Give an example of corporate social responsibility.
6. What is the difference between ethics and social responsibility?
7. Provide an example of a socially responsible business activity.
8. Can goodwill be bought? Explain.
9. What information can a business obtain from the EPA?
10. How can a positive corporate culture benefit the employees and the business?

Evaluate

Assign end-of-chapter activities.

Review Your Knowledge Answers

1. Honesty, integrity, responsibility, and confidentiality.
2. Following ethical behavior helps a marketer make fair decisions and develop positive customer relationships.
3. Customers have the right to expect a company to keep their information confidential. In order to maintain customer trust, you must keep information confidential.
4. Food and Drug Administration (FDA) and Consumer Product Safety Commission (CPSC)
5. Donating to nonprofits, recycling, supporting local businesses, using nonanimal testing, or supporting a cause like cancer research.
6. Ethics is doing what is right, and social responsibility is being sensitive to environment, social, and economic issues.
7. Examples include donating to nonprofits, recycling, supporting local businesses, using nonanimal testing, or supporting a cause like cancer research.
8. No. Goodwill is the advantage a business has due to its good reputation.
9. The EPA provides information about environmental-compliance rules and regulations. These laws vary by business sector. The EPA also has a vast amount of information devoted to environmental law and sustainable business practices.
10. It makes the company visible in a positive way to the community and to current and future employees.

Apply Your Knowledge

1. As a marketing professional, which ethical issues do you think will be most important for your career? List and explain your reasoning for each.
2. You have started your career as a marketing professional and realize the importance of having a personal code of ethics. Write a one-page summary describing the important topics that you will include in your personal code of ethics.
3. Identify a company that acts socially and ethically responsible. Conduct research on how its actions have influenced the marketing and sales of the company. Prepare a one-page written report.
4. When you begin working for a business, do you think you would be required to sign a confidentiality agreement? Why or why not?
5. As a new marketing professional, you are in the position of setting prices for products sold to other businesses. Research the laws regulating pricing. Write a one-page report on your obligations as a marketing professional as outlined in the laws.
6. As a new marketing professional, you understand the value of being socially responsible. List and describe three activities that you can undertake to show your responsibility to the community.
7. Look around your community and select a company who you think is socially responsible. What is this business doing to support the community?
8. A tornado has struck your town. The business you work for already supports a number of charities in the area. Should they react and assist with the disaster? Explain your answer.
9. Research proprietary information. What proprietary information might a marketing professional possess?
10. As a marketing professional, what activities could increase your business' environmental responsibility?

Check Your Marketing IQ

Now that you have finished the chapter, see what you learned about marketing by taking the chapter posttest. If you do not have a smartphone, visit the G-W Learning companion website.
G-W Learning mobile site: www.m.g-wlearning.com
G-W Learning companion website: www.g-wlearning.com

Common Core

College and Career Readiness

CTE Career Ready Practices. As a student and worker, you use technology skills every day to enhance your productivity. In your role as a marketing professional, traveling to tradeshows may be part of your job responsibilities. Describe the technology methods you would use to enhance your productivity while you are traveling.

Reading. Read a magazine, newspaper, or online article about a recent unethical business situation. Determine the central issues and conclusions of the article. Provide an accurate summary of the article, making sure to incorporate who, what, when, and how the unethical situation happened.

Writing. Go to the Environmental Protection Agency Protection website. How does the EPA help businesses protect the environment? Write an informative report consisting of several paragraphs to describe your findings.

Teamwork

Ethics are discussed in this chapter. Working with your team, make a list of five current ethical issues that have been in the news. Indicate if the ethics issues involve the owner, employees, or other specific individuals. Your team should give suggestions on how to remedy each ethics violation. Discuss your opinions with your class. What did you learn from this exercise?

G-W Learning Mobile Site

Visit the G-W Learning mobile site to complete the chapter pretest and posttest and to practice vocabulary using e-flash cards. If you do not have a smartphone, visit the G-W Learning companion website to access these features.

G-W Learning mobile site: www.m.g-wlearning.com

G-W Learning companion website: www.g-wlearning.com

Unit 1 Marketing Dynamics
Building the Marketing Plan

The best companies in the world make plans. They plan their marketing efforts; they plan for growth; they plan for hiring; they plan for profitability. As a future marketing manager, you need to plan as well. One way you begin planning is to do research about companies that you might like to create a marketing plan for in your marketing plan activity. Once you have selected a company to assume the role of marketing manager, you will begin the plan.

Part 1 Introduction

Objectives

- Set personal and SMART goals.
- Review the marketing plan template.

Directions

In this textbook, you will be exploring the world of marketing. As you learn about marketing and progress through the chapters, you will write a marketing plan. Step one of that process is to become acquainted with the marketing plan template you will use. Access the *Marketing Dynamics* companion website at www.g-wlearning.com. Download the data files as indicated for the following activities.

1. Unit Activity 1-1. SMART Goals. Create SMART personal and professional goals.
2. Open the data file called *MarketingPlanTemplate.docx*. Preview each section of the template in this data file. To familiarize your-self with the marketing plan format, read the instructions and questions that will guide you in the writing process. As you progress through the chapters, you will be directed to complete each section. However, the sections you complete in each activity may not be in the order listed in the document.
3. Ask your instructor where to save your documents. This could be on the school's network or a flash drive of your own. Save the marketing plan template as your own document to use for creating your Marketing Plan. Save the document as FirstnameLastname_MktPlan.docx (i.e., JohnSmith_MktPlan.docx).

Part 2 Identify Your Company

For this activity, you will assume the role of marketing manager for a company that you select. This is an important step. You will research potential companies and select one for which you will act as a marketing manager. Spend time now selecting the company that interests you and at which you will feel comfortable playing the marketing manager role. As you progress through this text, it will be your assignment to create a Marketing Plan for your company.

Objectives

- Identify a company for which you will assume the role as marketing manager.
- Create a title page for your Marketing Plan.
- Write a short business description for your business.
- Gather information about the target customers for your business.

Directions

1. Unit Activity 1-2. Research. Identify a company for which you will write a marketing plan. You will also find and study the business plan for your company. Much information found in the business plan will be helpful when completing the marketing plan.

2. Open the Marketing Plan document that you saved in Part 1. Locate the Title Page of the Marketing Plan. Complete the Title Page using the information you gathered in Activity 1-2. Key your company name, product, and your name. Leave the date blank until the Marketing Plan is completed. As you progress through the chapters, you will be directed to complete each section.

3. Locate the Business Description section of the Marketing Plan. Based on information in the business plan, list the company goals, vision and mission statements (if given), an overview of the business, and short descriptions of the products or services. This will be a short section: no longer than one page. It is permissible to condense this information. However, it is not acceptable to rewrite or recreate.

4. Locate the Situation Analysis section of the Marketing Plan. Begin writing the Target Market subsection. You will learn more details about target markets later in this text. For this exercise, record information about the customer to whom the business sells. This information can be found in the Target Market section of your company business plan. Write as much information about the targeted customer as is available in the business plan. You will continue adding to this section as the marketing plan develops.

5. Use the suggestions and questions listed in the template to help you generate ideas. Delete the instructions and questions when you are finished recording your responses. Proofread your document and correct any errors in keyboarding, spelling, and grammar.

6. Save your document.

You may use the sample business plan on the *Marketing Dynamics* companion website at www.g-wlearning.com. This business plan is written to be used as the basis for a marketing plan. The name of the file is Bus Plan_Sample.YoursinRetro.docx.

You may choose to require students to either work with a local business or publicly traded company. Students would need to be able to obtain a copy of the company's business plan.

Remember to remind students the importance of selecting a company that works for them. It will be challenging if they select a company, start a marketing plan, and realize it doesn't work for them.

Unit 2
Dynamics of the Economy

Chapters

6. Economic Principles and Systems
7. Market Forces and Economic Indicators
8. Business Cycles and the Role of Government
9. Global Trade

Eye-Catcher

Marketing Matters

There are many ways to send marketing messages to consumers. Any place where people can see a message is now a marketing venue. For example, the marketers at Hyundai clearly thought that sponsoring a racecar was a natural fit for their car brand—and they were right. A captive audience is a sure way to get your name in front of potential customers.

Marketing Core Functions Covered in This Unit

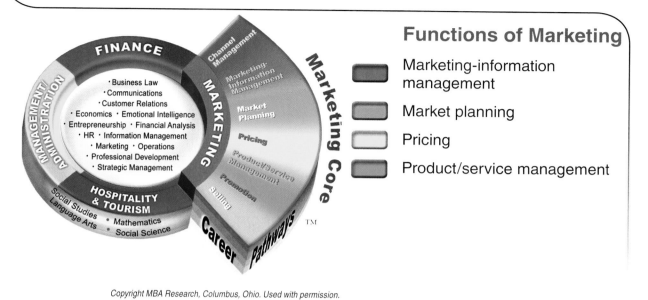

Functions of Marketing

- Marketing-information management
- Market planning
- Pricing
- Product/service management

Developing a Vision

Take a look around you. The state of our economy is in the news every day. Economics plays an important role in today's business. Successful marketers know how to use economic information and apply it to marketing strategies. Marketing a product in slow economic conditions may be difficult. Or, it may present opportunities. Understanding the marketing concept and how to apply it in good and bad conditions is crucial.

Marketing is global. Trade barriers are disappearing. Communication is improving. Opportunities exist to take product to other parts of the world. It is an exciting time to be a marketer.

6

Economic Principles and Systems

Section 6.1 Economics and Scarcity
Section 6.2 Economic Systems

"The most important single central fact about a free market is that no exchange takes place unless both parties benefit."

—Milton Friedman, Nobel-prize winning American economist

College and Career Readiness

Reading Prep
Before reading this chapter, read the opening pages for this unit and review the chapter titles. These can help prepare you for the topics that will be presented in the unit. What does this tell you about what you will be learning?

Check Your Marketing IQ

Before you begin the chapter, see what you already know about marketing by taking the chapter pretest. If you do not have a smartphone, visit the G-W Learning companion website.
G-W Learning mobile site: www.m.g-wlearning.com
G-W Learning companion website: www.g-wlearning.com

Explore
Assign the College and Career Readiness Reading Prep activity before students read the chapter. Reading Prep activities give students opportunity to apply the Common Core State Standards.

Engage
Assign the Chapter 6 pretest.

◇DECA Emerging Leaders

Creative Marketing Project, Part 1

Career Cluster and **Instructional Area** are not identified for this event.

Knowledge and Skills Assessed

The chapter representatives will demonstrate knowledge and skills needed to address the components of the project as described in the content outline and evaluation forms as well as learn/understand the importance of

- communications knowledge and skills—the ability to exchange information and ideas with others through writing, speaking, reading or listening;
- analytical knowledge and skills—the ability to derive facts from data, findings from facts, conclusions from findings and recommendations from conclusions;
- critical thinking/problem-solving knowledge and skills;
- production knowledge and skills—the ability to take a concept from an idea and make it real;
- teamwork—the ability to plan, organize and conduct a group project;
- the ability to evaluate group presentations; and
- priorities/time management—the ability to determine priorities and manage time commitments and deadlines.

Purpose

Designed for one to three chapter representatives, the project is a research study in the marketing field, planned, conducted, and reported by a DECA chapter, the use of which will measurably improve the marketing activities of an individual company, a group of companies (such as a shopping mall), an organization, a club, or the business community. All chapter members are encouraged to participate. The project may begin at any time after the close of the previous chartered association conference and run to the beginning of the next chartered association conference.

Procedure, Part 1

1. For Part 1 in this text, read the skills assessed and purpose of the event. Discuss these with your chapter members.
2. The written document will account for 60 points, and the oral presentation will account for the remaining 40 of the total 100 points.
3. The body of the written entry must be limited to 30 numbered pages, including the appendix (if an appendix is attached), but excluding the title page and the table of contents.
4. The Written Event Statement of Assurances must be signed and submitted with the entry. Do not include it in the page numbering.
5. Prior to the presentation, the judge will evaluate the written portion of the entry. The major emphasis of the written entry is on the content. Drawings, illustrations and graphic presentations (where allowed) will be judged for clarity.
6. The chapter representatives will present the project to the judge in a 15-minute presentation worth 40 points.
7. If there are any questions, ask your teacher to clarify.

Critical Thinking

1. How can your chapter benefit from participating in this project?
2. What strategy will be used identify the chapter representatives?

Visit www.deca.org for more information.

Section 6.1 Economics and Scarcity

Objectives

After completing this section, you will be able to
- **explain** the term *economics* and why it is important.
- **describe** how scarcity affects individuals and nations making economic choices.
- **list** the four major factors of production and give an example of each.

Key Terms

economics
supply and demand
scarcity
opportunity cost
factor of production
land
natural resource
labor
productivity
capital
capital good
infrastructure
technology
entrepreneurship

Web Connect

Search the Internet to find the three industries in your state that generate the most revenue. What is the most important factor of production to each of these industries: land, labor, or capital? Is your state well suited to provide these factors?

Critical Thinking

A nation's economic system turns factors of production into goods and services. List three major industries in the United States that lead the world in producing the best products and services.

Economics

Economics is a science that deals with examining how goods and services are produced, sold, and used. Economics is how people, governments, and companies make choices about using limited resources to satisfy unlimited wants. Consumers can purchase products and services from whomever they choose. Understanding how economics plays a role in the buying decisions of consumers helps marketers make better decisions.

Businesses must create a desirable product or service. The marketing team helps determine the reasons for customers to buy it from them. Supply and demand is the economic principle relating to the quantity of products available to meet consumer demand. Product prices are influenced by supply and demand. When demand is higher than the available resources, it is called scarcity.

Problem of Scarcity

Think about the things you need and want. For example, you may need an apple, a pen, or a new shirt. You may want to go to a movie, out to dinner with friends, or on a vacation. You may also want to buy someone a gift, give to a charity, or save money for the future.

Explore

Provide an opportunity for students to explore by assigning a hands-on activity. Review the vocabulary terms at the beginning of the section. Where have students encountered these terms before? Help students make educated guesses about the meanings of the terms with which they are least familiar.

Resource

Use the Chapter 6 presentation on the optional Instructor's Presentations for PowerPoint® CD as an outline for presenting the chapter.

Elaborate/Extend

Assign the College and Career Readiness Portfolio activity at the end of the chapter.

A shortage of fuel usually leads to long lines at the pumps and higher prices.

Lisa F. Young/Shutterstock.com

Can you afford everything you need and want right now? No. Why not? You do not have enough resources to meet all of your needs and wants. What are your resources? Your resources include time, money, and your ability to work to earn money. You do not have enough resources because of a problem called scarcity.

Both individuals and nations struggle with the problem of scarce, or limited, resources. One quality of a resource is that it can only be used once. For example, the dollar used to buy an apple cannot also be used to buy a pen. A tree that is used to make tables cannot also be used to make paper. This problem of scarcity requires people and nations to make economic choices.

Every economic decision has a cost. When you make a choice, you lose the opportunity to do the thing you did not choose. Economic decisions often have more than two options. An opportunity cost is the value of the best option you did *not* choose.

For example, suppose you have two free hours. You can watch TV or go to work and earn $20. If you watch TV, you will not earn $20. If you go to work, you will miss your favorite TV show. So, the opportunity cost of watching TV is $20. However, if you choose to work, the opportunity cost is missing your favorite TV program. You make your decision based on what is more valuable to you.

Nations also have many economic needs and wants, but most resources are scarce. As a result, nations have to make economic choices with bigger opportunity costs. For example, a nation might choose to spend money on its military instead of medical research. The opportunity cost is the medical research that was not conducted. Like individuals, nations also make economic decisions based on certain values. Governments make those decisions based on politics.

Factors of Production

Factors of production are the economic resources nations use to make products and supply services for their citizens. The factors of production are land, labor, capital, and entrepreneurship. Factors of production are also called *economic resources.*

Think about goods that you often use, such as athletic shoes. What was required to produce those shoes? Many economic resources were used to create them: cotton, rubber, shoe-fabricating machines, people running the machines, and a business owner.

These resources represent the four factors of production: land, labor, capital, and entrepreneurship, as shown in Figure 6-1. In this example, cotton and rubber represent the land resource. Workers provide the labor. The shoe-fabricating machines are the capital.

The business owner represents entrepreneurship by organizing the other three economic resources to operate the business.

Land

Land includes all of a nation's natural resources. **Natural resources** are raw materials found in nature. These can include soil, water, minerals, plants, and animals. Every good produced uses natural resources in some form. Many natural resources are scarce and take a very long time to replenish. Even developed nations like the United States have limited natural resources.

Figure 6-1 Production of athletic shoes requires land, labor, capital, and entrepreneurship.

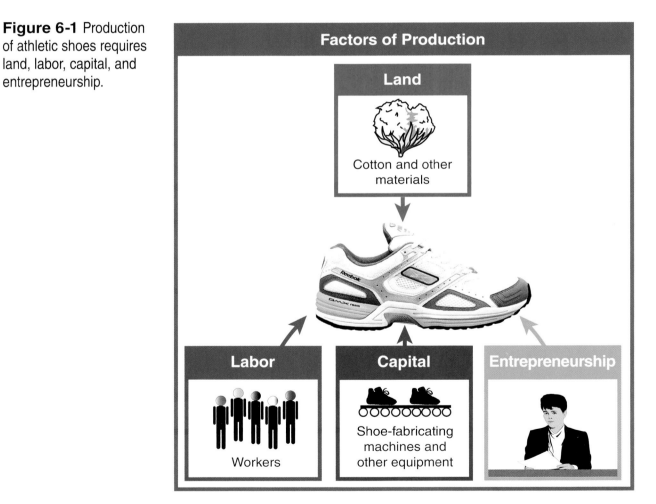

Explain

Review the factors of production and their importance to the economy.

Engage

Encourage a discussion about the importance of natural resources and products we need to survive.

Case in Point

Silly Bandz

Sales for Silly Bandz took off in 2006 when Brainchild Products founder, Robert J. Croak, introduced the rubber-band bracelets in colorful shapes. The bracelets quickly became a craze. From a small warehouse in Toledo, Ohio, Silly Bandz went from shipping 20 to 1,500 boxes a day in a very short time. Silly Bandz became the brand name for the bracelets as Kleenex is the brand name for tissues.

In general, the law of supply and demand states that when demand rises, prices also rise. There was a time in 2008 when the company could have easily increased the Silly Bandz price. The marketers, however, chose a pricing strategy that kept the price low. The marketers made that decision for two reasons. They wanted the product to remain an affordable alternative to video games and other expensive toys. And, the pricing would still beat competitors trying to get in on the bracelet trend. That strategy proved sound, especially in a poor economy. By 2010, Silly Bandz sales slowed, but remain stable. At just $5.00 for 24 Silly Bandz, parents could afford the low price to keep their children happy.

Natural resources are not equally distributed among nations. Some natural resources are found only in certain parts of the world. For example, South Africa has mines producing great quantities of diamonds and other gemstones. While the United States is rich in minerals like coal, lead, and zinc, it has no diamond mines.

The size of a nation also determines the quantity of a nation's natural resources. For example, Japan is four percent the size of the United States. Therefore, it has much fewer natural resources.

Labor

Labor is the work performed by people in businesses. **Productivity** is the amount of work a person can do in a specific amount of time, usually an hour. Another term for labor is *human resources.*

A nation can make up for a lack of natural resources if its people are very productive. For example, Japan has few natural resources. However, it has the world's third-largest economy. This is because Japanese workers are highly educated, skilled, and very productive.

Extend

Ask students to explain why productivity is important.

Capital

As a factor of production, **capital** is all of the tools and machinery used to produce goods or provide services. **Capital goods** are those products businesses use to produce other goods. Capital goods are used to make final products, which are then sold to consumers. For example, a shoe-fabricating machine is a capital good because its only purpose is to make shoes. The shoes are the final product. Consumers do not buy capital goods, they buy final products.

FYI

Capital is another business term with different meanings. It is often used as the short form of *financial capital,* which is money that is used to buy capital goods. As a result, capital can be used to refer to capital goods or money.

Infrastructure

Infrastructure is considered part of capital. **Infrastructure** consists of the transportation systems and utilities necessary in a modern

Extend

Make a list of capital goods. Ask: Why is capital important?

economy. Infrastructure is usually large and cannot be moved from place to place.

Transportation infrastructure includes highways, bridges, railroads, public transportation, seaports, and airports. Infrastructure provides the foundation on which modern industry is built. Utility infrastructure includes sanitation systems, electric power plants, water systems, and telecommunications services. Some infrastructure, such as the railroads and oil pipelines, were built by private companies. However, most infrastructure is built by state and federal governments.

Imagine you are looking for a place to build a factory. You have a choice between two areas. One area has excellent infrastructure access. It is close to major highways, railroads, and power plants. The other area has poor highway access and is very far from rail service. Where would you want to build your new factory? Your answer will likely be in the area with the better infrastructure.

Technology

Another part of capital as a factor of production is technology. **Technology** is the use of science to invent useful things or to solve problems. Countries can use early technology or advanced technology. The type of technology used has a major impact on an economy.

Most businesses choose to locate near large transportation hubs with good infrastructure to save on shipping costs.

Maksimilian/Shutterstock.com

Elaborate

Discuss the importance and cost of transportation to a business.

Explore

Review Figure 6-2. Ask for other suggestions to expand the information that is presented.

Early technology includes the six simple machines: lever, wedge, inclined plane, screw, pulley, and wheel and axle. Machines powered by people or animals are also examples of early technology. Early technology produced great productivity improvements in ancient times. However, in modern times, countries that only use early technology struggle to meet the basic needs of food and shelter for citizens.

More advanced technology includes industrial and digital technologies. *Industrial technology* is powered by steam and fuel combustion. For example, automobiles and jets are powered by fuel combustion, as are many factories. *Digital technology* uses electricity to control data. Examples include computers, smartphones, and the Internet. Countries using advanced technologies produce more goods and services than those using early technology.

Entrepreneurship

The final factor of production is entrepreneurship. Entrepreneurship is the willingness and ability to start a new business. Entrepreneurs organize the other three factors of production to produce a product or service and earn a profit. They are able to take financial and personal risks necessary to start and run a business.

From a small store to a large manufacturer, all businesses are started by entrepreneurs. For example, the entrepreneur Steve Jobs cofounded Apple, Inc. It became one of the most successful corporations in the world. The number and quality of entrepreneurs in a country have a major impact on an economy. Figure 6-2 summarizes the four factors of production.

Three Types of Economic Inputs			
Input	**Other Names**	**Categories**	**Examples**
Land	Natural resources Raw materials	Soil, water, minerals, plants, animals, climate	Mississippi River, fertile soil, coal, forests, salmon, temperate climate
Labor	Human resources Workers Entrepreneurs	Agricultural workers, construction workers, factory workers, miners, professionals, service workers	Farmers, electricians, steelworkers, teachers, managers, flight attendants, business owners
Capital	Capital goods Equipment Infrastructure Technology	Tools, equipment, machinery, buildings, vehicles, transportation systems, utilities	Scissors, oil drills, computers, office buildings, warehouses, tractors, airports, roads, sanitation systems
Entrepreneurship	Ownership Partnership Corporation	Business owners and partners	President, owner, founder

Goodheart-Willcox Publisher

Figure 6-2 A healthy economy needs all four factors of production.

Checkpoint 6.1

1. Discuss the concept of scarcity.
2. Explain the meaning of the phrase, "every economic decision has a cost."
3. Name the four factors of production.
4. What is the difference between final products and capital goods?
5. Why is entrepreneurship an important factor of production?

Build Your Vocabulary

As you progress through this text, develop a personal glossary of marketing terms which will help you build your vocabulary and prepare you for a career in marketing. Write a definition for each of the following terms, and add it to your personal marketing glossary.

economics
supply and demand
scarcity
opportunity cost
factor of production
land
natural resource
labor
productivity
capital
capital good
infrastructure
technology
entrepreneurship

Checkpoint Answers

1. You do not have enough resources to meet all of your needs and wants. Both individuals and nations struggle with the problem of scarce, or limited, resources. One quality of a resource is that it can only be used once.

2. When you make a choice, you lose the opportunity to do the thing you did not choose. There are often more than two options when faced with making an economic decision. An opportunity cost is the value of the best option you did *not* choose. You make your decision based on what is more valuable to you.

3. Four factors of production are land, labor, capital, and entrepreneurship.

4. Final products are purchased by consumers, while capital goods are used to make final products.

5. Entrepreneurs organize the other three factors of production to produce a product or service and earn a profit.

Build Your Vocabulary Answers

Definitions for these terms can be found in the glossary of this text.

Section 6.2 Economic Systems

Economic System Defined

A *system* is a way to manage, control, or organize something that follows a set of rules. For example, a computer system consists of input, a production mechanism, and output. The information or data keyed into the computer is the input. The production mechanism includes the computer hard drive, software programs, and the printer. The output is the physical or electronic document produced.

An **economic system** is an organized way in which a state or nation allocates its resources to create goods and services. Figure 6-3 shows some simple examples of systems.

Just like a computer system, an economic system has input, a production mechanism, and output. Recall that the factors of production are the economic resources or input of a nation. In Chapter 3, you learned that

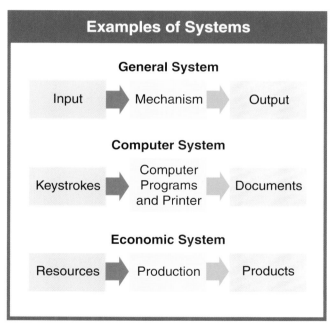

Goodheart-Willcox Publisher

Figure 6-3 An economic system turns resources into products.

production is any activity related to making a product. Production includes farming, mining, construction, manufacturing, and performing services. You will learn more about the production of goods in Chapter 15. **Economic input** includes the resources used to make products. **Economic output** is all the goods and services produced by an economic system during a specific time.

As discussed in the previous section, every nation has the problem of scarcity. Scarce resources limit the quantity of goods and services produced in any economic system. The problem of scarcity leads to three important economic questions every nation must answer, as shown in Figure 6-4:
- What should we produce?
- How should we produce it?
- Who should get the products?

FYI

Economic output is also called *Gross Domestic Product (GDP)*.

Types of Economic Systems

A nation's economic system develops around the way it deals with scarcity. Economists classify these systems as being a traditional, command, or market economy. In addition, most economies today are mixed. Mixed economies have elements of both a command and market economy.

The Three Economic Questions		
Economic Question	**Related Questions**	**Examples**
What should we produce?	Which goods, services, and ideas should we produce? How much of each product should we produce?	Should we produce consumer products or weapons for the military? Should we grow crops or raise cattle? Should we explore space or research a cure for cancer?
How should we produce it?	Who should produce each type of product? How shall we use our natural resources? What production techniques should be used?	Who should be a doctor and who should be a farmer? Should we generate electricity from coal, oil, or nuclear power? Should natural areas be preserved or used for mining? Should people or computers calculate the payroll?
Who should get the products?	How will the nation decide who gets each product? How should products be distributed?	Should the rich get all the products they want? Should the head of the government get whatever he or she wants? How should the nation provide for the poor? How should the country ration scarce resources in times of crisis?

Goodheart-Willcox Publisher

Figure 6-4 Economic systems develop around the way each country answers the three basic economic questions.

Elaborate/Extend

Provide an opportunity for students to exhibit their understanding of concepts in context of the material as it is presented. As time permits, have students read and discuss the special features in the chapter.

Elaborate

Compare and contrast economic input and economic output.

Green Marketing

Paper

Marketing efforts can use a lot of paper, so look for paper products that are safe for the environment. Paper manufacturers are always looking for new ideas to produce paper products from renewable sources. Currently, some paper is made from by-products of sugar cane instead of wood. Sugar cane biodegrades faster than wood, is less expensive, and is cleaner to use in the production process. Many office supply companies carry sugar cane paper with more new products to come. Other companies use recycled paper to create new paper products. Consider using recycled paper for your print marketing materials.

Traditional Economy

Tradition is a way of thinking, behaving, or acting used by a group of people for a long time. Societies based on tradition tend to use early technology, such as human- or animal-powered machines.

A **traditional economy** is one in which most citizens have just enough to survive. Elders of the society usually make economic decisions for the group based on tradition. Countries with traditional economies are often farm based with large rural populations. There is little to no manufacturing. Most people trade or barter for needed goods and services.

Traditional economies developed early in human history and there are very few left. Examples include the Bedouin people of the Middle East and the Inuit tribes in northern Canada.

Command Economy

In a **command economy**, the government makes all of the economic decisions. The government decides what, when, and how to produce products. For example, the government would decide how much land would be used to grow wheat. It would determine which resources will go to producing consumer goods and who gets the products. A command economy is also called a *centrally planned economy* because a central government makes all decisions.

One goal of a command economy is to make sure all citizens share limited resources equally. As a result, the government tries to make jobs available to everyone. It also provides other necessities like education, medical care, and housing.

Command economies are associated with two related political philosophies: communism and socialism. Both are characterized by central planning, collective ownership, and government control of the factors of production. One of the largest command economies of the 20th century was the former Soviet Union, which fell in 1991. Two that remain today are North Korea and Cuba.

Market Economy

The opposite of a command economy is a *pure market economy* with no government involvement in the economy. A **market economy** is one in which individuals are free to make their own economic decisions. The people decide what and how much to produce. They also choose what to buy based on how much money they have. The government does not set prices. Instead, the individuals in a marketplace determine prices by how much they are willing to pay for items. Due to that fact, a market economy is also sometimes called a *consumer economy*.

Elaborate/Extend

If students are using the optional *Marketing Dynamics* workbook, assign activities to engage active learning.

Explore

Ask students to research traditional, command, and market economies. Which do they think is most extreme?

FYI

Market economies developed in countries that chose a political philosophy called *democracy.* Citizens in democracies control the government through voting. Democracies allow important individual rights, including the right to own property and the freedom of speech.

The United States has maintained the largest market economy of the 20th and 21st centuries. However, it has never been a *pure* market economy. In fact, pure market economies do not exist. All countries have at least some government influence on economic decisions. Many countries have primarily market economies with three main features, as shown in Figure 6-5.

Three main features of a market economy are
• Both individuals and businesses can own private property.
• Individuals are free to make their own economic decisions.
• Market forces affect the economy.

Goodheart-Willcox Publisher

Figure 6-5 Businesses and competition thrive in market economies.

Private Property

A market economy is based on the right of individuals to own private property. They also have the freedom to do what they want with it. People can live on a property, start a business on it, or sell it. For example, individuals are free to use their money to buy equipment and make basketballs or buy farmland and grow wheat. In a command economy, the central government owns all of the property and decides how it is used.

Economic Freedom

Individuals are free to make their own economic decisions in a market economy. In

Resource/Evaluate

Assign the optional Chapter 6 test for **EXAM**VIEW® Assessment Suite as a formal assessment tool.

other words, each person decides what to buy, when to buy it, and how to use it. Citizens are also free to become entrepreneurs and start any legal business or enterprise. For this reason, a market economy is sometimes referred to as a *free-enterprise system* or *private enterprise.*

Individuals also make their own labor choices in a market economy. They can choose to work for themselves, a company, or not work at all. By contrast, in a command economy, the government controls labor. It decides which citizens will do which jobs. People are *not* free to choose their work or quit their jobs.

FYI

Other names for a market economy are *capitalism* or a *capitalist economy.*

Market Forces

The three major market forces are supply and demand, the profit motive, and competition. Unlike command economies, market forces affect market economies. Even though individuals are free to make economic decisions, market forces can influence their decisions. A market economy is often called a *free-market economy.* This is because market forces freely influence economic decisions. Figure 6-6 summarizes the main features of a market versus a command economy.

The Scottish philosopher Adam Smith was the first person to realize how a market economy works. In 1776, he published *The Wealth of Nations* that outlined his economic views. Smith believed that freedom of choice creates the market forces, which he described as an *invisible hand.* Market forces ensure that the right products are available at the right times, in the right quantities, and at the right prices.

Command and Market Economies		
Features	**Command**	**Market**
Who owns the economic inputs?	• Central government	• Individuals
Who answers the three economic questions?	• Central government	• Individuals
Who controls the economy?	• Central government	• Market forces
Main features	• Government ownership of land and capital • Government control of labor • Government control of all economic activity	• Private property • Economic freedom • Market forces: supply and demand, profit motive, competition
Political philosophy	• Communism • Socialism	• Democracy
Other names	• Centrally planned economy • Communist economy • Socialist economy • Welfare state	• Capitalism • Capitalist economy • Consumer economy • Free enterprise • Free market economy • Private enterprise

Goodheart-Willcox Publisher

Figure 6-6 Command and market economies differ in how the economic questions are answered and by whom.

Mixed Economies

Both a pure command economy and a pure market economy have weaknesses. A *pure command economy* is far too large and complex for a government to control all of a nation's resources. The lack of freedom removes all three essential market forces. Shortages tend to occur. As a result, command economies have historically failed to meet the needs of its citizens. To solve these problems, some command economies have moved to allow more individual freedoms.

A *pure market economy* is also not sustainable. Some government help is needed to provide products and services for the common good. As a result, nearly every modern economic system includes parts of both command and market economies. In a **mixed economy,** both the government and individuals make decisions about economic resources. In most countries, for example, public roads are built and maintained by government. The government also handles areas like law enforcement and national defense.

Some mixed economies have more government involvement, while others have more individual involvement. There are three types of mixed economies: mixed command, mixed socialist, and mixed market.

Mixed Command

A *mixed-command economy* is primarily command with some free-market principles. The Peoples' Republic of China continues to be a communist country with a command

Extend

Review Figure 6-6. Do students agree or disagree with the information?

economy. In 1978, however, the Chinese government began a program of economic reforms that included some qualities of a market economy.

China now allows some private business ownership, with limits, to create competition. There is also less government involvement in farming and industry. In 2010, the number of private businesses reached 7.5 million, or half of the businesses in China. However, private businesses employed only 20 percent of the workers.

Mixed Socialist

Many European countries, such as Sweden and France, are social democracies. A **social democracy** is a socialist system of government achieved by democratic means. The government, however, collects a large percentage of taxes from the citizens. It uses this money to make sure every citizen has a certain standard of living. The government also owns and operates some important major industries, such as telecommunications and the railroads.

In a mixed-socialist economy, both the market and command economic principles are fairly equal. The citizens in a social democracy vote for their government and have many individual rights. Entrepreneurship is also encouraged.

Mixed Market

The United States is often said to be a market economy, but it is clearly a mixed-market economy. A *mixed-market economy* has more free enterprise than command economic principles. While individuals have total business freedom, government still controls some major aspects of the economy.

Citizens elect government officials who pass laws and make economic decisions. These decisions are funded by some personal and business income taxes. Examples include public education, national defense, and various social programs, such as Social Security and Medicare. How significant is this government involvement? Government spending was about 20 percent of total US spending in 2011.

Economic reforms have helped the Chinese economy grow to the second largest in the world behind the United States.

pcruciatti/Shutterstock.com

College and Career Portfolio

Organization

As you collect items for your portfolio, you will need a method to keep the items clean, safe, and organized for assembly at the appropriate time. A large manila envelope works well to keep hard copies of your documents, photos, awards, and other items. Three-ring binders with sleeves are another good way to store your information. If you have a box large enough for full-size documents, it will work also. Plan to keep like items together and label the categories. For example, store the documents that illustrate your writing or computer skills together. Use notes clipped to the documents to identify each item and state why it is included in the portfolio. For example, a note on a newsletter you wrote might say, *Newsletter that illustrates desktop publishing skills.*

1. Select a method for storing hard copy items you will be collecting for your portfolio. *Note:* You will decide where to keep electronic copies in a later activity.

2. Write a paragraph that describes your plan for storing and labeling the items. Refer to this plan each time you add items to the portfolio.

Mixed-Economy Continuum

One way to look at modern economies is to see them on a continuum, as shown in Figure 6-7. On the left side of the continuum is the pure command economy. On the right side is the pure market economy. The economies of other nations fall at different points between the two extremes. Their positions on the continuum depend on the amount of control exercised by the government versus individuals. For example, Cuba and North Korea are closest to pure-command economies. Singapore and Hong Kong are closest to pure-market economies. The United States has more government influence than Singapore and Hong Kong, but more individual influence than France and Sweden.

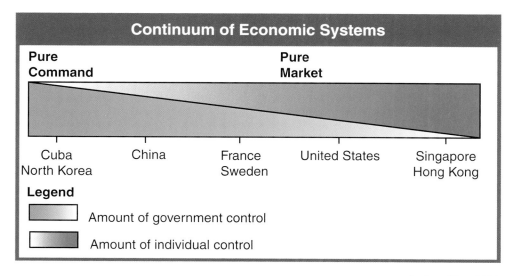

Figure 6-7 There are no pure-command or pure-market economies. The amount of individual and governmental control changes across the continuum.

Goodheart-Willcox Publisher

Engage

Ask a student to present the information in Figure 6-7.

The AMA partners with more than 30 organizations to offer enhanced content and benefits to members. For example, by partnering with a global consulting firm, the AMA is able to offer additional reports to members, including a guide to behavioral economics. Content and benefits from AMA partners are available to members. www.marketingpower.com

Checkpoint 6.2

1. What are the three basic economic questions about scarcity which need to be answered by every nation?
2. What are three basic economic systems that nations have developed to deal with the questions regarding scarcity?
3. What is the major difference between a command economy and a market economy?
4. List three major market forces.
5. Why are most economies mixed?

Build Your Vocabulary

As you progress through this text, develop a personal glossary of marketing terms which will help you build your vocabulary and prepare you for a career in marketing. Write a definition for each of the following terms, and add it to your personal marketing glossary.

economic system
economic input
economic output
traditional economy
command economy
market economy
mixed economy
social democracy

Evaluate

Assign the Checkpoint questions at the end of the section. Assess students' comprehension using the Checkpoint activity as a self-assessment tool.

Checkpoint Answers

1. Three basic economic questions about scarcity are: what should be produced; how should it be produced; and who should get the products?
2. Three basic economic systems are traditional, command, and market.
3. The government makes all the economic decisions in a command economy, while individuals make the economic decisions in a market economy.

4. Three major market forces are supply and demand, the profit motive, and competition.
5. Most economies are mixed because pure command economies fail as it is too complicated to centrally plan all the details of a national economy. Pure market economies cannot function without at least some government functions, such as to enact and enforce laws so people don't steal.

Build Your Vocabulary Answers

Definitions for these terms can be found in the glossary of this text.

Chapter Summary

Section 6.1 Economics and Scarcity

- Economics is a science that deals with examining how goods and services are produced, sold, and used. Economics reflects how people, governments, and companies make choices about using limited resources to satisfy unlimited wants.
- All individuals and nations have to face the problem of scarcity, since all resources are limited. Economies develop around the way a nation and its people deal with scarcity.
- The four major factors of production are land, labor, capital, and entrepreneurship.

Section 6.2 Economic Systems

- Economic systems are organized ways in which a state or nation allocates its resources to create goods and services. An economic system has input, a production mechanism, and output.
- Economists classify economic systems as being traditional economies, command economies, or market economies. In addition, most economics are mixed, meaning they have elements of both a command and market economy.

Review Your Knowledge

1. Describe natural resources.
2. Explain the word *system.*
3. Name the three main components of an economic system,
4. Define the word *tradition.*
5. Why might growth be difficult to achieve in a traditional economy?
6. Command economies are associated with which two political philosophies?
7. What other term is a market economy also known as?
8. Why is a pure market economy not sustainable?
9. Many European countries are classified as what type of economy?
10. Describe one way to look at modern economies.

Review Your Knowledge Answers

1. Natural resources are raw materials found in nature, such as soil, water, minerals, plants, and animals.
2. System is a way to manage, control, or organize something that follows a set of rules.
3. The three main components of an economic system are input, production, and output.
4. Tradition is a way of thinking, behaving, or doing something used by a group of people for a long time.
5. Growth might be difficult to achieve because people tend to perform economic activities based on tradition, or the way they have always been done. As a result, traditional economies rely more heavily on early technologies.
6. Two political philosophies associated with command economies are socialism and communism.
7. A market economy also known as a consumer economy because consumers ultimately determine which products are produced.
8. A pure market economy is not sustainable because some government help is necessary to provide products and services for the common good.
9. Many European countries are classified as a social democracy.
10. One way to look at modern economies is to see them on a continuum. On the left side of the continuum is the pure command economy. On the right side is the pure market economy. The various nations' economies fall at different points between the two extremes. Their positions on the continuum depend on the amount of control exercised by the government versus individuals.

Apply Your Knowledge

1. You selected a company for which to write a marketing plan. How do you think the term scarcity will impact your business?
2. Identify the factors of production that will impact you as marketing manager for the business you have selected.
3. Explain why you think it is important for a marketing professional to understand economics.
4. How will supply and demand impact your marketing plan?
5. How will scarcity determine if you have a career in marketing?
6. You are creating a marketing plan and evaluating consumers who might buy your product. Would it be helpful to have information about the opportunity costs of your potential customers? Briefly explain.
7. Explain *free enterprise* in your own words.
8. Do you think there is a need for a marketing manager in a command economy? Briefly explain.
9. Would a marketing manager be needed more in a command economy or a market economy? Briefly explain.
10. Give examples of how government regulations might affect the way you market a product in a mixed market economy.

Check Your Marketing IQ

Now that you have finished the chapter, see what you learned about marketing by taking the chapter posttest. If you do not have a smartphone, visit the G-W Learning companion website.

G-W Learning mobile site: www.m.g-wlearning.com

G-W Learning companion website: www.g-wlearning.com

Apply Your Knowledge Answers

Student answers will vary for questions 1–10.

Evaluate

Evaluate the students' understanding and knowledge. Assign the Chapter 6 posttest. The test may be accessed by using the QR code or going to the companion website. What questions were students able to answer that they couldn't when they took the pretest?

Common Core

College and Career Readiness

CTE Career Ready Practices. Working in teams is a part of workplace culture. Describe how you would work with a sister team in Germany. What cultures would you need to be aware of that might impact the working relationship?

Reading. Read a magazine, newspaper, or online article about the importance of marketing leadership in the business world. Use your prior knowledge about the topic as you complete the research. Determine the central ideas of the article and review the conclusions made by the author. Provide an accurate summary of your reading, making sure to distinguish among facts, reasoned judgment based on research findings, and speculation.

Writing. Conduct research on effective marketing strategies in a market economy. Write a clear informative report, consisting of several paragraphs, to describe your findings on the implications of positive or negative management strategies in the workplace.

Teamwork

Work as a team and create a comparative chart to describe the different types of economies. Give examples of countries for each type of economy different from those listed in the text. What did you learn from this experience?

G-W Learning Mobile Site

Visit the G-W Learning mobile site to complete the chapter pretest and posttest and to practice vocabulary using e-flash cards. If you do not have a smartphone, visit the G-W Learning companion website to access these features.

G-W Learning mobile site: www.m.g-wlearning.com

G-W Learning companion website: www.g-wlearning.com

Marketing Plan

At the end of Unit 1, students began writing a marketing plan. This is a project-based activity that appears at the end of each unit and was described in the teacher notes in Chapter 1.

The next section of the marketing plan will be completed at the end of this unit. The directions are specific as to which parts

of the marketing plan will be written at this time. Students will continue to develop their plans as the text progresses.

If you did not assign the marketing plan in Unit 1 but would like to begin the activity now, refer back to the teaching notes in Chapter 1 to prepare for this end-of-unit activity.

This activity requires research and time to complete.

7 Market Forces and Economic Indicators

Section 7.1 | Market Forces at Work
Section 7.2 | Economic Measures

"Walt Disney told his crew to 'build the castle first' when constructing Disney World, knowing that vision would continue to serve as motivation throughout the project. Oftentimes when people fail to achieve what they want in life, it's because their vision wasn't strong enough."

—Gail Blanke, president and CEO, Lifedesigns

College and Career Readiness

Reading Prep
Before reading this chapter, flip through the pages and make notes of the major headings. Compare these headings to the objectives. What did you discover? How will this help you prepare to read new material?

Check Your Marketing IQ

Before you begin the chapter, see what you already know about marketing by taking the chapter pretest. If you do not have a smartphone, visit the G-W Learning companion website.
G-W Learning mobile site: www.m.g-wlearning.com
G-W Learning companion website: www.g-wlearning.com

G-W Mobile

Explore
Assign the College and Career Readiness Reading Prep activity before students read the chapter. Reading Prep activities give students opportunity to apply the Common Core State Standards.

Engage
Assign the Chapter 7 pretest.

◇DECA. Emerging Leaders

Creative Marketing Project, Part 2

Career Cluster and **Instructional Area** are not identified for this event.

Procedure, Part 2

1. In the previous chapter, you studied the assessed skills and procedures for this event.
2. The presentation begins immediately after the introduction of the chapter representatives to the judge by the adult assistant. Each chapter representative must take part in the presentation.
3. At the beginning of the presentation, chapter representatives will spend no more than 10 minutes focusing on an explanation and description of the chapter's project. Each chapter representative may bring a copy of the written entry or note cards pertaining to the written entry and use as reference during the presentation.
4. The judge will spend the remaining five minutes questioning the chapter representatives. Each chapter representative must respond to at least one question posed by the judge.
5. The chapter representatives may use the following items during the oral presentation:
   - not more than three (3) standard-sized posters not to exceed 22 ½ inches by 30 ½ inches each. Participants may use both sides of the posters, but all attachments must fit within the poster dimensions.
   - one (1) standard-sized presentation display board not to exceed 36 1/2 inches by 48 1/2 inches.
   - one (1) desktop flip chart presentation easel 12 inches by 10 inches (dimensions of the page).
   - one (1) personal laptop computer.
   - cell phones/smartphones, iPods/MP3 players, iPads/tablets, or any type of a hand-held, information-sharing device will be allowed in written events, if applicable to the presentation.
   - sound, as long as the volume is kept at a conversational level.

6. Only visual aids that can be easily carried to the presentation by the actual chapter representatives will be permitted, and the chapter representatives themselves must set up the visuals. No set-up time will be allowed. Chapter representatives must furnish their own materials and equipment. No electrical power will be supplied.
7. Materials appropriate to the situation may be handed to or left with judges in all competitive events. Items of monetary value may be handed to but may not be left with judges. Items such as flyers, brochures, pamphlets, and business cards may be handed to or left with the judge. No food or drinks are allowed.
9. If any of these rules are violated, the adult assistant must be notified by the judge.

Project

This project might concern itself with finding new markets for local products, promoting the community's resources, increasing the trading area of facilities, increasing sales, increasing employment, providing better shopping facilities, solving problems or challenges affecting the marketing process, etc.

Critical Thinking

1. What problem will your chapter select?
2. What is the rationale for selecting the problem?

   Visit www.deca.org for more information.

Section 7.1 Market Forces at Work

Objectives

After completing this section, you will be able to
- **discuss** how market forces affect an economy.
- **describe** the principle of supply and demand.
- **identify** three ways a business can increase profits.
- **describe** how competition results in better products and lower prices.
- **explain** the role of the consumer in determining which products are sold.

Key Terms

market supply
market demand
law of supply and demand
equilibrium
profit motive
specialization
nonprice competition

Web Connect

Go to an auction website like eBay and observe the bidding on different items. Why might the bid prices for an item increase quickly and go very high? What might this tell you about the demand and supply for this item?

Critical Thinking

Name an industry with which you are familiar, such as video games or athletic shoes. Name at least two competitors in the industry. How does their competition affect you as a customer? Do you think the product quality, assortment, and prices would be the same if there were only a single company in each industry?

Market Forces

In Chapter 6, you learned that market forces are an important feature of a market economy. These forces include supply and demand, the profit motive, and competition. Recall that in a market economy, individuals are free to make their own economic decisions. Business owners decide what and how much to produce. Consumers decide what to buy based on how much money they have. However, these decisions are still influenced by those market forces.

Here is an example of market forces at work. Imagine the market for basketballs. Suppose the sport suddenly becomes even more popular and the demand for

basketballs rises. An increasing number of consumers will want the existing supply of basketballs, so prices will go up. Those who can afford the higher prices get the basketballs, and profits for manufacturers will rise.

However, market forces naturally work to adjust the supply and demand. The rising price of basketballs will encourage basketball manufacturers to increase their production levels. In addition, new companies might be attracted by the high profits and decide to enter that business. At this point, the supply of basketballs will increase and prices will go back down. Profits generally go down as well.

Market forces will continue affecting the market for basketballs. Basketball companies will compete with each other to increase their

Explore

Provide an opportunity for students to explore by assigning a hands-on activity. Review the vocabulary terms at the beginning of the section. Where have students encountered these terms before? Help students make educated guesses about the meanings of the terms with which they are least familiar.

Resource

Use the Chapter 7 presentation on the optional Instructor's Presentations for PowerPoint® CD as an outline for presenting the chapter.

profits. For example, some might find ways to improve their products and lower their costs. They may get more customers by offering better basketballs at lower prices. Consumers benefit and the successful companies will make more money. However, the companies that cannot compete will make less money and might have to exit the business.

This example is simplified. Markets can be much more complex in real life. And, market forces take time to achieve balance. However, it demonstrates three main market forces at work: supply and demand, profit, and competition.

Supply and Demand

Supply is the quantity of goods available for purchase. *Demand* is the quantity of goods that consumers want to purchase. Supply and demand can be viewed on the individual and market levels.

Individual supply is the quantity of a product available for purchase by any one supplier. *Individual demand* is the quantity of a product any one consumer wants to purchase.

However, it is market supply and market demand that act as a market force. **Market supply** is the total supply of every seller willing and able to sell a product. **Market demand** is the total demand of every person willing and able to buy a product. In this text, supply and demand is *market supply* and *market demand*.

Effect of Supply and Demand on Price

The **law of supply and demand** says that both supply and demand affect price. Generally, higher demand raises prices, while lower demand decreases prices. An increased supply of a product often lowers prices. When the supply of a product decreases, the price usually increases. **Equilibrium** is the point at which the supply equals the demand for a product.

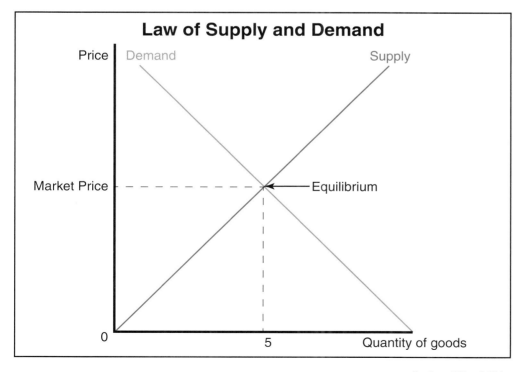

Figure 7-1 The effects of pricing on supply and demand.

Goodheart-Willcox Publisher

Case in Point

Walmart

Marketers have a complex job meeting consumer needs in a free-market economy. For example, Walmart must constantly evaluate which of more than 100,000 different products to stock on its shelves. In 2009, Walmart cut its product assortment by thousands of items. This was done to make stores appear less cluttered and operate more efficiently. However, customers did not react favorably to the changes and sales suffered. Customer feedback influenced Walmart to restock many of the discontinued items. Customers *voted* with their dollars and Walmart listened. If Walmart had not complied with the many customer requests, there is a good chance the company would have lost those customers completely because there are many other places to shop. This is a perfect example of a retailer following the marketing concept and working to create customer satisfaction.

Figure 7-1 shows that an equilibrium is reached at a market price where the quantity of the product demanded equals the quantity supplied. The law of supply and demand applies to a constant environment. A *constant environment* means that factors such as marketing, the economy, or social trends do not change.

In the previous basketball example, greater demand for basketballs drove the price higher at first. However, the supply increased when manufacturers increased production and new companies entered the market. The price then dropped.

How Demand Changes

The environment is rarely constant. Changes in marketing, the economy, and social trends can change demand. In fact, one of the major roles of marketing is to increase demand through promotion. For example, advertising a toy during the December gift-giving season can create high demand for that toy.

The condition of the economy can also increase or decrease demand. In good economies, consumers often have more money to spend. Therefore, the demand for many products goes up. In poor economies, consumers tend to spend less money. This means the demand for many products goes down.

Changes in society also affect demand. For example, the 20th century saw an increase in the number of women working outside the home. This change resulted in less time to prepare meals at home. That particular change created an increased demand for convenience foods.

In the earlier basketball example, a social trend might have caused the increase in demand for basketballs. For example, the success of Michael Jordan in the 1990s could have spurred an increase in the popularity of basketball. That trend might also help increase demand for basketballs.

Profit

Profit is another powerful market force. Recall that profit is the revenue from sales that exceeds the cost of producing and selling a product. Profit is the goal of most businesses. The following is the formula to determine profit.

sales − costs = profit

Suppose you own a basketball factory. Last year, your sales totaled $380,000. In order to make those sales, the costs of producing and selling the product were $345,000. These costs included rent, utilities, raw materials, maintenance, salaries, and marketing. Your profit is $35,000.

$380,000 sales − $345,000 costs = $35,000 profit

Explain

Discuss factors that cause changes in demand. Ask students for current examples.

Extend

Profit is a market force. Ask students why it is so powerful.

Profit motive is why people start and expand businesses: to earn profit. In the basketball example, increased profits led more people to enter the business. For existing companies, profits are increased by reducing expenses, increasing productivity, and/or increasing sales.

Reduce Expenses

Think about the basketball factory example. If the costs of doing business can be reduced, profits will increase. On the other hand, if expenses rise, profits decrease. If expenses rise too much, the business might lose money.

A business owner studies how much money is being spent for items like rent, raw materials, and maintenance. Reducing some of those expenses should increase profit, as long as sales remain the same. For example, a business might look for a place where rent is lower. Or, it might find lower-cost raw materials or ways to maintain machinery.

Increase Productivity

Another way to increase profits is to increase productivity. Recall that *productivity* is the amount of work a person can do in a specific amount of time, usually an hour. For example, in the basketball factory, a worker might produce ten basketballs per hour. If the same worker could make twenty basketballs in an hour, productivity would double. As a result, the factory would produce twice as many basketballs with the same labor cost. Lower costs generally lead to higher profits, as long as sales are stable.

There are two primary ways to increase productivity: increase efficiency and use new technology. One of the ways to increase efficiency is through specialization. **Specialization** is assigning workers to specialized tasks for increased efficiency.

Henry Ford is credited with being one of the first to use specialization in his company by using the assembly line. Before the assembly line was used in production, it took ten

Nearly all auto manufacturers and many other industries use the assembly line to keep productivity high and costs low.

Natalliya Hora/Shutterstock.com

Explain

Specialization is also known as *division of labor*.

Explore

Profit can be increased by reducing expenses and increasing productivity. Ask students for examples.

Ford workers to produce ten cars in one day. However, with an assembly line, each worker specialized in one-tenth of the car assembly and worked more efficiently. By working in this way, ten workers produced thirty cars in a day. The Ford assembly line increased productivity through efficiency. Specialization lowered manufacturing costs, making automobiles affordable for most people.

Using new technology is another way to increase productivity. Near the end of the 20th century, US productivity leaped forward with the widespread use of digital technology. This technology produced computers that helped workers do various jobs much faster than ever before. Computer technology actually changed the way business is done throughout the world.

Increase Sales

In the basketball example, forces outside the basketball manufacturing industry increased the demand for basketballs. However, a business can often do a great deal on its own to increase sales. Marketing can help to increase sales by developing programs to attract new customers. It may also encourage current customers to buy more of the same product. Advertising campaigns and rewards for frequent purchasers are examples of this strategy. Companies can also try to find new markets to sell their products.

FYI

Specialization is also referred to as *division of labor.*

Competition

While lower prices are an important way for business to compete, it is not the only way. Sometimes businesses use **nonprice competition,** or ways other than price, to win business. Nonprice competition methods include offering higher-quality products, better service, or more locations. You will learn more about competition in Chapter 11.

Good salespeople are critical to increasing sales, especially for big-ticket items.

Andresr/Shutterstock.com

Marketing Plan

At the end of Unit 1, students began writing a marketing plan. This is a project-based activity that appears at the end of each unit and was described in the teacher notes in Chapter 1.

The next section of the marketing plan will be completed at the end of this unit. The directions are specific as to which parts

of the marketing plan will be written at this time. Students will continue to develop their plans as the text progresses.

If you did not assign the marketing plan in Unit 1 but would like to begin the activity now, refer to the teaching notes in Chapter 1 to prepare for this end-of-unit activity.

Role of Consumers

Consumers play a critical role in a marketplace because they can determine which products are made or sold. When a large number of consumers buy a product, the demand for it goes up. When a large number of consumers decide they do not want a product, the demand for that product goes down.

In effect, consumers vote for products with their dollars. Successful businesses using the marketing concept respond to the demands of consumers based on product sales. They change their offerings to meet demand, which increases sales.

For example, suppose a new restaurant opens and a large number of people like it and visit many times. The restaurant will succeed and may eventually expand. However, if few people like the restaurant, it will eventually go out of business due to lack of customers.

Marketing professionals who seek certification can become a Professional Certified Marketer (PCM) through the AMA. PCM certification shows that you have mastered essential marketing standards and practices. Certification also reflects your goal of demonstrating that you are a professional in your field. www.marketingpower.com

Checkpoint 7.1

1. What are three market forces?
2. List two ways to think about supply and demand.
3. Describe profit.
4. What are two ways that businesses compete with one another?
5. What is the role of the consumer in the marketplace?

Build Your Vocabulary

As you progress through this text, develop a personal glossary of marketing terms which will help you build your vocabulary and prepare you for a career in marketing. Write a definition for each of the following terms, and add it to your personal marketing glossary.

market supply
market demand
law of supply and demand
equilibrium
profit motive
specialization
nonprice competition

Evaluate

Assign the Checkpoint questions at the end of the section. Assess students' comprehension using the Checkpoint activity as a self-assessment tool.

Checkpoint Answers:

1. The three market forces are supply and demand, profit, and competition.
2. Supply and demand can be viewed on the individual and market levels.
3. Profit is another powerful force in the marketplace. Recall that profit is the revenue from sales that exceeds the cost of producing and selling a product. Profit is the goal of most businesses.
4. Business can engage in both price or nonprice competition.
5. Consumers determine which products will be produced by voting with their dollars by making purchases.

Build Your Vocabulary Answers:

Definitions for these terms can be found in the glossary of this text.

Section 7.2 Economic Measures

Objectives

After completing this section, you will be able to
- **summarize** how the economy is measured using economic indicators.
- **explain** how the stock market can be an unreliable economic indicator.

Key Terms

indicator
gross domestic
   product (GDP)
economic growth
   rate
per capita GDP
standard of living
inflation
demand-pull inflation
cost-push inflation

inflation rate
consumer price
   index (CPI)
nominal GDP
real GDP
labor force
unemployment rate
full employment
stock market
stock market index

Web Connect

Find the website of the US Bureau of Economic Analysis and update the gross domestic product (GDP) data in Figure 7-1. How much has GDP grown since the end of 2011? What was the rate of change? Do consumers still make up over 70 percent of total spending in the economy?

Critical Thinking

Which economic indicator do you think gives the most accurate measure of the strength of the economy? Briefly explain your reason.

Economic Indicators

Market forces of supply and demand, profit motive, and competition influence the economic decisions of individuals and businesses. In a market economy, these decisions lead to the production of goods and services. But how do businesses know whether an economy is performing well? Can economic performance be measured? Why is it important?

The strength of the economy can be measured by using economic indicators. An indicator is a sign that shows the condition or existence of something. For example, temperature is a heat indicator. Heat is measured in degrees. A body temperature of 98.6°F is normal and indicates no fever. A temperature of 102°F is high and indicates a possible illness that might need medical attention. Economic indicators work in a similar way to temperature.

When economic indicators are normal, the economy is doing well. If the indicators are too high or too low, the economy might have problems. Business owners, government officials, and consumers often base economic decisions on the strength or weakness of an economy.

For example, suppose management wants to launch a new product. When is the best launch time to ensure its success? As a marketer, it is important to know if the type of new product sells better in a strong or weak economy. If the answer is a

Successful businesses follow economic indicators closely to help them make important business and marketing decisions.

Pressmaster/Shutterstock.com

strong economy, then it would be a mistake to launch it in a weak economy. You would save quite a bit of money by waiting until the economy turns around before launching.

The most widely followed indicators of the economy are gross domestic product (GDP), per capita GDP, inflation rate, and the unemployment rate. The stock market is another indicator, but falls into a different category.

Gross Domestic Product (GDP)

Gross domestic product (GDP) is the market value of all final products produced in a country during a specific time period. GDP is also called *economic output* and is measured in dollars. Imagine looking at the United States from a satellite and counting every final product made in the United States during a year. After adding up the dollar values of all these products, the sum is the national GDP.

Gross domestic product (GDP) is one of the most closely followed economic indicators. It is used by the White House and Congress to prepare the federal government budget. Large

companies consider GDP when preparing business plans and sales forecasts. Financial institutions use GDP as an indicator of economic activity, which can affect interest rates.

In 2011, the GDP for the United States was about $15.1 trillion. The Bureau of Economic Analysis (BEA) of the US Department of Commerce found at www.bea.gov keeps track of GDP.

GDP as Money Spent

There is another way to look at GDP. It is also the total amount of money spent in the economy to buy goods and services. The major spenders in the US economy are consumers, businesses, and various government agencies, as shown in Figure 7-2. Each can be viewed as a stream that flows into the river of GDP.

FYI

15 trillion is a 15 with 12 additional zeroes after it: 15,000,000,000,000.

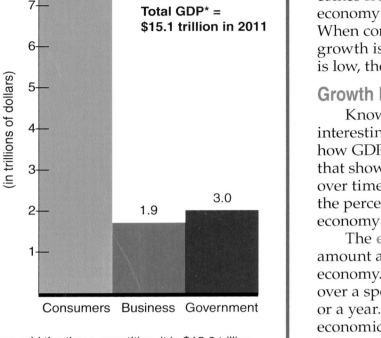

Contributors to GDP

Total GDP* =
$15.1 trillion in 2011

Consumers   Business   Government

Money Spent
(in trillions of dollars)

* If you add the three quantities, it is $15.6 trillion.
When economists calculate GDP, they include a
quantity called "net exports." That amount was
– $0.5 trillion in 2011.

Goodheart-Willcox Publisher

Figure 7-2 The major spenders in the US economy
are consumers, business, and government. Each group
contributes to GDP.

Consumer spending includes everything consumers buy for personal use, such as food, clothing, cars, medical care, and recreation. Business spending includes all purchases made for capital goods and construction. These might include things like computers, bulldozers, and warehouses. Business spending is also called *investment spending.*

Government spending includes spending by national, state, and local governments. Government agencies fund such things as

the national defense system, school lunch programs, police protection, and roads.

Notice that consumers spend the most and contributed over 70 percent of GDP in 2011. Because such a large percentage of GDP comes from consumer purchases, the US economy is often called a *consumer economy.* When consumer spending is high, economic growth is often strong. If consumer spending is low, the economy tends to be weak.

Growth Rate of the Economy

Knowing GDP at a given point in time is interesting. However, you also need to know how GDP changes over time. An indicator that shows how much something changes over time is called a *rate of change.* The larger the percentage rate of change, the faster the economy is changing—for better or worse.

The **economic growth rate** shows the amount and direction of growth of an economy. It is expressed as a percent change over a specific time period, such as a quarter or a year. In the United States, for example, economic growth over the long-term averages between 6 and 7 percent, including inflation. Many industrialized countries have growth rates in this range. Many fast-growing countries have growth rates that are higher.

High rates of economic growth indicate a strong economy. Lower rates of economic growth indicate a weakening economy. Sometimes economic growth turns negative and GDP falls, which is an indicator of serious economic weakness. For example, the GDP growth rate during the Great Recession of 2008 was negative, as shown in Figure 7-3.

The formula for growth rate of the economy is

[(GDP for time 2 – GDP for time 1)
÷ GDP time 1] × 100 = economic growth rate

FYI

The rate of change of GDP is often referred to
as the *growth rate of the economy.*

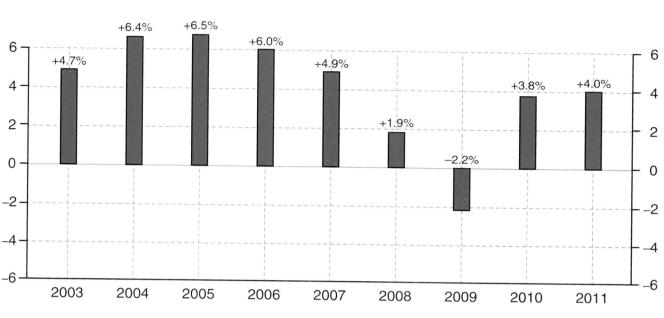

Figure 7-3 This chart shows the annual percentage change by quarter in the US GDP over the 10 years ending 2011.

For example, GDP was $15.1 trillion for 2011 and $14.5 trillion for 2010. The growth rate in 2011 was 4.1 percent:

[($15.1 trillion − $14.5 trillion) ÷ $14.5 trillion] × 100 = 4.1% economic growth rate

Per Capita GDP

The major spenders in the US economy are consumers. **Per capita GDP** is the GDP of a nation divided by its population. It shows how much economic output there is for each person in the country.

When per capita GDP is high, there is more economic output for the average person. High per capita GDP usually indicates a higher standard of living. **Standard of living** refers to the financial well-being of the average person in a country. For example, suppose the average person in one country

has a home, clothes, and food, but little else. Suppose the average person in a different country has a home, clothes, and food—plus a telephone, television, and car. The person in the second country is thought to enjoy a higher standard of living. One of the goals of a national government is to increase the standard of living for its citizens.

The following is the formula to calculate per capita GDP:

GDP ÷ total population = per capita GDP

For example, in 2011, the GDP for the United States was about $15.1 trillion and the population was about 312 million. The 2011 per capita GDP for the United States was about $48,397:

$15.1 trillion GDP ÷ 312 million people = $48,397 per capita GDP

Explore

Ask for a student volunteer to present Figure 7-3.

Citizens in countries with a high standard of living have much more disposable income.

Tupungato/Shutterstock.com

The United States has a high standard of living. The per capita GDP for countries around the world varies quite a bit. For example, per capita GDP in the Congo is $200, while it is $110,000 in Luxembourg. Of course, a standard-of-living measurement like per capita GDP does not consider important quality-of-life factors that are difficult to measure. Quality of life includes things like health, safety, environmental concerns, and political freedom.

Inflation Rate

Inflation is the term for a general rise in prices throughout the economy. In other words, if the price of only one product rises, it does not necessarily indicate inflation. However, if the prices of many products rise, inflation is present. The major effect of inflation is that it reduces the purchasing power of money.

Prices can rise in several ways. Increased demand can bring prices up. This is called demand-pull inflation because increasing demand pulls up prices. Prices can also rise when business costs go up and are passed on to consumers. This is called cost-push inflation because increasing business costs push up production costs and consumer prices.

The inflation rate is the rate of change of prices calculated on a monthly or yearly basis. It is expressed as a percent. Low inflation between 1 and 4 percent is usually not a problem for the economy.

However, problems can happen as inflation gets higher. For example, high inflation hurts those living on fixed incomes because they have less purchasing power. It also leads to higher interest rates, which hurts those needing loans. Inflation also tends to result in prices rising faster than wages, which hurts consumers. High inflation disrupts business and financial planning, and makes budgeting more difficult. It generally adds uncertainty to an economy.

Consumer Price Index

There are several indicators of inflation. However, the consumer price index is the most widely used. The consumer price index is a measure of the average change in the prices paid by urban consumers for typical consumer goods and services over time. It is compiled by the US Bureau of Labor Statistics (BLS). The group of typical consumer goods and services the BLS uses is called its *market basket.*

The BLS first compiled the prices in its market basket for a base time period between 1982 and 1984. The base index for that period of time was set at 100. Prices for the market basket are then compiled for subsequent periods and compared with previous time periods. For example, the CPI for 2011 was about 225. This figure means that 2011 prices were 125 percent higher than the prices for the same goods and services during the base index period. It also means that something costing $100 in 1983 would cost about $225 in 2011.

When the CPI is reported, the number value is often not given. Instead, CPI is expressed as the *percent change* between the current period and an earlier time period. That number is reported as the inflation rate, shown by the following formula:

$$[(\text{CPI time period 2} - \text{CPI time period 1}) \div \text{CPI time period 1}] \times 100 = \text{inflation rate}$$

For example, suppose you want to find the inflation rate for 2011. The exact CPI value for 2011 was 224.9 and was 218.1 for 2010. The inflation rate for 2011 is calculated to be 3.1 percent.

$$[(224.9 - 218.1) \div 218.1] \times 100$$
$$= 3.1\% \text{ inflation rate}$$

Levels of Inflation

Inflation is sometimes divided into four levels: low, moderate, severe, and hyperinflation. Each level is based on the inflation rate, as shown in Figure 7-4. Severe inflation is also called *double-digit inflation.*

Inflation in the United States has averaged around 3 percent annually over the last 100 years. The last period of severe inflation occurred during the three-year period 1979 to 1981. The inflation rate reached 13.6 percent in 1980. Since 1982, it has only been above 5 percent in two years. In 1982, it was 6.2 percent, and in 1990, it was 5.4 percent.

Hyperinflation is an extremely rapid, out-of-control rise in inflation. A country's currency is severely devalued by hyperinflation. The United States has never experienced hyperinflation, although there was a serious inflationary situation during the Civil War.

Levels of Inflation		
Level	**Inflation Rate**	**Effect on Economy**
Low	1% to 4%	Good. Economy and prices are stable.
Medium	4% to 9%	Some problems. Prices start rising faster than wages. Purchasing power falls.
Severe (double digit)	10% or higher	Economic problems increase. Purchasing power falls more quickly.
Hyperinflation	Over 1000%	Occurs rarely, but destroys the value of money and the economy. One of the most well-known instances of hyperinflation occurred in Germany after World War I.

Goodheart-Willcox Publisher

Figure 7-4 The terms for inflation levels are usually applied to changes that occur on a month-to-month or year-to-year basis.

Exploring Careers

E-commerce Director

Companies that conduct their business partly or entirely online have needs similar to companies that operate entirely from a specific physical location. However, the execution of those needs is quite different online. An e-commerce director manages the online retail activities of a company. This includes managing inventory, implementing business and marketing strategies, fulfilling online orders, and shipping products to customers. Other typical job titles for an e-commerce director are *online manager, online merchant,* and *e-commerce manager.*

Some examples of tasks that e-commerce directors perform include:
- organize the company website, or online storefront, to maximize the advantages of online selling;
- determine the keywords and product descriptions to maximize exposure to the appropriate audience;
- use electronic transaction services to process customer payments;
- perform online customer service tasks; and
- use financial or spreadsheet software to calculate sales and expenses.

E-commerce directors must be computer literate. They must understand how to build and maintain websites and how to effectively market products or services online. They should also have a solid financial background. Many jobs in this field require a degree in management or finance in addition to website development and management experience. For more information, access the *Occupational Outlook Handbook* online.

Effect of Inflation on GDP

Due to inflation, economic indicators from different time periods are not always comparable. The following, oversimplified example shows why this is so.

GDP is calculated on prices. To show the effect of inflation on GDP, imagine a country whose only product is bicycles. In 1984, the country made and sold only one bicycle at a price of $100. Therefore, the 1984 GDP for that country was $100. Now suppose that in 2011, the country still makes only one bicycle, but the price is $225 due to inflation. The GDP in 2011 is $225, so it *looks* like bicycle production has gone up. However, this was not the case; only one bicycle was made. GDP was only higher because of inflation.

Economists try to remove the effect of inflation on economic indicators. To do this, one year is chosen as a base year. The prices from that year are used to calculate the value of goods in all years. In the previous example, an economist might take the one bicycle produced in 2011 and use the 1984 price of $100 to get an inflation-adjusted GDP. Therefore, the GDP for both 1984 and 2011 would be $100.

Nominal GDP is calculated *without* adjusting for inflation, so it is the GDP in current dollars. Real GDP is calculated *with* an inflation adjustment, so it is GDP in constant dollars. When different GDP values for the same time period are shown, it is likely the difference between using real and nominal GDP.

Figure 7-5 shows GDP figures for 2011 and 2010. The first column shows *nominal GDP,* which is in current dollars and is not corrected for inflation. The second column shows *real GDP,* which is shown in 2005 dollars to correct for inflation. The last row shows nominal and real GDP growth for 2011.

How fast does real GDP in the United States usually grow? From 1929 to 2011, real GDP grew at average annual rate of

Extend
Explain the difference between *nominal GDP* and *real GDP*

Nominal vs. Real GDP		
	Nominal GDP	**Real GDP**
	In current dollars, **not** corrected for inflation	In 2000 dollars, corrected for inflation
Time 1: 2010	$14.5 trillion	$13.1 trillion
Time 2: 2011	$15.1 trillion	$13.3 trillion
GDP growth for 2011	4.1%	1.5%

Source: www.bea.gov

Figure 7-5 Real GDP has been corrected for inflation. It helps marketers to make more accurate comparisons from year to year.

3.2 percent. During this same period, *nominal* GDP grew at an average annual rate of 6.4 percent. Nominal GDP growth exceeded real GDP growth by 3.2 percent due to inflation.

Unemployment Rate

All people who are capable of working and want to work are called the **labor force.** The labor force does not include children, retired people, or those choosing not to work. The total labor force is divided between civilian and those in the military.

The civilian labor force is divided into two categories: employed and unemployed. *Employed* includes everyone who is working. *Unemployed* includes those who do not have a job but are actively looking for one. The **unemployment rate** is the percentage of the civilian labor force that is unemployed. The unemployment rate formula is:

(number of unemployed ÷ total civilian labor force) × 100 = unemployment rate

For example, in 2011 the total civilian labor force was 153,887,000. Of this number, 13,097,000 were unemployed. The unemployment rate at the end of 2011 was 8.5 percent.

(13,097,000 ÷ 153,887,000) × 100
= 8.5% unemployment rate

If every person who is willing and able to work has a job, the economy would be at **full employment.** Interestingly, the unemployment

Marketing Ethics

Advertising

As a marketer, you will be asked to write a sales message or other types of documents for your organization. Even though it may be tempting to focus on sales *hype* or other persuasive techniques to convey a message, remember to keep the information honest. Embellishing a message about a product or service and intentionally misrepresenting a product or service is unethical and may be illegal. Make sure to respect and follow the truth-in-advertising laws. Focus on the facts, and use your communication skills in a positive manner to create interest or demand for the product or service. Do a search on the Internet to find out more about truth-in-advertising laws.

Engage

Describe unemployment and how it has impacted your community in the last few years.

rate will still be about 4 percent even when at full employment. This is because there are always people who are not working for any number of reasons. They are entering and reentering the workforce or are between jobs. As a result, an unemployment rate between 4 and 5 percent indicates a healthy economy.

A rising unemployment rate indicates a weakening economy because it means businesses are not hiring. How high does the unemployment rate get in the United States? Over the last 30 years, it has only reached 10 percent during 1981, 1982, and 2009.

Many economists believe there is a trade-off between inflation and unemployment. When the unemployment rate is low, businesses often have to increase wages to keep good workers and hire new ones. This increases the cost of doing business, which means higher consumer prices.

Conversely, a high unemployment rate means wages remain the same or fall. So many people are looking for jobs that they are willing to work for less. While this may keep business costs and prices lower, fewer consumers have enough money to buy the products.

Stock Market and the Economy

A **stock market** is a system for buying and selling stocks or a place where stocks are bought and sold. *Stock* represents the right of ownership in a company. It is divided into *shares,* where each share represents a partial ownership. Buying partial ownership in a company is a form of investment. People who buy shares of stock in a company are called *stockholders.*

A rising stock market means the value of corporations is rising. Therefore, investors are positive about a strengthening economy. A falling stock market means the market value

NYSE Euronext is the corporation which owns the NYSE. However, when discussing US stock trading in New York, NYSE is the accepted name.

Songquan Deng/Shutterstock.com

Resource/Evaluate

Assign the optional Chapter 7 test for **EXAM**VIEW® Assessment Suite as a formal assessment tool.

Social Media

Identify SMM Goals

When using social media for your company, identify your goals. Do not become overwhelmed with attempting to use too many tools at once. Establish what the goal or goals will be. Are you using social media to communicate with customers, promote products, or get the name of the business in front of potential customers? There are many reasons to use social media in your marketing plan. By aligning your social media plans with your marketing and business goals, you will be able to focus on the top priorities and do a good job. Learn to accept that all of your ideas will not work. Do not become frustrated if you have several false starts in finding that social media idea that works well for your company. You will find the avenue that is successful by playing on your wins and losses.

of corporations is falling. So, investors are negative about the economy.

Stock markets constantly rise and fall. They do not always reflect the actual state of an economy at that time. History has shown that stock markets tend to peak right before a downturn in the economy. However, no one really knows when a market has peaked, so many are caught by surprise when markets fall.

Many economists consider the stock market a secondary economic indicator at best. It is a difficult indicator to rely on for many reasons.

- There is not just one stock market, but many stock markets.
- Each stock market may have more than one indicator.
- The different stock market indicators may go in different directions over a given period of time.
- Many people are confused by daily ups and downs in a stock market. It is better to look at longer-term trends over months and years.

The major US stock markets are the New York Stock Exchange (NYSE) and the National Association of Securities Dealers Automated Quotation Stock Market (NASDAQ). Each stock market has its own index. A **stock market index** tracks the performance of a certain group of stocks. These stocks represent a certain market or part of the US economy.

There are two well-known independent stock indexes. The first is the Dow Jones Industrial Average (DJIA). DJIA consists of 30 *blue-chip stocks* from the New York Stock Exchange. The second is Standard & Poor's 500 (S&P 500), which consists of 500 stocks from a variety of exchanges. Most newspapers and business websites quote the DJIA, S&P 500, NYSE, and NASDAQ. In addition, they may quote stock exchanges in other countries.

Evaluate

Assign the Checkpoint questions at the end of the section. Assess students' comprehension using the Checkpoint activity as a self-assessment tool.

Explore

Bring in a newspaper, or print from the Internet, a daily stock report. Distribute to students and review what the numbers mean.

Checkpoint 7.2

1. What is an economic indicator?
2. How is GDP measured?
3. Describe hyperinflation.
4. What is the difference between nominal and real GDP?
5. Name two categories of the labor force.

Build Your Vocabulary

As you progress through this text, develop a personal glossary of marketing terms which will help you build your vocabulary and prepare you for a career in marketing. Write a definition for each of the following terms, and add it to your personal marketing glossary.

indicator
gross domestic product (GDP)
economic growth rate
per capita GDP
standard of living
inflation
demand-pull inflation
cost-push inflation
inflation rate
consumer price index (CPI)
nominal GDP
real GDP
unemployment rate
full employment
stock market
stock market index

Chapter Summary

Section 7.1 Market Forces at Work

- There are three market forces at work: supply and demand, profit, and competition. Market forces affect the economy because they influence all decisions made by individuals.
- The law of supply and demand says that the greater demand for a given supply of a product, the higher the price. The lower the demand, the lower the price.
- Profit is the goal of most businesses. A business can increase profits by decreasing expenses, increasing profits, or increasing sales.
- Competition results in better products and lower prices for consumers. Because of competition, businesses often improve productivity so products can be sold at a lower price.
- Consumers ultimately determine which products are produced by voting with their dollars.

Section 7.2 Economic Measures

- The most widely followed economic indicators are GDP, per capita GDP, inflation rate, and unemployment rate. These indicators measure the strength of the economy.
- Many economists consider the stock market as a secondary economic indicator. There are two major stock markets in the US: New York Stock Exchange (NYSE) and the National Association of Securities Dealers Automated Quotation Stock Market (NASDAQ).

Review Your Knowledge

1. Describe a constant environment.
2. How can productivity be increased?
3. Who ultimately determines which products are produced in a market economy?
4. How can profits be increased?
5. What is competition and what is the result for the economy?
6. GDP can be considered money spent. Name the three spending streams of GDP.
7. How is the growth rate expressed?
8. Name two types of inflation.
9. Explain the idea that there is a trade-off between inflation and unemployment.
10. What does a rising stock market indicate?

Evaluate

Assign end-of-chapter activities.

Review Your Knowledge Answers

1. A constant environment is when there is no change in factors such as marketing campaigns, the economy, and social trends.
2. Productivity may be increased by increasing efficiency and using new technology.
3. Consumers ultimately decide.
4. Profits can be increased by decreasing expenses, increasing profitability, or increasing sales.
5. Competition is a contest between two or more businesses to get customers. The result is better products and lower prices.
6. Consumer spending, business spending, and government spending.

7. The growth rate is expressed as a percent of change over a specific time, such as a quarter or year.
8. Two types of inflation are demand-pull inflation and cost-push inflation.
9. When the unemployment rate is low, businesses often have to increase wages to keep good workers and hire new ones. This increases the cost of doing business, which means higher consumer prices. Conversely, a high unemployment rate means less pressure to increase wages because so many people are looking for jobs. While this may keep business costs and prices lower, fewer consumers have enough money to buy the products.
10. A rising stock market indicates that the market value of corporations is rising. Conversely, a falling stock market may mean the value of corporations is falling.

Apply Your Knowledge

1. What is the current inflation rate in the United States today? How would this influence your decisions to market a product?
2. Imagine you are a marketing manager for a professional sports team where the supply of tickets for each game exceeds the demand. How will this affect your marketing strategy?
3. What are the possible advantages and disadvantages of trying to increase the profits of a business by decreasing marketing expenses?
4. Do you think it is a better strategy to increase profits by increasing productivity or decreasing marketing expenses? Briefly explain.
5. How might your marketing strategy differ if you try to increase sales by encouraging current customers to buy more, instead of attracting new customers?
6. Do you think a good marketing plan is needed more in an industry which is more competitive or less competitive? Briefly explain.
7. What are the advantages of marketing luxury products in countries with a high per capita gross domestic product? Are there any disadvantages?
8. What are the challenges of marketing luxury products in countries with a low per capita gross domestic product? Are there any opportunities?
9. How might your marketing plan for a product be impacted during a period of high inflation, when the costs of your product are increasing rapidly?
10. What is the current GDP for the United States? How can you use that information as a marketing manager?

Check Your Marketing IQ

Now that you have finished the chapter, see what you learned about marketing by taking the chapter posttest. If you do not have a smartphone, visit the G-W Learning companion website.

G-W Learning mobile site: www.m.g-wlearning.com
G-W Learning companion website: www.g-wlearning.com

College and Career Readiness

Common Core

CTE Career Ready Practices. Employ valid and reliable research strategies as they apply to reflecting current information on GDP. Write a paragraph on your findings. Create a chart to show how GDP has fluctuated over the last 12 months.

Speaking. Participate in a collaborative classroom discussion about economic indicators. Ask questions to participants that connect your ideas to the relevant evidence presented.

Listening. Do an Internet search for *speeches made by Ben Bernanke,* who was appointed Chair of the US Federal Reserve Board in 2006. Select one speech and listen to it in its entirety. Present your findings and supporting evidence of the line of reasoning, organization, development, and style Mr. Bernanke used to prepare the information. Identify the target market and the purpose of the speech.

Teamwork

Working as a team, choose a restaurant with which you are all familiar and imagine you are in charge of marketing. Identify your closest competitor. List a major strength and weakness of your restaurant compared to this competitor. Then use that information to think of one idea to increase sales. This idea should take in account the current strength of the economy.

G-W Learning Mobile Site

Visit the G-W Learning mobile site to complete the chapter pretest and posttest and to practice vocabulary using e-flash cards. If you do not have a smartphone, visit the G-W Learning companion website to access these features.

G-W Learning mobile site: www.m.g-wlearning.com

G-W Learning companion website: www.g-wlearning.com

8 Business Cycles and the Role of Government

Section 8.1 Business Cycles
Section 8.2 Role of Government

"There is no royal flower-strewn path to success. And if there is, I have not found it, for if I have accomplished anything in life it is because I have been willing to work so hard."

—Madam C.J. Walker, creator of the modern African-American hair-care and cosmetics industry

College and Career Readiness

Reading Prep
Before reading this chapter, review the highlighted terms and definitions to preview the new content. Building a business vocabulary is an important activity to broadening your understanding of new material.

Check Your Marketing IQ

Before you begin the chapter, see what you already know about marketing by taking the chapter pretest. If you do not have a smartphone, visit the G-W Learning companion website.
G-W Learning mobile site: www.m.g-wlearning.com
G-W Learning companion website: www.g-wlearning.com

Explore

Assign the College and Career Readiness Reading Prep activity before students read the chapter. Reading Prep activities give students opportunity to apply the Common Core State Standards.

Engage

Assign the Chapter 8 pretest.

◇DECA Emerging Leaders

Sports and Entertainment MarketingTeam Decision-Making Event, Part 1

Career Cluster: Marketing
Instructional Area: Economics

General Performance Indicators

- Communications skills—the ability to exchange information and ideas with others through writing, speaking, reading, or listening
- Analytical skills—the ability to derive facts from data, findings from facts, conclusions from findings, and recommendations from conclusions
- Production skills—the ability to take a concept from an idea and make it real
- Teamwork—the ability to be an effective member of a productive group
- Priorities/time management—the ability to determine priorities and manage time commitments

Specific Performance Indicators

- Explain the concept of economic resources.
- Explain the principles of supply and demand.
- Discuss the global environment in which businesses operate.
- Identify factors affecting a business's profit.
- Explain factors affecting pricing decisions.
- Describe factors used by businesses to position corporate brands.
- Demonstrate connections between company actions and results.

Purpose

Designed for a team of two DECA members, the event measures the team's ability to explain core business concepts in a case-study format through a role-play. This event consists of a 100-question, multiple-choice, cluster exam for each team member and a decision-making case study situation. The Team Decision-Making Event provides an opportunity for participants to analyze one or a combination of elements essential to the effective operation of a business in the specific career area presented as a case study.

For the purposes of this text, you will be presented with the material for this event in two parts. Part 1 presents the knowledge and skills assessed and an overview of the event's purpose and procedure. Part 2 presents the remaining procedures and the event situation.

Procedure, Part 1

1. For Part 1 in this text, read both sets of performance indicators. Discuss these with your team members.
2. If there are any questions, ask your teacher to clarify.

Critical Thinking

1. What is the significance of performance indicators while preparing for the event?
2. What is your team's strategy to communicate effectively your response to the performance indicators?

Visit www.deca.org for more information.

Section 8.1 Business Cycles

Objectives

After completing this section, you will be able to
- **identify** the four stages of a business cycle.
- **explain** how economic indicators can be used to analyze the business cycle.

Key Terms

business cycle
expansion
peak
recession
depression

trough
economic recovery
leading indicator
lagging indicator
coincident indicator

Web Connect

What stage of the business cycle do you think the economy is in today? Support your answer with data on the gross domestic product (GDP) from the Bureau of Economic Analysis website. Find quarterly data on *real GDP*. Has it recently been increasing or decreasing?

Critical Thinking

Make a list of three businesses you would expect do well in the expansion stage of the business cycle. Make a list of three businesses that might do well in the recession stage of the business cycle.

Business Cycles

The market economy of the United States has been very successful and experienced growth over the years. Recall from Chapter 7 that the US gross domestic product (GDP) increased from $103.6 *billion* in 1929 to $15.1 *trillion* in 2011. This is an average annual growth rate of 6.4 percent, or real growth of 3.2 percent after adjusting for inflation.

However, GDP does not grow at the same rate every year. Market forces cause GDP growth to change from being above average in some years to below average in others. As a result, GDP moves in a pattern of cycles. During most years, GDP *expands,* or increases. However, in some years GDP *contracts,* or decreases. A **business cycle** is alternating periods of expansion and contraction in the economy.

US business cycles repeat over many years. This is shown on the graph on Figure 8-1, which shows the annual percent change in real GDP from 1929 to 2011. Note how the year-to-year growth in real GDP changes. In a number of years, the growth rate was negative, or economic output in the country declined.

While business cycles repeat, no two are exactly the same. Each cycle is a different length with different highs and lows. During the 20th century, business cycles averaged four years in length. Every cycle goes through the same four stages: expansion, peak, recession, and a trough. These are illustrated on the graph on Figure 8-2.

Expansion

An economic **expansion** is a period when GDP is rising. This is also called a

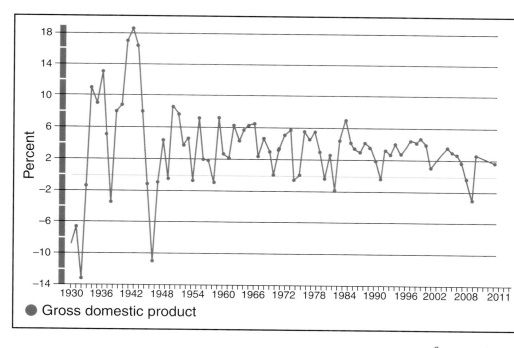

Figure 8-1 Real GDP grew at an average annual rate of 3.2 percent from 1929 to 2011. However, the graph shows the economy did not grow at this rate every year. In some years, the growth rate was higher or lower; and in some years, it was negative.

Source: www.bea.gov
Goodheart-Willcox Publisher

growth period. Expansions often start with an increase in consumer demand for goods and services. Businesses respond by increasing production and hiring more workers. More workers in an economy then demand more goods and services. GDP and the economy begin to grow and expand.

Peak

The **peak** is the highest point of a business cycle. It marks the end of an expansion. Consumer demand for goods and services starts to slow. Businesses respond by reducing production and cutting workers. GDP growth declines and the economy weakens.

An economic recession is beginning to form. Sometimes an expansion ends for a clear reason. For example, in 2008 a financial crisis caused the housing market to collapse, which led to the great recession. Other times the reason is not clear.

FYI

Many economists also define a recession more simply as two consecutive quarters (six months) of declining *real* GDP.

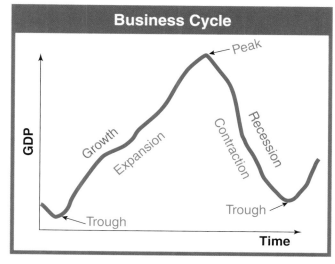

Goodheart-Willcox Publisher

Figure 8-2 One business cycle consists of the time from one trough to the next.

Explore

Ask a student to present Figure 8-1.

Economic recession is characterized by a high job-loss rate as a direct result of business losses.

JustASC/Shutterstock.com

Recession

A special department of the government, the National Bureau of Economic Research (NBER), studies economic indicators and determines the official start and end of recessions. The NBER defines a recession as a period of significant decline in total output, income, employment, and trade, usually lasting from six months to a year, and marked by widespread contractions in many parts of the economy. However, many economists often define a *recession* more simply as two consecutive quarters (six months) of declining *real* GDP.

Recessions vary in length and severity. Some are brief and mild. Others are long and severe. During the twentieth century, there were about 20 recessions. The United States recently suffered a severe recession from 2008–2009. It was fueled by a crash in housing prices and huge financial losses on defaulted mortgages. There was a decline in real GDP and unemployment reached 10 percent.

An economic contraction that is very severe and lasts a long time is called a depression. The last depression in the United States was the Great Depression. It began in 1929 and did not end until around 1940. During this period, real GDP declined over 25 percent and unemployment reached 25 percent. Many banks failed, people lost their homes, and poverty was widespread. Economists still disagree on the exact causes of the Great Depression. However, several factors are often mentioned: a stock market crash, reduced money supply, and declining business investment.

Trough

The trough is the lowest stage of a business cycle that marks the end of a recession. The period of expansion after a trough is also called an economic recovery. As with all turning points in a business cycle, it is not always clear why a recession ends. However, consumer demand for goods and services begins to increase, and GDP grows. The business cycle continues.

Case in Point

Hyundai

Marketing professionals study business cycles to help determine strategies to which consumers will react in a positive way. When the economy is stable, consumers are more willing to spend more money. When the economy is in a slump, though, consumers may not be willing or able to spend. However, businesses must continue generating revenue through all business cycles. Hyundai Motor Company is a good example of how a business can generate sales in a slow economy by using creative marketing techniques. The auto industry suffered losses during the great recession of 2008–2009. To keep sales moving during this slow economic period, Hyundai introduced an innovative sales program. The company advertised that buyers could purchase a new car and return the vehicle within a year if they lost their jobs—with no questions asked. Through a consumer-oriented marketing program, Hyundai strengthened its image and kept sales stable.

Economic Indicators and the Business Cycle

The economic indicators introduced in Chapter 7 are used to analyze business cycles. The indicators show which stage of the business cycle an economy is in and the stage coming next. This information can be valuable when making business decisions.

The relationship between different economic indicators and the business cycle is not always the same. As a result, indicators are commonly classified as being leading, lagging, or coincident.

- A *leading indicator* is one that changes *before* a change in economic activity.
- A *lagging indicator* is one that changes *after* a change in economic activity.
- A *coincident indicator* is one that changes at the *same time* as changes in economic activity.

Some important indicators that are widely used when analyzing the business cycle are GDP, inflation rate, unemployment rate, and the stock market. There are many others.

The AMA offers its members a variety of publications. AMA magazines and journals provide access to information about marketing topics, trends, and other industry information for marketing professionals. There are multiple publications from which members can select to help stay current and improve professional development. www.marketingpower.com

GDP

GDP is a *coincident indicator* of economic activity. When GDP is rising and the growth rate is increasing, it is a sign of economic expansion. Recall that the average growth rate of real GDP has been about 3.2 percent (6.4 percent in nominal terms) over the long term. When GDP is growing faster than average, the economy is strong. The economy is weakening when the rate of GDP growth is declining and falling below average. When GDP growth turns negative, it signals a recession.

Inflation Rate

The inflation rate is also considered a *coincident indicator* of economic activity. The inflation rate generally tends to rise during an economic expansion. This happens because increased consumer demand forces prices higher. In addition, more hiring during an expansion also tends to increase overall wages. Conversely, the inflation rate generally tends to decline during a recession. This is because consumer demand falls, which tends to lower prices. In addition, workforce cuts during a contraction also tend to decrease overall wages.

Unemployment Rate

The unemployment rate is a *lagging indicator* of economic activity. An economic expansion usually begins with rising consumer demand for goods and services. Businesses then respond by increasing production and eventually hiring more workers. The unemployment rate declines, but not until after the expansion has been underway for around six to nine months. Conversely, the unemployment rate rises during a recession, but not until after the contraction has started and been underway for a while.

This lagging relationship was evident during the great recession that started in 2008. Real GDP declined in the first quarter of 2008, but the unemployment rate remained steady at about 5.0 percent during that period. The unemployment rate eventually increased to 5.4 percent in the second quarter of 2008. It continued to rise and eventually peaked at 10.0 percent. However, the peak occurred in October, 2009, about four months after the recession had ended according to the National Bureau of Economic Research (NBER).

Stock Market

The stock market is considered by many to be a *leading indicator* of economic activity. This is because investors make decisions

The stock market is affected by many factors including the health of the global economy.

Evaluate

Assign the Checkpoint questions at the end of the section. Assess students' comprehension using the Checkpoint activity as a self-assessment tool.

based on what they believe will happen in the future. As a result, changing stock prices reflect expectations for changes in economic activity. Many believe a rising stock market will lead an economic expansion and a falling stock market will lead a contraction.

This leading relationship was evident during the great recession of 2008–2009. The stock market, as measured by the S&P 500, reached a peak in October, 2007. It began to decline about three months before the recession actually started. The S&P 500 eventually dropped over 40 percent. It troughed in March, 2009, and then started recovering about three months before the recession ended.

Checkpoint 8.1

1. What are the four stages of a business cycle?
2. How do many economists define a recession?
3. How are economic indicators classified?
4. How does an economic expansion usually begin?
5. Why is the stock market considered a leading indicator of economic activity?

Build Your Vocabulary

As you progress through this text, develop a personal glossary of marketing terms which will help you build your vocabulary and prepare for a career in marketing. Write a definition for each of the following terms, and add it to your personal marketing glossary.

business cycle
expansion
peak
recession
depression
trough
economic recovery
leading indicator
lagging indicator
coincident indicator

Section 8.2 Role of Government

Objectives

After completing this section, you will be able to
- **discuss** how the role of the US government has grown since the nation was founded.
- **explain** the various ways government is involved in our economy today.

Key Terms

laissez-faire
externality
fiscal policy
monetary policy

Web Connect

Visit the website of the Federal Reserve system. Who is the current chairman of the board of the Federal Reserve? How is the chairman appointed?

Critical Thinking

The government performs many roles in our economy. Which three roles do you think are most important? Why? Are there any functions you feel the government should *not* perform?

Evolving Role of Government

Market economies have been more successful and created more wealth than any other economic system. As discussed in Chapter 6, the foundation of a market economy is free choice by individuals. This implies that the government should not interfere with market forces at work. **Laissez-faire** is the economic policy allowing businesses to operate with very little interference from the government. It is a French term that means "let them do as they please."

The founding fathers of the United States saw a very limited economic role for the government. When writing the US Constitution, the founding fathers gave Congress limited economic powers. These included the power to collect taxes, borrow money, and regulate commerce with foreign nations and among states. Another was the power to coin money.

The US economy grew rapidly during the 1800s and had many successes. However, citizens, political leaders, and other interest groups saw problems with the market economy. For example, large companies were accused of controlling prices and interfering with competition. Working conditions and products were often said to be unsafe. The poverty level was often thought to be too high.

The government response to economic problems was mostly laissez-faire until the Great Depression, which started in 1929. The country suffered through a serious economic contraction, high unemployment, bank failures, and widespread poverty. Many thought the free-market economy had failed and

Explore

Provide an opportunity for students to explore by assigning a hands-on activity. Review the vocabulary terms at the beginning of the section. Where have students encountered these terms before? Help students make educated guesses about the meanings of the terms with which they are least familiar.

Engage

Use the Teamwork exercise at the end of the chapter to engage students with each other to solve a problem or make a group presentation.

Timberline Lodge on Mount Hood, Oregon, is an example of a New Deal construction project that created hundreds of jobs in the mid 1930s for skilled workers.

St Nick/Shutterstock.com

needed government help. By 1932, many thought the economy might never recover. Franklin Roosevelt won the1932 presidential election by pledging the government would take steps to end the depression. He campaigned with a "New Deal for America."

The *New Deal* greatly expanded the role of government in the economy. Massive government programs were started. The New Deal created government jobs, provided social benefits, and tried to combat the housing crisis. Perhaps the program most recognized today is Social Security. The country finally emerged from the Great Depression around 1940. However, economists still debate the effectiveness of the New Deal.

By the early 1940s, the government had created more than 100 new agencies. These agencies regulated trade, energy, product safety, aviation, traffic safety, and many others. The government also continued to manage the economy to try to reduce the negative impact of business cycles.

Current Economic Role of Government

There is still ongoing pressure for the government to be involved in the economy. Many want the government to address problems a market economy has created or cannot fix. Others think the role of government should be very limited. However, it is clear that the role of government has grown since the nation began.

Today, the government
- provides a legal framework;
- provides public goods and services;
- provides for social welfare;
- promotes competition;
- corrects for externalities; and
- manages the economy.

Legal Framework

Laws are made and enforced at all levels of government: national, state, and local. Laws are necessary in certain areas for a

Elaborate/Extend

Provide an opportunity for students to exhibit their understanding of concepts in context of the material as it is presented. As time permits, have students read and discuss the special features in the chapter.

Elaborate/Extend

If students are using the optional *Marketing Dynamics* workbook, assign activities to engage active learning.

Green Marketing

Energy Savings

It is a common practice in Europe to unplug equipment that is not in use, including lights and computers. A business can *save some green,* as in dollars, by going green. Up to 25 percent can be saved on energy costs by turning off and unplugging equipment at the end of the day. Less energy usage also reduces harmful effects on the environment. Consider creating an internal marketing contest for employees to make suggestions for using energy-saving techniques for the business.

market economy to function. For example, laws define and enforce property rights and provide for public safety. The US legal framework has expanded and now covers many other areas. Examples include restrictions on products or services considered harmful or immoral, workplace and product safety, minimum wages, and import quotas.

Public Goods and Services

The government provides some *public goods and services* because they do not fit well in a market economy. Public goods and services must be made available to everyone. It would be difficult for a private company to monitor usage and charge fees for them. As a result, government agencies provide the goods and services and collect taxes to pay for them.

Public education is a common example. A nation will generally be more productive and stable when its population is well educated. Education is expensive, though. If private schools were the only options, few could afford the cost of education. Other public

The US Congress meets in the Capitol building located in Washington, DC, to propose, discuss, and enact new laws.

Mesu Dogan/Shutterstock.com

services include roads, police and fire protection, postal service, and public parks.

Social Welfare

A market economy is impersonal because the main motives are money and profit. People with plenty of money can get what they want and need. This is not the case for people with little money. This group often includes retirees, the disabled, veterans, disaster victims, and the unemployed.

Over the years, social programs have provided benefits to individuals considered to be in need. The largest programs are Medicare and Social Security that benefit retirees and the disabled. Unemployment compensation provides some money to those who have lost their jobs. The Federal Emergency Management Agency (FEMA) gives disaster relief, such as during hurricane Sandy in 2012. There are many other programs at the federal, state, and local levels. Of course, there is an ongoing debate about who should receive government benefits and how much.

Competition

The United States has laws to promote fair competition. These laws are enforced by the US Federal Trade Commission, which was established in 1914. While we have laws intended to maintain competition in the market, determining when anti-competitive behavior takes place is often not clear and subject to interpretation.

Externalities

An **externality** is something that affects people not directly connected to an economic activity. For example, think of a factory that emits bad-smelling smoke that is harmful when inhaled. This is an externality that can cause discomfort and health problems for those living nearby.

Some externalities are positive, though. Suppose fireworks are released at a baseball stadium for the direct benefit of the fans who bought tickets. Many people outside the stadium can also see the fireworks even though they have not paid.

Federal, state, and local governments are responsible for building and maintaining most roads and the highway infrastructure.

Tim Roberts Photography/Shutterstock.com

College and Career Portfolio

Electronic File Organization

You will create both a print portfolio and an e-portfolio in this class. You have already decided how to store hard-copy items for your print portfolio. Now you need to create a plan for storing and organizing the electronic files for your e-portfolio.

Ask your instructor where to save your documents. This could be on the school network or a flash drive of your own. Think about how to organize related files into categories. For example, *school transcripts and diplomas* might be one category. *Awards and certificates* might be another category, and so on. Next, consider how you will name the files. The names for folders and files should be descriptive but not too long. This naming system is for your use. You will decide in a later activity how to present your electronic files for viewers.

1. Create a folder on the network drive or flash drive in which you will save your files.
2. Write a few sentences to describe how you will name the subfolders and files for your portfolio.
3. Create the subfolders to organize the files, using the naming system you have created.

The government imposes taxes and regulations to reduce many negative externalities, such as pollution. The EPA monitors compliance with environmental laws. Many cities ban smoking in some public places. Sometimes subsidies are given to encourage positive externalities, such as in areas that promote education.

Manage the Economy

Recall that market forces produce business cycles in an economy. The result is alternating periods of expansion and recession.

The government continues to take an active role in trying to manage and stabilize the economy so as to reduce the length and effects of recessions. This happens through both fiscal and monetary policies, as shown in Figure 8-3.

Fiscal Policy

Fiscal policy refers to the tax and spending decisions made by the president and Congress. Often, the government uses fiscal policy to try to smooth business cycles and lessen the impact of recessions. Tax and

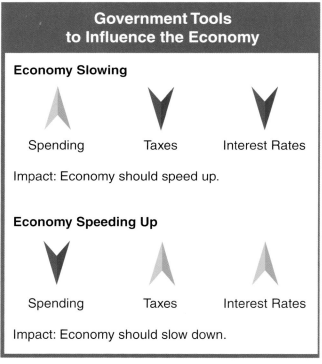

Goodheart-Willcox Publisher

Figure 8-3 The federal government uses spending, taxes, and interest rates to influence the economy.

Explore

The economy is in the news every day. Ask students to share what has happened this particular week that impacts the economy.

spending decisions are made to boost GDP and reverse an economic contraction.

GDP is made up of consumer, business, and government spending. Declining consumer demand can start a recession, which then spreads to businesses and deepens the contraction. To boost GDP and reverse a contraction, some economists believe the government should lower taxes.

The economic theory is that when taxes are low, consumers and businesses have more money to spend. However, there is no guarantee that lowering taxes will increase consumer or business spending. They might choose to save the extra money or pay off debt instead. Fiscal policy is clearly not an exact science. The exact type and amount of a tax reduction will impact spending results.

Some economists argue that another way to increase GDP is to increase government spending on goods and services. However, this policy also has potential problems. Where will the government get the extra money to spend? It could increase taxes. But, that might cause a decrease in consumer and business spending. More often, the government borrows to increase its spending. Of course, the money must be repaid at some time. This means higher taxes or less spending in the future.

Monetary Policy

Monetary policy is managing the economy through changes in the money supply and interest rates. Monetary policy is set by the Federal Reserve System. The Federal Reserve was started in 1913 and regulates the commercial banking system as the nation's central bank. Its goal is to maintain stable prices and moderate long-term interest rates, while also pursing maximum employment in the economy.

When the economy is sluggish, the Federal Reserve can use different tools to increase the growth of the money supply and help lower interest rates. The idea is that lower interest rates will make borrowing easier and induce more spending and investment. Likewise, the Federal Reserve can use tools to slow the growth of the money supply and increase rates if it believes the economy is growing too fast and inflation might result.

Many economists believe that monetary policy is more powerful than fiscal policy in impacting the course of the economy. However, like fiscal policy, monetary policy is not an exact science and its effectiveness is also open to debate.

FYI

The Federal Reserve is more commonly known as *the Fed.* As the central bank, it buys and sells US Treasury bonds and regulates the US credit system.

Evaluate

Assign the Checkpoint questions at the end of the section. Assess students' comprehension using the Checkpoint activity as a self-assessment tool.

Engage

Encourage a discussion about how the government manages our economy. Ask for current events that support this.

Checkpoint 8.2

1. What does the French term *laissez-faire* mean?
2. What economic event resulted in our government dramatically increasing its involvement in the economy?
3. Name the six major areas of government involvement in our economy today.
4. How does the government take an active role in trying to manage and stabilize the economy?
5. Fiscal policy refers to government decisions in what two areas?

Build Your Vocabulary

As you progress through this text, develop a personal glossary of marketing terms which will help you build your vocabulary and prepare for a career in marketing. Write a definition for each of the following terms, and add it to your personal marketing glossary.

laissez-faire
externality
fiscal policy
monetary policy

Checkpoint Answers

1. Laissez-faire means "let them do as they please."
2. The Great Depression of 1929.
3. (1) provide a legal framework, (2) provide public goods and services, (3) provide for social welfare, (4) promote competition, (5) correct for externalities, and (6) manage the economy.

4. The government takes an active role in trying to manage and stabilize the economy through fiscal policy and monetary policy.
5. Taxes and spending

Build Your Vocabulary Answers:

Definitions for these terms can be found in the glossary of this text.

Chapter Summary

Section 8.1 Business Cycles

- The four stages of the business cycle are expansion, peak, contraction, and trough.
- Economic indicators can be used to help identify which stage of the business cycle an economy is in and which stage is coming next. This information can be valuable when making business decisions.

Section 8.2 Role of Government

- The founders of the United States saw a very limited economic role for government. However, government involvement in the economy increased dramatically since the Great Depression.
- Today there is ongoing pressure for the government to be involved in a wide range of economic activities. These include such areas as our legal system, public goods, social welfare, competition, externalities, and management of the economy.

Review Your Knowledge

1. When do expansions often start?
2. What causes the GDP growth rate to change?
3. How long do most recessions last?
4. What type of role did the founders of the United States see for the government in the economy?
5. What impact did the Great Depression of 1929 have on the role of government in the economy?
6. Could our economy function without a legal framework? Why or why not?
7. What is a public good?
8. What is an externality? Why does the government try to correct for one?
9. Why might reducing taxes not provide a boost to GDP?
10. Who sets US monetary policy?

Apply Your Knowledge

1. Explain how marketing strategies differ if you are in the recession stage of a business cycle instead of the expansion stage.
2. Explain how the New Deal was intended to help the US economy in the Great Depression.
3. Imagine that you are on a marketing team, and your job is to help adjust your marketing plan based on changes in the business cycle. The economy is currently in a recession. What data might you analyze that would indicate the recession is ending?
4. Describe the current status of the business cycle in the United States today.
5. Imagine you are on a marketing team and believe the economy peaked a few months ago and is now beginning a recession stage. A member of your team disagrees. He says the economy is fine because the unemployment rate has not risen. What is your response?
6. What is the current unemployment rate for the United States?
7. You are the marketing manager for a business that provides private tutoring for high school students in a local school district. The school district just announced that it is starting a new program to provide free tutoring after school. How will this impact your business and marketing strategy?
8. Discuss the importance of public goods and services on your local economy.
9. In recent years the government has become more concerned that there is a negative externality connected to various high-calorie foods. What is this externality and why is it negative? Should you be concerned if you make or sell high-calorie foods? How would this affect your marketing strategy?
10. Who sets our country's monetary policy?

Check Your Marketing IQ

Before you begin the chapter, see what you already know about marketing by taking the chapter pretest. If you do not have a smartphone, visit the G-W Learning companion website.

G-W Learning mobile site: www.m.g-wlearning.com
G-W Learning companion website: www.g-wlearning.com

Common Core

College and Career Readiness

CTE Career Ready Practices. Most people in the United States act as responsible and contributing citizens. How can a person demonstrate social and ethical responsibility in times when disaster relief is needed in the community? Participate in a group discussion about how citizens can go beyond the minimum expectations of helping others in the community.

Reading. Read a magazine, newspaper, or online article about the current condition of the economy. Read for detail and determine the central ideas of the article. Review the conclusions made by the author. Provide an accurate summary of your reading, making sure to list the who, what, when, and how of this situation.

Writing. Conduct research on how many small businesses were forced to close in the past year due to the economy. Write a report consisting of several paragraphs to describe your findings and the implications for the economy.

Teamwork

Work as a team and pick a business for which you will be the marketing manager. First, identify the business cycle which your company is experiencing. Then discuss how your business will be impacted by changes in the business cycle. Next, make of list of the ways government involvement in the economy might affect your business. Explain how this situation affects the marketing plan for your business.

G-W Learning Mobile Site

Visit the G-W Learning mobile site to complete the chapter pretest and posttest and to practice vocabulary using e-flash cards. If you do not have a smartphone, visit the G-W Learning companion website to access these features.

G-W Learning mobile site: www.m.g-wlearning.com
G-W Learning companion website: www.g-wlearning.com

9 Global Trade

Section 9.1	Going Global
Section 9.2	Trade Regulations

"We must ensure that the global market is embedded in broadly shared values and practices that reflect global social needs, and that all the world's people share the benefits of globalization."

—Kofi Annan, former Secretary-General of the United Nations

College and Career Readiness

Reading Prep
As you read this chapter, determine the point of view or purpose of the author. What aspects of the text help to establish this purpose or point of view?

Check Your Marketing IQ

Before you begin the chapter, see what you already know about marketing by taking the chapter pretest. If you do not have a smartphone, visit the G-W Learning companion website.
G-W Learning mobile site: www.m.g-wlearning.com
G-W Learning companion website: www.g-wlearning.com

G-W Mobile

Explore

Assign the College and Career Readiness Reading Prep activity before students read the chapter. Reading Prep activities give students opportunity to apply the Common Core State Standards.

Engage

Assign the Chapter 9 pretest.

◇DECA Emerging Leaders

Sports and Entertainment Marketing Team Decision-Making Event, Part 2

Career Cluster: Marketing
Instructional Area: Economics

Procedure, Part 2

1. In the previous chapter, you studied the performance indicators for this event.
2. The event will be presented to you through your reading of the General Performance Indicators, Specific Performance Indicators and Case Study Situation. You will have up to 30 minutes to review this information and prepare your presentation. You may make notes to use during your presentation.
3. You will have up to 10 minutes to make your presentation to the judge, followed by up to five minutes to answer the judge's questions. You may have more than one judge. All members of the team must participate in the presentation as well as answer the questions.
4. Turn in all of your notes and event materials when you have completed the event.

Case Study Situation

You are to assume the roles of merchandise managers for Deluxe Linens, a popular brand of luxury bath towels. The **marketing manager (judge)** has asked your team to decide the best way the company should respond to rising cotton prices.

Deluxe Linens was introduced ten years ago when the economy was soaring and consumers had much more disposable income. The company sells luxury bath towels made from 100% cotton that are known for superior softness and absorbency. Deluxe Linens bath towels are sold in department stores and are moderately priced.

In the last year, continuous bad weather has resulted in smaller cotton crops overseas. Since all textiles worldwide are made from the same cotton crops, all textile companies are competing for the small supply of cotton. This has created a steady increase in cotton prices. Before the year is over, prices for cotton will be more than double the usual price.

Deluxe Linens cannot afford to pay the steep prices for cotton and still sell the merchandise at moderate prices. The marketing manager has come up with two possible solutions to the rise in cotton prices and wants you to determine which is the best option for Deluxe Linens. You can raise the price of Deluxe Linens' bath towels or switch to a less expensive cotton blend.

Your team will explain which solution you have chosen and the reasoning for the choice to the marketing manager in a meeting to take place in the marketing manager's office. The marketing manager will begin the meeting by greeting you and asking to hear your ideas. After you have explained your solution and reasoning and have answered the marketing manager's questions, the marketing manager will conclude the meeting by thanking you for your work.

Critical Thinking

1. How does the present economy affect a company's sales strategy?
2. What other option should the marketing manager consider in response to the rising prices?

Visit www.deca.org for more information.

Section 9.1 Going Global

Objectives

After completing this section, you will be able to
- **explain** the concept of globalization.
- **identify** reasons for global trade.
- **define** exports, imports, and the balance of trade.
- **explain** foreign exchange rates and their impact on global trade.

Key Terms

globalization
global economy
developed country
developing country
multinational
  corporation
export
import

balance of trade
trade surplus
trade deficit
currency
foreign exchange
  rate
floating currency

Web Connect

When doing business outside of the United States, knowing the value of the US dollar in those countries is vital. Do an Internet search for an online currency converter. Select five countries, and list the current value of one dollar. In which countries is the dollar worth more than it is in the United States? less?

Critical Thinking

In your role as marketing manager, do you think there would be any restrictions on marketing your product in a global market? Why or why not?

Globalization

Globalization is a popular term now, but it is not a new concept. **Globalization** occurs when nations become connected through freely moving goods, labor, and capital across borders. Sometimes this movement is referred to as *international trade*. Advances in technology and transportation now make it easier and quicker to conduct business in foreign countries. The result is more global trade and trading partners that rely on each other.

Different countries often have vastly different cultures. *Culture* is the shared beliefs, customs, practices, and social behavior of a particular group or nation. This means challenges for international business as well as for their marketers. When marketing to people in different cultures, it is important to understand the cultural preferences and economic

environments. One marketing technique may work well in one country but not in others. For example, personal dress is very specific in certain countries. Marketers must be aware of the culture before using photos of people dressed in a way that might be considered offensive.

When doing business across borders, labor laws also have to be considered. The United States has labor laws that apply to doing business in foreign countries. For example, the Child Labor Law does not allow children under the age of 14 to work. Businesses with overseas manufacturing plants must make sure that law is followed as well as any local labor laws. The US Bureau of International Labor Affairs (ILAB) and the Office of International Relations (OIR) exist to help businesses with both cultural differences and labor laws in other countries.

Explore

Provide an opportunity for students to explore by assigning a hands-on activity. Review the vocabulary terms at the beginning of the section. Where have students encountered these terms before? Help students make educated guesses about the meanings of the terms with which they are least familiar.

Resource

Use the Chapter 9 presentation on the optional Instructor's Presentations for PowerPoint® CD as an outline for presenting the chapter.

In addition, certain legal documents are required depending on the business type. For example, an exporting business may need weight, insurance, and place-of-origin certificates plus invoices and packing lists written in different languages. Businesses must also take into account longer shipping times and the added expenses of international shipping by rail, air, or water. There are professional shipping companies that specialize in international trade and can guarantee shipments.

Global Economy

The term **global economy** is the collective economic activity of every nation in the world. Today there are over 190 countries classified according to their level of economic development. They are called *developed* or *developing countries.*

Developed Countries

A **developed country** has a strong base of industrial production, good infrastructure, and a high standard of living. Many have a per capita GDP of over $20,000. Developed countries are also referred to as being *industrialized.* Examples include the United States, Japan, and western European countries.

The terms *global trade* and *international trade* are different terms for the same thing.

Developing Countries

A **developing country** has a lower standard of living, weaker infrastructure, and less industry than a developed country. Examples include many countries in the former Soviet Union, Latin America, Africa, and Asia. The standard of living in many developing countries is improving. As a result, they are often good markets to start or expand a business. There is great potential for the demand for goods and services to grow. Developing countries are also called *emerging markets.*

Multinationals

Globalization has increased with the growth of multinational corporations. A **multinational corporation** produces and sells products in foreign countries as well as inside its borders. Many large corporations are multinational.

For example, General Electric, General Motors, and Exxon Mobil are some

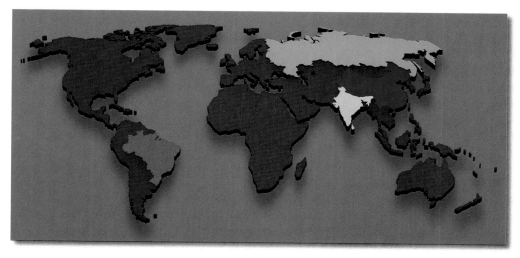

Currently, Brazil, Russia, India, and China (BRIC) are considered to be powerful emerging markets.

MAR Photography/Shutterstock.com

Explain
Discuss the difference between developed countries and developing countries.

Case in Point

Cadbury

Researching the market to implement the marketing concept of satisfying the customer is an important part of the marketer's job. Kraft Foods found this to be true when it introduced the Cadbury chocolate product to India. Kraft found two challenges in India. First, the hot, tropical weather made selling chocolate in stores without air conditioning very difficult. Second, Indian customers thought Cadbury chocolates were too expensive. Kraft needed to resolve both issues for Cadbury to achieve success in India. To address the weather issue, Kraft gave coolers to store owners so the product would not melt. To solve the pricing problem, Kraft repackaged the chocolate in smaller sizes to sell at lower price points. The marketing strategies worked. In 2011, Cadbury posted its highest sales and earnings ever in India, beating its competition there. The marketing concept succeeds—again.

well-known companies based in the United States. Many of the largest multinational companies are based in other countries. For example, the world's largest food company is Nestlé, which is based in Switzerland. Other large, foreign multinationals include Toyota, Sony, and Samsung, to name just a few.

Global Trade Advantages

Global trade has been growing fast. The value of goods that US companies bought and sold in foreign markets went from $34.4 *billion* in 1960 to $3.7 *trillion* in 2011. This is an average annual growth rate of 9.6 percent. Nations trade with each other for four important reasons: unique natural resources, unique products, lower prices, and growth opportunities.

Unique Natural Resources

Natural resources are not evenly divided among the nations. As a result, many nations do not have all of the natural resources they need. So, they must trade with other nations to get them. For example, Japan cannot grow enough wheat to meet its needs, so it buys wheat from other countries. The United States and China must buy oil from other countries to meet their needs.

Unique Products

Many nations make unique products not found elsewhere. For example, France is known for its fine lace products. Delft pottery is only produced in Holland. Guatemala makes vivid embroidered cloth.

One of the major unique products of a country is tourism. For example, people visit the Grand Canyon because there is no other place in the world like it. People visit the Eiffel Tower in Paris because it is unique.

Lower Prices

Sometimes the lower cost of labor in developing countries gives them a price advantage. For example, items like clothing and electronics can be produced at a much lower cost in some Asian countries.

Growth Opportunitis

Many companies expand into foreign markets to grow the business. This often occurs after a company achieves success at home. They then look for growth opportunities outside the country. For example, in 1957, J.W. Marriott opened his first hotel in the United States. When Marriott looked to grow in 1969, it

Extend

The United States has many global trade advantages. Ask students for examples.

opened the first foreign hotel in Acapulco, Mexico. By 1996, the company changed its name to Marriott International. It currently operates nearly 3,700 hotels in over 70 countries.

Exports and Imports

Goods that are sold to another country are called exports, as illustrated in Figure 9-1. Goods that are purchased from another country are called imports. Exports earn money for a country, while imports cost money. The balance of trade for a nation is the difference between its exports and imports as shown by the following formula.

exports – imports = balance of trade

More exports than imports result in a positive balance or trade surplus for a nation. More imports than exports result in a

negative balance or a trade deficit. For example, in 2011, US exports were $1.5 trillion. Imports were $2.2 trillion. The balance of trade was a $0.7 trillion deficit, meaning that imports were higher than exports.

exports $1.5 trillion – imports $2.2 trillion = trade deficit – $0.7 trillion

The United States enjoyed a trade surplus until 1971. However, over the last 40 years, the US annual balance of trade has been a surplus only two times. The amount of US trade deficit has also been increasing. The deficit grew from –$25.5 billion in 1980 to –$738.4 billion in 2011.

There is an ongoing debate about whether a trade deficit is good or bad for the US economy. Some economists believe a deficit is bad if it must always be paid for with borrowed money. In addition, imports hurt US employment.

United States Exports in 2011	
Country/Region	**Export Dollar Amounts**
Canada	$280,764,268,022
Mexico	197,543,674,806
China	103,878,554,773
Japan	66,168,328,820
United Kingdom	55,963,534,142
Germany	49,134,174,634
South Korea	43,505,004,799
Brazil	42,943,393,779
Netherlands	42,826,973,461
Hong Kong	36,512,581,188
World total*	**$1,480,552,124,563**

*The values given are for exports from the United States. The ten countries or regions represent 62.2 percent of the total US exports for all goods.

Figure 9-1
The top ten 2011 US exports.

Source: International Trade Administration

Extend

Encourage a discussion about imports and exports and the impact of on our economy.

Explore

Bring in the business section of a local newspaper. Discuss articles on the state of the economy.

Other economists believe a trade deficit is good because it reflects rising consumer income and confidence. In addition, they think our economy can benefit if we import capital goods and become more productive.

FYI

A central bank is a financial institution that oversees the money system in a nation. It regulates banks, lends money when commercial banks are unable to, and controls the money supply.

Foreign Exchange Rates

Global trade is complex because most countries have their own **currencies,** or money. There are over 160 different currencies in the world. For example, the currency of the United States is the US dollar. Japan uses the yen. The United Kingdom uses the pound. If you go to Japan and want to buy something, first you have to turn your US dollars into yen. Likewise, a Japanese citizen visiting the United States would turn yen into dollars.

The cost to convert one currency into another is called the **foreign exchange rate**. Exchange rates are necessary because currencies have different values relative to each other. Most currencies today are floating. **Floating currencies** mean that the exchange rate is set by the market forces of the supply and demand in the foreign exchange market. The *foreign exchange market (FOREX)* works like a stock market in which foreign currencies are bought and sold throughout the world. Central banks often trade in the foreign exchange market to influence exchange rates.

Every day more than $1.2 trillion of foreign currency is traded around the world. Over 80 percent of those transactions involve US dollars. Figure 9-2 shows a sample of five foreign currency exchange rates at year-end 2010 and 2011. The rates show what a unit of each foreign currency was worth in US dollars. For example, at year-end 2010, the price of one British pound was $1.547 in US dollars.

Sometimes the price of a foreign currency declines in US dollars. Figure 9-2 shows the decline from year-end 2010 to 2011 in the Canadian dollar, euro, and Mexican peso. The Canadian dollar dropped in value from $1.00 to $0.98. The Euro dropped from $1.325 to $1.295. The peso dropped from $.081 to $.072.

When the price of a foreign currency declines, it means the value of a US dollar has *strengthened.* The good news is that a stronger dollar can buy more foreign products. Imports become less expensive, which means lower prices. The bad news, though, is that our exports become more expensive to foreign buyers. This hurts US companies exporting products.

Figure 9-2 Foreign currencies tend to fluctuate.

Currency Exchange Rates: US Dollars per Foreign Unit		
Currency	**December 31, 2010**	**December 31, 2011**
British pound	$1.547	$1.547
Canadian dollar	$1.000	$0.981
European Union euro	$1.325	$1.295
Japanese yen	$0.012	$0.013
Mexican peso	$0.081	$0.072

Goodheart-Willcox Publisher

Doing business in a foreign country means dealing in foreign currencies. Currencies may or may not have exchange rates beneficial for a US-based company.

filmfoto/Shutterstock.com

Sometimes the price of foreign currency increases in US dollars. Figure 9-2 shows the value of the Japanese yen increased from $.012 to $.013. When the price of a foreign currency increases, the value of a US dollar has *weakened.* A weaker dollar buys fewer foreign products. A weaker dollar also brings both good and bad news for the US economy. The good news is that US exports are less expensive to foreign buyers. The bad news is that imports are more expensive, so prices are higher for American buyers.

The exchange rate of a currency is often considered an indicator of an economy's health. The higher a currency's value, the stronger the economy is relative to other countries. Of course, greater demand for a currency will cause its exchange rate to increase.

But, what causes the demand for a currency to increase? There are a number of factors, including the following situations.

- Greater demand for products in a country translates to more demand for its currency.

- Higher interest rates in a country make its investments and currency more attractive.
- Low inflation in a country makes the currency more attractive
- Countries with greater political stability have stable currencies which are more attractive.

In addition, central banks also buy or sell currencies to influence exchanges rates. When central banks influence exchange rates, it is called a *managed float.* A central bank hopes to manage the balance of trade in its country through managed float. Some currencies are highly managed, such as the Chinese yuan. Some are not, including the US dollar.

AMA Tip

The *Journal of International Marketing,* published by the AMA, features the latest research and findings on global marketing issues. Because the contributors come from both academic and business backgrounds, the journal addresses international marketing questions from both viewpoints. The journal is available to AMA members. www.marketingpower.com

Explore

Check currency exchanges today and compare to Figure 9-2. Discuss the impact of the economy on exchange values.

Explain

Discuss how the fluctuating currency impacts process on imports and exports.

Marketing Ethics

Integrity
Integrity is defined as the quality of being fair and honest. Integrity and ethics go together in both the personal and professional lives of workers. As a leader, the marketing professional helps establish the reputation of the business in the community. A marketing professional who displays integrity helps create a positive culture for the business, its customers, and the community.

Checkpoint 9.1

1. What is a developed country?
2. Identify four reasons why countries trade with one another.
3. What is the difference between an export and an import?
4. Why are exchange rates necessary?
5. How does a stronger US dollar help an American importer and hurt an American exporter?

Build Your Vocabulary

As you progress through this text, develop a personal glossary of marketing terms which will help you build your vocabulary and prepare for a career in marketing. Write a definition for each of the following terms, and add it to your personal marketing glossary.

globalization
developed country
developing country
global economy
multinational corporation
export
import
balance of trade
trade surplus
trade deficit
currency
foreign exchange rate
floating currency

Evaluate

Assign Checkpoint questions at end of section. Assess student comprehension using the Checkpoint activity as a self-assessment tool.

Checkpoint Answers

1. A developed country is a country that has a strong base of industrial production, good infrastructure, and a high standard of living.
2. Four reasons why a country might want to trade with another country are unique natural resources, unique products, lower prices, and growth opportunities.

3. Exports are goods sold to another country. Imports are goods purchased from another country.
4. Exchange rates are necessary because currencies have different values relative to each other.
5. A stronger US dollar makes imports less expensive and exports more expensive.

Build Your Vocabulary Answers

Definitions for these terms can be found in the glossary of this text.

Section 9.2 Trade Regulations

Objectives

After completing this section, you will be able to
- **explain** the reasons for trade regulations and identify three different types.
- **describe** the purposes of trade agreements and trading blocs.

Key Terms

embargo
trade sanction
tariff
quota
trade agreement
trading bloc
free trade zone

Web Connect

Perform online research to find guidelines on shipping marketing materials out of the country. These materials might include catalogs, brochures, or promotional items. Select a country for which you think your business might export a product. Then check the customs regulations for sending marketing pieces into that country. What did you learn?

Critical Thinking

Why do you think that governments of various countries impose trade restrictions? Do you think these laws are necessary? Why or why not?

Types of Trade Regulations

Governments regulate many aspects of foreign trade for various reasons. Most governments try to protect domestic companies from foreign competitors. They may also want to put pressure on foreign governments for political reasons. Or they want to prevent hazardous products from entering the country. Trade regulations include embargoes, tariffs, quotas, and import restrictions.

Embargoes

An **embargo** is a government order that prohibits trade with a foreign country. A *total embargo* is the most severe trade restriction. For example, in 1962, the United States restricted all trade and travel to Cuba. The total embargo was later relaxed.

Trade sanctions are embargoes affecting only one or several goods. Trade sanctions can prohibit the importation of a specific product for health reasons. For example, in 1989, the US government placed a trade sanction on beef from countries with cattle infected with mad cow disease. Both embargoes and sanctions are trade tools that can be used as foreign policy.

Tariffs

A **tariff** is a government tax on imported goods. A tariff may also be called a *duty, customs duty,* or *import duty.* There are two reasons for tariffs. One reason is to generate revenue for the government. Another reason

Most international airports have duty-free stores to attract travelers interested in saving sales taxes on goods.

is to protect domestic industries. Before the US government taxed incomes, its main source of revenue was from tariffs. Now tariffs are used mainly to protect domestic companies. Tariffs protect domestic companies because the taxes make competing imported products more expensive for consumers.

Quotas

A **quota** limits the amount of a product imported into a country during a specific period of time. For example, some products with US quotas include sugar, some textiles, tuna, dried milk, and anchovies. Import quotas are designed to protect domestic producers by limiting foreign competition.

Import Restrictions

Governments use import restrictions to protect the health and safety of citizens from dangerous imported products. The United States has laws controlling hazardous materials, firearms, and drugs coming into the country. There are also laws restricting plants, animals, and food that may carry pests or diseases. Endangered plant and animal species and products made from them are banned under the US Endangered Species Act.

Trade Relations

For many years, the disadvantages of foreign trade seemed to outweigh the advantages. Many countries wanted to be

Social Media

Twitter

Twitter is a useful tool for conversations with customers. You can connect in real time with customers who may be using your product or visiting your booth at an exhibit. Customers can find information instantly about the company, a product launch, or some other announcement you choose to make. Marketers can see what customers are saying about the company, the industry, or a topic that helps gather intelligence about the competition. Twitter gives you a chance to network and expand your customer base. It is easy to use and easy to set up an account. But remember that Twitter, like other social media tools, has strict guidelines on how to use their logo, buttons, and other trademarked information. Be ethical and follow the rules because social media is an important part of any marketing plan.

Elaborate/Extend

If students are using the optional *Marketing Dynamics* workbook, assign activities to engage active learning.

Elaborate/Extend

Provide an opportunity for students to exhibit their understanding of concepts in context of the material as it is presented. As time permits, have students read and discuss the special features in the chapter.

Some fruits and vegetables are not permitted to bring into some countries due to potential diseases they may carry.

Roman Samokhin/Shutterstock.com

self-sufficient. They did not want another country to cut off needed products in time of war. Countries also wanted to keep out lower-cost imports to protect domestic industries.

After World War II, though, foreign trade became more attractive. Many countries saw foreign trade as a way to speed up economic recovery. It promoted friendly relations and helped developing countries. In general, trade policies in recent years have become more open around the world. Global trade is freer than it has ever been. However, there are still many who believe import policies are harmful and argue for restrictions and policy changes.

Trade Agreements

A **trade agreement** is a document listing the conditions and terms under which goods are imported and exported between countries. Trade agreements are numerous and complex. For example, the United States currently has over 300 different trade agreements with other countries.

Explain

Trade relations are important for the success of the economy. Ask students for reasons why trade agreements are important.

The General Agreement on Tariffs and Trade (GATT) was signed by the United States and 23 other nations in 1947. Through GATT, member countries negotiated major reductions in tariffs and other trade barriers. In 1995, GATT was replaced by the *World Trade Organization (WTO)*. The WTO has 153 member countries. Its purpose is to provide a forum for member trade negotiations, to handle trade disputes, and to help developing countries.

Trading Blocs

A **trading bloc** is a group of countries joining together to trade as if they were one country, as shown in Figure 9-3. A trading bloc is usually a free-trade zone as well. A **free-trade zone** is a group of countries that have reduced or eliminated trade barriers among themselves.

The European Union is a major trading bloc and free-trade zone consisting of 27 European countries. The North American

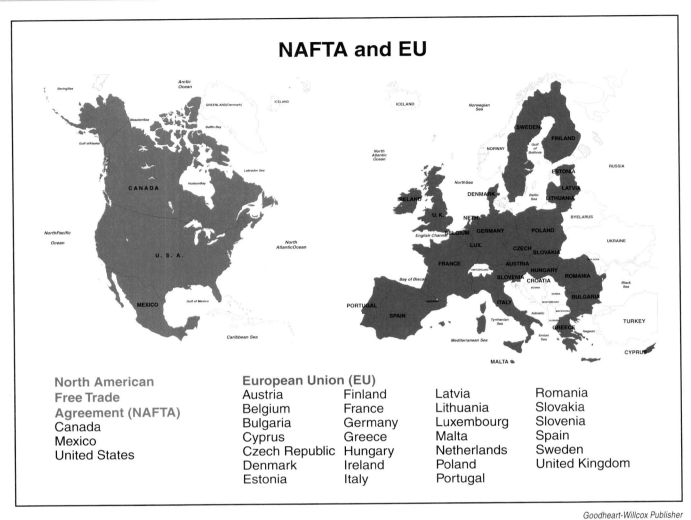

Goodheart-Willcox Publisher

Figure 9-3 NAFTA and the EU have free trade agreements among themselves.

Free Trade Agreement (NAFTA) created a
free-trade zone among the United States,
Canada, and Mexico. The Asia-Pacific
Economic Cooperation promotes free trade
and economic cooperation among its 21
member countries.

Exploring Careers

Market Analyst

A profitable product or service is one that customers want to buy. Companies rely on market analysts to find out what products or services people want and how much they are willing to pay for them. A market analyst researches market conditions, including public interest, potential competitors and their pricing, plus current sales. This information helps company executives make decisions about which products or services to offer. Typical job titles for these positions include *market analyst, market research analyst, market research consultant,* and *business development specialist.*

Some examples of tasks that market analysts perform include:

- gather information about selected products and product ideas;
- analyze data about customer preferences and buying habits to identify potential markets;
- monitor related industries and businesses; and
- forecast trends in sales and marketing.

Market analysts need to be able to analyze large amounts of data to find trends and other information. They evaluate not only the data but also the reliability of the data sources. Marketing analysts must be able to accurately communicate the information gained from the research to company executives so they can make good product decisions. A strong background in statistics is necessary, as well as the ability to use information-retrieval software. A bachelor degree is required for about 70 percent of the jobs in this field. For more information, access the *Occupational Outlook Handbook* online.

Checkpoint 9.2

1. Why do governments regulate international trade?
2. Identify four types of trade regulations.
3. How does a tariff protect a domestic company against foreign competition?
4. Has global trade generally become freer or more restrictive since World War II?
5. What agreement created a free-trade zone among the United States, Canada, and Mexico?

Build Your Vocabulary

As you progress through this text, develop a personal glossary of marketing terms which will help you build your vocabulary and prepare for a career in marketing. Write a definition for each of the following terms, and add it to your personal marketing glossary.

embargo
trade sanction
tariff
quota
trade agreement
trading bloc
free-trade zone

Checkpoint Answers

1. A country might regulate trade to protect domestic companies from foreign competitors, exert political pressure on foreign governments, or safeguard against the import of hazardous products.
2. A country can regulate foreign trade using embargoes, tariffs, quotas, and import restrictions.

3. A tariff makes an imported product more expensive.
4. Global trade has become freer.
5. The North American Free Trade Agreement (NAFTA).

Build Your Vocabulary Answers

Definitions for these terms can be found in the glossary of this text.

Chapter Summary

Section 9.1 Going Global

- Globalization is a process in which the economies of nations become connected. This happens through the free movement of goods, labor, and capital across national borders.
- Global trade has expanded rapidly. Nations participate in global trade for unique natural resources, lower prices, unique products, and growth opportunities.
- Goods that are sold to another country are called *exports*. Goods that are purchased from another country are called *imports*. The difference between exports and imports is called the balance of trade.
- A foreign exchange rate is the cost to covert one currency into another. Global trade is affected when the exchange rate increases or decreases, because this causes the prices of exports and imports to either increase or decrease.

Section 9.2 Trade Regulations

- Trade regulations are imposed in order to protect domestic companies from foreign competitors, to exert political pressure on foreign governments, and to prevent hazardous products from coming into a country. Trade regulations include embargoes, tariffs, and quotas.
- A trade agreement is a document that regulates how goods are imported and exported between countries. A trading bloc is a group of countries that join together to trade as one country.

Review Your Knowledge

1. What is the difference between a developed and developing country?
2. Why might a developing country be a good place to start or expand a business?
3. Give examples of a multinational corporation.
4. What is one major unique product of a country?
5. Explain a managed float.
6. Why does a stronger dollar bring both good and bad news for the US economy?
7. What is the most severe trade restriction that a government can order?
8. What is a trade agreement?
9. What is the purpose of the World Trade Organization (WTO)?
10. Why is a trading bloc created?

Evaluate

Assign end-of-chapter activities.

Review Your Knowledge Answers

1. A developed country has a stronger base of industrial production, better infrastructure, and a higher standard of living as compared to a developing country.
2. Because the standard of living in developing countries is often improving, there is great potential for the demand for goods and services to grow.
3. Examples of a multinational corporation are General Electric, General Motors, and Exxon Mobil.
4. One major unique product of a country is tourism.
5. A managed float is a situation in which central banks influence exchange rates by trading on the foreign exchange market.

6. A strong dollar makes imports less expensive, which benefits American buyers. However, it also makes exports more expensive, which hurts US companies that sell to foreigners.
7. The most severe trade restriction is a total embargo.
8. A trade agreement specifies the conditions and terms under which goods between two or more nations are imported and exported.
9. The purpose of the World Trade Organization (WTO) is to provide a forum for member trade negotiations, handle trade disputes, and assist developing countries.
10. A trading bloc is a group of countries that join together to trade as if they were one country. They are formed to make trading easier among the member countries.

Apply Your Knowledge

1. As a marketing manager for a company which sells sunglasses, how might your marketing plan differ if you are selling in a developing country instead of a developed country?
2. A restaurant chain that specializes in Stromboli sandwiches is considering opening restaurants in a foreign country. However, it is discovered that Stromboli sandwiches are virtually unknown there. Identify a potential advantage and disadvantage of expanding into this new market.
3. As a marketing manager for a multinational company, your strategy will be to sell to foreign countries. Research a company that you may want to export to and the required documents needed in that country.
4. Imagine you are a marketing manager for a retail store that sells athletic apparel. One of your best sellers is a line of authentic Premier League soccer jerseys, which are imported from the United Kingdom. The US dollar was recently weakened against the British pound. How will this affect your marketing strategy for this product?
5. A US company makes candy and uses large amounts of sugar. How will quotas on imported sugar affect the price of the product and the marketing plan?
6. Create a table of the current exchange values similar to the example in this chapter. Evaluate the buying power of the dollar today.
7. Research embargoes for the United States. What did you learn?
8. How does tourism affect the economy of the United States?
9. Research the history of the euro. Which countries changed their currency to adopt the euro? What other information did you find?
10. Research a country with an economy that is dependent on tourism. Why has tourism become so important? What other industries are significant to that country, if any?

Check Your Marketing IQ

Now that you have finished the chapter, see what you learned about marketing by taking the chapter posttest. If you do not have a smartphone, visit the G-W Learning companion website.

G-W Learning mobile site: www.m.g-wlearning.com
G-W Learning companion website: www.g-wlearning.com

College and Career Readiness

Common Core

CTE Career Ready Practices. You may have been taught to treat others how you would like to be treated. This is often called *the golden rule.* Working well with others who have a background different from yours may also require that you learn to treat others as *they* wish to be treated. Conduct research on the Internet about cultural differences related to personal space, time, gestures, body language, and views of authority figures. List four differences and how you would approach each.

Speaking. Research the features of some currencies used around the world. Compile information about the aspects of each type of currency that helps to prevent counterfeiting. Also include the denominations made available, the materials used in making the currency, the features of the currency that help to identify the country it represents, and any other interesting information you find. Use this information, along with what you already know about the features of US currency, to create a world currency. Using various elements (visual displays, written handouts, technological displays), present your currency to the class. Explain why you chose the features you did.

Listening. Active listening means that you are fully participating as you process what others say. Practice active listening skills while listening to a broadcast business report on the radio, on television, or podcast. Pick a single story about international business. Write a report in which you analyze the following aspects of the story: the audience for the speaker, point of view, reasoning, stance, word choice, tone, points of emphasis, and organization.

Teamwork

Working with your team, research import quotas for the United States. Name the products, quantities, and any other information you can find. What did you learn from this exercise?

G-W Learning Mobile Site

Visit the G-W Learning mobile site to complete the chapter pretest and posttest and to practice vocabulary using e-flash cards. If you do not have a smartphone, visit the G-W Learning companion website to access these features.

G-W Learning mobile site: www.m.g-wlearning.com

G-W Learning companion website: www.g-wlearning.com

Marketing Plan

Teaching notes have been provided in Chapters 1–4 to prepare you for assigning the marketing plan activity. This is a project-based activity that appears at the end of each unit. Students were directed at the end of Unit 1 to begin writing a marketing plan. The marketing plan will be written based on a business plan. If you opt to assign this activity to your students, you will need to prepare in advance and locate a business plan for them to use.

There are several options for locating a business plan.

Sample business plans are readily available on the Internet. The website www.bplan.com site has many business plans from which to choose. You may preselect a business or assign students to visit the site and select a business that is of interest to them.

You may choose to require students to either work with a local business or publicly traded company. Students would need to be able to obtain a copy of the company's business plan.

Remember to remind students the importance of selecting a company that works for them. It will be challenging if they select a company, start a marketing plan, and realize it doesn't work for them.

This part of the marketing plan calls for students to research economic conditions for the company they have selected to write a marketing plan. The economy plays an important role in business and the marketing functions. In order for students to complete a realistic marketing plan, they will need to get to know the company well through personal interviews, web pages, or other research. This can be a major research activity. Or if you prefer, you can direct students to find only the information they need to complete this part of the plan.

Unit 2
Dynamics of the Economy
Building the Marketing Plan

As a famous philosopher said, "A journey of a thousand miles begins with a single step." The first step of your journey as a marketer is your marketing plan. You will make many revisions to the plan as you proceed through the text chapters. So, remember there are no right or wrong answers to any of the activities that you complete. You have reviewed the parts of the marketing plan and are now ready to begin writing your own plan. Keep in mind that you are writing a draft as you complete each section of your marketing plan. You will revise each section or subsection multiple times as you conduct more research and learn more about your business and industry.

Economic Conditions

Objectives

- Evaluate current economic conditions and the impact on your business.
- Explore the impact of inflation on your business.

Directions

In this activity, you will begin developing the **Situation Analysis** section of the marketing plan. The  Situation Analysis is a snapshot of the environment in which a business has been operating over a given time, usually the last 12 to 16 months.

Access the *Marketing Dynamics* companion website at www.g-wlearning.com. Download the data file for the following activity.

1. Unit Activity 2-1. **Research**. In this activity, you will examine the current economic conditions of the country or region where the business operates, inflation, and business cycles.

2. Open your saved marketing plan document.
3. Locate the Situation Analysis section of the plan. In your role as a marketing manager for the company you selected, how do you think the current economic conditions would influence the marketing of your product or business? Assume your role as the marketing manager and provide information about the state of the economy and its impact on the business. Complete the introduction for this section.
4. How does inflation impact the marketing of your product or business? As marketing manager, provide information about the current inflation rate and its impact on the business. Continue adding information to the introduction for this section.
5. How does the current business cycle impact the marketing of the product that your business offers? As marketing manager, provide information about the current business cycle and its impact on your business.
6. Use the suggestions and questions listed to help you generate ideas. Delete the instructions and questions when you are finished recording your responses. Proofread your document and correct any errors in keyboarding, spelling, and grammar.
7. Save your document.

Unit 3

Marketplace Dynamics

Chapters

Eye-Catcher

Annette/Shaft/Shutterstock.com

Marketing Matters

Have you ever thought of the Internet as a marketplace? A market or marketplace is the world of trade. Nowhere are more goods and services traded than online. Amazon.com exists only online. There are no Amazon stores you can visit, yet it is one of the largest providers of products and services in the world. Think about other kinds of marketplaces in which marketers must compete for business.

Marketing Core Functions Covered in This Unit

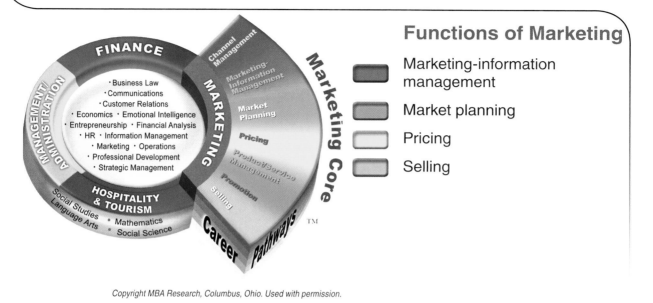

Functions of Marketing

- ■ Marketing-information management
- ■ Market planning
- □ Pricing
- □ Selling

Developing a Vision

Customer demand and competition are driving factors in the marketplace. Consumer buying habits change daily. New competition for customer dollars makes a business work harder. A business must take an objective look at the market through the eyes of the buyer as well as the competition. Consumer preferences and competitive information are learned through market research.

Research also forces marketing to be efficient and target the correct audience. Understanding the customer is the key to marketing success. Is your target business-to-consumer (B2C)? Or is your target business-to-business (B2B)? Focused marketing helps businesses meet their sales and profit goals.

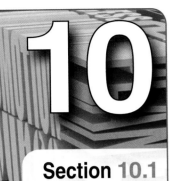

10 Marketing Research

| Section 10.1 | Determine Research Needs |
| Section 10.2 | Conduct the Research |

"If we only have great companies, we will merely have a prosperous society, not a great one. Economic growth and power are the means, not the definition, of a great nation."

—Jim Collins, American economics author

College and Career Readiness

Reading Prep
Before reading this chapter, read the quote on the chapter opening page. How does this quote relate to what is being presented in the content?

Check Your Marketing IQ

Before you begin the chapter, see what you already know about marketing by taking the chapter pretest. If you do not have a smartphone, visit the G-W Learning companion website.
G-W Learning mobile site: www.m.g-wlearning.com
G-W Learning companion website: www.g-wlearning.com

G-W Mobile

Explore
Assign the College and Career Readiness Reading Prep activity before students read the chapter. Reading Prep activities give students opportunity to apply the Common Core State Standards.

Engage
Assign the Chapter 10 pretest.

◇DECA Emerging Leaders

Professional Selling Events, Part 1

Career Cluster: Marketing
Instructional Area: Not identified for this event.

Knowledge and Skills Assessed

The participant will demonstrate knowledge and skills needed to address the components of the project as described in the definitions and evaluation forms as well as learn/understand the importance of

- communications knowledge and skills—the ability to exchange information and ideas with others through writing, speaking, reading or listening;
- analytical knowledge and skills—the ability to derive facts from data, findings from facts, conclusions from findings and recommendations from conclusions;
- critical thinking/problem-solving knowledge and skills;
- production knowledge and skills—the ability to take a concept from an idea and make it real;
- priorities/time management—the ability to determine priorities and manage time commitments; and
- how to apply selling principles and techniques to the business environment.

Purpose

Designed for individual DECA members, participants will organize and deliver a sales presentation for one or more products and/or services while demonstrating skills needed for a career in sales. The guidelines and evaluation form for each Professional Selling Events career category will be exactly the same. However, each career area will deliver a sales presentation for a different product described in the Products/Services and Target Customer Descriptions section. Products, services, and target markets are identified annually.

Procedure, Part 1

1. For Part 1 in this text, read the skills assessed and purpose of the event.
2. The objective for the sales presentation is for the participant to assume the role of salesperson making a presentation to a potential **buyer (judge).** Prior to ICDC, the participant will prepare a sales presentation for the product/service and target market customers described.
3. The participant will make a 20-minute sales presentation to the judge worth 100 points.
4. The presentation begins immediately after the introduction of the participant by the adult assistant to the judge.
5. The participant will spend no more than 15 minutes setting up visual aids and delivering the sales presentation. The participant may bring presentation notes to use during the sales presentation.
6. The judge will spend the remaining five minutes questioning the participant.
7. If there are any questions, ask your teacher to clarify.

Critical Thinking

1. What role does marketing research play in the preparation?
2. Why are new products and services important to business/industry?

Visit www.deca.org for more information.

Section 10.1 Determine Research Needs

After completing this section, you will be able to
- **describe** the importance of marketing research.
- **identify** the two types of research data.

marketing research	focus group
data	survey
database	diary
primary data	variable
research sample	secondary data
qualitative data	chamber of
quantitative data	commerce
interview	trade association

Visit the website of the US Census Bureau. Find the link for *State and County Quick Facts*. Select your state. What type of useful information can you find for your state? Explain why this information would be helpful when writing a marketing plan.

As you conduct market research, there will be many variables that will influence the approach you take to gathering information. List some variables you would need to consider when researching the customers most likely to buy your product or service.

Why Use Marketing Research?

It makes sense that the best way to make a profit is through the marketing concept, or customer satisfaction. Satisfying the needs and wants of target market customers leads to customer satisfaction. Logically, the businesses doing a better job of meeting those needs will sell more than the competition.

So, how do businesses define their target markets? How can they learn about the needs and wants of their customers? What motivates people to buy? Where do businesses get information about the competition? How do businesses learn about new opportunities? All of these questions can be answered through marketing research.

Marketing research is gathering and analyzing information to help make good marketing decisions. Marketing research is an important part of market planning, which is one of the seven functions of marketing. All good marketing plans refer to the marketing research that helped form the goals, strategies, and tactics.

As shown in Figure 10-1, marketing research helps businesses to: define primary customers; learn about the competition; and identify growth opportunities.

Types of Research Data

Data are the pieces of information gained through research. A **database** is an organized collection of data most often in digital

Three Areas of Marketing Research		
Marketing Research	**Purpose**	**Sample Question**
Customer	Learn about customers so that the company can meet customers' needs	What is my customers' favorite snack food?
Competition	Learn about competition so that the company can beat the competition	Does my competitor's product have better features than mine?
Opportunity	Learn about new opportunities so that the company can grow	Which market is growing the fastest?

Goodheart-Willcox Publisher

Figure 10-1 The purpose of marketing research is to learn as much as possible about customers, competitors, and opportunities to develop marketing plans and make marketing decisions.

form. One database common to most businesses is its customer database. A customer database contains contact information about current customers. Some companies also have databases for people who might become customers. Depending on the company, a database may also contain buying habits or other information.

Another type of database is the marketing research database. A marketing research database contains the results of marketing research. There are two types of data collected through research: secondary and primary.

Primary Data

Primary data are pieces of information collected by you or your organization. Primary data may come from internal sources, such as customers, customer service reps, or salespeople. For example, a chef is collecting primary data by asking diners in his restaurant if they like his new chicken dish.

Primary research must be done properly for the data to be accurate. For example, the right people have to be asked the right questions. A research sample represents the group of people or target market on which the research is done. The responses from a smaller

group of people reflect those of the larger population. However, the sample size must be large enough for the results to be valid.

The *sample size* is the number of people in the research sample. Many national surveys use 1,000 people to get useful information about national attitudes and opinions. The people who choose samples and analyze results are statisticians and marketing researchers.

Primary data can be qualitative or quantitative, as shown in Figure 10-2. Qualitative data provide insight into what people think about a topic. Qualitative data come from research questions that require judgment; not *yes* or *no* answers from a few people. This type of data needs answers from a larger sample size. It can provide a lot of detailed information. Quantitative data are the facts and figures from which conclusions can be drawn.

Marketers can collect primary data themselves. Or, they may hire a marketing research firm to collect it. Large businesses often collect their own marketing data. Over 50 percent of manufacturers have their own marketing research departments.

Businesses hire marketing research firms if they do not have in-house researchers or the project is large. In some cases, the added cost is worth the expected results. Marketing research is a big business. Some of the larger

Elaborate/Extend

Assign the College and Career Readiness Portfolio activity at the end of the chapter.

Explore

Ask students if they have participated in any type of market research such as an online survey. If they have, ask them to describe the experience.

Figure 10-2 Both types of data are useful for different reasons.

Differences Between Qualitative and Quantitative Data	
Senior Class Qualitative Data	**Senior Class Quantitative Data**
Community minded	467 members participate in community activities
Lots of school spirit	55% of males and 45% of females attend school functions
Value learning	73% are college-bound; 14% are work-bound; 13% are military-bound

Goodheart-Willcox Publisher

marketing research companies include A.C. Nielsen, Arbitron, J.D. Power and Associates, Gallup, and Yankelovich.

The most common ways to collect primary research data are observation, interviews, surveys, diaries, and experiments, as shown in Figure 10-3. Research that has not yet been analyzed is called *raw data*. Researchers analyze the raw data to draw conclusions. The conclusions then help marketers make good decisions.

Observation

In the observation method, the researcher watches people or situations and records facts. The key to getting good information through observation is to make sure the subjects do not know they are being observed. Their behaviors must be real and not influenced by the observer.

For example, a business may want to test its window displays. A researcher could use the observation method to sit in front of the store and observe reactions to the displays.

Figure 10-3 The method used to gather primary research data is very important. Different methods may lead to different conclusions and business decisions.

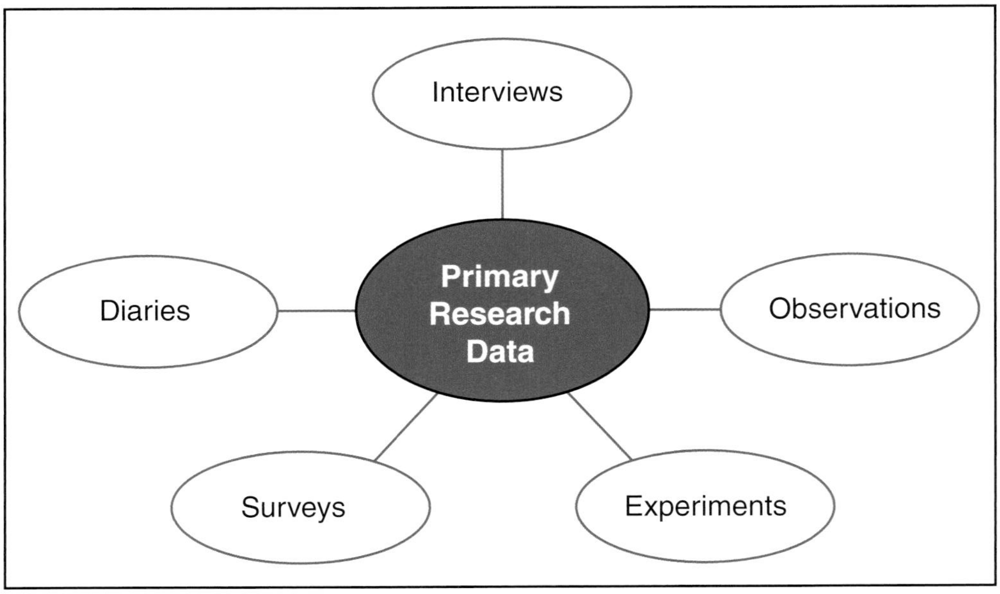

Goodheart-Willcox Publisher

Engage

Market research is a topic that many students will find interesting. Lead a discussion about different tools that are used to find data.

Explore

Bring in samples of survey tools. Many of these come in the mail or online. Critique each. Have students create a survey tool.

FYI

A Likert scale is often used in marketing re-search to gather data about attitudes. People are asked how much they agree or disagree with a given statement. Each response is assigned a number to help researchers analyze the data. Likert scales usually have three, five, or seven responses from which to choose.

Raw data might include the following:
- how many people walked by;
- how many people looked at the store windows;
- the number entering the store; and
- the number leaving with purchases.

Another form of observation many companies use is the secret shopper. A *secret shopper* is a person hired by a company to visit its place of business and observe the quality of service. Secret shoppers may also buy products to test the staff. The employees do not know which customers, if any, are secret shoppers. Secret shoppers report their experiences in writing to the business. They report good service and any problems.

Interview

An **interview** is a formal meeting between two or more people to obtain certain information. In marketing, interviews provide insight into the thoughts and opinions of people about a product or business. When interviews are done with a group of people, it is called a **focus group.** Focus groups usually consist of six to nine people brought together to discuss a specific topic. They are almost always paid for their time. A focus group is run by one person who asks questions and keeps the group focused. Focus groups are often recorded on video. They may be watched in real time by others from behind a one-way mirror. Focus groups are useful for gaining information based on how people in the group interact with each other.

Survey

A **survey** is an organized study in which people are asked the same questions. A survey can be given in person, over the telephone, by mail, or online. The success of a survey depends on asking the right ques-tions, in a random order, to the right group

Case in Point

Netflix

Is marketing research always correct? Quite simply, no. There are incorrect decisions based on incomplete research from which a marketer can learn valuable lessons. A good example is Netflix. In 2011, Netflix split its streaming services and DVD-by-mail service into two separate companies. Netflix thought the streaming video business was different from the DVD business. So, the two businesses should be separate to better address spe-cific customer needs. A new DVD company was created called Qwikster, because according to Netflix CEO, Reed Hastings, "it refers to quick delivery."

Netfix continued as the streaming video business. Customers were unhappy with the Qwikster name as well as the business split. Customers wanting both DVD and streaming video had to visit separate websites. To make matters worse, Netflix increased rental fees. After losing customers and getting negative press, Netflix went back to its old business model and abandoned Qwikster. Hastings said, "There is a difference between moving quickly, which Netflix has done very well for years, and moving too fast, which is what we did in this case."

Explain
Describe a focus group, how it is monitored, and how the information is used.

of people. The questions should not suggest answers or be biased in any way.

Diary

A **diary** is a written record of the thoughts, activities, or plans of the writer during a given period of time. Market researchers use diaries in much the same way. Marketing diaries are given to a sample of people to learn about their activities. Researchers most often use diaries to study how people use their time and spend their money. Diaries can use an open- or forced-choice response format—or a combination of both.

An *open format* allows people to write whatever they want about their experiences. It allows people to give more feedback. Open-format diaries take a long time to analyze, which makes them too costly for most research projects.

A *forced-choice format* is more like a multiple-choice test where only one answer can be chosen from several options. A forced-choice diary is much easier to analyze, but has much less feedback. Diaries have a number of advantages and disadvantages as shown in Figure 10-4.

Using Diaries in Market Research	
Advantages of Diaries	**Disadvantages of Diaries**
• Ability to collect sensitive information that a participant may not provide in an interview • Greater reliability because participants are not asked to recall information • Supplements other research methods including the interviews	• Expensive method of research • Overly conscientious participants who write too much • Large dropout rate of about 40 percent immediately after the initial interview • Inaccurate participant responses

Goodheart-Willcox Publisher

Figure 10-4 While diaries can give researchers a tremendous amount of information, they are not appropriate for all research purposes.

Experiment

In the experiment method, the researcher sets up two situations that differ in only one variable to compare the results. A **variable** is something that changes or can be changed. For example, the researcher might count the number of people passing by and how many enter the store. The store then changes the window display. The new window display is the variable. The researcher will again count the number of people passing by and how many enter the store. Analyzing this data might show if the different window display influenced the number of people entering the store.

Taste tests are also common product experiments. Researcher may use observation, survey, and experiment methods to get the most valid data.

Secondary Data

Secondary data already exists and can be found in a variety of sources. Someone has collected that data for other reasons, but anyone can use it. For that reason, secondary data are usually easier to find and less expensive than primary data.

If the data already exists, there is no need to go through the time and expense of collecting primary data. Due to this fact, most marketers look for secondary data first. However, for secondary data to be useful, it should relate to the research topic and be timely. In general, secondary data older than five years is not useful.

Sources for secondary data can include your business records; government, business, and academic sources; trade associations; and the Internet.

Business Records

Every business collects data in many forms that can be used for different purposes.

The data include sales records, customer databases, financial statements, and marketing records. Business records are the best place to start when learning about current customers and their buying behaviors.

Government Sources

Federal, state, and local governments collect an enormous amount of data. Marketers can easily find information about the economy, industries, and the population. The US Census Bureau is a good place to start for free, recent information. There are many government agencies that are also good resources, as shown in Figure 10-5.

Market-Research Sources

Many businesses collect data that can be used by others for marketing-research purposes. Some is available at no or low cost on company websites. Other forms may be costly. Research firms, such as Dun & Bradstreet, collect data in order to sell it to other businesses.

State and local chambers of commerce are also good sources for free secondary data. A **chamber of commerce** is a group of businesses whose main purpose is to encourage local business development. They can often provide current information about other area businesses and the local economy.

Academic Sources

Universities, community colleges, and local libraries are great resources for secondary data. Colleges and their libraries can help marketers find databases and research done by the schools. Most universities also have small-business organizations on campus that provide secondary data. Local libraries house books, business directories, magazines, journals, newsletters, newspapers and other free resources.

Trade Associations

A **trade association** is an organization of people in a specific type of business or industry. The members of a trade association

Federal Governmental Agencies	
Agency	**Website**
FedWorld (search for government information)	www.fedworld.gov or www.usasearch.gov
International Trade Administration	www.trade.gov
US Bureau of Economic Analysis	www.bea.gov
US Bureau of Labor Statistics	www.stats.bls.gov
US Census Bureau	www.census.gov
US Department of Commerce	www.commerce.gov and www.quickfacts.census.gov
US Federal Reserve (for economic research and data)	www.federalreserve.gov/econresdata
USA.gov (for business and nonprofit data and statistics)	www.usa.gov

Figure 10-5 Secondary research gathered from governmental sources is generally reliable.

College and Career Portfolio

E-portfolio File Formats

Your e-portfolio may contain documents you have created. Scanned images of items, such as awards and certificates, may also be included. You need to decide which file formats you will use for electronic documents. You could use the default format to save the documents. For example, you could use Microsoft Word format for letters and essays. You could use Microsoft Excel format for worksheets. Someone reviewing your e-portfolio would need programs that open these formats to view your files. Another option would be to save or scan documents as PDF (portable document format) files. These files can be viewed with Adobe Reader software and some other programs. Having all of the files in the same format can make viewing them easier for others who need to review your portfolio.

1. Search the Internet and read articles to learn more about PDF documents. Download a free program, such as Adobe Reader, that opens these files.
2. Practice saving a Microsoft Word document as a PDF file. *Note:* Use the *Save As* command. Refer to the *Help* link, if needed.
3. Create a list of the format(s) you will use to store your electronic files.

---

work together to help each other succeed. Information from a trade association may be free to anyone—or free only to members. Depending on the source, sometimes it is available for a fee.

Some information can also appear on association websites. For example, the National Grocers Association posts results from various surveys on its website. Businesses can compare themselves to others of similar size and location by using trade association data.

Industry publications, also called *trade journals,* are magazines or newsletters focusing on a specific industry. Many trade associations publish trade journals. The journals usually cover a wide range of topics of interest to those in the industry. One example of a trade journal is the National Retail Federation publication, *STORES Magazine.*

Internet

Internet search engines make all types of marketing research easier and quicker

to find. Information about any topic can be found online. The Internet is especially helpful in the area of competitive research. Marketers learn about the competition, their marketing mixes, and promotions by viewing their websites. Internet sources do need to be verified, though. Open-source websites and business websites ending in .com or .net may or may not have correct information. More trustworthy sites tend to be those ending in .gov or .edu.

Secret shoppers may also be called *mystery shoppers.* Mystery shopping can be a full-time job. Research firms can hire and manage mystery shoppers, sending them to many different companies during a day.

Checkpoint 10.1

1. What will market research help to accomplish?
2. Why do many researchers and entrepreneurs use secondary data first?
3. Name three sources of primary data.
4. Explain the difference between qualitative and quantitative data.
5. Why do researchers look for secondary data first rather than primary data?

Build Your Vocabulary

As you progress through this text, develop a personal glossary of marketing terms which will help you build your vocabulary and prepare you for a career in marketing. Write a definition for each of the following terms, and add it to your personal marketing glossary.

marketing research
data
database
primary data
research sample
qualitative data
quantitative data
interview
focus group
survey
diary
variable
secondary data
chamber of commerce
trade association

Checkpoint Answers

1. Market research helps to define primary customers, identify growth opportunities, and learn about the competition.
2. Secondary data is usually inexpensive and easy to find. In some cases, secondary data are free, such as the census data.
3. Responses should include three of the following: interviews, surveys, diaries, experiments, or observation.
4. Qualitative data provides insight into what people think about a topic, while quantitative data consists of facts and figures from which conclusions can be drawn.

5. If data already exists and it can be used, there is no need to go to the time or expense of collecting primary data.

Build Your Vocabulary Answers

Definitions for these terms can be found in the glossary of this text.

Section 10.2 Conduct the Research

Objectives

After completing this section, you will be able to
- **describe** the marketing research process.
- **discuss** trend research.
- **explain** how marketers use a marketing-information system.
- **summarize** reasons why marketing research might be unreliable.

Key Terms

hypothesis
data mining
trend
marketing trend
social trend
demographics
demographic trend
product trend
marketing-information
   system (MkIS)
database marketing
fad
order bias

Web Connect

Perform an Internet search on the marketing research process. Read about formal and informal processes and how they differ. Make notes on your findings.

Critical Thinking

In your marketing plan, you will segment the larger market by geographic, demographic, psychographic, and behavioral traits. List the factors that are most important when deciding which customers to target.

Marketing Research Process

Marketers collect many types of research data. It may be data about new opportunities, potential customers, trends, competition, or pricing, to name just a few. Data can be gathered in both formal and informal ways.

For example, the owner of a gift shop walks around her store talking with customers. She informally learns what her customers think of the products and services. Another example is when a salesperson notices his sales are down. He starts asking his customers questions about the product and what they are buying instead.

Research can also be formal. A survey may be given to current clients or a focus group held to test a new product. Both types of data can help people understand what customers really want and need. Choosing which form of research to use depends on the problem to be solved.

The formal research process is very similar to the scientific method.
1. Define the problem.
2. Conduct background research.
3. State a hypothesis.
4. Develop a research plan.
5. Collect the data.
6. Analyze the data.
7. Draw conclusions.
8. Make recommendations.

Explore

Provide an opportunity for students to explore by assigning a hands-on activity. Review the vocabulary terms at the beginning of the section. Where have students encountered these terms before? Help students make educated guesses about the meanings of the terms with which they are least familiar.

Engage

Use the Teamwork exercise at the end of the chapter to engage students with each other to solve a problem or make a group presentation.

Define the Problem

All research begins by defining the problem or situation. Start by asking the questions for which you need answers. For example, questions might include the following:

- How is the competition promoting its products?
- What products or services will make the business more competitive?
- What are the demographics of the best customers?

There are many more questions to answer as your research continues.

Conduct Background Research

Before collecting data, learn as much about the problem as possible. Personal interviews with current and potential customers can be helpful. You can also conduct Internet research to learn about the competition or other industry problems. Find out anything that could help to understand the marketing challenge.

State a Hypothesis

A **hypothesis** is a statement that can be tested and proved either true or false. A hypothesis is always stated in the positive. For example, if you are marketing smartphones, the hypothesis might be: "Customers buy smartphones because smartphones make them feel trendy." It is a good idea to test the hypothesis first before creating a marketing plan based on it. Research will either confirm or disprove a hypothesis. Plans can then be changed if the hypothesis does not test well.

Develop a Research Plan

A research plan includes all of the steps to take when testing a hypothesis. You will decide if you will conduct primary research, use secondary research, or both. Research costs money, so build this into the marketing budget. If you are doing primary research, decide the best way to gather it. If secondary research will be used, identify the type of data needed and where it can be found.

If the research plan calls for collecting a great amount of data, storage of that data is also an important part of the plan.

Andreas Weiss/Shutterstock.com

Green Marketing

Batteries

Marketing professionals who are technologically aware will stay on top of the latest trends in equipment to make their jobs more efficient. However, it is important to respect the environment when using equipment that requires batteries. The batteries in cell phones and other portable devices are hazardous and will harm the environment if discarded in a landfill. Batteries should always be properly recycled by a reputable organization and never thrown in the regular trash. To be environmentally informed and save money, consider using rechargeable batteries. Rechargeable batteries can be used many times over, saving both money and trips to the store to purchase disposable batteries. If your company sells products that use batteries, consider placing information on the package encouraging customers to use recyclable batteries.

Collect the Data

Depending on the research plan, the actual data collection may be done by you or others. Make sure there is enough time to gather the data needed.

Analyze the Data

Raw data, by itself, is useless. Analyzing data makes it useful. This involves studying the data for patterns, organizing it into graphs and charts, and comparing it with previous studies. Analyzing the data helps to draw conclusions about the hypothesis and make sound business decisions.

Analysis may be done manually or through a software program. **Data mining** is searching through large amounts of digital data to find useful patterns or trends. All data must be analyzed and explained to help make sound business decisions.

Draw Conclusions

Research conclusions are made based on data analysis. For example, "Customers buy smartphones because smartphones make them feel trendy." Did the research confirm or disprove the hypothesis? If not, start the process over with a different hypothesis.

If the research confirms the hypothesis, you may decide to move forward with

marketing smartphones using that concept. However, more research may be needed. For example, is feeling trendy the *most important* reason customers buy cell phones? If not, then basing a decision to market smartphones on that hypothesis may not be a good decision.

Make Recommendations

Once research conclusions are reached, making a business recommendation is the next step. The results of marketing research are often shared with others in the company. Therefore, marketing researchers usually write the results, conclusions, and recommendations in a formal report.

FYI

Statistical analysis is a mathematical technique for analyzing the collected data.

Trend Research

One of the major goals of marketing research is to spot good business opportunities that support growth. One way to do this is to look for new trends. In general, a **trend** is an emerging pattern of change. Trends tend to be long lasting.

A **marketing trend** is the pattern of change in consumer behavior that leads to changes in the marketing mix. Trend research often combines research on customers, competition, and possible opportunities. This information is important to marketers. It helps them adjust product, price, place, and promotion to meet new trends.

A number of marketing firms specialize in researching and predicting trends. Faith Popcorn and her company, BrainReserve, is one of the best-known trend researchers. BrainReserve has successfully predicted some major trends before they happened. For example, it predicted the fast growth of social media and of local farmers' markets.

Popcorn noticed a trend several years ago that she called *small indulgences*. The underlying cause of this trend is that consumers are very stressed by their busy lives. They want to reward themselves. The trend showed a change in consumer-buying behavior: they are willing to spend money on small luxuries. An example of a successful product based on this trend is designer sunglasses, which average $150 a pair. Sunglass Hut profited from this growing trend. It now has over 1,900 stores worldwide with annual gross sales of over $4 billion.

There are many types of trends. Social, demographic, and product trends are of particular interest to marketers. Successful marketers

To this day, the hula-hoop craze that swept the country in 1958 remains one of the biggest fads in American history. Twenty million were sold in the first four months.

Cheryl Casey/Shutterstock.com

Elaborate/Extend

If students are using the optional *Marketing Dynamics* workbook, assign activities to engage active learning.

Resource/Evaluate

Assign the optional Chapter 10 test for **EXAM**VIEW® Assessment Suite as a formal assessment tool.

notice trends early and help their businesses offer products to meet new wants or needs.

Social Trends

Social trends are the patterns of change in society. Social trends often lead to changes in consumer behavior. One of the major social trends of the 20th century was the increase in the number of working mothers. This social trend resulted in the need for more child care and more convenience foods. Companies that jumped on this trend by providing child care or developing easier foods to prepare were successful.

Demographic Trends

Demographics are the qualities, such as age, gender, and income, of a specific group of people. **Demographic trends** are changes the size of different segments of the population. Marketers are very interested in demographic trends because they often mean changes in product preferences. Marketers looking to grow their companies are interested in several recent demographic trends.

One trend is the increase in the population over age 65. As the Baby Boomer generation ages, this group of people has time, money, and possible health concerns. Travel, health care, and financial services companies are finding new, stable markets for their products and services.

Another trend is the increase in ethnic populations, particularly the African-, Latino-, and Asian-American markets. These markets are growing in size and buying power. Businesses catering to the specific needs and wants of these groups are also growing.

Product Trends

Product trends are the changes in current product features or new products being developed. Marketers must know product trends to meet customer needs. For example, the trend in electronic devices is toward smarter and

smaller devices with more interactivity. This means consumers are buying more touch-screen products that serve multiple functions.

Trends are different from fads. A **fad** is something that is very popular for a short time and dies out quickly. Trends happen over a long period of time and affect large numbers of people. What products can you think of that were fads?

AMA Tip

The AMA provides valuable, relevant information to members and nonmembers through its Facebook and Twitter pages. Posts include links to articles and groundbreaking research, fun infographics, and updates from local AMA chapters. www.marketingpower.com

Marketing-Information System (MkIS)

A **marketing-information system (MkIS)** is the organized system of gathering, sorting, analyzing, evaluating, and distributing information for marketing purposes. The data gathered through marketing research is used to create a marketing-information system. Marketing research is part of the market planning and marketing-information management functions of marketing.

Some marketing-information systems are complex, while others are simple. Each business decides which system works best for the company needs, as shown in Figure 10-6. Company records, competitor information, and customer databases are part of any MkIS.

Database marketing consists of gathering, storing, and using customer data for marketing directly to customers based on their histories. Database marketing makes *customer relationship management (CRM)* easier and more effective. Recall that CRM is a system to track contact and user information for current and potential customers. CRM databases can help build stronger customer relationships. For example, some companies store credit-card purchase information in their MkIS. This data helps marketers make offers to those customers based on products they already purchased. Customers feel like the company knows them and what they want or need.

Reliability of Marketing Research

The results of any research are only as good as the research process. Sometimes, the results of marketing research can be misleading. If market research is done incor-

Marketing-Information System Example	
Gather	Input customer contact databases, customer purchases, primary product research data.
Sort	Sort data by customer, zip codes, products purchased, purchase months.
Analyze	Determine how many customers bought the products during each month by zip code.
Evaluate	Based on analysis, change current product and marketing mixes. Shift budgets to increase personalized marketing efforts.
Distribute	All MkIS data and reports are sent to mid-level managers and above for decision-making purposes.

Goodheart-Willcox Publisher

Figure 10-6 Businesses use the data gathered through marketing research to create a marketing-information system.

rectly, the results are flawed. Research results that are wrong will lead to poor business decisions.

There are many examples of companies that have incorrectly conducted research. Market research may be unreliable for a number of reasons. Reasons can include problems with the research sample, question structure, data analysis, or reporting errors. Make sure to follow the proper research process and your results should be reliable.

Research Sample

A number of errors may come from using a poor research sample. The sample size may be too small. The sample may include people who are not in the targeted market, or the wrong target market used. A poor research sample means the data will be incorrect.

Question Structure

Order bias is the skewing of results caused by the order in which questions are placed in a survey. For example, responders tend to select the first few answers from a list and overlook the rest. So, order bias happens if answer choices for questions are *not* rotated among all surveys given. Questions using vague or misleading language or that assume certain knowledge may also skew results. Any of these things can influence how a person answers questions.

Data Analysis

Raw data is neither right nor wrong. When analysis is done incorrectly, however, errors occur. For example, simple math errors are common. Sometimes, the usefulness of marketing research depends on the person explaining the results. A person familiar with the business, customers, and market might explain research results better than one who is unfamiliar. Some researchers will say that a *gut feeling* has given them better results than costly marketing research.

Reporting Errors

The most common reporting error is misrepresenting the research results. This means that reported results are incomplete or inaccurate. If a report format is too simple, for example, crucial data may be left out. A reporting error could be as simple as poor grammar and sentence structure. Or, it could be as complex as choosing poor visuals to show results. Even the best research and best analysis cannot survive reporting errors.

Checkpoint 10.2

1. What is the first step in the research process?
2. What is the purpose of a research plan?
3. Why do marketers need to track product trends?
4. Describe the difference between a trend and a fad.
5. Why is order bias a concern for marketing researchers?

Build Your Vocabulary

As you progress through this text, develop a personal glossary of marketing terms which will help you build your vocabulary and prepare you for a career in marketing. Write a definition for each of the following terms, and add it to your personal marketing glossary.

hypothesis
data mining
trend
marketing trend
social trend
demographics
demographic trend
product trend
marketing-information system (MkIS)
database marketing
fad
order bias

Chapter Summary

Section 10.1 Determine Research Needs

- Marketing research is important so that businesses can meet the needs of customers. Marketing research results provide businesses with information about their primary customers' needs and wants, their competition, and their growth opportunities.
- The two types of research data are primary and secondary. Primary data is collected firsthand by the researcher. Secondary data already exists and can be found through a variety of sources.

Section 10.2 Conduct the Research

- The marketing research process consists of eight steps: 1. Define the problem. 2. Conduct background research. 3. State a hypothesis. 4. Develop a research plan. 5. Collect the data. 6. Analyze the data. 7. Draw conclusions. 8. Make recommendations.
- Trends tend to be long lasting. Trend research helps marketers adjust their businesses and promotional efforts to take advantage of new trends.
- A marketing-information system (MkIS) is an organized system of gathering, sorting, analyzing, evaluating, and distributing information gathered through marketing research. This data will then help a business better tailor their marketing efforts to meet customer needs.
- Marketing research can sometimes be unreliable because the results may be faulty if the research was incomplete or incorrect. Following proper research processes can ensure your results are reliable.

Review Your Knowledge

1. Why is marketing research important to a marketer?
2. What is the difference between primary and secondary data?
3. Give an example of each of the five ways to collect primary data.
4. List the five sources of secondary data and give an example of each.
5. What is the difference between formal and informal research?
6. List and describe the steps in the research process.
7. Describe a marketing-information system (MkIS).
8. Explain trend research and why it is important to marketing.
9. Describe the four areas in which problems most commonly occur in marketing research.
10. What is the most common reporting error when conducting research?

Evaluate

Assign end-of-chapter activities.

Review Your Knowledge Answers

1. A marketer would want to do marketing research because the results will define the primary customers and their needs, reveal the competition, and identify growth opportunities.
2. Primary data are pieces of information collected by you or your organization, while secondary data consists of information that already exists and can be found in a variety of sources.
3. Examples of collecting primary data are through observation, interviews, surveys, diaries, and experiments.
4. Five sources of secondary data are business records, such as sales records and customer databases; the government sources, such as the US Census Bureau; business sources, such as state or local chambers of commerce; academic sources, such as a university college library; and trade sources, such as a trade journal.

5. Formal research follows a structured process very similar to the scientific method, while informal research might consist of simply walking around a store talking to customers.
6. The steps in the research problem are: 1. Define the problem. 2. Conduct background research. 3. State a hypothesis. 4. Develop a research plan. 5. Collect the data. 6. Analyze the data. 7. Draw conclusions. 8. Make recommendations.
7. A marketing-information system is an organized system of gathering, sorting, analyzing, evaluating, and distributing information gathered through marketing research.
8. Trend research is important because it combines research on customers, competition, and possible opportunities to help marketers adjust their businesses and promotional efforts to take advantage of new trends.
9. Problems can occur in the research sample, in the question structure, in data analysis, and in reporting.
10. Misrepresenting vital research findings is the most common reporting error.

Apply Your Knowledge

1. In an earlier unit, you identified a company for which you are creating a marketing plan. As a marketer, give some reasons why you would need primary data to market products for your company.
2. Why would you need secondary data for your marketing efforts?
3. For your selected business, where would you go to get secondary data about the products you are marketing?
4. Explain how qualitative and quantitative data are important for your marketing plan.
5. How would you conduct informal research about customers for your product?
6. You may decide that primary data is important in order to get feedback for your product so that you can help the development team create a relevant product for the business. To collect data, you may choose to use observation, interviews, surveys, diaries, or experiments. For this activity, draft a survey of questions in a format that would encourage responses from the individuals who would be solicited for input.
7. Assume your company is creating a new customer database. What types of information would you suggest that the database include?
8. Identify trade associations that you might consider joining.
9. What product trends would you have to address as a marketer?
10. What kind of research do you think your competitors are conducting?

Check Your Marketing IQ

Now that you have finished the chapter, see what you learned about marketing by taking the chapter posttest. If you do not have a smartphone, visit the G-W Learning companion website.
G-W Learning mobile site: www.m.g-wlearning.com
G-W Learning companion website: www.g-wlearning.com

Common Core

College and Career Readiness

CTE Career Ready Practices. It is important to act as a responsible and contributing citizen. For every action, there is a reaction whether it is immediately seen or not. There are positive and negative consequences for different actions and inactions. Make a list of five things that you have done for which there were either positive or negative consequences. Put a plus sign (+) beside the positive outcomes and a minus sign (–) beside the negative outcomes. What could you have done differently that would have changed each outcome?

Reading. Locate different research plans and read them to note the similarities. Identify sections of the research plans that are unique and creative. After reading, be prepared to present your findings to your class.

Writing. Write a two- to three-page report on why marketing research projects might fail. Explain how you will make sure your research does not experience the same problems.

Teamwork

Working with a teammate, investigate different types of rating scales used in marketing, such as Likert scales, semantic differential scales, or behavior intention scales. Create a chart and describe the key characteristics of these scales and how marketers use them. Share your findings with your class.

G-W Learning Mobile Site

Visit the G-W Learning mobile site to complete the chapter pretest and posttest and to practice vocabulary using e-flash cards. If you do not have a smartphone, visit the G-W Learning companion website to access these features.

G-W Learning mobile site: www.m.g-wlearning.com
G-W Learning companion website: www.g-wlearning.com

11

Competition

Section 11.1	Economics of Competition
Section 11.2	Identify the Competition

"If you don't like something, change it; if you can't change it, change the way you think about it."

— Mary Engelbreit, illustrator and founder of Mary Engelbreit Studios

College and Career Readiness

Reading Prep
Before reading this chapter, observe the objectives for each of the two sections. Keep these in mind as you read, and focus on the structure of the author's writing. Was the information presented in a way that was clear and engaging?

Check Your Marketing IQ

Before you begin the chapter, see what you already know about marketing by taking the chapter pretest. If you do not have a smartphone, visit the G-W Learning companion website.
G-W Learning mobile site: www.m.g-wlearning.com
G-W Learning companion website: www.g-wlearning.com

G-W Mobile

Explore
Assign the College and Career Readiness Reading Prep activity before students read the chapter. Reading Prep activities give students opportunity to apply the Common Core State Standards.

Engage
Assign the Chapter 11 pretest.

◇DECA Emerging Leaders

Professional Selling Event, Part 2

Career Cluster: Marketing
Instructional Area: Not identified for this event.

Procedure, Part 2

In the previous chapter, you studied the skills assessed and procedures for this event.

1. The participants may use the following items during the oral presentation:
    - visual aids appropriate for an actual sales presentation.
    - not more than three standard-sized posters not to exceed 22 ½ inches by 30 ½ inches each. Participants may use both sides of the posters, but all attachments must fit within the poster dimensions.
    - one standard-sized presentation display board not to exceed 36 ½ inches by 48 ½ inches.
    - one desktop flip chart presentation easel 12 inches by 10 inches (dimensions of the page).
    - one personal laptop computer.
    - cell phones, smartphones, iPods, MP3 players, iPads, tablets, or any type of a hand-held, information sharing device will be allowed in written events *if* applicable to the presentation.
    - sound, as long as the volume is kept at a conversational level.
2. Only visual aids that can be easily carried to the presentation by the actual participants will be permitted, and the participants themselves must set up the visuals. No set-up time will be allowed. Participants must furnish their own materials and equipment. No electrical power will be supplied.
3. Materials appropriate to the situation may be handed to or left with judges in all competitive events. Items of monetary value may be handed to but may not be left with judges. Items such as flyers, brochures, pamphlets, and business cards may be handed to or left with the judge. No food or drinks are allowed.
4. If any of these rules are violated, the adult assistant must be notified by the judge.

Products/Services and Target Customer Description

For this event, you will assume the role of sales representative for a company that manufactures bicycle tires. A major bicycle manufacturer is taking meetings with tire manufacturers to hear their sales pitches to be the tire supplier for the company's new entry-level mountain bike. You have a meeting scheduled with the bicycle manufacturer's supply chain manager to pitch your company's products and price points.

Critical Thinking

1. What key points will you include in your presentation?
2. Based on your presentation, what visual aids will you bring? How will you use them?

Visit www.deca.org for more information.

Section 11.1 Economics of Competition

Market Structure

As you learned in Chapter 4, *competition* is two or more businesses attempting to attract the same customers. **Market structure** is how a market is organized based on the number of businesses competing for sales in an industry. The four basic market structures are oligopoly, monopoly, perfect competition, and monopolistic competition.

A **monopoly** is a market structure with one business that has complete control of a market's entire supply of goods or services. Monopolies prevent healthy competition. An **oligopoly** is a market structure with a small number of large companies selling the same or similar products.

Perfect competition is characterized by a large number of small businesses selling the same products at the same prices. It would be the ideal market structure, but is unrealistic.

In contrast, **monopolistic competition** is a large number of small businesses selling similar, but not the same, products at different prices. It is also known as *imperfect competition*. Most companies operate in monopolistic competition or oligopoly market structures. No one company can sell all of the products or control the prices. Each competitor works to make its products more appealing or to offer lower prices to win customers. As a result, consumers get better products at competitive prices.

FYI

The SBA offers business guides by industry. These guides provide valuable information targeted toward a specific business. By reading these guides, marketers can learn information about their industries and compare their businesses to similar ones.

Competition in Different Economic Systems

Business is not always conducted the same in every country. In some countries, their economic systems may limit or even forbid competition. Depending on the location of a business, it may operate within a market, command, traditional, or mixed economy. Competition is a key element of both market and mixed economies. Wise marketers study the economies of the countries in which they do business to market the business correctly.

Market Economy

Recall that in a market economy, individuals can own private property. They also have the freedom to do what they want with it. People can live on a property, start a business on it, or sell it.

The products and services offered by companies in a market economy are those customers choose to buy. Buying and selling with few government restrictions defines a market economy. In a pure market economy, no businesses would be owned or controlled by the government. This means *no* country has a pure market economy.

Command Economy

In a command economy, the government decides which goods are produced, how much is produced, and the prices. Most industries are publically owned. There is little or no competition. In a command economy, the government acts as a monopoly.

Businesses in a command economy do not compete for customers. There can be shortages of popular products. Some economists think that part of the reason command economies are not successful is the lack of competition. Competition motivates businesses to improve their products and services.

Traditional Economy

A traditional economy is one in which most citizens have just enough to survive. Most people trade or barter for needed goods and services. There is little to no manufacturing or

Traditional economies tend to be rural and farm based.

wdeon/Shutterstock.com

Social Media

Sharing Information

There are over 250 million active Twitter users and growing, out of 500 million accounts. If you decide to use Twitter as a communication tool for your company, you will need to create a business account through someone's personal account. Once you have a Twitter account for the business, review the case studies on the site to learn how best to optimize your tweets. For example, the American Red Cross created a national Twitter account, @RedCross. However, it soon realized that local Red Cross chapters also needed to interact with their local community members. So, the Red Cross leadership encouraged local chapters to create their own accounts. Post useful information on your business Twitter account so community members will want to share that information with others in their networks. The ability to share information is one of the most powerful business uses of social media as a marketing tool.

formal businesses, so there is no competition. Money is scarce and property is held by families to be passed on to the next generations.

Mixed Economy

A mixed economy is one in which both the government and individuals make decisions about providing goods and services. Most developed countries, including the United States, have some form of mixed economy. Most businesses are privately owned. However, the government owns and runs some businesses for the citizens' welfare. Some examples of publicly owned institutions in a mixed economy include the US Post Office, the French national health system, or any public education system.

Antitrust Laws

In the 1800s, the US government did little to regulate businesses. As a result, business leaders in a number of industries created monopolies. These leaders worked together to remove their competition, set prices, and control distribution, which is called collusion. The government created the term antitrust in an effort to fight the big corporate trusts that operated as monopolies.

Explore

Bring in examples of antitrust cases that have been in the news.

As a result, federal and state governments passed antitrust laws. The goal of antitrust laws is to make sure that markets remain open and competitive. They prevent corporate trusts from
*   buying out competitors;
*   setting high prices as a group to block fair competition;
*   forcing customers to sign long-term agreements; and
*   forcing customers to buy unwanted products in order to receive the wanted goods.

Antitrust laws cover the prevention of monopolies and illegal cooperation between companies to fix prices. The first of these laws, the *Sherman Antitrust Act of 1890*, removed limits on competitive trade and kept companies from monopolizing markets. It was used in 1911 to end the Standard Oil Company monopoly of the oil industry. As a result, Standard Oil was divided into 30 competing companies. In 1914, the *Clayton Antitrust Act* gave the federal government more power to detect companies in the early stages of creating corporate trusts and prevent it.

Many public utilities, such as electricity, natural gas, and water, are allowed to operate as monopolies because it is the most cost efficient. However, utility rates and operations are regulated mostly by state governments to protect consumers from high prices and poor service. Telephone service was once a regulated monopoly operated by AT&T, but was broken up by the US government in 1974 into smaller, regional companies. The antitrust suit brought by the government against AT&T caused many changes in the telephone industry. That antitrust lawsuit also let private companies compete in the growing mobile phone service industry. Today there is much more competition than in past years.

Antitrust laws also prevent one company from buying up all the companies in the same business. For example, if one athletic shoe manufacturer tried to buy all of the other large athletic shoe companies, it would become a monopoly. Antitrust laws prevent

this from happening. However, antitrust laws are not the only laws governing competition. The following laws also govern competition:

- The *Federal Trade Commission Act of 1914* regulates business activities to prevent unfair competition.
- The *Robinson Patman Act of 1936* prohibits price discrimination so that all businesses have the same opportunity to purchase the same amount and type of product at the same price.
- The *Celler-Kefauver Antimerger Act of 1950* protects competitors from takeovers if the takeover would harm competition.

Checkpoint 11.1

1. Name the four basic market structures.
2. Most companies operate in which market structures?
3. Compare and contrast how business property is owned within the four economic systems.
4. What do antitrust laws prevent corporate trusts from doing?
5. Explain the Sherman Antitrust Act of 1890 and the Clayton Antitrust Act in 1914.

Build Your Vocabulary

As you progress through this course, develop a personal glossary of marketing terms and add it to your portfolio. This will help you build your vocabulary and prepare you for a career. Write a definition for each of the following terms, and add it to your personal marketing glossary.

market structure
monopoly
oligopoly
perfect competition

monopolistic competition
collusion
antitrust

Section 11.2 Identify the Competition

Objectives

After studying this section, you will be able to
- **describe** direct and indirect competitors.
- **explain** market share and why it is important to marketers.
- **describe** how to create a competitive advantage in business.
- **identify** how to analyze competitive information.
- **prepare** a SWOT analysis.

Key Terms

direct competitors
indirect competitors
market share
market size
market-share leader
competitive
    advantage
unique selling
    proposition (USP)
price competition
nonprice competition
feature
benefit

Web Connect

Visit the website of the Federal Trade Commission. Select a current news article posted on the home page. Write a summary of your findings to share with the class.

Critical Thinking

Competition helps consumers have access to more choices and better-quality products. Explain what this means and why it happens.

Who Are the Competitors?

As a marketer, one of your tasks is to understand the competition. Knowing exactly what the competition is doing helps marketers make decisions about how to market their products or companies. Identifying competitors helps in your market planning efforts, which is one of the functions of marketing. There are two types of competitors: direct and indirect.

Direct competitors are companies that sell products or services identical or very similar to the ones you sell. For example, if your company provides car maintenance and repair services, there are other companies providing the same services. The businesses compete against each other directly.

Indirect competitors offer different, but similar, products or services that could also meet customer needs. The products or services sold by indirect competitors might substitute for your products. For example, if your business sells fruit smoothies, an indirect competitor may be a store selling frozen yogurt. The businesses compete for the same customers, but not directly.

Market Share

How can a business tell how well it is doing compared to its competitors? One way is to look at market share. **Market share** is the percentage of the total sales that one business

Explore

Provide an opportunity for students to explore by assigning a hands-on activity. Review the vocabulary terms at the beginning of the section. Where have students encountered these terms before? Help students make educated guesses about the meanings of the terms with which they are least familiar.

Engage

Use the Teamwork exercise at the end of the chapter to engage students with each other to solve a problem or make a group presentation.

has in a specific market. Market share is based on the size of the market. **Market size** is the total sales per year for a specific product.

Sales can be measured in a number of ways, such as in dollars or the number of items sold. Most businesses look at market share in terms of total sales dollars. Calculating market share is shown in Figure 11-1. The market share formula follows.

(company sales ÷ total sales in market) × 100 = percent market share

For example, suppose the market size for one food product is $100 million. That is, each year, the total sales of that product is $100 million. Three companies make the product.

- The Big Company sells $75 million of the product each year; its market share is 75 percent.
- The Medium Company sells $20 million; its market share is 20 percent.
- The Small Company sells $5 million; its market share is 5 percent.

Market share is useful for comparing the companies with each other. It shows the relationship of the companies to each other, as shown in Figure 11-2.

Calculating Market Share

Formula

$$\frac{\text{company sales}}{\text{total sales in market}} \times 100 = \text{percent market share}$$

Data
Total Sales in Market = $100 million
Big Company Sales = $75 million
Medium Company Sales = $20 million
Small Company Sales = $5 million

Big Company

$$\frac{\$75 \text{ million}}{\$100 \text{ million}} \times 100 = 75\%$$

Medium Company

$$\frac{\$20 \text{ million}}{\$100 \text{ million}} \times 100 = 20\%$$

Small Company

$$\frac{\$5 \text{ million}}{\$100 \text{ million}} \times 100 = 5\%$$

Goodheart-Willcox Publisher

Figure 11-1 This simplified example shows how market share is calculated.

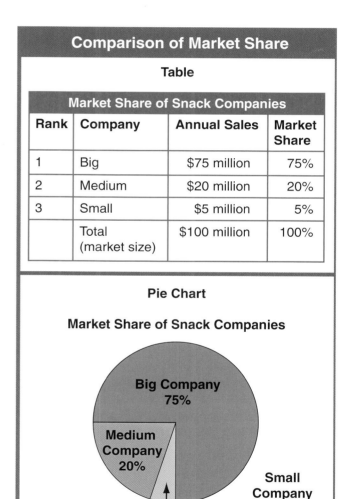

Comparison of Market Share

Table

Market Share of Snack Companies			
Rank	Company	Annual Sales	Market Share
1	Big	$75 million	75%
2	Medium	$20 million	20%
3	Small	$5 million	5%
	Total (market size)	$100 million	100%

Pie Chart

Market Share of Snack Companies

Big Company 75%
Medium Company 20%
Small Company 5%

Goodheart-Willcox Publisher

Figure 11-2 Market share can be shown as tables or charts to show the competitive relationship of companies in the market.

Case in Point

UPS

The marketing concept plays an important role in every business, especially for businesses that have been around for a while. Satisfying the customer is the number one priority for any successful business.

At the turn of the 21st century, the shipping giant UPS was concerned about FedEx taking market share. So in 2002, UPS launched a new marketing campaign to capitalize on its well-known brown UPS logo. What Can Brown Do for You?^{SM} was launched with the idea that any employee in the company, including the CEO, could provide service to any customer.

The campaign was a huge success. But, UPS did not stop there. Ten years later, I Love Logistics® was launched to show that the company serves not only domestic needs but also meets global needs. A new program was also launched for consumers. UPS My Choice ^{SM} is a membership program allowing customers the convenience of managing their home deliveries online. These are just three ways that UPS stresses the marketing concept of satisfying the customer. It is important to tell your customers that they are the number one reason you are in business.

Market-share leaders are the companies with the largest combined market share. For example, the two market-share leaders in this example have a 95 percent market share. Some research shows that market-share leaders are more profitable and successful than companies with smaller market shares. A business goal of many companies is to increase market share, which makes it a marketing goal as well.

Competitive Advantage

The **competitive advantage** of a product or business is offering better value, features, or service than the competition. The competitive advantage is the answer to the question: "Why would customers want to buy this product from this business instead of from a competitor?" Having an advantage over competitors tends to increase sales, which is necessary for most companies to make a profit.

Another way to think of competitive advantage is as a unique selling proposition that can be used in promotions and sales efforts. A **unique selling proposition (USP)** is the

statement summarizing the special features or benefits of a product or business. An example of a USP might be, "Turf Brothers' lawn services are guaranteed to have the lowest prices in the area—or your money back." A USP may be based on price as well as nonprice factors.

Price Competition

Price competition occurs when a lower price is the main reason for customers to buy from one business over another. For businesses competing on price, the focus is to make more sales by offering the lowest prices. For example, many gas stations compete through their pricing. Many customers buy fuel on price alone. However, others think it is not worth driving around to find the lowest price.

It is important to know the advantages or your products or business. If there are no advantages, the business may fail due to lack of sales.

Nonprice Competition

Although price is important, many companies, especially smaller ones, cannot afford to compete on price alone. A competitive advantage based on factors other than price is called nonprice competition. Some businesses choose to provide better service or exclusive brands to beat the competition. For example, the department store Nordstrom is known for its great customer service and the traits of a product that serve as an advantage for the customer.

Nonprice competition may also focus more on the features and benefits of a product or service, rather than the price. Features are facts about a product or service. Benefits are the traits of a product that serve as an advantage for the customer.

For example, an ad may say, "Our shampoo with conditioner makes your hair shiny and manageable in half the time." The feature is that the shampoo has a conditioner. The benefit is getting shiny, manageable hair in half the normal time. The consumer knows right away why he or she should use the product.

Other nonprice features may include extended hours, gift wrapping, or custom orders. The benefits of these services are that they save time and are convenient.

Competitive Analysis

Just like in sports, it is important for marketers to analyze their competitors. It helps them learn the best way to compete with each one. As a marketer, you first need to know what products your competitors are selling and their pricing. You also need to know the features and benefits of the products and how they are sold. It is also important to monitor the promotions of all competitors. In other words, you need to know their marketing mix to be able to compete with them.

Complete a *competitive analysis*, as shown in Figure 11-3, to gather this information. List the names of the competitors and the data for comparison. Information about price, features, benefits, and other details help marketers learn some strategies of the competition. Once you gather the information, analyze it to decide how your business is better than the others.

There are many ways to collect information about your competition. The important thing to keep in mind is ethics. Avoid tactics that put customers in an uncomfortable position to provide you with information about a competitor.

Competitive Analysis				
Variables	**Your Company**	**Company A**	**Company B**	**Company C**
price	$28–$50	$40–$100	$30–$60	$20–$80
monogram	yes	yes	no	no
sizes	S–XL	S–XL	S–XXL	S–XXL
designers	Well-known	High end	Knockoffs	Well-known and knockoffs
special order	No	Yes	No	Yes
continental USA shipping	$0	$4–$6	$5.00 flat fee	$2.99

Goodheart-Willcox Publisher

Figure 11-3 When creating a competitive analysis, choose the relevant variables in your business and then choose the top competitors to analyze.

Elaborate/Extend

If students are using the optional *Marketing Dynamics* workbook, assign activities to engage active learning.

Explain

Competitive analysis is an important exercise that all businesses perform to evaluate competition. Select a product and walk through an analysis.

Websites

The most obvious way to learn about your competition, of course, is to visit their websites. Read about their featured products and social media comments that discuss customer strategies. Sign up for their newsletters, like them on Facebook, and follow them on Twitter.

Competitor Product

One of the most efficient ways to evaluate product of the competition is to buy it. You can analyze the price you paid, the packaging, and review benefits and features.

Trade Shows

Trade shows are great places to learn information. The competition will probably have catalogs, brochures, and other information at their exhibits. Pick up their marketing pieces, listen to them talk to customers, and even ask questions. Competitors are not always hostile—sometimes friendly relationships grow between competitors. Some marketing managers swap products with their competitors.

Sales Team

Your sales team will be one of the most important sources of competitive information. Sales people develop relationships with their customers. They will more than likely hear comments about products and sales strategies of the competition.

SWOT Analysis

After you have analyzed the competition, you will analyze your company's product or services. As you learned in Chapter 4, a *SWOT analysis* helps a company identify its strengths, weaknesses, opportunities, and threats.

- Strengths—internal factors that give your company a competitive advantage

Marketers can share information and learn from each other at trade shows.

Marketing Plan

At the end of this unit, students will write the next phase of the marketing plan. They will focus on competitive information for their business. It will be necessary for them to refer to this chapter for examples of a competitive analysis grid and the SWOT analysis.

Marketing Ethics

Technology
Marketers have a responsibility to use technology in an ethical manner. Using software downloaded from the Internet without a license is unethical and illegal. It is important to set an example for coworkers and obtain licenses for any technology used in the business.

- Weaknesses—internal factors that place your company at a disadvantage relative to competitors
- Opportunities—external factors that provide chances for your company to increase profits
- Threats—external factors that threaten your company's growth or ability to make profits

A SWOT analysis helps determine marketing strategy as well as product development strategies. An example of a SWOT analysis is shown in Figure 11-4.

AMA Tip

The AMA offers conferences for its members. By attending conferences, marketing professionals can network, participate in professional development opportunities, and learn the latest trends and happenings in the field.
www.marketingpower.com

SWOT Analysis for Your Company			
Strengths	**Weaknesses**	**Opportunities**	**Threats**
Well-known designers Competitive pricing Free shipping to continental USA Monogramming option	Our designers do not offer XXL Cannot take special orders Lacking promotional plan Current inventory limited	Find designers offering XXL Take special orders Partner with local organizations for increased brand presence Expand product line and offer more customization options	Recession impacting customer disposable income Continued growth of online retail clothing stores Rumored that Company A will also go into lower-priced market Companies B and C's high-end-designer knockoffs priced competitively

Goodheart-Willcox Publisher

Figure 11-4 A SWOT analysis is an important part of a marketing plan.

Evaluate
Assess student comprehension using the Checkpoint activity as a self-assessment tool.

Explain
SWOT analysis is an important part of a marketing plan. Walk through an example and explain how these are created.

Exploring Careers

Advertising and Promotions

One of the most basic needs of any company is to let the public know what it offers. Companies rely on advertising and promotional events to inform potential customers about their products and services. Advertising and promotions managers plan and coordinate advertising programs, promotional materials, and coupons. They also organize contests and other events to help make people aware of a company's products and services. Typical job titles for these positions include *advertising manager, promotions director, promotions manager, marketing and promotions manager,* and *advertising sales manager.*

Some examples of tasks that advertising and promotions managers perform include:

- plan advertising and promotional campaigns to increase public awareness and increase sales of products or services;
- review and approve layouts and advertising copy, including audio and video scripts;
- coordinate or direct a campaign team to meet the company's campaign goals; and
- prepare budgets for advertising or promotional campaigns.

Advertising and promotions managers must have a strong knowledge of various types of media production and communication techniques. They must understand how to use written, oral, and visual media effectively to promote specific products and services. They should also have a basic knowledge of sales and marketing principles, including strategies and tactics for creating interest in a company's products or services. Most advertising and promotions manager positions require a bachelor degree. Many also require experience and knowledge both in the type of product or service the company sells and in advertising or promotions techniques. For more information, access the *Occupational Outlook Handbook* online.

Checkpoint 11.2

1. What is a common way to measure sales?
2. Name two ways to compete with another business.
3. Name five ways to collect information about competitors.
4. What important facts are included in a competitive analysis?
5. Why is a SWOT analysis important for a marketer?

Build Your Vocabulary

As you progress through this course, develop a personal glossary of marketing terms and add it to your portfolio. This will help you build your vocabulary and prepare you for a career. Write a definition for each of the following terms, and add it to your personal marketing glossary.

direct competitors   unique selling proposition (USP)
indirect competitors   price competition
market share   nonprice competition
market size   feature
market-share leader   benefit
competitive advantage

Checkpoint Answers

1. A common way to measure sales is dollars of goods sold or number of items sold.
2. Price competition or nonprice competition are ways businesses compete.
3. Five ways to collect information about competitors are by reading about them on the Internet, buying and examining their products, attending a trade show to gain information, talking with the sales team about customer comments regarding competitors, and by performing competitive and SWOT analyses.
4. Important facts that are included in a competitive analysis are the competitors' names; information about their products, such as price, features, and benefits; and how the products are distributed.
5. A SWOT analysis helps determine marketing and product development strategies.

Build Your Vocabulary Answers

Definitions for these terms can be found in the glossary of this text.

Chapter Summary

Section 11.1 Economics of Competition

- The four basic market structures are monopoly, oligopoly, perfect competition, and monopolistic competition.
- Direct competitors are businesses that sell similar products. Businesses may operate in a market, command, traditional, or mixed economy.
- Antitrust laws are created by the government in an effort to make sure that markets are competitive. Two well-known laws are the Sherman Antitrust Act of 1890 and the Clayton Antitrust Act in 1914.

Section 11.2 Identify the Competition

- Direct competitors are companies that sell products or services identical or very similar to the ones you sell. Indirect competitors offer different, but similar, products or services that could also meet customer needs.
- Market share is one business' percentage of the total sales in a specific market. Market share is an indicator for a business to tell how well it is doing compared to its competitors.
- To create a competitive advantage in business, a company must offer a greater value, better features, or better service than offered by the competition. Creating a unique selling proposition (USP) is a way to highlight special features and benefits of a company or product.
- A competitive analysis involves gathering information about other companies such as price, features, and benefits. This information is then analyzed to determine how the business can best compete with each of the competitors.
- A SWOT analysis helps a company identify its strengths, weaknesses, opportunities, and threats. The SWOT analysis also helps a company determine marketing strategies and product development strategies.

Review Your Knowledge

1. Explain which type of market structure is characteristic to the United States.
2. Why is competition good for the consumer?
3. What role do antitrust laws play in the economy?
4. Compare and contrast direct competition and indirect competition.
5. What is the difference between market size and market share?
6. What question does the competitive advantage answer?
7. Describe unique selling proposition (USP) and why it is important to a marketer.
8. Why is a competitive analysis created as a marketing activity?
9. Name several ways of finding information about the competitor.
10. Why is a SWOT analysis completed as part of the marketing plan?

(continued)

Apply Your Knowledge

1. We live in a mixed economy. Describe what that means to you as a marketing professional and how it impacts your job responsibilities.
2. As a marketer, it is important for you to understand business laws. Research laws about truth in advertising. What were your results?
3. You have selected the business for which you are writing a marketing plan. List three direct competitors of your products or services.
4. List three indirect competitors for your products or services.
5. Who are the market leaders among your competition?
6. Research to find out what you anticipate the market share to be for your products or services.
7. List and describe three competitive advantages for your products or services.
8. Describe nonprice competition factors for your products or services.
9. List three strengths of your products or services.
10. List three weaknesses of your products or services.

Check Your Marketing IQ

Now that you have finished the chapter, see what you learned about marketing by taking the chapter posttest. If you do not have a smartphone, visit the G-W Learning companion website.

G-W Learning mobile site: www.m.g-wlearning.com

G-W Learning companion website: www.g-wlearning.com

5. Market size is the total sales per year for a specific product, while market share is one business' percentage of the total sales in a specific market, and is based on market size.

6. The competitive advantage answers the question, Why would customers what to buy this product from this business instead of from a competitor?

7. A unique selling proposition (USP) is a statement that highlights a company's or product's special features or benefits. It is important because it provides the competitive advantage for promotions and sales.

8. A competitive analysis provides a company with information about its competitors' marketing strategies, which in turn helps the company to determine its best marketing mix.

9. Information can be found about the competitor through websites, product, trade shows, and sales teams.

10. A SWOT analysis is useful because it helps a company identify its strengths, weaknesses, opportunities, and threats, which are important to take into account when determining marketing strategies.

Apply Your Knowledge Answers

Student answers will vary for questions 1–10.

Apply Your Knowledge Teaching Tip

Please note that the Apply Your Knowledge Questions prepare students for the next installment of the marketing plan they are writing at the end of each unit. These questions help them assume the role of a marketing manager and begin applying concepts learned in the chapter.

Marketing Plan

At the end of this unit, students will write the next phase of the marketing plan. They will focus on competitive information for their business. You may choose to complete the plan at the end of this unit. However, you may prefer to assign the Marketing Plan activity now so that students can complete if as they progress through each chapter.

Evaluate

Evaluate the students' understanding and knowledge. Assign the Chapter 11 posttest. The test may be accessed by using the QR code or going to the companion website. What questions were students able to answer that they couldn't when they took the pretest?

Common Core

College and Career Readiness

CTE Career Ready Practices. A successful marketer demonstrates creativity and innovation. Whether you see problems as challenges or opportunities, they often require creative thinking to solve them. Many new inventions are the result of attempting to solve a problem. Describe a competitive situation that faced a business where a problem led to the creation of a new way of doing things or a new invention.

Speaking. Create a presentation about the marketing concept using your choice of digital media. Find examples of slogans or other competitive marketing tools to enhance understanding and to add interest to your presentation. Take turns with your classmates in making a presentation.

Listening. Hearing is a physical process. Listening combines hearing with evaluating. As your classmates make their presentations on the marketing concept, listen and then evaluate each presenter's point of view and use of digital media.

Teamwork

Working with your team, select a product that you know well. Find two companies that make the product. Create a competitive analysis using a spreadsheet. What did you learn from this exercise?

G-W Learning Mobile Site

Visit the G-W Learning mobile site to complete the chapter pretest and posttest and to practice vocabulary using e-flash cards. If you do not have a smartphone, visit the G-W Learning companion website to access these features.

G-W Learning mobile site: www.m.g-wlearning.com

G-W Learning companion website: www.g-wlearning.com

12 Targeting a Market

Section 12.1 Identify the Market
Section 12.2 Segment the Market

"The aim of marketing is to know and understand the customer so well that the product or service fits him or her and sells itself."

—Peter F. Drucker, author, management consultant, and professor

College and Career Readiness

Reading Prep
As you read the chapter, determine the point of view or purpose of the author. What aspects of the text help to establish the purpose or point of view?

Check Your Marketing IQ

Before you begin the chapter, see what you already know about marketing by taking the chapter pretest. If you do not have a smartphone, visit the G-W Learning companion website.
G-W Learning mobile site: www.m.g-wlearning.com
G-W Learning companion website: www.g-wlearning.com

Explore

Assign the College and Career Readiness Reading Prep activity before students read the chapter. Reading Prep activities give students opportunity to apply the Common Core State Standards.

Engage

Assign the Chapter 12 pretest.

◇DECA Emerging Leaders

Marketing Communications Team Decision-Making Event, Part 1

Career Cluster: Marketing
Instructional Area: Communication Skills, Selling

General Performance Indicators

- Communications skills—the ability to exchange information and ideas with others through writing, speaking, reading, or listening
- Analytical skills—the ability to derive facts from data, findings from facts, conclusions from findings, and recommendations from conclusions
- Production skills—the ability to take a concept from an idea and make it real
- Teamwork—the ability to be an effective member of a productive group
- Priorities/time management—the ability to determine priorities and manage time commitments
- Economic competencies

Specific Performance Indicators

- Explain the nature of effective verbal communications.
- Employ communication styles appropriate to target audience.
- Make oral presentations.
- Explain the nature and scope of the selling function.
- Discuss motivational theories that impact buying behavior.
- Explain the key factors in building a clientele.
- Explain the role of customer service as a component of selling relationships.

Purpose

Designed for a team of two DECA members, the event measures the team's ability to explain core business concepts in the format of a case study in a role-play. This event consists of a 100-question multiple-choice cluster exam for each team member and a decision-making case study situation. The Team Decision-Making Event provides an opportunity for participants to analyze one or a combination of elements essential to the effective operation of a business in the specific career area presented as a case study.

For the purposes of this text, you will be presented with the material for this event in two parts. Part 1 presents the knowledge and skills assessed and an overview of the event's purpose and procedure. Part 2 presents the remaining procedures and the event situation.

Procedure, Part 1

1. For Part 1 in this text, read both sets of performance indicators. Discuss these with your team members.
2. If there are any questions, ask your teacher to clarify.

Critical Thinking

1. Explain the difference between General and Specific Performance Indicators.
2. What role do performance indicators play in regard to the team's analysis and presentation?
3. Based on the purpose of the event, describe your team's strategy for communicating during your presentation to the judge.
4. Discuss two benefits of completing this activity with a team member.
5. Work with your team member to determine three strategies for effectively reviewing the information on this page in an actual competitive event.

Visit www.deca.org for more information.

Section 12.1 Identify the Market

Objectives

After completing this section, you will be able to
- **compare and contrast** mass markets and target markets.
- **describe** the marketing mix for a target market.
- **differentiate** between mass marketing and target marketing.

Key Terms

market
mass market
target market
niche market
mass marketing
target marketing

Web Connect

Do an Internet search for *marketing research companies.* Select one company and read the home page. What types of services does the company offer?

Critical Thinking

Mass marketing can be useful for certain types of businesses. For what types of businesses do you think mass marketing could create positive results?

Markets

The term market can mean a number of different things. However, in the world of marketing, market means the people who might buy something. Markets are the focus of all marketing efforts. Markets can be large or small, broad or narrow. What they all have in common is they include the particular types of customers most likely to buy certain products or services. It is these groups the marketers want to reach to increase sales, earn profits, and stay in business.

Mass Market

A mass market is the overall market or group of people who might buy a product or service. Products that appeal to nearly everyone have mass markets. For example, everyone who wants a car and can afford to buy one is part of the mass market for cars. This means the mass market for cars is nearly everyone old enough to drive who has a source of income. However, the markets for *specific* cars are different from the market for cars in general.

Think of the current markets for cars. Can you imagine a car manufacturer making one car that would meet the needs of every person in the mass market? Think about the many different needs customers have for their cars. For example, one group wants a sports car for driving vacations. Another group wants a minivan to hold a team of kids and all of their soccer gear. Yet another group wants a pickup truck for business purposes. In other words, the mass market consists of

Explore

Provide an opportunity for students to explore by assigning a hands-on activity. Review the vocabulary terms at the beginning of the section. Where have students encountered these terms before? Help students make educated guesses about the meanings of the terms with which they are least familiar.

Resource

Use the Chapter 12 presentation on the optional Instructor's Presentations for PowerPoint® CD as an outline for presenting the chapter.

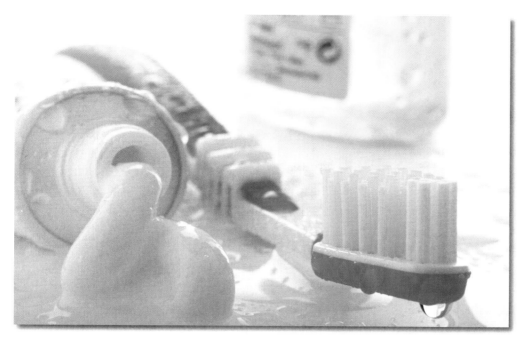

Good dental care is a common goal for nearly everyone. Therefore, using mass market methods for promoting dental products make the most sense.

zigozigo/Shutterstock.com

many customer groups with different needs, wants, and product preferences.

Consumer markets are diverse. That is why marketers spend so much time, effort, and money to determine the best markets for their products or businesses. They do not want to waste marketing dollars on people who do not want or need their products.

Target Market

A **target market** is the specific group of customers at which a company aims its products and services. These are the people whose wants and needs are fulfilled by the products or services a business offers. They are also the people most likely to buy the products or services. Target markets have four characteristics:

- clearly defined wants and needs that the business can meet;
- money to buy the product;
- willingness and ability to buy the product; and
- enough customers to be profitable.

Correctly choosing the best target market is one of the most important decisions a marketer makes. In fact, selecting the wrong target market means the business loses an opportunity for success in a different one.

Many businesses select more than one target market. However, each one selected must meet the four characteristics of a target market. If these characteristics are not met, the business will probably not meet its sales goals.

A **niche market** is a piece of the target market that is very narrow and specific. Niche markets are often created by businesses looking for a market segment whose needs are not being met. Often, a niche market can be very profitable. Niche markets can be small or large, but they are very specific, as illustrated in Figure 12-1.

If a target market is too small, the business may not be able to sell enough products to make a profit.

Market Examples
Mass market: All people who like water sports.
Target market: People who take vacations for water-sport activities.
Niche market: Scuba divers in the Caribbean.

Goodheart-Willcox Publisher

Figure 12-1 This figure provides an example of a mass, target, and niche market.

Marketing Mix for a Target Market

What makes a marketing mix unique for a given target market? One or more of the four Ps are changed to meet the unique needs and wants of a certain target market. The *product* can be changed by adding new features. The *price* can be changed to match new features. The *place* where a product is offered can be changed. For example, an Internet website can be added as a way for customers to obtain the product. Last but not least, the *promotion* can be changed to appeal more to that group of people. Marketers help businesses choose a unique marketing mix based on different target markets.

Product Strategies

Product strategies include all the decisions made about which products to offer. Keep in mind that the term *product* includes goods, services, and ideas. Product strategies include decisions about quality, quantity, size, color, features, technical support, packaging, warranties, brand name, and image.

Price Strategies

Price strategies include all of the decisions made about product pricing. Price strategies include decisions about the desired profit, discounts, and selling prices. Pricing can also have an impact on the image of a product.

Place Strategies

Place strategies include all of the decisions made about where the product will be sold. It includes decisions about how to transport the product, warehousing, inventory control, and order processing.

College and Career Portfolio

Certificates

You have identified the types of items you might place in your portfolio. You will begin adding items in this activity and add other items as you continue this class. Locate certificates you have received. For example, a certificate might show that you have completed a certain training class. Another certificate might show that you can keyboard at a certain speed. You might have a certificate that you received for taking part in a community project. Include any certificates that show tasks completed or your skills or talents. Also, create a document that lists each certificate along with when you received it. Briefly describe your activities, skills, or talents related to each certificate.

1. Scan these documents to include in your e-portfolio. Use the file format you selected earlier.
2. Using the naming system you created earlier, give each document an appropriate name. Place each certificate and the list in an appropriate subfolder for your e-portfolio.
3. Place the hard-copy certificates and list in the container for your print portfolio.

Extend
Review the components of the marketing mix.

Evaluate
Assign Checkpoint questions at end of section. Assess student comprehension using the Checkpoint activity as a self-assessment tool.

Explain
Discuss the pros and cons of mass marketing. Ask for examples of why a company would mass market.

Promotion Strategies

Promotion strategies include all of the decisions made about how to promote the product. It includes decisions about advertising, such as the type of ads and where to place them. It also includes decisions about personal selling, customer service, publicity, promotional events, and store design and layout.

Mass Marketing versus Target Marketing

Mass marketing uses one marketing mix of product, price, place, and promotion for a product. Mass marketing ignores customer differences. The market is viewed as an unsegmented group. It assumes that everyone has exactly the same wants and needs for the product. When using mass

marketing tools, such as television, everyone in the larger group gets the same promotional message.

However, customers are different. There are many groups of customers with differing needs. Sending everyone the same message may be inefficient, though. Mass marketing might miss the best customers and waste marketing funds.

The opposite of mass marketing is target marketing. Using unique marketing mixes for different target markets is called **target marketing.** Marketing budgets and energy are put to work where sales are most likely to happen, which is the target market.

Target marketing does have challenges, though. If the target market turns out to be too small, there may not be enough customers to make a profit. If the wrong market was chosen, the opportunity to make a profit from a different market was missed. Segmenting the market can help reduce some of these challenges.

Checkpoint 12.1

1. Name two markets that may be a part of the marketing strategy.
2. What are the four characteristics of a target market?
3. Explain how one or more of the four Ps are changed to meet the unique needs and wants of a certain target market.
4. Explain the idea behind mass marketing.
5. What is the relationship between segmenting a market and target marketing?

Build Your Vocabulary

As you progress through this course, develop a personal glossary of marketing terms and add it to your portfolio. This will help you build your vocabulary and prepare you for a career. Write a definition for each of the following terms, and add it to your personal marketing glossary.

market

mass market

target market

niche market

mass marketing

target marketing

Checkpoint Answers

1. Two markets that may be a part of the marketing strategy are mass markets and target markets.
2. The four characteristics of a target market are clearly defined wants and needs that the business can meet; money to buy the product; willingness and ability to buy the product; and enough customers in the market to be profitable.
3. The *product* can be changed by adding new features. The *price* can be changed to match the new level of features. The *place* where a product is offered can be changed. For example, an Internet website can be added as a way for customers to obtain the product. Last but not least, the *promotion* can be changed to appeal more to

a certain target market. Marketers help businesses choose a unique marketing mix based on different target markets.
4. A mass marketing strategy looks at the market as an unsegmented group and assumes that everyone has exactly the same wants and needs. Everyone gets the same promotional message, which may not be the best message for the target market.
5. Segmenting a market involves dividing a larger market into smaller groups, allowing marketers to determine which of these groups will become the target market. They can then develop strategies and tactics to appeal specifically to that market, or target marketing.

Build Your Vocabulary Answers

Definitions for these terms can be found in the glossary of this text.

Section 12.2 Segment the Market

Market Segmentation

You learned about the concept of market segmentation in Chapter 4. Markets can be segmented in countless ways. The segments are determined by different variables. Recall that a variable is something to which a changing value can be assigned. The variables used for market segmentation are geographic, demographic, psychographic, and behavioral, as shown in Figure 12-2. Within those groups, customer types can be even further refined by using additional variables. Research has found that customers in the same market segments have similar buying patterns and behaviors.

Explore

Provide an opportunity for students to explore by assigning a hands-on activity. Review the vocabulary terms at the beginning of the section. Where have students encountered these terms before? Help students make educated guesses about the meanings of the terms with which they are least familiar.

Geographic Segmentation

Segmenting a market based on where customers live is called **geographic segmentation**. It also includes how far they will travel to do business. Customers can be segmented by region, climate, or population density.

Region

Customer needs for products can vary based on where they live. Customers in one area often need different products from those in other areas. For example, people in countries that drive on the right side of the road must have cars with steering wheels on the left. Vehicles sold in countries where people drive on the left side must have steering wheels on the right.

Engage

Use the Teamwork exercise at the end of the chapter to engage students with each other to solve a problem or make a group presentation.

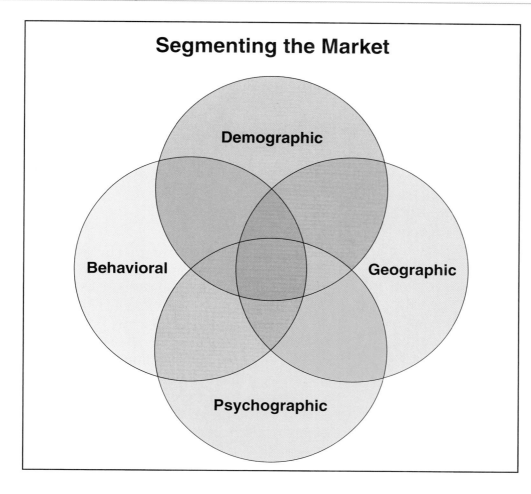

Segmenting the Market

Demographic

Behavioral

Geographic

Psychographic

Goodheart-Willcox Publisher

Figure 12-2 Market segmentation is based on different variables.

Therefore, a company producing cars for the global market would segment it by countries needing left-side and right-side steering wheels.

Climate

Climate has a huge impact on what customers need. Customers who live in climates where it never gets colder than 60°F (15.5°C) do not need warm coats. Customers who live where the average winter temperature is 20°F (–6.7°C) need warm coats. Therefore, a coat manufacturer might segment the market based on average winter temperatures.

Population Density

Customers may be grouped according to the population density of where they live. These geographic segments are urban, suburban, and rural. If a product appeals to people working on a ranch, the target market may be rural. If a product appeals to people who live in larger cities, the target market is urban.

Demographic Segmentation

Recall that demographics are the qualities, such as age, gender, and income, of a specific group of people. Demographic segmentation is dividing the market of potential customers by their personal statistics. The United States takes a census every ten years. A *census* is a count of the people in a country made by the government on a regular basis. Some of the census data

Elaborate/Extend

If students are using the optional *Marketing Dynamics* workbook, assign activities to engage active learning.

collected includes age, gender, income, ethnicity, education level, occupation, marital status, and family size. The government agency that performs the census is the US Census Bureau.

Age

Age is a common segmentation variable because people at different ages have different needs and wants. For example, babies require special food. So, a number of companies specialize in making baby food. Clothing is another area directly affected by age.

Different age groups often like or want different products. An important age variable is generation. A **generation** is a group of people born during a certain time in history, as shown in Figure 12-3. The period of history in which a group of people grew up in has a major effect on their attitudes, wants, and needs. For example, if you were born in the late 1990s or first part of the 21st century, you are part of Generation Z. People in Generation Z have a high interest in electronic products and information.

One of the largest generations is the Baby Boomers. These are the people born between 1946 and 1964. The Baby Boomers were influenced by television in the 1950s, the

countercultural movement of the 1960s, and the Vietnam War in the late 1960s and early 1970s. Marketers like to target this generation because it is large, distinct, and wealthy.

Generation Z is also called the *iGeneration.*

Gender

Customers are often grouped by gender because men and women tend to have different needs and wants. There are products and services preferred by men, women, or both. For example, spa services are more popular with women, while more men buy hand tools. However, if a company is selling hand tools, it does not mean it will ignore women as potential customers. In fact, there may be a market for hand tools targeted to women, just like there may be a market for men's spa services.

Income

People with similar income levels often buy similar types of products. The two categories of income in which marketers are interested are disposable and discretionary. **Disposable income** is the take-home pay a

Figure 12-3 People in the same generation tend to have similar characteristics, needs, and wants.

Generations	
Generation name	**Born between years (approximate)**
Greatest Generation	1901–1925
Silent Generation	1926–1945
Baby Boomer Generation	1946–1964
Generation X	1965–1983
Generation Y	1984–1995
Generation Z	1996–2010

Goodheart-Willcox Publisher

Green Marketing

Green Certification

Many businesses are focused on offering products and services that respect the environment. If you work for such an organization, consider having your products certified as sustainable. There are various organizations, such as *Green Seal,* that use rigid criteria to evaluate products for sustainability. If a product meets all of the requirements, it earns an official green seal of approval. A product with a seal of approval sends the message that your company values preserving the environment and this can be used in marketing campaigns.

person has available to dispose of, meaning spend. Usually, disposable income is used for the necessities of life: food, clothing, shelter, and transportation.

Discretionary income is the remaining take-home pay after life necessities are paid for. Discretionary income is the money people can spend at their discretion, or however they want. Discretionary income is often spent on wants versus needs, such as entertainment, vacations, or dining out.

Ethnicity

The United States is composed of people from many ethnic backgrounds. The need for jeans does not vary by ethnic background. However, needs for other products may vary with ethnic heritage. For example, a person of Chinese heritage may want specific Chinese cooking ingredients, such as dried squid and yellow bean paste.

Many people enjoy products related to the ethnic heritage of other people. For example, people from many ethnic backgrounds enjoy cooking and eating Chinese food. Depending on the product, marketers can be successful by segmenting the market by ethnicity. They offer products to meet the needs of a specific ethnic group and the wants of people interested in that ethnic group.

Education Level

Education level is another way to segment a market. A person with a high school education may have very different wants or needs than someone with a bachelor degree. Somebody with a bachelor degree may have very different wants or needs than someone with a doctoral degree.

Occupation

People in different jobs often have similar wants and needs based on the job type. The terms *blue collar* and *white collar* are common. *Blue collar* generally refers to a job in which a person must wear work clothes or protective gear. *White collar* usually refers to a job in an office environment where business clothing is required. A person's job may affect his or her buying behavior.

Marital Status

Marital-status categories are married, single, widowed, divorced, or separated. Marital status can influence purchases, such as houses, vacations, and food. A single person, for example, may purchase a smaller house and travel more often than a married couple.

Family Size

Marketers have found that the needs and wants of a one-person household differ from those with parents and children. As a result,

This photo represents a Baby Boomer target market who also likes to golf. What products or services could be marketed to that group?

Monkey Business Images/Shutterstock.com

marketers often segment the market based on family size. For example, many convenience food manufacturers have developed single-serving packaging to meet the needs of single-person households.

Psychographic Segmentation

Psychographics are data about the preferences or choices of a group of people. Customers have psychological and emotional characteristics that affect their buying habits. **Psychographic segmentation** is dividing the market by certain preferences or lifestyle choices. When targeting psychographic markets, knowing the values, attitudes, activities, and interests that affect purchases is crucial. Psychographic information about target markets is very useful for marketers when planning a marketing mix.

Values and Attitudes

Believe it or not, customers can be segmented by their values and attitudes. **Values** are what a person believes in. An **attitude** is how a person feels about something. For example, customers who feel fashionable clothing is important may shop at high-end, name-brand stores. However, customers who want to save money may be more likely to shop at discount stores. Customers who value the environment may choose to buy a hybrid-engine car over an SUV.

Consumer values, attitudes, and lifestyles can be difficult to measure. In order to group people in this way, marketing researchers can give surveys. One well-known consumer-behavior research tool is the VALS™ survey. VALS was developed by the SRI Consulting Business Intelligence research company. The survey uses a *Likert scale* asking respondents to rate how strongly they agree or disagree with statements. The 40 VALS survey statements are designed to measure the attitudes, interests, and opinions of survey takers.

The following statements are from the VALS survey.

- "I follow the latest trends and fashions."
- "I would rather make something than buy it."
- "I consider myself an intellectual."

After taking the survey, each person is found to have two primary buying characteristics. These characteristics are based on answers to statements measuring the resources and innovation plus the ideals, achievements, and self expression of survey takers.

For example, one group is called *Achievers*. This group is concerned about status, has a mid-level income, buys premium products, and watches an average amount of TV. Another group is called *Survivors*. This group is concerned with safety, has a lower income, tends to be brand loyal, and watches a more-than-average amount of TV.

The VALS survey results show what motivates people to buy. Results can also predict different consumer buying behaviors, as shown in Figure 12-4. Marketers and other businesspeople making marketing mix decisions find these results quite useful.

Figure 12-4 The VALS™ survey divides US adults into eight segments.

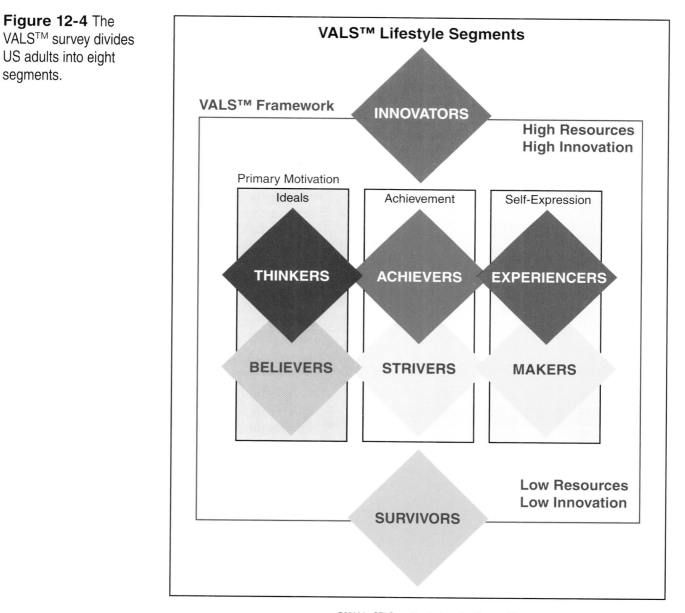

Explore

Assign students to research VALS surveys and bring in an example.

Case in Point

Spanish Television

Demographics are important when targeting a market. By dividing larger markets into smaller, more targeted markets, companies can better meet the needs of those customers and earn a profit. Recent research shows the need for Hispanic media is growing rapidly in the United States. The US Census Bureau reveals that the Hispanic population has increased by more than 40 percent in the last century. The US Latino population is made up of American-born Latinos and immigrants.

This mix of generations looks for Spanish-language programming that preserves their culture and incorporates some aspects of American culture. Latinos want quality entertainment and news programs. They also want a variety of programming choices. Media providers have jumped at the opportunity to appeal to the Hispanic target market. Telemundo, Univision, and Fox offer Spanish television programming, some with English subtitles. The media providers are constantly researching the audience to determine which type of shows are preferred. This growing Latino market is inspiring competition for quality amongst the media providers.

Activities and Interests

People who like the same activities or have the same interests or hobbies tend to have similar buying patterns. Activities and interests can include sports, hobbies, traveling, or attending cultural events, to name a few. For example, the market segment of people who enjoy basketball will tend to buy basketball-related items and attend basketball games.

Behavioral Segmentation

Customers differ in how they use products. **Behavioral segmentation** divides a market by the relationships between customers and the product or service. Behavioral variables include benefits sought, usage rate, buying status, brand loyalty, and special occasions.

Benefits Sought

Many customers choose the same products, but often for entirely different reasons. One customer may want a computer with a great gaming platform. A second customer may want a computer with a great sound system to play music. A third customer may only want a computer to check e-mail. All of these customers are buying a computer, but each is seeking a different benefit from the product.

Usage Rate

The **usage rate** is how often a customer buys or uses a product or service. Usage rates are classified as heavy, moderate, light, and nonuser. A *heavy usage rate* means the person buys the product often. A *light usage rate* means the person rarely buys the product. A *moderate usage rate* falls somewhere between heavy and light. A *nonuser usage rate* means the person never buys the product. Marketers send different messages to people based on how often they buy the product.

Buying Status

Buying status describes when a customer will buy a product or service. The most common are potential, first time, occasional, and regular. A *potential customer* is

Resource/Evaluate

Assign the optional Chapter 12 test for **EXAM**VIEW®
Assessment Suite as a formal assessment tool.

one who has not bought the product, but is thinking about it. A *first-time customer* is one who has bought the product once. An *occasional customer* is one who rarely buys the product. A *regular customer* is one who buys the product often or on a predictable basis.

Brand Loyalty

Customers vary in how loyal they are to a brand or store. As amazing as it might seem, for many businesses 80 percent of total sales tend to come from 20 percent of the customers. This is called the *80/20 rule.*

Loyal customers are generally the source of most company sales. As a result, marketers often segment the market based on degree of loyalty. For example, airlines have frequent-flier programs to reward customers who often fly on that airline. Programs give them free tickets or other merchandise after flying so many miles. Other businesses also use loyalty programs to increase sales.

Customer Profile

Once marketers have divided a market into segments, they choose which segments to target for marketing purposes. They analyze the segments to determine which ones have the most sales potential.

Once the market segments are chosen, a customer profile is created for each segment. A **customer profile** is a detailed description of the typical consumer in a market

segment. The profile includes geographic, demographic, psychographic, and behavioral characteristics about this typical customer.

For example, some businesses decide to sell luxury items that appeal to people with fairly high incomes and specific values. Marketing research can determine which areas of the country have the highest average incomes. It can also find other traits of people who buy luxury goods, such as their attitudes, values, occupations, or education level. The customer profile for luxury items reflects all of these variables.

Accurate customer profiles help determine the best promotional strategies. By knowing who is most interested in company products, promotional dollars can be used wisely. Instead of wasting money on mass-market advertising, the product or service is promoted only to those in the target markets. A typical customer profile is shown in Figure 12-5.

AMA Tip

AMA Connect brings the marketing community together in an online forum. Members engage in question-and-answer sessions about new marketing practices and business challenges. By joining *AMA Connect,* members receive access to various group blogs, discussion forums, file sharing, and wikis. www.marketingpower.com

Explore
Have students list the various factors that would be used to create a customer profile.

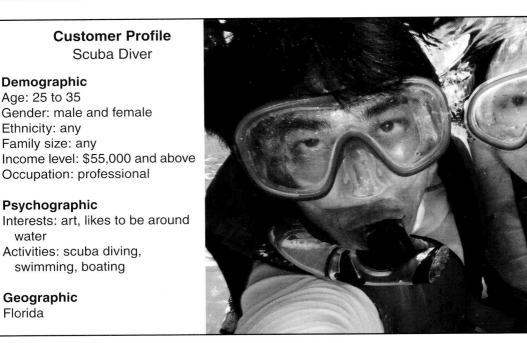

Customer Profile
Scuba Diver

Demographic
Age: 25 to 35
Gender: male and female
Ethnicity: any
Family size: any
Income level: $55,000 and above
Occupation: professional

Psychographic
Interests: art, likes to be around
    water
Activities: scuba diving,
    swimming, boating

Geographic
Florida

Goodheart-Willcox Publisher

Figure 12-5. A sample customer profile for a diving shop in Florida.

Checkpoint 12.2

1. List the variables for market segmentation.
2. Explain the difference between disposable and discretionary income.
3. What is a VALS™ survey used for?
4. Describe the different types of usage rates.
5. Explain the significance of brand loyalty.

Build Your Vocabulary

As you progress through this course, develop a personal glossary of marketing terms and add it to your portfolio. This will help you build your vocabulary and prepare you for a career. Write a definition for each of the following terms, and add it to your personal marketing glossary.

geographic segmentation
demographic segmentation
generation
disposable income
discretionary income
psychographics
psychographic segmentation

value
attitude
behavioral segmentation
usage rate
buying status
customer profile

Checkpoint Answers

1. The variables for market segmentation are geographic, demographic, psychographic, and behavioral.
2. Disposable income is take-home pay a person has available to dispose of or spend, usually on the necessities of life. Discretionary income is the remaining take-home pay after life's necessities have been paid for, to be used for wants rather than needs.
3. A VALS™ survey is a consumer-behavior research tool that uses a Likert scale to rate respondent answers.
4. The different types of usage rates are heavy usage rate, which means that the consumer often buys the product; moderate

usage rate, which means that the consumer sometimes buys the product; light usage rate, which means that the consumer rarely buys the product; and nonuser usage rate, which means that the consumer never buys the product.
5. Brand loyalty is significant because loyal customers are generally the source of most company sales. For many businesses, 80 percent of the sales come from only 20 percent of the customers.

Build Your Vocabulary Answers

Definitions for these terms can be found in the glossary of this text.

Chapter Summary

Section 12.1 Identify the Market

- A mass market is the overall market or group of people who might buy a product or service. A target market is the specific group of customers at which a company aims its products and services.
- The marketing mix for a target market is always unique and based on the wants and needs of the consumers in that target market. Product, price, place, and promotion can be adapted to meet the target market.
- Mass marketing looks at the market as an unsegmented group and uses the same promotional message for everyone. Target marketing determines its target customers and creates a unique marketing mix for that target group.

Section 12.2 Segment the Market

- Markets can be segmented by many variables. The variables used for market segmentation are geographic, demographic, psychographic, and behavioral.
- Customer profiles help determine the effective promotional strategies for marketers. By knowing who is most interested in the company products, promotional dollars can be used wisely.

Review Your Knowledge

1. What do all markets have in common?
2. Explain how niche markets are created.
3. List three commonly used geographic variables.
4. List five commonly used demographic variables.
5. Why do marketers use generations to segment a market?
6. Why might a marketer segment the market based on family size? Give an example.
7. List four commonly used psychographic variables.
8. Why might a marketer segment the market based on activities? Give an example.
9. List four commonly used behavioral variables.
10. How might a marketer segment a market based on buying status?

Evaluate

Assign end-of-chapter activities.

Review Your Knowledge Answers

1. All markets have particular types of people or businesses most likely to buy certain products or services.
2. Niche markets are often created by businesses looking for a market segment whose needs are not being met.
3. Three commonly used geographic variables are region, climate, and population density.
4. Five commonly used demographic variables are age, gender, income, ethnicity, and education level.
5. The period of history that a group of people grew up in has a major effect on their attitudes, wants, and needs. Marketers use generations to segment a market because different age groups tend to have different product preferences.
6. A marketer would segment the market based on family size because a small household has quite different needs and wants from a large household. For example, a food manufacturer would develop a single-serving food item for a household of one, and a family-serving food item for a household of four.
7. Four commonly used psychographic features are values, attitudes, activities, and interests.
8. A marketer would segment the market based on activities because different people have different interests, and as such are going to make different purchases. For example, a manufacturer of basketball equipment is going to target people who enjoy playing basketball.
9. Four commonly used behavioral variables are benefits sought, usage rate, buying status, and brand loyalty.
10. The different types of customers are potential customers, who have not yet purchased the product but are considering it; first-time consumers, who have just purchased the product for the first time; occasional customers, who have purchased the product more than once, but only infrequently; and regular customers, who purchase the product on a regular basis.

Apply Your Knowledge

1. In earlier chapters, you identified the product or service for which you are creating a marketing plan. Which demographic factors will you use to identify your target market?
2. Which geographic factors will you use to identify your target market?
3. Which psychographic factors will you use to identify your target market?
4. Which behavioral factors will you use to identify your target market?
5. Describe the customer for your business.
6. As you do research for your company, you will follow the research process. Select a research topic and write a hypothesis statement.
7. One way to collect data is to use a survey tool for your customers to give feedback. Develop a survey that you might use for your business to find out what types of products your customers need or want.
8. Describe the mass market for your company.
9. Identify a potential niche market for your product.
10. What added value do you bring as a marketing manager to a business?

Check Your Marketing IQ

Now that you have finished the chapter, see what you learned about marketing by taking the chapter posttest. If you do not have a smartphone, visit the G-W Learning companion website.

G-W Learning mobile site: www.m.g-wlearning.com
G-W Learning companion website: www.g-wlearning.com

Apply Your Knowledge Answers

Student answers will vary for questions 1–10.

Marketing Plan

At the end of this unit, students will write the next phase of the marketing plan. Please note that the Apply Your Knowledge Questions prepare students for the next installment of the marketing plan that they are writing at the end of each unit.

These questions help them assume the role of a marketing manager and begin applying concepts learned in the chapter.

Evaluate

Evaluate the students' understanding and knowledge. Assign the Chapter 12 posttest. The test may be accessed by using the QR code or going to the companion website. What questions were students able to answer that they couldn't when they took the pretest?

Common Core

College and Career Readiness

CTE Career Ready Practices. Marketing professionals, by nature, are creative. Describe why you think you are a creative person. Give an example of how your creativity can help generate ideas as you target a market.

Reading. Using active reading skills, read this chapter closely to determine what is being expressed on each page. Once you finish reading, write specific inferences you can make based on the content. Cite specific paragraphs to support your conclusions.

Writing. Write a narrative to develop the steps you would take in identifying a target market. Focus on your writing style and tone while selecting the right words to express your thoughts. Use well-chosen details, and structure the events in a logical sequence.

Teamwork

Working with teammates, select a product that you know well. Create a customer profile using the geographic, demographic, psychographic, and behavioral variables for market segmentation. Describe the experience of creating a customer profile and the amount of work that was required.

G-W Learning Mobile Site

Visit the G-W Learning mobile site to complete the chapter pretest and posttest and to practice vocabulary using e-flash cards. If you do not have a smartphone, visit the G-W Learning companion website to access these features.

G-W Learning mobile site: www.m.g-wlearning.com

G-W Learning companion website: www.g-wlearning.com

CHAPTER

13

Business-to-Consumer (B2C) Marketing

| Section 13.1 | Influences on Consumer Purchasing |
| Section 13.2 | Consumer Decisions |

"Doing emotional due diligence is just as important as doing financial due diligence. It is actually people that make money and lose money, not Excel spreadsheets."

—Halla Tomasdottir, cofounder of Audur Capital financial services

College and Career Readiness

Reading Prep

Before reading this chapter, read the opening pages for Unit 3 and review the chapter titles. These can help prepare you for the topics that will be presented in the unit. What does this tell you about what you will be learning?

Check Your Marketing IQ

Before you begin the chapter, see what you already know about marketing by taking the chapter pretest. If you do not have a smartphone, visit the G-W Learning companion website.

G-W Learning mobile site: www.m.g-wlearning.com
G-W Learning companion website: www.g-wlearning.com

G-W Mobile

Explore

Assign the College and Career Readiness Reading Prep activity before students read the chapter. Reading Prep activities give students opportunity to apply the Common Core State Standards.

Engage

Assign the Chapter 13 pretest.

◇DECA Emerging Leaders

Marketing Communications Team Decision-Making Event, Part 2

Career Cluster: Marketing
Instructional Area: Communication Skills, Selling

Procedure, Part 2

In Chapter 12, you studied the performance indicators for this event.

1. The event will be presented to you through your reading of the General Performance Indicators, Specific Performance Indicators, and Case Study Situation.
2. You will have up to 30 minutes to review this information and prepare your presentation. You may make notes to use during your presentation.
3. You will have up to 10 minutes to make your presentation to the judge, followed by up to five minutes to answer the judge's questions. All members of the team must participate in the presentation, as well as answer the questions.
4. Turn in all of your notes and event materials when you have completed the event.

Case Study Situation

You are to assume the role of sales team for FIT FOR LIFE, a new health club located next door to a large hospital. The **manager (judge)** of FIT FOR LIFE has called upon your team to describe a sales and marketing strategy to sell memberships to the 1,000 employees who work at the hospital.

FIT FOR LIFE is a 24-hour health club equipped with a running track, racquetball and tennis courts, swimming pool, exercise equipment, and numerous fitness classes. Since FIT FOR LIFE is open 24 hours, seven days a week, it is highly accessible to medical employees who work any shift at the hospital.

The manager of FIT FOR LIFE wants to obtain memberships from the majority of hospital employees. The manager of FIT FOR LIFE has asked your team to develop a sales and marketing strategy that will convince hospital employees to join the health club. Your team has been called upon to describe an effective sales presentation for hospital employees. Your team must describe special incentives you will offer to encourage hospital employees to attend the sales presentation and special promotional events offered by FIT FOR LIFE to sign up new members.

Your team must describe the types of communication that will be the most effective for recruiting health club members. Your presentation should include the following topics: communication, oral presentation, building clientele, motivational theories, customer service, and product features.

You will present your sales strategy to the manager of FIT FOR LIFE in a meeting to take place in the manager's office. The manager of FIT FOR LIFE will begin the meeting by greeting you and asking to hear your ideas. After you have presented your information about a sales strategy to sell health club memberships and have answered the manager's questions, the manager of FIT FOR LIFE will conclude the meeting by thanking you for your work.

Critical Thinking

1. Which features should be emphasized by FIT FOR LIFE that are attractive to hospital workers?
2. Why should FIT FOR LIFE'S hours of operation be emphasized in the meetings with hospital employees?

Visit www.deca.org for more information.

Section 13.1 Influences on Consumer Purchasing

Objectives

After completing this section, you will be able to
- **explain** the business-to-consumer (B2C) market.
- **describe** the psychological influences that impact consumer purchasing.
- **explain** how social influences impact consumer purchasing.
- **discuss** situational influences on consumer purchasing.

Key Terms

consumer behavior
psychological influence
hierarchy of needs
self-actualization
motive
motivate
buying motive
social influence
reference group
peer pressure
word-of-mouth
publicity
situational influence

Web Connect

Do an Internet search on the topic *emotional buying motives* or *Maslow's Hierarchy of Needs*. Select two of the articles you find. Write a brief summary of each and explain how the information can help marketers.

Critical Thinking

After studying Maslow's Hierarchy of Needs, do you agree or disagree with this theory? Write a paragraph describing your opinion.

Business-to-Consumer (B2C) Market

Recall that many businesses sell mostly to consumers. The consumer market is very different from the business market. B2C marketers need to understand *why* people buy and use their products or services to create the ideal marketing mix. Therefore, they study **consumer behavior**, or the actions taken by people to satisfy their needs and wants including what they buy.

Many things can influence consumer buying behavior, especially since every consumer is different. How do marketers know what is influencing the consumers in their target markets? They perform marketing research.

Psychological Influences

Think about your most recent purchase. Maybe it was a music download or the latest book by your favorite author. Why did you make the purchase? What influenced you to make the purchase? Maybe it was psychological influences. **Psychological influences** are the influences that come from within a person or why a person has specific needs and wants.

Explore

Provide an opportunity for students to explore by assigning a hands-on activity. Review the vocabulary terms at the beginning of the section. Where have students encountered these terms before? Help students make educated guesses about the meanings of the terms with which they are least familiar.

Resource

Use the Chapter 13 presentation on the optional Instructor's Presentations for PowerPoint® CD as an outline for presenting the chapter.

Hierarchy of Needs

In the 1950s, psychologist Abraham Maslow was trying to understand why people behave the way they do. He developed what is now referred to as Maslow's Hierarchy of Needs. Maslow's theory states that unsatisfied needs motivate people to act. However, not all needs are equal. There is a hierarchy of needs, or some needs that must be satisfied before others. Maslow noticed that people tend to fulfill physical needs first before fulfilling others less critical for survival. The needs for security, love and acceptance, esteem, and self-actualization are then fulfilled in that order. Maslow presented this hierarchy of needs in pyramid form, as shown in Figure 13-1.

According to Maslow, the strongest needs are physical. These needs *must* be met in order to survive, such as having enough air, water, and food. The next level of need is for security. People need to be safe from physical harm and have financial security. After security are the needs for love and acceptance, which are also called *social needs*. People need to feel accepted by others and that they are part of a group. The next level of need is for esteem. People need to feel self-confident and that others respect them. The last level of need is for self-actualization. Self-actualization is the need to express a person's true self through reaching personal goals and helping others.

Maslow's Hierarchy of Needs also explains human behavior as it relates to buying behaviors. For example, if a person is hungry, he or she will seek food before any other product. This need is partly the reason why so many malls provide food courts. People will not be interested in buying other things when they are hungry.

From a marketing viewpoint, the lower levels of the pyramid have the largest markets. Everyone needs to eat, but very few people focus on their self-actualization needs. Many marketers use Maslow's theory to develop

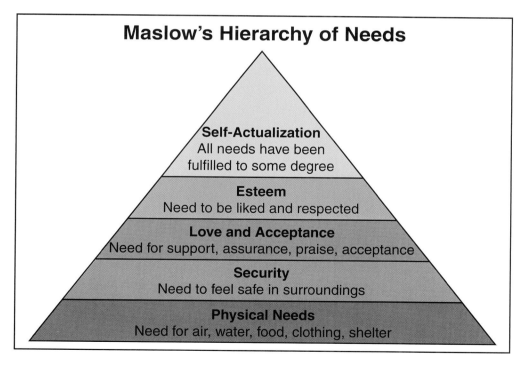

Figure 13-1 Abraham Maslow believed physical needs must be met before all other needs and wants.

Goodheart-Willcox Publisher

products that fulfill certain needs. They also focus promotions on how the products meet those needs. For example, smartphones meet several needs—safety, acceptance, and esteem. Smartphones promotions focus on how they easily keep people connected, up-to-date, and safe any place in the world.

Transferring Needs into Wants

The human mind usually transforms needs into wants. For example, any type of food, including bread and water, can satisfy hunger. However, most people turn the need for food to satisfy hunger into the want for a certain food. With so many food choices, hunger can be satisfied in thousands of different ways.

In the modern consumer market, many products satisfy more than one need. In a choice between products, consumers usually choose the product satisfying the most needs and wants. For example, you may want a car to satisfy the need for work transportation. If a certain car make and model also impresses your friends, you might purchase that one over another.

People are not always aware of all of their needs. However, they usually know their wants. For example, a person may want a certain brand of clothing. The underlying need might be acceptance by peers who only wear that clothing brand. Marketers can use their understanding of the different needs of customers to increase sales. They can develop products and promotions to satisfy unconscious needs as well as the conscious wants.

Sometimes new products can create needs. For example, before Sony invented the Walkman portable audio player, people were unaware of a need for such a device. Once the product was created, many people decided they needed a portable audio device with headphones.

Needs and Wants as Buying Motives

When a need is not satisfied, it turns into a drive. Another term for drive is motive. A **motive** is an internal push that causes a person to act. The strongest motives are based on the most pressing needs or wants.

Case in Point

Illinois Department of Transportation (IDOT)

It pays to do market research—not only for businesses, but for government agencies. In 2004, the Illinois Department of Transportation (IDOT) set out to decrease the number of work zone fatalities in the state. IDOT decided primary research was the best way to collect data. First, a legislatively mandated program was put in place in work zones. To gather data, IDOT used speed-radar photo enforcement (SPE) vans with down-the-road and across-the-road radar. The speeds obtained from the down-the-road radar are displayed on top of the SPE van. This warns drivers to slow down. The across-the-road radar measures the speeds against the speed limit. If the driver is speeding, cameras take a picture of the driver and the license plate for ticketing purposes. Based on the statistics gathered, the State of Illinois launched educational campaigns and increased law enforcement in work zones. Crashes and fatalities decreased significantly and remain low. The American Association of State Highway and Transportation Officials recognized "Speed Photo Enforcement in Illinois Work Zones" as a high-value research project at the regional level.

To **motivate** is to provide the internal push that results in action.

A **buying motive** is the reason a consumer seeks and buys a product or service, as shown in Figure 13-2. Marketers and researchers work hard to learn why some people are motivated to buy certain products, while others are not. Understanding different buying motives is particularly helpful when creating promotions. It also helps salespeople working with potential customers.

Social Influences

Social influences are those influencers from the society in which a person lives. Social influences are conveyed through the people around you. Family, friends, classmates, and other groups to which you belong are social influences. A **reference group** is a group of people who influence buying decisions. A person may have different reference groups for different types of purchases.

Many consumers are unaware of their own reference groups. For example, by default, the people in a neighborhood may be considered a reference group. In other cases, a consumer may consciously choose a reference group. For example, some people choose to dress or look like their favorite actors or actresses. This means they will only buy things that are similar to those worn by the celebrities.

Marketers learn about social influences through research. This information helps them determine what products and promotions appeal to the customers. Social influences can be organized into three categories: culture, family, and peers.

Culture

Culture is a very strong influence on buying decisions because it affects many aspects of life. The ethnic group and social class in which people grow up form their cultural influences. It provides them with an initial set of values, beliefs, and behaviors. The culture consumers are most familiar with often informs their attitudes about products, credit, and shopping. For example, if you grew up in a primarily Hispanic environment, you might prefer buying tortillas to

Types of Buying Motives		
Buying Motives	**Basis**	**Examples**
Physical motives	Physical needs	Food, shelter, health and well-being, protection from harm, safety, relaxation, relief from stress
Psychological motives	Psychological and social needs	Friendship, respect, appreciation, love, reputation, distinction, prestige, importance, recognition, enjoyment, fun
Rational motives	Logical reasoning	Features, quality, durability, dependability, price
Emotional motives	Emotions, impulse, instincts	Popularity, acceptance, romance, thrill seeking, adventure, anxiety, fear, prestige, recognition
Product motives	Features of product	Features, quality, design, color, brand
Patronage motives	Features of a specific store	Location, reputation for reliability and quality, positive image in community, atmosphere, service

Goodheart-Willcox Publisher

Figure 13-2 There are many ways to think about buying motives. This table shows several ways.

Engage

Ask students for opinions on how consumers make decisions to purchase. How does this influence marketing techniques that are used?

Explain

Review Figure 13-2 and discuss each buying motive.

Marketing Ethics

Communication

Ethical communication is very important in both the business and personal life of market-ers. Distorting information for your own gain is an unethical practice. Honesty, accuracy, and truthfulness should guide all communications. Ethically, communication must be presented in an unbiased manner. Facts should be given without distortion. If the information is an opinion, label it as such. Do not take credit for ideas that belong to someone else; always credit your sources.

sliced bread. The culture you grew up in may also affect your ideas of what is appropriate to buy, eat, wear, and do.

Cultural influences also come from the media, including TV, movies, and social media. Because so many people are watching and experiencing the same things, the media exert social influence without trying.

Family

Family is one of the major influences on all consumers. The adults in a family, particularly parents and grandparents, pass on their values, religion, and behaviors to their children. Your family also influences your buying behavior. You learn how to be a consumer from your parents, siblings, and other family members.

Children often buy the same brands as their parents because those brands are familiar. For example, suppose your family always buys Crest toothpaste. It is quite likely that you will buy Crest toothpaste, too. In addition, many people ask family members for product recom-mendations. For example, people ask family for recommendations on cars, clothing, and furni-ture. They will also ask for recommendations of services, such as doctors, auto mechanics, restaurants, and hotels.

Cultural influences are often the strongest in many areas of life includ-ing buying decisions.

kRie/Shutterstock.com

Peers

Another influence on consumer-buying behavior is friends and other peers. Class-mates, coworkers, and members of other groups or organizations also serve as reference groups for many people. Friends are very influential because of the human need for acceptance and esteem. Peer pressure is the social influence exerted on an individual by their peers. Peer pressure may be strong or mild. It does, however, create the feeling that you must do the same things as other people in a social group. Often, buying the right music, clothing, or car gives teens the feelings of belonging and self-confidence.

People often ask friends and other peers for product and service recommendations. In addition, people often talk about the products and services they have bought. Word-of-mouth publicity is the informal conversation people have about their experiences with a business and its products. For example, when people have a great meal at a restaurant, they tend to tell their friends and family about it. When people have a bad experience with a business or product, they tell family and friends about the negative experience also. Word-of-mouth publicity can positively or negatively affect buying decisions.

Situational Influences

Situational influences are the influences that come from the environment. Situational influences that can affect buying choices include the weather, store location, time of day, or available sales promotions. The mood, physical condition, and finances of a buyer at the time of a potential purchase are also situational influences. For example, perhaps you need more computer paper, but it is raining and you do not have transportation. That situation may help you decide to put off buying the computer paper. However, if you have a 25 percent discount coupon expiring the next day, you may find a way to make the purchase.

It is important for marketers to understand how situational influences affect consumer behavior. This information helps them to develop marketing strategies that enhance purchases of their products.

Social Media

Blogs

Web logs, or *blogs* as they are known, are websites maintained by an individual who regularly posts about certain topics or gives opinions. Blogs typically provide information or news about subjects that the blogger chooses to discuss. The entries are posted in a reverse chronological order so that the line of communication is easy to follow. People who want to follow a blog must subscribe to gain access to it. Some blogs are written on a daily basis, others are updated less frequently. Blog followers may also comment on any posts. Business blogs are generally used to share information with current or potential customers. There is no maximum word count, so blogs allow your customers, and you, to communicate freely. Many people follow blogs to look for product information, seek jobs, or learn more about a company. Blogs are indexed on search engines, which is great for business promotion. And, as an added benefit, the messages are permanently posted, so readers can go back at any time to review information.

Consumer behavior research helps marketers learn about important trends that affect product development decisions.

Ryan Jorgensen-Jorgo/Shutterstock.com

Checkpoint 13.1

1. How do consumer needs turn into wants?
2. Why are buying motives analyzed so closely by marketers?
3. How does culture influence buying decisions?
4. Why is word-of-mouth publicity important to marketers?
5. Name examples of situational influences.

Build Your Vocabulary

As you progress through this course, develop a personal glossary of marketing terms and add it to your portfolio. This will help you build your vocabulary and prepare you for a career. Write out a definition for each of the following terms, and add it to your personal marketing glossary.

consumer behavior
psychological influence
hierarchy of needs
self-actualization
motive
motivate

buying motive
social influence
reference group
peer pressure
word-of-mouth publicity
situational influence

Checkpoint Answers

1. The human mind usually transforms needs into wants. For example, any type of food, including bread and water, can satisfy hunger. However, most people turn the need for food to satisfy hunger into the want for a certain food.
2. Marketers and researchers work hard to learn why some people are motivated to buy certain products, while others are not. Understanding different buying motives is particularly helpful when creating promotions. It also helps salespeople working with potential customers.

3. Culture influences buying decisions because ethnic group and social class provide individuals with an initial set of values, beliefs, and behaviors that influences purchases.
4. Word-of-mouth publicity can positively or negatively affect buying decisions.
5. Examples of situational influences are weather, store location, time of day, or sales promotions.

Build Your Vocabulary Answers

Definitions for these terms can be found in the glossary of this text.

Section 13.2 Consumer Decisions

After completing this section, you will be able to
- **explain** the decision-making process of consumers.
- **differentiate** among the four levels of purchase decisions.
- **discuss** how consumers make purchases.

value
impulse buying decision
routine buying decision

limited decision-making process
extensive decision-making process

Perform an Internet search for the definition of *consumer* and *customer*. Compare and contrast the two in a few sentences.

This section covers the consumer decision-making process. Do you personally use these steps when making a purchase? Why or why not?

Consumer Decision-Making Process

How does a consumer make the decision to buy a particular product or service? Marketers think that many consumers use the five-step decision-making process shown in Figure 13-3. Depending on the consumers and what they are buying, each of these steps may be short or long. In some cases, one or more steps may even be skipped. However, some form of each step is considered by most consumers before, during, and after a purchase.

Awareness of Need or Problem

The first step in the decision-making process is defining the problem or situation.

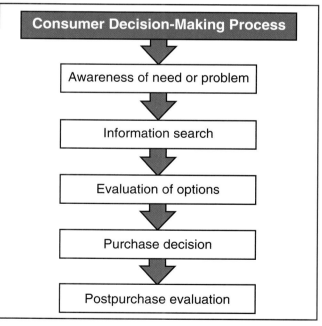

violetkaipa/Shutterstock.com

Figure 13-3 The decision-making process is much like the scientific process and can be used to make any type of decision.

Exploring Careers

Trade Show Management

Have you ever been to a trade show or industry exhibition? These huge gatherings allow companies to show the public—especially prospective customers—their latest products. Companies purchase booth space to showcase and even demonstrate their wares. Organizing these enormous events is the job of the trade show manager. Coordinating everything from the location of the event to the logistics of getting all company products into the exhibit area, a good trade show manager is critical to the success of the event. Typical job titles for these positions include *trade show manager, events manager, conference manager, conference planner,* and *director of events.*

Some examples of tasks that trade show managers perform include:

- Inspect the event facility to make sure it offers everything needed for the trade show.
- Meet with the staff at the chosen location to work out details of the event.
- Monitor event activities to make sure they comply with all applicable laws and ordinances.
- Ensure the safety and security of the exhibits and all of the people, including participants, vendors, and the public.
- Arrange for any equipment and services needed by the participants, such as electricity, tables, chairs, and monitors or other display devices.

Trade show managers need excellent organizational skills. They must be able to understand the requirements for a show or event and coordinate all of the necessary details to make it successful. In addition, they must have good management skills. In most cases, a bachelor degree is required to be a trade show manager, although a highly experienced applicant may be accepted without a degree. Knowledge and skills related to trade shows may also be required. On-the-job training is sometimes offered. For more information, access the *Occupational Outlook Handbook* online.

If there were no problems or unanswered questions, a decision would be unnecessary. Consumers first become aware of a problem when there is a need or want to be satisfied. For example, winter is coming and you realize your old coat no longer fits. So, you need to buy a new one.

Information Search

After the consumer recognizes a need or want, the search for information about how to fulfill the need begins. At this stage, consumers draw on past experiences and may ask family and friends for recommendations. Many consumers conduct product research on websites, look at advertisements,

and read product reviews. If the risk of buying the wrong product is low, then the search for information is short.

In the winter coat example, you may use every form of product research to make the best coat-purchase decision. This may be because the risk of buying the wrong coat would be high. Coats are expensive, you will wear it often, you want the right brand, and it may need to last several years.

Evaluation of Options

After product information is gathered, the purchase options are reviewed. At this stage in the decision-making process, a number of things are considered. The price,

Engage

The problem-solving model was used in market research. How does Figure 13-3 compare to the market research model?

value, brand, features, and benefits for each purchase option are weighed against each other. Value is the relative worth of something. For consumers, value may be tied to price and brand. For example, perhaps you found four good options for a new winter coat. When evaluating each one, you might consider whether it is a good value for the price. You may be willing to spend more on a name brand your friends also wear. Or, you may prefer certain features, such as a hood or fleece lining.

Purchase Decision

Once a purchase is decided, the consumer then chooses where and when to buy it. At this point, consumers may decide to look for the best price, which will determine where the item will be purchased. Or, consumers may decide to postpone the purchase to a later date, perhaps for financial reasons. There may also be other external factors that impact where and when purchases are made. For example, if you started looking for a winter coat in the summer, prices may be lower than in the fall. Some stores may not carry the coat you want and you end up buying it online. Or, you may choose to wait until the coat goes on sale after the holidays.

Postpurchase Evaluation

After a purchase, consumers compare the recent purchase with earlier ones. Every situation is different, but each consumer has some expectations of their shopping experience. The purchase either matches, beats, or falls below those expectations. Consumers may like or dislike the product, store, or service they received. Good business owners and marketers make sure customers are satisfied with a purchase because it ensures repeat business. For example, perhaps the coat you bought was poorly made and several seams ripped after a few wearings. Upon returning it to the store, the manager apologized and gave you a new

Making a buying decision sometimes requires help from others.

bikeriderlondon/Shutterstock.com

coat of your choosing. Your evaluation of the store is positive, but it is unlikely you will buy that brand again.

Levels of Buying Decisions

Have you ever noticed that it often takes longer to buy a pair of athletic shoes than it does to buy a tube of toothpaste? Some purchases require more research and thought than others. The level of decision making varies both with the consumer and what they seek to purchase. Large, expensive products tend to require quite a bit of research and planning. Smaller, less expensive products tend to require little research and planning before purchase.

Some consumers have a harder time making decisions than others. Often, these consumers will take much longer researching their first purchase of a product. After they become familiar with the product, it becomes easier to make more purchases of it. There are four levels of decision making for purchases: impulse, routine, limited, and extensive, as shown in Figure 13-4.

Buying Decision Levels
Impulse Purchase = No prior planning; spur of the moment purchase
Routine Purchase = Little thought or planning; familiar products purchased often
Limited Decision Making = Some research and planning needed; new purchase
Extensive Decision Making = A lot of research, time, and planning; usually an expensive product or service

Goodheart-Willcox Publisher

Figure 13-4 Some buying decisions involve little thought and no research, while other buying decisions may involve a great deal of thought and research.

Impulse Purchases

A purchase made with no planning or research is called an impulse buying decision. For example, you are waiting in the checkout line in a grocery store. A display of key chains, including one with your name on it, is on the counter. You put it in your cart without giving it a second thought. You did not consciously plan to buy a key chain, but the urge to buy one with your name on it suddenly became powerful. You did not use any steps in the decision-making process to buy the key chain. Marketers often place product displays near a checkout counter to encourage impulse purchases.

Routine Purchases

A routine buying decision is a purchase made quickly and with little thought. For example, think about how you buy shampoo. You probably do not think about the buying decision very much. You go into the store, locate the brand you use, and buy it. Routine buying decisions are made when the consumer has experience with the product or prefers a certain brand. Products purchased routinely include groceries, cosmetics, cleaning products, and other inexpensive items. Sometimes, expensive items are also purchased in a routine way. For example, if you usually buy a specific brand and size of running shoes, the buying decision is routine.

Limited Decision Making

The limited decision-making process is one requiring some amount of research and planning. This process is used when buying unfamiliar products or those only bought occasionally. For example, suppose you need to buy a coffeemaker for the school store. You have never bought one before. It is not an expensive purchase, but you want to buy the best coffee-

Routine purchases are easy because decisions can be made quickly.

Monkey Business Images/Shutterstock.com

maker for the money. Therefore, you research coffeemakers in the library, using the *Consumer Reports* magazine. You also research coffeemakers on the Internet. You list the options, their features, and their prices. At that point, you choose the best coffeemaker for the price and buy it. You just went through a limited decision-making purchase process.

Extensive Decision Making

An **extensive decision-making process** involves a great deal of research and planning. It is usually used when buying higher-priced items. For example, imagine you are ready to buy your first car. This purchase will have a major impact on your daily life, safety, and finances. You will analyze your budget to determine what type of car you can afford. You may have to start planning for this purchase a year or more to save for a down payment. You may perform much Internet research, visit many car dealerships, and test-drive a number of cars. If you decide on a used car, you will have a mechanic examine it before buying it. You will also have to research

and purchase auto insurance. The process just described is an example of an extensive decision-making process.

The *AMA Journal of Public Policy and Marketing* focuses on the relationship between marketing and public interest by addressing a wide range of topics. Article topics focus on business and government and include nutrition and public health, corporate social responsibility, antitrust, copyrights and trademarks, and the implications of public policy decisions. The journal is available to AMA members. www.marketingpower.com

Consumer Purchases

Once a buying decision has been made, the actual purchase takes place. Impulse and routine purchases are made in retail stores and online. Sometimes a customer is just browsing with no intention to purchase. However, they may see a new product or one offered for a great price, so they buy it.

Online purchases continue to grow. Marketers of products sold online need to be aware of the selling techniques that appeal to Internet shoppers. They will differ from in-store selling techniques that attract browsers, such as signage or displays. For example, many shoppers rely on search engines, such as Google, Bing, and Yahoo, to look for products. Marketers should understand how to design and write copy for a website so the product shows up early in the search-return list. Each search engine has tools available to help marketers with their sales efforts.

Many consumers are comfortable doing online product research for purchases involving limited and extensive decision making. Some will purchase the products online, but many prefer to see, touch, and examine important purchases in a store or dealership before buying.

Regardless of where a purchase is made, *sales transactions* are calculated the same. Most states require sales tax from retail sales. *Sales tax* is a certain percentage of the selling price added to the final selling price of the good or service. The sales tax is paid to the state by the business owner even though it is collected from the customers. Each state has very different sales tax rates for different categories of goods.

When items are bought that need to be shipped, such online or dealership purchases, these costs are also added to the final selling price. These additional costs are called *shipping and handling charges* or *delivery fees*. Consumers have three ways of paying for purchases: cash, credit cards, or loans. When paying with cash, consumers often do not have the exact amount of the sale. For example, if an item with sales tax is $17.56, many people would give the cashier a $20 bill. The cashier then *makes change* by giving the customer the remaining amount after the purchase price is taken out. In this case, the cashier would give the customer $2.44.

Checkpoint 13.2

1. List several ways in which a consumer might search for information on a product.
2. Explain how the value of one product could vary for different consumers.
3. List factors that could influence when a consumer purchases a product.
4. Give some example of routine buying-decision purchases.
5. Explain the steps in the extensive decision-making process a consumer might take in making a large purchase, such as a car.

Build Your Vocabulary

As you progress through this course, develop a personal glossary of marketing terms and add it to your portfolio. This will help you build your vocabulary and prepare you for a career. Write out a definition for each of the following terms, and add it to your personal marketing glossary.

value
impulse buying decision
routine buying decision

limited decision-making process
extensive decision-making process

Evaluate

Assign Checkpoint questions at end of section. Assess student comprehension using the Checkpoint activity as a self-assessment tool.

Checkpoint Answers

1. In order to search for information on a product, a consumer might ask family and friends, conduct online research, look at advertisements, or read product reviews.
2. Each consumer has a different opinion about what the most important aspect of the product is. For example, with a jacket, one consumer might value a hood, another may value the type of material it is made from, and yet another may value the brand name.

3. A few factors that could influence when a consumer purchases a product are when the consumer thinks the price will be lowest and when the consumer can afford it.
4. Examples may include groceries, cosmetics, cleaning products, gasoline, or other inexpensive items.
5. Steps include analyzing his or her budget, planning the purchase to begin saving for it, performing Internet research, and visiting several dealerships to compare prices and test-drive different cars.

Build Your Vocabulary Answers

Definitions for these terms can be found in the glossary of this text.

Chapter Summary

Section 13.1 Influences on Consumer Purchasing

- The business-to-consumer (B2C) market relies heavily on consumer behavior. B2C marketers study consumer behavior to understand how to satisfy consumers' wants and needs.
- The psychological influences that impact consumer purchasing are wants and needs. Maslow's Hierarchy of Needs theory states that unsatisfied needs motivate people to act. However, not all needs are equal, and some needs must be satisfied before others.
- Social influences are conveyed through the people around you. Social influences that impact consumer purchasing are culture, family, and peers.
- Situational influences are influences that come from the environment and affect purchasing actions. This information helps marketers develop strategies that enhance purchases of their products.

Section 13.2 Consumer Decisions

- The decision-making process of consumers typically involves five steps: 1. Becoming aware of a need or problem; 2. Searching for information; 3. Evaluating options; 4. Deciding on a purchase; 5. Evaluating the purchase afterwards.
- Some purchases require more research and thought than others. The four levels of purchase decisions are impulse, routine, limited, and extensive.
- Once a buying decision has been made, the actual purchase takes place either online, in a store, or at a dealership. Regardless of where a purchase is made, sales transactions are calculated the same. Sales tax and other charges are added to the final selling price.

Review Your Knowledge

1. Describe the different types of needs in Maslow's Hierarchy of Needs.
2. How do marketers learn about social influences on a target market?
3. Name and describe three social influences that impact consumer decision making.
4. Why are friends influential on consumer-buying behavior?
5. Explain the importance of social influences on consumer decision making.
6. Compare and contrast social influences with situational influences.
7. List the five steps in the consumer decision process.
8. Why is the postpurchase evaluation an important step in the decision-making process?
9. Describe the four levels of purchase decision making.
10. Why is extensive decision making more involved than other decision-making processes?

Apply Your Knowledge

1. As a marketing professional, how can you create customer needs and wants into buying motives for your product or service?
2. Consider the product or service that you are marketing. How would you define the reference group that influences a majority of your target market?
3. Give an example of word-of-mouth marketing that might influence purchase of your product or service.
4. Describe how your customers would evaluate the decision to purchase your products.
5. How can you make sure that your customers have access to information needed to purchase your products?
6. Create a flowchart for the decision-making process that your customers may use. Identify the details for each step that would exemplify a typical customer to whom you would market.
7. In your opinion, what do you think customers would say in their postpurchase evaluation of your product or service?
8. Do you have any products for your chosen company that are considered impulse items? If so, describe them.
9. Explain how routine buying decisions by customers influence your marketing plans.
10. Do any of your products require the customer to use an extensive decision-making process? If yes, describe the situation.

Check Your Marketing IQ

Now that you have finished the chapter, see what you learned about marketing by taking the chapter posttest. If you do not have a smartphone, visit the G-W Learning companion website.

G-W Learning mobile site: www.m.g-wlearning.com
G-W Learning companion website: www.g-wlearning.com

Apply Your Knowledge Answers

Student answers will vary for questions 1–10.

Marketing Plan

At the end of this unit, students will write the next phase of the marketing plan. Please note that the Apply Your Knowledge Questions prepare students for the next installment of the marketing plan that they are writing at the end of each unit. These questions help them assume the role of a marketing manager and begin applying concepts learned in the chapter.

Evaluate

Evaluate the students' understanding and knowledge. Assign the Chapter 13 posttest. The test may be accessed by using the QR code or going to the companion website. What questions were students able to answer that they couldn't when they took the pretest?

Common Core

College and Career Readiness

CTE Career Ready Practices. There will be instances in which you will need to use critical thinking skills to solve a problem. One way to approach a problem is to create a pros and cons chart. Imagine that you have to decide which vendor to use for a promotion. Place all of the positive things about the vendor under the *pro* side and all the negative things on the *con* side. Circle the items on your list that you consider the most important. Did the pros and cons chart help you make a decision? Why or why not?

Speaking. Select three of your classmates to participate in a discussion panel. Acting as the team leader, name each person to a specific task such as timekeeper, recorder, etc. Discuss the topic of impulse buying and its effect on the consumer. Keep the panel on task and promote democratic discussion.

Listening. Active listeners know when to comment and when to remain silent. Practice your listening skills while your teacher presents a lesson. Participate when appropriate and build on his or her ideas.

Teamwork

Working with your team, select a well-known product that is marketed to consumers. Outline the decision-making process that you anticipate customers will experience when buying this product.

G-W Learning Mobile Site

Visit the G-W Learning mobile site to complete the chapter pretest and posttest and to practice vocabulary using e-flash cards. If you do not have a smartphone, visit the G-W Learning companion website to access these features.

G-W Learning mobile site: www.m.g-wlearning.com

G-W Learning companion website: www.g-wlearning.com

CHAPTER

14 Business-to-Business (B2B) Marketing

| Section 14.1 | Business Customers |
| Section 14.2 | B2B Buying Decisions |

"Don't be afraid to take time to learn. It's good to work for other people. I worked for others for twenty years. They paid me to learn."

—Vera Wang, American fashion designer

College and Career Readiness

Reading Prep
As you read this chapter, stop at the section checkpoints and take time to answer the questions. Were you able to answer them without referring to the chapter content?

Check Your Marketing IQ

Before you begin the chapter, see what you already know about marketing by taking the chapter pretest. If you do not have a smartphone, visit the G-W Learning companion website.
G-W Learning mobile site: www.m.g-wlearning.com
G-W Learning companion website: www.g-wlearning.com

G-W Mobile

Explore
Assign the College and Career Readiness Reading Prep activity before students read the chapter. Reading Prep activities give students opportunity to apply the Common Core State Standards.

Engage
Assign the Chapter 14 pretest.

◇DECA Emerging Leaders

Principles of Marketing Event

Career Cluster: Marketing
Instructional Area: Information Management

Performance Indicators

- Assess information needs.
- Demonstrate basic database applications.
- Obtain needed information efficiently.
- Store information for future use.

Purpose

Designed for first-year DECA members who are enrolled in introductory-level principles of marketing/ business courses, the event measures the individual's ability to explain core business concepts in the format of a content interview in a role-play. This event consists of a 100-question, multiple-choice, business administration core exam and a content interview. Participants are not informed in advance of the performance indicators to be evaluated.

Procedure

1. The event will be presented to you through your reading of these instructions, including the Performance Indicators and Interview Situation. You will have up to 10 minutes to review this information to determine how you will handle the role-play situation and demonstrate the performance indicators of this event. During the preparation period, you may make notes to use during the role-play situation.
2. You will have up to 10 minutes to role-play your situation with a judge. You may have more than one judge.
3. You will be evaluated on how well you meet the performance indicators of this event.
4. Turn in all your notes and event materials when you have completed the role-play.

Interview Situation

You are to assume the role of candidate for an internship at the national headquarters of Project Smile, a non-profit business dedicated to providing cleft lip and palate repair to children whose families are unable to afford the corrective surgery. You have submitted your résumé to the intern in the marketing department who is responsible for soliciting and acknowledging monetary donations from the general public. The **marketing manager (judge)** has invited you in for a face-to-face interview. This interview will be used to measure your knowledge and understanding of an aspect of the business. The marketing manager wants to make sure you understand the role that the donor database plays in the business's ability to raise the necessary funds.

In the first part of your interview, you will assess the information needs of the business as it relates to soliciting and acknowledging donations. In addition, you must explain how database management can facilitate the information needs of the business and how this produces accurate business records and provides for proper customer receipts. Your presentation should also address the additional performance indicators listed on the first page of this event. Following your explanation, the marketing manager will ask you to respond to additional questions.

The interview will take place in the marketing manager's office. The marketing manager will begin the interview by greeting you and asking to hear your ideas on how proper operation of the donor database can help to raise the funds needed by the business. After you have provided your explanation and have answered the marketing manager's questions, the marketing manager will conclude the interview by thanking you for your presentation.

Critical Thinking

1. How will the marketing manager use this interview?
2. What are you to do in the first part of your interview?
3. What is the relationship between the performance indicators identified and your presentation with the marketing manager?
4. Match information in the role-play with each performance indicator.
5. What is one question the marketing manager may ask about information management at Project Smile? How will you respond?

Visit www.deca.org for more information.

Section 14.1 Business Customers

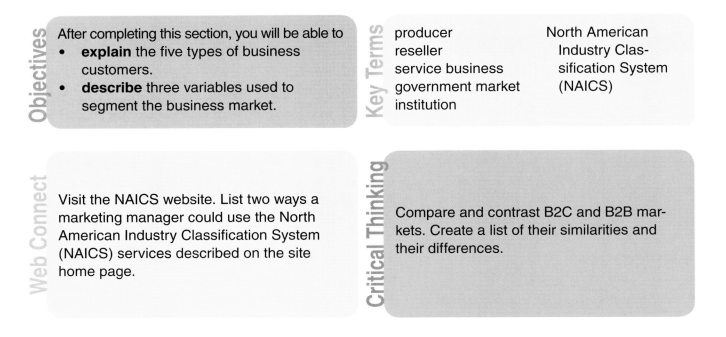

Objectives

After completing this section, you will be able to
- **explain** the five types of business customers.
- **describe** three variables used to segment the business market.

Key Terms

producer
reseller
service business
government market
institution

North American Industry Classification System (NAICS)

Web Connect

Visit the NAICS website. List two ways a marketing manager could use the North American Industry Classification System (NAICS) services described on the site home page.

Critical Thinking

Compare and contrast B2C and B2B markets. Create a list of their similarities and their differences.

Who Are Business Customers?

Recall from Chapter 3 that businesses selling primarily to other businesses are called *business-to-business (B2B) companies*. There are some companies, such as Staples or FedEx, that sell to both B2C markets and B2B markets. However, most companies sell to one market or the other. The business market can be grouped into five categories: producers, resellers, service businesses, governments, and institutions, as shown in Figure 14-1.

Producers buy raw materials and equipment, which they use to make products and product components. Producers are also called *manufacturers*.

Resellers buy finished products to resell them to consumers. Retail stores are in the reseller category. Both producers and resellers may also buy distribution and warehousing services.

Service businesses are those providing services to consumers or other businesses, such as leasing companies or law firms. Service businesses may need to buy very specific products to operate their businesses, such as cars, equipment, or tuxedos to rent.

The **government market** includes national, state, and local government offices and agencies. They buy a wide variety of products, from airplanes to paper and computers. Governments also buy services, such as education and medical care.

Institutions include public and private nonprofit organizations. These include schools,

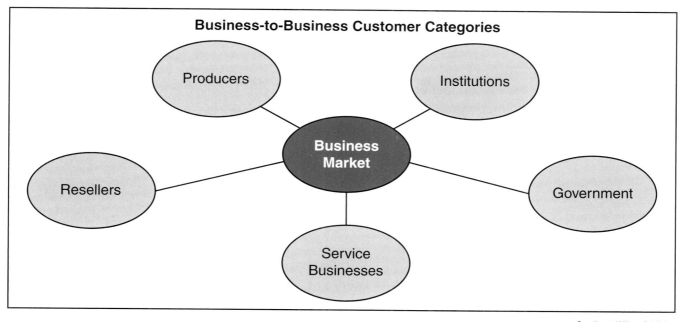

Figure 14-1 Each type of business or organization buys very different products.

Goodheart-Willcox Publisher

hospitals, museums, and charities such as United Way or the American Cancer Society. Much like the government, institutions also buy a wide variety of products and services.

Segment the Business Market

In some ways, targeting business-market segments is similar to targeting consumer-market segments. Variables are used to segment the customers, and then a customer profile is created. B2B marketers use customer profiles to determine the best marketing mix. Common variables used to segment business customers are business type, customer size and location, and product use, as shown in Figure 14-2.

Business Type

Different types of businesses naturally have different needs. The same types of

businesses usually need similar products and services. For example, most financial institutions buy ATMs, security systems, and vaults. Businesses making and selling these products have at least one target market—all financial institutions.

Segmentation Variables for the Business Market	
Variable	**Example**
Business Type	• Producer/reseller/govern-ment/institution • North American Industry Classification System (NAICS)
Business Size and Location	• Independent store • Chains over 100 stores
Product Use	• Structural beams/auto-mobiles/appliances/cans

Goodheart-Willcox Publisher

Figure 14-2 B2B marketers use different variables to segment their markets.

Case in Point

Cisco

As a world leader in networking, Cisco provides services to business customers including corporations, and governments. Cisco provides limited products, such as Wi-Fi routers, to the consumer market. Its largest market, by far, is selling to resellers who in turn, sell or provide the services to the end users. Like other business-to-business (B2B) companies, Cisco has been very successful marketing to the business customer. That is why they are known as the market leader in networking.

However, Cisco has taken networking a step further. The company wants to make sure their business customers know how to resell the Cisco product lines. Cisco created a marketing program for their business customers to use, in turn, to sell to *their* customers. Cisco offers a step-by-step guide to empower their reseller customers and help them to be successful by using Cisco tools. Checklists, templates, and resources are provided so resellers can easily create their own marketing programs. Details on customer databases and how to segment the market are provided. The program is called Cisco Marketing Fundamentals— and it is working very well. Cisco understands the marketing concept of customer satisfaction.

There are many ways to define types of businesses. Producers, resellers, services, governments, and institutions may be too broad to help define a target market. The **North American Industry Classification System NAICS** (pronounced nākes) is a numerical system used to classify businesses and collect economic statistics. Figure 14-3 lists the major industrial categories in NAICS.

This system was developed by the US, Canadian, and Mexican governments for trade purposes. Marketers use the unique NAICS codes to identify different business market segments. Most B2B marketers use NAICS. More information on NAICS is available through the US Census Bureau.

FYI

NAICS is a source for targeted marketing lists for both B2C and B2B markets.

NAICS Business Classifications	
11	Agriculture, Forestry, Fishing and Hunting
21	Mining
22	Utilities
23	Construction
31-33	Manufacturing
42	Wholesale Trade
44-45	Retail Trade
48-49	Transportation and Warehousing
51	Information
52	Finance and Insurance
53	Real Estate Rental and Leasing
54	Professional, Scientific, and Technical Services
55	Management of Companies and Enterprises
56	Administrative and Support and Waste Management and Remediation Services
61	Educational Services
62	Health Care and Social Assistance
71	Arts, Entertainment, and Recreation
72	Accommodation and Food Services
81	Other Services (except Public Administration)
92	Public Administration

Goodheart-Willcox Publisher

Figure 14-3 Each major NAICS category is subdivided into smaller, more specific categories.

College and Career Portfolio

Community Service

Community service is an important quality that interviewers expect in a candidate. Serving the community shows that the candidate is well rounded and socially aware. In this activity, you will create a list of your contributions to nonprofit organizations. Many opportunities are available for young people to serve the community. You might volunteer for a community clean-up project. Perhaps you might enjoy reading to residents in a senior-living facility. Maybe raising money for a pet shelter appeals to you. Whatever your interests, there is sure to be a related service project.

In this activity, you will create a list of your community service activities. Remember that this is an ongoing project. Plan to update this list when you have new activities to add.

1. List the service projects or volunteer activities in which you have taken part. Give the organization or person's name, the dates, and the activities that you performed. If you received a certificate or award related to this service, mention it here.
2. Give the document an appropriate name, using the naming system you created earlier. Place the file in your e-portfolio.
3. Place a hard copy of the list in the container for your print portfolio.

Business Size and Location

Large businesses have different needs than small businesses. Therefore, B2B marketers often find it useful to segment markets based on business size. Variables such as annual sales and number of employees, offices, or customers can be used to classify businesses by size.

In addition, the geographic location of some businesses may include or exclude them from a target market segment. Businesses that sell products regionally or globally impact how the marketers will segment its markets.

For example, suppose your business sells commercial cleaning products. Your customers will have varying needs for cleaning products. A big-box business with thousands of stores has very different cleaning needs than a small, local hardware store. The big-box company will need large quantities of cleaning items and a system to distribute the products to each store. The small hardware store may need only several products in small quantities.

Product Use

Business customers vary in the way they use products, especially raw materials and product components. B2B marketers target sales efforts to companies with similar uses for their products, even when not in the same business category.

For example, the market for steel is quite large. However, businesses use steel in many ways. Four of the many uses for steel are as structural beams, truck bodies, kitchen appliances, and school lockers. Steel suppliers would find it useful to segment customers into groups based on how the steel is used. Business customers use the products they buy to make new products, resell to customers, or to operate the business.

Explore

Assign students to research NAICS codes. Why are they important?

This farming business must purchase equipment, seed, and fertilizer from different suppliers to keep the business running.

Elize Lotter/Shutterstock.com

Make New Products

Many businesses buy products to make new products. These types of businesses are often referred to as *producers* or *manufacturers.* Producers buy raw materials and other products from suppliers to form them into different goods for the consumer market. For example, a company that makes water bottles must buy sheets of plastic from a plastic supplier. It then forms the sheets of plastic in different bottle forms and sells the products to retailers.

Resell to Customers

Retail businesses buy finished goods to sell to their consumers. Most retailers buy

goods from other businesses called *vendors.* The stores then resell those goods to make a profit. These goods are the *inventory* of the stores. For example, sporting goods stores buy water bottles from suppliers to sell to consumers who use them.

Operate the Business

Every business needs goods and services to run the business. Most businesses buy equipment and office supplies they need to operate. For example, an accounting firm buys ten computers for its accountants. Those computers are used to run the business; they are not sold by the business. The product of the accounting firm is accounting services.

Checkpoint 14.1

1. What is another name for producers?
2. In which business market category are retailers classified?
3. Give an example of a public or private nonprofit organization.
4. How are business-to-business market segments similar to consumer marketing segments?
5. How do business customers use the products they purchase?

Build Your Vocabulary

As you progress through this course, develop a personal glossary of marketing terms and add it to your portfolio. This will help you build your vocabulary and prepare you for a career. Write out a definition for each of the following terms, and add it to your personal marketing glossary.

producer
reseller
service business
government market
institution
North American Industry Classification System (NAICS)

Checkpoint Answers

1. Another name for producers is *manufacturers*.
2. Retailers are resellers.
3. Examples of a public or private nonprofit organization include schools, hospitals, museums, and charitable organizations such as United Way or the American Cancer Society.
4. B2B market segments are similar to consumer-marketing segments because in both, variables are used to segment the markets and then create a customer profile.
5. Business customers use the products they buy to make new products, resell to customers, or in operating the business.

Build Your Vocabulary Answers

Definitions for these terms can be found in the glossary of this text.

Section 14.2 B2B Buying Decisions

Objectives

After completing this section, you will be able to
- **identify** three influences on business-to-business buying.
- **describe** B2B buying decisions versus B2C.
- **explain** the two types of organizational buyers in business purchasing.

Key Terms

internal influence
external influence
situational influence
business purchasing
organizational buyer
supplier
purchasing agent

inventory
buyer
bid

Web Connect

Imagine that you are the purchasing agent for a business. You need to find a source for a business product. Name your type of business and the product needed for that business. For example, a restaurant needs plates and silverware. Use the Internet to research and find a supplier for that product.

Critical Thinking

Purchasing is not a function of marketing. However, all functions of a business must work together to be successful. Give your viewpoint about how a marketing manager would work with purchasing agents or buyers in a business.

B2B Buying Influences

The needs of an organization are the primary influencer of B2B buying decisions. However, there may be additional influences on the final purchases. These influences can be grouped into three categories: internal, external, and situational.

Internal

Internal influences are are a motivator or change factor that comes from within the business itself. Internal influences include the structure, goals, and management team of a company. For example, one company might have a president who values innovation. That company will be willing to use new vendors or develop new products. Another company might

have a president who does not like change. That president could be less likely to approve the purchase of new products from new vendors.

External

External influences are a motivator or change factor from outside the business. External influences include business competition, new technology, or product trends. For example, if a competitor comes out with a new product, a business might decide to create a similar one. This means the business will need new goods, materials, and services to develop that product.

Situational

Situational influences are those from the environment in which the business exists. Situational influences include the economy,

Because the B2B salesperson has fewer customers than the B2C salesperson, more time can be spent with them to build solid, long-term relationships.

Franck Boston/Shutterstock.com

political environment, and regulations or laws. For example, if the economy is strong, a business might be more likely to expand. An expanding business will buy more goods and services. In a poor economy, sales may decrease, so purchases will also decrease.

B2B versus B2C Buying Decisions

Business customers have very different buying needs and motives than consumers. A typical consumer buys products or services to use personally. However, a business buys products to manufacture new products, resell, or use for its operations.

A B2B sale may take a long time to close and is often based on relationship selling. The salesperson may only have a few customers. A department store salesperson, however, may have hundreds of customers.

Consumers generally purchase enough goods to last a reasonable amount of time. The purchases are typically of a quantity and size that can be stored in the home. In contrast, resellers buy large quantities of inventory that is stored for selling to their customers. For that reason, businesses usually buy in greater volume than the average consumer.

Like B2C, some B2B purchases can be made on the Internet, often from international companies. Businesses have levels of buying decisions similar to three levels of consumer decisions as seen in Chapter 13. However, there is generally no impulse buying in the business market.

New Purchase

A *new purchase* is a decision to buy a new product requiring a great deal of research and thought. New purchases are challenging as the business does not have experience making that particular buying decision. The business will probably create product specifications outlining exactly what the business expects for this new product. This is similar to the extensive decision-making process of consumers.

Repeat Purchase

Many businesses purchase the same items on a regular basis. A *repeat purchase* is a buying decision that requires little research

and thought. For example, a business that makes computers continues to renew a vendor contract for computer parts. Repeat-purchase decisions occur when the buyer is satisfied with the product, vendor, and terms of sale. This is similar to the limited decision-making process of consumers.

Modified Purchase

Often something occurs to make a buyer less satisfied with a product or vendor he or she has been using. A *modified purchase* is a decision to buy a familiar product that needs some changes or modifications. The current vendor, as well as other vendors, may be given an opportunity to supply the modified product. This is similar to the routine buying decisions of consumers.

Business Purchasing

Business purchasing is the activity of acquiring goods or services to accomplish the

A pharmacy is a good example of a business that makes many repeat-purchase decisions based on medicines that must always be kept on hand.

Federico Marsicano/Shutterstock.com

Elaborate/Extend

If students are using the optional *Marketing Dynamics* workbook, assign activities to engage active learning.

goals of an organization. In Chapter 3, you learned that the term *organization* is another term for business. Businesses buy a wide variety of goods and services depending on their different needs.

Larger businesses usually have purchasing departments because so many large purchases are made. The person who buys products for a business is often called an **organizational buyer**. There are two types of organizational buyers: purchasing agents and buyers. A business that sells to organizational buyers is called a **supplier** or a *vendor*.

Purchasing Agents

In companies with purchasing departments, **purchasing agents** buy goods and services the company needs internally to operate its business. These departments are staffed with specialized *purchasers*, which is another term for purchasing agents. Purchasing agents often need technical knowledge about the company products or production processes. For example, a purchaser for a manufacturer must know a great deal about the raw materials and equipment used for producing the products.

Purchasers must also buy the furniture, fixtures, equipment, and supplies needed to run the business. Purchasing agents research where to get the best products at the best prices. Purchasing departments may also be called *procurement*.

In smaller businesses, it is not always clear who makes the final buying decisions. There is often more than one person involved. Written approval is generally needed to make large purchases. Sometimes the people making the decision are obvious, such as the company president or vice president. Sometimes, they are not obvious. For example, the person who knows the department needs best may choose which computers are purchased. That person may be a manager or an administrative assistant. A purchase order similar to the one shown in Figure 14-4 is used to officially place an order with a vendor. Copies of a purchase order should be kept for business records.

Buyers

Purchasing agents buy goods and services the company needs to operate. However, resellers purchase products that the business will not use, but resell to customers. The goods a business has on hand to sell to customers are called its **inventory.** The person responsible for planning and ordering inventory is usually called the **buyer.** However, sometimes the terms *purchaser* and *buyer* are used for the same purpose. Other terms for buyers are *professional buyer, retail buyer,* and *merchandise manager.*

The buyer in a retail business is very important. Decisions about what goods to purchase for resale have a major effect on the success of the business. Much planning goes

---

Green Marketing

Electronic Newsletters

One valuable marketing strategy is sending monthly newsletters to current and potential customers. Consider turning paper newsletters into electronic newsletters. The electronic format can cut printing and paper costs and decrease paper waste. In fact, some companies only use interactive newsletters to provide a greater level of content and customer participation.

J&J Flowers		PURCHASE ORDER		
123 Main Street Tampa, FL 33601 Phone: (813) 555-1234 Fax: (813) 555-1235				

PO #: 003725			Date: 03/31/20--	

Vendor Name/Address:	Vendor ID:	Customer ID:
Magnolia Floral Wholesale 9807 Second Avenue Atlanta, GA 30060 (678) 555-1236	24	1068A

SHIPPING METHOD	SHIPPING TERMS	DELIVERY DATE
Ground	Received by 05/01/20--	05/01/20--

Item	Job	Description	Qty	Unit Price	Line Total
013188	12	4″ by 4″ square vase	24	3.70	88.80
011088	12	4.5″ by 10″ cylinder bowl vase	60	11.25	675.00
012488	12	12″ by 5″ curved vase	48	6.15	295.20

1. Please send two copies of your invoice.
2. Enter this order in accordance with the prices, terms, delivery method, and specifications listed above.
3. Please notify us immediately if you are unable to ship as specified.
4. Send all correspondence to:
   J&J Flowers
   Email: judy@J&Jflowerstampa.com
   Fax: (813) 555-1235

Subtotal	1,059.00
For resale? (Yes)/ No Tax ID: 12-3456789 Sales Tax	—
Shipping	126.95
Total Net 30 days	**$1,185.95**

Authorized by: *Judy Jackson*	Date: 3/31/20--

Figure 14-4 A purchase order should include all pertinent information to process the order.

into purchasing inventory for a business. For example, retailers spend an average of 70 cents of every dollar in sales on inventory. If the wrong inventory is purchased, customers may not buy enough for the business to make a profit. Depending on the type of business, inventory may be purchased daily, weekly, monthly, or less often.

Bid Process

In a small business, the owner might also buy both the inventory and items needed for operations. However, in larger businesses, a merchandise manager or purchasing agent might handle all of the purchasing duties.

Explain

Bring in samples of purchase orders so students can review and analyze.

Engage

Most companies use a bid process whenever they make a purchase. Ask students why they think this is a good process or bad one.

Purchasing agents and organizational buyers go through the same basic decision process as consumers. However, there are usually more people involved in each decision. The quantities of products purchased and total amounts paid are usually large.

Due to amount of money invested in business purchases, a formal bidding process is often used. A **bid** is a formal written proposal that lists all the goods and services that will be provided, their prices, and timeline. Often, the buyer must obtain two or more bids, compare each, and choose the best one. Analyzing bids can take a long time. Decisions often also need written approval by more than one person in the company.

The buyer and the supplier often develop a partnership-type of relationship. The buyer needs the supplier to be successful. In addition, the supplier needs the buyer as a customer in order to be successful. It is in the interest of both to work well with each other. A form similar to the one shown in Figure 14-5 can be used to monitor the track record of vendors and suppliers over time. You will learn more about the purchasing process in Chapter 21.

FYI

Many businesses and organizations need to purchase costly services, such as architectural, legal, or telecommunications. To invite companies to submit formals bids for the business, purchasers create a Request for Proposal (RFP). The RFP lists the necessary experience and details required to fulfill the expected work. Companies hoping to win the business provide formal bids answering each requirement listed in the RFP.

Vendor Evaluation Form

Vendors	Date	Availability of products	Quality	Reliability	On-time delivery	Damages or discrepancies	Service	Price
Vendor #1								
Vendor #2								
Vendor #3								
Vendor #4								

Goodheart-Willcox Publisher

Figure 14-5 Rating vendors will help you evaluate which companies to do business with.

Evaluate

Assign Checkpoint questions at end of section. Assess student comprehension using the Checkpoint activity as a self-assessment tool.

Checkpoint 14.2

1. List the three factors that decide a business purchase.
2. List the three levels of buying decisions that a business might make.
3. What are two types of organizational buyers?
4. Explain the job of a purchasing agent.
5. Why are many businesses required to use a formal bidding process?

Build Your Vocabulary

As you progress through this course, develop a personal glossary of marketing terms and add it to your portfolio. This will help you build your vocabulary and prepare you for a career. Write out a definition for each of the following terms, and add it to your personal marketing glossary.

internal influence
external influence
situational influence
business purchasing
organizational buyer
supplier
purchasing agent
inventory
buyer
bid

Chapter Summary

Section 14.1 Business Customers

- The business market can be grouped into five categories: producers, resellers, service businesses, governments, and institutions. These businesses provide goods and services for customers as well as buy goods and services for use by the business.
- Targeting business-to-business market segments is similar to targeting consumer-market segments. For both markets, variables are used to segment the customers, and then create a customer profile. Common variables used to segment business customers are business type, customer size and location, and product use.

Section 14.2 B2B Buying Decisions

- The needs of an organization are the primary influencer of buying decisions. These influences can be grouped into three categories: internal, external, and situational.
- Businesses have levels of buying decisions similar to three levels of consumer decisions. Those buying levels are new purchases, repeat purchases, and modified purchases.
- There are two types of organizational buyers: purchasing agents and buyers. Purchasing agents make purchases for internal use for the organization. Buyers make purchases of product to resell to customers.

Review Your Knowledge

1. Name the five categories of the business market.
2. What types of products do government offices buy?
3. Who created the NAICS codes and why?
4. How do B2B marketers segment markets?
5. Businesses that buy products to make new products are classified in which business market category?
6. How does the business buying motive differ from a consumer buying motive?
7. Give an example of an internal influence that impacts the purchasing decision.
8. Compare and contrast the three levels of buying decisions that a business might make.
9. What is the difference between a purchasing agent and buyer?
10. What is an RFP?

Evaluate

Assign the end-of-chapter activities.

Review Your Knowledge Answers

1. The five categories of the business market are producers, resellers, service businesses, governments, and institutions.
2. Governments buy a wide variety of products, from airplanes to paper and computers. Governments also buy services, such as education and medical care.
3. The NAICS codes were developed by the US, Canadian, and Mexican governments for trade purposes.
4. B2B marketers often find it useful to segment markets based on business size. Variables, such as annual sales and number of employees, offices, or customers can be used to classify businesses by size. In addition, the geographic location of some businesses may include or exclude them from a target market segment.
5. Businesses that buy products to make new product are classified as producers.
6. Business customers use the products they buy to make new products, resell to customers, or in operating the business.

Consumers buy products to use.

7. Internal influences that impact the purchasing decision include the company's structure, its goals, and the management team.
8. New purchases are challenging as the business does not have experience making that particular buying decision. The business will probably create product specifications outlining exactly what the business expects for this new product. Repeat-purchase decisions occur when the buyer is satisfied with the product, vendor, and terms of sale. Often something occurs to make a buyer less satisfied with a product or vendor he or she has been using so a modified purchase is necessary.
9. A purchasing agent purchases goods to be used internally by the company. A buyer makes purchases of goods that will be resold to customers.
10. Purchasers create a Request for Proposal (RFP) to invite companies to submit formal bids for the business. The RFP lists the necessary experience and details required to fulfill the expected work. Companies hoping to win the business provide formal bids answering each requirement listed in the RFP.

Apply Your Knowledge

1. In earlier chapters, you identified the product or service for which you are creating a marketing plan. Which NAICS code applies to your company?
2. What kinds of services does NAICS provide as marketing tools?
3. Identify the product or service you are marketing. Assume your company is a business-to-business model and describe the customer profile.
4. Assume your company is in the B2B market. How would the information on its website differ from a website for a company in the B2C market?
5. Think about an institutional organization for which you are familiar. Make a list of the ten most important purchases the purchasing agent would need to make. Write a short explanation for each item you listed.
6. You have been asked by the buyer to help create an approval system for bids. Make a list of the steps you think should be a part of the approval process.
7. What kind of information can marketing provide to buyers in a business?
8. Describe specific internal influences that a buyer for your business might encounter. Describe specific external influences that a buyer for your business might encounter.
10. Describe specific situational influences that a buyer for your business might encounter.

Check Your Marketing IQ

Now that you have finished the chapter, see what you learned about marketing by taking the chapter posttest. If you do not have a smartphone, visit the G-W Learning companion website.

G-W Learning mobile site: www.m.g-wlearning.com
G-W Learning companion website: www.g-wlearning.com

Apply Your Knowledge Answers:

Student answers will vary for questions 1–10.

Marketing Plan

At the end of this unit, students will write the next phase of the marketing plan. Please note that the Apply Your Knowledge Questions prepare students for the next installment of the marketing plan that they are writing at the end of each unit. These questions help them assume the role of a marketing manager and begin applying concepts learned in the chapter.

Evaluate

Evaluate the students' understanding and knowledge. Assign the Chapter 14 posttest. The test may be accessed by using the QR code or going to the companion website. What questions were students able to answer that they couldn't when they took the pretest?

Common Core

College and Career Readiness

CTE Career Ready Practices. Being creative and innovative are two characteristics that most marketing professional possess. Whether you see problems as challenges or opportunities, they often require creative thinking to solve them. Many new inventions come from trying to solve a problem. Describe a situation in your life or in history in which a problem led to the creation of a new way of doing things or a new invention.

Listening. Passive listening is casually listening to someone speak. Passive listening is appropriate when you do not have to interact with the speaker. Search the Internet for a presentation on purchasing for an organization. After it has played, evaluate what you heard and write down what you remembered from the presentation. How many points could you note?

Speaking. There are many instances when you will be required to persuade the listener. When you persuade, you convince a person to take a course of action which you propose. Prepare for a conversation with a classmate to persuade that person to approve your idea for hiring a new vendor for your company.

Teamwork

Working with teammates, create a list of ten businesses that sell to both consumers and businesses. Note any differences that the products may take in each of these markets.

G-W Learning Mobile Site

Visit the G-W Learning mobile site to complete the chapter pretest and posttest and to practice vocabulary using e-flash cards. If you do not have a smartphone, visit the G-W Learning companion website to access these features.

G-W Learning mobile site: www.m.g-wlearning.com

G-W Learning companion website: www.g-wlearning.com

Unit 3 **Marketplace Dynamics**

Building the Marketing Plan

No business exists in a vacuum. Competition is everywhere, especially through the Internet. Markets and customer preferences change. To compete and be successful, marketing managers must have the most current information about their customers' wants and needs to fulfill them. Marketers must also know everything about their business competitors. Research is vital to a marketing team to help the business thrive and grow.

Part 1 **Research the Competition**

Objectives

*   Identify and research the main competitors for your business.
*   Create a competitive analysis.

Directions

In this activity, you will develop the subsection of Situation Analysis that addresses your competition. Access the *Marketing Dynamics* companion website at www.g-wlearning.com. Download data files as indicated for the following activities.

1. Unit Activity 3-1. Competition. As marketing manager for your company, it is important to recognize the competition.
2. Unit Activity 3-2. Competitive Analysis. Use this document to create a competitive analysis grid that will be included in the Appendix of your Marketing Plan.
3. Open your saved Marketing Plan document.
4. Locate the Situation Analysis section, then the Competition subsection. Make notes on the research you did for the competition, and refer the reader to the Appendix for the competitive analysis.
5. Save your document.

Part 2 **Complete a SWOT Analysis**

Objectives

*   Assess your company's strengths, weaknesses, opportunities, and threats.
*   Create a SWOT Analysis for your company.

Directions

In this activity, you will assess your business as it compares to the competition to continue creating the Situation Analysis. Access the *Marketing Dynamics* companion website at www.g-wlearning.com. Download data files as indicated for the following activities.

1. Unit Activity 3-3. Company Assessment. Complete the research necessary to do a SWOT analysis.
2. Unit Activity 3-4. SWOT Analysis. Use this document to create a SWOT analysis that will be included in the Appendix of your marketing plan.
3. Open your saved marketing plan document.
4. Locate the Situation Analysis section, and then the Competition subsection. Make notes on the research you did and refer the reader to the Appendix for the SWOT analysis.
5. Use the suggestions and questions listed in the marketing plan template to help you generate ideas. Delete the instructions and questions when you are finished recording your responses. Proofread your document and correct any errors in keyboarding, spelling, and grammar.
6. Save your document.

Part 3 **Determine the Target Market**

Objective

- Identify the target market for your company's.

Directions

In this activity, you will conduct research to determine who is most likely to purchase your products or services, or your target market(s). Access the *Marketing Dynamics* companion website at www.g-wlearning.com. Download the data file as indicated for the following activity.

1. Unit Activity 3-5. Target Market Analysis. Based on the products and services of your company, define your target market. Who are the people or businesses most likely to buy from your business?
2. Open your saved marketing plan document.
3. Locate the Situation Analysis section, then the Target Market subsection. Make notes on the research you did and refer the reader to the Appendix for the target market analysis.
4. Use the suggestions and questions listed in the marketing plan template to help you generate ideas. Delete the instructions and questions when you are finished recording your responses. Proofread your document and correct any errors in keyboarding, spelling, and grammar.
5. Save your document.

Part 4 **Complete a Customer Profile**

Objective

- Define a typical customer within your target market to create a customer profile.

Directions

Information about your target market's needs and product preferences is very important to any marketing plan. In this activity, you will create a customer profile representative of the target market for your business. Access the *Marketing Dynamics* companion website at www.g-wlearning.com. Download the data file as indicated for the following activity.

1. Unit Activity 3-6. Customer Profile. Use this document to create a customer profile containing as much information as possible about your typical target market customer including product preferences.
2. Open your saved marketing plan document.
3. Locate the Situation Analysis section, then the Target Market subsection. Make notes on the research you did and refer the reader to the Appendix for the customer profile.
4. Use the suggestions and questions listed in the marketing plan template to help you generate ideas. Delete the instructions and questions when you are finished recording your responses. Proofread your document and correct any errors in keyboarding, spelling, and grammar.
5. Save your document.

Marketing Plan

This part of the marketing plan calls for students to research competition for the company they have selected to write a marketing plan. Students will have an opportunity to create grids and surveys that will be placed in the appendix of the plan. In order for students to complete a realistic marketing plan, they will need to get to know the company well through personal interviews, web pages, or other research. This can be a major research activity. Or if you prefer, you can direct students to find just the information they need to complete this part of the plan.

Product Dynamics

Chapters

Eye-Catcher

Jeff Schultes/Shutterstock.com

Marketing Matters

To marketers, product can mean a number of things. Product can be a consumer good, business service, brand, store, person, or even a website. Product is anything with an identity that needs attention brought to it through marketing efforts. For example, Macy's is a department store chain that sells many thousands of products. However, Macy's is also a product with its own logo and brand identity. Here, the marketers for Macy's flagship store in New York City are positioning it as *the world's largest store*.

Marketing Core Functions Covered in This Unit

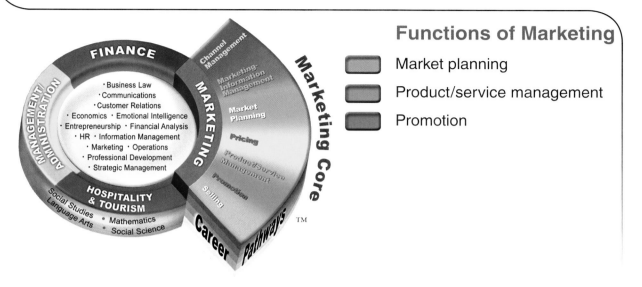

Functions of Marketing

- Market planning
- Product/service management
- Promotion

Developing a Vision

A marketer would not have a job if product did not exist. Product is the heart of any business. Product is the starting point for the marketing mix. Price, place, and promotion only happen because a business has a product or service to sell. New offerings are important for a business to remain competitive. By reviewing the life cycle of current products, it can be determined what is necessary to sustain profits and generate growth.

However, marketing decisions do not end here. Success depends on customer recognition and awareness. Branding is how a marketer distinguishes product in the marketplace. Creating a branding strategy can determine the success or failure for a business.

15 Products and Services

Section 15.1 | What Is Product?
Section 15.2 | Product Planning
Section 15.3 | Product Life Cycles

"Innovation has nothing to do with how many research and development dollars you have. When Apple came up with the Mac, IBM was spending at least 100 times more on R&D. It's not about money. It's about the people you have, how you're led, and how much you get it."

—Steve Jobs, cofounder of Apple, Inc.

College and Career Readiness

Reading Prep
Before reading this chapter, go to the end of the chapter and read the summary. The chapter summary highlights important information presented in the chapter. Did this exercise help you prepare to understand the content?

Check Your Marketing IQ

Before you begin the chapter, see what you already know about marketing by taking the chapter pretest. If you do not have a smartphone, visit the G-W Learning companion website.
G-W Learning mobile site: www.m.g-wlearning.com
G-W Learning companion website: www.g-wlearning.com

G-W Mobile

Explore

Assign the College and Career Readiness Reading Prep activity before students read the chapter. Reading Prep activities give students opportunity to apply the Common Core State Standards.

Engage

Assign the Chapter 15 pretest. The test may be accessed by using the QR code or going to the companion website. Discuss which questions students were unable to answer

◇DECA Emerging Leaders

Principles of Hospitality and Tourism Event

Career Cluster: Hospitality and Tourism
Instructional Area: Economics

Performance Indicators

- Explain the principles of supply and demand.
- Describe the functions of prices in markets.
- Explain the concept of economic resources.
- Identify factors affecting a business's profit.

Purpose

Designed for first-year DECA members who are enrolled in introductory-level principles of marketing/business courses, the event measures the individual's ability to explain core business concepts in the format of a content interview in a role-play. This event consists of a 100-question, multiple-choice, business administration core exam and a content interview. Participants are not informed in advance of the performance indicators to be evaluated.

Procedure

1. The event will be presented to you through your reading of these instructions, including the Performance Indicators and Interview Situation. You will have up to 10 minutes to review this information to determine how you will handle the role-play situation and demonstrate the performance indicators of this event. During the preparation period, you may make notes to use during the role-play situation.
2. You will have up to 10 minutes to role-play your situation with a judge. You may have more than one judge.
3. You will be evaluated on how well you meet the performance indicators of this event.
4. Turn in all your notes and event materials when you have completed the role-play.

Interview Situation

You are to assume the role of candidate for a business operations manager position at the Plaza Hotel, a 500-room hotel located five blocks from the site of the upcoming Super Bowl. You have submitted your résumé and have been invited in for a face-to-face interview with the **human resources director (judge).** This interview will be used to measure your knowledge and understanding of an aspect of business. The human resources director wants to make sure you understand economic concepts necessary for setting prices and profit goals before offering you the business operations manager position.

In the first part of your interview, you will explain the principles of supply and demand, pricing implications for hospitality and tourism-related businesses and the additional performance indicators listed on the first page of this event. Following your explanation, the human resources director will ask you to respond to additional questions.

The interview will take place in the human resources director's conference room. The human resources director will begin the interview by greeting you and asking to hear your ideas on economic principles that influence prices and profits. After you have provided your explanation and have answered the human resources director's questions, the human resources director will conclude the interview by thanking you for your presentation.

Critical Thinking

1. How are hotel prices impacted by a city hosting the Super Bowl?
2. Why should the hotel monitor the prices charged by competing hotels for the Super Bowl?

Visit www.deca.org for more information.

Section 15.1 What Is Product?

Objectives

After completing this section, you will be able to
- **define** product.
- **describe** the elements of product.
- **explain** how the characteristics of services differ from those of goods.

Key Terms

feature	warranty
option	guarantee
quality	intangible
usage	inseparability
direction	variability
installation	perishability
packaging	

Web Connect

Visit the website of an automobile manufacturer or dealer. Select a vehicle that you would like to buy. Describe the basic product and the available options. What target market do the options appeal to? How does the availability of these options give the car a competitive edge?

Critical Thinking

Recall a product you or a family member used *before* reading the directions. What was the outcome? Why did you or the family member choose to not read the directions first?

Understanding Product

In Chapter 2, you learned that a product is anything that can be bought or sold. Product is the primary *P* of the marketing mix because it is the first element of the marketing mix to be decided. The other marketing mix decisions—place, price, and promotion, are based on the product decision. If you do not have a product to sell, you do not need the other elements of the marketing mix.

A product is whatever the business sells to satisfy customer needs. That product can be a good, a service, or an idea. Recall that goods are physical products; services are activities performed by others; and ideas are concepts.

What does a customer actually buy when he or she buys a product? When you buy an automobile, are you buying just metal, cloth, plastic,

and glass formed into a machine? Or, are you are really buying the ability to safely and easily travel from one place to another? You may also be buying independence and prestige.

Many products are combinations of both goods and services. Imagine that you are having a nice dinner in a restaurant. What is the product of that restaurant? Is it a good or a service? Actually, it is both. The food itself is a tangible good. The restaurant atmosphere and its food preparation and presentation are services for which you pay.

FYI

The need-satisfying quality of a product is considered a *product benefit*.

Explore

Provide an opportunity for students to explore by assigning a hands-on activity. Review the vocabulary terms at the beginning of the section. Where have students encountered these terms before? Help students make educated guesses about the meanings of the terms with which they are least familiar.

Resource

Use the Chapter 15 presentation on the optional Instructor's Presentations for PowerPoint® CD as an outline for presenting the chapter.

Products can be seen as being on a continuum, or a range, as shown in Figure 15-1. On the left end, the products are pure goods. On the right end, the products are pure services, for example, tutoring. In between are the products with varying combinations of goods and services.

Product Elements

Products have some elements that can be changed to meet customer needs. These elements can be organized into three categories: features, usage, and protection, as shown in Figure 15-2. Marketers work closely with the product development team to determine which elements are important to the target market(s).

Features

Features are facts about a product or service. For example, the physical features of a smartphone include its size and color. Depending on the product, some features may also include additional services. For example, other features of the smartphone

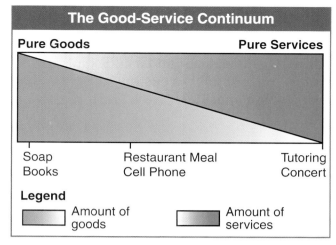

Goodheart-Willcox Publisher

Figure 15-1 Many products are a combination of goods and services. Where would some of the products you use fit on this continuum?

could be the available apps and data plans. The marketer decides which features to include in a product. The features of a product include its options and quality.

Options

An *option* is a feature that can be added to a product by customer request. Many products have a basic design to which some

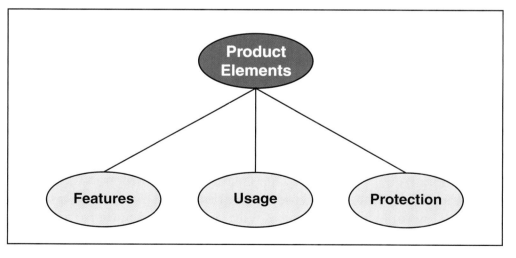

Goodheart-Willcox Publisher

Figure 15-2 Marketers consider many elements when making product decisions.

features can be added. Sometimes, options are called *optional features*. For example, options on an automobile might include a sunroof, leather seats, and a GPS. Options enable the customer to customize the product to his or her specific needs and wants.

Quality

Quality is the degree of a product's excellence. There are three general quality levels: premium, moderate, and value. Price and quality are often directly related.

Premium Quality. *Premium quality* is the highest level of quality available in products. Premium-quality products usually have the highest prices. This is because they have the highest quality of materials and artisanship.

For example, the US Department of Agriculture (USDA) assigns quality standards to certain food products, such as meat or eggs. Quality standards describe the entire range of quality for a product. The number of quality grades varies by product. The USDA Prime or Grade AA symbol means that the product meets the highest level of product-quality standards. In clothing, high-end designer brands tend to offer the highest quality.

Moderate Quality. *Moderate quality* is the middle range of product quality. It usually combines good-quality materials with moderate prices. For example, the USDA Choice or Grade A symbol means that the product meets the middle level of product-quality standards. Most department-store clothing brands are typically of moderate quality.

Value Quality. *Value quality* is an adequate level of product quality. Value-quality goods are typically functional. For example, the USDA Select or Grade B symbol means that the product meets the lowest level of product-quality standards. Discount-store clothing brands are usually of value quality.

Alhovik/Shutterstock.com

Premium-quality goods are often stamped or labeled with a guarantee to emphasize the quality.

Usage

Usage means the way something is used. Many products are designed to be assembled, installed, or used in a very specific way. Marketers make product decisions about how to help customers use the product correctly. If customers do not know how to properly use a product, they might become frustrated and dissatisfied. They may return the product or just never buy it again. Product usage includes the available directions, installation, and technical support.

Directions

Directions are the steps that must be carried out in a specific order to complete a task successfully. Clear directions are an essential part of many products. Some products with directions include furniture needing assembly, electronic devices, and software.

Social Media

Facebook Pages

With more than 1 billion users, Facebook is becoming a must for most businesses, both large and small. Like other social media platforms, business pages on Facebook must be created through a current personal user with an active e-mail address. Personal users create *time lines.* Businesses, organizations, and brands create *pages* to share their stories and connect with people. Like time lines, you can customize business pages by adding apps, posting stories, hosting events, and more. People who *like* your business page will get your updates in their news feeds.

The best way to use social media is to engage customers, not as just another website with products for sale. It is important to understand that building a Facebook business page will *not* automatically drive current or potential customers to your business' website. There are thousands of business pages with less than 100 fans. It is important to drive customers to *like* your Facebook page and interact with you on a regular basis. After they *like* your business on Facebook, continue to give them reasons to return and tell others about it. Facebook also offers analytics to help businesses track how many people visit the page, visitors' demographics, and other important marketing information.

Simple products may include one sheet of assembly directions. Directions for complex products are often in the form of an owner manual or user guide. Some companies provide classes or seminars to help customers learn to use their products. Computer software companies and home supply stores often provide such classes.

Installation

Installation is the act or process of making a good ready for use in a certain place. Installation is a service offered with many large or complex items. Products that require installation include appliances, carpeting, plumbing fixtures, and landscaping, to name a few. Although some customers prefer to install their own goods, many want an expert to install goods for them.

Technical Support

Technical support is the people available to help customers with any equipment or electronic problems. The availability of technical support is often very important to customers who buy complex products.

Complex consumer products include software, cable TV, and Internet service. Many home products now include a computer that directs its functions, such as appliances and home security systems. These products can develop problems from time to time in both the computerized parts of the products as well as the functional parts. Many companies selling such products offer technical support. Complex business products can include factory equipment and telecommunications systems.

Protection

Some products are fragile and some could be dangerous if not used correctly. Both the products and the users may need some form of protection. Protection is a broad category that includes safety inspections, packaging, warranties, and maintenance and repair services.

Explain
Ask students the difference between directions and instructions. Why is it important to understand the difference?

Elaborate
Why is technical support an important part of marketing?

Often, directions and user guides for complex products are also available online.

Safety Inspections

Most companies ensure product safety through internal quality control during the manufacturing process. Some products, though, also have laws mandating certain safety standards. For example, the National Highway Traffic Safety Administration regulates safety standards for automobiles. Automobile manufacturers must meet the minimum safety standards for their products to pass inspections before sale.

The safety standards for some products are set by the government through special agencies. For example, the USDA regularly inspects many food products for safe consumption. Marketers often promote product safety features because they may influence buying decisions.

Packaging

Packaging protects products until customers are ready to use them. For example, appropriate packaging is critical to keeping most food products fresh and healthful. Also, many fragile products, such as computers and lamps, must be carefully packaged to prevent damage.

The packaging of consumer products is often designed to make them easier to stack or display. It may also protect the product from theft. For example, small items are often placed in large or bulky packages to make it harder for shoplifters to hide the items.

Packaging choices that might affect buying behavior, such as design, color, and materials, are part of the marketing function. For example, using plastic bottles instead of glass for beverages and child-safety caps for medicines is important to many consumers.

Packaging also has information about the product, such as content labeling, nutritional information, and weight. Some packaging contains directions about potential safety

Companies use internal quality control inspections to ensure the safety of prducts.

Extend

Encourage a discussion on packaging, its importance, and why it is costly.

Marketing Ethics

Responsible CRM

Marketing uses customer relationship management (CRM) software in which contact information is recorded about each customer. This information has been given to the company for their specific use. It is unethical and irresponsible for a marketer to sell this list to another company unless every customer has given permission to sell his or her information.

issues from improper use. For example, the USDA requires that safe-handling instructions appear on all packages of raw and partially cooked meat and poultry. This function of packaging helps prevent the spread of food-borne illnesses.

Warranties and Guarantees

A **warranty** is a written document stating the quality of a product and promising to correct specific problems that might occur. Often, customers are concerned that an expensive item will not perform as expected. Therefore, many marketers provide warranties to assure customers of the quality and reliability of a product. For example, all new and many used automobiles have warranties. The warranty promises that the manufacturer will replace or repair some parts if they break within a certain mileage or length of time.

A **guarantee** is a promise that a product has a certain quality or will perform in a specific way. A guarantee is similar to a warranty but is not a written document. The term *guarantee* is usually used in promotions, such as "Satisfaction guaranteed, or your money back." Services often advertise guarantees. For example, some carpet cleaning services guarantee customer satisfaction or they will reclean the carpet at no charge.

Maintenance and Repair Services

Large, complex machinery, especially in the B2B market, requires regular maintenance to remain safe and in good working order. Many consumer products also require regular maintenance, such as vehicles.

When marketers develop a product that requires maintenance and repair services, they must also plan for the services. The availability of these services can affect buying decisions. Marketers are involved in helping to determine which services are necessary. For example, when purchasing a car, there are many dealer choices. Some consumers might choose the dealership with the most convenient service department or the manufacturer that includes free regular maintenance services.

Characteristics of Services

While services are also considered products, they are different from goods in four important ways. Services are intangible, inseparable, variable, and perishable. These characteristics of services can present special challenges for those who market services.

Service features are the tasks that will be completed as part of a certain service. For example, a checking account might include online banking options and interest paid on balances.

Extend
Clarify the difference between a warranty and guarantee. Which do students think is most important?

Explore
Bring in examples of warranties for the students to compare and contrast. What did they learn from this activity?

Today, services account for approximately 70 percent of GDP in the United States.

dotshock/Shutterstock.com

Intangibility

Services are **intangible,** meaning something that cannot be touched, tried out before purchase, or returned. For example, when shopping for clothing, you can feel the material and choose a color or style. You can also try on the item for proper fit. However, when seeking a service, such as event planning or legal help, you are buying the expertise of the provider.

Intangibility also presents some promotional challenges to marketers of services. Sometimes, it is difficult to show a picture of the service or give the customer a sample. As a result, marketers often try to make an intangible service seem tangible. One well-known promotional slogan for insurance services is "You're in Good Hands with Allstate." The

Allstate insurance logo is an image of two hands cupped in a supportive way much like a safety net. The slogan and image make the insurance seem more like a friend helping you in times of need.

Inseparability

Inseparability means that the creation of the service cannot be separated from its use. In other words, the service cannot be separated from the person who performs it. For example, suppose you get a haircut. The haircut does not exist until the stylist cuts your hair. Because services are inseparable from the provider, customers often think of the service and the service provider as one and the same.

Caregivers provide very important services that are inseparable from the service provider.

Monkey Business Images/Shutterstock.com

Variability

Variability means each service is nearly always unique. The service only exists once and is rarely repeated in exactly the same way. For example, you may receive a bad haircut from one stylist and a great cut from another stylist at the same salon. The product of the hair salon is not just the haircut. The service providers are also viewed by consumers as part of the service/product. So, consumers often equate the stylist with the service.

Variability can give rise to concerns about service quality and uniformity because every person is different. It is very hard to make sure that each service provider gives exactly the same quality of service. For this reason, there are *certifications*, or rigorous training programs, for many service providers.

Even with certification, providers will still perform the same services in different ways. For example, when a good hair stylist stops working for a salon, his or her clients often follow. This is because clients know exactly how the stylist performs. They do not want to take a chance on going to a different stylist. Effective training and careful monitoring of customer satisfaction and feedback can help maintain high service standards.

Perishability

Perishable refers to a physical product that will spoil or decay quickly if not used. Perishable items cannot be stored long. When applying the term **perishability** to services,

it means that because services are intangible, they cannot be stored for later use. For example, once a concert is over, the tickets have no value. Some services also require appointments to be made with the provider, such as with doctors or dentists.

Perishability can create business and marketing challenges, because unused services are simply wasted sales opportunities. For example, empty airplane or theater seats cannot be stored and sold later. There is usually only one opportunity to sell time-and-place-specific services.

Checkpoint 15.1

1. A product is whatever the business sells to satisfy customer needs. What form can a product take?
2. What is premium quality, moderate quality, and value quality?
3. What role does packaging play for a product?
4. Explain the term *service features.*
5. What is a perishable product?

Build Your Vocabulary

As you progress through this course, develop a personal glossary of marketing terms and add it to your portfolio. This will help you build your vocabulary and prepare you for a career. Write a definition for each of the following terms, and add it to your personal marketing glossary.

feature
option
quality
usage
direction
installation
packaging

warranty
guarantee
intangible
inseparability
variability
perishability

Evaluate

Assign Checkpoint questions at end of section. Assess student comprehension using the Checkpoint activity as a self-assessment tool.

Checkpoint Answers

1. A product can be a good, a service, or an idea.
2. Premium quality is the highest level of quality available, moderate quality is the middle range of product quality, and value quality is an adequate level of product quality.
3. Packaging protects a product until ready for use, makes a

product easier to stack or display in a store, protects a product from misuse, and provides product information.
4. Service features are the tasks that will be completed as part of a particular service. For example, a checking account might include online banking options and interest paid on balances.
5. Perishable is a physical product that will spoil or decay quickly if not used.

Build Your Vocabulary Answers

Definitions for these terms can be found in the glossary of this text.

Section 15.2 Product Planning

After completing this section, you will be able to
- **define** product strategy.
- **describe** the product mix.
- **explain** why product/service management is a function of marketing.

product planning
product mix
product line
product item
product width
product depth
consumer product
convenience good
shopping good
specialty good
business product
product/service management
product manager
category manager

Visit the website of a company that manufactures a large number of consumer products, such as Procter & Gamble, Kraft, or General Electric. List their product lines and the individual brands in each line. Do they sell a different line of products in foreign countries?

Choose a familiar product and think about all of the raw materials that went into the making of that product. After you list them, research how the product is made. Was your list correct?

Product Strategy

Recall that *product strategy* is all of the decisions made about a given product. The first decision made by any business is to select which products it will offer. Some businesses offer only one product or service, such as carpet cleaning or furnace repair. However, many businesses sell more than one type of product.

Product planning is the process of deciding which product elements to include that will appeal to the target market. These decisions are made with the target customer profile in mind. Product planning helps marketers make product decisions to distinguish their products from others.

Product Mix

A **product mix** is all of the products and services that a business sells. Small businesses may only sell a few products, while large corporations can offer thousands of different products. Usually the product mix consists of products and services that relate to each other in some way. For example, the product mix for a local stationery store may include specialty paper, greeting cards, pens, and printing custom invitations.

Products are generally organized into product lines. A **product line** is the group of closely related products within the product mix. For example, a shoe store may sell several different lines of shoes, such as athletic, dress, and casual shoes.

The product lines of this bath department include towels, rugs, and bath accessories.

Galina Barskaya/Shutterstock.com

A **product item** is the specific model, color, or size of products in a line. For example, the product items in a shoe store will include the different styles, colors, and sizes of shoes. Perhaps the store has five identical, size-nine brown shoes. They are not considered different items, but the quantity (five) of one item (size-nine brown shoes).

The **product width** is the number of product lines a company offers. **Product depth** is the number of product items within a product line. As discussed in an earlier chapter, products are grouped by those sold mainly to consumers and those sold mainly to businesses. Some goods and services are used by both groups.

Consumer Products

Consumer products are those sold to consumers for their personal use, as in B2C. The three basic categories of consumer products are convenience goods, shopping goods, and specialty goods, as shown in Figure 15-3.

Convenience goods are goods that are usually bought often with little effort and for immediate use. Convenience goods include most grocery items and gasoline. The target market for convenience goods is broad and may only be limited by location.

Shopping goods are goods usually purchased after making the effort to compare price, quality, and style in more than one store. Shopping goods are purchased less often than convenience goods. They include more expensive, durable items such as appliances and furniture. The target markets for specialty goods are narrower and are defined by demographics and price preference.

Specialty goods are unique items that consumers are willing to spend considerable time, effort, and money to buy. Examples of specialty products include a unique sports car or rare antiques. Specialty goods have the smallest target markets because fewer people have the time, money, or desire to expend the effort to find unique goods.

Business Products

Business products are items sold to businesses to keep them operating, as in B2B. The target markets for business products are based primarily on the business type and how the products are used. Business products tend to fall into one of the following six categories.

Raw materials are natural or man-made materials that become part of a manufactured product. Raw materials include substances such as wood, plastic pellets, or metal. They are sold to various manufacturers for different uses.

Process materials are used in product manufacturing, but are not identifiable in the final product. Process materials include products such as food preservatives or industrial glue. They are sold to different product manufacturers.

Component parts become a part of a finished product but are already assembled. Component parts are items like computer chips, tires, or switches. They are sold to companies that produce final products, such as car or computer manufacturers.

Major equipment is the large machines and other equipment used for production purposes, such as furnaces, cranes, or conveyors. Every size and type of manufacturing company needs different equipment. So, the type of machinery actually determines which companies need it.

Office equipment and supplies are products for basic office needs. These products may include computers, calculators, paper, pens, and other office items. Every type of business needs these products.

Business services are the tasks necessary to keep the business running. Business services can include such activities as building maintenance, equipment repair, or accounting. Different businesses require different services, so target markets for services vary greatly.

FYI

Each category of business product has a different marketing strategy.

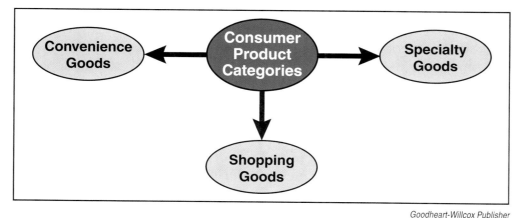

Figure 15-3 The categories of consumer products are important because they are marketed very differently.

Goodheart-Willcox Publisher

Every piece of this fuel refinery company started as a business product. Someone in this company was responsible for buying the products used to create the business as well as run the business.

Christian Lagerek/Shutterstock.com

Product/Service Management

The organizational structure that manages the development, marketing, and sale of a product or products is called **product/service management.** Successful marketers constantly review their product mixes to determine if those products are meeting the market demands. Companies may choose to change the product mix by adding or removing products. They may also create brand new products or change existing products to meet different customer needs.

A **product manager** is a marketing professional who guides the selection of products and oversees the marketing and sales of those products. The product manager is one part of the team responsible for company profits. A **category manager** performs the same functions as a product manager but is responsible for an entire category of products.

Product managers work closely with many areas in a company to make sure profit goals are met. For example, they may get constant updates on the profits or losses for each product from accounting. Product managers help the sales team learn how to sell products to different markets. They help prepare product sales forecasts and monitor inventory levels.

Since part of managing products is driving successful promotions, product managers also work closely with the advertising department or an outside ad agency. Underlying all of these functions, product managers need current and accurate marketing research based on the right variables. It is the research that justifies a large capital investment to develop any new products that are needed. New product development is discussed in more detail in the next chapter.

Evaluate

Assign Checkpoint questions at end of section. Assess student comprehension using the Checkpoint activity as a self-assessment tool.

Explore

If possible, ask someone in a marketing position to speak to the class about the different roles a product manager or category manager plays in a company.

Exploring Careers

Public Relations

Presenting a positive image to customers and others is important to the success of an organization. People who work in public relations (PR) help businesses and other organizations make a favorable public impression, which is part of marketing's responsibility. Typical job titles for these positions include *public relations director, communications specialist, community affairs manager,* and *press secretary.* Public relations professionals may work for businesses, government agencies, or other organizations.

Some examples of tasks that PR professionals perform include:

- Work with others to promote the organization's image, activities, or brands.
- Prepare press releases, write newsletters, maintain blogs, give presentations, and answer questions from the media or the public.
- Arrange for company executives to give speeches or presentations, which they may also help to write.
- Work with community groups or charities the organization sponsors.

PR professionals need strong communications and human-relations skills. Computer skills in word processing, desktop publishing, and webpage creation are also important. A bachelor degree in communications, public relations, marketing, or related studies is required for many jobs in this field. Managers and directors may be required to have several years of work experience in public relations. For more information, access the *Occupational Outlook Handbook* online.

Checkpoint 15.2

1. List the basic categories of consumer products.
2. List the different categories of business products.
3. Which are purchased less often—shopping goods or convenience goods?
4. What are business services?
5. Why do specialty goods have the smallest target markets?

Build Your Vocabulary

As you progress through this course, develop a personal glossary of marketing terms and add it to your portfolio. This will help you build your vocabulary and prepare you for a career. Write a definition for each of the following terms, and add it to your personal marketing glossary.

product planning	convenience good
product mix	shopping good
product line	specialty good
product item	business product
product width	product/service management
product depth	product manager
consumer product	category manager

Section 15.3 Product Life Cycles

Product Stages

Part of the product-management process includes reviewing the product life cycle. The product life cycle is the stages a product or a product category goes through from its beginning to end. The complete life cycle of a product can be long or short. For example, certain products, such as computers or cell phones, can have a short life cycle due to rapidly changing technology. Depending on the product, the length of each stage within the life cycle also varies.

Marketers are always reviewing which stage of the product life cycle their products are in. This is due to the fact that marketing efforts differ for products in each stage. Figure 15-4 illustrates the four product life cycle stages: introduction, growth, maturity, and decline.

Introduction Stage

The introduction stage is the time when a new product is first brought to the market. Usually, very few people know about the product. At this stage in the life cycle, marketers focus heavily on promotions explaining the new product and its benefits. Sales tend to be low until more people learn about why they should buy the product. Profits are also lower in the introduction stage due to low sales and higher costs.

Production costs for a new product tend to be higher because, until demand increases, fewer are made. In addition, the company has already invested a large amount of money on market research, product development, production, and promotion. The company expects the investment will be recovered as the product begins to sell. Profits tend to rise

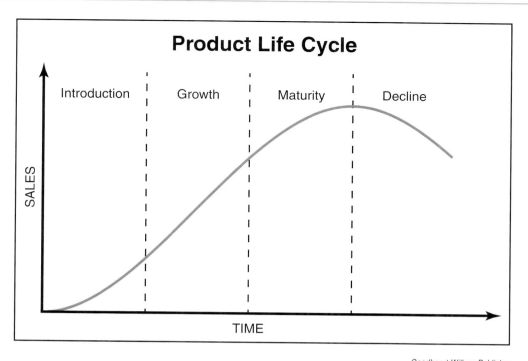

Figure 15-4 A product life cycle is based on the overall industry sales of that product over time.

Goodheart-Willcox Publisher

later in the product life cycle due to increased sales and decreased production costs.

Growth Stage

The **growth stage** is the period in which product sales increase rapidly. To keep product sales high, new models of the product may be introduced. Modifications may also be made to the product to keep customers interested or meet new needs.

As the product becomes more successful, competitors enter the market. Now there are many companies competing for customers. During the growth stage, marketers focus on promotions distinguishing their brands from the competition. They also use strategies to build brand loyalty.

FYI

Marketers may focus on adding features to products in the growth stage of the product life cycle. New product features should provide new benefits and beat the competition.

Maturity Stage

The **maturity stage** occurs when product sales are stable. Sales are no longer increasing quickly, nor are they decreasing. Maturity can happen when the market becomes saturated with a product or when a newer, better product is introduced to fill the consumer need. A **saturated market** is one in which most of the potential customers who need, want, and can afford a product have bought it. No more people will buy in a saturated market unless their current product runs out, breaks, or the market expands.

During the maturity stage, competition for customers is very intense. At this stage, marketers look for new ways a product could be used. Or, they identify new markets for the product to avoid losing revenue.

Decline Stage

Mature products eventually enter the decline stage. Product sales begin to decrease during the **decline stage**. If sales decline

Case in Point

L.L. Bean

Listening to the customer is an important marketing task. Customer input about new products usually leads to corporate success. L.L. Bean is a retail company well known for listening to its customers. It has a process for interviewing product users and performs follow-up meetings for user feedback. To test product quality and performance, L.L. Bean has a team of 1,300 independent field testers who personally test products under various conditions and report results to the company.

Also unique to the industry, the company has its own independent lab for testing and revising products until they meet the most stringent standards. Products continue to be tested, even while they are in the marketplace, to ensure the highest quality. And it does not stop there. Customer service is also considered an extremely important component of the business. Employees are trained to provide outstanding customer service whether on the telephone, in person, or through social media. In the words of president Chris McCormick, "Superior customer service has always been and always will be the cornerstone of our brand and heritage and an attribute that differentiates us from the rest of the pack. It goes back to L.L.'s golden rule of treating customers like human beings."

rapidly, marketers may advise the company to stop making or selling the product. Decline often occurs when a new technology is growing rapidly, so the older products become obsolete quickly.

Deciding whether a product is truly at the end of its life cycle can be tricky for marketers. A decline in sales does not always mean the product is in the decline stage. For example, in an economic recession, sales for big-ticket items like cars may decline quickly because consumers need to save money. However, that does not mean that cars are at the end of their life cycle.

Product Life Cycles Impact the Marketing Mix

Recall that the *product/service management marketing function* determines which products a business should offer as well as how to market them. Frequent review of products to determine their life cycle stages is part of the product/

service management function of marketing. Knowing the life cycle stage of their products helps marketers develop effective marketing-mix strategies, as shown in Figure 15-5.

Some businesses choose to offer products that are in a certain life cycle stage. For example, discount stores may buy a large amount of discontinued products at the end of the product life cycle. Because the life cycle for these products is nearly over, the business can buy them for an extremely low price. And, due to the low cost, the business can still make a profit when reselling the goods at discount-store prices.

After a product completes its life cycle, a new product or service may be needed to replace lost revenue. Marketers, however, must take care when they evaluate an individual product.

Product

As a business matures, the market needs and wants may change. Therefore, the product mix may need adjustment to remain

Explore

Ask students to name other products that are marketed for various uses, such as baking soda.

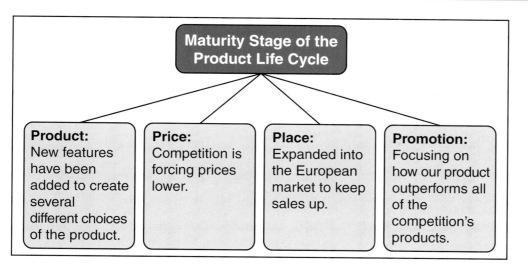

Goodheart-Willcox Publisher

Figure 15-5 This product, for example, is in the maturity stage of the product life cycle.

competitive. One option to keep sales from declining is to develop new uses for the current product. A classic example is Arm & Hammer baking soda. The original use for baking soda was as an ingredient in homemade baked goods. As fewer people baked at home, baking soda sales declined. Through market research, Arm & Hammer found that some customers were using baking soda to deodorize refrigerators, clean rugs, and brush their teeth. Arm & Hammer began to market its baking soda as an essential cleaning product, and sales rose. Arm & Hammer now sells products, such as toothpaste and laundry detergent, with baking soda as the differentiating feature.

Price

Marketers use different pricing strategies at varying stages of the product life cycle. For example, during introduction, prices are often higher because the product is new and there is no competition. Plus, the business needs to recoup its development costs. During the maturity stage, however, prices are often lowered because there is more competition to force competitive pricing strategies. During the decline stage, prices are often at their lowest to stimulate slow sales.

Explore

Ask students to select a product that has changed either in form or delivery. Direct them to draw a flow chart of the product life cycle for that product.

Place

One way to prevent declining sales in a maturity stage is to search for new markets that need or want the product. This search may lead marketers to expand into the global market. Or, marketers may look for a new delivery system, such as through the Internet.

Some countries may not yet have products that are popular in the United States. However, before launching a product in a foreign market, marketers must perform market research. Research is necessary to determine if the new market would be large enough to be profitable for the company.

Promotion

Promotions and the marketing message change throughout the product life cycle. During the introduction stage, promotions inform customers about the product, explain its benefits, and persuade them to buy. During the growth and maturity stages, promotions make the case for customers to choose one seller over another. During the decline stage, promotions often focus on low prices to increase sales.

Engage

Give examples of a product that is in decline and how they are promoted.

For example, before 1984, few people knew about inline skates. Then the Rollerblade® company introduced inline skating as a cool, new sport to sell its brand of inline skates. To gain customer notice and get customers to try the new skates, Rollerblade gave free inline skates to rental shops in trendy Venice Beach, California. Needless to say, the product entered the growth stage quickly after the introductory promotion.

In the introduction stage of the product life cycle, one producer usually takes the lead in introducing, marketing, and selling the new product. For the inline skate category, that leader was Rollerblade. Once Rollerblade made inline skates popular, competitors started entering the market. There are now many manufacturers, including K2 Skates and numerous foreign companies.

AMA members have the option to earn the organization's prestigious credential of Professional Certified Marketer (PCM). To earn the title, members must pass a rigorous exam and keep their certification current by attending AMA conferences and other continuing education opportunities. PCM certification helps professional marketers stand out in a competitive job market.
www.marketingpower.com

Checkpoint 15.3

1. What is the focus of marketers during the introduction stage of a new product?
2. What takes place during the maturity stage?
3. At what stage in the product life cycle are prices generally at a high level?
4. What do marketers focus on during the introduction stage of a product?
5. Name one way to prevent declining sales in a mature stage of a product.

Build Your Vocabulary

As you progress through this course, develop a personal glossary of marketing terms and add it to your portfolio. This will help you build your vocabulary and prepare you for a career. Write a definition for each of the following terms, and add it to your personal marketing glossary.
product life cycle
introduction stage
growth stage
maturity stage
saturated market
decline stage

Evaluate

Assign Checkpoint questions at end of section. Assess student comprehension using the Checkpoint activity as a self-assessment tool.

Checkpoint Answers

1. Marketers focus heavily on promotions explaining a new product and its benefits at this stage in the life cycle.
2. During the maturity stage, competition for customers is very intense; product sales are stable.
3. During introduction, prices are often higher because the product is new and there is no competition.
4. During the introduction stage, marketers focus on promotions to inform customers about the product, explains its benefits, and persuade them to buy.
5. One way to prevent declining sales in a mature stage is to search for new markets that need or want the product.

Build Your Vocabulary Answers

Definitions for these terms can be found in the glossary of this text.

Chapter Summary

Section 15.1 What Is Product?

- A product is anything that can be bought or sold. Product is the primary *P* of the marketing mix because it is the first element of the marketing mix to be decided.
- Tangible products, or goods, have many elements that can be changed to meet customers' needs. These elements can be organized into three categories: features, usage, and protection.
- While services are also considered products, they are different from tangible goods in four important ways. Services are intangible, inseparable, variable, and perishable.

Section 15.2 Product Planning

- Product strategy consists of all the decisions made about the product. It starts with the decision about which product to offer and progresses to decisions about the various elements of the product. Product planning is the process of deciding which features and services a product will have.
- A product mix is all of the products and services that a business sells. A product line is the group of closely related products within the product mix, and the product width is the number of product lines a company offers.
- The organizational structure that manages the development, marketing, and sale of a product or products is called product/service management.

Section 15.3 Product Life Cycles

- The product life cycle is the stages a product or a product category goes through from its beginning to end. The four stages of the product life cycle are introduction, growth, maturity, and decline.
- Frequently reviewing products to determine their life-cycle stages is part of the product/service management function. Knowing which life cycle stage their products are in helps marketers develop effective marketing mix strategies.

Review Your Knowledge

1. Name the elements of a tangible product.
2. What is the purpose of technical support in an organization?
3. Name the characteristics of services.
4. What is the difference between a product line and product width?
5. Give an example of a convenience good.
6. Define raw materials.
7. Why is product management an important responsibility for marketers?
8. Name two positions that are generally responsible for product management in an organization.
9. When is competition generally intense for a product?
10. Which function of marketing includes frequent review of product to determine life cycle stages?

Apply Your Knowledge

1. In earlier chapters, you identified the product or service for which you are creating a marketing plan. What is the product or service you will be marketing? Is it for a business-to-business market or business-to-consumer market?

2. If you are marketing a product, there are three elements on which you will focus: features, usage, and protection. Create a chart for each product that you are marketing and define each one of the elements as they pertain to the product. If you are marketing a service, create a chart for each service that describes its characteristics of intangible, inseparable, variable, and perishable.

3. Your business will more than likely offer a warranty or guarantee. Describe the protection that is offered for your product or service. Create a document for the warranty or guarantee if none exists on the website of your business.

4. Write a set of directions or instructions on how to use your product.

5. Describe the packaging for your product and why it is important.

6. Describe the product mix for your business.

7. Describe the product line for your business.

8. If you are marketing consumer products, which category do your products fit: convenience goods, shopping goods, or specialty goods? If you are marketing business products, which category do your products fit?

9. Draw an illustration for your product to show its life cycle.

10. Search a job search website, such as CareerOneStop at www.ajb.dni.us or www.monster.com, for jobs as a product manager or category manager. Choose a job that appeals to you. What are the qualifications for the job? What does a person in the job do? Would you like this job? Explain why or why not.

6. *Raw materials* are natural or man-made materials that become part of a manufactured product. Raw materials include substances such as wood, plastic pellets, or metal. They are sold to various manufacturers for different uses.

7. Successful marketers constantly review their company's product mix to determine if those products are meeting the market demands. Companies may choose to change the marketing mix by adding or removing products. They may also create brand new products or change existing products to meet different customer needs.

8. Two positions that are generally responsible for product management in an organization are product managers or category managers.

9. During the maturity stage, competition for customers is very intense. At this stage, marketers look for new ways that customers might use a product.

10. Frequently reviewing products to determine their lifecycle stages is part of the product and service management function of marketing.

Apply Your Knowledge Answers

Student answers will vary for questions 1–10.

Apply Your Knowledge Teaching Tip

At the end of this unit, students will write the next phase of the marketing plan. Please note that the Apply Your Knowledge Questions prepare students for the next installment of the marketing plan that they are writing at the end of each unit. These questions help them assume the role of a marketing manager and begin applying concepts learned in the chapter. If your class is not participating in the marketing plan activity at the end of the unit, Apply Your Knowledge questions can be used by directing students to select a business of their choice and answer each question about that business.

Marketing Plan

The marketing plan is now taking shape. The activities for this unit are time-consuming. You may want to assign the first part of the marketing plan as students finish this chapter. Or, you may prefer for them to do the entire activity at the end of the unit.

Check Your Marketing IQ

Now that you have finished the chapter, see what you learned about marketing by taking the chapter posttest. If you do not have a smartphone, visit the G-W Learning companion website.

G-W Learning mobile site: www.m.g-wlearning.com
G-W Learning companion website: www.g-wlearning.com

College and Career Readiness

Common Core

CTE Career Ready Practices. Everyone has a stake in protecting the environment. Taking steps as an individual to be more environmentally conscious is a behavior of responsible citizens. From a business standpoint, it may also help a company be more profitable. What things can marketers do in the workplace to save energy or other resources?

Reading. Read a magazine, newspaper, or online article about product life cycles. Measure the validity of the article and the evidence that is presented. Provide an accurate summary of your reading, making sure to incorporate the *who*, *what*, *when*, and *how* of this situation.

Writing. Gather relevant information from multiple print and digital resources that discuss product strategy. Assess the credibility of each source and integrate your findings in several paragraphs.

Teamwork

Following directions can be a challenging assignment. Working with a teammate, test your ability to write clear directions. Each person should write steps on how to fill a gas tank. Exchange your directions with your teammate. Which set of directions was more complete?

G-W Learning Mobile Site

Visit the G-W Learning mobile site to complete the chapter pretest and posttest and to practice vocabulary using e-flash cards. If you do not have a smartphone, visit the G-W Learning companion website to access these features.

G-W Learning mobile site: www.m.g-wlearning.com
G-W Learning companion website: www.g-wlearning.com

Evaluate

Evaluate the students' understanding and knowledge. Assign the Chapter 15 posttest. The test may be accessed by using the QR code or going to the companion website. What questions were students able to answer that they couldn't when they took the pretest?

16 New Product Development

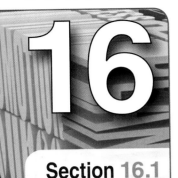

Section 16.1	New Products
Section 16.2	New Product Development Process

"People shop and learn in a whole new way compared to just a few years ago, so marketers need to adapt or risk extinction"

—Brian Halligan, CEO and cofounder of HubSpot

College and Career Readiness

Reading Prep
Before reading this chapter, look at all of the illustrations. Illustrations help readers visualize the situations presented in the content. What can you predict will be covered in the chapter?

Check Your Marketing IQ

Before you begin the chapter, see what you already know about marketing by taking the chapter pretest. If you do not have a smartphone, visit the G-W Learning companion website.
G-W Learning mobile site: www.m.g-wlearning.com
G-W Learning companion website: www.g-wlearning.com

G-W Mobile

Engage
Assign the Chapter 16 pretest. The test may be accessed by using the QR code or going to the companion website. Discuss which questions students were unable to answer.

Explore
Provide an opportunity for students to explore by assigning a hands-on activity. Assign the College and Career Readiness Reading Prep activity before students read the chapter. Reading Prep activities give students opportunity to apply the Common Core State Standards.

◇DECA Emerging Leaders

Buying and Merchandising Team Decision-Making Event, Part 1

Career Cluster: Marketing
Instructional Area: Product/Service Management Promotion

General Performance Indicators

- Communications skills—the ability to exchange information and ideas with others through writing, speaking, reading, or listening
- Analytical skills—the ability to derive facts from data, findings from facts, conclusions from findings, and recommendations from conclusions
- Production skills—the ability to take a concept from an idea and make it real
- Teamwork—the ability to be an effective member of a productive group
- Priorities/time management—the ability to determine priorities and manage time commitments
- Economic competencies

Specific Performance Indicators

- Describe factors used by marketers to position products.
- Explain the nature of product/service branding.
- Describe the use of grades and standards in marketing.
- Explain the nature of a promotional plan.
- Coordinate activities in the promotional mix.
- Explain the role of promotion as a marketing function.
- Demonstrate connections between company actions and results.

Purpose

Designed for a team of two DECA members, the event measures the team's ability to explain core business concepts in the format of a case study in a role-play. This event consists of a 100-question, multiple-choice, cluster exam for each team member and a decision-making case study situation. The Team Decision-Making Event provides an opportunity for participants to analyze one or a combination of elements essential to the effective operation of a business in the specific career area presented as a case study.

For the purposes of this text, you will be presented with the material for this event in two parts. Part 1 presents the knowledge and skills assessed and an overview of the event's purpose and procedure. Part 2 presents the remaining procedures and the event situation.

Procedure, Part 1

1. For Part 1 in this text, read both sets of performance indicators. Discuss these with your team members.
2. If there are any questions, ask your teacher to clarify.

Critical Thinking

1. Explain the relationship between the specific performance indicators and the case study situation.
2. Discuss with your team member how you will incorporate the performance indicators in your presentation.

Visit www.deca.org for more information.

Section 16.1 New Products

Objectives

After completing this section, you will be able to
- **define** new products.
- **list** the six categories of new products.
- **explain** why creativity is important in new product development.
- **describe** why new products can be risky.

Key Terms

new product
repackaging
repositioning
creativity

Web Connect

Visit the website of the Product Development & Management Association. How can membership in this organization help you in a career in product development and management?

Critical Thinking

Over the years, marketing has taken a more active role in new product development. How do you think this evolution happened? Why do you think that marketers should contribute to developing new product for a business?

What Products Are *New*?

It has been said that "there is nothing new under the sun." If this statement is true, then no products could really be considered *new*. Often, a small change to an existing product is considered to be a new product. However, because new technology has changed the way the world works, there are more really new products than ever before. For practical purposes, a **new product** is a product that is different in some way from existing products. That difference may be minor or major.

New products may replace those at the end of their life cycles. Often, new products are developed to meet a specific need, such as the polio vaccine or a shampoo to reduce dandruff. Others are developed to meet a

new want, such as faster computers or equipment for a new sport. Most new products, though, are minor variations of existing products. For example, many familiar foods are recreated with less fat, sugar, or fewer carbohydrates for health reasons. Would you consider these foods to be new products?

New Product Categories

Many marketers believe that products created to meet a real need have a better chance of success than products whose usefulness must be sold as much as the product itself. When new products are needed, there are six categories of new products, as shown in Figure 16-1.

Explore

Provide an opportunity for students to explore by assigning a hands-on activity. Review the vocabulary terms at the beginning of the section. Where have students encountered these terms before? Help students make educated guesses about the meanings of the terms with which they are least familiar.

Resource

Use the Chapter 16 presentation on the optional Instructor's Presentations for PowerPoint® CD as an outline for presenting the chapter.

FYI

Another term for new-to-the-world is *really new*.

New-to-the-World Products

Really new products are either new inventions or products with never-seen-before technology. No one knows how they work. The marketing strategy for new-to-the-world products is to explain what they are, how they work, and why people should buy them. The cost and risk of developing really new products or technology is great. However, when a new-to-the-world product is successful, the rewards are also great.

For example, hybrid and electric engines used completely new technology for fueling cars that saved fossil-fuel gasoline. The Toyota Prius and Chevy Volt were developed with the new engines for the target market interested in saving the environment and money on fuel. Both cars proved successful. However, there are many new cars, such as the AMC Gremlin and the DeLorean, that were short-lived for various reasons.

Minor Product Variations

Because really new products are so risky, many companies choose to develop varia-tions on current or past successful products. These variations should improve function of the existing product. Such products become *improved* and *revised* versions of the originals, and are advertised as such. For example, Proctor and Gamble regularly uses the marketing strategy of introducing new and improved versions of its products.

Repackaging, or using new packaging on the same product, is a another common way to create a new product. The product stays the same; only the packaging is different, making it more efficient or attractive. For example, Dean Foods took an ancient product, milk, and repackaged it in a new form called the Milk Chug. The Milk Chug is a plastic, resealable, single-serving bottle. The new name and single-serving packaging allows the product to compete directly with other single-serve drinks. Plus, it is more convenient than the old cardboard or glass containers.

Add New Product Lines

Sometimes companies wish to produce or sell products that are new to the company, but familiar to customers. The markets for the products already exist, so adding a new product line may be less risky. A company may enter the established market by offering new-to-the-company product lines. For example, a fabric manufacturer may decide

New Product Categories
• New-to-the-World Products
• Minor Product Variations
• Add New Product Lines
• Add to Existing Product Lines
• Reposition Existing Product Lines
• Offer a Less Expensive Version of a Current Product

Figure 16-1
There are six categories of new products.

Keith Bell/Shutterstock.com

College and Career Portfolio

School Work

Your portfolio should contain items related to your school work. These items might include report cards, transcripts, or honor roll reports. Diplomas or certificates that show courses or programs you completed should also be included. At some point, you will likely apply for a particular job or volunteer position. At that time, list the classes you took that helped prepare you for the job or volunteer position. Describe the activities you completed or topics you studied in these classes that relate to the job or volunteer duties. This information will be helpful when you apply for the position by letter or talk with an interviewer.

1. Identify a job or volunteer position for which you could apply. Write a paragraph that gives the classes you took and activities completed that relate to the position. You can use this document as a model when you are actually ready to apply for a position.
2. Scan other documents related to your school work, such as grade reports, transcripts, and diplomas. Place the model paragraph and other documents in your e-portfolio.
3. Place hard copies in the container for your print portfolio.

---

to start producing sewing patterns or a line of clothing to grow sales. The customer may already be familiar with the company. Adding new a product would not be totally unexpected.

Add to Existing Product Lines

Some companies may only need to add items to existing product lines to keep the product mix current and sales up. This marketing strategy adds to the product depth, or the number of items within the product line. For example, perhaps a shoe store wants to attract younger customers. In addition to the old, reliable styles, it would add some new trendy styles and feature them in the store windows.

Reposition Existing Products

Repositioning is marketing an existing product in a new way to create a new position in the minds of customers to increase sales. Many existing products can end

up being valuable for other uses than the original one. A classic example of successful repositioning is Kleenex. The thin paper tissues were developed in 1924 as a disposable towel for removing makeup. However, by 1926, customer feedback showed that most people were using the product to blow their noses. Kleenex began advertising the product as a disposable handkerchief and product sales doubled.

Offer a Less Expensive Version of a Current Product

It costs a lot of money to develop a new product. However, sometimes companies find ways to make a current, popular product for less. Lower costs would reduce the selling price, so the new version can be marketed as a *reduction in price* or *price reduction*. This is a good way to introduce a less-expensive version of an expensive product. For example, new technology is improving how solar cells are manufactured, cutting costs by up to

Elaborate/Extend

Assign the College and Career Readiness Portfolio activity at the end of the chapter.

Explore

Review each of the new product categories. Ask students for examples of products that meet the criteria.

half. For solar-panel manufacturers, cheaper solar cells mean solar panels can be made at a reduced cost. They can take advantage of a great marketing opportunity to increase sales through a reduction in price.

Creativity

Creativity is the ability to make new things or think of new ideas. One of the keys to successful new product development and target marketing is creativity. In marketing, the ideas can be completely new or a new twist to an old idea. Creativity is often considered a talent, and some people are naturally creative. However, creativity is also a set of skills that can be developed. There are some techniques that can develop creativity in anyone:

- Brainstorm ideas about the product to be developed or the need to be fulfilled. Let your mind float free. Then list as many

The road to creativity is varied. Try new things to find out what you are good at; it might be surprising.

Blend Images/Shutterstock.com

Extend/Elaborate

Ask students to share their creative interests. Have a volunteer to record these responses on the chalkboard. Then ask: What are some ways to explore these creative interests?

Green Marketing

Company Policies

Many companies today find that being good stewards of the environment can help increase sales and profits. This is because consumers often hold companies in higher regard when they act responsibly and have environmentally-friendly policies. These policies are often marketed as part of public relations campaigns.

ideas as you can. Do not cross out any idea, even ones that seem silly.

- Ask questions of people with the same needs you want the new product to fulfill. Use critical thinking skills to find solutions to the problems presented.
- Participate in new activities. Trying new things can stimulate creativity. Take art, foreign language, or improvisational acting classes to get out of your comfort zone.
- Create a mind map. Start by writing down a central topic or word. Next, link related terms or ideas around the central word. Each word can branch to other words. It provides a visual way of seeing how these ideas are linked.
- Keep a journal to jot down new ideas whenever you get them. Look for inspiration everywhere. Review your journal when developing new products or product promotions.

New products fail for many reasons. One of the main reasons for a failed product is the lack of planning and research. The product did not meet a market need, was unappealing, or a better product came out at the same time. Some well-known failed products include the Ford Edsel, the Sony Betamax, and the Lisa and Newton computers from Apple.

Try using the *six hats* technique to stretch your creativity. It involves looking at a problem from six differing viewpoints. This exercise produces more ideas than if you only looked at the situation from one or two points of view.

Risk of New Products

Each year, over 25,000 new consumer products hit the market. More than 75 percent of these new products fail. A failed product can be very costly. For example, a large corporation might invest $20 million to develop, produce, advertise, and introduce a new product. If the product fails, most of that investment is lost. In some cases, product failure can ruin a business.

Checkpoint 16.1

1. Why are new products developed?
2. List the six categories of new products.
3. How can repackaging create a new product?
4. Give an example of a product that was successfully repositioned.
5. Can creativity be developed?

Build Your Vocabulary

As you progress through this course, develop a personal glossary of marketing terms and add it to your portfolio. This will help you build your vocabulary and prepare you for a career. Write a definition for each of the following terms, and add it to your personal marketing glossary.

new product
repackaging
repositioning
creativity

Checkpoint Answers

1. New products replace those at the end of their life cycles. Often, new products are developed to meet a specific need, such as the polio vaccine or a shampoo to reduce dandruff. Others are developed to meet a new want, such as faster computers or equipment for a new sport.
2. The six categories of new products are new-to-the-world, minor product variations, add new product lines, add to existing product lines, reposition existing products, and offer a less expensive version of a current product.
3. The product stays the same; only the packaging is different, making it more efficient or attractive.
4 Kleenex was developed in 1924 as a disposable towel for removing makeup. However, by 1926, customer feedback showed that most people were using the product to blow their noses. Kleenex began advertising the product as a disposable handkerchief and product sales doubled.
5. Yes. Creativity is often considered a talent, and some people are naturally creative. However, creativity is also a set of skills that can be developed.

Build Your Vocabulary Answers

Definitions for these terms can be found in the glossary of this text.

Section 16.2 New Product Development Process

Objectives

After completing this section, you will be able to
- **describe** the role of marketing in new product development.
- **list** and explain the steps in the new product development process.

Key Terms

image
brand
prototype
trial run
test marketing

virtual test market
reverse engineering
commercialization
release date
trade show

Web Connect

Which cities are often used for test marketing? Use an Internet search engine to find out. Use the keywords "cities used for test marketing." List the top five cities and explain why they are good for test marketing purposes. If you were test marketing a new product, which city would you use? Why?

Critical Thinking

Think of a new product that you have bought or seen. In what ways was this product new? In what ways was it similar to existing products?

Marketing Role in New Product Development

Identifying the best products to meet target-market needs sounds simple. However, much thought and planning is necessary before making final product decisions. Marketing plays an important role in new product development. Marketing does the research, tests the product, and creates the promotional strategies. Marketing, along with the sales team, is the all-important *direct link* between a company and its customers.

Marketing research is critical to planning and developing new products to meet customer needs and wants. A new product must also be able to fulfill company profit goals. Marketing research is necessary to make sure a new product or service is the best business decision.

Many products might be able to fulfill some needs or wants. How do marketers help a business decide exactly which new products to make or sell? There are two questions that marketers must answer during the new product development process.
1. Will the target market customers buy the product?
2. Can the company produce and sell the product profitably?

New Product Development

The new product development process generally follows seven steps, as shown in Figure 16-2. For example, first, the idea for a new product, such as an iPad, had to be

Explore

Provide an opportunity for students to explore by assigning a hands-on activity. Review the vocabulary terms at the beginning of the section. Where have students encountered these terms before? Help students make educated guesses about the meanings of the terms with which they are least familiar.

Engage

Use the Teamwork exercise at the end of the chapter to engage students to solve a problem or make a group presentation.

New Product Development Process

Steps 1, 2, 3 • Idea generation • Idea screening • Business analysis	 *Yuri Arcurs/Shutterstock.com*	In the earliest stages, ideas are generated, researched, and screened. A business analysis examines projected costs and sales.
Steps 4, 5 • Product design • Test marketing	 *vovan/Shutterstock.com*	Details of how to produce the product are further examined followed by production. The next stage allows the company to test the product in various markets.
Step 6 • Commercialization	 *michael rubin/Shutterstock.com*	The new product is then introduced. Trade shows and announcements of release dates are used to trigger customer interest.
Step 7 • Evaluation	 *lev radin/Shutterstock.com*	The company must then monitor the success of the product based on sales, customer interest, and other business goals.

Goodheart-Willcox Publisher

Figure 16-2 Each step in the new product development process must be completed to ensure success.

Case in Point

3-D TV

New products do not always prove to be successful. Even though market research was completed and the product seemed like a winner, some products never make the cut. For example, the 3-D television that requires glasses for viewing was launched at the Consumer Electronics show in 2010. Sales for the early versions of 3-D TV were low. It turns out that many people do not like wearing 3-D glasses to watch television. They feel the glasses are bulky and restraining. Viewing fatigue is common, and multitasking with 3-D glasses is nearly impossible. To complicate the situation further, very few television programs are produced in the 3-D format. Producers of television shows need special equipment to film programs in 3-D, which adds to the production cost. And of course, the end user pays a premium for the high-end TV.

So, is having the latest, greatest *new-to-the-world* product a guaranteed moneymaker? In some situations, yes, but not for the makers of 3-D televisions requiring glasses. However, this situation inspired newer technology for 3-D TVs to be developed that does *not* require glasses for viewing.

---

conceived and analyzed. Then, it would go through an extensive design phase. Next, the product would enter a testing phase. After successful testing, the product is introduced and sold. The success of any product is evaluated on an ongoing basis.

Idea Generation

What new product or product improvement would make sense for the business? Where do companies find the ideas for a new or improved product? Product ideas are usually the result of observation, trend research, customers, and brainstorming.

Observation

Observation is a common source of product ideas. A marketer observes his or her environment and looks for unfilled customer needs. Sometimes, a customer cannot find a product to meet a personal need. Often, that need turns into an idea for a new product.

Trend Research

Many large companies hire marketing research firms that specialize in trend

research and new-product ideas. For example, trend research shows that Americans want more healthy choices when dining out. For this reason, many restaurants have added more entrée salads and other heart-healthy choices to their menus. Trend research does not always have to be formal or expensive, though. Marketers can conduct their own secondary research that identifies the latest trends that apply to their industries.

Customers

Customer input and feedback is critical for companies that follow the marketing concept. The sales staff is a great source for new-product ideas because they are in constant contact with customers. Salespeople hear customers' ideas, their unmet needs, complaints, and suggestions about how to improve products. Some companies have a formal process for salespeople to submit product ideas.

Brainstorming

Use the creative process of brainstorming to focus on new product ideas. Include all of the people in an organization who have knowledge about the target market and their needs. Also include those people who understand the business and its processes. A product manager is the most likely person to lead a formal brainstorming session.

Idea Screening

Once a list of new product ideas is generated, they must be reviewed. The goal of idea screening is to choose the best and hopefully the most profitable ideas before making a large capital investment. Idea screening looks at the new product ideas from the customer viewpoint. Gather as much information as possible by talking to other people in the industry. This is a time to conduct primary and secondary research to learn whether the product will meet customer needs and wants. Pay attention to your social media discussions in your target market. Notice what is trending as well as their concerns or complaints. Will any of your new product ideas address their concerns?

Discuss your best new product ideas with potential customers in the target market. Send surveys or hold focus groups to discover if those products will actually meet the needs of the market. If the first new product idea does not test well, develop another one. For example, before movies are released to the public, they are screened by groups of target market viewers. The movie writers and producers use the feedback from those viewers to make any changes to the parts of the movie that tested poorly.

Business Analysis

A business analysis of a new product idea looks at the projected costs and forecasts product sales. Does the company have the necessary people, expertise, equipment,

and money to develop and promote the new product? Even a nonprofit organization must determine whether it can afford a new product.

Analysis includes researching the cost of revising a current product or bringing a new product to market. Market research should help determine if the product can generate enough sales to cover costs and make the desired profit. All companies should do a detailed financial analysis of any new-product plan.

Any new product must also align with the company image, mission, and goals. An image is the idea that people have about someone or something. Many companies choose to develop a specific image through their brand, which marketers help to create.

A brand is a name, term, or design that sets a product or business apart from its competition. For example, Jaguar has the image of a company that builds luxury sports sedans. A truck would not fit the Jaguar corporate identity. The American Cancer Society (ASC) has a mission to cure and prevent cancer and provide support to cancer patients and families. Any product or service that does not meet a part of the ACS mission should not even be considered.

AMA Tip

The American Marketing Association Foundation uses marketing as a vehicle for social change by offering resources to nonprofit marketers, awarding scholarships to marketing students, and acknowledging marketer excellence. Nonprofit organizations benefit from grants, conferences, and a specialized nonprofit marketing boot camp. The foundation also promotes marketing research by offering resources and special support to marketing students pursuing doctoral degrees.
www.themarketingfoundation.org

New products should also meet company goals. For example, Jaguar had a goal to expand its market by appealing to a more price-conscious group of consumers. To meet this goal, Jaguar could have considered creating a new line of less expensive vehicles, such as trucks. However, the Jaguar brand is associated with luxury vehicles, and trucks do not fall into that category. To expand its market, Jaguar developed the X-Type, a less expensive version of its premium luxury car.

FYI

The image of a company is also known as its *corporate brand.*

Product Design

After proving the new product meets a need in the market and company profit goals, designing the product comes next. This is the stage where the product idea becomes a reality. During the design phase, details of how to produce the product are planned. For goods, numerous product designs are completed and evaluated. To evaluate services, they are usually tried out on a few potential customers.

Determining the product brand is also part of the design phase. The name, image, logo, slogan, and packaging of the good or service are usually created at this stage.

Goods

A **prototype** is a working model of a new product for testing purposes. Product designers experiment with the prototype to determine if it performs as expected. If any problems are found, they are fixed before full-scale production. Prototypes are especially important for any product with moving parts.

For example, Toyota had a goal to develop a new car that used much less gas and saved natural resources. To accomplish that goal, Toyota engineers developed an entirely new hybrid engine: one powered by both gas and electricity. This meant the engine delivered more miles per gallon (mpg) and used far less fuel than other cars. The design team built a prototype and tested it for performance and safety before full-scale production. Toyota's first hybrid car, the Prius, was very successful and remains a best seller in its vehicle class.

Marketers also use prototypes to get customer feedback before the final design is chosen. Large companies may create several prototypes for a single product, each with different features. Researchers will have customers within the target market test the different prototypes—often through focus groups. The tester responses help marketers determine which prototype and features will sell the best. Creating prototypes can be expensive, however. To save money, a product manager may choose to create a prototype of only one of the designs. Once the prototype is researched and approved, the product can go into full production.

Services

A service business usually goes through a period during which the details of providing a new service are planned. Training the service providers is also an important step to perform before the business opens. Depending on the service, a physical location is chosen and the business may perform trial runs. A **trial run** consists of testing the service on a few select customers to make sure that everything runs smoothly. A trial run is like a dress rehearsal for a business. For example, a restaurant might start serving meals to small groups before the grand opening to work out any problems in food preparation, timing, or service.

Explore

Ask if any student has been a part of a test marketing group.

Trade shows and conferences are great places for industry businesses to introduce new products directly to their target markets.

arindambanerjee/Shutterstock.com

Test Marketing

Due to the expense and potential risk of failure, many companies do not immediately start producing a new product in large numbers. This is especially true for products that will be sold on the national or global level. Test marketing introduces a new product to a small portion of the target market, one city for example, to learn how it will sell. Test marketing can test the entire marketing mix—product, place, price, and promotion.

Customer responses in the test market help marketers solve unexpected problems. Test marketing may also determine whether or not to produce the product on the mass level. For example, Peoria, Illinois has long been a test-market city for many new products. It has a representative population of the overall Midwestern market, and the media prices for advertising are inexpensive. Over the years, companies such as Hellman's, Google, and Enceutical Corp, Inc. have tested new products and services in Peoria.

Many smaller companies cannot afford to test market new products, however. The latest development in test marketing is virtual test

markets. Virtual test markets are computer simulations of consumers, companies, and market environments. Products can be tested in different virtual test markets for a fraction of the cost of live test marketing. However, the lack of personal feedback makes virtual test marketing results less reliable than live test marketing.

While test marketing products can save money by working out problems before production, it does have a downside. There is the risk that competitors can buy your product and copy it through reverse engineering. Reverse engineering is taking apart an object to see how it was made—usually in order to produce something similar. Some companies reverse engineer existing products to copy or enhance them without the expense or developing their own products. They may be able to produce a better product before yours is finalized and on the market.

Commercialization

The *introduction stage* of the product life cycle is also called commercialization. Management chooses a release date to make the new product available for sale. Promotion is critical at this point and often starts before the product is released. The production and shipping functions must have the product ready for shipment and in the stores by the release date.

For example, the seventh Harry Potter book, *Harry Potter and the Deathly Hallows,* was set for release at 12:01 a.m. on July 21, 2007. The book publisher, Scholastic, Inc., had to make sure that the books were printed and delivered to thousands of stores before the release date. Anticipation and promotion of the book started months earlier when the release date was announced. Many bookstores planned parties for the release date of the book, and it set a record for preorders. A record-breaking 12 million copies went on sale at midnight, July 21. The book sold more in one weekend than any Hollywood movie at that time.

Often, new products are introduced at industry trade shows to monitor customer response. A trade show is a large gathering of businesses for the purpose of displaying products

for sale. There are trade shows for every industry and type of B2C product. For example, the annual North American International Auto Show (NAIAS) is held in Detroit. Since 1989, over 1,300 new vehicles were introduced at the NAIAS.

There are also trade shows for B2B products. For example, the National Retail Federation (NRF) holds an annual convention called Retail's Big Show. Manufacturers introduce retailers to every kind of new product.

Evaluation

All businesses, including institutions and governments, need to know if their products are successful. It is important to evaluate both new and existing products often. The success of a product is based how it met the sales and other goals set for the product during the business analysis. The marketing department shares responsible for determining the success of products.

Checkpoint 16.2

1. What two questions do marketers need to answer during the new product development process?
2. List the seven steps of the new product development process.
3. How do salespeople help with the new product development process?
4. What is the function of the business analysis step in the new product development process?
5. What can test marketing new products or services accomplish?

Build Your Vocabulary

As you progress through this course, develop a personal glossary of marketing terms and add it to your portfolio. This will help you build your vocabulary and prepare you for a career. Write a definition for each of the following terms, and add it to your personal marketing glossary.

image
brand
prototype
trial run
test marketing

virtual test market
reverse engineering
commercialization
release date
trade show

Checkpoint Answers

1. Will the target market customers buy the product and can the company produce and sell the product profitably?
2. The seven steps of the new product development process are idea generation, idea screening, business analysis, product design, test marketing, commercialization, and evaluation.
3. Salespeople hear customers' ideas, their unmet needs, complaints, and suggestions about how to improve products. Some companies have a formal process for salespeople to submit product ideas.
4. A business analysis of a new product idea looks at the projected costs and forecasts product sales.
5. Customer responses in the test market help marketers solve unexpected problems. Test marketing may also determine whether or not to produce the product on the mass level.

Build Your Vocabulary Answers

Definitions for these terms can be found in the glossary of this text.

Chapter Summary

Section 16.1 New Products

- A new product is a product that is different in some way from existing products. That difference may be minor or major.
- The six categories of new products are new-to-the-world, minor product variations, add new product lines, add to existing product lines, reposition existing products, and offer a less expensive version of a current product.
- One of the keys to successful new product development and target marketing is creativity. In marketing, the ideas can be completely new or a new twist to an old idea.
- New products fail for many reasons. One of the main reasons for a failed product is the lack of planning and research.

Section 16.2 New Product Development Process

- Marketing plays an important role in new product development. Marketing does the research, tests the product, and creates the promotional strategies.
- The seven steps of the new product development process are idea generation, idea screening, business analysis, product design, test marketing, commercialization, and evaluation.

Review Your Knowledge

1. Why do companies develop a new product based on a successful product?
2. What is the benefit of offering a less expensive version of a current product?
3. Why would a company want to add new product lines?
4. List four techniques that may help a person develop his or her creativity.
5. What role does marketing play in new product development?
6. Why should new product ideas be screened?
7. Why are prototypes made for some new products?
8. At what stage does a new product idea become a reality?
9. Why might a new product be reverse engineered by another company?
10. How might smaller companies carry out test marketing for new products?

Apply Your Knowledge

1. In earlier chapters, you identified the product or service for which you are creating a marketing plan. Research your company. What is the newest product or service that has been added to one of its product lines?

2. Have you seen the newest product designs? Use the keywords *best product designs of the year* in an Internet search engine. Look for new product ideas that your company might use as a springboard to expand their offerings. What did you find?

3. After reviewing product offerings from your company, do you see any gaps in product lines? Are the product offerings competitive?

4. A number of companies specialize in helping businesses develop new products. Conduct a search online for *new product development firms.* Choose one company and write a report on what it does, the process used, how it works with businesses, and the new products it helped develop.

5. Describe the role you would play in new product development for your company. Make a list of bullet points of your talents, skills, and experiences that you would bring to the product development process.

6. Your company may offer only goods or goods and services. Think of a new service your company might offer. Hint: Think of a service business you use. What new services might you suggest to add?

7. Name a product that your company offers that could be repositioned simply by changing the packaging. Describe the changes you would make.

8. Industrial designers are key professionals in new product development. Use library resources and the Internet to find out what an industrial designer does. Visit the website of the Industrial Designers Society of America. Click on the *About* link and then *Industrial Design: Defined.* What skills, abilities, and education do industrial designers need?

9. Obtain the annual report for your company. Many annual reports can be found online. List the new products that were launched this year. Are sales increasing, decreasing, or stable?

10. Based on research, which trade shows would you recommend your business attend to showcase its products?

Check Your Marketing IQ

Now that you have finished the chapter, see what you learned about marketing by taking the chapter posttest. If you do not have a smartphone, visit the G-W Learning companion website.

G-W Learning mobile site: www.m.g-wlearning.com
G-W Learning companion website: www.g-wlearning.com

9. Some companies reverse engineer existing products to copy or enhance them without the expense or developing their own products. They may be able to produce a better product before yours is finalized and on the market.

10. Many smaller companies cannot afford to test market new products. The latest development in test marketing is virtual test markets.

Apply Your Knowledge Answers

Student answers will vary for questions 1–10.

Apply Your Knowledge Teaching Tip

At the end of this unit, students will write the next phase of the marketing plan. Please note that the Apply Your Knowledge Questions prepare students for the next installment of the marketing plan that they are writing at the end of each unit. These questions help them assume the role of a marketing manager and begin applying concepts learned in the chapter. If your class is not participating in the marketing plan activity at the end of the unit, Apply Your Knowledge questions can be used by directing students to select a business of their choice and answer each question about that business.

Marketing Plan

The marketing plan is now taking shape. The activities for this unit will be time-consuming. You may want to assign one section of the marketing plan as students finish this chapter. Or, you may prefer for them to do the entire activity at the end of the unit.

Common Core

College and Career Readiness

CTE Career Ready Practices. As discussed in this text, environmental awareness is important in the workplace. Decisions that marketing managers make could have an impact on social and economic situations in the community. Give an example of a decision that a marketing manager might make that would have a positive impact on the community.

Listening. Research the positives and negatives of working as a marketing professional. Use the Internet to find videos of at least three speeches or news broadcasts that discuss the opportunities in the marketing profession. Listen for specific information and compare and contrast the speakers' information, points of view, and opinions. How are they similar and/or different? Using the information presented, create a list of pros and cons that you might encounter when starting a career in marketing.

Speaking. Working in small groups, develop a list of regulations that you would like to have in your classroom and your reasoning for each one. Develop a presentation in which you attempt to persuade your classmates to adopt your classroom regulations. Then, develop a separate presentation in which you attempt to persuade your teacher, acting as a member of the school board, to adopt your regulations. How will you alter your presentations for these two different audiences?

Teamwork

Working with a team, think of a product that you use every day that was once a new technology, for example, telephone, cell phone, television, or automobile. Research this product on the Internet. Find out when the product was invented. Who invented it? Why? How was it originally promoted? How is it promoted now?

G-W Learning Mobile Site

Visit the G-W Learning mobile site to complete the chapter pretest and posttest and to practice vocabulary using e-flash cards. If you do not have a smartphone, visit the G-W Learning companion website to access these features.

G-W Learning mobile site: www.m.g-wlearning.com

G-W Learning companion website: www.g-wlearning.com

17 Branding

Section 17.1 | Brand Elements
Section 17.2 | Power of the Brand

"I've never felt like I was in the cookie business.

I've always been in a feel-good feeling business.

My job is to sell joy. My job is to sell happiness.

My job is to sell an experience"

—Debbi Fields, founder of Mrs. Fields Bakeries

College and Career Readiness

Reading Prep
Before reading this chapter, go to the Review Your Knowledge section at the end of the chapter and read the questions. This exercise will prepare you for the content that will be presented in this chapter. Review questions at the end of the chapter to serve as a self-assessment to help you evaluate your comprehension of the material.

Check Your Marketing IQ

Before you begin the chapter, see what you already know about marketing by taking the chapter pretest. If you do not have a smartphone, visit the G-W Learning companion website.
G-W Learning mobile site: www.m.g-wlearning.com
G-W Learning companion website: www.g-wlearning.com

G-W Mobile

Explore
Provide an opportunity for students to explore by assigning a hands-on activity. Assign the College and Career Readiness Reading Prep activity before students read the chapter. Reading Prep activities give students opportunity to apply the Common Core State Standards.

Engage
Assign the Chapter 17 pretest. The test may be accessed by using the QR code or going to the companion website. Discuss which questions students were unable to answer.

◇DECA Emerging Leaders

Buying and Merchandising Team Decision-Making Event, Part 2

Career Cluster: Marketing
Instructional Area: Product/Service Management
Promotion

Procedure, Part 2

1. In the previous chapter, you studied the performance indicators for this event.
2. The event will be presented to you through your reading of the General Performance Indicators, Specific Performance Indicators, and Case Study Situation. You will have up to 30 minutes to review this information and prepare your presentation. You may make notes to use during your presentation.
3. You will have up to 10 minutes to make your presentation to the judge followed by up to five minutes to answer the judge's questions. You may have more than one judge. All members of the team must participate in the presentation, as well as answer the questions.
4. Turn in all of your notes and event materials when you have completed the event.

Case Study Situation

You are to assume the roles of marketing specialists for Shopmart, a national discount retail chain. The **CEO of Shopmart (judge)** has asked you to develop a strategy to raise customer awareness of the store's private-label brand to ultimately increase sales and increase profit margins.

Shopmart is one of several large national discount retail chains across the country. The store sells a wide variety of merchandise such as: household items, clothing, health and beauty products, electronics, small furniture, and seasonal items. While merchandise sales have been steady, the past two quarters have not shown any significant increases.

The CEO of Shopmart is now focusing on the store's private label brand, *Match*. The Shopmart health and beauty department offers all major brand name products consumers expect to find, plus the additional private label brand, *Match*. Priced from 5 percent to 20 percent less than the national brands, *Match* products are just as effective as national brands. Sales of *Match* brand health and beauty products should be higher than what they are, given the economic crisis in the country. The CEO has asked you to develop a strategy to raise awareness of the *Match* brand to Shopmart customers, which will increase sales.

The CEO warns that price alone does not create customer loyalty to a brand. Please consider the following product qualities. Your strategy should:
* meet customer needs;
* exude quality; and
* deliver a positive experience.

You will explain your strategy to the CEO in a meeting to take place in the CEO's office. The CEO will begin the meeting by greeting you and asking to hear your ideas. After you have explained your strategy and answered the CEO's questions, the CEO will conclude the meeting by thanking you for your work.

Critical Thinking

1. How does your strategy create differentiation from the competition?
2. If successful, what other departments could use the *Match* brand?

Visit www.deca.org for more information.

Section 17.1 Brand Elements

What Makes a Brand?

Recall that a *brand* is what sets a product or business apart from its competitors. All products, services, and businesses have a brand—whether the owners realize it or not. Some are stronger and more effective than others. The brand is a result of everything a customer sees, hears, and experiences. A positive brand experience can ensure the success of the product. The opposite is true as well. A product or business with negative brand image, for any reason, has a harder time overcoming it to remain profitable.

Brands are created through both tangible and intangible elements. Often, the tangible elements of a brand are the first experience a consumer has with a product. For example, many people see new products in grocery or other retail stores. Some may first see print or television ads. Just like people make a first impression, how a product looks, is packaged, and presented also makes a first impression.

Intangible brand elements include customer expectations, their feelings about the brand, as well as their direct interactions with it. Recall that image is the idea that people have about someone or something. Brands can convey a variety of images, such as prestige, value, or trendiness.

Tangible Brand Elements

The tangible elements of a brand are its name, graphic design elements, and tagline or slogan. Those are the brand elements that can be seen and heard. Marketers consider each tangible element very carefully to make sure they reflect the desired brand image.

The Canon logo is a unique graphic treatment of the name.

Name

A **brand name** is the name given to the product consisting of words, numbers, or letters that can be read and spoken. Sometimes choosing the right name for a product can guide the product strategy and other marketing mix decisions. For example, a vacation resort was developed on Hog Island in the Bahamas. However, the resort did not take off until the island name was changed to Paradise Island.

Graphic Design Elements

One of the most powerful aspects of a brand is the graphic design elements. These elements appear in packaging, on labels, and form the logo. A **logo** is the picture, design, or graphic image that represents a brand. A logo may also be called a *brand mark.* A logo can be a graphic symbol like the Nike swoosh or the red target symbol for Target. It may also be the name of the company or product without a symbol.

Symbols tend to work best when they evoke some aspect of the product. Part of the

reason the Nike swoosh is so effective is that it evokes a sense of movement and power. Or, it can simply be the name with a special graphic treatment or unique typeface, such as the IBM, Citibank, and Dell logos.

Another graphic design element sometimes used for branding purposes is trade characters. A **trade character** is an animal, real or fictional person, or object used to advertise a good or service. Effective trade characters symbolize the product, service, or company. These trade characters become so closely associated with the good or service that they can actually become the brand. The Jolly Green Giant, Uncle Sam, and Morris, the cat are all successful trade characters.

Tagline

A **tagline**, or slogan, is a phrase or sentence that summarizes some essential part of the product or business. Marketers recognize that a catchy phrase or memorable tagline can strengthen a brand. For example, Nike tagline, "Just Do It," appears in every form of advertising and promotion. It is so

This image of Uncle Sam (U.S.) was introduced in 1916 to represent the United States of America.

memorable that "Just Do It," along with the swoosh symbol, has become a strong brand identifier for Nike.

A tagline or slogan set to music is called a jingle. Jingles are used for radio, television, or even Internet advertising purposes. An example of a jingle is Chili's "I want my baby-back ribs." More recently, companies are purchasing the rights to popular songs to represent their brands. The music also becomes a very identifiable part of the overall brand.

Metaphors are often used in advertising as a way to enhance the perceived value of a product. Value is the relative worth of something to a person. A metaphor is a word or phrase for one thing used in reference to a very different thing in order to suggest a similarity. An example of a metaphor is describing someone who is "drowning in paperwork."

An advertising metaphor may also combine a phrase with an image to strengthen the message. For example, Geico Insurance advertises its services as "So easy a caveman could do it." Tropicana promotes its orange juice as "Your daily ray of sunshine."

Intangible Brand Elements

Intangible brand elements include the implied promise of the brand, the consistency of the brand, and customer perceptions of brand image. Intangible elements of a brand are hard to measure because they cannot be seen or heard.

Brand Promise

What will consumers get when they purchase a product or service from your brand? In its simplest form, a brand is the promise made to consumers that may or may not be included in the graphics or tagline. Consumers develop expectations for a brand based on how it is promoted and priced. When customers pull hard-earned money out of their pockets to purchase something, they assume their expectations will be met.

AMA Tip

The purpose of conducting a brand perception survey is to understand how your brand is viewed in the market, what brand attributes are preferred by customers, and to identify how your customers competitively position your products/services. It will also help to pinpoint which purchasing criteria your customers value most. The AMA has a free, downloadable Brand Perception Survey template for its members to use as part of the AMA Marketer's Toolkit. www.marketingpower.com

Extend

Consider showing an advertisement from television or playing a radio advertisement. Ask students to critique the effectiveness of the ad.

Extend

Discuss the intangible brand elements that appeal to customers.

1000 Words/Shutterstock.com

The brand promise of Apple, represented by the well-known apple logo, is innovation and quality in personal electronics.

Brand Consistency

Brand consistency means that the product or service is the same whenever and wherever you buy it. For example, when you go to a Chili's restaurant, you expect the same menu, prices, décor, and service at every location across the country. As a marketer, if your brand fails to meet consumer expectations at any time, it may eventually run into problems. It is the failed expectations that customers tend to remember and discuss with others.

Customer Perceptions of Brand Image

Have you ever heard the saying, "Perception is everything"? This saying could be written about branding. **Perception** is the mental image a person has about something. Perception also includes feelings about a product or company.

For example, what are your perceptions about these entirely different brands: BP, Microsoft, Levis, Coach, or Walmart? Just saying their names can evoke certain feelings based on your perception of the image of the company.

The perceptions of brand image are formed in three ways, as shown in Figure 17-1. Because perception is so critical to brand success, marketers use every tool and technique they can to enhance the image of their brand.

When marketing an intangible service, using a metaphor can make it seem more personal.

How Customer Perceptions of Brand Image Are Formed
Personal experience
Hearing about the experiences of others with the brand
How the brand is promoted

Goodheart-Willcox Publisher

Figure 17-1 Customers can have different brand perceptions based on their personal values.

Product Brand Types

There are three types of product brands: national, private label, and generic. Each type of brand is specific to the company that creates and owns it.

Marketing Ethics

Expense Accounts

Marketing professionals may have an expense account at their places of employment. An expense account is to be used when it is necessary to buy a meal for a client or for other company-related expenses in your job description. Personal expenses should *not* be charged against your business expense account. It is unethical to charge your employer for expenses that were not related to customers or other company business.

Elaborate

Define *perception* and how its meaning varies from customer to customer.

Explain

Ask for definitions of *national brands, private label brands,* and *generic brand.* What is the perception of each?

National

A **national brand** is one created by a manufacturer for its own products. It may also be called a *manufacturer's brand.* National brands are probably the most familiar ones because they are carried by many large and small retail stores. For example, Diesel clothing, Cover Girl make-up, and Frye boots are all well-known national product brands. For example, if you want certain national-brand jeans, such as Levis, Lee, or Guess, you must go to a retailer that carries them, such as Sears, Macy's, or Dillard's. Some manufacturers also have their own retail stores to exclusively sell their own brands.

Private Label

Private-label brands are products owned by and created specifically for large retailers. Private-label products are only sold by one retailer. For example, Abercrombie & Fitch stores only carry Abercrombie-label products. You cannot buy any other brands at Abercrombie & Fitch; nor could you buy Abercrombie clothing at any other retailer. Macy's has 17 private-label brands across different departments including Charter Club, Bar III, and Epic Threads. These product brands are advertised as "only available at Macy's."

Generic

A consumer product that lacks a widely recognized name or logo is a **generic brand**. Generic brands are not advertised, and it is not obvious who manufactured them. With no promotional costs to recoup, generic brands can cost up to 50 percent less than similar brand-name products.

Many products are made and sold for less in a generic-brand format. For example, most prescription and over-the-counter medicines are also available in generic forms. Grocery stores, in particular, create and sell many generic brands of packaged foods and other products. Generic brands appeal to value-conscious consumers.

Private-label brands are also called *store brands* or *dealer brands.*

Generic brands do not carry a popular brand name or logo. Many products, including clothing and shoes, are sold as generic brands.

Le Do/Shutterstock.com

Exploring Careers

Customer Relationship Management

Customer relationship management (CRM) professionals help create and maintain a company's image by planning and directing activities to improve the company's relationship with its customers. A customer relationship manager also helps others within the business to maintain good customer relationships. Typical job titles for these positions include *customer relationship manager, custom relations manager,* and *customer service director.*

Some examples of tasks that CRM professionals perform include:

- listen to recordings of an individual representative's customer interactions and score the interaction based on company criteria;
- develop, run, and maintain customer retention programs;
- maintain customer databases and analyze data for trends; and
- work with IT department to keep databases current.

CRM professionals spend most of their time communicating with company executives, customers, and the sales force, so good communications skills are important. Good management skills and strong analytical, technical, and mathematical abilities are helpful in these positions. CRM positions require a bachelor's degree, with many also asking for prior CRM experience. For more information, access the *Occupational Outlook Handbook* online.

Checkpoint 17.1

1. Give examples of a tangible element of a brand.
2. What is another name for a logo?
3. Give an example of a metaphor.
4. Explain brand consistency.
5. List the three types of brands.

Build Your Vocabulary

As you progress through this course, develop a personal glossary of marketing terms and add it to your portfolio. This will help you build your vocabulary and prepare you for a career. Write a definition for each of the following terms, and add it to your personal marketing glossary.

brand name
logo
trade character
tagline
jingle
value

metaphor
perception
national brand
private-label brand
generic brand

Checkpoint Answers

1. The tangible elements of a brand are its name, graphic design elements, and tagline or slogan.
2. Another name for a logo is a brand mark.
3. An example of a metaphor is "drowning in paperwork," although student answers may vary.
4. Brand consistency means that the product or service is the same whenever and wherever you buy it.

5. The three types of brands are national, private label, and generic. Each type of brand is specific to the company that created and owns it

Build Your Vocabulary Answers

Definitions for these terms can be found in the glossary of this text.

Section 17.2 Power of the Brand

Objectives

After completing this chapter, you will be able to
- **discuss** how branding relates to product identity.
- **explain** ways to protect a brand.
- **describe** personal branding.

Key Terms

brand equity
corporate social
  responsibility
brand loyalty
intellectual property

trademark
service mark
personal brand

Web Connect

Visit the US Patent and Trademark Office website. Click on *Search for Trademarks*, then click on *Basic Word Mark Search (New User)*. Enter the name of a famous brand. Explore the registrations that appear and then answer these questions. Who owns the trademark? Has anyone else applied for it? What is the date and number of the current registration? Which elements does the trademark cover?

Critical Thinking

Think about your personal brand objectively. Write a paragraph about what makes you different and sets you apart in a way that may be attractive to some employers. If that is difficult, ask some friends or family members who know you well to help you identify your personal brand.

Branding and Identity

Have you ever asked someone to pass you a Kleenex? In some product categories, one brand becomes so powerful that it replaces the generic category name. The Kleenex brand name has replaced *disposable facial tissues*. Another example of a powerful brand is Google. Most people now refer to using a search engine as *googling*. Google has literally become a verb, and the company was only started in 2001. All companies dream of creating a brand as powerful as Google.

The true power of a brand lies in its ability to influence purchasing behavior. **Brand equity** is the value of having a well-known brand name. The brand equity of both Google and Kleenex is priceless. Branding helps marketers promote

products to increase sales. Marketers hope their branding efforts will achieve the following goals:
- create a unique brand identity;
- contribute to the positive image of the brand; and
- inspire brand loyalty and repeat sales.

Unique Brand

Many companies often use product features to sell a product. However, product features can easily be copied by the competition and are rarely unique. Recall that a benefit is the need-satisfying ability of the product. In order to make a brand stand out from the competition, marketers learn which product benefits are valued by different target market customers. Marketing research plays a large part in creating unique brands.

Explore

Provide an opportunity for students to explore by assigning a hands-on activity. Review the vocabulary terms at the beginning of the section. Where have students encountered these terms before? Help students make educated guesses about the meanings of the terms with which they are least familiar.

Engage

Use the Teamwork exercise at the end of the chapter to engage students to solve a problem or make a group presentation.

Google is one of the most recognized brands in the world.

Annette Shaff/Shutterstock.com

The key to a unique brand is creating products and promotions that appeal to the needs and wants of your target market. For example, most computers now have very fast processing capabilities. That feature is common. However, some customers want fast processing to play video games. Other customers need the computer for heavy multimedia use, such as pictures and music. Depending on the target market, the computer promotions will focus on different benefits.

Positive Image

Developing a unique brand does not always translate into a positive brand image, however. Recall that a positive brand image is tied directly to customer perception. All marketers want their brands perceived in a positive light to keep sales up. One way to accomplish this goal is to align the brand with a positive message.

Corporate social responsibility is the actions of a business to further social good. It goes beyond profit interests and legal requirements for a business. Examples include donating to nonprofits, recycling, or supporting a cause like cancer research. The brand of a company reflects its image in the community. For this reason, many companies participate in visible community and charitable events.

For example, Sony Pictures partners with nonprofits and other organizations that promote environmental causes. Among others, Sony donates money and encourages employees to participate in Conservation International and the Natural Resources Defense Council.

Some large corporations buy the *naming rights* for sports stadiums and other public places to show their support for a community. For example, Conseco is an Indiana-based insurance company. When the city of Indianapolis built a new sports arena, Conseco paid $90 million for the privilege of having its name on it for 20 years. By having its name on this arena, Conseco is promoting its brand as one that supports sports and the economic well-being of the State of Indiana. Conseco hopes that people attending events

Brand loyalty occurs when a product meets the needs and expectations of a customer. If the customer's experience is positive, he or she will often decide to make a repeat purchase with the same brand in the future.

at the Conseco Fieldhouse will perceive the company positively. This positive image may lead some people to think of Conseco when they need insurance.

Brand Loyalty

Research has shown that it costs four times as much to create a new customer as it does to keep an existing one. **Brand loyalty** is a situation in which the customer will only buy a certain brand of product. If that brand is not available, the customer will search elsewhere for it—or not buy the product at all. Brand-loyal customers are the best customers, because brand loyalty means repeat purchases. This is one very good reason to create brands that inspire loyalty.

Brand loyalty occurs when the product, service, or business consistently meets customer needs and expectations. This creates a strong relationship between the customer and the brand. A unique brand

with a positive image may impact brand loyalty. However, customer experience with the brand is the main factor in brand loyalty. For example, some people will only buy a General Motors (GM) car because they have had a positive experience with GM makes and models. Others will never consider buying a GM car due to a negative experience or perception of GM.

If customers have a negative experience at any time, the chance for a repeat purchase drops drastically. For example, customers who receive poor service at a certain restaurant are much less likely to return. Plus, people who have had bad experiences with a product often discuss their dissatisfaction with other people. This is how negative perceptions about a brand can spread quickly and be hard to change. Successful marketers understand why excellent customer service is vital for brand loyalty. Any negative experiences must be turned around to keep customers satisfied.

Elaborate/Extend

If students are using the optional *Marketing Dynamics* workbook, assign activities to engage active learning.

Engage

Ask students how they perceive brand loyalty. To which products are they loyal?

Heinz bought the naming rights for Heinz Field in Pittsburgh, Pennsylvania, which now prominently displays the company logo.

StacieStauffSmith Photos/Shutterstock.com

Brand Protection

A brand is only valuable if competitors cannot copy it. In business, a brand is considered the intellectual property of its owner and should be protected from theft. **Intellectual property** is something that comes from a person's mind, such as an idea, invention, or process. Certain intellectual-property laws protect the unique phrases, symbols, and designs associated with brands. Many companies also choose to protect their brands by registering them with the United States Patent and Trademark Office (USPTO).

Trademarks and Service Marks

A **trademark** protects taglines, names, graphics, symbols, or any unique method to identify a product or company. A **service mark** is similar to a trademark, but it identifies a service rather than a product. Trademarks and service marks do not protect the product, itself, from theft. They only protect the ways in which the product is described. The symbols ™ for trademark or ℠ for service mark can be used without USPTO registration.

Trademark Registration

Ownership of all intellectual property including brands is implied. However, registering the trademark or service mark with the USPTO is recommended for increased protection. Once a trademark or service mark has been registered, the symbol ® can be used with the mark, as shown in Figure 17-2. These symbols notify the public that the creator claims exclusive rights to the brand and its use.

The term *trademark* is often used to refer to both trademarks and service marks.

Correct Usage of Trademark Symbols	
TM	Trademark, not registered
SM	Service mark, not registered
®	Registered trademark

Goodheart-Willcox Publisher

Figure 17-2 Graphic marks are the symbols that indicate legal protection of intellectual property.

Generic names cannot be registered trademarks. For example, the words *disposable facial tissue* cannot be trademarked. Many current brand names are used in place of product categories, though. Examples include Band-Aid, Styrofoam, and Xerox. The generic usage of the name attests to the popularity of the brand.

On the other hand, when a brand name becomes a generic name, the brand no longer has legal trademark protection. It can be used by anyone. Many now-familiar generic names began as trademarked brand names.

Examples include aspirin, thermos, granola, and zipper.

Most marketers want to protect their brands and the investments made in them. Losing trademark protection is not desirable. To help distinguish the brand from the generic category, marketers often use the word *brand* along with the name. For example, Kleenex is often advertised as "Kleenex-brand tissue." In the case of Google, the company protected its brand by striking deals with the publishers of Oxford and Merriam-Webster dictionaries. The dictionary definition of *google* is now "using the

When given a choice of brands, you want customers that are brand loyal so they will choose your product first.

Lightspring/Shutterstock.com

An example of intellectual property protection is on the Converse website: "All trademarks, service marks and trade names (e.g., the CONVERSE name, the Star and Chevron Design and the Chuck Taylor Ankle Patch) are trademarks or registered trademarks of Converse Inc."

Christopher Halloran/Shutterstock.com

Google search engine to obtain information on the Internet."

FYI

A global brand means that at least 20 percent of the product is sold outside of its home country.

Personal Branding

Imagine you as a product and your name as the brand. Your **personal brand** is the sum of the differences between you and those around you. When your school principal hears your name, what image comes to his or her mind? What image would you like him or her to have of you? Think about what makes you special. This will help to shape your own personal brand identity in the way you want.

Resource/Evaluate

Assign the optional Chapter 17 test for **EXAM**VIEW®
Assessment Suite as a formal assessment tool.

The easiest way to understand the concept of personal branding is through celebrities. Celebrities are defined by what people think about them. These perceptions are based on how the stars look, their behaviors, and what they support. In effect, the celebrity becomes a unique brand.

Some well-known people, such as Jennifer Lopez and Jessica Simpson, create their own product lines. They automatically bring their personal brands to the products. Or, a celebrity is hired by a company to help endorse its brand. Most often, the celebrity chosen has a personal brand with which the company wants to be associated. Examples of this include William Shatner for Priceline and Emma Stone for Revlon.

Many job seekers have personal websites to display their résumés, portfolios, and other accomplishments. At the very least, most have profiles on professional networking sites like LinkedIn. How you look and sound online determines your personal brand even before a personal interview.

Explain

Personal branding is important to all of us. Ask a student to explain what personal branding means.

Taylor Swift has a personal brand *and* she represents the brands of several different products.

The purpose of developing your own personal brand is the same as the purpose of a product brand. Your brand should positively distinguish you from the rest of the competition.

In the competitive world of job searching, the concept of personal branding is very important. It should also persuade the potential employer to buy your product, meaning hire you.

Social Media

Using Apps on Facebook

According to Facebook, there are over 550,000 active apps businesses can use on the Facebook platform. More are being offered daily. Many were created to improve business practices or more efficiently integrate Facebook into a company's operations. For example, there are surveys, contacts, blogging, testimonials, contests, and sweepstakes apps, to name just a few. YouTube, Twitter, or Flickr have apps that automatically embed information you posted on those sites into your Facebook business page. Many business apps are free. Often, fee-based apps offer a basic service at no charge. Another option is to look into having your own custom apps created specifically for the needs of your business. Many large brands use custom apps because they enhance the user experience. When your users are happy, they will interact more with your page, and that can mean more business. Search the Internet to find the apps that will work best for marketing your business on Facebook.

Case in Point

Jell-O and State Farm

Catch phrase, tagline, slogans—multiple words for a product line that consumers remember and connect with a product. A great slogan that people remember can sell a product for years to come. However, creating a slogan that fits and sells a product is no easy feat. There are slogans that have been around for years that are living proof people will remember a product with a catchy phrase. "There is always room for Jell-O" is a good example of brand longevity. Jell-O first came to market in 1902 claiming to be "America's Most Famous Dessert." "Please don't squeeze the Charmin!" became popular in 1964 and was used in campaigns until 1985. In 1971, famous American songwriter Barry Manilow wrote State Farm's musical jingle, "Like a good neighbor, State Farm is there." Baby boomers related well to it, and State Farm still uses the same jingle today. Slogans create emotional buying experiences for customers that they remember. If customers can recognize a slogan or hum a jingle, branding has done its job.

Checkpoint 17.2

1. What is the key to a unique brand?
2. How can businesses show social responsibility through a brand?
3. Why is brand loyalty important for businesses?
4. What is the difference between a trademark and a service mark?
5. What is the importance of personal branding.

Build Your Vocabulary

As you progress through this course, develop a personal glossary of marketing terms and add it to your portfolio. This will help you build your vocabulary and prepare you for a career. Write a definition for each of the following terms, and add it to your personal marketing glossary.

brand equity
corporate social responsibility
brand loyalty
intellectual property
trademark
service mark
personal brand

Checkpoint Answers

1. The key to a unique brand is creating products and promotions that appeal to the needs and wants of your target market.
2. The brand of a company reflects its image in the community. Examples include donating to nonprofits, recycling, supporting local businesses, or supporting a cause like cancer research. For this reason, many companies participate in visible community and charitable events.

3. Brand loyalty means repeat purchases for a business.
4. A trademark protects a product or company. A service mark protects a service provided rather than a product.
5. Personal branding distinguishes you from other people and may be useful when searching for a job.

Build Your Vocabulary Answers

Definitions for these terms can be found in the glossary of this text.

Chapter Summary

Section 17.1 Brand Elements

- A brand is what sets a product or business apart from its competitors. There are two elements of a brand: tangible elements and intangible elements.
- There are three types of brands: national, private label, and generic. Each type of brand is specific to the company that created and owns it.

Section 17.2 Power of the Brand

- The true power of a brand lies in its ability to influence purchasing behavior. Successful branding creates a unique brand identity, contributes to the positive image of the brand; and inspires brand loyalty and repeat sales.
- A brand is only valuable if competitors cannot copy it. In business, a brand is considered the intellectual property of its owner and should be protected from theft.
- A personal brand is the sum of the differences between you and those around you. Think about what makes you special. This will help you shape your own personal brand identity in the way you want.

Review Your Knowledge

1. Explain the purpose of a brand.
2. What is the most powerful aspect of a brand?
3. What are the intangible elements of a brand?
4. Why is a brand considered a promise to customers?
5. How are brand perceptions formed?
6. What are three goals that a brand should achieve?
7. Give an example of a corporation buying naming rights to show community support.
8. When does brand loyalty occur?
9. When can the registered symbol be used with a trademark or service mark?
10. How can a person create a personal brand?

Evaluate

Assign the end-of-chapter activities.

Review Your Knowledge Answers

1. A brand is what sets a product or business apart from its competitors. The brand is a result of everything a customer sees, hears, and experiences. A brand image can be positive or negative.
2. The most powerful aspect of a brand is the graphic design elements. These elements appear in packaging, on labels, and form the logo.
3. The intangible elements of a brand include the implied promise of the brand, the consistency of the brand, and customer perceptions.
4. A brand is considered a promise to customers because they develop expectations based on how the product is promoted and priced. When they pull their hard-earned money out of their pockets and purchase something, they assume their expectations will be met.
5. Brand perceptions are formed in three ways: personal experience, hearing about someone else's experiences, and how the brand is promoted.

6. Branding efforts should achieve a unique brand identity, contribute to the positive image of the brand; and inspire brand loyalty and repeat sales.
7. An example of a corporation buying naming rights to show community support is Conseco, an Indiana-based insurance company, paying to have its name on a sports stadium.
8. Brand loyalty occurs when the product, service, or business consistently meets customer needs and expectations.
9. Once a trademark or service mark has been registered with the USPTO, the symbol ® can be used with the mark.
10. Consider the image you want to present. Think about what makes you special. This will help you shape your personal brand identity in the way you want.

Build Your Vocabulary Answers

Definitions for these terms can be found in the glossary of this text.

Apply Your Knowledge

1. Describe the tangible elements of your company's brand, including its name, graphic design elements, and tagline or slogan.
2. What types of branding decisions were made for your company? Are they effective? If not, what are recommendations to improve the brand and its image?
3. What is your company's brand promise? In other words, describe what customers expect when they purchase a product or service from your brand?
4. Suppose you were a marketer for a company providing a consumer service. Choose a service you know well, and write two metaphors for that service that could be used in promotions.
5. It is important for marketers to know the general perception of the company's brand among the customer base. How would you go about learning about the perceptions of your customers?
6. As a marketer, how does the branding of your company products help you to make decisions about the three other Ps?
7. What does social responsibility have to do with creating a brand identity? What are some ways that you, as a marketer, can help to reinforce your company image as it relates to social responsibility?
8. Think about the brand loyalty for the products your company sells. What percentage of customers do you think are brand loyal? How could you increase brand loyalty for your products?
9. Is any part of your company brand trademarked? Describe the process for trademarking a part or all of the tangible parts of your company brand.
10. Write a résumé that highlights your personal brand.

Check Your Marketing IQ

Now that you have finished the chapter, see what you learned about marketing by taking the chapter posttest. If you do not have a smartphone, visit the G-W Learning companion website.

G-W Learning mobile site: www.m.g-wlearning.com
G-W Learning companion website: www.g-wlearning.com

College and Career Readiness

Common Core

CTE Career Ready Practices. Responsible citizens consider the environmental, social, and economic impacts of decisions that are made. As a marketing professional, how could you show corporate responsibility when participating in the branding strategy for your company? List three ways that you can demonstrate your corporate responsibility.

Reading. Carefully consider the use of the term *corporate responsibility.* What does this term mean to you? Do you think the term readily conveys its meaning to the reader? Why or why not?

Writing. Using the Internet, research a successful branding story. Cite the company and create a narrative that describes circumstances that lead to a successful branding strategy. Be sure to include the relevant details that contributed to the success of the brand. Pay close attention to the sequence of events as you develop your narrative.

Teamwork

Working with a teammate, choose a corporation that makes consumer products, such as Liz Claiborne, Inc. or Procter & Gamble. Use library resources or the Internet to research the company brands. Make a poster or use presentation software to show the different brands made by the company you chose. Include the brand name, logo, and slogan for each brand. Were you surprised by any of the brands that the company owns?

G-W Learning Mobile Site

Visit the G-W Learning mobile site to complete the chapter pretest and posttest and to practice vocabulary using e-flash cards. If you do not have a smartphone, visit the G-W Learning companion website to access these features.

G-W Learning mobile site: www.m.g-wlearning.com

G-W Learning companion website: www.g-wlearning.com

Unit 4 **Product Dynamics**
Building the Marketing Plan

Without products to sell, there would be no businesses. As the marketing manager for your company, you must decide not only what products or services to offer, but why yours are better than those sold by the competition. Describing your products and their competitive advantages is an important part of the marketing plan. Marketers help create solid, positive brand identities to ensure the success of the business.

Part 1 **Product**

Objectives

- List the products or service offered by your business.
- Complete a features and benefits chart for each one.
- Determine the unique selling proposition (USP) for each one.

Directions

In this activity, you will complete the Competition portion of the Situation Analysis section. In addition, you will begin the Marketing Strategies section by describing your Product Strategies. Access the *Marketing Dynamics* companion website at www.g-wlearning.com. Download the data file as indicated for the following activity.

1. Unit Activity 4-1. Product. Describe the products or services your business will offer. Discuss the features and benefits for each and write your unique selling proposition (USP).
2. Open your saved marketing plan document.
3. Locate the Marketing Strategies section and start the Product Strategies portion. Use the suggestions and questions listed in the marketing plan template to help you generate ideas. Delete the instructions and questions when you are finished recording your responses. Proofread your document and correct any errors in keyboarding, spelling, and grammar.
4. Save your document.

Part 2 **Branding**

Objectives

Describe the brand and show the tangible brand elements.

- Explain how the current branding strategy supports the product or company.
- Make recommendations for improving the branding strategy.

Directions

In this activity, you will complete the portion of the Marketing Strategies section that describes your Product Strategies. Access the *Marketing Dynamics* companion website at www.g-wlearning.com. Download the data file as indicated for the following activity.

1. Unit Activity 4-2. Branding. Analyze the branding strategies that are currently in place for your product or company, and recommend ways to improve the branding program for a stronger brand identity.
2. Open your saved marketing plan document.
3. Locate the Marketing Strategies section and complete the portion under Product Strategies that relates to branding. Use the suggestions and questions listed in the marketing plan template to help you generate ideas. Delete the instructions and questions when you are finished recording your responses. Proofread your document and correct any errors in keyboarding, spelling, and grammar.
4. Save your document.

Unit 5

Price Dynamics

Chapters

Eye-Catcher

Oleksiy Mark/Shutterstock.com

Marketing Matters

In marketing, price may change everything. For many customers, the price of a product they want determines the one they choose to buy. For other customers, value and quality are more important than price alone. And, a small group of people actually prefer higher prices. Through the use of QR codes, marketers make it easy for customers to compare prices anytime, anywhere. Marketing is truly all around us.

Marketing Core Functions Covered in This Unit

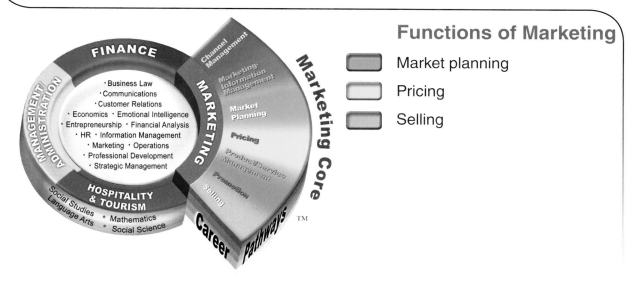

Functions of Marketing

- Market planning
- Pricing
- Selling

Developing a Vision

Price—what does it mean? To one buyer, it may mean value. For other buyers, price may mean quality. To one seller, it may mean profit. To other sellers, price may mean competition. There is no single answer. Price has different meanings to everyone depending on their situations.

For a marketer, creating the correct pricing model that is effective for both buyers and sellers is a challenge. Marketers must study economic conditions to create realistic pricing structures. Product life cycles must be considered. Government regulations must also be followed. Pricing is a complicated task for even the most experienced marketing professionals.

18 Price

Section 18.1 Importance of Price

Section 18.2 Governmental Influences on Pricing

"A business that makes nothing but money is a poor business."

—Henry Ford, founder of Ford Motor Company

College and Career Readiness

Reading Prep
As you read this chapter, take notes on the important points you want to remember. Record key terms and ideas. Is this helpful in understanding the material?

Check Your Marketing IQ

Before you begin the chapter, see what you already know about marketing by taking the chapter pretest. If you do not have a smartphone, visit the G-W Learning companion website.

G-W Learning mobile site: www.m.g-wlearning.com
G-W Learning companion website: www.g-wlearning.com

Explore

Assign the College and Career Readiness Reading Prep activity before students read the chapter. Reading Prep activities give students opportunity to apply the Common Core State Standards.

Engage

Assign the Chapter 18 pretest. The test may be accessed by using the QR code or going to the companion website. Discuss which questions students were unable to answer.

◇DECA Emerging Leaders

Sports and Entertainment Marketing Team Decision-Making Event, Part 1

Career Cluster: Marketing
Instructional Area: Selling/Pricing

General Performance Indicators

- Communications skills—the ability to exchange information and ideas with others through writing, speaking, reading, or listening
- Analytical skills—the ability to derive facts from data, findings from facts, conclusions from findings, and recommendations from conclusions
- Production skills—the ability to take a concept from an idea and make it real
- Teamwork—the ability to be an effective member of a productive group
- Priorities/time management—the ability to determine priorities and manage time commitments
- Economic competencies

Specific Performance Indicators

- Discuss motivational theories that impact buying behavior.
- Explain key factors in building a clientele.
- Explain factors affecting pricing decisions.
- Explain the role of customer service as a component of selling relationships.
- Describe word-of-mouth channels used to communicate with targeted audiences.
- Explain the concept of marketing strategies.
- Identify factors affecting a business's profit.

Purpose

Designed for a team of two DECA members, the event measures the team's ability to explain core business concepts in the format of a case study in a role-play. This event consists of a 100-question, multiple-choice, cluster exam for each team member and a decision-making case study situation. The Team Decision-Making Event provides an opportunity for participants to analyze one or a combination of elements essential to the effective operation of a business in the specific career area presented as a case study.

For the purposes of this text, you will be presented with the material for this event in two parts. Part 1 presents the knowledge and skills assessed and an overview of the event's purpose and procedure. Part 2 presents the remaining procedures and the event situation.

Procedure, Part 1

1. For Part 1 in this text, read both sets of performance indicators. Discuss these with your team members.
2. If there are any questions, ask your teacher to clarify.

Critical Thinking

1. Work with your team members to determine three strategies for effectively reviewing the information on this page.
2. Identify present day examples that illustrate effective application of each performance indicator.
3. Generate a list of creative ways to discuss, explains and describe when required to do so in a presentation.

Visit www.deca.org for more information.

Section 18.1 Importance of Price

Objectives

After completing this section, you will be able to
- **explain** the concept of price.
- **identify** and describe factors that affect pricing.
- **describe** how product, place, and promotion may affect pricing decisions.

Key Terms

value proposition
list price
selling price
manufacturer's suggested retail price (MSRP)
unit pricing
fixed expense
variable expense
elastic demand
marginal utility
law of diminishing marginal utility
inelastic demand

Web Connect

Do an Internet search for *pricing strategies*. List three websites that addressed the topic. What important advice did these sites offer?

Critical Thinking

To be competitive, it might be necessary to offer multiple pricing options to your customers. What are some of the criteria you would consider for special pricing? Why?

What Is Price?

As you learned earlier, *price* is the amount of money requested or exchanged for a product. Every business faces the challenge of correctly pricing goods and services. The price
- must cover the costs of producing and selling the product;
- should generate the desired level of profit for the business; and
- must be what customers are willing to pay for the product.

As a function of marketing, marketers use price to establish and communicate the value of products. As you learned in Chapter 17, *value* is the relative worth of something to a person. Some marketers use price to influence customer perception. The **value proposition** explains the value of the product over others that are similar. Value may also be a part of the brand promise. Customers may be willing to pay more if they believe in the value of the product or service.

Marketers need to know the value that customers place on their products. Market research helps them to learn this information. Individual customers often place different values on the same product. You might think that a friend is crazy for paying $125 for a pair of shoes. Yet, you might not think anything of paying $125 for a front-row concert ticket. What you value is different from what your friend values. The price you are willing to pay for the same products also differs because of your values.

Price is just as important in the B2B market as it is to consumers.

Photodiem/Shutterstock.com

Pricing Types

Most businesses have several tiers, or levels, of pricing. The **list price** of a product is the established price printed in a catalog, on a price tag, or in a price list. The list price does not include any discounts. The **selling price** is the actual price paid for a product, after any discounts or coupons are deducted.

Discounts are shown as a percentage, such as a *40 percent discount*. Discounts may also be shown as a dollar figure, such as *$20 off.*

Suppose you are shopping for a jacket. You find a jacket you like with a price tag that reads $50. You have a $10-off coupon, so you actually pay only $40 for the jacket. In this case, the list price is $50. The selling price is $40. If there are no discounts or coupons, the selling price is the same as the list price.

Another type of price is the MSRP, which is often associated with car buying. The **manufacturer's suggested retail price (MSRP)** is the price recommended by the manufacturer. Some manufacturers, such as Coach, require a retailer to sell at MSRP. Others, however, do not require the retailer to use the MSRP as the list price.

Price is often considered the dollar amount listed on a price tag of a good. However, there are many other terms used for the price of services. The *tip* paid to a server at a restaurant is part of the price of a meal. *School tuition* is the price of attending a school. *Admission* is the price paid for entrance to amusement parks and theaters. A *donation* is the price for attending a charitable event. The price for a loan is called *interest*. The price for seeing a professional, such as a doctor or lawyer, is called a *fee*. The price of transportation, such as for an airline ticket, is called a *fare*.

FYI

The selling price may also be called the *market price*.

Sale pricing can bring more customers to a store and increase product sales.

Unit Pricing

Unit pricing allows customers to compare prices based on a standard unit of measure, such as an ounce or a pound. The unit prices are posted on shelving labels under the items. In some states, unit pricing is required by law to help consumers make good buying decisions.

Retailers often price items by the package. For example, a bag of grapes might be priced at $1.99. If there are 8 ounces of grapes in the bag, the unit price is $0.249 per ounce. The shelf would display the total price of $1.99 *and* the unit price of $0.25 per ounce.

Other grocery items, such as bottles of shampoo or containers of oatmeal, show *per-unit prices* as well. Since packages come in so many different sizes, it would be difficult for consumers to compare the real price without the unit price. The larger the overall package, the more expensive it is. However, the per-unit price of larger packages is generally less expensive. For example, a 10-ounce bottle

Magicinfoto/Shutterstock.com

Explore

There are laws in some states that require the unit price be listed for products in stores. Is your state one of those that has this law?

of shampoo maybe priced at $4.99, which is $0.50 per ounce. A 27-ounce bottle of the same shampoo might be priced at $8.99, which means the unit price falls to $.033 per ounce. Which is the better value? As a result, many stores voluntarily use unit pricing to encourage customers to buy the larger size and increase sales.

Factors That Affect Price

Many factors affect the price of a product, as shown in Figure 18-1. The following factors can affect price: company goals, expenses, customer perception, competition, economic conditions, government regulations, product life cycle, and supply and demand.

Company Goals

Marketers must set prices that are consistent with the overall company goals. The image a company projects is in part determined by the prices it charges. High prices tend to create an image of high-end products. Low prices often create an image of discount products.

Marketers must be sure the image created by the pricing matches the company goals outlined in the business and marketing plans. For example, some companies want to project a bargain-value image. These companies offer less expensive products to keep prices as low as possible. In contrast, other companies want to project a high-end image of luxury and would offer higher-quality products. Therefore, the cost of these products would be priced a great deal higher than those in bargain stores.

Company goals may also vary by product. For example, a retailer may have a large number of goods that did not sell well. The retailer might lower the price of these goods so that they would sell faster.

Expenses

All products and services have certain expenses related to their creation and distributing them to the end user. These costs influence the price that is set for that product or service because a profit is made only after all

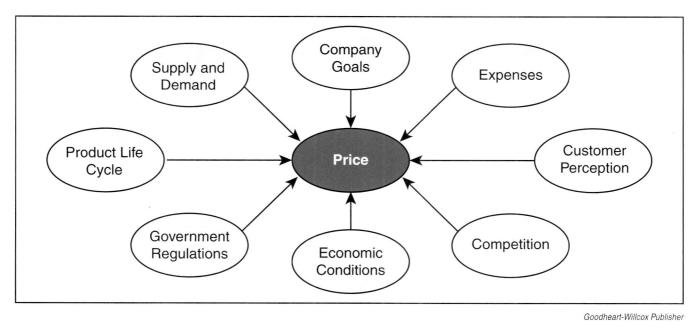

Goodheart-Willcox Publisher

Figure 18-1 Pricing is a dynamic marketing activity influenced by a number of factors.

Case in Point

Microsoft

Many consumers continue to use their favorite products because the products are familiar and keep the consumers in their comfort zones. In order for a company to keep product sales up, marketers may suggest newer versions of the products. It is up to the marketers to craft campaigns that convince consumers to trade up to the newer version or model of a product they already own.

The Microsoft marketing mix is a good example of how to convince consumers it is time to switch—by making a great introductory offer. Microsoft released its new operating system, Windows 8, in October, 2012. To encourage users to upgrade from their current Windows system right away, Microsoft offered a low *promotional price* to grab the attention of PC owners. It offered a Windows 8 operating-system download for less than 20 percent ($69) of the $199 MSRP. A boxed version was also available for the same price. However, that low, introductory price was only good through February, 2013. Was the promotional offer the key to success? Maybe. Windows 8 sales are reported to be higher than the Windows 7 version release in 2009.

of the expenses are covered. There are two basic types of expenses: fixed and variable, as shown in Figure 18-2.

Fixed expenses are those that do not change and are not affected by the number of products produced or sold. For example, fixed expenses may include rent, insurance, and marketing salaries that stay the same each month. Variable expenses are those that change based on the activities of the business. For example, variable marketing expenses might include advertising or sales commissions that may vary monthly.

The price of the product has to at least cover the fixed and variable expenses related to that product. For manufacturers, price has to cover the cost of making the goods and marketing them to customers. For retailers, the price has to cover the cost of buying the goods and reselling them to consumers.

A marketer may temporarily lower a price to near, at, or below cost to meet competition or to increase market share. In some states, though, it is illegal to sell products at a price below cost. However, a company cannot always price at or below cost, because there would be no profit. A company is likely to go out of business unless it makes a profit. Most companies today are looking for ways to maintain quality and keep prices stable while

Monthly Operating Expenses	
Fixed Expenses	**Variable Expenses**
• Insurance • Mortgage • Phone • Rent • Salary • Marketing salaries	• Advertising • Fees • Office supplies • Utilities • Miscellaneous • Sales commissions

Goodheart-Willcox Publisher

Figure 18-2 Profits come only after both fixed and variable expenses are met.

still making a profit. They are achieving this goal by reducing expenses.

Customer Perception

Customers often perceive price as showing the value or quality of a product. Have you ever wondered what was wrong with a product because the price was so low? If you said *yes*, then the price influenced your perception of the quality of the product. Sometimes, customers believe that a high price means a better-quality product, which is not always the case.

On the other hand, products also can be priced too high. When the price of a product is too high, customers may not buy it. Their perception of the product is that it is not worth the money. In this situation, the marketer can lower the price to see if customers will then buy the product.

Competition

Marketers should always be aware of the prices of the competition. You might decide to match the competition or set higher or lower prices than your competitors. Marketers constantly monitor the prices of their competitors because these prices may change. If a competitor suddenly lowers its prices, that could negatively impact sales for your business if you do not respond in some way.

As discussed in Chapter 11, *price competition* is competing on the basis of price alone. *Nonprice competition* is having a competitive advantage based on factors other than price. Companies that compete based on price, such as airlines, change their prices frequently. Usually, when one seller lowers prices, other competitors are quick to lower their prices.

Some companies, such as department stores, rarely change pricing unless it is for a special offer or a sale. Nonprice competition is often used to build brand loyalty. If customers prefer a brand, they are not easily influenced by a lower price to buy another brand. For example, if you are loyal to one brand of jeans, you probably would not buy a different brand just because the price was lower.

Economic Conditions

Economic conditions change. One day the economy seems stable. The next day the stock market may fall and the economy takes a turn for the worse. As you learned in Chapter 8, business cycles affect the prices of many products. Prices tend to rise during good economic times, or expansion. During expansion, most people are employed and have money to spend, so demand for products tends to increase. When demand rises, prices also typically rise.

Prices tend to fall during bad economic times, or recession. During a recession, unemployment rises and many people have less money to spend. Demand for products generally decreases during a recession. When demand falls, prices also typically fall.

However, some product prices are not affected by business cycles. For example, the prices of luxury items tend to stay the same regardless of the business-cycle stage. Business cycles usually impact the wealthy less. So, even during economic downturns, they have the money to spend on luxuries.

Product Life Cycle

The stage of a product in the product life cycle affects its pricing strategies. Often, the price of a brand new product is high. The manufacturer wants to recover some of the new product development costs. Plus, only one company is usually making the new product, so the supply is low—but demand may be high. Other times, new products are introduced at very low prices so people will

Green Marketing

Electronic Equipment

A variety of electronic equipment, such as computers, cell phones, and other tools are necessary to enable a business to run efficiently. Care must be taken to keep equipment clean and maintained on a regular basis. Avoid chemical cleaners when removing the smudge marks from an LCD or TV screen or a computer monitor. Chemical cleaners may ruin some equipment finishes, and some are bad for the environment. Look for environmentally-friendly cleaners that will not harm equipment to protect your investment as well as the environment.

try the product. After the sales increase, the prices are raised.

During the growth stage, more competitors enter the market, and the price of a high-priced new product usually falls. This is especially true for technology products, such as computers and smartphones.

During the maturity and decline phases of a product, prices are usually lowered. The lower prices help a declining product generate more sales.

Supply and Demand

The law of supply and demand is tied directly to price, as shown in Figure 18-3. When demand is high and the supply is low, marketers usually raise prices. Customers are willing to pay higher prices for products they really want. When demand is low and supply is high, marketers usually cut prices to increase sales. Customers are often willing to buy more of a product when the price is low.

Price can also affect the demand for some products. For example, higher prices tend to lower the demand because fewer people can afford the product. In contrast, lower prices tend to raise the demand. However, for some products, demand is not affected by price. *Demand elasticity* is the degree to which price changes demand. The demand for some products is very elastic; that is, the demand

changes when the price changes. The demand for other products tends to remain constant; that is, demand does *not* change when the price changes.

Elastic Demand

Elastic demand is product demand in which the percent change in demand is greater than the percent change in price. Think of a rubber band. A rubber band is elastic; its size changes with the amount of pressure applied. For many products, demand is elastic like a rubber band. The higher the price, the lower the demand.

For example, if the prices of your favorite clothing brand become too high, your demand for that brand will drop. You would buy it less often—or not at all. Luxury products that you do not really need tend to have elastic demand. Products that have cheaper substitutes also tend to have elastic demand. For example, if the price of beef goes up, you can substitute chicken. The demand for beef is elastic.

Similarly, when prices for products with elastic demand are lowered, the demand rises. In other words, as the price of the product falls, consumers tend to buy more of that product. For example, if the price of beef goes down, you may buy more beef. However, there will come a point at which no matter how low the price, you will not buy any more. You have already bought as much

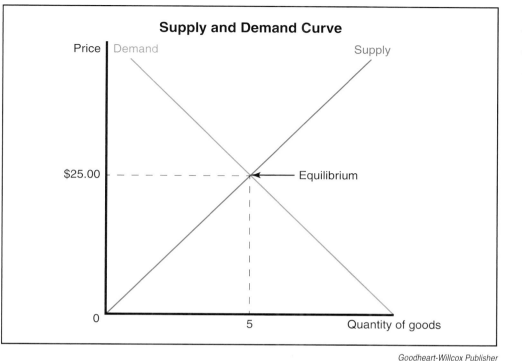

Supply and Demand Curve

Goodheart-Willcox Publisher

Figure 18-3 In theory, when supply meets demand, the market price is stable.

beef that will fit in your freezer. Even if the price goes lower, you will not buy any more because you cannot use any more.

Recall that *utility* defines the characteristics of a product that satisfies human wants and needs. The consumer gains satisfaction from the product when it is used. **Marginal utility** is the additional satisfaction gained by using one additional unit of the same product. For example, when you eat an ear of corn, you get satisfaction, or utility. If you eat a second ear of corn, you get a bit more satisfaction, which is its marginal utility. As you continue to eat, you begin to feel full. The second ear of corn does not give you as much satisfaction as the first. If you continue to eat more ears of corn, each additional one gives you little or no added satisfaction. This is an example of the law of diminishing marginal utility. The **law of diminishing marginal utility** states that consuming more units of the same product decreases the marginal utility from each unit.

FYI

The law of diminishing marginal utility explains why a marketer can only lower prices to a certain level to increase sales. After a certain point, consumers do not need or cannot use additional units of the product, regardless of the price.

Inelastic Demand

Inelastic demand is product demand that is *not* affected by price. Think of a metal ring. A metal ring is hard and inelastic. Its size does not change, no matter how hard you pull on it. The demand for certain products does not drop when the price rises. For example, basic food products, such as milk and bread, have inelastic demand because they are necessities.

Medicines also tend to have inelastic demand. For example, suppose you must take a particular medication daily to stay healthy. Will your demand for that medica-

Extend

Compare and contrast elastic demand with inelastic demand.

The marginal utility of each ear of corn decreases as the number eaten increases.

tion change if the price rises? No, you will find a way to afford the higher price because without the medication, you would become very ill. Brand loyalty also can create inelastic demand. For example, you may like only one brand of shampoo. Your demand for that shampoo is inelastic because you will not buy another brand, even if it is cheaper.

Some products have both elastic and inelastic demand, depending on the situation. For example, perhaps you drive a car to school every day. Suppose the price of gasoline doubles. You may be likely to decrease your demand for the expensive gasoline by bicycling to school most days or carpooling. In this case, your demand for gasoline is elastic.

However, suppose that you are driving on a limited-access highway. You notice that your fuel gauge is on empty. You must pull into the only gas station in the area within 50 miles. The price of gas at this station is double what you usually pay. Will your demand change? No, you must have gas in order to reach your destination. You will pay the extra price. In this case, the demand for gasoline is inelastic because it is a necessity.

Product, Place, and Promotion Decisions

As you learned earlier, the decisions marketers make about a marketing mix influence each other. Pricing decisions influence those made about product, place, and promotion. And, the decisions made about product, place, and promotion affect pricing decisions as well. Product, place, and promotion decisions can be difficult to change. Pricing, however, can be easily changed to meet the competition or address changes in the economy.

Product

Product decisions can be influenced by price decisions, particularly in the types of materials used in the product. For example, sweatshirts can be made from 9-ounce fabric or 11-ounce fabric. The 11-ounce fabric is heavier and more expensive to produce. If the product decision is to produce a lower-priced sweatshirt line, then the less expensive 9-ounce fabric would be used to keep the price down.

Place

Place decisions are also affected by pricing decisions. If your products are low-priced, you will want to find a low-cost method of shipping or distributing them. For example, if you sell a product over the Internet for $4.99, it would not make sense to charge an additional $6.00 for shipping. On the other hand, if you sell a $10,000 diamond to a customer overseas, you would most likely ship it by air. The extra expense of airfreight would be worth it to get the diamond quickly and safely to the customer.

Promotion

Price decisions often affect the promotion decisions made by marketers. Price plays a part in both the message used to appeal to the target market and the marketing budget. For example, when prices are lowered, promotions should advertise the new, competitive pricing. In addition, some higher-priced products, such as fine jewelry, may generate a higher profit for the business. The higher profits might allow marketers more funds for promotions to increase sales and generate even more profit.

Checkpoint 18.1

1. List the factors that affect price.
2. List two pricing levels.
3. Why is unit pricing important?
4. Why is the law of marginal utility important for marketers to understand?
5. Name two of the basic types of expenses.

Build Your Vocabulary

As you progress through this text, develop a personal glossary of marketing terms and add it to your portfolio. This will help you build your vocabulary and prepare for a career as a marketing professional. Write a definition for each of the following terms, and add it to your personal marketing glossary.

value proposition
list price
selling price
manufacturer's suggested retail price (MSRP)
unit pricing
fixed expense

variable expense
elastic demand
marginal utility
law of diminishing marginal utility
inelastic demand

Section 18.2 Governmental Influence on Pricing

Objectives

After completing this section, you will be able to
- **list** five unfair pricing practices some businesses may attempt to use.
- **discuss** pricing laws that protect businesses and consumers.
- **explain** how and when the government may attempt to control some prices.

Key Terms

bait and switch
price-fixing
price discrimination
deceptive pricing
predatory pricing
loss leader
price gouging
price ceiling
price floor

Web Connect

You are the marketing manager for the business for which you are writing a marketing plan. Conduct research on the Internet about how products similar to yours are typically priced. What did you learn about the pricing process?

Critical Thinking

Given the nature of your business, which pricing laws or regulations are relevant? Why were those laws put in place?

Unfair Pricing Practices

Both businesses and consumers are affected by unfair and unethical pricing practices. Businesses that use unfair pricing practices are breaking laws in addition to being unethical. Unfair pricing practices are usually reported to authorities by unhappy customers. The best-case scenario for these businesses is decreasing sales and profits. In the worst-case scenario, owners may have to pay costly fines and the business may fold. These following pricing practices are both harmful to consumers and illegal.

- **Bait and switch:** the practice of advertising one product with the intent of persuading a customer to buy a more expensive item when they arrive in the store.

- **Price-fixing:** a group of competitors get together and set the price for a specific product, which is usually high.
- **Price discrimination:** when a company sells the same product to different customers at different prices based on personal characteristics.
- **Deceptive pricing:** pricing products in a way to intentionally mislead a customer is illegal.
- **Predatory pricing:** setting very low prices to remove competition, such as foreign companies that price their products below the same domestic ones to drive the domestic companies out of business.

Some US states have their own laws against additional pricing practices. However, there are no federal laws banning these practices, so they are enforced on the state

Explore

Provide an opportunity for students to explore by assigning a hands-on activity. Review the vocabulary terms at the beginning of the section. Where have students encountered these terms before? Help students make educated guesses about the meanings of the terms with which they are least familiar.

Engage

Use the Teamwork exercise at the end of the chapter to engage students to solve a problem or make a group presentation.

College and Career Portfolio

Skills and Talents

Your portfolio should contain samples of your work that show your skills or talents. Now is the time to start collecting these items. You can decide which documents to include later when you prepare your final portfolio. Look at past school or work assignments you have completed. Select a book report, essay, poem, or other work demonstrating your writing talents. Include a research paper, letter, electronic presentation, or other items that illustrate your business-communication skills. Also, look for projects that show your skills related to critical thinking, time management, and problem solving. Have you completed a long or complicated project? Write a description of the project and explain how you managed various parts of the assignment to complete it on time. Include samples from the completed project. What career area interests you most? Select completed work from classes that will help prepare you for jobs or internships in that area.

1. Save the documents that show your skills and talents in your e-portfolio. Remember to place the documents in an appropriate subfolder.
2. Place hard copies in the container for your print portfolio.

level. As a marketer, make sure to know the pricing laws for your state.

Twenty-two US states have *sales-below-cost (SBC) laws* that ban loss-leader pricing. A **loss leader** is pricing an item much lower than the current market price or the cost of acquiring the product. The purpose of loss leaders is to draw customers into a business by advertising a product for a very low price. The business hopes that once in the store, consumers will buy other products to make up for the lost profit. Some state laws consider loss-leader pricing to be predatory and misleading pricing practices.

Thirty-four US states have laws that protect consumers from price gouging practices. **Price gouging** is the raising of prices on certain kinds of goods to an excessively high level during an emergency. The state laws consider price gouging a form of price fixing.

Pricing Laws

There are state and federal laws that regulate pricing to prevent unfair pricing policies and practices used by some businesses. The government also prevents the forming of monopolies, which interfere with the workings of a market economy. Recall that a monopoly takes place when a company controls the market for a single product and is the only seller of a product or service. As a result, a monopoly usually sets unfair high prices that hurt consumers. A list of specific laws that regulate or affect pricing are shown in Figure 18-4.

AMA Tip

Staying aware of current marketing research helps marketers make informed decisions based on reasonable predictions. For example, a recent article in the AMA *Journal of Marketing Research* explained in detail the effect of gasoline prices on consumer grocery-shopping behaviors. Marketers who read this article will know how to respond quickly to rises in gasoline prices in order to maximize grocery sales. Check out your school library and the AMA website to find more information from marketing and business journals. www.marketingpower.com

Elaborate/Extend

Provide an opportunity for students to exhibit their understanding of concepts in context of the material as it is presented. As time permits, have students read and discuss the special features in the margins.

Elaborate/Extend

If students are using the optional *Marketing Dynamics* workbook, assign activities to engage active learning.

Laws That Regulate Pricing		
Law	**What It Regulates**	**When It Might Be Used**
Sherman Antitrust Act (1890)	This law regulates price-fixing.	The gasoline stations in your town all collude to charge the same price for gasoline.
Clayton Antitrust Act (1914)	Passed in 1914, this law makes price discrimination illegal.	Your school store ordered 100 widgets from a company and was charged $4.00 a widget. The school store manager finds out that another store ordered 100 widgets from the same company and was charged $3.50 a widget.
Robinson-Patman Act (1936)	This law strengthened the Clayton Act by specifically prohibiting a seller from charging different prices to different customers for the same product and same quantity.	This law helps small retailers compete against large chains. The same types of discounts, financing, etc., have to be offered to both large and small retailers.
Wheeler Lea Act (1938)	This law prohibits deceptive advertising of prices. Companies cannot advertise that their prices are lower unless they can prove it; they cannot advertise lowered prices unless the original price was higher; and list prices cannot be used in reference to a sale price unless the product was actually sold at the list price.	You see a pair of shoes on sale for $45.99; however, you were in the same store last week before the sale, and they were $45.99.
Unit-Pricing Laws	These laws vary from state to state. Retailers must display pricing that shows the price of an item per unit. Most packaged items are priced per package, which makes it hard to compare the prices of certain items, particularly grocery items.	The price of a 32-ounce bottle of shampoo is $5.99. A sign on the shelf should state that it costs 19 cents an ounce.
Minimum Price Laws or Sales-Below-Cost, Laws	These laws vary from state to state. Retailers cannot sell a product for less than its cost.	A retailer buys running shoes from the manufacturer for $20; it cannot resell them for less than $20.
Federal Trade Commission Price Advertising Guidelines	Guidelines prohibit any deceptive or bait-and-switch advertising	This law prohibits advertising that makes unsubstantial claims about health or safety, such as sunscreen that "reduces the risk of skin cancer."

Goodheart-Willcox Publisher

Figure 18-4 The federal government passed a number of laws to prevent monopolies and promote fair price competition.

Explain

Identify specific examples of each type of illegal pricing activity. Ask students to share experiences they have had with one or more of these pricing practices.

Elaborate/Extend

If students are using the optional *Marketing Dynamics* workbook, assign activities to engage active learning.

Governmental Price Controls

The government may also intervene in the pricing of some products in an attempt to control the economy or help consumers. Price controls are often set when the public becomes alarmed about a fast-growing rate of inflation. Most economists believe price controls can sometimes help suppliers and/or consumers. However, price controls can actually worsen the very problems the government is trying to solve.

The government may set maximum prices called **price ceilings** for certain goods and services it thinks are being priced too high. The government may believe that consumers need some help to purchase the products. Price ceilings on some products are often set during war times when there may be shortages that could drive prices unreasonably high. However, price ceilings can also cause the very shortages the government is trying to prevent. The existing businesses or producers have to accept a lower price than they would otherwise set for their goods or services, and many are likely to leave the business. For example, the government set a price ceiling for gasoline in 1973 when the price of oil nearly doubled. However, the price ceiling actually created a gas shortage, which created long lines at the pumps due to rationing.

Price floors are minimum prices set by the government for certain goods and services that it thinks are being priced too low. Price floors are set to help the producers. However, if the price floor is set higher than

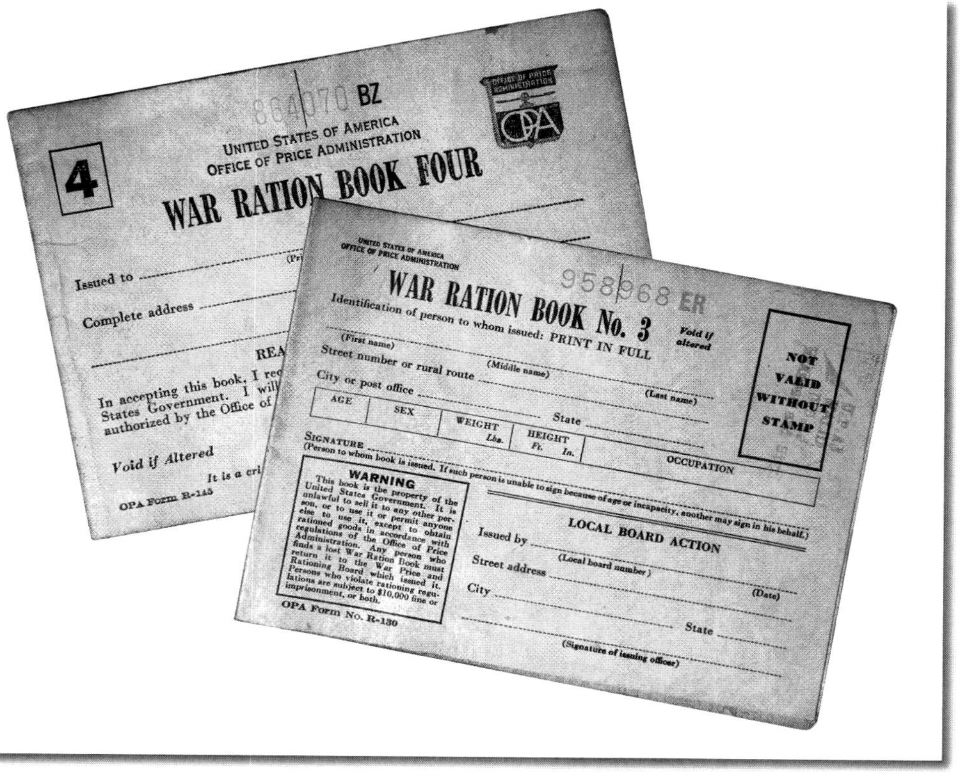

This picture shows two food and commodity ration books from World War II when US price ceilings and rationing were in effect.

Resource/Evaluate

Assign the optional Chapter 18 test for **EXAM**VIEW® Assessment Suite as a formal assessment tool.

Extend

Ask for student opinions of why price ceilings and floors are important to consumers.

the market price, a surplus situation will occur. A surplus happens because consumers will not buy the higher-priced products. As a result, many products are unsold. In many cases, a surplus situation also forces the government to buy the excess inventory to prevent rampant waste.

Governments sometimes set price floors for agricultural products to protect farmers from price drops.

Checkpoint 18.2

1. Give examples of unfair pricing practices.
2. Describe the purpose of the Sherman Antitrust Act.
3. Who creates pricing laws?
4. What is the purpose of pricing laws?
5. What happens if a price floor is too high?

Build Your Vocabulary

As you progress through this course, develop a personal glossary of marketing terms and add it to your portfolio. This will help you build your vocabulary and prepare you for a career. Write a definition for each of the following terms, and add it to your personal marketing glossary.

bait and switch
price-fixing
price discrimination
deceptive pricing
predatory pricing
loss leader
price gouging
price ceiling
price floor

Evaluate

Assign the Checkpoint questions at the end of the section. Assess students' comprehension using the Checkpoint activity as a self-assessment tool.

Checkpoint Answers

1. Examples of unfair pricing practices are bait and switch, price-fixing, price discrimination, deceptive pricing, and predatory pricing.
2. The Sherman Antitrust Act (1890) regulates price-fixing.

3. Pricing laws are created by both state and federal governments.
4. Pricing laws regulate pricing to prevent unfair pricing policies and practices used by some businesses.
5. If the price floor is set higher than the market price, a surplus situation will occur.

Build Your Vocabulary Answers

Definitions for these terms can be found in the glossary of this text.

Chapter Summary

Section 18.1 Importance of Price

- Price is the amount of money requested or exchanged for a product. Pricing types include list price, selling price, and manufacturer's suggested retail price.
- Many factors affect the price of a product. Some factors include company goals, expenses, customer perception, competition, economic conditions, government regulations, product life cycle, and supply and demand.
- Pricing decisions influence those made about product, place, and promotion. Pricing can easily be changed to meet competitive challenges and address economic changes.

Section 18.2 Governmental Influence on Pricing

- Both business customers and consumers are affected by unfair and unethical pricing practices. Businesses that use unfair pricing practices are breaking laws in addition to being unethical.
- There are state and federal laws that regulate pricing to prevent unfair pricing policies and practices used by some businesses. The government also prevents the forming of monopolies, which interfere with the workings of a market economy.
- The government may also intervene in the pricing of some products to control the economy, protect consumers, or help producers. The government may set price ceilings and price floors to regulate fair pricing practices.

Review Your Knowledge

1. What is value?
2. What is the purpose of a value proposition?
3. Why would a business use bait-and-switch tactics?
4. Describe how supply and demand affect pricing.
5. Give an example of the diminishing marginal utility of a product.
6. How does pricing impact product, place, and promotion decisions?
7. What is the difference between deceptive pricing and price discrimination?
8. Which pricing practices are illegal at the federal level and which are only banned by some US states?
9. What is the effect of a monopoly on pricing?
10. Why are governmental price controls created?

Evaluate
Assign the end-of-chapter activities.

Review Your Knowledge Answers
1. Value is the relative worth of something to a person. Some business owners use price to establish and communicate the value of a product in the minds of consumers. Value may also be a part of the brand promise.
2. A value proposition explains the value of the product over others that are similar. Individual customers often place different values on the same product.
3. A business would use bait-and-switch tactics to get customers in their place of business but try to sell them a different, more expensive item than the one advertised.
4. The law of supply and demand is tied directly to price. When demand for a product is high and the supply is low, marketers usually raise prices. When the demand is low and supply is high,

marketers usually cut prices to increase sales. Customers are often willing to buy more of a product when the price is low.
5. When you eat an ear of corn, you get satisfaction, or utility. If you eat a second ear of corn, you get a bit more satisfaction, which is its marginal utility. The second ear of corn does not give you as much satisfaction as the first. If you continue to eat more ears of corn, each additional one gives you little or no added satisfaction.
6. Product decisions can be influenced by price decisions, particularly in the types of materials used in the product. Place decisions are also affected by pricing decisions. If your products are low-priced, you will want to find a low-cost method of shipping or distributing them. For high-priced products, shipping will be more costly. Price decisions often affect the promotion decisions made by marketers in both the message used to appeal to the target market and possibly the marketing budget.

Apply Your Knowledge

1. In earlier chapters, you identified the product or service for which you are creating a marketing plan. Create a chart of the major products or services that you are responsible for marketing. Create three columns: list price, selling price, and MSRP. Calculate the percentage of difference among each price. Is the difference a consistent percentage?
2. What is the unit price for each of your products?
3. The following factors affect price: company goals, expenses, customer perception, competition, economic conditions, government regulations, product life cycle, and supply and demand. Describe how you think these factors influence pricing for your products or services.
4. Make a list of the fixed and variable expenses that impact the product or services you sell.
5. How do you think customers perceive the prices for your products? Does price contribute to your image?
6. How does marginal utility apply to your products?
7. Explain how product, place, and promotion influence the pricing of your products.
8. Which pricing laws influence your business?
9. Are there any recent examples of businesses similar to yours that have violated pricing laws?
10. Does your business use any loss leaders? If so, describe them and when they are used.

Check Your Marketing IQ

Now that you have finished the chapter, see what you learned about marketing by taking the chapter posttest. If you do not have a smartphone, visit the G-W Learning companion website.

G-W Learning mobile site: www.m.g-wlearning.com
G-W Learning companion website: www.g-wlearning.com

7. Price discrimination is selling a product to different customers at different prices. Deceptive pricing is pricing that is misleading. Both practices are illegal.

8. Bait and switch, price-fixing, price discrimination, deceptive pricing, and predatory pricing have federal laws that prevent them. Some US states have laws that ban loss-leader pricing and price gouging.

9. A monopoly controls the market for a single product and can set whatever price it wants. As a result, a monopoly usually sets unfairly high prices, which hurts the consumers.

10. Price controls are often set when the public becomes alarmed about a fast-growing rate of inflation.

Apply Your Knowledge Answers

Student answers will vary for questions 1–10.

Evaluate

Evaluate the students' understanding and knowledge. Assign the Chapter 18 posttest. The test may be accessed by using the QR code or by going to the companion website. What questions were students able to answer that they could not answer when they took the pretest?

Common Core

College and Career Readiness

CTE Career Ready Practices: To become career ready, it will be important to learn how to communicate clearly and effectively by using reason. Create an outline that includes information about the importance of unit pricing. Consider your audience as you prepare the information. Using the outline, make a presentation to your class.

Speaking: Participate in a collaborative classroom discussion about the role of supply and demand on pricing. Ask questions to participants that connect your ideas to the relevant evidence that has been presented.

Listening: Do an Internet search for oral presentations on product-pricing strategies. Select one speech and listen to it in its entirety. Present your findings and supporting evidence of the line of reasoning, organization, development, and style the speaker used to prepare his or her information. Identify the target market and the purpose of the speech.

Teamwork

Working as a team, research *price wars.* Select one industry that appeals to the team. Create a chart that gives the industry, business, year of the price war, and any other relevant information. Create a presentation that describes what happened and the implications for consumers.

G-W Learning Mobile Site

Visit the G-W Learning mobile site to complete the chapter pretest and posttest and to practice vocabulary using e-flash cards. If you do not have a smartphone, visit the G-W Learning companion website to access these features.

G-W Learning mobile site: www.m.g-wlearning.com
G-W Learning companion website: www.g-wlearning.com

19 Price Strategies

Section 19.1	Importance of Price
Section 19.2	Strategic Pricing
Section 19.2	Credit

"The bitterness of poor quality is remembered long after the sweetness of low price has faded from memory"

—Aldo Gucci, the late Italian designer and former chairman of Gucci®

College and Career Readiness

Reading Prep
Before reading this chapter, think about the chapter title. What does the title tell you about what you will be learning? How does this chapter relate to information you already know?

Check Your Marketing IQ

Before you begin the chapter, see what you already know about marketing by taking the chapter pretest. If you do not have a smartphone, visit the G-W Learning companion website.
G-W Learning mobile site: www.m.g-wlearning.com
G-W Learning companion website: www.g-wlearning.com

G-W Mobile

Explore
Provide an opportunity for students to explore by assigning a hands-on activity. Assign the College and Career Readiness Reading Prep activity before students read the chapter. Reading Prep activities give students opportunity to apply the Common Core State Standards.

Engage
Assign the Chapter 19 pretest. The test may be accessed by using the QR code or going to the companion website. Discuss which questions students were unable to answer.

◇DECA Emerging Leaders

Sports and Entertainment Marketing Team Decision-Making Event, Part 2

Career Cluster: Marketing
Instructional Area: Selling/Pricing

Procedure, Part 2

1. In the previous chapter, you studied the performance indicators for this event.
2. The event will be presented to you through your reading of the General Performance Indicators, Specific Performance Indicators, and Case Study Situation. You will have up to 30 minutes to review this information and prepare your presentation. You may make notes to use during your presentation.
3. You will have up to 10 minutes to make your presentation to the judge followed by up to 5 minutes to answer the judge's questions. You may have more than one judge. All members of the team must participate in the presentation, as well as answer the questions.
4. Turn in all of your notes and event materials when you have completed the event.

Case Study Situation

You are to assume the roles of business managers at Emerald Crest Country Club, an exclusive membership-based club. The **club owner (judge)** has asked you to recommend changes to keep the club from closing its doors.

Emerald Crest Country Club is located in an affluent suburb of a large metropolitan area. Constructed in the 1980s, the club does not have the rich history that other country clubs in the area have but does offer the same amenities. Members of the club are treated to valet service, a pristine 18-hole golf course, two Olympic-sized swimming pools, eight tennis courts, a fitness center, a full-service restaurant, lounge, and a ballroom with catering services. These fantastic amenities are only offered to club members. No public options for utilizing club services are allowed.

To become a member of Emerald Crest Country Club, applicants must pay a one-time $5,000 application fee. After approval from a criminal background check and credit report, members pay an annual fee of $15,000. Members must also spend $100 per quarter in the club's restaurant to maintain membership.

In the last five years, new membership has decreased by 20% and membership renewal has decreased by 15%. The club owner does not want to close the club. However, to remain open, changes must be made. The club owner has asked you to determine what changes should be made. The following are options the club owner is considering:

- waiving application fee;
- new member campaign;
- reducing services offered;
- allowing the public into the club on certain days;
- renting ballroom/catering for non-club events; and
- other revenue generating ideas.

You will make your recommendations to the club owner (judge) in a meeting to take place in the owner's office. The club owner will begin the meeting by greeting you and asking to hear your recommendations. After you have made your recommendations and have answered the owner's questions, the club owner will conclude the meeting by thanking you for your work.

Critical Thinking

1. Will making these changes lessen our reputation?
2. Why is it important to run a credit report on prospective members?
3. Are country clubs becoming old fashioned?

Visit www.deca.org for more information.

Section 19.1 Importance of Price

Objectives

After completing this section, you will be able to
- **describe** business pricing objectives.
- **explain** why the break-even point is important when pricing products.

Key Terms

pricing objective
volume pricing
gross profit
return on investment (ROI)
net profit
total assets
return on marketing investment (ROMI)
break-even point

Web Connect

Conduct online research about the typical markup percentage in your industry and for the main product of your company. What is the range? Which markup do you feel will work best in your market and still meet profit goals?

Critical Thinking

Marketers must make pricing decisions based on expected sales and profits. Does raising the price of an item always lead to higher revenues? Explain your answer.

Pricing Objectives

The price of a product or service plays a major role in determining whether the product and the company are successful. For that reason, it is important that companies set pricing objectives. Pricing objectives are the goals defined in the business and marketing plans for the overall pricing policies of the company. Pricing objectives may be based on both the short- and long-term goals of the company.

Pricing objectives change and are often revised regularly. The price must be at a level that encourages customers to purchase the product. However, price must also be at a level that generates profits for the business. Pricing objectives fall under two categories: maximize sales and maximize profit.

Explore

Provide an opportunity for students to explore by assigning a hands-on activity. Review the vocabulary terms at the beginning of the section. Where have students encountered these terms before? Help students make educated guesses about the meanings of the terms with which they are least familiar.

Maximize Sales

Maximizing sales is a pricing objective based on offering the lowest price possible to get the largest number of customers to buy the product. There are different ways this can be accomplished. Two ways are to increase market share and establish volume pricing.

Increase Market Share

Recall that *market share* is the percentage of total sales in a market held by one business. Increasing market share by gaining more customers is one way to maximize sales. For example, a marketing goal might be to increase market share from 10 percent to 13 percent. In order to increase market share, the company has to find additional customers. Finding more customers usually means taking them away from the competition. Marketers might lower prices or offer discount coupons or other incentives to achieve that goal.

Resource

Use the Chapter 19 presentation on the optional Instructor's Presentations for PowerPoint® CD as an outline for presenting the chapter.

FYI

When you hear the phrase, *what the market will allow*, it is referring to pricing products as high as possible before sales fall due to the price.

Establish Volume Pricing

Volume pricing is lowering the list price based on the higher number of units purchased at the same time, as shown in Figure 19-1. Lower prices generally lead to increased sales. The strategy behind volume pricing is to give the buyer a price incentive to purchase more at one time and receive the per-item discount.

Maximize Profit

Gross profit is the amount of profit before subtracting the costs of doing business. Maximizing profit is a pricing objective that means generating as much revenue as possible in relation to total cost. A marketer charges the highest price a customer will pay before deciding that the price exceeds the value for customers. The high-end jewelry industry is one in which maximizing profit per sale is the pricing objective.

Improve Return on Investment (ROI)

Return on investment (ROI) is a common measure of profitability based on the amount earned from the investment

made in the business. ROI is expressed as a percentage. The better a company is at investing in itself to increase profit, the more profit will be generated. A high ROI typically indicates a profitable company. Marketers are very aware of ROI because profitability is always both a corporate and marketing goal.

Simple ROI is determined by dividing net profit after taxes by total assets. **Net profit** is what is left after all company expenses are subtracted from total revenue. Everything the company owns is its **total assets**. For example, if a business has a net profit after taxes of $50,000 and assets of $150,000, the ROI is 33 percent.

$$\frac{\text{net profit after taxes}}{\text{total assets}} = \text{ROI}$$

$$\frac{\$50,000}{\$150,000} = 33\,\%$$

Improve Return on Marketing Investment (ROMI)

For many years, companies did not measure the impact of marketing on their businesses. However, companies now routinely calculate the return on marketing investment (ROMI). **Return on marketing investment (ROMI)** is a measurement showing the overall effectiveness of a marketing campaign or yearly budget. The *marketing investment* is the dollars spent on that campaign. Companies use a variety of metrics to measure ROMI, such as those shown in Figure 19-2.

Volume Pricing Example			
Number Purchased	Price per Item	Total Sales	Volume Pricing Savings
10	Up to 12: $9.99	$ 99.90	0
30	13–36: $8.99	$269.70	$ 30.00
100	72– 100: $7.99	$799.00	$200.00

Figure 19-1
In volume pricing, the unit price decreases as the volume increases, which should automatically increase sales.

Goodheart-Willcox Publisher

Explain

Ask students to explain the difference between return on investment (ROI) and return on marketing investment (ROMI). Students should demonstrate an understanding of the terms.

Figure 19-2 ROMI data help marketers make better decisions about how to spend their marketing budgets.

Return on Marketing Investment (ROMI) Metrics
• **New customer:** the cost of acquiring new customers, market share comparisons, customer awareness levels of brand or campaigns
• **Product:** level of customer satisfaction, first-time users, ease of product use, or ease of learning how to use the product
• **Customer retention:** the retention and abandonment rates of different customer groups, brand loyalty, repeat sales, referral rates.

Goodheart-Willcox Publisher

The basic formula for the ROMI of a particular campaign follows.

$$\frac{\text{gross profit} - \text{marketing investment}}{\text{marketing investment}} = \text{ROMI}$$

The following example shows how to determine ROMI. Suppose your marketing class project were to sell yearbooks using a new marketing campaign. The class sent home notices, paid for an ad on the school website, and placed ads in the print and online versions of the school newsletter. They also placed an ad in the fall sports program and sent an e-mail to all parents through the school Listserve. Those activities cost the class $1,000, which is the marketing investment. The class sold 700 books at $50 each for $35,000 in sales. The cost of each yearbook was $40; so 700 books sold times $40 equals $28,000. The gross profit was $7,000 ($35,000 minus $28,000). The marketing investment was $1,000. The ROMI for this investment would be 60 percent.

$$\frac{\$7,000 - \$1,000}{\$1,000} = 600\%$$

Break-Even Point

Pricing strategically is a balancing act for marketers because both profit and sales goals are important. In order to make a profit, prices must be set high enough to cover the costs and make a profit. However, if the product is priced too high, customers and sales may be lost. If the price is set too low,

the costs may not be covered, which means the company could take a loss.

When does a product start making profit? A product starts making profit after the **break-even point,** or the point at which revenue from sales equals the costs. The break-even point is often expressed as the number of items that must be sold to recover the money spent to create or buy them. At this point, the company is not losing or making money, it is breaking even. Any revenue made from sales after the break-even point is profit. The break-even point formula is

$$\frac{\text{cost} \times \text{number of units}}{\text{selling price}} = \text{break-even point}$$

For example, the marketing manager is responsible for a product line of lawn mowers and recently ordered 100 units of a new model. Each lawn mower costs the business $140. The pricing plan is to sell the mowers for $250 each. By following the formula, 56 lawn mowers would need to be sold just to reach the break-even point.

$$\frac{\$140 \text{ cost} \times 100 \text{ units sold}}{\$250 \text{ selling price}} = 56 \text{ units (break-even point)}$$

Marketers must be able to calculate the break-even point of their products to price them correctly, forecast sales, and estimate potential profit. A change in the selling price directly affects the forecasted sales numbers, the break-even analysis, and expected profits.

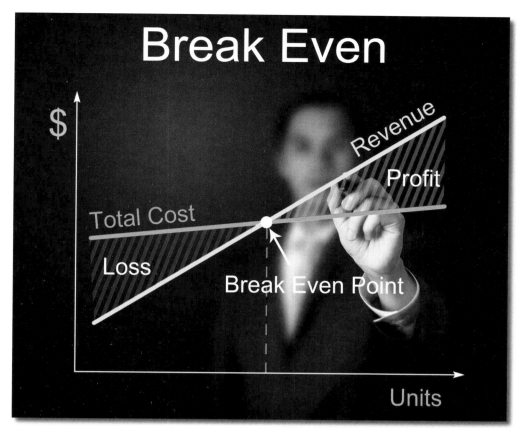

Marketers often create several break-even analyses for different price points before determining the best one.

Dusit/Shutterstock.com

Checkpoint 19.1

1. What are the categories of pricing objectives?
2. Name two ways that a business could maximize sales.
3. How can marketers use return on marketing investment (ROMI) information?
4. Why is it difficult for marketers to price products strategically?
5. Name three reasons marketers should know the break-even point for their products.

Build Your Vocabulary

As you progress through this course, develop a personal glossary of marketing terms and add it to your portfolio. This will help you build your vocabulary and prepare you for a career. Write a definition for each of the following terms, and add it to your personal marketing glossary.

pricing objective
volume pricing
gross profit
return on investment (ROI)

net profit
total assets
return on marketing investment (ROMI)
break-even point

Checkpoint Answers

1. Pricing objectives fall under two categories: maximize sales and maximize profit.

2. Two ways that a business could maximize sales are to increase market share or set lower prices to increase sales.

3. The ROMI data that marketers gather help them make better decisions about how to spend their marketing budgets.

4. It is difficult to price strategically because both profit and sales goals are important. In order to make a profit, prices must be set high enough

to cover the costs and make a profit. However, if the product is priced too high, customers and sales may be lost. If the price is set too low, the costs may not be covered, which means no profit is made.

5. Marketers must be able to calculate the break-even point of their products to price them correctly, forecast sales, and estimate potential profit.

Build Your Vocabulary Answers

Definitions for these terms can be found in the glossary of this text.

Section 19.2 Strategic Pricing

Objectives

After completing this section, you will be able to
- **explain** three approaches to setting the base price of a product.
- **describe** psychological- and discount-pricing strategy techniques and explain why they are used.
- **discuss** price-setting options.

Key Terms

base price
cost-based pricing
markup
keystone pricing
demand-based pricing
competition-based pricing
psychological pricing
web-based pricing software

Web Connect

Choose an item of clothing you may need to buy. Find four e-tailing websites that sell the item and compare the prices and the product choices. Is there a correlation between price and quality? From which e-tailer would you buy and why?

Critical Thinking

Some online stores charge shipping and handling for their items; others do not. How do you think shipping and handling costs affect buying decisions? How might shipping and handling charges affect a business and its pricing policies?

Determine the Base Price

The **base price** of a product is the general price at which the company expects to sell the product. To establish the base price for products or services, three different approaches may be used. They are cost-, demand-, and competition-based pricing.

Cost-Based Pricing

Cost-based pricing is a method that uses the cost of the product to set the product selling price. The first step is to accurately determine the actual cost to the business of the item. Next, the markup is added. **Markup** is the amount added to the cost of a product to determine the base price. Markup can be expressed as a dollar amount or as a percentage. Regardless of the method, the following equation expresses cost-based pricing.

$$\text{cost} + \text{markup} = \text{price}$$

Determining Price Using the Percentage-Markup Method

Using a *percentage markup* is the most common way to determine a base price. Management decides the percent of profit necessary for each item. The percentage markup for each product is turned into a dollar figure and added to the cost. Most retail businesses use the percentage markup method because it guarantees a consistent level of profit. The formula to determine base price when using the percentage-markup method is:

$$(\text{cost} \times \%\text{markup}) + \text{cost} = \text{price}$$

Explore

Provide an opportunity for students to explore by assigning a hands-on activity. Review the vocabulary terms at the beginning of the section. Where have students encountered these terms before? Help students make educated guesses about the meanings of the terms with which they are least familiar.

Engage

Use the Teamwork exercise at the end of the chapter to engage students to solve a problem or make a group presentation.

The average grocery store markup percentage is around 12 percent.

For example, perhaps the company business model states that it must make a 40 percent profit on all sales. To achieve a 40 percent markup, each $140 lawn mower would have to be priced at $196.

$140 cost × 40% markup = $56

$56 + $140 cost = $196 price

Determining Price Using the Keystone-Pricing Method

Keystone pricing is doubling the total cost of a product to determine its base price. Many retail businesses use keystone pricing because it is an easy way to create a 100-percent markup on the cost. The formula for keystone pricing is:

cost × 2 = price

For example, under keystone-pricing method, the $140 lawnmower would be priced at $280.

$140 cost × 2 = $280 price

Determining Price Using the Dollar-Markup Method

In the previous example, the cost for lawn mowers is $140 each. Suppose the company decides it must make $156 after costs on each mower. This method of markup is called *dollar markup* because it is expressed as a dollar amount, not a percentage. Using the dollar-markup pricing method, the base price would be $296.

$140 cost + $156 dollar markup = $296 price

Demand-Based Pricing

Demand-based pricing is a pricing strategy based on what customers are willing to pay. It is also called *value-based pricing* and reflects customer perceptions of the value of a product. Demand-based pricing is a short-term pricing strategy. It is most effective when the product is unique or there is a high demand for it.

Dollar Tree

One important responsibility of marketing is to set a pricing strategy. A price that is too high will deter customers from buying. A price that is too low will have a negative impact on profits. Sometimes, a simple pricing strategy works as well as a strategy that might be more complex. One example of simple pricing is the Dollar Tree chain. Products at Dollar Tree are priced at one dollar or less. Name brand items are sold in their stores that might cost more elsewhere. The Dollar Tree brand name reflects its pricing strategy, so customers know exactly what they will spend. The four Ps are clearly defined: product, one item for a dollar; price, one dollar; place, Dollar Tree; and promotion, all products for one dollar. Dollar Tree is a good example of a complete marketing strategy that works. Dollar Tree continues to grow and post profits as the largest single-price-point company in the United States.

For example, perhaps a small local business is the only one nearby selling new bracelets popular with middle school students. The students could order the bracelets online for $7 plus shipping for a $10 total, but they would not arrive for weeks. However, the local marketer can charge $12 for the bracelets and earn a higher profit per sale—at least until demand drops.

Competition-Based Pricing

Competition-based pricing is a pricing strategy based primarily on what the competitors charge. The marketer makes a decision to price above, below, or at the price of the competition depending on the pricing objective. To effectively use a competition-based pricing strategy, marketers monitor the prices of competitors often and adjust price as necessary.

Sometimes, when local competitors are matching prices, a price war will begin. During a price war, one company lowers its price. When a competitor sees this, it lowers its price on the same product. The original company will then lower its price, and so on. Competition-based pricing does not take into account the cost of producing the product and may not provide enough, or any, profit.

Adjust the Base Price

The last step in pricing products is to select which pricing strategy will work best for the product or service. Marketers tend to use one or more of the psychological- or discount-pricing strategies depending on the situation or product type.

Psychological Pricing

Psychological pricing strategies are pricing techniques that create an image of a product and to entice customers to buy. These techniques are most often used by marketers working for retail companies (B2C). Some common B2C psychological pricing techniques include odd, even, prestige, price lining, BOGO, and bundling.

Odd Pricing

Odd pricing sets the prices to end in an odd number such as 5 or 9. Prices such as $9.99, $99.95, and $19,995 convey an image of a bargain. Discount-store prices and sale items usually end in odd numbers. A shopper might think of these prices as $9.00, $99.00, and $19,000, even though the prices are actually closer to $10, $100, and $20,000, respectively.

Online businesses, such as eBay and Amazon, that can sell products for less than brick-and-mortar stores, have created more pressure for businesses to price competitively.

pio3/Shutterstock.com

Even Pricing

Even pricing sets the sale price so it ends in an even number, most often 0. Prices might be set at $40, $100, or $14,000. Customers see the even number and think the product is better than one priced for value. Even pricing conveys quality.

Prestige Pricing

Prestige pricing is setting prices high to convey quality and status. Customers see a higher price and think the product is better than lower-priced competing products. High-end fashion designers and car manufacturers often use prestige pricing.

Price Lining

Price lining is setting various prices for the same type of product to indicate different levels of quality. For example, appliance stores often use price lining. For example, a dishwasher with three features may be priced at $350, a dishwasher with four features at $400, and a dishwasher with five

or more features at $500. Price lining gives customers options and allows them to choose the features and value they want based on their needs and budgets.

Buy One, Get One (BOGO)

The buy one, get one (BOGO) pricing technique gives customers a free or reduced-price item when another is purchased at full price. Depending on the promotion, the items may be the same or similar. Some stores have *buy two, get one free* promotions and other similar offers. The BOGO technique conveys savings and value.

Bundling

Bundling combines two or more services or products for one price. Bundling can reduce the overall price when compared to buying the items separately. For example, a clothing store might bundle a $10 hat and a $20 T-shirt for a single price of $25. This bundled price saves the customer $5, and the store has sold two items instead of one. Bundling conveys savings and value.

Discount Pricing

In the retail businesses, when items are discounted from the list price, they are *on sale*. Marketers for companies that sell to other businesses (B2B) use different discount pricing strategies as pricing techniques. The five most popular B2B discount pricing strategies marketers use are shown in Figure 19-3.

Cash Discount

A *cash discount* is usually a percentage removed from the total invoice amount. It is offered to encourage a customer to pay a bill early. A cash discount often shows up in a format similar to *2/10, net 30*. The *2* reflects the percentage off the invoice total. The *10* indicates the number of days the customer has to pay the bill to receive the discount. The *30* stands for the number of days the customer has to pay the bill without receiving a penalty. This discount would be read, "2 percent off if paid within 10 days, otherwise the entire bill is due in 30 days." Cash discounts encourage customers to pay bills early, which help the cash flow of the business.

Tungphoto/Shutterstock.com

Most consumers are attracted to buy-one-get-one-free (BOGO) offers.

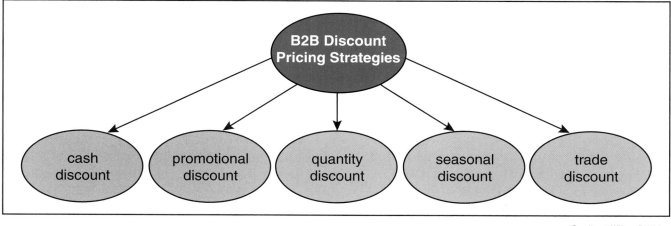

Goodheart-Willcox Publisher

Figure 19-3 B2B discount pricing strategies differ from those used by B2C marketers.

Social Media

LinkedIn

LinkedIn is a professional networking social media website. Like other social media, individuals must set up a company page, but can post as the company separately. Anyone can create a LinkedIn profile at no charge and then invite others to join their circles. For a fee, businesses can post open jobs on the site. Any LinkedIn member can search for and apply to the posted positions. LinkedIn provides a vehicle for employers to promote themselves as an employer of choice. Creating a professional network provides businesses the opportunity to recruit candidates as well as obtain referrals for job applicants. By using key words to target skill sets or other criteria, qualified candidate profiles can be reviewed with the opportunity to contact candidates directly or the people who know them. LinkedIn also offers professional groups in which you can represent your company and network with others in your industry. It is an opportunity to market your company without a major financial investment. The site offers solutions and tips to help employers make the most of the vehicle as well as other support.

Promotional Discount

A *promotional discount* is given to businesses that agree to advertise or promote a manufacturer's product. The discount may be a dollar amount or a percentage of the product order. When you see a product advertised in an ad sponsored by a manufacturer, the retail store probably got a promotional discount on that product.

Quantity Discount

A *quantity discount* offers a reduced per-item price for larger numbers of an item purchased. Many companies offer quantity discounts as an incentive for buying more product. The more the customer buys, the more money he or she saves on each item. For example, if a customer buys 48 sweatshirts, the price may be $22 per shirt. If the customer buys 96 shirts, however, the price may be $18 per shirt.

FYI

A quantity discount is another term for volume pricing.

Seasonal Discount

If retailers buy goods well in advance of the season, they are often given a seasonal discount. For example, buyers for goods sold in the December gift-giving season will often place orders the January before. They are buying 11 months before the goods are sold to take advantage of lower prices. Similarly, summer clothing orders are placed at least six months in advance of the season. Seasonal discounts help manufacturers plan production and reduce inventories.

Trade Discount

A *trade discount* is not really a discount. It is actually the way that manufacturers quote prices to wholesalers and retailers. Some manufacturers suggest retail prices for their products (MSRP). The MSRP is often used as a list price. The manufacturer then offers the wholesaler or retailer a percentage off the list price. A trade discount may be 20 percent or more off the list price.

Set the Price

After taking all of the steps in the price-setting process as shown in Figure 19-4, you are ready to set the price. Review the mission statement and goals for the business to make sure the proposed price is in line with business and profit goals. Many businesses use **web-based pricing software,** or technology that helps businesses to maximize profit by pricing products correctly. Using technology to automate pricing also makes the process efficient and saves time in price monitoring.

Remember that pricing objectives and strategies may change as a business grows. Also, take into account that most businesses cannot sell every product at the list price. Some products may be put on sale, some on permanent clearance, and some donated to a charity.

Process for Setting a Price
1. Establish price goals. - Maximize profits - Maximize sales
2. Estimate demand, costs, and needed profit by product.
3. Study the competition.
4. Choose a pricing approach to determine base price.
5. Fine tune price by using pricing strategies and techniques.

Goodheart-Willcox Publisher

Figure 19-4 The steps for setting prices are typically taken in this order.

Checkpoint 19.2

1. List the steps to take for setting a price.
2. Why do many retail businesses use keystone pricing?
3. What does the *2/10, net 30* cash discount mean?
4. What is the advantage of offering quantity discounts?
5. Why would a business use technology tools to help set prices?

Build Your Vocabulary

As you progress through this course, develop a personal glossary of marketing terms and add it to your portfolio. This will help you build your vocabulary and prepare you for a career. Write a definition for each of the following terms, and add it to your personal marketing glossary.

base price
cost-based pricing
markup
keystone pricing

demand-based pricing
competition-based pricing
psychological pricing
web-based pricing software

Section 19.3 Credit

Offering Credit

Credit is an agreement or contract to receive goods or services before actually paying for them. Issuing credit to customers has a direct impact on pricing. In addition, marketers view credit as a customer convenience and benefit. The **debtor** is the individual or business who owes money for goods or services received. The **creditor** is the individual or business to whom money is owned for goods or services provided.

The **debtor-creditor relationship** is a legal relationship existing between the two parties. This relationship is based on good faith that both parties will uphold their end of the agreement. The debtor must repay the creditor based on the terms. This relationship can be enforced by law because it is a contract. In addition, the US government has a number of laws that protect consumers who attempt to get credit or already have it, as shown in Figure 19-5.

Consumer Credit

Consumer credit is credit given to individual consumers by a retail business. Consumer credit can be in the form of a loan or proprietary credit cards, such as Macy's or Dillard's. Proprietary credit cards may only be used in the stores issuing them.

If the business sells big-ticket items like appliances or cars, consumer credit may be offered in the form of an installment loan. An **installment loan** is a loan paid in regular payments, or installments, with interest until

US Consumer Credit Laws	
Truth in Lending Act (1968)	Requires disclosure of all finance charges on consumer credit agreements and in advertising for credit plans.
Fair Credit Reporting Act (1970)	Protects individuals from consumer reporting agencies sending inaccurate credit reports. Gives individuals the right to examine and correct their own credit histories.
Equal Opportunity Act (1975)	Protects consumers from discrimination based on sex, marital status, race, national origin, religion, age, or the receipt of public assistance.
Fair Debt Collection Practices Act (1978)	Protects consumers against unfair methods of collecting debts.
Fair Credit Billing Act (1986)	Protects consumers from unfair billing practices. Consumers can dispute credit card billing errors.
Credit Card Accountability, Responsibility, and Disclosure (CARD) (2009))	Requires credit providers to mail bills at least 21 days before the due dates. They also must give at least 45 days' advance notice of rate hikes or any other important changes to the credit card agreement and at least 30 days' notice prior to an account closure. The law includes special provisions regarding credit cards issued to minors. Credit providers may not offer credit card accounts to minors who have no proof of financial means to pay debts incurred unless there is a cosigner over age 21 who has the ability to pay. The law also requires any advertisements for free credit reports to make clear that free credit reports are available under federal law.

Goodheart-Willcox Publisher

Figure 19-5 These laws protect consumers from unfair credit policies or billing practices.

the loan is paid in full. Installment loans are called *secured loans.* Secured loans require *collateral,* an asset pledged to guarantee the loan will be repaid. If the loan is not repaid, the asset can be taken by the creditor and sold to recoup the cost of the loan.

Some businesses extend credit by accepting debit or credit cards from their customers. It is sometimes preferable to accept bank cards, such as MasterCard and Visa. An advantage of accepting these cards is that the retailer transfers the responsibility for collecting the money owed to the bank. The bank provides a *financial service* by collecting the money owed for the sale directly from the customer and then pays the business. This service is *not* free for the retailer or the customer. For the retailer, the bank adds a service charge to each purchase made on one of its debit or credit cards. For the customer, he

or she must pay monthly interest on unpaid balances to the bank issuing the credit card.

Trade Credit

Trade credit is granting a line of credit to another business for a short period of time to purchase its goods and services. Trade credit is often used by established businesses. The line of credit extended is most often 30 or 60 days. This means that the purchase is interest free for 30 or 60 days. Full payment is expected at the end of the time period. If the bill is paid in full by the specified date, no interest is charged. However, if the bill is not paid or not paid in full by the specified date, interest charges begin to accumulate. Due dates for trade credit repayment must be carefully monitored to maintain adequate cash flow and avoid interest charges.

Explain

Ask: What are secured loans? Clarify responses as needed.

Explore

Ask students to explore the Internet to research information about trade credit. Students should compile their findings in a chart.

Customer Service

No matter how hard a company works to provide excellent quality products or services, customers will occasionally have questions or complaints. How they are handled can have a huge effect on the success of the company—for better or worse. Customer service reps present an image of the company to the people they assist. Typical job titles for these positions include *customer service representative, customer service specialist, hub associate, account service representative,* and *call center representative.*

Some examples of tasks customer service professionals perform include:

- provide product or service information to customers in person or by telephone;
- keep records of customer comments, complaints, and the actions taken to resolve the issues;
- solve customer problems by exchanging merchandise, offering a refund, or making adjustments to charges;
- refer unresolved issues to the appropriate departments for further research; and
- recheck to make sure customer problems were solved and they are satisfied.

People skills are of utmost importance for customer service professionals. They must be active listeners, giving their full attention to what the customer is saying. They also must have the ability to speak well and persuasively. Critical thinking skills to negotiate solutions for the customer and the company are necessary. Most customer service positions require a high school diploma and up to a year of on-the-job training. Prior experience in working with the public is also helpful. For more information, access the *Occupational Outlook Handbook* online.

Costs of Credit

There are multiple costs involved when businesses extend or accept credit. These costs may directly affect pricing of product. These are only a few of the costs of extending credit.

- If credit or debit cards are accepted, the business will have to pay transaction fees to the institution that issued the card.
- If trade credit is extended to businesses, cash is tied up that could be used to operate the business.
- Some customers may not pay their credit, which means that the net income for the business will be decreased.
- Credit requires additional paperwork, which takes management or employee time to process.

For these reasons, many businesses add an additional percentage, or markup, to the sales price of products to cover the cost of credit. Cost of credit is a variable expense that influences the pricing decisions for products. It is part of the overhead necessary for doing business.

Rewards and Risks of Extending Credit

When credit is extended to customers, there are obvious rewards. The most obvious reward is the generation of sales. Research shows that people will often spend more when using a credit card than if they are paying cash. While there are many rewards

Credit cards are a customer convenience and necessary when shopping online.

to offering consumer or trade credit, there are also risks. If a customer fails to pay a bill on time, it may cause a cash flow problem for the business.

Rewards

Offering credit through credit cards, installment loans, or trade credit can create a steady income for the business. Another reward of extending credit to customers is building customer loyalty. **Customer loyalty** is the continued and regular patronage of a business even when there are other places to purchase the same or similar products. There are many reasons that customers are loyal to

a business, but one of them is convenience. Customers appreciate using a bank card for in-store or Internet purchases. Businesses that offer credit tend to generate more sales than if they only accepted cash.

Risks

Credit risk is the potential of credit not being repaid. Businesses or consumers that cannot pay their credit debts may risk legal action being taken against them.

Creating debt for the business is similar to creating debt for an individual. If the business does not have cash to pay what is owed, the owner could get in financial trouble and have to close the business. A credit card debt of a business will show up on personal credit reports and affect the credit rating of the owner. During the Great Recession, many businesses had to close their doors because they were overextended on their credit cards or could not pay other credit debt.

For example, many people lost their jobs during the recession of the early 21st century. The number of unemployed people who could not repay their credit bills put many businesses at risk.

For those customers who do not eventually pay their debts, it may be necessary for the creditor to incur costs and hire a collection agency. A **collection agency** is a company that collects past-due bills for a fee. Businesses may also attempt to get payment for debt under a certain amount of money through small claims court, depending on the state. Collecting bad debts, however, creates additional expenses for the business and, in turn, decreases income.

FYI

Businesses that cannot pay their credit bills risk the possibility of bankruptcy that can lead to either restructuring the business or closing its doors.

Reducing Credit Risk

Each business must decide if extending credit to customers is a good business decision. Some businesses choose to only accept cash or checks to avoid the associated transaction fees. When granting credit to customers, it is important to establish a credit process that reduces risk.

Create a Credit Policy

Having a credit policy in place can help guide the process of extending credit. Credit policies vary by the type of credit extended to businesses or individual customers.

Before extending credit, it is important to establish dollar figures for the amount of credit that will be extended for installment loans and trade credit. Specific terms of repayment, interest rates, late fees, penalties, and actions for nonpayment should be established. Employees should always ask for customer identification when accepting credit cards to help avoid credit card fraud. Credit limits and guidelines should be set for how much credit the business can afford to extend. Most importantly, when extending credit, the cash flow of the business should be monitored.

Require a Credit Application

If providing credit to customers through installment loans or with a business credit card, it is important to check the financial backgrounds of the applicants. Customers should complete an application that shows credit history, work history, and other information necessary to qualify for credit. Depending on the loan amount or trade credit extended, the business may also request financial statements that show net worth and financial status. Bank statements should also be requested.

Obtain a Credit Report

Before extending credit, it is important to learn the credit history of an applicant. A credit history may provide information about his or her likelihood of repaying the credit. A **credit report** is a record of a business or person's credit history and financial behavior. It shows:

- the number and types of credit accounts and indicates any that are past due;

- how promptly credit cards statements and loans were paid off in full;
- if other bills, such as rent, taxes, or utilities, were paid on time;
- current total outstanding debts; and
- the available credit left on credit cards and home equity loans.

Credit reports are issued by credit bureaus. A **credit bureau** is a private firm that maintains consumer credit data and provides credit information to businesses for a fee. There are three national credit-reporting agencies: Equifax, Experian, and TransUnion LLC.

Evaluate the Information

Once information is obtained about the customer, the company evaluates the credit worthiness of each applicant based on the *three Cs of credit*. The three Cs of credit are shown in Figure 19-6.

If approved for credit, give the customer a copy of your credit policies. This is necessary so that the customer knows what his or her responsibilities are to pay off the credit. Included may be payment schedule, interest, and late payment penalties. The *Truth in Lending Act* requires that businesses convey all of that information to customers before the first transaction. If the customer is *not* approved for credit, convey that message as well.

Three Cs of Credit
• Character: the individual or business has a good record of repaying bills on time.
• Capacity: the individual or business has a good employment history or business earnings.
• Capital: the individual or business has a positive net worth.

Goodheart-Willcox Publisher

Figure 19-6 The three Cs of credit are used to determine the ability of an applicant to repay the extended credit on time.

Manage Accounts Receivable

One very important financial-management task is to keep track of when the accounts receivable are due or overdue. The accounts receivable are the amounts owed to a company by its customers. This activity is critical to keeping cash flow at the level that will pay bills so the business can remain open. Customers who are late making payments should be sent reminders urging them to pay.

An **accounts receivable aging report** shows when accounts receivables are due as well as length of time accounts have been outstanding. An aging report typically shows receivables as current, 30 days, 60 days, 90 days, and 120 days and over. The purpose of an aging report is to indicate which receivables are more urgent to collect because they have been past due longer.

AMA Tip

Checkpoint 19.3

1. What is credit?
2. Installment loans are taken out to finance what types of purchases?
3. Why should the due dates for trade credit repayment be carefully monitored?
4. Why would a business risk extending credit?
5. List five ways business can reduce credit risk?

Build Your Vocabulary

As you progress through this course, develop a personal glossary of marketing terms and add it to your portfolio. This will help you build your vocabulary and prepare you for a career. Write a definition for each of the following terms, and add it to your personal marketing glossary.

debtor
creditor
debtor-creditor relationship
consumer credit
installment loan
trade credit
cost of credit
customer loyalty
credit risk
collection agency
credit report
credit bureau
accounts receivable aging report

Checkpoint Answers

1. Credit is an agreement or contract to receive goods or services before actually paying for them.
2. Installment loans are taken out to finance large, big-ticket items, such as appliances or cars.
3. Due dates for trade credit repayment must be carefully monitored to maintain adequate cash flow and avoid interest charges.
4. Offering credit through credit cards, installment loans, or trade credit can create a steady income for the business. Another reward of extending credit to customers is building customer loyalty.
5. Five ways a business can reduce credit risk are to create a credit policy, require a credit application, obtain a credit report, evaluate the information, and manage accounts receivable.

Build Your Vocabulary Answers

Definitions for these terms can be found in the glossary of this text.

Evaluate

Assign the end-of-chapter activities.

Chapter Summary

Section 19.1 Importance of Price

- The price of a product or service plays a major role in determining whether the product and the company are successful. Pricing objectives are created based on maximizing sales and maximizing profits.
- The break-even point is important when pricing products. A product begins making a profit after the break-even point is reached.

Section 19.2 Strategic Pricing

- The base price of a product is established using cost-based pricing, demand-based pricing, or competition-based pricing. Businesses select the method which is most applicable to the products they are selling.
- Managers use psychological- or discount-pricing strategies to adjust the base price. By using these techniques, it is hoped to encourage increased numbers of sales.
- Many businesses use pricing software or other technology to maximize profit by pricing products correctly. To make a profit, a business should be sure the proposed price is in line with business and profit goals.

Section 19.3 Credit

- *Credit* is an agreement or contract to receive goods or services before actually paying for them. Issuing credit to customers has a direct impact on pricing. Businesses may offer consumer or trade credit, depending on its customers.
- The cost of credit to a business is a variable expense. The more it costs a business to provide credit, the more the business should charge for a good or service to recoup the credit costs.
- While there are many rewards to offering consumer or trade credit, there are also risks. Research shows that people will often spend more when using a credit card than if they are paying cash. However, if a customer fails to pay a bill on time, it may cause a cash-flow problem for the business.
- Five ways a business can reduce credit risk are to create a credit policy, require a credit application, obtain a credit report, evaluate the information, and manage accounts receivable.

Review Your Knowledge

1. What does a high return on investment (ROI) mean to a business?
2. What is the reason to use volume pricing?
3. Suppose you were marketing a product priced at $500. Perhaps at some point you realize that the break-even point was higher than you expected, and you think that you cannot sell enough of the item to break even. What could you do?
4. Explain how simple return on investment (ROI) is determined.
5. How is the break-even point for a product usually shown?

Review Your Knowledge Answers

1. A high ROI typically indicates a profitable company.
2. The strategy behind volume pricing is to give the buyer a price incentive to purchase more at one time and receive the per-item discount.
3. Lower the price to the point that it stimulates enough sales to break even or make a profit.

4. Simple ROI is determined by dividing net profit after taxes by total assets. Net profit is what is left after all company expenses are subtracted from total revenue. The cash value of everything the company owns is its total assets.
5. The break-even point is often expressed as the number of items that must be sold to recover the money spent to create or buy them. At this point, the company is not losing or making money, it is breaking even.

6. Explain when marketers would choose to use demand-based pricing.
7. What is the biggest drawback to using a competition-based pricing approach?
8. List four psychological pricing techniques.
9. List the five most popular B2B discount pricing strategies used by marketers.
10. How does extending credit influence pricing of product?

Apply Your Knowledge

1. Pricing objectives are the goals defined in the business and marketing plans for the overall pricing policies of the company. What are the pricing objectives for your company?
2. Explain how your pricing policies affect the company image.
3. Research the typical markup percentage for the products in your industry. What is the markup percentage of the merchandise your company sells? If it is different from the typical markup, explain why.
4. What types of discounts are offered by your company? Explain each type of discount and why it is a good pricing strategy.
5. Discuss the types of psychological pricing your company uses. Explain why you chose those techniques.
6. Think about the types of promotional discounts you might be able to negotiate from manufacturers or other vendors. How would they affect your company pricing policies?
7. Research the term *economies of scale* as it applies to your industry. How does your company take advantage of economies of scale?
8. Companies use a variety of metrics to measure the return on marketing investments (ROMI). Which metrics will you use to measure your ROMI?
9. Perform a job search for a *cost/price analyst* on a job-search website, such as CareerBuilder or Monster. Browse through the available jobs and choose one. What does the person in this job do? What are the job duties and education requirements? Would you like this job? Explain why or why not.
10. Does your company offer credit to its customers? If so, what forms of credit are provided, and do you think offering the credit provides enough customer benefits to justify the cost? Explain your position.

6. Demand-based pricing is a short-term pricing strategy. It is most effective when the product is unique or there is a high demand for it.
7. Competition-based pricing does not take into account the cost of producing the product and may not provide enough, or any, profit.
8. Student answers should include four of the following psychological pricing techniques including odd, even, prestige, price lining, BOGO, and bundling.
9. The five most popular B2B discount pricing strategies marketers used are cash, promotional, quantity, seasonal, and trade discount.

10. There are multiple costs associated with extending credit, such as paying transaction fees to the institution that issued a credit card, debt that customers may not repay, and additional paperwork that takes management or employees time to process.

Apply Your Knowledge Answers

Student answers will vary for questions 1–10.

Marketing Plan

Your students are approaching the halfway point in completing the marketing plan. This would be a good time to summarize and review what has been completed to this point.

Check Your Marketing IQ

Now that you have finished the chapter, see what you learned about marketing by taking the chapter posttest. If you do not have a smartphone, visit the G-W Learning companion website.

G-W Learning mobile site: www.m.g-wlearning.com

G-W Learning companion website: www.g-wlearning.com

Common Core

College and Career Readiness

CTE Career Ready Practices. Create a Venn diagram to show the relationship between pricing factors and pricing objectives. Where do the circles overlap? What do you think this overlap signifies? What would a diagram with a lot of overlap tell you? What about one with little or no overlap?

Reading. Using independent research and the information contained in the chapter, write a report in which you analyze how different pricing strategies affect the consumer market. As needed, derive meaning of the environmental print and use visual and contextual support to confirm understanding. Use support from classmates and your teacher as needed to help understand the material. Cite specific evidence from the text and your research to support your understanding of these strategies of pricing.

Writing. Conduct a short research project on Internet-auction companies. Using information from multiple sources, write a report on the impact Internet-auction companies have on traditional retailers.

Teamwork

Working with a teammate, research the topic *pricing ethics.* Select a pricing topic that illustrates unfair or unethical pricing of a product. Why was the case you found determined to be unethical? Share your findings with the class.

G-W Learning Mobile Site

Visit the G-W Learning mobile site to complete the chapter pretest and posttest and to practice vocabulary using e-flash cards. If you do not have a smartphone, visit the G-W Learning companion website to access these features.

G-W Learning mobile site: www.m.g-wlearning.com

G-W Learning companion website: www.g-wlearning.com

Evaluate

Evaluate the students' understanding and knowledge. Assign the Chapter 19 posttest. The test may be accessed by using the QR code or by going to the companion website. What questions were students able to answer that they could not answer when they took the pretest?

Unit 5 **Price Dynamics**
Building the Marketing Plan

Pricing products correctly can mean the difference between success and failure for many businesses. Owners look to marketing professionals to help them with the pricing process. In your role as a marketing manager for the company you selected, you will be involved in pricing decisions. Make sure your pricing is competitive and aligns with the company's financial goals. Often a company's financial goals also help marketers to set marketing goals. You will be making decisions about markup, pricing strategies, and techniques for setting the base and final prices.

Part 1 **Marketing Objectives**

Objectives

- Find and list the company's financial goals.
- Determine pricing objectives for your company.
- Determine the company's marketing goals.

Directions

In this activity, you will develop the Marketing Objectives section of the marketing plan. The marketing objectives are the goals a business wants to achieve during a given time, usually one year, by implementing the marketing plan. They include both financial and marketing goals. Access the *Marketing Dynamics* companion website at www.g-wlearning.com. Download the data file for the following activity.

1. Unit Activity 5-1. Marketing Objectives. First, find and list the financial goals of the company for your marketing plan. Then, determine and list the company pricing objectives. Explain how the pricing objectives relate to the overall financial goals of the company. Then, list the marketing goals you wish to accomplish or begin to accomplish in the coming year. Remember to write them as short- or long-term SMART goals.
2. Open your saved marketing plan document.

3. Locate the Marketing Objectives section of the plan. Then complete the Marketing Goals and Company Financial Goals subsections. Use the suggestions and questions listed to help you generate ideas. Delete the instructions and questions when you are finished recording your responses. Proofread your document and correct any errors in keyboarding, spelling, and grammar.
4. Save your document.

Part 2 **Price**

Objectives

- Determine the base price for one company product.
- Research the product prices of your competitors.
- Determine the pricing strategy and technique to set the final price.

Directions

In this activity, you will continue writing the Marketing Strategies section of the marketing plan. The marketing strategies are the decisions made about product, price, place, and promotion. Access the *Marketing Dynamics* companion website at www.g-wlearning.com. Download the data file for the following activity.

1. Unit Activity 5-2. Price. Select one product or service you market for your company. First, determine the cost to the company. Next, determine the markup needed to make the profit your company wants. Then use the correct formula from Chapter 19, Section 2 to set the base price. Show your math. Research and list the prices of the competition. Describe the pricing strategy and the technique to set the final price for your product or service.
2. Open your saved marketing plan document.
3. Locate the Marketing Strategies section of the plan. Complete the Price Strategies subsection. Use the suggestions and questions listed to help you generate ideas. Delete the instructions and questions when you are finished recording your responses. Proofread your document and correct any errors in keyboarding, spelling, and grammar.
4. Save your document.

Unit 6

Place Dynamics

Chapters

Eye-Catcher

Frontpage/Shutterstock.com

Marketing Matters

Supply chain managers must select channel members based on the needs of the producers. However, some larger producers have their own trucks for transportation, which reduces the number of channel members. Walmart is an example of a producer that is also a private carrier. Not only do the Walmart trucks provide product transportation, but they also serve as a marketing vehicle by increasing name recognition.

Marketing Core Functions Covered in This Unit

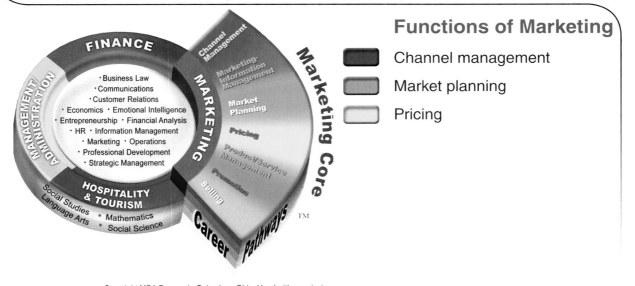

Functions of Marketing

- Channel management
- Market planning
- Pricing

Developing a Vision

Have you ever thought about how your iPod got from Apple to you? A marketing team at Apple had a lot to do with you getting your iPod when you wanted it, in the place you wanted to buy it, and for the price you were willing to pay. A major challenge for marketing is distribution of product. The channel of distribution is the *path* that the product takes from the producer to the end user. The supply chain is the *people* who move the goods.

Supply chain management is an important marketing activity that focuses on the marketing concept of customer satisfaction. This involves getting the product to you, the end user, as quickly and efficiently as possible.

CHAPTER

20 Place

Section **20.1** Channels of Distribution
Section **20.2** Physical Distribution
Section **20.3** Managing the Channel of Distribution

"The Internet is becoming the town square for the global village of tomorrow."

—Bill Gates, cofounder of Microsoft

College and Career Readiness

Reading Prep
In preparation for reading the chapter, read a newspaper or magazine article on marketing and advertising to customers. As you read, keep in mind the author's main points and conclusions.

Check Your Marketing IQ

Before you begin the chapter, see what you already know about marketing by taking the chapter pretest. If you do not have a smartphone, visit the G-W Learning companion website.
G-W Learning mobile site: www.m.g-wlearning.com
G-W Learning companion website: www.g-wlearning.com

Explore

Assign the College and Career Readiness Reading Prep activity before students read the chapter. Reading Prep activities give students opportunity to apply the Common Core State Standards.

Engage

Engage the student by providing an activity or question that will connect students to what they already know. Assign the Chapter 20 pretest. The test may be accessed by using the QR code or going to the *Marketing Dynamics* companion website. Discuss which questions students were unable to answer.

◇DECA Emerging Leaders

Hospitality Services Team Decision-Making Event, Part 1

Career Cluster: Hospitality and Tourism
Instructional Area: Market Planning

General Performance Indicators

- Communications skills—the ability to exchange information and ideas with others through writing, speaking, reading, or listening
- Analytical skills—the ability to derive facts from data, findings from facts, conclusions from findings, and recommendations from conclusions
- Production skills—the ability to take a concept from an idea and make it real
- Teamwork—the ability to be an effective member of a productive group
- Priorities/time management—the ability to determine priorities and manage time commitments
- Economic competencies

Specific Performance Indicators

- Identify information monitored for marketing decision making.
- Explain the concept of marketing strategies.
- Explain the nature of marketing plans.
- Explain the role of situational analysis in the marketing planning process.
- Describe factors used by marketers to position products/services.
- Explain the role of customer service as a component of selling relationships.
- Explain the role of ethics in human resources management.

Purpose

Designed for a team of two DECA members, the event measures the team's ability to explain core business concepts in the format of a case study in a role-play. This event consists of a 100-question, multiple-choice, cluster exam for each team member and a decision-making case study situation. The Team Decision-Making Event provides an opportunity for participants to analyze one or a combination of elements essential to the effective operation of a business in the specific career area presented as a case study.

For the purposes of this text, you will be presented with the material for this event in two parts. Part 1 presents the knowledge and skills assessed and an overview of the event's purpose and procedure. Part 2 presents the remaining procedures and the event situation.

Procedure, Part 1

1. For Part 1 in this text, read both sets of performance indicators. Discuss these with your team members.
2. If there are any questions, ask your teacher to clarify.

Critical Thinking

1. In a business, what information should be monitored for effective decision making?
2. Explain how marketing strategies and marketing plans impact marketing decisions.
3. What is the role of situational analysis in the marketing planning process?
4. Describe various factors marketers use to position products/services. Why are the factors important?
5. Discuss with your team member why performance indicators about the role of customer service and ethics might be included.

Visit www.deca.org for more information.

Section 20.1 Channels of Distribution

Objectives

After completing this section, you will be able to
- **describe** the supply chain and the role intermediaries play.
- **compare** and **contrast** the channels of distribution for business-to-consumer (B2C) markets and business-to-business (B2B) markets.

Key Terms

supply chain
intermediary
brick-and-mortar
e-tailer
agent
channel of
  distribution
direct channel

indirect channel
retailer channel
wholesaler channel
agent/broker
  channel
industrial good

Web Connect

Choose a consumer product that you use. Perform Internet research to trace the supply chain for that product. Find out the specific channel members for that product. How did that product get from the producer to the consumer?

Critical Thinking

Think about all the products at your school. How do you think all of the desks, science equipment, sports equipment, marketing and business equipment and supplies arrived at your school? Identify three companies from which your school might have bought products and the path these items might have taken.

Place Is the Supply Chain

Place is one of the four Ps of marketing. Recall that in marketing, *place* refers to the activities involved in getting a product or service to the end user. Place decisions involve determining when, where, and how products get to customers. Place is also known as *distribution*.

A **supply chain** are the businesses, people, and activities involved in turning raw materials into products and delivering them to end users. Physical distribution is a part of the larger process of the supply chain involved in getting products to end users. The supply chain for some businesses can be very short. For other businesses, it can be rather lengthy.

Intermediaries

The people or businesses between the manufacturers or producers and the end users in the supply chain are called **intermediaries.** The intermediaries are also called *channel members*. There are several types of intermediaries, including wholesalers, retailers, and agents.

Wholesalers

A *wholesaler* purchases large amounts of goods directly from manufacturers. The wholesalers stores the products and then resell them in smaller quantities to various retailers. In the B2B supply chain, wholesalers are often called *distributors*. Wholesalers provide many important functions. Wholesalers usually buy prod-

Explore

Provide an opportunity for students to explore by assigning a hands-on activity. Review the vocabulary terms at the beginning of the section. Where have students encountered these terms before? Help students make educated guesses about the meanings of the terms with which they are least familiar.

Resource

Use the Chapter 20 presentation on the optional *Instructor's Presentations for PowerPoint® CD* as an outline for presenting the chapter.

Both brick-and-mortar stores and e-tail websites are intermediaries that provide transactional functions.

David P. Lewis/Shutterstock.com

ucts in bulk and then resell them in smaller quantities to other companies. Some wholesalers provide promotional support. Wholesaling services often include the warehousing, or storage, and the transportation of goods.

Retailers

A *retailer* buys products either from wholesalers or directly from manufacturers. The retailer then resells the products to consumers, also called *end users*. Retailers perform many important functions including promotion, selling, offering credit, and handling returns. Many retailers have physical stores, but some do not. **Brick-and-mortar** is the term for a physical store.

A *nonstore retailer* is a business that sells directly to consumers through ways other than in a retail store. Nonstore retailers include catalogs, direct sales, and e-tailers. **E-tailers** are retailers that sell through the Internet. Some retailers sell in both brick-and-mortar stores and online.

Some nonstore retailers have sales representatives who either sell products to customers in their homes or by telephone. Avon, Tupperware, Miche, and Mary Kay have long used their own sales representatives to sell products instead of opening stores. These direct-sales companies also sell to consumers on their websites.

Agents

An **agent** is someone working on the behalf of another party. Agents are also known as *brokers.* An agent may be hired by either the buyer or the seller. The goal of this intermediary is to create a favorable exchange for both buyer and seller. Agents can be used anywhere in the supply-chain process. They are especially useful in facilitating international trade.

The Internet is also considered an intermediary. The Internet provides a link between businesses that create or resell the products and the end users.

Role of Intermediaries

Intermediaries serve three functions to help ensure the goods are in the right place at the right time.

The *transactional function* is typically the sales and marketing activities for the business. The intermediary contacts customers and provides information about the products.

The *logistics function* is physically moving products from the manufacturers to distributors, retailers, or end users. The intermediary makes sure that the product moves through the supply chain. This includes transportation such as trucking, rail, or other shipping options.

The *facilitating function* is the final part of the supply chain. This involves the actual selling of the product or service to the end users. The end user could be consumers or businesses.

Intermediaries are important to the supply chain process. Intermediaries can add substantial value to a business by providing specialized services the business may not be able to afford. Intermediaries help increase the number of end users a producer can reach, increase market share for the producer, and help to reduce some costs by sharing responsibilities.

For example, think of an apple you ate recently. As shown in Figure 20-1, the apple started out in an apple orchard owned by an apple farmer: the producer. The apple farmer sold the apples to an apple buyer: an intermediary. The apple buyer sold apples to the local grocery store: an intermediary. You, as a consumer, visited the grocery store

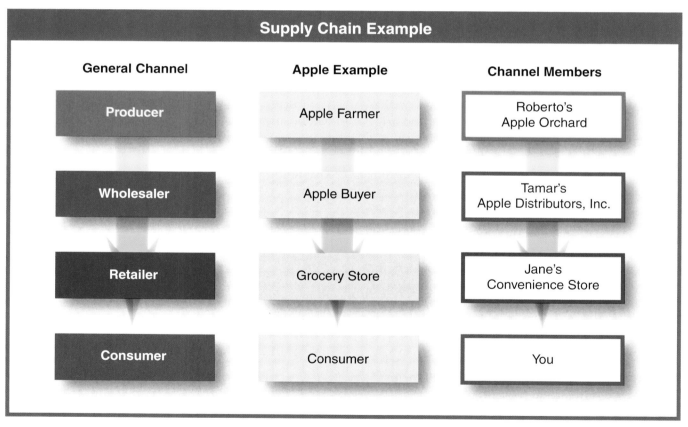

Figure 20-1 The most common supply chain for consumer goods includes a producer, wholesaler, and retailer before reaching the consumer.

Explore

Ask students for examples of logistics companies in their community.

Explain

Discuss Figure 20-1. Ask students for other examples of getting a product to the consumer.

and bought the apple. You could have bought the apple directly from the apple farmer. However, the apple buyer and the grocery store made the apple more convenient for you to buy when you wanted it.

Distribution Channels

A major part of the place decision is selecting the channel of distribution. A channel of distribution is the *path* that goods take through the supply chain. The supply chain is the *people* who move the goods. Distribution is not free. There are many costs associated with getting products to the end users. These distribution costs increase the prices charged for goods or services. Therefore, it is important to find efficient ways to move products that keep costs under control.

You can visualize each step in the channel of distribution as being one of the links in the supply chain. The supply chain is visualized vertically, with the raw material at the top and the final customer at the bottom. Products start at the top and move from link to link to reach the final customer. Figure 20-2 shows an example of a distribution channel. Depending on the product, the distribution channel can be direct, or short. On the other hand, it can be indirect, or long.

Direct Channel of Distribution

A direct channel is the path of selling goods or services directly from a manufacturer to end users without using intermediaries. Many companies sell products directly to consumers from their websites. Services usually have a very short path: from the service provider directly to the customer. For example, a childcare business provides services directly to the parent or guardian of the child.

Indirect Channel of Distribution

An indirect channel uses intermediaries to get the product from the manufacturer to the end users. Manufactured goods often have very long and complex paths. This is due, in part, to the hundreds of raw materials and manufactured parts often needed for manufacturing products. Warehousing, shipping, and retail intermediaries also add to the length of indirect-channel paths.

Distribution Channels for B2C Market

There are four channels of distribution for consumer goods. They include the direct, retailer, wholesaler, and agent broker channels, as shown in Figure 20-3.

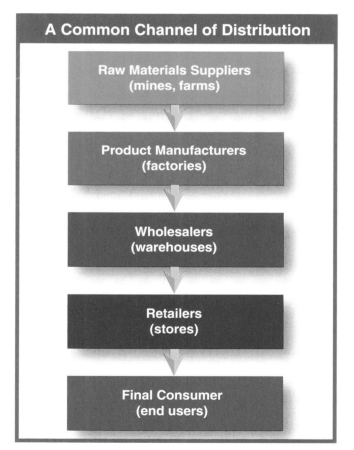

Goodheart-Willcox Publisher

Figure 20-2 Each segment of the supply chain follows the channel of distribution.

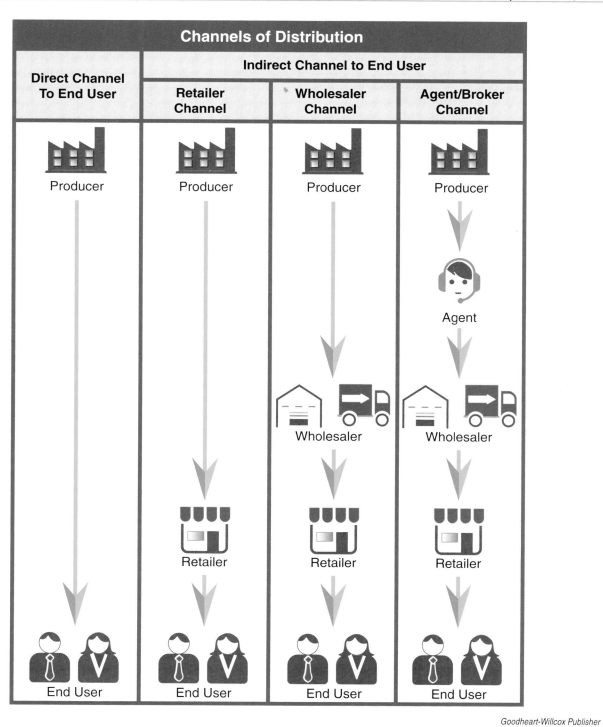

Figure 20-3 The channel of distribution for consumer goods may be very short (direct) or very long (indirect) using several intermediaries.

Case in Point

Clothing Traceability Project

Supply chains are becoming global for many types of products. The mission of the Clothing Traceability project is to help consumers "visualize the clothing supply chain—essentially where and how a garment is made and the people involved throughout the process." For example, designer Laurie Siegel uses Quick Response (QR) codes attached to her designs. When scanned, the QR code takes consumers to a *sourcemap*, or a global map of the supply chain for that garment. For Siegel, the sources of the fibers, producers, and shippers start in Bolivia and India and end in the countries where her collection is sold in retail stores. For people interested in sustainability, the Clothing Traceability project provides added value.

The Clothing Traceability project uses software on **sourcemap.com,** which began as a project at the Massachusetts Institute of Technology (MIT). Sourcemap.com is the first open-sourced collection of global supply chains. Any person or organization can show the story behind their products and calculate an environmental footprint. As a marketer, think about making your supply chain available for viewing to current and potential customers.

The *direct channel* in the B2C is when a consumer buys goods or services directly from the producers or manufacturers. Buying a computer online from Dell is an example of a direct channel purchase.

The **retailer channel** is the path of selling goods from the producer to the retailer, then the retailer to the consumer. An example is a customer buying a product from a sporting goods store. The producer sells to the sporting goods store, which then sells to the consumer. The retailer channel is an indirect channel.

The **wholesaler channel** is the path the product takes from the producer, to a wholesaler, and the retailer before reaching the end user. For example, a producer manufactures paper goods. The producer sells the goods to a wholesaler who in turns sells to retailers. The retailer then puts the goods in the store and sells to the consumer. The wholesaler channel is an indirect channel.

The **agent/broker channel** is the path of selling in which the producer hires an agent to sell to the wholesaler. Some producers do not want to assume the responsibility of selling or shipping products. Those producers will contract with an agent to handle the products after production. The agent never takes possession of the goods, just facilitates the path from the producer to the wholesaler. The agent/broker is the longest indirect channel in the B2C market.

Distribution Channels for B2B and Industrial Market

Goods used in the production of other goods or consumed by a business are called **industrial goods.** All businesses use industrial goods—to either manufacture goods or operate the business. There are four channels of distribution for the B2B and industrial market, just like there are four B2C channels. These channels are illustrated in Figure 20-4.

The *direct channel* is getting the product from the producer to the end user, which is business or government. No intermediaries are used. The industrial user might be

Explain

Industrial goods are different than consumer goods. Ask for examples of each.

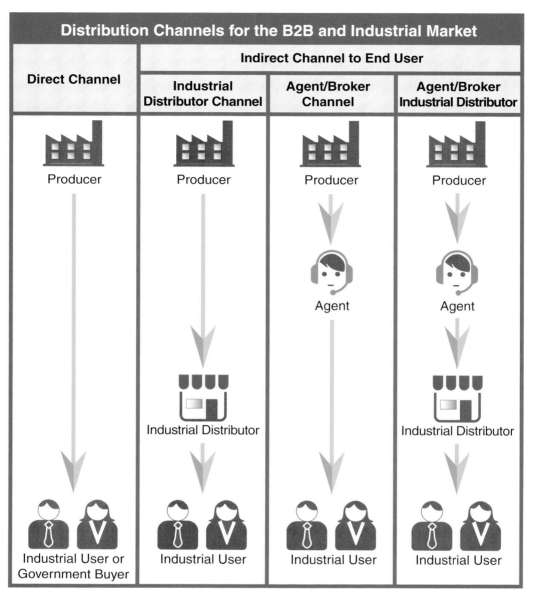

Distribution Channels for the B2B and Industrial Market

Direct Channel	Indirect Channel to End User		
	Industrial Distributor Channel	Agent/Broker Channel	Agent/Broker Industrial Distributor
Producer	Producer	Producer	Producer
		Agent	Agent
	Industrial Distributor		Industrial Distributor
Industrial User or Government Buyer	Industrial User	Industrial User	Industrial User

Goodheart-Willcox Publisher

Figure 20-4 The direct channel of distribution is the most common method for industrial goods.

purchasing steel to build a new headquarters for a company. A company may be purchasing computers to use in day-to-day operations. The direct channel of distribution is the most common method for industrial goods.

In the *industrial distributor channel,* an industrial distributor performs the same services as a wholesaler in the B2C market.

The difference is usually in the variety of products carried. Most industrial distributors specialize in one area. For example, an industrial distributor may focus on after-market car parts or chemicals used in the production of paint. The end users in the B2B and industrial markets buy products directly from the industrial distributor.

In the *agent/broker channel,* a producer uses an agent to assume the full responsibility of selling, storing, and shipping products. The end users in the B2B and industrial markets buy products directly from the agent/broker.

The *agent/broker industrial distributor channel* combines both of the agent and distributor channel and is the longest. The producer first contracts with an agent/broker to find the best industrial distributors to provide the selling, storage, and shipping services. In this channel, the B2B and industrial market end users buy products directly from the industrial distributor.

AMA Tip

Just like your favorite retailers know that online shopping is sometimes easiest, the American Marketing Association offers plenty of online events for busy marketing professionals. The AMA's Virtual Xchange Events bring together key speakers, companies and professionals to participate in highly interactive forums, lounges, and resource centers. Participants network by exchanging virtual business cards and can even win great prizes. Papers, presentations, and videos from Virtual Xchange Events are also available online after the event. www.marketingpower.com

Checkpoint 20.1

1. Describe the importance of the supply chain in the four Ps of marketing.
2. List three types of intermediaries.
3. What are the three functions that intermediaries serve?
4. What are the types of distribution channels for the B2C market?
5. What are the types of distribution channels for the B2B market?

Build Your Vocabulary

As you progress through this course, develop a personal glossary of marketing terms and add it to your portfolio. This will help you build your vocabulary and prepare you for a career. Write a definition for each of the following terms, and add it to your personal marketing glossary.

supply chain
intermediary
brick-and-mortar
e-tailer
agent
channel of distribution
direct channel
indirect channel
retailer channel
wholesaler channel
agent/broker channel
industrial good

Section 20.2 Physical Distribution

Objectives

After completing this section, you will be able to
- **describe** the distribution strategies of transportation, storage, and utility.
- **explain** product ownership in the distribution channel.

Key Terms

bulk-breaking
freight forwarder
transportation
private carrier
common carrier

pipeline
private warehouse
public warehouse

Web Connect

Choose a company you like that has an online store. If you were to order something from that business, what shipping companies are available to deliver your order? Why do you think that the business uses those specific shipping companies?

Critical Thinking

Divide a sheet of paper into two columns. In the left column, list all of the ways that you think a product can move from a producer to the end user. In the right column, list why you think a producer might use that method.

Distribution

Physical distribution is one of the most important parts of place. The selling function helps to transfer ownership to the end user. However, the physical distribution actually gives the end user possession of the goods. Physical distribution also plays a competitive role in product promotion. It makes products available where needed, correctly fills orders, and provides on-time delivery.

Distribution influences the final price of the product and company profitability. Distribution strategies include decisions about transportation, storage, and utility costs. The goal is to provide the best distribution services for the lowest cost. This efficiency helps to keep customer prices lower.

Breaking bulk is one efficiency that intermediaries can provide. **Bulk-breaking**

is the process of separating a large quantity of goods into smaller quantities for resale. An intermediary buys goods in bulk and then breaks the bulk into smaller quantities of goods. For example, it is easier and cheaper to ship a bushel of apples rather than 100 separate apples. The grocery store buys apples by the bushel and then sells them to customers a few at a time.

Another efficiency provided by an intermediary are the services of freight forwarders. A **freight forwarder** is a company that organizes shipments. It is not a shipper or carrier; it functions as an agent.

Freight forwarders generally combine shipments from various companies. They combine the shipments and hire a transportation company to move them as one large shipment. By putting these smaller shipments together, money is saved for the companies shipping the goods.

Freight forwarders are also called *cargo agents*.

Transportation

Transportation is the physical movement of products through the channel of distribution. Transportation decisions impact the price of the product and the length of time it takes to reach the end user. The cost of transportation can add up to 10 percent to the price of the product.

Each type of transportation has different costs, efficiencies, and time constraints. For example, a less expensive and slower mode of transportation may be used to ship large quantities of durable products. However, when shipping perishable goods, a more expensive, faster mode of transportation may be necessary.

There are six main methods of transportation as shown in Figure 20-5. Transportation methods are road, rail, air, water, pipeline, and digital.

Transportation Modes for Distribution		
Transportation Mode	**Advantages**	**Disadvantages**
Road	• Can deliver door to door • Flexible schedules • Can be modified for specific cargo (i.e., refrigerator trucks)	• Weather delays • Traffic delays • Maintenance problems
Rail	• Send large quantities over long distances • Inexpensive • Can carry trucks closer to the destination • Can be modified for cargo (flatbed railcars for intermodal containers)	• Slower method of transportation • Minimal destination flexibility • Needs a second mode of transportation to get to final destination
Air	• Fastest mode of transportation • Less chance of damage to items • Can save on warehousing as products arrive as needed	• Most expensive • Weather delays • Maintenance problems • Needs a second mode of transportation to get to final destination
Water	• Send large quantities over long distances • Can be modified for cargo (i.e., tankers for oil) • Inexpensive	• Slowest method • No destination flexibility • Needs a second mode of transportation to get to final destination
Pipeline	• Not subject to weather delays • Fewer maintenance issues • Low operating costs	• Can only carry products that flow (i.e., gasoline) • Expensive to build • Leaks linked to environmental damage • Needs a second mode of transportation to get to final destination
Digital	• Low to no operating cost • Easy access • Very fast delivery	• Only for electronic products or services

Goodheart-Willcox Publisher
Source: 2007–2010 Census Statistical Abstract

Figure 20-5 There are pros and cons for each method of transportation.

Elaborate/Extend

Provide an opportunity for students to exhibit their understanding of concepts in context of the material as it is presented. As time permits, have students read and discuss the special features in the margins.

Explore

Ask: As a marketer, which mode of transportation would be a first choice for your marketing plan?

Green Marketing

As a marketer, it will be necessary to find phone numbers and other contact information for suppliers and customers. Instead of using a print directory, consider using an online resource. Notify the company that sends print directories that the business no longer needs a print copy. However, if a print directory is needed, recycle it when the new copy is available. By recycling these directories, we can save thousands of tons of paper each year and save space in the landfills.

Road

Road transportation includes any motor vehicle that moves products on highways and roads. Vehicles used are trucks, buses, vans, and automobiles.

Trucking is the most common method of distribution in the United States. Trucks are a flexible mode of transportation and can be modified to carry a specific type of cargo. For example, refrigerated trucks are designed to carry products that must be kept cold. Trucks that transport canned beverages are structured to hold the cases, so they will not get broken in transit. Trucks that transport cars are designed to fit as many cars as possible on one truck. Many other types of trucks are designed for the specific product that they carry.

Some large companies, such as Kroger, own their own trucks. Products are shipped daily from company warehouses across the country to the local stores. A **private carrier** is a company that transports its own goods. Other companies hire independent trucking firms to move their products. Independent trucking companies are called **common carriers** or *contract carriers.*

The main advantage of using motor vehicles to deliver products is door-to-door delivery. Vehicles can be scheduled to deliver at a specific place during a specific time period. This advantage is useful for restaurants, which must receive food products at specific times.

There are disadvantages to shipping by motor carriers. Delays caused by traffic, bad weather, or maintenance problems can impact delivery. Road transportation can also be more costly than rail or water transportation. Motor carriers may be subject to weight limits on interstate highways.

Rail

Rail transportation is the second most often used mode of transportation in the United States. Rail transportation is one of the least expensive modes of transportation and is good for long-distance shipping of large, bulky items. Shipping long distances by rail takes about the same amount of time as freight shipped by trucks.

Steel, cars, and coal are often transported by rail. Refrigerated railcars carry perishable items, such as vegetables. Tankers can be fitted on railcars to carry flammable and hazardous materials, such as chemicals or fuel.

Flatbed railcars can carry shipping containers and truck trailers. From the train, each container or trailer can be taken off and trucked to its destination. The contents of the container or truck trailer are not unloaded or reloaded. Thus, there is less chance for goods to be damaged during the train-to-truck transfer. Using the train-truck combination also combines the lower cost of train transportation with the door-to-door advantage of truck transportation.

Engage
Ask: Are there any other factors that should be considered when choosing transportation that are not listed in this text?

Another leader in transportation is DHL, serving 220 countries and territories with over 83,800 vehicles.

Erasmus Wolff/Shutterstock.com

A major disadvantage to rail is that there is no destination flexibility. Trains can only go where there are railroad tracks. However, very few events stop or slow down a train.

Air

Air transportation is the most expensive and least often used method of transporting products. Many private transportation companies offer air services. UPS and FedEx are well-known names.

High-value, low-weight items are often shipped by air. An example is emergency medicines that must arrive quickly at the destination. Air shipments are also used for some perishable goods. Perishable goods spoil quickly, such as fresh flowers.

Shipping by plane is used when delivery time must be short and the higher transportation cost can be justified. Government contracts, especially, have strict delivery dates for their vendors to deliver finished goods. Parts for the manufacturing of the goods must be delivered on time. Also, the finished goods must be shipped on time. Shipping costs are not spared for these business deals.

The speed of air transportation can sometimes save on inventory costs. Holding expensive or perishable goods in a warehouse is costly. Products can spoil, plus warehouse space costs money. For these reasons, the cost of air transportation can be offset by the savings on inventory storage.

A disadvantage of air transportation is the high cost. Once a product arrives at an airport, it still needs to be delivered to its final destination. Road companies called *air cargo companies* specialize in delivering air cargo.

Water

Water transportation includes ocean-going ships, inland ships, and coastal ships. Ships are also called *freighters. Ocean-going ships* transport products across the ocean, normally between countries. *Inland ships* use rivers and the Great Lakes to transport products. *Coastal ships* move products up and down the coastline of a country. In the United States, coastal ships move products up and down the Pacific and Atlantic coastlines.

Ships can be modified for the type of cargo they carry. *Tankers* are ships designed

The containers on this cargo ship hold goods from many different producers.

specifically for transporting petroleum oil. *Barges* are large holding vessels that are towed or pushed.

Container ships are ships designed to hold large metal shipping containers for cargo shipped long distances. It is easier to load and unload one large metal container than many small boxes. Containers allow large quantities of goods to travel long distances without being unpacked. Containers can be transferred from a ship to a truck or flatbed railcar to continue to their destinations.

The low cost of water transportation must be weighed against the disadvantages. Water transportation is also the slowest option. Hurricanes and monsoons at sea can also impact the delivery of products.

Products arrive at a port, rather than at specific delivery addresses. The products delivered to a port must then be transported by another mode of transportation. This is usually done by using road or rail transportation and generally increases the final shipping cost. Security has also become an issue. New security programs check cargo entering the United States to prevent import fraud and terrorism.

Explore

Assign students to research container ships. How large are they? For what purposes are they used? Who uses container ships? How long does it take for the product to arrive to its destination?

Pipeline

A **pipeline** is a line of connected pipes that are used for carrying liquids and gases over a long distance. Products carried through pipelines move slowly but continuously. Pipelines are limited in what they can carry, such as liquid or oil products. However, the products are safe from damage or theft. Also, they are not subject to delivery delays due to bad weather.

Building a pipeline is expensive, but the cost to operate it is small. Leaks rarely occur. However, when there is a leak, the risk of environmental damage is great.

FYI

The most famous pipeline in the United States is the Alaskan pipeline, which is 800 miles long. It stretches from Prudhoe Bay, Alaska to Valdez, Alaska. The Alaskan pipeline represents almost 40 percent of the 2,000 miles of pipelines in the United States.

Convenience and lower pricing affect the choice between digital and physical products.

Olaf Speier/Shutterstock.com

Digital

Digital transportation is gaining in popularity as more people download books and music onto personal media devices, electronic readers, and smartphones. Digital transportation is inexpensive and uses the Internet to transport the product from the producer to the end user. Products can be shipped instantly after an order is placed.

Storage

Storage is also critical to the strategy for place. Products need protection from weather, theft, and damage. Retail and manufacturing businesses need areas to store physical inventory. This may increase distribution costs, which will affect the final product pricing. If a business does not have enough storage space in the facility, it will need to rent, lease, or build space.

Large companies, such as Crate and Barrel and Sears, have their own warehouse facilities. **Private warehouses** are those owned by a company for storage of their own goods.

Smaller companies may lease storage space from **public warehouses** that offer space to any company. Or, they use wholesalers to store products until they are needed. Some public warehouse facilities provide delivery to the end user. By using this type of warehousing service, a business can reduce inventory-storage costs and losses due to damage or theft. However, some companies prefer not to

Intermediaries, such as agents or brokers, provide services necessary to the channel of distribution of many businesses, such as these shippers of oil.

use storage facilities but stagger the delivery of inventory. By issuing a purchase order for a large quantity of product, they can negotiate when inventory is delivered. The manufacturer will make and hold the products in storage until the ship date.

Utility

In Chapter 3, you learned that *utility* is the attribute that makes a product capable of satisfying a need or want. Four of the five types of utility—place, time, possession, and form—are associated with distribution. Based on the specific product or service, some utility costs will be necessary and directly affect place strategies; others will not apply.

Place Utility

Place utility means placing products where they are needed and are useful. For example, if you sell sunscreen lotion, it makes sense to have it available at the beach where people who need it can buy it.

Time Utility

Time utility is getting a product delivered to the end user when it is needed. Timing is everything. If the product is late, the business could lose a customer and goodwill is damaged.

Possession Utility

Possession utility is the satisfaction that a customer receives from owning a product or receiving a needed service. An example of possession utility is owning a car you have wanted for a long time.

Form Utility

Form utility is added when a business changes the form of something to make it more useful. For example, an auto manufacturer turns steel, plastic, fabric, and glass into an automobile. The materials needed to produce a product must be delivered to the manufacturers. In a service business, the production of the service itself provides the utility.

Ownership

Physical distribution involves responsibilities associated with the transfer of ownership of products from the producer to the end user. The original owner is at the beginning of the distribution channel. The final owner is the end user at the end of the distribution channel.

Most, but not all, of the intermediaries take ownership of the product as it moves through the channel of distribution. Agents/brokers never take ownership of the products.

When ownership is transferred to intermediaries in the distribution channel, each one assumes the risk and responsibility for the product. The new owner is the one who will suffer any loss if the product is damaged or lost. For that reason, producers must use caution when hiring intermediaries to transport their products to the end user.

Checkpoint 20.2

1. Name two transportation efficiencies provided by intermediaries.
2. Which mode of transportation is used most often?
3. What are the six main methods of freight transportation?
4. Which forms of utility are associated with distribution?
5. What happens when intermediaries in the channel of distribution assume ownership of products?

Build Your Vocabulary

As you progress through this course, develop a personal glossary of marketing terms and add it to your portfolio. This will help you build your vocabulary and prepare you for a career. Write a definition for each of the following terms, and add it to your personal marketing glossary.

bulk-breaking
freight forwarder
transportation
private carrier
common carrier
pipeline
private warehouse
public warehouse

Section **20.3** Managing the Channel of Distribution

Objectives

After completing this section, you will be able to
- **describe** supply chain management and the role of a supply chain manager.
- **define** the three levels of distribution.
- **discuss** place decisions for global businesses.
- **explain** the importance of managing channel members.

Key Terms

supply chain
  management
supply chain
  manager
intensive distribution
selective distribution
exclusive distribution

export management
  company

Web Connect

Conduct Internet research on the job title *supply chain managers*. Read the job description for the position. Is this a position that would interest you? Why or why not?

Critical Thinking

It takes a lot of coordination to get a product from the producer to the ultimate consumer. What are some things that might happen to a product as it moves through the channel of distribution?

Supply Chain Management

Supply chain management is coordinating the events happening throughout the supply chain. It may also be called *channel management*.

Effective supply chain management results in the following benefits:
- streamlined inventories;
- lower operating costs;
- timely product availability; and
- increased customer satisfaction.

The **supply chain manager** is the person who coordinates and monitors all the activities from the building of the product to delivery to the end user. After the product moves through the supply chain to the distribution stage, the manager makes place decisions. The supply chain manager must make

choices about how to best get its products to the end users. Before deciding which channel of distribution to use, several factors must be considered, as shown in Figure 20-6.

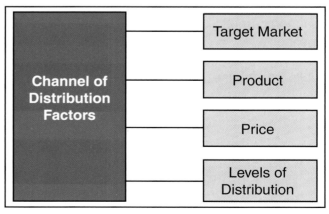

Goodheart-Willcox Publisher

Figure 20-6 These factors must all be considered when choosing the best channel of distribution.

Explain

Review Figure 20-6. Ask for a volunteer to explain the factors that are listed above and their importance.

Target Market

First, objectives must be identified for the distribution channel. Answering the *who, when, where, why,* and *how* about the target market is the first step.

• Who is the target market?
• When does the customer buy?
• Where do they go to buy?
• Why do they buy?
• How do they buy?

Once these questions are answered, the supply chain manager can begin to weigh the choice of a direct channel or indirect channel to get the product to the end user.

Product

Product considerations are important when selecting the channel of distribution. The product itself will help to determine how it should be transported. If a product has a short shelf life or is perishable, it will need to be handled differently than a staple clothing item like jeans. Product life cycle is also important. Winter coats and summer bathing suits have different seasonal opportunities for selling. So, they must be shipped early or in the most efficient manner to get them to the final retailer on time.

Price

The method of transportation will influence the price that the end user pays for the product. If the product must be shipped quickly, transportation costs may be high. This means the final price of the product may be higher. The opposite may also be true, and prices can be kept low by using less costly shipping options.

Levels of Distribution

The level of distribution plays a role in the channel that is selected. The three levels of distribution are intensive, selective, and exclusive.

Intensive Distribution

Intensive distribution places product in every potential sales situation possible. A manufacturer, wholesaler, or retailer may want to have as much exposure as possible. Producers and distributors of convenience goods often choose intensive distribution systems. For example, candy, gum, milk, and bread are found at many different locations.

Selective Distribution

Selective distribution is selecting the specific places that the manufacturer or whole-

Marketing Ethics

Collusion

It is unethical and illegal for intermediaries to participate in acts of collusion. *Collusion* occurs when channel members work together to eliminate competition by misleading supply chain managers, setting prices, or other fraudulent activities. Unethical businesses sometimes collude with other businesses so that they can dominate the marketplace. Collusion is not only unethical, it is illegal.

Extend

Give examples of each level of distribution. Why is each level important to marketing?

saler wants the product to be sold. Only select channel members are used. This method is used most often with shopping goods or brands with an exclusive image. For example, Coach products can only be found at high-end department stores or Coach retail stores.

In selective distribution, a retailer has just enough locations to adequately serve the target market. Selective-market coverage usually means there will be several stores in a market area. A selective retailer might locate one store in each major shopping mall. For example, Old Navy has a selective market approach.

Exclusive Distribution

Exclusive distribution occurs when there is only one channel member, or distributor of products, in a market area. Exclusive distribution traditionally occurs with highly technical or complex products that are expensive. An exclusive-distribution retailer

has only one store to serve the entire market area.

For example, there is only one Rolls Royce-Bentley automobile dealer in the Chicago area. These retailers can use the exclusive approach because their customers are willing to travel to buy these special products.

Global Distribution

Marketers working for companies that buy, sell, or distribute products globally have more complex place decisions. Some products can only be shipped by air. For products that can be shipped by water, the ports chosen as the transportation hubs help global companies save on distribution costs. For example, Panama has often used a transportation hub for companies in the Americas. It is centrally located and ships must go through the Panama Canal to reach some continents. Some other global companies have franchises

This cargo container ship is going through the Panama Canal to get from the Atlantic to the Pacific Ocean.

Explain
Global distribution can be very profitable but complex. Ask students to explain the issues a marketer might have with global markets. Clarify responses as needed.

or joint ventures with local companies in foreign countries that assist with distribution.

Many US businesses use intermediaries to help with foreign trade and distribution. An export management company is an independent company that provides support services, such as warehousing, shipping, insuring, and billing on behalf of the business. They are also called *export trading companies.* These companies also help US businesses with foreign customs offices; documentation; and sizing, weights, and measurement conversions. Export management companies can be either local or foreign-owned, and are paid by commission or a fee.

Cultural Differences

Cultural beliefs, customs, and social behaviors often differ from those in the United States. When doing business in a foreign country, it is important to fully understand its culture. For example, in some Asian countries, a business card must be treated with utmost respect. It should be taken with both hands, carefully reviewed for a few seconds, and put in a shirt pocket or business card holder. Never put someone's business card in your pants pocket. Doing so would offend your counterpart since you would be sitting on his or her card.

Communication

Even though English is considered a universal business language, not every person speaks it. It is important to learn the language of the country or have a reliable interpreter. Patience is needed when communicating with people who do not speak the same language as you. Incorrect word choice or even a different inflection can send the wrong message. Nonverbal communication may also be different. In the United States, shaking your head from side to side means *no.* However, in some countries, shaking your head from side to side means *yes.* It is important to understand accepted body language for the countries in which you are doing business.

Labor Issues

Marketers must know the laws that apply to global trade and distribution. These laws and

---

College and Career Portfolio

You have collected documents that show your skills and talents. However, some skills and talents are not shown effectively using only documents. Do you have a special talent in an area such as art, music, or design? Have you taken part in volunteer activities? Create a video to showcase your talents and activities. For example, if you are an artist, create a video that shows your completed works. If you are a musician, create a video with segments from your performances. If you have taken part in a volunteer or service activity, create a video that shows and tells viewers about it. Suppose you volunteer with a group that helps repair homes for elderly homeowners. The video could show scenes from the worksites and comments from the residents. Note: Make sure you have permission to include other people in your video.

1. Place the video file in an appropriate subfolder for your e-portfolio.
2. Print a few screen shots from the video. Create a document that describes the video. State that the video will be made available upon request or tell where it can be viewed online. Place the information in the container for your print portfolio.

regulations apply to all businesses. However, they can be especially important to companies operating globally to protect their businesses.

It is important to know that some countries have poor working conditions. Some countries employ children or have businesses that pay extremely low wages. There are US laws and policies to prohibit imported products from countries abusing human rights. In addition, some products are simply against the law to import from certain countries. Consult the Bureau of International Labor Affairs under the DOL. It is also wise to seek advice from attorneys and others specializing in international business. Because importing and exporting is important to the US economy, there are many agencies to provide support, as shown in Figure 20-7.

Channel Members

In a direct channel of distribution, the channel members are just the producer and the end users. For indirect distribution channels, however, there may be a number of intermediaries. To maintain efficiencies, the members must be selected, motivated, and evaluated.

Select Channel Members

Once the channel of distribution is chosen, the best channel members must be selected. When choosing channel members with whom to work, the following factors should be reviewed.
- Number of years the channel member has been in business.
- What product lines the channel member carries.
- Reputation in the business.
- Previous experience with the producer.
- Financial stability.
- Quality of the sales force and customer service.

Motivate Channel Members

Once a channel member is selected, it is necessary to keep that intermediary

Government Agencies
US Department of Commerce (DOC). The DOC promotes US interests by helping businesses export US goods and services. It helps businesses know foreign countries' laws, regulations, and tariffs. It also helps businesses to form joint ventures.
US Customs and Border Protection (CPB). The CPB enforces the laws for importing and exporting products. It also inspects all packages coming from foreign countries.
Environmental Protection Agency (EPA). The EPA oversees the laws for potentially hazardous imports and exports to ensure safety. Pesticides, fuels, and lead-free paints, especially on items for small children, are just a few of the products it regulates.
Small Business Administration (SBA). The SBA provides small businesses the information needed to safely import and/or export products.
US Embassies. The US embassies in other countries help US entrepreneurs understand and follow local laws and customs.

Figure 20-7 These government agencies can also help you understand global trade issues.

Goodheart-Willcox Publisher

Engage
Have students discuss the process of selecting channel members. Remind them that price is not the only factor.

motivated. Producers need their channel members to promote, sell, and distribute their products to make a profit. In order to motivate channel members, producers may offer special deals, premiums, and sales contests to maintain long-term relationships.

If more than one channel member is necessary to carry out distribution, the supply chain manager will be in charge of supervising them. There is always a possibility of conflict between two channel members over issues, such as exclusive distribution rights for one intermediary and not the other. Or, one channel member may feel the other is not doing their job well. It is important that the supply chain manger maintain control and keep all lines of communication open.

Evaluate Channel Members

After channel members are in place and performing, they must be evaluated. The supply chain manager must set measurable performance standards for evaluation. Standards may include prompt delivery, cooperative advertising, meeting sales quotas, service quality, treatment of lost or damaged goods, and overall satisfaction. Most producers annually review their contracts with channel members. They replace members who perform poorly. If a current channel member has competitive pricing and meets or exceeds expectations, the supplier remains. If it does not meet expectations, it may be replaced.

Warehouses are often vital parts of the distribution channel.

Maxim Blinkov/Shutterstock.com

Checkpoint 20.3

1. Name four benefits of supply chain management.
2. What is the first step in identifying the best channel of distribution?
3. What are the three levels of distribution?
4. What is an important distribution decision for global companies with products that can be shipped by water?
5. After channel members are in place and performing, what does the supply chain manager do?

Build Your Vocabulary

As you progress through this course, develop a personal glossary of marketing terms and add it to your portfolio. This will help you build your vocabulary and prepare you for a career. Write a definition for each of the following terms, and add it to your personal marketing glossary.

supply chain management
supply chain manager
intensive distribution
selective distribution
exclusive distribution
export management company

Checkpoint Answers

1. The benefits of supply chain management are streamlined inventories, lower operating costs, timely product availability, and increased customer satisfaction.
2. Answering the *who, when where, why, and how* about the target market is the first step.
3. The three levels of distribution are intensive, selective, and exclusive.
4. For products that can be shipped by water, the ports chosen as the transportation hubs help global companies save on distribution costs.
5. The supply chain manager evaluates the channel members on a set of measurable performance standards.

Build Your Vocabulary Answers

Definitions for these terms can be found in the glossary of this text.

Evaluate

Assign end-of-chapter activities.

Chapter Summary

Section 20.1 Channels of Distribution

- A supply chain is the businesses, people, and activities involved in turning raw materials into products and delivering them to end users. The people or businesses between the manufacturers or producers and the end users in the supply chain are called intermediaries.
- A channel of distribution is the path that goods take through the supply chain. The supply chain is the people who move the goods.

Section 20.2 Physical Distribution

- Physical distribution plays a competitive role in promoting products by providing on-time delivery, making products available where they are needed, and correctly filling orders. Distribution strategies include transportation, storage, and utility costs.
- When ownership is transferred to each intermediary in the distribution channel, risk and responsibility for the product is assumed. The new owner is the one who will suffer any loss if the product is damaged or lost.

Section 20.3 Managing the Channel of Distribution

- Supply chain management is coordinating the events happening throughout the supply chain. The supply chain manager is the person who coordinates and monitors all the activities from the manufacturer of the product to delivery to the end user.
- The level of distribution plays a role in the channel that is selected. The three levels of distribution are intensive, selective, and exclusive.
- Marketers working for companies that buy, sell, or distribute products globally have more complex place decisions. Cultural differences and communication are also important considerations when doing business in foreign countries.
- Indirect distribution channels may use a number of intermediaries. To maintain efficiencies, the members must be selected, motivated, and evaluated.

Review Your Knowledge

1. What is another term for an intermediary?
2. What is the difference between an agent and a wholesaler?
3. Do retailers only sell in brick-and-mortar stores or online?
4. What is the difference between a direct and an indirect channel of distribution?
5. Which indirect channel of distribution is the longest in the B2C market?
6. What is the most expensive mode of transportation used to distribute products?
7. How are private and public warehouses different?
8. Which type of utility places products where they are needed and are useful?
9. Which type of utility gets a product delivered to the end user when it is needed?
10. Name three criteria for choosing channel members.

Review Your Knowledge Answers

1. Another term for an intermediary is a channel member.
2. An agent does not take possession of the goods, but a wholesaler generally does.
3. No. Some retailers sell in both brick-and-mortar stores and online.
4. A direct channel has no intermediaries, while indirect channels do.

5. The agent/broker is the longest indirect channel in the B2C market.
6. Air is the expensive mode of transportation.
7. Private warehouses are those owned by a company for storage of their own goods. Public warehouses offer storage space to any company.
8. Place utility places products where they are needed and are useful.

Apply Your Knowledge

1. In earlier chapters, you identified the product or service for which you are creating a marketing plan. Research supply chain management for your product. Identify the various channel members in the supply chain. Describe the role of each member.
2. Draw a flowchart that identifies the specific channel members that are required to get the product from the producer to the end user. Use the information you found by completing Question 1.
3. Intermediaries serve three functions: transactional, logistical, and facilitating functions. Describe how your channel members serve these functions.
4. Conduct a SWOT analysis of the six types of transportation modes as to which mode of transportation would be most effective in moving your product to the end user. Write a paragraph summary with the SWOT analysis defending your choice.
5. Describe how a freight forwarder could help facilitate transportation of products for your business.
6. There are four types of utility that are associated with distribution—place, time, possession, and form. Describe how utility impacts your business.
7. Contact a local business and arrange for an interview with a supply chain manager. Create a list of questions to ask the person about what his or her responsibilities are and what challenges they face in managing the supply chain. Share your findings with the class.
8. Research current trends in supply chain management for your business. Write several paragraphs to reflect your findings.
9. What is the level of distribution in your business? Should it be changed? If so, why?
10. How would you motivate and evaluate the members in your channel of distribution.

Check Your Marketing IQ

Now that you have finished the chapter, see what you learned about marketing by taking the chapter posttest. If you do not have a smartphone, visit the G-W Learning companion website.
G-W Learning mobile site: www.m.g-wlearning.com
G-W Learning companion website: www.g-wlearning.com

9. Time utility gets a product delivered to the end user when it is needed.
10. Students can choose any three of the following: number of years the channel member has been in business; what product lines the channel member carries; reputation in the business; previous experience with the producer; financial stability; or quality of the sales force and customer service.

Apply Your Knowledge Answers

Student answers will vary for questions 1–10.

Marketing Plan

At the end of this unit, students will write the next phase of the marketing plan. Please note that the Apply Your Knowledge questions prepare students for the next installment of the marketing plan that they are writing at the end of each unit. These questions help them assume the role of a marketing manager and begin applying concepts learned in the chapter. If your class is not participating in the marketing plan activity at the end of the unit, Apply Your Knowledge questions can be used by directing students to select a business of their choice and answer each question about that business. A good example to use for supply chain management information is Target. Visit their corporate website or do a search for Target distribution and supply chain.

Common Core

College and Career Readiness

CTE Career Ready Practices. Read the Marketing Ethics features presented throughout this text. What role do you think ethics and integrity play in channel management? Think of a time when you used your ideals and principles to make a decision. What process did you use to make the decision? Did your decision have any consequences?

Reading. Select several articles that discuss supply chain management for well-known businesses such as Target or Walmart. What common theme did you observe about distribution that the companies you select have in common?

Writing. Undertake research on the Internet regarding digital transportation. What do you think are the advantages and disadvantages of this trend? What type of business could benefit from digital transportation? Create a 200-word news story or blog post detailing what your research revealed.

Teamwork

Form a team of three members. Create a chart with three columns: intensive distribution, selective distribution, and exclusive distribution. Identify two or three businesses for each category. Make a list of reasons for each company as to why you think they chose that type of distribution.

G-W Learning Mobile Site

Visit the G-W Learning mobile site to complete the chapter pretest and posttest and to practice vocabulary using e-flash cards. If you do not have a smartphone, visit the G-W Learning companion website to access these features.

G-W Learning mobile site: www.m.g-wlearning.com

G-W Learning companion website: www.g-wlearning.com

Evaluate

Evaluate the students' understanding and knowledge. Assign the Chapter 20 posttest. The test may be accessed by using the QR code or by going to the companion website. What questions were students able to answer that they could not answer when they took the pretest?

21

Purchasing and Inventory Control

Section 21.1 | Purchasing
Section 21.2 | Inventory Management

"The miracle of your mind isn't that you can see the world as it is. It's that you can see the world as it isn't."

—Kathryn Schulz , author of *Being Wrong: Adventures in the Margin of Error*

College and Career Readiness

Reading Prep
Recall all the things you already know about purchasing and inventory. As you read, think of how the new information presented in the text matches or challenges your prior understanding of the topic. Think of direct connections you can make between the old material and the new material.

Check Your Marketing IQ

Before you begin the chapter, see what you already know about marketing by taking the chapter pretest. If you do not have a smartphone, visit the G-W Learning companion website.
G-W Learning mobile site: www.m.g-wlearning.com
G-W Learning companion website: www.g-wlearning.com

Explore

Provide an opportunity for students to explore by assigning a hands-on activity. Assign the College and Career Readiness Reading Prep activity before students read the chapter. Reading Prep activities give students opportunity to apply the Common Core State Standards.

Engage

Engage the student by providing an activity or question that will connect students to what they already know. Assign the Chapter 21 pretest. The test may be accessed by using the QR code or going to the *Marketing Dynamics* companion website. Discuss which questions students were unable to answer.

◇DECA Emerging Leaders

Hospitality Services Team Decision-Making Event, Part 2

Career Cluster: Hospitality and Tourism
Instructional Area: Market Planning

Procedure, Part 2

1. In the previous chapter, you studied the performance indicators for this event.
2. The event will be presented to you through your reading of the General Performance Indicators, Specific Performance Indicators, and Case Study Situation. You will have up to 30 minutes to review this information and prepare your presentation. You may make notes to use during your presentation.
3. You will have up to 10 minutes to make your presentation to the judge followed by up to five minutes to answer the judge's questions. You may have more than one judge. All members of the team must participate in the presentation, as well as answer the questions.
4. Turn in all of your notes and event materials when you have completed the event.

Case Study Situation

You are to assume the role of a management team at WHITE BEAR RESORT, an upscale resort located in a very popular tourism/recreation area. The **owner (judge)** of WHITE BEAR RESORT has asked you to develop a strategy to deal with a natural disaster which occurred last week.

WHITE BEAR RESORT located on picturesque Lake Loraine, is a destination vacation resort featuring 720 rooms, four restaurants, a 200,000 square foot indoor water park, fitness center, spa, tennis courts, boating, Jet Skis, parasailing, rock climbing, a championship golf course, and a mini-golf course. Targeted to middle- and upper-income customers, WHITE BEAR RESORT is an all-suite resort charging $325 to $475 per night during the peak summer season. The resort employs mostly part-time and seasonal employees. Only 20% of the employees are full time. Located in the Loraine Valley, the region forms one of the top family vacation destinations in the United States.

Loraine Valley is an enormous vacation and recreation area with three outdoor water parks, an amusement park, go-kart tracks, scenic boat tours, horseback riding, a thrill show, two shopping districts, several nightclubs, and two casinos. Yearly, the area boasts an estimated five million annual visitors who pump over $1 billion into the local economy.

Last week, a dam holding back the water to Lake Loraine burst and the entire lake emptied into local rivers—turning Lake Loraine into one giant mud hole. The lake is expected to remain empty for more than a year. News of the unusual event was widely reported on television and radio and WHITE BEAR RESORT has experienced a cancellation of 30% of their summer reservations in less than a week.

With Lake Loraine now empty, all boating and other lake activities have been cancelled. The remainder of WHITE BEAR RESORT'S operation is unaffected, however. In fact, 90% of all Loraine Valley attractions will operate as usual this summer. Nonetheless, many visitors to WHITE BEAR RESORT are canceling their upcoming summer reservations.

The owner has asked to meet with you to hear your ideas on the following:
- a plan to try to get those who have already cancelled to reconsider their cancellations.
- a strategy that WHITE BEAR RESORT can implement to reduce the number of future cancellations and draw in new customers.

If it becomes necessary to reduce the workforce, how should those decisions be made and from which areas of operation should they come? Be as complete and specific as possible.

You will present to the owner of WHITE BEAR RESORT in a meeting to take place in the owner's office. The owner will begin the meeting by greeting you and asking to hear your ideas. When you have finished your presentation and have answered the owner's questions, the owner will conclude the meeting by thanking you for your work.

Critical Thinking

1. Other than reducing personnel, are there any other areas that WHITE BEAR RESORT can look at to reduce overall expenses?
2. Should we mention the fact that Lake Loraine is currently empty in any of our advertising? Why or why not?

Visit www.deca.org for more information.

Section 21.1 Purchasing

Objectives

After completing this section, you will be able to
- **explain** the importance of the purchasing process.
- **describe** the steps involved in managing the purchasing process.

Key Terms

inventory
electronic data
    interchange (EDI)
reorder point
product specification
    sheet
economy of scale
purchase order (PO)

packing slip
receiving record
invoice
quality control

Web Connect

Perform online research to find the general purchasing process in your company's industry. Does the general purchasing process you find apply to your business? Create a flow chart for each showing each step of the purchasing process as it applies to your company.

Critical Thinking

As a marketing professional, you will be making place decisions. You just learned about product and price in the previous units and place in the previous chapter. Choose a product that you would like to market and discuss how place and the right amount of inventory would be important to the success of the product.

Purchasing Process

The purchasing process is very important to all businesses. In Chapter 14, you learned that *purchasing agents* are the individuals responsible for purchasing goods and services the company needs internally to operate its business. Purchasing agents are involved in the production process of the business, so they can plan how much material is needed to keep the company running. **Inventory** is the assortment or selection of items that a business has in stock. For producers and manufacturers, inventory may include raw materials to produce a finished product.

You also learned that *buyers* in a retail organization are the individuals responsible for making purchases of merchandise. *Merchandise* consists of goods purchased with the intent of reselling to customers. For a retailer or wholesaler, inventory is merchandise that will be sold to customers. Buyers for a retail business create a *merchandise plan* that includes the details of product the business will need for a specified time period.

Managing the Purchasing Process

Much of the purchasing process takes place electronically to maximize efficiency and easily maintain records. **Electronic data interchange (EDI)** is the standard transfer

Explore

Provide an opportunity for students to explore by assigning a hands-on activity. Review the vocabulary terms at the beginning of the section. Where have students encountered these terms before? Help students make educated guesses about the meanings of the terms with which they are least familiar.

Resource

Use the Chapter 21 presentation on the optional Instructor's Presentations for PowerPoint® CD as an outline for presenting the chapter.

of electronic data for business transactions between organizations. Transactions can include orders, confirmations, and invoices.

The specific steps in the purchasing process are shown in Figure 21-1.

Identify Inventory Needs

For a retailer, the type and quality of merchandise purchased depends on the goals of the business as stated in the marketing plan. Retail and service businesses must be aware of the changes in customer needs and wants. In order to maintain a successful business, inventory must be adjusted to meet those needs. Before placing orders for merchandise, for example, buyers must study the target market. Marketers help the buyers know which products are popular, how often are they purchased, and about new trends. This information is important because inventory must be purchased before a business needs it.

Ongoing sales projections help determine the correct quantity of inventory needed to meet customer needs. If a business has been in operation for a few years, it is important to use actual sales history to determine inventory needs. A business should avoid being out of stock of any items and missing sales opportunities. Moreover, a business does not want to fail to meet customer needs by not having the latest products. It is necessary to have a reorder point for each item. The **reorder point** puts a control in place to trigger placing an order *before* the inventory gets too low. However, a business also needs to avoid purchasing too much inventory in the event sales projections were incorrect. Inventory management is discussed in greater detail in the next section.

Identify Vendors

Recall that vendors, or suppliers, are companies that sell products to other businesses. Depending on the products needed,

The Purchasing Process
1.   Identify inventory needs.
2.   Identify vendors.
3.   Select the vendor.
4.   Negotiate the purchase.
5.   Make the purchase.
6.   Receive the order.
7.   Pay the invoice.
8.   Evaluate the vendor.

Goodheart-Willcox Publisher

Figure 21-1 The purchasing process includes eight very different steps.

there may be many vendors from which to choose. The service and product quality and pricing can greatly differ by vendor. Buyers can check with other business contacts in their industry for vendor recommendations. The Better Business Bureau (BBB) also provides reports on vendor standings.

Select the Vendor

Buyers select vendors based on several criteria. In addition to price, other considerations include vendor quality, delivery time, and service. After comparing vendors, buyers choose the ones that meet the ongoing needs of the business. Developing good relationships with vendors is extremely important. A vendor with whom a buyer has a good relationship may be more willing to provide help when needed. This can be very important if there is a specific product that will be highlighted in an upcoming marketing campaign.

Negotiate the Purchase

Negotiation involves getting a good price and payment schedule for the goods as well as timely delivery. Most organizations are

Identifying inventory and supply needs is the first step in a business purchasing process.

required to get a number of bids from different vendors. Choosing the best bid can be a complex process. Organizations do not automatically choose the lowest-price bid. A bid includes a combination of goods and services. The buyer will choose the bid that provides the best combination of goods and services for the price. In other words, the buyer decides which bid provides the best value for the company.

Buyers ask vendors for a product specification sheet which describes the merchandise selected for purchase. A **product specification sheet** provides product facts including sizes, colors, materials, and weights. When used for bidding purposes, it should also include pricing, payment terms, delivery, and other issues important to making a purchase decision. After the price and terms are negotiated, buyers request an official bid stating the terms of purchase.

Quality and Value

The quality of products a business can offer ranges from high-end and expensive

to low-end and inexpensive. The key to negotiating for quality is to insist on *value,* or getting the highest quality for the lowest possible price. Remember, a business must still mark up the price it paid for items to earn a profit on customer sales. The choice of product quality also depends on how much the target market is willing to pay for certain items.

It is wise for buyers to understand how quality and price affect value in their industries to negotiate the best deals. Sometimes vendors offer higher-quality merchandise for very good prices to encourage a business to also buy inexpensive items. Depending on the vendor, this area is open for negotiation.

Economies of Scale

Most vendors offer *quantity discounts,* or a reduced per-item price based on the quantity purchased, to encourage larger orders. The greater the quantity purchased, the lower the per-unit price. This practice is similar to buying household items in bulk because the

Extend

Bring in samples of specs sheets, packing slips, and purchase orders for student to review.

Engage

Discuss economy of scale. For buyers, it is important to the profitability of the business.

price per item is lower than when buying only one. It is usually more cost effective for businesses to purchase inventory in larger quantities to obtain the lower unit prices.

After markup to the list prices, the profit margin on the goods sold is greater. Quantity discounts are based on the economy of scale. **Economy of scale** is the decrease in unit cost of a product resulting from large scale manufacturing operations. The efficiency of production increases as more of a product is made. This in turn reduces the cost per piece.

Economies of scale also occur in other business functions. For example, the per-item shipping-and-handling cost on larger orders may be less than when purchasing fewer products. Transportation costs can be spread over the total cost of all the products purchased and not just one item.

Make the Purchase

After choosing the vendor, the next step is completing a purchase order for the product. A **purchase order (PO)** is the form a buyer sends to the vendor to officially place an order. It lists the negotiated quantities, varieties, and prices for the products ordered. The purchase order includes the company information and the product, shipping, and payment details, as shown in Figure 21-2.

POs should be consecutively numbered so the record-keeping system remains sequential. Copies of the PO are made for business records and for the vendor.

Receive the Order

Tracking purchases is an important step to make sure shipments are correct and delivered when promised. When a shipment of goods is received, it includes a **packing slip** that lists the contents of the box or container. The person receiving the shipment should immediately verify the contents by comparing them to the packing slip. The confirmation process ensures that everything received also agrees with the PO.

A **receiving record** is the form on which all merchandise received is listed as it comes into the place of business. After receiving and inspecting the shipment, the details are recorded on a receiving record and filed for future use. Sometimes the contents will not match the packing slip. Other products may have become damaged in the shipping process. In those cases, the receiving record is used to help the vendor correct an order.

Marking is the process of attaching the price to each item that will be sold. Once goods are received and checked, they are

---

Case in Point

Best Buy

Inventory management is a critical part of every business. Without it, retailers would have a challenge meeting customer needs. But at times, even the best inventory management strategies do not always keep a business from running out of stock. However, companies that are prepared for stockout situations can win big points with customers. Best Buy is an example of a well-orchestrated inventory management plan. During the holiday season, Best Buy offers free home delivery if a customer wants to buy a product that is out of stock in the store. And as a bonus, Best Buy also matches Amazon's online prices. This gives customers two more reasons to shop at Best Buy. This policy is the marketing concept at its best. Best Buy hits a homerun with both pricing and place.

Extreme Sporting Goods					
123 Main Street Tampa, FL 33601 Phone: (813) 555-1234 Fax: (813) 555-1235		**PURCHASE ORDER**			

PO #: 003725			**Date:** 03/31/20--		
Vendor Name/Address: Salt Lake Wholesale 9807 Second Avenue Atlanta, GA 30060 (678) 555-1236		**Vendor ID:** 24	**Customer ID:** 1068A		

SHIPPING METHOD	SHIPPING TERMS		DELIVERY DATE		
Ground	Received by 05/01/20--		05/01/20--		

Item	Job	Description	Qty	Unit Price	Line Total
013188	12	Extreme water bottles	24	3.70	88.80
011088	12	Small camping packs	60	11.25	675.00
012488	12	12-pack DC golf balls	48	6.15	295.20

1. Please send two copies of your invoice.	Subtotal				1,059.00
2. Enter this order in accordance with the prices, terms, delivery method, and specifications listed above.	For resale? Yes / No	Tax ID: 12-3456789		Sales Tax	—
	Shipping				126.95
3. Please notify us immediately if you are unable to ship as specified.	**Total**	Net 30 days			**$1,185.95**
4. Send all correspondence to: Extreme Sporting Goods E-mail: extremesport@esg.com Fax: (813) 555-1235	Authorized by: *Carl Jackson*			Date: 3/31/20--	

Figure 21-2 It is important that the purchase order form include the necessary information.

usually marked with tickets or UPC codes. These tickets record the price and also serve as inventory tracking information

Merchandise is then placed in a stockroom where it is stored until needed. Stocking happens when the merchandise is moved from the storage area to the sales area.

Pay the Invoice

An **invoice** is the vendor bill requesting payment for goods shipped or services

provided. After an order is shipped, the vendor sends an invoice to the buyer. The invoice lists the goods purchased, the amount owed, and payment terms. Before paying an invoice, the buyer makes sure that the costs and payment terms listed on the invoice match those on the PO. In addition, the buyer must verify that the receiving record matches the invoice.

Most vendors expect payment either upon receipt of goods or within 30 days. Recall from Chapter 19 that some vendors offer a *cash discount* to encourage businesses to pay invoices early. Larger businesses often have a formal process for payment and approval of invoices that includes management. After approval, the buyer submits invoices to accounting for payment.

Evaluate the Vendor

The person or department responsible for receiving shipments helps buyers to evaluate vendors. Checking the merchandise received for any damages, shortages, or overages is crucial. At this point, the business is performing quality control. **Quality control** is the activity of checking goods as they are produced or received to ensure the quality meets expectations. If a vendor continues to be reliable and provides value and consistent product quality, then the vendor can be used again.

A good time for a buyer to evaluate vendors is after receiving their invoices. A form similar to the one shown in Figure 21-3 can be used to monitor the track record of vendors over time. A rating scale is helpful to score the criteria.

The AMA offers members exclusive access to *best-practice articles* written by industry experts. These best-practice articles are primers on core marketing topics. They instruct marketing professionals on the fundamentals of areas such as interactive marketing, advertising, brand management, marketing strategy, and customer relations. Best-practice articles provide overviews of essential concepts and tips for applying this knowledge to achieve marketing success.
www.marketingpower.com

Vendor Evaluation Form								
Vendors	**Date**	**Availability of products**	**Quality**	**Reliability**	**On-time delivery**	**Damages or discrepancies**	**Service**	**Price**
Vendor #1								
Vendor #2								
Vendor #3								
Vendor #4								

Goodheart-Willcox Publisher

Figure 21-3 Rating vendors helps to evaluate which companies are worth doing business with again.

Exploring Careers

Webmaster

Most companies have a website through which they do at least some of their marketing and selling. Logically, a website that looks interesting and is easy to use will be more successful than a poorly designed one. A webmaster manages the website development, design, and maintenance after it becomes active. Other typical job titles for webmasters include *information technology (IT) manager, website manager,* and *corporate webmaster.*

Some examples of tasks that webmasters perform include:

- work with web-development teams to provide an easy-to-use interface and solve usability issues;
- install updates and upgrades as needed;
- troubleshoot web page and server problems, keeping downtime to a minimum;
- implement and monitor firewalls and other security measures; and
- update content and links as requested or needed by the company.

Webmasters must be proficient in application-server software, graphics software, and web-page-creation software. They need a good understanding of graphic design and website design. If the website is used for sales, they must also be familiar with the company products or services, as well as electronic payment process and software. Most jobs in this field require an associate degree in web design or a related field—or training in a vocational school. Related job experience is also helpful. For more information, access the *Occupational Outlook Handbook* online.

Checkpoint 21.1

1. List the eight steps in managing the purchasing process.
2. Why is establishing a reorder point an important part of managing inventory?
3. Explain why the cost per unit decreases as the number of items manufactured increases.
4. Why is it important to track shipped items?
5. When is it most important for the receiving record to be accurate?

Build Your Vocabulary

As you progress through this text, develop a personal glossary of marketing terms and add it to your portfolio. This will help you build your vocabulary and prepare you for a career as a marketing professional. Write a definition for each of the following terms, and add it to your personal marketing glossary.

inventory
electronic data interchange (EDI)
reorder point
product specification sheet
economy of scale

purchase order (PO)
packing slip
receiving record
invoice
quality control

Checkpoint Answers

1. The eight steps in the purchasing process are: identify inventory needs, identify vendors, select the vendor, negotiate the purchase, make the purchase, receive the order, pay the invoice, and evaluate the vendor.
2. Any business should avoid being out of stock of any items and missing sales opportunities. A reorder point puts a control in place to trigger placing an order *before* the inventory gets too low.
3. Economy of scale is the decrease in unit cost of a product resulting from large scale manufacturing operations. The efficiency of production increases as more of a product is made.
4. Tracking purchases is an important step to make sure shipments are correct and delivered when promised.
5. Products may have become damaged in the shipping process. In those cases, the receiving record is used to help the vendor correct an order.

Build Your Vocabulary Answers

Definitions for these terms can be found in the glossary of this text.

Section 21.2 Inventory Management

After completing this section, you will be able to
- **explain** inventory management.
- **describe** inventory-control systems.
- **explain** the role of sales forecasting in inventory management.
- **determine** how to prevent inventory shrinkage.

inventory management
buffer stock
stockout
physical inventory
perpetual inventory-
  control system
manual-tag system
unit-control system
point-of-sale (POS)
  software
radio frequency
  identification (RFID)

periodic inventory-
  control system
just-in-time (JIT)
  inventory-control
  system
80/20 inventory rule
turnover rate
inventory shrinkage
internal theft
external theft

Choose two types of businesses, such as home electronics and automobile dealerships. Research the average stock turnover rate for the two industries. Are they similar or different? Why do you think they are similar or different?

Two of the main reasons for inventory shortages are employee theft and shoplifting. How can the marketing department help a company reduce the amount of employee theft and shoplifting in the company?

Manage the Inventory

Every business wants to maximize profits. Managing inventory correctly is one key factor in keeping costs down while maintaining enough products on hand for maximum sales. **Inventory management** is ordering the goods, receiving them into stock on arrival, and paying the supplier or vendor. It also includes managing the costs of shipping, storage, and the other tasks while keeping the costs associated with the inventory low. Inventory management is usually the responsibility of the supply chain manager. When managing inventory, there are three factors that need to be considered:
- lead time;
- stock needs; and
- carrying costs.

Lead Time

It takes time for vendors to process an order and send it to the business. *Lead time* is the total time it takes from placing an order until it is received. Lead time could be days, months, or longer, depending on the product and vendor. The product may need to be made or assembled or the vendor may not have enough of the product in stock when the order is placed. Lead time must be taken into consideration when planning for inventory purchases.

Stock Needs

Forecasting sales is always a challenge for business. It can be difficult to gauge how much product is needed each day or month of a selling season. To help avoid running out of inventory, stock may be maintained as a buffer or cushion. **Buffer stock**, also known as *safety stock*, is additional stock kept above the minimum amount required to meet forecasted sales. This helps prevent the business from running out of stock. Some businesses anticipate that certain products sell more on a seasonal basis. For example, many more barbeque grills are sold in the summer than in the winter. *Anticipation stock* is the necessary extra stock of products that sell more in certain seasons.

Carrying Costs

Carrying costs are directly related to carrying, or holding, inventory and are part of inventory management. These are the costs that must be controlled as they directly affect profit. Carrying costs include the following.

- *Capital costs* are related to borrowing cash from lenders to purchase inventory from vendors.
- *Handling costs* are related to the physical handling of the inventory and any necessary clerical work.
- *Storage costs* are paid for renting warehouse space or building a company-owned warehouse.
- *Inventory-risk costs* include the cost of inventory shrinkage, slow-moving

inventory, damaged or obsolete inventory, and nonselling merchandise that must be destroyed or donated for a tax write-off.

- *Inventory insurance costs* include premiums and taxes that are calculated as a percentage of the inventory value.

The cost of carrying inventory is often described as a percentage of the inventory value, as shown in Figure 21-4. Carrying costs can usually run between 24 percent and 48 percent of the inventory value per year. Businesses use this percentage to help them determine how much profit can be made on current inventory.

Inventory-Control Systems

There are three primary types of retail inventory-control systems: perpetual, periodic, and just-in-time. Every business has different inventory needs, so the supply chain manager chooses the system that best fits the goals of the company business plan. A **stockout** is running out of stock.

No matter which inventory-control system a business uses, it is important to conduct a physical inventory once or twice a year. A **physical inventory** is an actual count of all items in inventory at that time. It is used to verify the inventory-control system counts. If there are differences in the counts, the physical count is considered accurate. The records of the inventory-control system must be adjusted to reflect the physical count.

No inventory system is flawless because it cannot record theft, vendor returns, or damaged products.

Calculating Inventory Carrying Rate and Costs

1. Add up the annual inventory costs:
   Example:
   $1,200 = storage
   $2,000 = handling
   $2,500 = clerical
   $5,000 = obsolete, damaged, and dead products (markdowns and losses)
   <u>$4,000</u> = theft
   $15,000 total inventory costs

2. Divide the inventory costs by the inventory value:
   Example:
   $15,000 ÷ $100,000 = 15%

3. Add the percentages for insurance and taxes:
   5% = insurance premiums as a percentage of inventory value
   <u>6%</u> = taxes as a percentage of inventory value
   11%

4. Add all of the percentages:
   15% + 11% = 26%
   inventory carrying rate = 26% (or .26)

5. Multiply the inventory value by the inventory carrying rate: carrying costs = $100,000 × .26 = $26,000

Figure 21-4 This is an example of how to determine the costs of carrying inventory.

Goodheart-Willcox Publishe

Perpetual Inventory

A **perpetual inventory-control system** is a method of counting inventory that shows the quantity on hand at all times. The system records the receipt of goods into stock and all merchandise sales. There are two types of perpetual inventory systems—manual and computerized.

Manual Perpetual Inventory-Control System

In a *manual perpetual inventory-control system,* the inventory is calculated by physically counting and recording individual items. A person records each item that comes into inventory and each item that goes out of inventory as a sale or vendor return. This information is recorded on a spreadsheet or entered into a software program. The important part to note is that the inventory is done manually, *not* electronically.

One example of a manual perpetual inventory-control system is the manual-tag system that some small retailers use. A **manual-tag system** simply tracks sales by removing price tags when the products are sold. The retailer keeps the tags and uses them to deduct the sales from the inventory. Another example of a manual perpetual inventory-control system is the **unit-control system,** which uses a visual determination to decide when more stock is needed. This can be done by actually *eyeballing* the inventory to see if the inventory looks low. It may also be done by using bin tickets. A *bin ticket* is a tiny card placed by the product. It lists the stock number, description, minimum and maximum quantities, and cost in a code known only by store employees. A set number of bin tickets are placed with the merchandise. Each time a unit is sold, a bin ticket is removed. When the supply of bin

Explain

Discuss the meaning of *perpetual.* Ask why a business would prefer this method of inventory control.

The supply chain manager is usually responsible for inventory control.

wong yu liang/Shutterstock.com

tickets gets low, it is a visual signal to order more inventory.

In both manual-tag and unit-control systems, the reorder point is determined manually. The business must then place POs and hope the lead time is acceptable. A manual perpetual inventory-control leaves a business open to human errors and can be an inefficient use of time.

Computerized Perpetual Inventory-Control System

While manual systems have their place, most businesses use a *computerized inventory-control system* for more control and information. Computerized inventory-control systems are an important part of EDI. Inventory software programs track incoming inventory and sales. The software can run sales and inventory reports to track costs, track sales by salesperson or by category, and manage sales tax by state. Daily sales reports can also be generated making it easier to balance the cash drawer. The software may also analyze profit by items sold. Some software can automatically reorder standard products.

Most retail businesses use cash registers with point-of-sale software. **Point-of-sale (POS) software** electronically records each sale when it happens by scanning product bar codes. When the product *bar code* is scanned, the merchandise is immediately deducted from inventory. So, management always has a current inventory count.

POS software allows different reorder points to be entered for various products. Depending on the system, it automatically alerts an owner when it is time to order more merchandise, or it immediately places the order. This prevents stockouts and helps the business run efficiently. POS systems also improve pricing accuracy, which eliminates the human error factor of keying in information. Another computerized inventory system is the radio frequency identification system. **Radio frequency identification (RFID)** is a system that uses computer chips attached to inventory items and radio frequency receivers to track inventory. You may be familiar with the computer chip that is placed under the skin of the family pet. This chip identifies the pet and its owner when scanned. This is a type of RFID system. Many businesses use RFID systems to track inventory as it moves within a building and while it is stored in trailers outside a manufacturing plant.

Periodic Inventory-Control System

A **periodic inventory-control system** involves taking a physical count of merchandise at regular periods, such as weekly or monthly. The business actually counts everything that is in inventory and compares those numbers to the reorder points. Taking physical inventories is time-consuming, so it is only done at intervals. Because the count is only completed at given times, the actual inventory is not accurate on a day-to-day basis. A periodic inventory-control system is typically used by small businesses or businesses without inventory software.

Just-in-Time (JIT) Inventory-Control System

Carrying too much inventory can reduce the profitability of a company. The **just-in-time (JIT) inventory-control system** keeps a minimal amount of production materials or sales inventory on hand at all times. JIT was developed in Japan by Toyota to reduce the costs of carrying inventory. Manufacturing companies use JIT most often.

In a JIT system, materials are made available *just in time* for the next link in the supply chain to use them. For a JIT system to be successful, each company in the supply chain must coordinate each activity and be flexible when necessary. When JIT works well, both manufacturers and retailers can save time and money. A retail business using JIT tracks sales and only orders the least amount of stock necessary for any given point in time. A manufacturing company using JIT makes sure raw materials are delivered right before they are needed in the assembly process.

Inventory can easily be tracked as it arrives in a facility or store by scanning bar codes. Product counts are automatically updated in the inventory system.

Ditrijs Dmitrijevs/Shutterstock.com

Social Media

Using Social Videos in Business

Social videos posted on YouTube or other sites can actively engage viewers, which is good for business. YouTube has the ability for users to talk about videos by asking questions, giving comments, sharing, and requesting additional information from the content creator. For example, you can include links, Q&As, or comments about precise moments in the video. These features create an opportunity for dialogue between you and the viewers. In addition, on YouTube, marketers can buy pay-per-click advertising to promote their videos. This option is a great way to help videos reach a specific target audience and make an impression.

One important thing for marketers to remember: videos do not always have to specifically promote your company or product. Videos are also a great way to position the company as a go-to expert in your industry. When something important happens, such as new technology or how a disaster has affected customers, create a video offering the latest information or advice. People will be searching for content on that topic, so any videos can take advantage of the interest. Make sure your video can easily be passed along to others. Video content can also be repurposed into website content, blog posts, e-books, webinars, or other marketing formats. This allows content to last longer and reach different audiences in a variety of ways.

Ideally, it would finish producing goods just before they are shipped to customers.

Advantages of JIT are increased efficiency, reduced waste, reduced storage space, and freed up cash for other purposes. Another advantage of a JIT system is that it reduces losses and possible damage to products sitting on shelves or with expirations dates. A disadvantage of JIT is when products arrive late, or products are not available when they should be. The lack of product on hand would mean sales could be lost. If raw materials are late in arriving for any reason, a manufacturing production line may even be shut down. For companies needing smaller amounts of goods, they may not meet the minimum order amount or shipping costs may be too high. Also, if projected sales are too low, then the advantages of JIT are not achieved.

Sales Forecasting to Manage Inventory

The business must determine the correct amount of money to invest in inventory each year. Sales forecasting based on previous sales history is one way to plan for upcoming inventory needs. It is usually done a year in advance, depending on the type of business. Most businesses then review actual weekly sales and adjust the sales projections, which will also impact inventory orders.

A typical sales projection may look like the one shown in Figure 21-5 for The Computer Shack. This forecast is for the projected number of units sold per month for one year. The yearly sales projection is 16,885 laptop units and 3,380 desktop computers units. Sales forecasts after the first year in business are based on the previous sales history and current market conditions.

The Computer Shack Unit Sales Forecast for 20--												
	Jan.	Feb.	Mar.	Apr.	May	June	July	Aug.	Sep.	Oct.	Nov.	Dec.
Laptops	1,000	1,200	1,250	1,300	1,320	1,111	1,345	1,450	1,454	1,460	1,975	2,020
Desktops	300	200	210	210	225	175	200	250	250	300	500	560

Goodheart-Willcox Publisher

Figure 21-5 The marketer for The Computer Shack knows that if this sales forecast is accurate, the store must have at least those numbers of laptops and desktops available for sale.

80/20 Inventory Rule

Many businesses use the 80/20 rule to forecast sales to have enough inventory on hand. The **80/20 inventory rule** states that 80 percent of the sales for a business come from 20 percent of its inventory. The *productive inventory* is the 20 percent of the inventory that produces the most sales. The 80/20 inventory rule helps a buyer determine which merchandise to keep in stock at higher levels and which products to keep at a minimum. The buyer will then need to decide how much to purchase in advance and when to place the orders.

Turnover Rate

When forecasting inventory, another factor to consider is the turnover rate of stock. A **turnover rate,** or *turnover ratio,* is the number of times inventory has been sold during a time period, usually one year. A *ratio* is a way to see how two numbers compare with each other.

The following shows an example of using the turnover-rate formula. A business has a cost of merchandise sold of $120,000 for the previous year. The cost of merchandise sold includes beginning inventory, plus any inventory purchased during the year, minus ending inventory. The business has stated that the average inventory of merchandise on hand at the end of the year was $50,000. To calculate turnover rate, use the following:

$$\frac{\text{cost of goods sold}}{\text{average inventory value}} = \text{turnover rate}$$

$$\frac{\$120,000}{\$50,000} = 2.4 \text{ turnover rate}$$

The turnover rate for this business is 2.4. Is that number good? It depends on the business. This ratio indicates that inventory has been turned a total of 2.4 times during the year. A turnover rate is a good indicator of how effectively a business is managing its inventory. A high turnover rate generally indicates higher sales and more productive inventory. Depending on the industry, a business may benefit from ordering high-turnover products in larger quantities to save shipping costs and lower the price per unit. Merchandise with a low-turnover rate means the inventory is sitting on the shelves longer and is nonproductive.

Inventory Shrinkage

When the annual physical inventory is completed, the results are compared against the perpetual inventory. The two inventories are rarely exactly the same. The physical inventory usually shows fewer items in stock than the perpetual inventory indicates.

The difference between the perpetual inventory and the actual physical inventory is called **inventory shrinkage.** There are three main causes for inventory shrinkage.

Small items that are easy to hide are targets for shoplifters.

Steve Lovegrove/Shutterstock.com

- Data input errors can occur during receiving, stocking, or selling.
- Product damage, or breakage, may occur when products are being moved from receiving dock to storage to store shelves.
- Theft can be from people working in the store or outsiders, such as customers or burglars. Theft is the largest cause of inventory shrinkage.

Internal Theft

Internal theft is committed by employees of a store, a supplier, or a delivery company. It is the source of most inventory shrinkage. To prevent internal theft, overhead cameras and other surveillance devices can be used. These devices monitor employee behavior, receiving docks, warehouses, backrooms, and cash registers. Improved hiring procedures can also eliminate employees who may commit theft. Requiring police checks of job applicants can be effective. Also, training employees to be more aware and active can help theft prevention.

Engage

Theft is an important topic for business owners. Explain the difference between internal theft and external theft.

External Theft

External theft is stealing by people who are not employed or otherwise associated with the retailer. This includes shoplifting and burglary.

Shoplifting is the stealing of merchandise from a store by a person posing as a customer. Small, high-priced goods are common targets for shoplifting. Examples are jewelry and electronic devices. They are easy to take from stores. They bring cash when sold illegally. Shoplifting has increased because there are fewer salespeople in stores. Plus, there are more organized professional shoplifting gangs than ever before. Shoplifting is a serious crime, punishable by fine or time in prison. Anyone with a record of shoplifting should not be employed in retail stores.

Retail stores are crime targets. This is due partly because they have easy public access, available cash, and are open after dark. Often the few employees on duty in the store are busy in different locations. To discourage crime, closed circuit television and video

Explain

Ask students to discuss ways a business owner can prevent loss of inventory.

security systems may be installed. Sensing devices placed on merchandise, ringing alarms, and security guards also help to prevent theft. The obvious presence of security measures cuts down on stealing.

External theft also includes credit card fraud, check fraud, and computer fraud. Computer fraud by hackers who adjust accounts can be reduced by using blocking methods, such as encryption.

Loss Prevention

Loss prevention is the term used for programs designed to prevent loss of company assets. These assets could be merchandise, money, or other property. Such programs help businesses recognize, prevent, and monitor theft problems. Security personnel is part of the loss prevention program. Other security procedures involve accident and fire prevention and emergency response plans.

Checkpoint 21.2

1. What three factors must be considered when purchasing inventory?
2. Why is the 80/20 inventory rule important?
3. What percentage of inventory is considered productive inventory?
4. List at least two benefits of a computerized inventory-control system.
5. State the formula used to calculate turnover rate.

Build Your Vocabulary

As you progress through this text, develop a personal glossary of marketing terms and add it to your portfolio. This will help you build your vocabulary and prepare you for a career as a marketing professional. Write a definition for each of the following terms, and add it to your personal marketing glossary.

inventory management
buffer stock
stockout
physical inventory
perpetual inventory-control system
manual-tag system
unit-control system
point-of-sale (POS) software

radio frequency identification (RFID)
periodic inventory-control system
just-in-time (JIT) inventory-control system
80/20 inventory rule
turnover rate
inventory shrinkage
external theft
internal theft

Chapter Summary

Section 21.1 Purchasing

- The purchasing process consists of ordering the necessary goods and materials, receiving them into stock on arrival, and paying the supplier or vendor. Much planning goes into purchasing inventory for a business.
- The eight steps in the purchasing process are: identify inventory needs, identify vendors, select the vendor, negotiate the purchase, make the purchase, receive the order, pay the invoice, and evaluate the vendor.

Section 21.2 Inventory Management

- Inventory management is the process of buying and storing inventory while keeping the costs associated with the inventory low. When purchasing and managing inventory, there are three factors that need to be considered: lead time, stock needs, and carrying costs.
- There are three primary types of retail inventory-control systems: perpetual, periodic, and just-in-time. It is a good idea to start a formal inventory system to avoid a stockout.
- Sales forecasting based on previous sales history is one way to plan for upcoming inventory needs. Many businesses use the 80/20 rule to forecast sales to have enough inventory on hand. When forecasting inventory, another factor to consider is the turnover rate of stock.
- The difference between the perpetual inventory and the actual physical inventory is called inventory shrinkage. Data input errors, product damage, and internal and external theft are three main causes of inventory shrinkage.

Review Your Knowledge

1. Name four criteria buyers use when selecting vendors.
2. How should a buyer negotiate for quality?
3. Why should a buyer try to have good relationships with his or her vendors?
4. List three EDI transactions important in inventory purchasing and management.
5. When is the best time for a buyer to evaluate vendors?
6. Which type of business would use a periodic inventory-control system?
7. What is the difference between the manual-tag and unit-control inventory systems?
8. When would a business use an RFID inventory system?
9. What is the largest source of inventory shrinkage?
10. Explain loss prevention.

Evaluate

Assign the end-of-chapter activities.

Review Your Knowledge Answers

1. Buyers use the price, reliability, delivery time, and service as criteria for vendor selection.
2. The key to negotiating for quality is to insist on *value,* or getting the highest quality for the lowest possible price.
3. A vendor with whom a buyer has a good relationship may be more willing to provide help when needed. This can be very important if you have a specific promotion or product you want to highlight in an upcoming marketing campaign.
4. EDI transactions can include orders, confirmations, and invoices.
5. A good time for a buyer to evaluate vendors is after receiving their invoices.
6. A periodic inventory-control system is typically used by small businesses or businesses without inventory software.
7. A manual-tag system simply tracks sales by removing price tags when the products are sold. The unit-control system relies on a visual determination of when more stock is needed.
8. Many businesses use RFID systems to track inventory as it moves within a building and while it is stored in trailers outside a manufacturing plant.
9. Internal theft is the source of most inventory shrinkage.
10. *Loss prevention* is the term used for programs designed to prevent loss of merchandise, money, and other company assets. Loss prevention consists of strategies developed to recognize, prevent, and monitor theft problems.

Apply Your Knowledge

1. In earlier chapters, you identified the product or service for which you are creating a marketing plan. Determine the merchandise your business carries in inventory. Make a list of the inventory your business carries.

2. Every retail business relies on good vendors who are dependable. For each product in your inventory list, find two potential vendors who appear reliable and offer reasonable pricing.

3. Every company needs a receiving record that is specific to that business. Research receiving records on the Internet and find several examples that might work for your type of business. Create a receiving record for your company.

4. As a marketer, you have been requested to help create a product specification sheet that will be used to replenish inventory. Make a list of the specifications that you think are important to include on the sheet.

5. Research purchase-order forms online and find several examples that might work for your business. Use those examples to help you create a purchase order for your business.

6. Which type of inventory-control system do you think your business should use? Give your opinion of the type of inventory-control you would recommend and the reasons for your recommendations.

7. Based on the information in the business plan for your business, create an estimated sales forecast for the top-selling products for the upcoming year.

8. For your business, list the items you think will have a low turnover rate and those you think will turn over quickly.

9. As a marketer, what steps might you recommend the business take to increase the stock turnover while still keeping inventory at adequate levels.

10. Research the general level of inventory shrinkage in your industry. What do you recommend the company do to help minimize each of the different forms of inventory shrinkage: data input, product damage, and theft.

Check Your Marketing IQ

Now that you have finished the chapter, see what you learned about marketing by taking the chapter posttest. If you do not have a smartphone, visit the G-W Learning companion website.

G-W Learning mobile site: www.m.g-wlearning.com
G-W Learning companion website: www.g-wlearning.com

Common Core

College and Career Readiness

CTE Career Ready Practices. An individual working in supply chain management needs to understand the channel of distribution. Inventory management may be the responsibility of the supply chain manager. Describe how applying technology to inventory management could enhance productivity for the business.

Speaking. Analyze the process of negotiating a purchase. What advice would you give a channel manager on how to get a good price for inventory? Research successful negotiations. Make a presentation on your findings.

Listening. Informative listening is the process of listening to gain specific information from the speaker. Interview a person who works in sales and ask them about the 80/20 rule. How does this rule impact their sales forecasting? Make notes as the person explains the relationship. Evaluate the speaker's point of view and reasoning. Did you listen closely enough to write accurate facts?

Teamwork

Working with a teammate, select a merchandising business with which you are familiar. Focus on one type of product that consumers may buy from the business. Create a flow chart for the purchasing process that the business might use. Use graphics to illustrate each step. Share your flow chart with the class.

G-W Learning Mobile Site

Visit the G-W Learning mobile site to complete the chapter pretest and posttest and to practice vocabulary using e-flash cards. If you do not have a smartphone, visit the G-W Learning companion website to access these features.

G-W Learning mobile site: www.m.g-wlearning.com

G-W Learning companion website: www.g-wlearning.com

Unit 6 **Place Dynamics**

Building the Marketing Plan

Place, or distribution, decisions are some of the most important decisions marketers can help their businesses make. Place activities can affect pricing as well as how the end users receive your products and how they experience the company. Every retail or service business has inventory it must purchase and store. The purchasing and inventory management processes directly impact the bottom line of the company, so controlling those costs is vital to making a profit.

Part 1 **Supply Chain**

Objectives

- Describe the supply chain for your company.
- Explain the channel of distribution as it pertains to the marketing and company goals.

Directions

In this activity, you will continue writing the Marketing Strategies section of the marketing plan. The marketing  strategies are the decisions made about product, price, place, and promotion. Access the *Marketing Dynamics* companion website at www.g-wlearning.com. Download the data file for the following activity.

1. Unit Activity 6-1. Supply Chain. A supply chain is the businesses, people, and activities involved in turning raw materials into products and delivering them to end users. Show the supply chain and the distribution channel for your company. Explain how they contribute to the marketing and company goals in the marketing plan.
2. Open your saved marketing plan document.

3. Locate the Marketing Strategies section of the plan. Start writing the Place Strategies subsection. Use the suggestions and questions listed to help you generate ideas. Delete the instructions and questions when you are finished recording your responses. Proofread your document and correct any errors in keyboarding, spelling, and grammar.
4. Save your document.

Part 2 **Inventory Management**

Objectives

- Explain the purchasing process and inventory management systems for the business for which you are writing the marketing plan.

Directions

In this activity, you will continue writing the Marketing Strategies section of the marketing plan. The marketing strategies are the decisions made about product, price, place, and promotion. Access the *Marketing Dynamics* companion website at www.g-wlearning.com. Download the data file for the following activity.

1. Unit Activity 6-2. Purchasing and Inventory Management. Create a flowchart showing the purchasing process for your business. After performing online research, identify several computerized inventory-control systems that may work well for your particular business. List the pros and cons of each, and select the one you think is the most efficient.
2. Open your saved marketing plan document.
3. Locate the Marketing Strategies section of the plan. Complete the Place Strategies subsection. Use the suggestions and questions listed to help you generate ideas. Delete the instructions and questions when you are finished recording your responses. Proofread your document and correct any errors in keyboarding, spelling, and grammar.
4. Save your document.

Promotion Dynamics

Chapters

Eye-Catcher

Marketing Matters

Promotion is the heart of marketing. It is drawing positive attention to the product and increasing awareness. Often, that means thinking outside of the box. For example, Mister Red, Rosie Red, and Gapper are the mascots of the Cincinnati Reds baseball team. These colorful mascots promote the Reds at many events and functions in Cincinnati and around the country. They are fun, happy, and effective marketing representatives for the team.

Bill Florence/Shutterstock.com

Marketing Core Functions Covered in This Unit

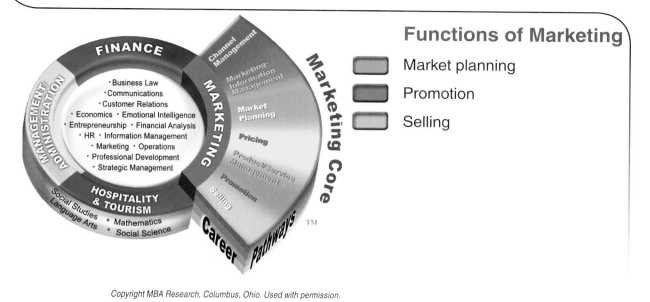

Functions of Marketing

☐ Market planning

☐ Promotion

☐ Selling

Developing a Vision

Marketers are challenged daily to find new ways to communicate with customers. Without knowledge, customers will not know the product exists. Without customers, a business will not make money.

Product knowledge happens through promotion. Product promotion is the activity that informs, persuades, and reminds customers to buy a good or service. Marketers use all of the promotional mix elements to give information. Advertising, sales promotions, public relations, and personal selling make up the mix. By combining these elements in a co-ordinated manner, marketers can push product information to the customers. This is known as Integrated Marketing Communications (IMC).

22 Communication Process

Section 22.1	Communication Basics
Section 22.2	Types of Communication
Section 22.3	Listening and Reading with a Purpose

"Successful innovation is not a single break-through. It is not a sprint. It is not an event for the solo runner. Successful innovation is a team sport; it's a relay race."

—Quyen Nguyen, professor of surgery and director of the Facial Nerve Clinic at the University of California

College and Career Readiness

Reading Prep
As you read this chapter, take notes on the important points you want to remember. Record information in the form of an outline to help you understand the material covered.

Check Your Marketing IQ

Before you begin the chapter, see what you already know about marketing by taking the chapter pretest. If you do not have a smartphone, visit the G-W Learning companion website.
G-W Learning mobile site: www.m.g-wlearning.com
G-W Learning companion website: www.g-wlearning.com

G-W Mobile

Explore
Assign the College and Career Readiness Reading Prep activity before students read the chapter. Reading Prep activities give students opportunity to apply the Common Core State Standards.

Engage
Assign the Chapter 22 pretest. The test may be accessed by using the QR code or going to the companion website. Discuss which questions students were unable to answer.

◇DECA Emerging Leaders

Hospitality and Tourism Professional Selling Event, Part 1

Career Cluster: Hospitality and Tourism
Instructional Area: Not identified for this event.

Knowledge and Skills Assessed

The participant will demonstrate knowledge and skills needed to address the components of the project as described in the definitions and evaluation forms as well as learn/understand the importance of

- communications knowledge and skills—the ability to exchange information and ideas with others through writing, speaking, reading or listening;
- analytical knowledge and skills—the ability to derive facts from data, findings from facts, conclusions from findings and recommendations from conclusions;
- critical thinking/problem-solving knowledge and skills;
- production knowledge and skills—the ability to take a concept from an idea and make it real;
- priorities/time management—the ability to determine priorities and manage time commitments; and
- how to apply selling principles and techniques to the business environment

Purpose

Designed for individual DECA members, participants will organize and deliver a sales presentation for one or more products and/or services while demonstrating skills needed for a career in sales. The guidelines and evaluation form for each Professional Selling Events career category will be exactly the same. However, each career area will deliver a sales presentation for a different product described in the Products/Services and Target Customer Descriptions section. Products, services and target markets are identified annually.

Procedure, Part 1

1. For Part 1 in this text, read the skills assessed and purpose of the event.
2. The objective for the sales presentation is for the participant to assume the role of salesperson making a presentation to a **potential buyer (judge).** Prior to ICDC, the participant will prepare a sales presentation for the product/service and target market customers described above.
3. The participant will make a 20-minute sales presentation to the judge worth 100 points.
4. The presentation begins immediately after the introduction of the participant to the judge by the adult assistant.
5. The participant will spend no more than 15 minutes setting up visual aids and delivering the sales presentation. The participant may bring presentation notes to use during the sales presentation.
6. The judge will spend the remaining five minutes questioning the participant.
7. If there are any questions, ask your teacher to clarify.

Critical Thinking

1. How will you use Knowledge and Skills Assessed to prepare for your presentation?
2. Why is it important to review information, such as the Purpose and Procedure?

Visit www.deca.org for more information.

Section 22.1 Communication Basics

Objectives

After completing this section, you will be able to
- **describe** the six elements of the communication process.
- **explain** barriers to effective communication.

Key Terms

communication process
sender
encoding
transmission
channel
receiver
decoding
feedback
barrier
diversity
multicultural society
multigenerational
sending barrier
receiving barrier

Web Connect

Written communication requires the use of Standard English. Do an Internet search for the definition of *Standard English*. Share your findings with the class.

Critical Thinking

Reflect on a recent communication that you had with a friend. Identify how the message was sent and received. What form did the message take, and what was the reason for the communication. Was your communication effective? Why or why not?

What Is Communication?

How would you define communication? For you, communication might involve sending a text message, talking on the phone, or waving to a friend. *Communication* is the process of sending and receiving messages that convey information, ideas, feelings, and beliefs.

The **communication process** is a series of actions on the part of the sender and the receiver of the message. The communication process has six elements: sender, message, channel, receiver, translation, and feedback, as shown in Figure 22-1.

Sender

The person who has a message to communicate is called the **sender**. The sender can be one person, a group of people, a business, or another type of organization. Marketing professionals send many promotional messages. They must also send business messages to people inside and outside of the organization. For example, if you were the marketing director for a company that sells smartphones, you would be the sender of promotional messages to existing and potential customers to buy your products.

Message

The message is a critical part of the communication process. As you develop your marketing message, it is necessary to keep the receiver, or target audience, in mind. You must answer two questions:

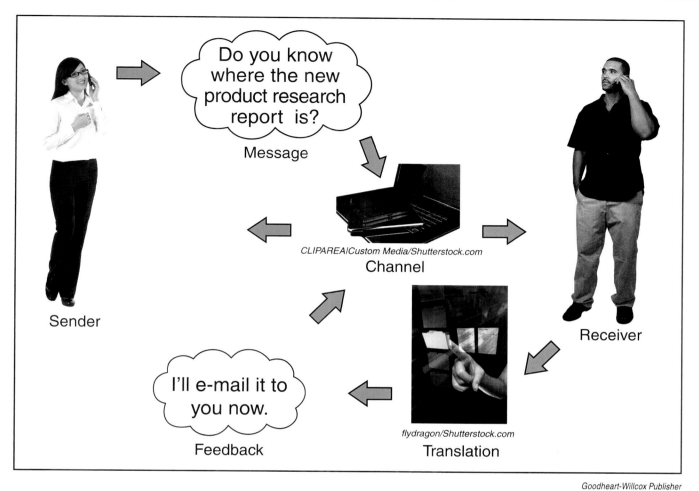

CLIPAREA/Custom Media/Shutterstock.com

flydragon/Shutterstock.com

Goodheart-Willcox Publisher

Figure 22-1 As a marketer, you will be communicating with customers, vendors, and people within your company.

- What do you want to communicate?
- How do you want to communicate?

When you create a message, you are encoding it. **Encoding** is the process of turning the idea for a message into symbols that are communicated to others. Most people convert their messages into a language of written or spoken words and symbols the readers can understand. In order for a language to be understood, the receiver, as well as the sender, must know the language. For instance, if you sent an e-mail written in English to someone in China who did not know English, that person would have no idea what was in the message.

As a marketer creating promotional materials for smartphones, you would carefully construct a message that the target market could understand. The goal of the message might be to inform current customers about new product upgrades. The content of the message would contain that information. A message that is not clear or understood by the reader would be an ineffective use of marketing dollars.

Channel

Once the message is encoded, it is ready to be sent. The act of sending of a message is called **transmission.** The **channel** is how the message is transmitted, such as face-to-face conversation, telephone, e-mail, text, or any other vehicle.

As a marketer, you select the channels for your messages based on the type of promotion or correspondence. For example, direct-marketing channels can include messages in catalogs, direct-mail pieces, telemarketing activities, interactive media, and home-shopping TV programs.

Receiver

The person who gets a message is the *receiver.* The receiver can be one person or many people. For example, the target audience of the smartphone promotional brochure could be hundreds of receivers. The number of receivers who watched your advertisement for smartphones on TV could be in the tens of thousands.

Translation

Decoding occurs in the mind of the receiver. *Decoding* is translating the message into terms that the receiver can understand. Decoding is usually seen as the process of understanding a message. Keep in mind that the message is not technically *received* if the receiver does not understand the content of the message.

FYI

A *language* is a common system of symbols used to communicate meaning. Messages can be transmitted in one of the spoken languages, such as English, Spanish, Chinese, or Russian. Messages can also be transmitted in language systems that do not rely on speech. Nonspeech systems include Braille, American Sign Language, Morse code, and *semaphore,* which is a visual signal using lights, flags, or mechanical arms.

Feedback

Marketing communication has a goal. The general goal is to persuade the receiver to request more information or make a purchase. *Feedback* is the response of the receiver to a message, and it concludes the communication cycle. Feedback may be positive or negative. Surveys often provide a way for customers to provide feedback about a company.

Marketers need feedback to determine if a promotional message was effective. For example, perhaps you placed an advertisement for a new smartphone model in the local newspaper. A potential customer saw the ad in the newspaper, went to the store, and bought that smartphone. The feedback

©California Milk Advisory Board

Marketing messages are often clever or humorous to draw attention to them, like this one for the California Milk Advisory Board.

is the purchase of the smartphone by the customer.

Barriers to Effective Communication

Barriers are things that prevent clear, effective communication. They may occur in written, verbal, and nonverbal communication. When people come together in the workplace, a variety of communication barriers may arise.

We live in a *global society* in which the market is diverse. **Diversity** means having people in a group or organization who are of different races or who have different cultures. *Culture* is the shared beliefs, customs, practices, and social behavior of a particular group or nation. A **multicultural society** is a society consisting of people from many cultures. A diverse, multicultural society is a market made of groups of people with different needs and wants.

The multicultural society, as well as the global society, has a direct impact on marketing because of various languages that are spoken. Communicating in different languages can present a *language barrier.* As a marketer, you may be working with

businesses in other countries. It cannot be assumed that everyone speaks English. It may be necessary for you to learn the language or hire an interpreter for communication.

Your company may be selling products internationally. This could mean that your promotional materials, packaging, and other marketing efforts may require assistance from a professional who understands the languages and cultures of those countries where you are selling products.

Multigenerational describes people of different generations in the same place, such as living in the same home or working together in the same office. People from different generations tend to have different interests, views, and needs, which can also create communication barriers.

The number of people in the United States over the age of 65 has increased from 12.3 million in 1950 to 35 million in 2000. By the year 2050, the number is expected to increase to 80 million. This demographic change has a major impact on marketing efforts. Marketing opportunities have been growing in the areas of health-care services, recreation, tourism, retirement housing, cosmetic products, and cosmetic surgery.

The six steps in the communication process can create potential barriers for a sender, receiver, or both.

Green Marketing

Presentations

As a marketer, you may make presentations to the management team at some point in your career. Your presentations will often include important marketing and financial documents and other information for the audience to know. Consider the environmental cost of the paper and ink needed for lengthy reports and other documents. Distribute hard copies of the important information necessary to the presentation, but instead of printing everything, e-mail the full documents. Your audience will appreciate having the essential facts in front of them and less paper to file after the meeting.

Sending Barriers

Sending barriers can occur when the sender says or does something that causes the receiver to tune out the message. This can happen when the receiver simply does not understand what the sender is saying. The words used may be unfamiliar to the receiver. Such misunderstandings cause daily problems—ranging from minor events to serious, costly errors. Additional ways the sender might cause barriers include:

- using poor grammar or spelling;
- overlooking typographical and formatting errors;
- presenting visually unattractive text or inappropriate graphics;
- assuming too much or too little about what the receiver already knows; and
- using inappropriate language, such as slang, jargon, or phrasing that is too formal or too informal.

How can the sender overcome these types of barriers? The sender has responsibility to the receiver to make sure the message is clear and understood. Figure 22-2 offers good communication tips senders should keep in mind.

Receiving Barriers

Receiving barriers can occur when the receiver says or does something that causes a message to *not* be received as intended. These barriers can be just as harmful to the communication process as sending barriers. The receiver has responsibility to give attention and respect to the sender. Most receiving barriers can be overcome with a little self-awareness.

- For written marketing documents, make sure you read each word that has been written.
- Take responsibility for getting clarification if you do not understand the message.
- While *hearing* is an innate ability, except in the case of a physical disability, *listening* is a conscious action. For example, if you are reading while engaged in a telephone conversation, you are not actively listening. Active listening is discussed later in this chapter.
- Give feedback to let the sender know you received the message. Ask questions, or give information if needed.

Although senders are responsible for sending clear messages, listeners should be ready to recognize unclear messages. A listener who is willing to accept responsibility for getting clarification is a more effective communicator.

Figure 22-2 Think of every marketing activity as an opportunity to improve communication for the benefit of the customers.

Communication Tips for Marketers
• For written marketing documents, follow the standard rules for writing, grammar, spelling, and formatting. A well-written and properly formatted document sends a positive message.
• Address people properly and as appropriate for the situation.
• For face-to-face communication, maintain a positive attitude, smile, and be interested in the conversation.
• Do not assume too much or too little about what the receiver already knows.
• Select the appropriate format for your message, such as an e-mail or a phone call, based on the situation.
• Ask for feedback from the receiver to see if your message came across clearly.

Goodheart-Willcox Publisher

Extend

Ask a student to present Figure 22-2.

Evaluate

Assign the Checkpoint questions at the end of the section. Assess students' comprehension using the Checkpoint activity as a self-assessment tool.

Checkpoint 22.1

1. What are the six elements of the communication process?
2. Give an example of a channel.
3. Where does decoding occur?
4. What is the difference between hearing and listening?
5. How does a language barrier affect marketing?

Build Your Vocabulary

As you progress through this text, develop a personal glossary of marketing terms and add it to your portfolio. This will help you build your vocabulary and prepare for a career as a marketing professional. Write a definition for each of the following terms, and add it to your personal marketing glossary.

communication process
sender
encoding
transmission
channel
receiver
decoding
feedback
barrier
diversity
multicultural society
multigenerational
sending barrier
receiving barrier

Checkpoint Answers

1. The six elements of the communication process are sender, message, channel, receiver, translation, and feedback.
2. A channel can be face-to-face conversation, telephone, e-mail, text, or any other vehicle.
3. Decoding occurs in the mind of the receiver.
4. While *hearing* is an innate ability, except in the case of a physical disability, *listening* is a conscious action.
5. The multicultural society, as well as the global society, has a direct impact on marketing because of various languages that are spoken. As a marketer, you may be working with businesses in other countries. It cannot be assumed that everyone speaks English. It may be necessary for you to learn the language or hire an interpreter for communication.

Build Your Vocabulary Answers

Definitions for these terms can be found in the glossary of this text.

Section 22.2 Types of Communication

Objectives

After completing this section, you will be able to
- **explain** the importance of written communication skills.
- **describe** verbal communication skills that are important in the workplace.
- **identify** the role nonverbal communication plays in marketing.

Key Terms

written
  communication
writing process
four Cs of writing
memo
report

verbal
  communication
telephone etiquette
nonverbal
  communication
body language

Web Connect

Nonverbal communication is very important in the business world. Do an Internet search for *nonverbal communication*. Cite five instances where nonverbal communication could influence a decision you make as a marketing professional.

Critical Thinking

Take a few minutes to think about how you communicate with your friends. What communication skills do you use? Now think about the people with whom you have more formal relationships, such as teachers or coaches. How does your communication style differ with your friends compared to people who are professional contacts?

Written Communication

Marketers use a variety of communication techniques. **Written communication** is the recording of words through writing or keying to communicate. Many decisions must be made when developing a written marketing message. Words are very powerful. Think of the effect of the word *SALE* posted in the window of your favorite store. That one word will cause you and others to enter the store, look at merchandise, and possibly buy something.

The main verbal tool that a marketer has is the choice of words, as indicated in Figure 22-3. The words chosen depend on the target market, the purpose of the message, and the desired response from the

Tone in Writing	
Example	**Tone**
We look forward to your response to our inquiry.	Friendly
You must respond immediately.	Cold

Goodheart-Willcox Publisher

Figure 22-3 Tone in writing is usually determined by word choice.

receivers. Words carry most of the information in marketing communication. Imagine watching a TV commercial without sound. Imagine a print ad without any words. Very few images are strong enough to carry a marketing message without any words. Those that can, such as the apple icon used by Apple computers, are strong in part due to the advertising words that preceded them.

Explore

Provide an opportunity for students to explore by assigning a hands-on activity. Review the vocabulary terms at the beginning of the section. Where have students encountered these terms before? Help students make educated guesses about the meanings of the terms with which they are least familiar.

Engage

Compare and contrast written, verbal, and nonverbal communication. Why are these important to marketing?

The **writing process** is a set of sequential stages for each writing task. The process includes prewriting, writing, post writing, and publishing. Using these stages when creating a marketing message helps marketers achieve the **four Cs of writing**, or clear, concise, courteous, and correct communication.

- *Prewriting.* Define the customer profile for your target audience. Plan the content of your message and the purpose of the communication.
- *Writing.* Create the draft of your message and revise until you are satisfied with the result.
- *Post writing.* The message is written, and it is wise to have someone review it and give feedback. Proofread the final draft.
- *Publish.* You are ready to send the e-mail, go to the printer, or publish the message in the appropriate format.

Many marketers send a variety of written documents—from letters and memos to formal reports and proposals. The appearance of your written documents is as important as the contents. Make sure to use the computer software programs and templates designed to help you write professional-looking documents. If your written documents are sloppy or if the paper is dirty or ragged, the impression is negative. Even if you do not have a budget for fancy covers or binding, you can still make sure a document is crisp, well formatted, and clean.

Marketing Promotions

Marketers write a variety of marketing promotions. These promotions include advertising pieces, items for sales promotions, press releases, media kits, sales brochures, and scripts for personal selling. These elements are described in more detail in Chapter 23.

Elaborate/Extend

Assign the College and Career Readiness Portfolio activity at the end of the chapter.

Business Correspondence

Standard business communication is a letter printed on company letterhead. *Letterhead stationery* has the name and address of the company printed at the top of the page. The company letterhead often includes the logo of the company. Marketers may need to write a number of different types of correspondence including business inquiries, thank-you notes, and informational letters. A sample business letter is shown in Figure 22-4.

The standard business letter has eight parts as follows:
- date: date the letter was written;
- inside address: name, title, and address of the receiver;
- salutation: greeting;
- body: message;
- complimentary close: closing lines;
- signature: name and title of sender;
- notation: may indicate initials of the person who keyed the letter, if other than the writer;
- enclosure: to note additional information is included.

Memos

A **memo** is a brief message sent to someone within an organization. A memo usually deals with only one topic or issue. The term *memo* is short for memorandum. Memos usually have a standard format as shown in Figure 22-5. The word *memo* or memorandum appears at the top of the page.

The parts of a memo include:
- to: person or persons who will receive the memo;
- from: sender name;
- date: date that the memo was written;
- subject: brief description of the topic, the shorter the better;
- body: message; and
- notations: indicate specifics to the reader, such as who was copied on the memo, and if there are any attachments.

Explain

Memos are not used as very frequently, as e-mail has replaced them. Ask students why they would choose to use a memo instead of an e-mail.

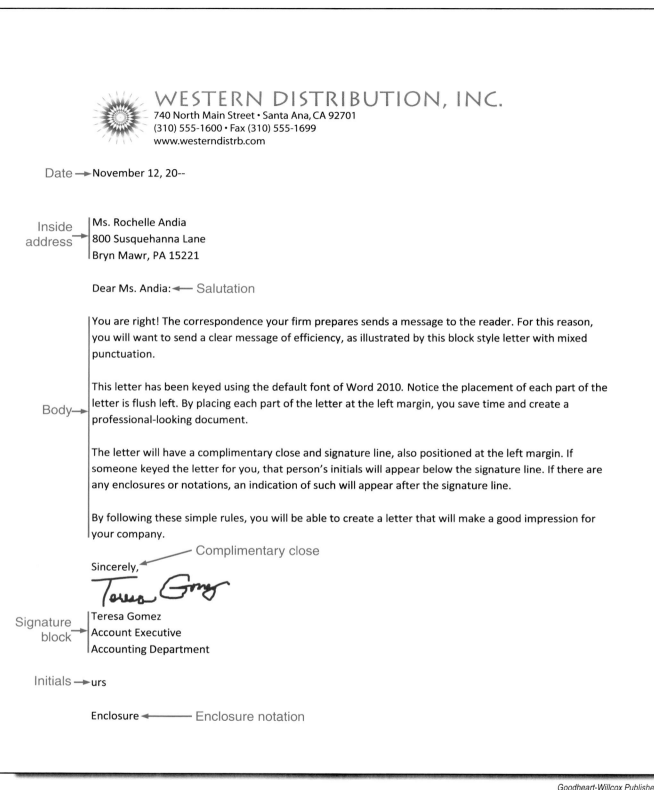

Figure 22-4 This example of a business letter shows the eight standard parts.

An e-mail may also be considered a form of business communication. Businesses generally have policies for using e-mail as well as disclaimers and other guidelines. Figure 22-6 shows an example of an e-mail in business style. E-mail is formatted similarly to a printed memo.

Reports

A **report** is a longer discussion of a topic presented in a structured format. Reports often include references to research. The marketing plan is an example of a report. Reports are often written to present new ideas, propose solutions to problems, or summarize work completed.

Planning is the most important stage of preparing any kind of report. Planning involves focusing on the subject and outlining the content. First, identify the purpose and audience for the report. Next, outline the content so that it flows logically and is easily understood. After writing the draft, edit and revise the report as often as necessary.

The specific format and length depends on the type of report, its purpose, and the receivers. Many departments submit reports at regular time intervals, such as weekly, monthly, or quarterly.

Verbal Communication

In addition to written communication, marketers are expected to have good verbal-communication skills. **Verbal communication** is speaking. *Tone of speech* refers to the feeling conveyed to the receiver from the way words are spoken. Tone can vary from

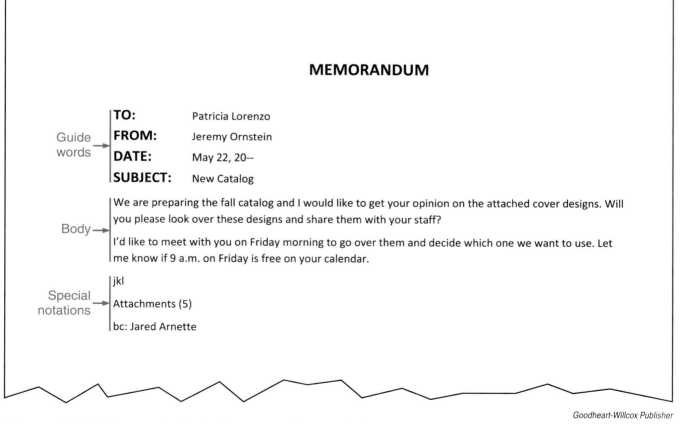

Goodheart-Willcox Publisher

Figure 22-5 This example of a business memo is properly formatted.

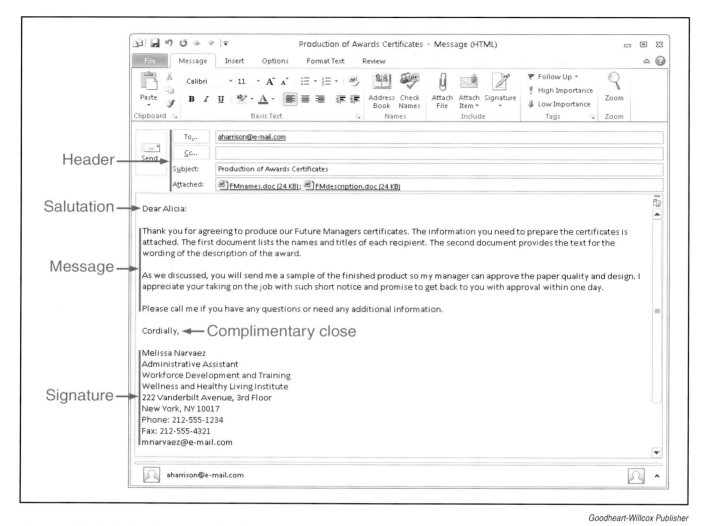

Figure 22-6 Professional e-mails reflect well on every employee.

warm to cold, friendly to hostile, humorous to serious, casual to professional, formal to informal. Words carry with them emotional value. Both the words and the tone marketers choose should convey the message and emotion you want.

Verbal communication in the workplace includes speaking to customers and others outside the company as well as coworkers. There are many instances when you may be asked to speak *informally,* such as to customers on the telephone. There will also be *formal* speaking opportunities, such as making a speech in front of an audience.

General Speaking Skills

The following guidelines will help you improve your verbal-communication skills.

- Use *Standard English:* the English language, grammar, and spelling generally used in professional writing.
- Speak clearly: if you speak too softly or mumble, practice saying each word more clearly and projecting your voice. If you tend to run your words together, speak more slowly. Make sure there is nothing in your mouth, such as chewing gum, while you are speaking.

Elaborate/Extend

If students are using the optional *Marketing Dynamics* workbook, assign activities to engage active learning.

Case in Point

Fisher-Price

Marketers focus on the importance of communication and the success of a business. Clear, concise, accurate product information is important for each piece of communication that reaches the customer. However, the information sent out is not always good news. For example, product recalls can damage the reputation that marketers work so hard to build. In addition, product recalls can be time-consuming.

In 2013, Fisher-Price voluntarily recalled its Newborn Rock 'N Play Sleepers™ due to the risk of infant exposure to mold. The marketers posted the recall information on Facebook and Twitter. The Fisher-Price website has a page dedicated to *Product Recalls & Safety Alerts* where all product recall information is listed. Companies are socially and legally responsible for communicating information about products that have been placed on the recalled products list by the US government. Make sure all of your communications efforts consider the best interests of your customers and follow consumer protection laws.

- Make eye contact: looking directly at the audience or receiver will help them get involved in what you are saying.
- Ask relevant questions.
- Develop a friendly tone: your tone of voice can either attract or repel your audience.
- Eliminate distracting habits: physical habits, such as hair twirling, knuckle cracking, or saying "um" or "you know" too often are highly distracting for listeners.

- Use the greeting specified by your company.
- When making a call, plan the message in advance.
- Have paper and pen available for taking messages or notes.

If you need to leave a voice-mail, speak slowly and pronounce each word clearly. Give the phone number at the beginning of the message and again at the end. Say the numbers distinctly. When leaving your name, spell it out.

Telephone Skills

The telephone, including landlines and mobile phones, is one of the major vehicles of communication at work. Good telephone skills are essential for success in marketing. When making and receiving calls, good telephone etiquette, or using good manners on the telephone, is important. The following guidelines will help you improve your telephone skills.

- Smile when you answer the phone.
- Speak clearly and in a normal tone of voice; avoid using a speaker phone when others are present.

Presentation Skills

A *presentation* is a formal speech that presents information to the receiver. The receiver may be one person or many. Many presentations have the added goal of persuading the receiver. For example, a sales presentation tries to persuade the receiver to buy the product. A product development team may present a new product idea to executive management. The goal is to persuade the company to develop the new product.

Many elements go into a successful presentation. A critical aspect is holding the attention and interest of an audience. Often, visual aids are helpful. In a sales presentation, the product being sold can be demonstrated. In other types of presentations, slide shows that include charts, tables, and diagrams can be used. A presentation involves the same basic work as any other communication. Plan, prepare the content, and then give the presentation.

FYI

Communication technology systems are a broad category of technology used for advanced forms of communications. Presenters may need to speak to a wide group of people in many different locations. They can use meeting websites, webinar software, or videos to make these presentations.

Nonverbal Communication

Nonverbal communication refers to actions, as opposed to words, that send messages. When you speak, nonverbal messages are sent through gestures, facial expressions, posture, and other actions. Marketers and those people representing the company must be very aware of what their nonverbal communications are telling receivers. If the message is positive, but the tone or mannerisms are negative, the entire message may be lost.

Body language is nonverbal communication through facial expressions, gestures, body movements, and body position. Facial expressions include smiles, frowns, raised eyebrows, and eye contact. Eye contact occurs when two people look directly into each other's eyes. It might only last a moment. Gestures include handshakes, waving,

pointing, or a shoulder shrug. Body movements include trembling, stepping closer, and turning your back on a person. Body position includes straight posture, leaning back in a chair, and slouching.

Remember that face-to-face, nonverbal communication barriers can include

- distracting mannerisms;
- facial expressions that conflict with the words spoken;
- inappropriate dress or conduct;
- sarcastic or angry tone of voice; and
- speaking too softly or too loudly.

In these situations, verbal messages may be lost or undermined by competing nonverbal messages. Marketers without a good grasp of the purpose for communicating may send a confusing or ineffective message.

AMA Tip

AMA TV is a bimonthly, online program featuring the latest in marketing trends and career information. The episodes deliver unique content in a fast-paced, entertaining format. For example, a recent episode highlighted the growing startup community in Chicago and offered advice to job seekers on their social-media profile pictures. AMA TV is available to members and nonmembers. www.marketingpower.com

Resource/Evaluate

Assign the optional Chapter 22 test for **EXAM**VIEW® Assessment Suite as a formal assessment tool.

Evaluate

Assign the Checkpoint questions at the end of the section. Assess students' comprehension using the Checkpoint activity as a self-assessment tool.

Checkpoint 22.2

1. What is the main tool a marketer uses to communicate?
2. What is the writing process?
3. When is a memo used?
4. What is workplace verbal communication?
5. Give examples of nonverbal communication.

Build Your Vocabulary

As you progress through this text, develop a personal glossary of marketing terms and add it to your portfolio. This will help you build your vocabulary and prepare for a career as a marketing professional. Write a definition for each of the following terms, and add it to your personal marketing glossary.

written communication
writing process
four Cs of writing
memo
report
verbal communication
telephone etiquette
nonverbal communication
body language

Checkpoint Answers

1. The main verbal tool a marketer uses his or her choice of words.
2. The writing process is a sequence of writing tasks.
3. A memo is used when sending a message to someone within an organization.
4. Workplace verbal communication includes speaking to customers and others outside the company as well as speaking to coworkers.
5. Examples of nonverbal communications are facial expressions, gestures, body movements, and body position.

Build Your Vocabulary Answers

Definitions for these terms can be found in the glossary of this text.

Section 22.3 Listening and Reading with a Purpose

Objectives

After completing this section, you will be able to
- **discuss** listening skills and why they are important to marketers.
- **explain** what it means to read with a purpose.

Key Terms

active listening
passive listening
empathy
prejudice
active reading

skimming
scanning
reading for detail

Web Connect

Enter *cultural difference in nonverbal communication* into a search engine. Explore the types of cultural differences. Choose a country you might visit for business. Make a list of recommendations and information to help business visitors act appropriately.

Critical Thinking

Are you a good listener? Analyze your listening skills. Write a list of the things you do well when listening to someone. Write a list of the things you do while listening that may be receiving barriers. What did you learn from this exercise? What might you change?

Listening Skills

Hearing is a physical process. Listening is an intellectual process that combines hearing with evaluation. Effective listening is an active process, as shown in Figure 22-7. **Active listening** takes place when the listener is focused on what is being said. Active listeners usually give nonverbal feedback to the speaker. For example, when listeners smile, nod their heads, make eye contact, or say, "I see," speakers know the message is received. Active listening is needed in the communication process, especially for marketing professionals.

The opposite of active listening is passive listening. **Passive listening** takes place when the listener hears the message, but does not pay attention to what is being said. The passive listener lets the words wash over him

Tips for Becoming an Active Listener
• Think about the purpose of a presentation before, during, and after it.
• Evaluate what you hear by relating the information to what you already know, or your prior knowledge.
• Take notes when necessary.
• If possible, make eye contact with the speaker to show attention.
• Ask relevant questions and make comments when appropriate.
• At formal presentations, sit close to the speaker, such as in the front of the room.
• Fight distractions; never engage in texting or answering a phone call when listening to another person.
• Concentrate on the speaker.

Goodheart-Willcox Publisher

Figure 22-7 Active listening makes speakers feel valued, which is very important in marketing.

Explore

Provide an opportunity for students to explore by assigning a hands-on activity. Review the vocabulary terms at the beginning of the section. Where have students encountered these terms before? Help students make educated guesses about the meanings of the terms with which they are least familiar.

Extend

Call on a student and have this student ask you the same question twice, i.e. "What is tonight's homework assignment?" The first time the student asks you the question, provide an example of passive listening. The second time, demonstrate active listening skills.

from the speaker. Several of his or her points are likely to be missed. When listening, focus on the speaker, listen carefully, and then plan your response *after* the speaker finishes. For example, salespeople may lose sales if they are too busy planning their responses instead of listening to customer needs.

Reading with Purpose

Reading is one of the main ways to learn new information. As a marketer, you will read research reports, business e-mails, and promotional pieces. An essential part of reading is comprehension. It is important to comprehend what is being read. Active reading is as important as active listening. Active reading takes place when the reader is thinking about what he or she is reading. Active reading is a learned skill that takes practice to perfect. The following suggestions can help improve reading comprehension.

Have a Purpose

It often helps to frame your purpose for reading something as a question. Think about what question this particular material will answer for you. You will have better comprehension if you know *why* you are reading. For example, you may be reading a research document to learn why consumers view one product as better than another.

Skim, Scan, or Read for Detail

Skimming is quickly glancing over the entire document to identify the main ideas. Start by reading the headings and captions and looking at any pictures. People often skim when they have a limited amount of time to read a lot of material.

Scanning is moving the eyes quickly down the page to find specific words and phrases. Usually, scanning is done when the reader is looking for a certain topic. If more details are needed, read the material more carefully.

Depending on the material, marketers skim, scan, or read for detail to increase comprehension.

Dmitrijs Dmitrijevs/Shutterstock.com

Reading for detail involves reading all of the words and phrases and considering their meanings. Reading for detail takes much longer than skimming or scanning.

Focus on the Words

Focusing on the words and their meanings helps to keep distracting thoughts out of your mind. Try to see in your mind's eye what the words are describing. Look up unfamiliar words in the dictionary.

Read for Meaning

Make sure you understand what you are reading as you go along. Picture what the words are describing. Review the concepts in your mind. Take notes. If you own the book, highlight key concepts. Evaluate what you have read to make sure you understand the content.

Checkpoint 22.3

1. How can you let a speaker know that you are paying attention?
2. What is a careless listener?
3. What are the four common types of interference that can occur at work?
4. Name four suggestions that can help you improve your reading comprehension.
5. How can you read for meaning?

Build Your Vocabulary

As you progress through this text, develop a personal glossary of marketing terms and add it to your portfolio. This will help you build your vocabulary and prepare for a career as a marketing professional. Write a definition for each of the following terms, and add it to your personal marketing glossary.

active listening
passive listening
empathy
prejudice
active reading
skimming
scanning
reading for detail

Checkpoint Answers

1. You can let the speaker know that you are paying attention by smiling, nodding your head, making eye contact, or saying, "I see."
2. A careless listener is someone who pays attention to only part of what is being said. This type of selective listening leads to misunderstanding or taking words out of context.
3. The following types of interference that often occur at work are interruptions, assumptions, prejudice, and planning a response.
4. The following suggestions can help you improve your reading comprehension: Have a purpose; skim, scan, or read for detail; focus on the words, and read for meaning.
5. You can read for meaning by understanding what you are reading as you go along. Picture what the words are describing. Review the concepts in your mind. Take notes. If you own the book, highlight key concepts.

Build Your Vocabulary Answers

Definitions for these terms can be found in the glossary of this text.

Evaluate

Assign the end-of-chapter activities.

Chapter Summary

Section 22.1 Communication Basics

- Communication is the process of sending and receiving messages that convey information, ideas, feelings, and beliefs. The communication process is a series of actions between the sender and the receiver of the message. The communication process has six elements: sender, message, channel, receiver, translation, and feedback.
- Barriers in the communication process are anything that prevents clear, effective communication. They may occur in written, verbal, and nonverbal communication.

Section 22.2 Types of Communications

- Marketers send a variety of written documents. When creating a marketing message, the writing process helps marketers achieve the four Cs of writing: clear, concise, courteous, and correct communication.
- Verbal communication is speaking to communicate. Workplace verbal communication includes speaking to customers and others outside the company, as well as speaking to coworkers.
- Nonverbal communication refers to actions, as opposed to words, that send messages. When you speak, nonverbal messages are sent through gestures, facial expressions, posture, and other forms of body language.

Section 22.3 Listening and Reading with a Purpose

- Hearing is a physical process. Listening is an intellectual process that combines hearing with evaluation. Listening barriers cause interference when listening to customers, vendors, or co-workers. Interruptions, assumptions, prejudice, and planning a response are some forms of interference that may occur at work.
- As a marketer, you will read and research, business e-mails, various reports, and endless promotional pieces created by you or others. Active reading takes place when the reader gives careful thought to what is being read. This is a learned skill that takes practice to perfect.

Review Your Knowledge

1. Before communicating a message, what two questions should a marketer ask?
2. When is a message technically received?
3. Why is the language used in communication so important?
4. Name four types of senders of a message.
5. Who performs the encoding and decoding of messages? When does it occur?
6. Explain why the tone of speech is just as important as the words.
7. Define *Standard English.*
8. Name three types of listeners.
9. Why is empathy important for a marketer?
10. Compare and contrast skimming, scanning, and reading for detail.

Review Your Knowledge Answers

1. What do you want to communicate, and how do you want to communicate?
2. When the receiver decodes and understands the content of the message.
3. Most people convert their messages into a language of written or spoken words or symbols the readers can understand.

In order for a language to be understood, the receiver, as well as the sender, must know the language.
4. The sender can be one person, a group of people, a business, or other type of organization.
5. Encoding is performed by the sender; it occurs when the message is created. Decoding is performed by the receiver; it occurs when the message is received.

Apply Your Knowledge

1. Create a flowchart of the communication cycle. Next, customize the steps for sending a promotion to your customers.
2. Explain why people from different cultures and different generations can pose marketing challenges.
3. Identifying appropriate channels of communication is an important business skill to learn. Sometimes it is important that a record of communication is made. Other times, documenting information is not necessary. Identify which channel of communication should be used for the following situations (letter, formal e-mail, casual e-mail, text, memo, or phone call).
    A. asking a colleague where to find information about a company organization chart
    B. confirming a meeting time for a presentation
    C. summary of minutes from a marketing meeting
    D. telling someone to meet you at the front door in five minutes
    E. forwarding information to a client
4. Ask a close friend or family member to describe your nonverbal communication skills. Ask the person to be honest and give you both the positive and negative things he or she observes. Take some time to review the notes and think about the feedback; then, meet with the person to discuss your viewpoint of the observations. Talk about areas of strength and where you would like to improve.
5. Record four important things you learned in Section 22.3. For each, write a paragraph about how you can use this information in communicating your message as a marketer. Share your responses with the rest of the class during an open discussion.
6. Written communication requires the use of Standard English. Create a list of at least 20 words or phrases in texting language. For each, write out the correct form in Standard English.
7. In an earlier unit, you selected a company for which you are creating a marketing plan. As a marketing professional, you will write many pieces of communications for your business. Imagine that you are preparing for a sales training event. Your job will be to train the sales team on how to sell the features and benefits of your product. Make a list of the sending barriers you could potentially encounter. How would you overcome these barriers?
8. The marketing team is sometimes responsible for creating the script that the company employees use when they answer the phone. Sometimes it is as simple as directing the person to state his or her name. Write the script that your company should use when answering the telephone. Make a list of the receiving barriers you may encounter.
9. Explain how a marketing professional could use empathy when listening to a customer complaint at a trade show.
10. You have just hired a marketing coordinator for your team. What would you tell this person about the importance of communication?

Check Your Marketing IQ

Now that you have finished the chapter, see what you learned about marketing by taking the chapter posttest. If you do not have a smartphone, visit the G-W Learning companion website.

G-W Learning mobile site: www.m.g-wlearning.com

G-W Learning companion website: www.g-wlearning.com

College and Career Readiness

Common Core

CTE Career Readiness Practices. Communication is an important part of the job for any marketing professional. Cite ways that you can use technology to enhance and improve your communication skills.

Listening. Practice active-listening skills while listening to your teacher present a lesson. Were there any barriers to effective listening? Evaluate the point of view of your teacher and the material presented.

Reading. Read an article about marketing in a newspaper or magazine. Analyze the structure of the material. How do the sentences and paragraphs relate to the article as a whole?

Teamwork

Meet with your teammates and analyze the communication process. Describe a recent situation where each of you observed (or created) a sending barrier and a receiving barrier. Get feedback from your teammates on what caused the barrier and what you could have done differently to avoid it.

G-W Learning Mobile Site

Visit the G-W Learning mobile site to complete the chapter pretest and posttest and to practice vocabulary using e-flash cards. If you do not have a smartphone, visit the G-W Learning companion website to access these features.

G-W Learning mobile site: www.m.g-wlearning.com

G-W Learning companion website: www.g-wlearning.com

Section 23.1 Promotional Campaigns
Section 23.2 Promotional Mix

"People shop and learn in a whole new way compared to just a few years ago, so marketers need to adapt or risk extinction."

—Brian Halligan, co-author or Inbound Marketing, CEO of Hubspot

**College
and Career
Readiness**

Reading Prep
Before reading this chapter, preview the illustrations. Translate the technical information in the illustrations into words. Assess the extent to which the illustrations support the content.

Check Your Marketing IQ

Before you begin the chapter, see what you already know about marketing by taking the chapter pretest. If you do not have a smartphone, visit the G-W Learning companion website.
G-W Learning mobile site: www.m.g-wlearning.com
G-W Learning companion website: www.g-wlearning.com

Explore
Assign the College and Career Readiness Reading Prep activity before students read the chapter. Reading Prep activities give students opportunity to apply the Common Core State Standards.

Engage
Assign the Chapter 23 pretest. The test may be accessed by using the QR code or going to the companion website. Discuss which questions students were unable to answer.

⬥DECA Emerging Leaders

Hospitality and Tourism Professional Selling Event, Part 2

Career Cluster: Hospitality and Tourism
Instructional Area: Not identified for this event.

Procedure, Part 2

1. In the previous chapter, you studied the skills assessed and procedures for this event.
2. The participants may use the following items during the oral presentation:
   - visual aids appropriate for an actual sales presentation.
   - not more than three (3) standard-sized posters not to exceed 22 ½ inches by 30 ½ inches each. Participants may use both sides of the posters, but all attachments must fit within the poster dimensions.
   - one (1) standard-sized presentation display board not to exceed 36 ½ inches by 48 ½ inches.
   - one (1) desktop flip chart presentation easel 12 inches by 10 inches (dimensions of the page).
   - one (1) personal laptop computer.
   - cell phones/smartphones, iPods/MP3 players, iPads/tablets, or any type of a hand-held, information-sharing device will be allowed in written events *if* applicable to the presentation.
   - sound, as long as the volume is kept at a conversational level.
3. Only visual aids that can be easily carried to the presentation by the actual participants will be permitted, and the participants themselves must set up the visuals. No set-up time will be allowed. Participants must furnish their own materials and equipment. No electrical power will be supplied.
4. Materials appropriate to the situation may be handed to or left with judges. Items of monetary value may be handed to but may not be left with judges. Items such as flyers, brochures, pamphlets and business cards may be handed to or left with the judge. No food or drinks allowed.
5. If any of these rules are violated, the adult assistant must be notified by the judge.

Products/Services and Target Customer Description

You will assume the role of tour operator on the Caribbean island of St. Thomas. Each year, tens of thousands of cruise ship passengers tour the island and participate in various tour excursions. A new cruise ship will begin porting weekly in St. Thomas beginning in a few months. The cruise line wants to work with local tour operators to sell shore excursions to passengers and is currently meeting with tour operators to hear their sales pitches. You have a meeting scheduled with the cruise ship's shore excursion manager to pitch your tour packages and price points.

Critical Thinking

1. What research will you conduct about the new cruise ship prior to your meeting?
2. How will you differentiate your tour packages and price points from competitors?
3. What question(s) should you ask the cruise ship's store excursion?

Visit www.deca.org for more information.

Section 23.1 Promotional Campaigns

Objectives

After completing this section, you will be able to
- **describe** why promotion is marketing communication.
- **identify** the three goals of a promotional campaign.
- **discuss** the four stages of the buying process.
- **explain** the importance of promotional strategies.

Key Terms

integrated marketing
   communications
   (IMC)
promotional
   campaign
product promotion
institutional
   promotion
persuasion
AIDA
push promotional
   concept
pull promotional
   concept

Web Connect

Do an Internet search on *pull promotional strategy* and *push promotional strategy*. Write a paragraph describing each and how they should be used in promotional campaigns.

Critical Thinking

Effective communication skills will play a role in a marketing professional being promoted within an organization. Make a list of the communication skills you think are important to be considered for a promotion.

Promotion Is Marketing Communication

In Chapter 22, you learned about the importance of the communication process. Promotion is considered *marketing communication.* Marketers use the communication process to craft a clear message that will be understood by the receivers, or target market. Using the communication process is key to creating effective promotions.

Most people think of promotion as just advertising. However, promotion is much more than that. Promotion can be broadly described as communications from an organization to its customers and the public. Therefore, everything a business says about itself is a form of promotion.

Integrated marketing communications (IMC) combines all forms of marketing communication in a coordinated way. This means that advertising, sales promotion, public relations, direct marketing, personal selling, and electronic promotions must all work together to strengthen the brand. Using IMC makes a marketing budget much more effective.

The coordination of marketing communications to achieve a specific goal is a **promotional campaign.** Campaigns may run for a limited time or be ongoing. While there are many types of promotional campaigns, they generally fall into two categories: product or institutional promotions. A **product promotion** is promoting specific products or services, as illustrated in Figure 23-1. Most promotional campaigns are product promotions.

Explore

Provide an opportunity for students to explore by assigning a hands-on activity. Review the vocabulary terms at the beginning of the section. Where have students encountered these terms before? Help students make educated guesses about the meanings of the terms with which they are least familiar.

Resource

Use the Chapter 23 presentation on the optional Instructor's Presentations for PowerPoint® CD as an outline for presenting the chapter.

Goodheart-Willcox Publisher

Figure 23-1 In this ad, the business is promoting its services.

In contrast, an **institutional promotion** focuses on promoting the company rather than its products, as shown in Figure 23-2. These promotions are designed to create a favorable view of the brand and increase awareness. Hopefully, increased awareness will also lead to more sales.

Promotional Goals

Promotions have three goals: to inform, to persuade, or to remind people about the business or its products. Some promotions do one thing, while others may do all three. Good promotions reach the target market with a message they value.

Goodheart-Willcox Publisher

Figure 23-2 In this ad, the business is promoting its support of local charities to create goodwill.

Explore

Assign students to research integrated marketing communications and find examples of companies that use this approach. What is the advantage of IMC?

Inform

Promotions that *inform* tell people something they want or need to know. Brochures, ads, e-mails, or catalogs make customers aware of the latest offerings. Businesses want to keep current and potential customers informed about

- existing products;
- new products;
- new features on existing products;
- how to use or assemble products;
- safety issues that may affect the use of a product;
- charities and cultural organizations the business supports; or
- events the business sponsors in the community.

Persuade

Persuasion uses logic to change a belief or get people to take a certain action. The end goal of most promotions is to *persuade* people to buy a product. Information is given about product features and consumer benefits. The target market must consider the purchase worthwhile. Otherwise, the message is not persuasive. Rebates, loyalty programs, or new product samples may persuade customers to take action.

Remind

Messages that *remind* are those appearing in multiple places over a period of time. The first few times a person sees the message, they may not remember it. So, reminder messages are provided. For example, when watching TV programs, think about how many times you see the same the commercial. By showing it often, the goal of the marketer is to strengthen the message in the mind of the viewer.

AIDA

If the main function of promotion is to increase sales, wise marketers design promotions that encourage customers to buy. Some experts believe that a customer goes through four stages of a buying process

Figure 23-3 AIDA is a four-step process that can help a marketing professional reach the target customer in any promotional campaign.

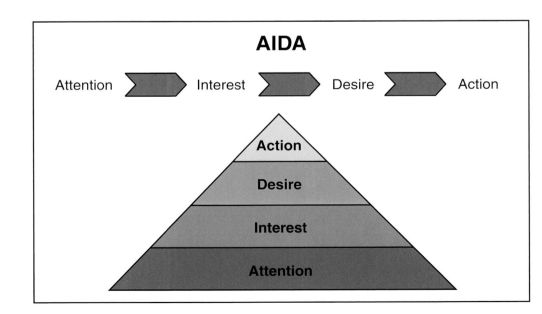

Goodheart-Willcox Publisher

Extend

Invite a panel of local business people or an advertising professional to share a promotional campaign with your students.

Explain

Have students compare and contrast messages that inform, persuade, and remind.

iQoncept/Shutterstock.com

Many businesses offer rewards to ensure customer loyalty.

before making a purchase. One model, AIDA, is shown in Figure 23-3. **AIDA** stands for customer attention, interest, desire, and action.

AIDA helps to integrate the different elements of the promotional mix. The AIDA model is used a bit differently for each element, though. For example, a printed piece should be attractive and easy to read with clear reasons to buy the product. In personal selling, the salesperson must be professional, engaging, and able to answer questions.

Attention

Getting the customer to look at the product or promotion is the first step in the AIDA process. The advertisement must capture the customer's attention. You should use design or sound elements to gain the attention of viewers and listeners. Then, make sure the customer knows exactly what your company offers.

Interest

The customer has to be interested in the business or product to make a purchase. Before making a purchase, all buyers want to know how the product can make their lives easier or better. Identify the features and benefits most important to the customer.

Explain

If the promotion is in print, conclude with a call to action. A call to action should be on every promotional piece.

Show that your company is interested in their specific needs.

Desire

Encourage the customer to sample, use, or touch the product, so they can experience and want it. Demonstrate the product, if possible. Make sure customers have a positive view of the company. If not, customers will not purchase the product, no matter how much they want it.

Action

Make it convenient for customers to buy. Explain exactly how, where, and when the product can be bought. Give purchase incentives or discounts.

The ultimate goal is to get the customer to purchase the product or request more information. If the promotion is print, close the piece with a call to action. If the situation is personal selling, always ask the customer for his or her business.

Promotion Strategies

Promotions are an important part of any marketing plan. They can be costly and a large part of the marketing budget. Recall from Chapter 4 that promotion strategies are decisions about which selling, advertising, sales promotions, and public relations activities to use in the promotional mix.

Most marketing plans include a one-year promotional plan. The *promotional plan* includes the promotional mix of personal selling, advertising, sales promotions, and public relations activities. These topics will be discussed in greater detail later in the next section. The steps to create any promotional plan are the same, though, as shown in Figure 23-4.

Promotion strategies involve choosing the best promotional mix for the budget. Each dollar spent on promotions should

Figure 23-4 As with any other business activity, a promotional plan should be carefully implemented in order to be successful.

Promotional Plan Steps
1. Identify the goals and objectives for the promotion: create SMART goals that can be measured.
2. Identify the target market: use research, sales information, and other sources to decide which people are most likely to purchase.
3. Develop the message of the campaign: determine the theme and desired actions to be taken.
4. Select the promotional mix that meets the campaign goals and best reaches the target market.
5. Establish the budget for the campaign: make sure all the elements of the promotional mix are addressed.
6. Implement the campaign: create the action plan.
7. Use metrics to evaluate the campaign: determine what, if anything, could be improved for the next campaign.

Goodheart-Willcox Publisher

provide a return on the marketing investment (ROMI). You learned earlier that *metrics* are ways to measure the effectiveness of a promotion. Most marketers consider which metrics to use when budgeting for promotions. Metrics can be as basic as keeping track of the number of website hits during a promotion, or as complex as tracking the number of products sold during a promotion. Sales tracking can help marketers learn which promotions influenced sales the most.

Businesses with great products may fail without a solid promotion strategy. Promotions create customer demand in two ways. Sales are made by either pushing the products *to* the customers or pulling the customers *in* to buy the products.

The **push promotional concept** involves taking the product directly to the customer. Depending on the type of business, push promotions may be different. For example, trade shows, visual merchandising displays, and sales calls are all examples of the push promotional concept. However, a push promotion for a manufacturer may include offering discounts and sales promotions. These promotions would serve to push products through the supply chain to the retailers.

The **pull promotional concept** involves using promotions to make customers actively seek out the product. A pull promotion in retail may be to use discounts and promotional items to pull customers into the stores. The pull promotional concept takes advantage of supply and demand. If customers want a product, the retailers will stock it.

Sometimes marketers will use both forms of promotion. For example, new businesses often use push promotions to create interest and be competitive. The first promotion for a new business may be a launch, or push, to introduce its goods or services. Once the business or product is established, a pull promotion could also be used.

The AMA offers a Social Media GPS podcast series to assist marketers with social media strategy and promotions. The series features a range of social media experts, authors, and bloggers. Each episode covers a specific element of social media marketing in fourteen minutes, so the podcasts work well for busy marketing professionals. AMA podcasts are available to members. www.marketingpwer.com

Checkpoint 23.1

1. Explain how promotion relates to communication.
2. How is a product promotion different than an institutional promotion?
3. List the three goals of promotion.
4. Why should marketers consider the AIDA model when planning promotions?
5. When would a marketer use both the push and the pull promotional concepts?

Build Your Vocabulary

As you progress through this course, develop a personal glossary of marketing terms and add it to your portfolio. This will help you build your vocabulary and prepare you for a career. Write a definition for each of the following terms, and add it to your personal marketing glossary.

integrated marketing communications (IMC)
promotional campaign
product promotion
institutional promotion
persuasion
AIDA
push promotional concept
pull promotional concept

Checkpoint Answers

1. Promotion is considered marketing communication.
2. A product promotion is promoting specific products or services, while an institutional promotion is promoting the company.
3. Promotions inform, or tell people something they want or need to know; persuade people to buy a product; or remind customers of previously conveyed product information.
4. If the main goal of promotion is to increase sales, wise marketers design promotions that help customers buy by using the four steps of the AIDA model.

5. Sometimes marketers will use both forms of promotion. For example, new businesses often use push promotions to create interest and be competitive. The first promotion for a new business may be a launch, or push, to introduce its goods or services. Once the business or product is established, a pull promotion could also be used.

Build Your Vocabulary Answers

Definitions for these terms can be found in the glossary of this text.

Section 23.2 Promotional Mix

Objectives

After completing this section, you will be able to:
- **identify** and discuss examples of the four elements of the promotional mix.
- **describe** electronic promotions and how marketers use different types for different reasons.

Key Terms

preselling
circulation
direct mail
event marketing
press release
press kit
press conference
personal selling
electronic promotion

quick response (QR) code
blog
uniform resource locator (URL)
search engine optimization (SEO)
viral marketing
mobile app

Web Connect

Use the Internet to research *best viral marketing campaigns* for the past year. Make a list of the top four promotions. Do you remember seeing any of the campaigns? If so, why did they stand out? Did watching any of these promotions result in you purchasing the advertised product?

Critical Thinking

Why do you think viewership on the three major television networks is down? Is this good or bad for marketers and the advertising industry?

Elements of the Promotional Mix

There are many ways to promote a business or its products or services. Recall that the *promotional mix* is a combination of the elements used in a promotional campaign. It can include advertising, sales promotion, public relations, and personal selling, as shown in Figure 23-5. All of the promotional elements are rarely used at the same time.

Advertising

Advertising is any nonpersonal communication paid for by an identified sponsor. Traditional advertising includes print and

broadcast media. However, other media may be used in an advertising campaign. For many marketers, advertising is the key part of a promotional campaign. Ads provide the features and benefits about a product, including the price, description, and *wow* factors. Effective advertising is aimed toward the *target market*, or people most likely to buy the product. Marketers find that advertising is sometimes a good way to presell products. **Preselling** is creating interest and demand for a product before it is available for sale.

Advertising is an expensive piece of the promotional mix. A creative person must write and design the ad plus physically create the final piece. Some companies have a creative person on staff to complete these tasks. However, some marketing teams hire

Explore

Provide an opportunity for students to explore by assigning a hands-on activity. Review the vocabulary terms at the beginning of the section. Help students make educated guesses about the meanings of the terms with which they are least familiar.

Explain

Have a student review the components of the promotional mix.

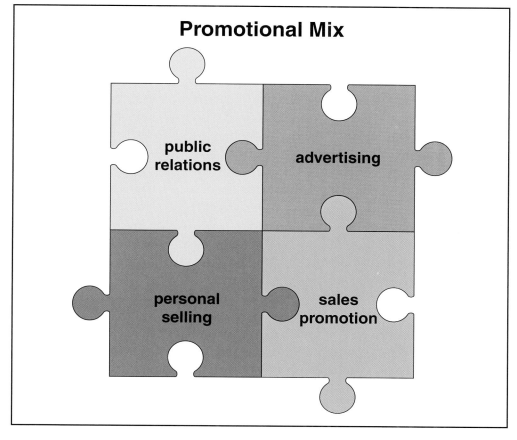

Promotional Mix

public relations

advertising

personal selling

sales promotion

Figure 23-5 Today, busy shoppers need to see more than one or two messages to inform, persuade, or remind them to make a purchase.

Goodheart-Willcox Publisher

outside resources, such as an advertising agency, for this work. However, advertising costs do not end there. They also include the prices paid for the space or time in which the ads will appear. Chapter 24 goes into much more detail about advertising.

Print Media

Print media is one of the most effective forms of advertising. It includes all tangible promotional messages. Newspapers, magazines, and directories are print media. Print also includes direct mailings, outdoor signage, and transit promotion.

The cost to place print ads in newspapers, magazines, and directories is based on circulation and ad size. Circulation is the number of copies distributed to subscribers and stores for

sale. Direct-mail costs include cost of creating the mailer, the number of pieces printed, and mailing costs. Other print-media outlets determine price by the average number of people who will see the ad in a month.

Newspapers. A newspaper is a daily or weekly publication printed on inexpensive paper. It is usually discarded after reading. Newspapers are bought by many different people, so they do not fit any specific target market. Consumers often rely on newspaper advertising for information on sales, new products and stores, and coupons. Although print newspaper sales have declined, newspapers are still a viable advertising medium.

Consumers often look at newspaper ads to learn about new products and current sales. There are *coupon clippers* who physically

Exploring Careers

Copywriter

Have you ever wondered how the people in radio, television, or other live commercials think of what to say? Actually, they rarely have to think about it. The company image is too important to allow the people in those commercials to say whatever pops into their heads. The job of a copywriter is to write the advertising and marketing messages a company uses to promote its goods or services. A good copywriter presents the products in the best possible way, encourages people to buy them, and uses a *hook*—an angle or scenario to help people remember the company. Other job titles for a copywriter may include *marketing writer, advertising copywriter, advertising writer, advertising associate,* and *web content writer.*

Some examples of tasks that copywriters perform include

* consult with experts in the company to learn about the product or service to be advertised;
* write advertising copy for use in written publications and print, broadcast, or online media;
* present written drafts to clients or company executives for approval;
* edit copy based on feedback received from the company; and
* work with the company's art department or director to develop visuals.

Copywriters must obviously have excellent wirting skills, with a vocabulary and style to communicate persuasively. They should present information about products and services in an appealing way. They should also have a sound understanding of principles of sales and marketing. Most copywriting jobs require a bachelor degree. For more information on this job, access the *Occupational Outlook Handbook* online.

---

cut newspaper coupons to save money on products. Coupons generally have a promotion code that indicates where the coupon originally appeared. Marketers use different promotion codes to track consumer response to ads and coupons.

Magazines. Magazines are printed weekly, monthly, or quarterly—usually on high-quality paper. Magazines are purchased by people in specific target markets based on their interests. People tend to keep magazines longer than newspapers. Therefore, magazine ads, just like the articles, can be repeatedly seen by readers. The value of more expensive magazine ads can be higher than newspaper ads, even though the circulation is lower.

Directories. Businesses and individuals still use print telephone directories. These directories list names, addresses, and phone numbers in alphabetical order. Directo-

ries are given to all households and businesses, so they are not targeted publications. Included in most phone books are the Yellow Pages for business listings, advertisements, and coupons. Yellow Pages ads can be affordable for a small promotional budget. Phone books are used repeatedly, so an ad is seen many times.

Direct Mail. An advertising message sent through the US Postal Service to current or potential customers is called **direct mail**. It can be highly targeted. Direct mail includes catalogs, brochures, postcards, and letters. The same message is usually sent to everyone. Marketers often use customer databases for the contact information. To reach new customers, marketers purchase target-market address lists from companies that sell mailing lists. Some marketers use an outside *direct-mail house* to manage direct mailings.

Elaborate/Extend

Provide an opportunity for students to exhibit their understanding of concepts in context of the material as it is presented. As time permits, have students read and discuss the special features in the margins.

Engage

Ask students how they feel about direct mail. Do they consider it as junk mail? Why?

In recent years, the number of direct-mail pieces has decreased in favor of electronic campaigns. Electronic campaigns are less expensive than print mailings and may be received faster.

Outdoor Signage. Outdoor billboards have been used as a form of advertising since the 19th century. They are placed where an audience on the move can see them. Billboards can be an affordable advertising method to display promotional messages 24 hours a day. The only way to target billboards is by location.

Outdoor signage can be print or electronic. *Digital billboards* change images every four to 10 seconds. Messages from one or more advertisers may be flashing on the same sign, which can be distracting for drivers. Some states have banned all billboards, including Maine, Vermont, Hawaii, Alaska, and 10 counties in Florida. A number of cities have banned digital billboards. Other forms of outdoor advertising include skywriting, blimps, and hot air balloons.

Transit Promotion. Transit advertising is found on the outside or inside of buses, taxis, subways, and commuter trains. Transit ads have high visibility to a narrow market. They are generally an inexpensive way to reach an often captive audience. Putting information on company vehicles is another inexpensive way marketers can promote a business.

Broadcast Media

There are two forms of broadcast media: television and radio. Radio and television ads, or commercials, reach a large number of people daily. Even though commercials are typically 15-, 30-, or 60-second messages, they can be costly.

Television. The most expensive form of advertising is television because it reaches the most people. Similar to other forms of advertising, TV commercials are designed to appeal to specific target markets. Making TV commercials is much like making short movies, which makes the cost of using it for advertising high.

Billboards can be located near roads or in the middle of big cities, such as these Times Square billboards for Broadway shows in New York City.

SeanPavonePhoto/Shutterstock.com

Elaborate/Extend

If students are using the optional *Marketing Dynamics* workbook, assign activities to engage active learning.

Engage

Ask students which form of promotion they think is the most effective.

Commercial time can be bought on the national or local level. Local-television advertising is more affordable because it only reaches local viewers.

Infomercials are paid product demonstrations. Infomercials are longer than commercials, usually 30 minutes. This type of programming is watched by some consumers and can be a good way to sell a new product. Infomercials tend to run at times with low viewership, so the costs may be less than some commercials.

Radio. Radio is an affordable advertising option to reach local customers. Radio advertising is typically much less expensive than television. There are many radio stations. They play music or have talk programs that attract very different target markets. For example, classical music and talk radio stations tend to have older listeners. Rock and pop music stations have more listeners in the teen and young-adult markets. Radio is an effective way to reach certain groups of people.

FYI

Outdoor signage is better known as *billboards.*

Sales Promotion

Marketers create sales promotions to encourage customers to buy a product as soon as possible. A sales promotion can include coupons, rebates, promotional items, samples, loyalty programs, contests and sweepstakes, trade shows, and displays.

Coupons

A *coupon* is a printed or electronic offer giving a discount on products bought before a certain date. Coupons are customer incentives to buy a new product or increase sales of current products. Because they cannot be used after the expiration date, coupons create a sense of urgency.

Rebates

A *manufacturer's rebate* is a return of a portion of the purchase price of an item. Unlike coupons, rebates are received *after* a product is purchased. Rebates also have expiration dates. Manufacturers offer rebates to encourage customers to purchase a product during a certain time frame. By offering rebates, manufacturers can also capture customer data for future campaigns or market research.

Social Media

Using #Hashtags on Twitter

Familiarize yourself with the hashtag symbol (#) and use it often in your business tweets. Twitter converts any word or URL with a hashtag in front of it into a searchable term. For example, if your business wanted to promote its new product called OrcaWater, you would type **#OrcaWater** in every tweet to create a searchable stream of relevant tweets about that product. Event organizers often use a hashtagged term to keep all tweets about the event in a single, searchable stream. Anyone searching Twitter for one of your topics can find all tweets containing your hashtagged word in a single location. These are the people you can connect with to turn them into followers of your business if they are not already following you. In addition, you may choose to use long-standing hashtagged terms relating to your business in your own tweets to become part of that stream of tweets. You can also search the Twitter database for hashtagged questions pertaining to your business or topics of your expertise.

Engage

Ask: Which is the better offer—a $5 rebate or a $5-off coupon for a product. Ask them to do the math that includes sales tax on the purchase.

To receive a rebate, the customer is required to complete a form and mail it to the manufacturer. Increasingly, the rebate process can happen online. The manufacturer then sends a check for the rebate amount to the buyer. However, it may take months for the customer to receive a rebate.

Promotional Items

Promotional items are given away to remind customers about a business and its products. The business name, address, phone number, and website are often printed on the items. Marketers choose useful items as reminders. They hope the customers will remember the company when making the next purchase. Promotional items can include inexpensive things, such as key chains, calendars, pens, and pencils. They may also be more expensive items, such as blankets, calculators, or books. Marketers sometimes call them *marketing premiums*.

Samples

When introducing a new product, companies may offer free product samples to encourage customers to try the new items. Samples give customers the product experience; hopefully they like the product and will purchase it. Product samples are often given in stores, such as food samples in markets. They may also be small, individual samples sent by direct mail, such as those sent by cosmetic companies.

Loyalty Programs

Many companies reward customers for their continued business through loyalty programs. Loyalty programs can take many forms. The most common ones revolve around giving customers a free product or service after making a certain number of purchases. For example, a juice store may give a small card that is punched every time a smoothie is purchased. After 12 punches,

Marketers use inexpensive promotional items as give-aways. When these items are used often, many people will see the marketing message.

Alfie Photography/Shutterstock.com

Explore

Ask students if they have submitted a rebate. Increasingly, rebates are submitted and processed online.

Explain

Data indicates that a significant percentage of rebates (about 40%) are never submitted.

the next smoothie is free. Customers like the free products, and loyalty programs often encourage repeat sales.

Contests and Sweepstakes

Contests and sweepstakes are tools that encourage people to visit a store or provide contact information. These promotional tools help marketers capture data for future campaigns or market research purposes. In *contests*, customers must do something to win, such as submit a video of themselves using the product. *Sweepstakes* are games of chance where prizes are given to randomly selected winners from a number of entries.

Trade Shows

Many businesses, large and small, exhibit at industry trade shows and conventions. Marketers attend trade shows to introduce new products or sell existing products to potential customers. Trade shows provide a face-to-face opportunity to talk with customers, gather sales leads, and give a promotional item or sample of a product or service.

Marketers often use event marketing strategies at trade shows. **Event marketing** is a promotional activity that encourages customers to participate rather than just observe. For example, conducting a cooking

demonstration allows people to interact with the demonstrator and the product.

Displays

Visual merchandising is displaying merchandise in strategic locations where customers can clearly see the product. Retail stores use displays to build product awareness. Attractive visual merchandising can tempt potential customers to purchase. Many stores display merchandise at the checkout counter to increase sales. These are called *point-of-purchase (POP) displays*.

Public Relations (PR)

In Chapter 2, you learned that public relations (PR) consists of the marketing activities promoting goodwill between a company and the public. Unlike advertising, public relations is unpaid media coverage. Public relations is classified as either proactive or reactive.

Proactive public relations is when the company presents itself in a positive manner to build an image. Companies issue PR communications to explain their contributions to the community, environment, and other socially responsible activities.

Reactive public relations is used to counteract a negative public perception about the company. Negative media publicity can be received for

---

Marketing Ethics

Promotional Items

One responsibility marketers have is to choose and purchase marketing premiums, or promotional items, such as T-shirts or coffee mugs. Seek respected premium vendors that have been in the business for some time. Inquire to see if they will allow you contact current customers as references. Avoid buying merchandise that does not come from a reliable source because the items may be counterfeit or made illegally in another country. Ensure your vendors follow acceptable labor and environmental practices.

Resource/Evaluate

Assign the optional Chapter 23 test for **EXAM**VIEW®
Assessment Suite as a formal assessment tool.

any number of reasons. Marketers need to take action to reestablish the positive image of the company. A good example of reactive public relations is the BP efforts to help clean up the Gulf of Mexico after its 2010 oil spill.

Established businesses may hire PR managers or specialists to coordinate media communications. In general, most public relations activities cost little or are free. It takes time to create the PR materials, but the only other cost may be printing. Some forms of PR include press releases, press kits, and press conferences.

FYI

Publicity is the unpaid coverage received when a newsworthy business, person, or product is featured in the media.

Press Release

A **press release**, or *news release*, is a story featuring useful company information written by the company PR contact. Press releases are sent to selected media that will reach the target market. Many industry associations can help guide this process. The media will only publish information in a press release it considers newsworthy.

Press releases announce new products, locations, businesses, and community events. They can also provide information about the company's revenue and earnings, business partnerships, and new employees. Press releases have a specific format. They should not look like an article or advertisement. The media will not run promotional information for free.

Press Kit

A **press kit** is a packet of information sent to the media about a new business

opening or other major business events. Press kits can include marketing materials, photos, videos, frequently-asked-questions (FAQ) sheets, and other important information. Many companies create *green press kits* that include only web-delivered information rather than printed materials to save paper.

Press Conference

A **press conference** is a meeting set by a business or organization in which the media is invited to attend. Press conferences are called to make major announcements that affect a large number of people. Large press conferences may be televised and covered by major print and broadcast media. Smaller press conferences may just include local media.

Personal Selling

Personal selling is any direct contact between a salesperson and a customer. Customers appreciate face-to-face interaction when making a buying decision. While the other pieces of the promotional mix are important, most customers prefer personal contact. Many companies have sales representatives who have direct contact with customers. Chapter 26 covers personal selling in greater detail.

Electronic Promotion

Electronic promotion is any promotion that uses the Internet or other technology like smartphones. It may also be called *digital marketing*. Nearly every element of the promotional mix can be electronic. Even personal selling can now be conducted online through video chatting. Marketers can easily track electronic promotions online.

QR codes are an inexpensive way for marketers to make special digital offers or promote a business.

bloomua/Shutterstock.com

FYI

Many consumers like electronic promotions and have come to expect them. Marketers like electronic promotions because they are generally low cost and can be updated quickly.

An *integrated marketing communication* combines electronic and traditional promotions for a wider audience appeal. For example, a print brochure is sent to a customer describing the features and benefits of the product. The brochure includes a QR code for the customer to scan and go directly to the product web page. **Quick response (QR) codes** are bar codes that, when scanned with a smartphone, connect the user to a website or other digital information.

Web Presence

Having a web presence is more than simply creating a website and hoping people will visit it. Websites have many uses. A website is an informational and promotional link for current customers. Potential customers should also be able to easily find it. For some marketers, the website is the primary way the company interacts with the public.

A **blog** is a website in a journal format created by a person or organization. The term *blog* is short for web log. The marketer usually makes regular posts on the company blog. It is a good way to connect with current or potential customers for any reason. A blog can be linked to the main business website or function as a stand-alone site.

Prior to designing a website, marketers decide what the site should do for the business. Some objectives might be to:
- advertise the business;
- sell products and services;
- provide cutting-edge industry information;
- capture client information;
- reach a global audience; or
- present a socially responsible image.

Depending on the site objectives, the web designer makes certain choices about how it looks and functions. For example, so customers can buy a product online, the website may need

Explain

Find a video of a press conference on the Internet for students to watch and observe. What did they learn?

Explore

This textbook includes QR codes. What do students think about a textbook that uses them?

a shopping cart. It may need a way for people to sign up for an electronic newsletter. Regardless of the site objectives, all marketers want to make sure their websites can be easily found through searching.

Search engines sift through all websites related to the search term and provide a list of websites from which to choose. Search engines include sites like Google, Yahoo, and Bing, among others. Every website and web page has a uniform resource locator. A **uniform resource locator (URL)** is the unique address of a document, page, or website on the Internet. The search engines provide a URL list of the best matches for a search term.

How do businesses happen to be at the top of a list returned by a search engine? **Search engine optimization (SEO)** is the process of indexing a website to rank it higher on the return list when a search is conducted. This process includes adding special coding and typical search terms to the website text. SEO helps increase the chances of higher rankings on any Internet search engine.

Online Advertising

Online advertising is placing ads on websites where typical viewers are the target market for the business. Marketers must know which websites will best reach the market. It is also important to know if dollars spent on digital advertising are providing value by delivering customers. There are many types of web advertising available, as shown in Figure 23-6.

Marketers often purchase key search terms on the different search engines, which is called *paid SEO*. Small text ads show up on the side of the URL lists when those purchased terms are used in a search. Advertisers are charged by the number of people who click on that small ad, which is a link to the main website. Most search engines have tracking metrics, such as Google AdWords for ads purchased on Google. The metrics provide daily reports that track how many people clicked on an ad or made a purchase because of an ad.

Social Media

Social media is an Internet platform that connects people with similar interests. Social-media sites create online communities where information, ideas, messages, pictures, and videos are shared. Businesses can also connect to people through social media. Marketers can take advantage of social-media sites to make special offers to different groups of people. They can also create a dialogue with people about products, suggestions, and other topics of interest.

Viral marketing, or *buzz marketing,* is information about products that customers or viewers are compelled to pass along to

Types of Web Advertising
• **Floating ads** literally float across or around the screen and disappear in seconds.
• **Banner ads** are placed at the top of a website, typically in a box, and look similar to a print ad.
• **Pop-up ads** literally pop up when a website is clicked open; customers can typically close these on the screen or block them completely.
• **Pop-under ads** are similar to pop-up ads, but they appear after the web page is closed; customers can typically close these on the screen or block them completely.
• **Demonstration videos** are posted on free video-sharing websites.

Goodheart-Willcox Publisher

Figure 23-6 Make sure the form of online advertising you use does not annoy website visitors, which is often the case with some pop-up and pop-under ads.

Case in Point

T-Mobile

Marketers have found that using different elements of the promotional mix can create successful marketing campaigns. Marketers can stretch their budgets by using both traditional and less expensive nontraditional methods such as online videos. These integrated campaigns are unique and achieve desirable results by going viral. Viral videos can mean low-cost advertising for the company.

One example of a company that has successfully used nontraditional means to expand its brand is T-Mobile. Since the T-Mobile products appeal to consumers of every age, the company decided to focus on viral-video marketing efforts. At various times, the company has used surprise flash mobs and other buzz-marketing techniques on YouTube™ and Twitter to achieve that goal. Along with traditional ads, T-Mobile created entertaining viral videos that were a hit in the global marketplace. By using memorable social-media campaigns, T-Mobile conveys a clear message of its products.

others. Both are more current terms for *word-of-mouth advertising.* Now that so much interaction happens through the Internet, word-of-mouth advertising seems like an outdated term. Social media is the basis of viral marketing because sharing is built into the platforms and shows quick results.

Marketers can post product videos and invite customers to share comments and feedback through a website, blog, or tweets. When people feel they are a valued part of a community, they will give testimonials and provide insight for others. Viral marketing works when people are electronically spreading the word about your product.

FYI

Guerrilla marketing utilizes low-cost, unconventional marketing tactics, like flash-mob videos that yield maximum results, to promote a product.

Each form of social media comes with its own rules and regulations. Business accounts must be opened by a personal user with a verifiable e-mail address. Before launching a

social-media campaign, it may be necessary to research the options and seek professional assistance. Networking, video sharing, and mobile apps are some ways marketers use social media in their promotional plans.

Networking

Professional networking sites, such as LinkedIn®, can be an effective way to promote a business to other professionals. Social networking sites, such as Facebook and Twitter, provide opportunities for businesses to create a company page. A marketer can post targeted messages, customer testimonials, and special offers to the community that *likes* its Facebook page. Twitter provides instant access to current and potential customers via 140-character posts. Pictures can also be posted.

Locational social-media platforms, such as Foursquare and Yelp, appeal to customers looking for businesses in specific locations. They are excellent tools for any business to attract nearby customers by offering discounts or specials.

Video Sharing

Videos can also be shared through websites, blogs, and e-mails. YouTube is the best-known video-sharing website. Anyone can post a video at no cost. YouTube is a good site to post product demonstrations, creative ads, and other interesting activities people will want to share. It also has the ability for customers to comment and recommend products or services.

Mobile Applications

Social-media sites are increasingly viewed on mobile devices, such as smartphones and tablets. Mobile applications software, or **mobile apps,** are software applications developed for use by mobile devices. Mobile apps must be downloaded to the device to work. Ringtones, GPS, and games are examples of apps. Social media and mobile advertising, in particular, are growing rapidly as viable marketing outlets, shown in Figure 23-7.

Many companies use QR codes linked to apps that market certain products or services. Promotions encourage customers to download the app by visiting the website. Marketers hope that if their company apps are on consumer phones, their websites will be visited often. Repeat visits to the website may increase sales.

The native app is another form of mobile apps that businesses use. A *native app* is one that resides on the mobile device rather than on the website. Native apps, such as calendars, games, and maps, are created and sold to customers. In addition to promotional purposes, native apps create a new form of revenue.

E-mail Campaigns

E-mail can be an effective way to provide information, new product updates, or announce sales. However, if not used correctly, it can quickly create a negative image of a business. Some unwanted e-mails are viewed like junk mail or telemarketer phone calls.

Spam

Unsolicited e-mail is called *spam* and reflects poorly on any business sending it. The last thing marketers want to do is offend a customer. One way to avoid being labeled a spammer is to send e-mails only to people giving their e-mail for promotional purposes.

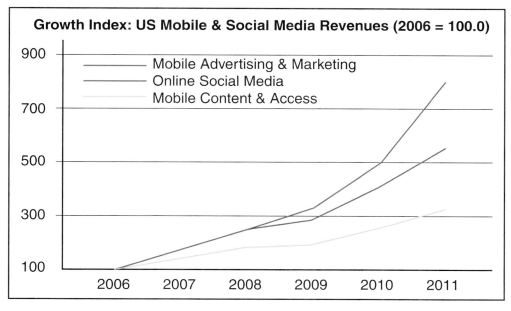

Figure 23-7 Experts predict that mobile and social media advertising will continue to grow as more and more people buy smartphones.

Source: PQ Media US Mobile & Social Media Forecast 2012–2016

Before conducting an e-mail campaign, research e-mail etiquette and the 2004 CAN-SPAM Act. This act is enforced by the Federal Trade Commission (FTC) and allows individuals to report companies sending spam. E-mails that violate the CAN-SPAM Act rules are subject to penalties of up to $16,000.

E-mail Tips

In order to get the most from e-mail campaigns, consider a few simple suggestions. Most companies push their e-mails out between midnight and 6:00 a.m. hoping to catch people first thing in the morning. However, many people simply delete their morning e-mails because of the number they receive. Consider sending e-mails between 10:00 a.m. and 3:00 p.m. People are more likely to take the time to read and respond to e-mails when their inboxes are not overfilled.

The subject line of an e-mail is critical. E-mail etiquette suggests that your company name appear in the subject line. It is also important to know that some words trigger filters that automatically send e-mails with those words to spam folders. Words like *free, act now, offer,* or *credit* will almost always trigger spam filters.

Keep the e-mail message or offer short and to the point. When a customer opens an e-mail, it should take them no more than 15–20 seconds to understand it. Avoid too many graphics or other elements that may cause the e-mail to open slowly.

Checkpoint 23.2

1. How is advertising different from publicity?
2. Describe the components of a press kit.
3. Why is search engine optimization (SEO) important to marketers?
4. Why might a marketer buy magazine advertising rather than newspaper advertising?
5. How can marketers avoid sending spam?

Build Your Vocabulary

As you progress through this course, develop a personal glossary of marketing terms and add it to your portfolio. This will help you build your vocabulary and prepare you for a career. Write a definition for each of the following terms, and add it to your personal marketing glossary.

preselling
circulation
direct mail
event marketing
press release
press kit
press conference
personal selling

electronic promotion
quick response (QR) code
blog
uniform resource locator (URL)
search engine optimization (SEO)
viral marketing
mobile app

Checkpoint Answers

1. Advertising is paid for by an identified sponsor and publicity is unpaid media coverage.
2. Press kits can include marketing materials, photos, videos, frequently asked questions (FAQ) sheets, and other important information.
3. SEO helps increase the chances of higher rankings on any Internet search engine.
4. Magazines are more highly targeted publications. People tend to keep magazines longer than newspapers. Therefore, magazine ads, just like the articles, can be repeatedly seen by readers.

5. One way to avoid being labeled a spammer is to send e-mails only to people giving their e-mail for promotional purposes.

Build Your Vocabulary Answers

Definitions for these terms can be found in the glossary of this text.

Evaluate

Assign the end-of-chapter activities.

Chapter Summary

Section 23.1 Promotional Campaigns

- Promotion is considered marketing communication. Promotions generally fall into two categories: product or institutional promotions.
- The three goals of a promotional campaign are to inform, persuade, or remind people about the business or its products.
- Some experts believe that a customer goes through four stages of a buying process before making a purchase. These four stages complete the AIDA model, which stands for customer attention, interest, desire, and action.
- Promotion strategies involve choosing the best promotional mix for the budget. Each dollar spent on promotions should provide a high return on the marketing investment (ROMI).

Section 23.2 Promotional Mix

- The four elements of the promotional mix include advertising, sales promotion, public relations, and personal selling. All of the promotional elements are rarely used at the same time.
- Electronic promotion is any promotion that uses the Internet or other technology like smartphones. It includes having a web presence, online advertising, and social media and e-mail campaigns.

Review Your Knowledge

1. How can understanding the communication process help make promotion activities more effective?
2. What is the difference between institutional and product promotion?
3. What are the four elements of the promotional mix?
4. What is the difference between proactive and reactive public relations?
5. Which of the four components of the promotional mix do most customers prefer?
6. Explain *paid SEO* advertising.
7. What is the difference between a mobile app and a native app?
8. How are advertisers charged for search engine advertising?
9. What are the three broad categories of mobile and social media?
10. Which words in an e-mail subject line can trigger spam filter?

Review Your Knowledge Answers

1. Understanding the communication process helps marketers craft a clear message that will be understood by the receiver, or target market.
2. An institutional promotion promotes the company and a product promotion promotes the company's products and services.
3. The four elements of the promotional mix are advertising, public relations, sales promotion, and personal selling.
4. Proactive PR is when the company presents itself in a positive light, and reactive PR is used to counteract a negative public perception about the company.
5. Most customers prefer personal selling.

6. Marketers often purchase key search terms on the different search engines, which is called *paid SEO*. Small text ads show up on the side of the URL lists when those purchased terms are used in a search.
7. A mobile app resides on a website and a native app resides on the mobile device.
8. Advertisers are usually charged by the number of people who click on the ad or eventually make a purchase.
9. These include mobile advertising and marketing, mobile content and access, and online social media.
10. Words like *free, act now, offer, or credit* will almost always trigger spam filters.

Apply Your Knowledge

1. In an earlier chapter, you selected a company for which you are writing a marketing plan. You will be creating a promotional campaign for your chosen business. Decide if you will create an institutional promotional campaign or product promotion campaign.
2. Promotional goals include informing, persuading, or reminding customers of the product or brand. Select the goal that will be appropriate for your business. List the information that you need in order to use this approach.
3. Imagine your promotional campaign will use all elements of the promotion mix. The budget will be a part of the overall marketing plan. Decide how much money you would like to have appropriated to your campaign.
4. Select a theme for your campaign. You may also decide to use a slogan, theme colors, or other items to tie the campaign together.
5. For the advertising element of the campaign, select one media you will use.
6. For the sales promotion element of the campaign, select at least one strategy that you will use.
7. Write a press release for your product or service.
8. You will train the sales team to sell your product. Make a list of the features and benefits that you will use as part of the training script. Using the script you created for the sales presentation, make the presentation yourself. Record and upload it to YouTube to use as a training video.
9. Outline a social media plan for your business.
10. Create a flowchart to outline the planning and execution process of the promotional plan.

Check Your Marketing IQ

Now that you have finished the chapter, see what you learned about marketing by taking the chapter posttest. If you do not have a smartphone, visit the G-W Learning companion website.

G-W Learning mobile site: www.m.g-wlearning.com
G-W Learning companion website: www.g-wlearning.com

Common Core

College and Career Readiness

CTE Career Ready Practices. Marketing professionals must behave in an ethical manner at all times. Misrepresentation of the company would put the business in jeopardy. Outline ways that a marketing professional can be a responsible employee when creating a promotional campaign.

Reading. Read a magazine, newspaper, or online article about a sales promotion for a business or product that caused negative customer reaction. Determine the central ideas of the article and review the conclusions made by the author. Provide an accurate summary of your reading, making sure to incorporate *who, what, when,* and *how* content of the situation.

Writing. Conduct research on effective sales strategies. Select either positive or negative sales strategies as your focus. Write an informative report, consisting of several paragraphs to describe your findings of the implications of positive or negative sales strategies on a business.

Teamwork

Working with a teammate, select an advertisement for a product with which you are familiar. Analyze the advertisement. List the theme, features, benefits, and call to action. How would you rate the quality of the piece? What would you do differently?

G-W Learning Mobile Site

Visit the G-W Learning mobile site to complete the chapter pretest and posttest and to practice vocabulary using e-flash cards. If you do not have a smartphone, visit the G-W Learning companion website to access these features.

G-W Learning mobile site: www.m.g-wlearning.com

G-W Learning companion website: www.g-wlearning.com

CHAPTER

24

Advertising

Section 24.1 Advertising Campaigns
Section 24.2 Creating Effective Ads

"One customer well taken care of could be worth more than $10,000 in advertising"

—Jim Rohn, American entrepreneur, author, and motivational speaker.

College and Career Readiness

Reading Prep
Before you begin reading this chapter, try to find a quiet place with no distractions. Make sure your chair is comfortable and the lighting is adequate.

Check Your Marketing IQ

Before you begin the chapter, see what you already know about marketing by taking the chapter pretest. If you do not have a smartphone, visit the G-W Learning companion website.
G-W Learning mobile site: www.m.g-wlearning.com
G-W Learning companion website: www.g-wlearning.com

G-W Mobile

Explore
Assign the College and Career Readiness Reading Prep activity before students read the chapter. Reading Prep activities give students opportunity to apply the Common Core State Standards.

Engage
Assign the Chapter 24 pretest. The test may be accessed by using the QR code or going to the companion website. Discuss which questions students were unable to answer.

◇DECA Emerging Leaders

Business Operations Research Events, Part 1

Career Cluster and **Instructional Area** are not identified for this event.

Skills Assessed

The participants will demonstrate skills needed to address the components of the project as described in the content outline and evaluation forms as well as learn/understand the importance of

- communications skills—the ability to exchange information and ideas with others through writing, speaking, reading, or listening;
- analytical skills—the ability to derive facts from data, findings from facts, conclusions from findings and recommendations from conclusions;
- critical thinking/problem-solving skills;
- production skills—the ability to take a concept from an idea and make it real;
- teamwork—the ability to be an effective member of a productive group
- priorities/time management—the ability to determine priorities and manage time commitments and deadlines; and
- identification of competitive conditions within market areas.

Purpose

Designed for a team of one to three DECA members, the Business Operations Research Events provide an opportunity for participants to demonstrate skills needed by management personnel. The Business Operations Research Events consist of two major parts: the written document and the oral presentation by the participants. The guidelines for each of the Business Operations Research Events will be exactly the same in each career category. However, each area will be treated separately as a competitive event

For the purposes of this text, you will be presented with the material for this event in two parts. Part 1 presents an overview of the event's purpose and procedure. Part 2 presents the remaining procedures and the research topic.

Procedure, Part 1

1. For Part 1 in this text, read the skills assessed and purpose of the event. Discuss these with your team members.
2. The written document will account for 60 points and the oral presentation will account for the remaining 40 of the total 100 points.
3. The body of the written entry must be limited to 30 numbered pages, including the appendix (if an appendix is attached), but excluding the title page and the table of contents.
4. The Written Event Statement of Assurances must be signed and submitted with the entry. Do not include it in the page numbering.
5. If there are any questions, ask your teacher to clarify.

Critical Thinking

1. Identify the various activities or careers addressed by each Business Operations Research Event. How do they connect to career clusters?
2. What are the benefits of learning to conduct research pertaining to business operations in different career areas?

Visit www.deca.org for more information.

Section 24.1 Advertising Campaigns

Objectives

After completing this section, you will be able to
- **define** advertising.
- **explain** the steps for developing a successful advertising campaign.

Key Terms

advertising campaign   posttesting
lead time
reach
frequency
pretesting

Web Connect

Select a product advertisement that has recently captured your attention. Does the product have a website? Facebook page? Mobile app? Which elements of the promotional mix have been used in the campaign? List each promotional element and describe how it was used.

Critical Thinking

Your generation is called the *Z generation* or *iGeneration*—in part due to the amount of time you spend communicating on electronic devices. If you were a marketer, what might be the best ways to reach people in your age group? What might be the best ways to reach adults in their 40s and 50s? Are there any similarities?

What Is Advertising?

As you learned in Chapter 23, advertising is one element of the promotional mix. *Advertising* is any nonpersonal communication paid for by an identified sponsor. In other words, the same message is given to all receivers. In the past, there was little or no interaction between senders and receivers of advertisements. However, with electronic promotions, advertising is becoming increasingly interactive. It is now possible to receive a digital message and buy the product with one click.

Advertising is a daily influence in our lives. It is everywhere people look—on streets, computers, phones, television, and radio. Advertising can change beliefs and attitudes about products and help people make buying decisions. It may create positive or negative feelings about a product or a company.

The main purpose of advertising is to *persuade* receivers to buy a product or accept an

idea. It can also *inform* customers about product and services and *remind* them to take action.

Recall that *institutional* advertising promotes the brand or the company. It is sometimes also called *corporate* advertising. *Product* advertising promotes specific products or services.

In 2011, over $496 billion was spent on advertising worldwide. By 2015, marketers are predicted to spend $603 billion worldwide. In the United States, over $158 billion was spent on advertising in 2011. Figure 24-1 shows how the dollars were spent in the various media plus projections through 2016.

An advertisement is a single advertising message paid for by an identified sponsor, often called an *ad* in print media and a *commercial* or *spot* in broadcast media.

Explore

Review the vocabulary terms at the beginning of the section. Where have students encountered these terms before? Help students make educated guesses about the meanings of the terms with which they are least familiar.

Engage

See how many corporate ads students can name without researching.

US Total Media Ad Spending, by Media, 2011–2013 (billions)						
	2011	2012	2013	2014	2015	2016
TV	$ 60.66	$ 64.54	$66.35	$68.54	$69.91	$73.05
Digital	$ 31.99	$ 37.31	$42.50	$47.77	$51.95	$55.25
—Mobile	$ 1.45	$ 2.61	$ 4.41	$ 6.62	$ 9.20	$11.87
Print	$ 35.84	$ 34.33	$33.10	$32.34	$31.79	$31.50
—Newspapers	$ 20.69	$ 19.14	$17.97	$17.25	$16.73	$16.40
—Magazines	$ 15.15	$ 15.19	$15.13	$15.09	$15.05	$15.10
Radio	$ 15.20	$ 15.50	$15.73	$16.00	$16.08	$16.13
Directories	$ 8.17	$ 7.48	$ 6.90	$ 6.38	$ 5.93	$ 5.53
Outdoor	$ 6.40	$ 6.80	$ 7.09	$ 7.34	$ 7.56	$ 7.76
Total	$158.26	$165.96	$171.66	$178.37	$183.23	$189.23

Figure 24-1 If actual US advertising expenditures follow these predictions, businesses will increase advertising spending by nearly 20 percent over five years.

Source: eMarketer, Sep 2012

Develop a Successful Advertising Campaign

An **advertising campaign** is a coordinated series of linked ads with a single idea or theme. The advertising campaign is one piece of the overall promotional campaign. Some media are more appropriate than others depending on the product and the target market. There is no one medium or mix of media that is the best to use for all advertising situations. Advertising campaigns should be well-planned to be effective and stay within the budget. Figure 24-2 shows the steps for creating successful advertising campaigns.

Steps for Creating an Advertising Campaign
1. Set campaign goals.
2. Select the target audience.
3. Establish the budget.
4. Identify the media.
5. Create the message.
6. Measure the responses.
7. Evaluate results.

Goodheart-Willcox Publisher

Figure 24-2 Marketers will have more effective advertising campaigns by following each step carefully.

Set Campaign Goals

Marketers should clearly define the goals for any advertising campaign. The goals should be specific and measurable to know if the campaign was effective. For example, campaign goals might include a specific sales goal or to increase brand awareness by 10 percent.

Select the Target Audience

It is important to identify the audience for the product or the message. Gather as much data as possible about your target market. The target market will help determine the message and the media for the campaign. For example, you may choose to target women, ages 25 to 49, who shop in a certain area.

Establish the Budget

The ad campaign budget must be established before media is chosen. Advertising dollars are just one part of the promotional budget. It is important to be clear on the amount allocated for advertising in particular. For example, a marketer may want to run TV ads, but the budget cannot support the cost.

Identify the Media

An important step in planning is selecting the appropriate media for a campaign. Marketers must be able to determine which media will best communicate the message and reach the target market. However, cost is also a factor to stay within the budget. Each form of media has advantages and disadvantages, as shown in Figure 24-3.

Pros and Cons of Different Media Forms			
Media Type	**Medium**	**Pros**	**Cons**
Broadcast	Television	• Visual and audio • Messages can be clever, creative, and entertaining • Most-watched medium • May impact popular culture • Influences consumers	• Fragmented audiences • *Zipping*, or channel surfing during commercials • *Zapping*, or fast forwarding or skipping commercials • High number of spots per commercial break • Most expensive medium
Broadcast	Radio	• Highly targeted markets • Personal and intimate medium • Relatively low cost of production and running ads • Increased frequency • Short lead time	• Clutter • Only auditory • Number of radio stations—difficult to determine which is most effective • Difficult to achieve high reach • Ease of channel surfing
Print	Magazines	• High reproduction quality • Long ad life—magazines kept longer • Possible higher reach—share or give away magazines • Highly targeted markets	• Long lead time • High costs of production and ad space • Ad clutter • Declining readership • Most magazines published monthly
Print	Newspapers	• Provide detailed message • Flexible by geographic need • Short lead time • Readers have higher incomes and education levels	• Print audiences declining—by 2043, predicted newspapers will no longer exist • Discarded daily • Expensive to reach target audience • Hard to target a specific market
Print	Directories	• Directories kept for a year or more • Efficiently reaches those needing the service	• Cannot change an ad for one year • Limited readership for some directories • May be expensive
Print	Billboards	• Low cost • High frequency • Flexible by geographic need • 24/7 message	• Hard to measure viewer demographics • Low reach • Short message; only five-second average length of viewing
Electronic	Online	• Popular communication • Simple to track effectiveness • Cost effective • Interactivity • Changes made quickly • Both audio and visual • Short lead time • Link to other websites	• Fragmented search engines • Limited Internet access for some • Hard to measure target markets • Potential of hacking and/or identity theft • Possible service interruptions

Goodheart-Willcox Publisher

Figure 24-3 It is the responsibility of the marketer to determine the best media to meet the campaign goals and stay within budget.

Case in Point

E*TRADE

Creating an advertising campaign that is unforgettable is the goal of every marketer. However, competing for the fragmented attention of consumers is challenging. Yet, there are creative advertising campaigns that grab attention and get people emotionally involved, talking about, and engaged with the company. Those campaigns tell a story—a story that not only captures your attention but also stays with you. For example, E*TRADE Financial Corporation is a holding company that includes online discount brokerage services for individual investors. During Superbowl XLII in 2007, E*TRADE ran commercials in which a talking baby made its debut. In each of the ads, the baby gave investing advice to his parents. The ads were clever, unusual, and humorous—a winning combination for memorable advertising. The rest is history.

E*TRADE still runs talking-baby commercials. The baby continues to give financial advice and checks his E*TRADE account before naptime. According to researcher ABX, the E*TRADE baby TV spots outscore all of its competitors, including Scottrade, Charles Schwab, Fidelity, and TD Ameritrade. The advertising campaign also gets high marks on branding metrics, such as message, relevance, and likability. Most importantly, the campaign continues to deliver results for the company. Since 2007, new customers continue to grow on a quarterly basis. Many things might change at E*TRADE over the years, but the talking baby is here to stay.

The **lead time** for an ad is the time between reserving the ad space and when it actually runs. Lead times vary by medium. The lead time to run an ad in a national magazine could be a month or more. The lead time to run an ad in the local newspaper, though, might only be 24 hours. For example, perhaps a campaign goal is to increase sales during the holiday season. Marketers must have the ad materials ready for placement well before that time.

Cost is also a factor when selecting media. The cost of one full-page ad in a magazine might be as much as $50,000. But, a small ad in the local paper may only cost $500 because fewer people will see the ad.

Marketers must also know their ads are seen by the expected number of people in the target market. **Reach** is the number of viewers expected to see an ad. **Frequency** is the number of times the ad appears before the customer. Reach and frequency numbers help to determine the cost of some media.

Explain

Lead time may be needed to write the ad, create the ad, and decide where to place the ad. These steps take time.

Reach and frequency metrics measure ad effectiveness. The more often a person sees an ad, the better the chance the message will be remembered. However, a point can occur where viewers *tune out* the message after seeing it too many times.

Create the Message

Effective campaigns deliver a marketing message that is valuable to the customer. The unique selling proposition (USP) should be at the heart of the campaign. The message usually provides information that customers need about a business or product. For example, price, features, benefits, new items, store location, hours, and sale pricing are often included in advertising.

Measure Responses

Successful marketers create metrics for each campaign to measure its success. Would you spend money if you did not know

Explain

Ask students to explain the importance of using Standard English in advertisements. Then, review the importance of grammar when writing a message. Slang is not always accepted by the audience, so proper communication techniques should be used.

what you would be getting? Probably not. However, advertising is often purchased without metrics in place. Measuring effectiveness in terms of dollars and cents may sometimes be difficult. If necessary, hire a marketing research firm to help you.

Some campaigns seem easy to measure. For example, for a product ad, a marketer might track the number of advertised items sold in a three-day period. Or, the overall increase in product sales for the week after the ad appears could be tracked. In fact, sometimes neither method is accurate. Can you guess why?

In the first method, customers who did not see the ad might happen to purchase the item. Those who saw the ad might wait weeks before buying. In the second method, there is no way of knowing whether any increase in sales was due to that ad. One way to be sure an ad influenced sales is to tie item purchases to a coupon. This method is often used in product advertising.

However, not every advertising campaign has a goal of increased product sales. For example, a marketing goal may be to increase brand awareness or appeal to a new target market. Researchers specializing in advertising have ways to determine whether a campaign achieves other goals. Advertising research can be divided into two stages: pretesting and posttesting.

Pretesting measures the effectiveness of an ad *before* it is seen by the general public. Ads are pretested during development to test different concepts or messages. Pretesting is often done by conducting focus groups and interviewing shoppers. The interviews determine whether that sample of consumers understands the message and/or will buy the product. If the sample group understands and likes the ad, it can be predicted the campaign will be successful.

After a campaign is over, posttesting can determine whether nonsales goals were met. Posttesting usually measures changes in brand awareness or attitudes toward the brand after a campaign. For example, large companies often conduct telephone surveys both before *and* directly after a broadcast campaign airs. This technique measures changes in awareness that can be tied to the advertising.

Evaluate Results

Marketers must be able to determine if the campaign results were worth the marketing investment. Marketers can use a variety of metrics to measure return on marketing investment (ROMI), which was discussed in Chapter 19. Some of the most common marketing metrics include the following:

- *New-customer metrics* measure market share, cost of acquiring new customers, customer awareness levels, and brand awareness.
- *Customer-retention metrics* measure customer retention and abandonment rates, brand loyalty, return visits, and the likelihood to refer a brand.
- *Product metrics* measure overall customer satisfaction, ease of learning and using a product, and first-time user satisfaction.

Marketers choose the best metrics to determine ROMI based on the campaign goals. After evaluating the results, they report what could be changed for the next campaign to increase effectiveness.

AMA Tip

The American Marketing Association offers marketers the opportunity to advertise in *Marketing News*, its top marketing magazine. Business leaders also take advantage of the AMA directories listing marketing firms that specialize in every area of marketing. For example, a marketer might consult the AMA Customer Satisfaction Firms directory to help improve customer satisfaction. www.marketingpower.com

Checkpoint 24.1

1. What is advertising?
2. What are the three main advertising media types?
3. What is the function of reach and frequency in media?
4. What does an advertising message provide to readers?
5. What are the three most common marketing metrics?

Build Your Vocabulary

As you progress through this course, develop a personal glossary of marketing terms and add it to your portfolio. This will help you build your vocabulary and prepare you for a career. Write a definition for each of the following terms, and add it to your personal marketing glossary.

advertising campaign
lead time
reach
frequency
pretesting
posttesting

Evaluate

Assign the Checkpoint questions at the end of the section. Assess students' comprehension using the Checkpoint activity as a self-assessment tool.

Checkpoint Answers

1. Advertising is any nonpersonal communication paid for by an identified sponsor. It is one element of the promotional mix.
2. Broadcast, print, and electronic media are the three types of media.
3. Reach and frequency numbers help to determine the cost of some media. Reach and frequency measure ad effectiveness.
4. The message usually provides information that customers need about a business or product. For example, price, features, benefits, new items, store location, hours, and sale pricing are often contained in advertising.
5. The three most common marketing metrics are new-customer, customer-retention, and product metrics.

Build Your Vocabulary Answers

Definitions for these terms can be found in the glossary of this text.

Section 24.2 Creating Effective Ads

Objectives

After completing this section, you will be able to
- **describe** how an advertisement is created.
- **explain** how advertising benefits society.

Key Terms

advertising agency
creative plan
headline
hook
copy
action word
typography
typeface

weight
art
layout
white space
signature
Advertising Self-
   Regulatory Council
   (ASRC)

Web Connect

Conduct an online search for how to create an effective advertisement. What did you learn from your research? Write a list of procedures to create an advertisement that will capture customer attention.

Critical Thinking

Think about all of the advertisements you have seen or heard in the last 24 hours. Make a list of the ones you remember. Why do you think you remembered those specific advertisements and not others? Did you respond by purchasing the product advertised? Why or why not?

Creating the Advertisement

Large companies usually have advertising departments that create the various elements in the promotional mix. Advertising departments fall under the overall marketing division in these companies. Other businesses, both large and small, may choose to use outside resources to create their promotions. Freelance graphic designers and copywriters are hired to perform those services.

Some companies, however, use an advertising agency. An **advertising agency** is a firm that creates ads, commercials, and other parts of promotional campaigns for its clients. Typically, the advertising manager

from the marketing team is the *client*, or primary contact for the advertising agency. The manager works with an agency account representative to produce ad campaigns. The client makes agency assignments through the account rep. He or she manages the agency staff. The staff creates and delivers the assigned creative services.

The advertising manager works closely with the account rep to develop a creative plan for the agency. A **creative plan** outlines the goals, primary message, budget, and target market for different ad campaigns.

The ad agency will have a copywriter who writes the message. A graphic designer chooses the visual graphics and creates the overall design. A layout artist or broadcast production manager delivers the final ad or commercial. A media buyer purchases print ad space and broadcast commercial time on behalf of the client. The ad agency bills the clients for work performed on an hourly basis.

Regardless of who creates the ads, they generally include the same elements. The classic structure for an ad has four elements: headline, copy, graphics, and the signature, as shown in Figure 24-4.

Headline

A **headline** consists of the words designed to grab attention so viewers will read the rest of the ad. Headlines usually appear in large type or have some other attention-getting graphic element. A general rule recommends that headlines have no more than seven words.

The headline uses words to call attention to the ad, much like a lure on a fishing hook. Copywriters hope that by reading the headline, a person is hooked into reading the rest of the ad. In fact, the aspect of an ad that grabs attention is often called the **hook.**

Research shows that over 80 percent of readers only read headlines. Because of this fact, many advertisers think the headline is the most important part of the ad.

Copy

Copy is ad text that provides information and sells the product. In advertising, copy refers to the words in the ad. The term *body copy* is often used to refer to the words that explain the product and give added information. The person who writes advertising copy, including the headlines, is called a *copywriter.*

The headline and body copy should work together. The headline attracts attention, while the body copy presents the selling message. Body copy should be brief and clearly give reasons to purchase the product. It should provide any information needed to locate the product and make the buying decision. The most effective advertising copy does the following.

Creates Intrigue

Copywriters use words to arouse interest, curiosity, and desire. Words like *new, hottest, free, limited offer, sale, bonus,* and *special offer* may be intriguing to readers.

Appeals to the Senses

It is hard to make products seem real on a printed page. Copywriters use descriptive words so the reader can almost see, hear, taste, feel, or smell the product.

Sounds Newsworthy

Stating the *who, what, when, where, why,* and *how* of a product can make the copy sound newsworthy. Include data, such as statistics, performance results, case histories, comments from satisfied customers, and quotes from experts.

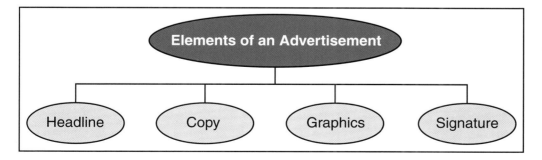

Goodheart-Willcox Publisher

Figure 24-4 There are no hard-and-fast rules for where each element appears. However, most ads begin with the headline.

Uses Action Words

Action words are verbs that tell the readers what to do. These call-to-action words include *save, join, get, buy, come in, visit, call, e-mail,* and *register,* to name a few. They are joined by adverbs suggesting when or how to act, such as *now, toll-free,* and *today.*

Graphics

Graphics provide visual interest. The graphics are often the first part of the ad a reader notices, especially when colorful or unusual. Those in the advertising industry argue about whether the graphics or the headline is most important. Actually, the two must work together to attract the reader. Graphics include typography, art, and layout.

Typography

Typography is the visual aspect of the words printed on a page. Typography includes decisions about typeface, size, and weight. A **typeface** is a particular style for the printed letters of the alphabet, punctuation, and numbers. There are hundreds of typefaces from which to choose.

A second aspect of typography is size. Letters can vary in size from small to very large. Larger letters have more emphasis. Headlines are usually larger than body copy. In a long headline, some words may be larger than others. Size makes these words stand out and emphasizes the key ideas.

The third aspect of typography is weight. **Weight** in typography refers to the thickness and slant of the letters. There are three weights: *regular, italic,* and *bold.* Size and weight are both used to make some words more prominent. Headlines are usually bold and appear in the largest size.

Color may also impact headlines and advertising copy. White or yellow letters on a dark background can make the words stand out. Words in red also pop out. Blue is often used to attract attention, but has a serious look and suggests reliability, as illustrated in Figure 24-5.

Art

Art is all of the elements that illustrate the message of an ad. Art includes drawings, photographs, charts, and graphs. Logos, shapes behind print, and abstract images or designs are also considered art. The art used in advertising should be consistent with the brand. In fact, art sometimes helps to define a brand if it is used properly.

A product photograph is the most common type of advertising art. Grocery, fashion, and automobile ads use product photos to make products look attractive. Businesses that sell services also use art to convey the idea of the service. Photos may also show people using the service.

Green Marketing

Reusable Bags

When looking for marketing premium items to give to customers, consider a reusable bag with your company imprint. Reusable bags save thousands of pounds of landfill waste every year. While there are different schools of thought on this topic, it is generally accepted that plastic bags take nearly 1,000 years to degrade. Additionally, discarded plastic bags can pose threats to wildlife and contaminate the soil. As a marketer, also think about the possibility of using recyclable packaging as a product benefit.

Elaborate/Extend

Provide an opportunity for students to exhibit their understanding of concepts in context of the material as it is presented. Have students read and discuss the special features in the margins.

Engage

Using the computer, demonstrate the various fonts and sizes that could be used for an advertisement.

Figure 24-5 This Cisco ad strategically uses two shades of blue in the headline, signature, and copy.

Most people are attracted to photos of other people, particularly children. Celebrities, such as sports figures and actors, are often used in advertising because they are well-known. Shocking, surprising, or amazing art may also act as a hook. Well-executed drawings are often as effective as photographs.

Layout

Layout is the arrangement of the headline, copy, and art on a page. An ad may have a great headline and fascinating art. However, if they are not placed attractively on the page, the ad might be ineffective.

One of the most useful layout tools is white space. White space is the blank areas on a page where there is no art or copy.

Explore

Visit a stock photo website. Demonstrate how a researcher might select a photo for an advertisement.

White space acts as a frame for the message. It can also separate the parts of an ad so they stand out. Ads with little white space appear cluttered and are hard to read. Graphic designers are tasked with creating ads that are easy to read so the message will be received.

Another term for typeface is *font*. The traditional, most flexible, and widely used typeface is *Times Roman*. It is used in many newspapers, magazines, and books because it is easy to read.

Signature

The signature identifies the person or company paying for the ad. Signatures usually include the company name and logo. It may also include the company slogan or tagline. The ad signature completes an advertisement much like a signature ends a letter. An ad signature may also include location and contact information, such as website, phone number, and street address.

Advertising and Society

While advertising clearly benefits business, it also can benefit society. Advertising can
- help increase employment to keep up with demand for advertised products;
- stimulate competition among businesses so they offer the best products at the lowest prices;
- encourage consumers to seek a higher standard of living;
- speed up the acceptance of new products;
- inform consumers and businesses about product choices;

Engage

Encourage a discussion about ethics and how advertising can play a positive or negative influence in a person's life.

- provide revenue to pay for broadcast programming and print vehicles; and
- may help people learn about health and social issues.

Advertisers have legal and ethical obligations to consumers and business customers. They are responsible for providing honest, accurate information. For example, advertisers make promises in their ads and commercials. These promises encourage people to buy products or services. Misleading or false ads sometimes make promises that are not kept. As a result, laws and regulations were passed to protect buyers from deceptive and improper advertising practices. These laws regulate advertisers what they can and cannot say.

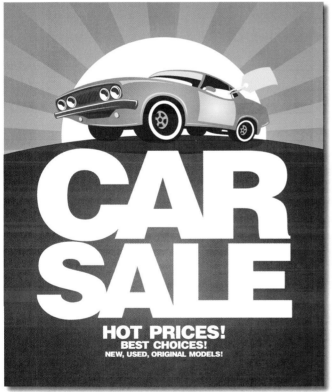

Olena Pantiukh/Shutterstock.com

Think about the information that needs to be added to this basic advertisement to keep it from being misleading or deceptive.

Laws and Regulations

Many laws govern the advertising industry. Some of these laws established federal agencies that monitor the actions of advertisers. These agencies also enforce the laws and regulations. The main agency is the Federal Trade Commission (FTC). Other agencies that regulate advertising include the Food and Drug Administration (FDA), and the Federal Communication Commission (FCC). The US Patent and Trademark Office and the Library of Congress also monitor certain advertising and licensing rules. It is the responsibility of marketers to know the laws and regulations for their businesses.

Figure 24-6 lists some of the areas these agencies monitor.

Self-Regulation

Most industries self-regulate advertising in addition to following the law. The advertising industry, however, leads the way in self-regulation. It has many organizations dedicated to monitoring advertising practices. The **Advertising Self-Regulatory Council (ASRC)** establishes the policies and procedures for advertising self-regulation.

The ASRC also includes the National Advertising Division (NAD), Children's Advertising Review Unit (CARU), and National Advertising Review Board (NARB). The Electronic Retailing Self-Regulation Program (ERSP) and Online Interest-Based Advertising Accountability Program regulate Internet advertising. The self-regulatory systems in advertising are administered by the Council of Better Business Bureaus.

The *Better Business Bureau (BBB)* promotes fair advertising and selling practices across all industries. Local BBBs are found in most large cities. They keep records of all advertising and selling complaints. The Council of Better Business Bureaus reviews complaints and recommends solutions.

Associations within the advertising industry also have codes of ethics and standards of practice to monitor member advertising practices. The American Association of Advertising Agencies and the American Advertising Federation work to maintain high advertising standards. The various media outlets also have advertising standards. Each newspaper and magazine sets standards for the kind of advertising it will accept. The network television stations have some of the strictest advertising standards. These standards may change to reflect the changes in public viewpoints.

Ethics

Even with federal laws in place, advertisers have a great deal of freedom. Ethics begin where the law ends. In Chapter 5, you learned that *ethics* are rules of behavior based on ideas about what is right and wrong. Advertising ethics follow the rules of truth and accuracy at all times.

Sometimes it is hard to tell what is ethical. A company may learn it has behaved unethically only after the reaction to its advertising. For example, it is legal for a lumber company to advertise home-repair

services after a natural disaster. However, the company should be careful *not* to give the impression it is using the disaster for gain.

Social Responsibility

Recall from Chapter 5 that social responsibility is behaving with sensitivity to social, environmental, and economic issues. A business also has a duty to help others and to improve society in general.

For example, Pedigree® donates one bowl of dog food to animal shelters every time someone likes its Facebook page. The goal of Pedigree is to donate 4 million bowls of dog food, enough to feed every shelter dog in America for one day.

Several national professional organizations in the advertising industry work with advertisers to help them help their communities. Examples include the Ad Council, American Association of Advertising Agencies, and American Advertising Federation. Through these organizations, advertisers donate time and money for civic events and community projects. They often create professional ads and commercials free of charge for these events.

Federal Advertising Investigations
• Allegations of misrepresentation, omission, or misleading information in advertising
• Problems with word usage in vague phrases; for example, phrases like *highest performance* when it cannot be proven
• Information on food-product labels; for example, food labeled *fat free* must contain less than 0.5 grams of fat per serving
• Product claims; for example, if a product label reads *Made in USA*, the product must be almost entirely made in the United States
• Unfair advertising; for example, taking advantage of children, who cannot make valid choices

Figure 24-6 Agencies that regulate advertising take action against businesses that advertise in unacceptable ways.

Goodheart-Willcox Publisher

Evaluate

Assign the Checkpoint questions at the end of the section. Assess students' comprehension using the Checkpoint activity as a self-assessment tool.

Explain

Discuss corporate social responsibility. Ask students for examples.

College and Career Portfolio

Technical Skills

Your portfolio should not only showcase your academic accomplishments, but the technical skills you have. Are you exceptionally good working with computers? Do you have a talent for playing a musical instrument? Technical skills are very important. Interviewers will want to know what talents and skills you have that may relate to the open position.

1. Write a paper that describes the technical skills you have acquired. Describe the skill, your level of competence, and any other information that will showcase your skill level.
2. Save the document file in your e-portfolio folder. Create a subfolder named *Skills*. Save a document for each skill with the file names *Skills01*, *Skills02*, etc.
3. Place a printed copy in the container for your print portfolio.

Checkpoint 24.2

1. What is the first step to creating an advertisement?
2. What is the function of a headline?
3. What are the three elements of typography?
4. Why were laws created to regulate advertising?
5. How are the self-regulatory policies and procedures in advertising created and administered?

Build Your Vocabulary

As you progress through this course, develop a personal glossary of marketing terms and add it to your portfolio. This will help you build your vocabulary and prepare you for a career. Write a definition for each of the following terms, and add it to your personal marketing glossary.

advertising agency
creative plan
headline
hook
copy
action word
typography
typeface
weight
art
layout
white space
signature
Advertising Self-Regulatory Council (ASRC)

Checkpoint Answers

1. Developing the creative plan is the first step in creating an advertisement.
2. The headline uses words to grab the attention of the reader, like a lure on a fishing hook. When the reader reads the headline, he or she is hooked, either into reading the rest of the ad or buying the product.
3. The three elements of typography are typeface, size, and weight.
4. Misleading or false ads sometimes make promises that are not kept or promote harmful products. As a result, laws and regulations were passed to protect buyers from deceptive and improper advertising practices. These laws tell advertisers what they can and cannot say.
5. The Advertising Self-Regulatory Council (ASRC) establishes the policies and procedures for advertising self regulation. The self-regulatory systems in advertising are administered by the Council of Better Business Bureaus.

Build Your Vocabulary Answers

Definitions for these terms can be found in the glossary of this text.

Chapter Summary

Section 24.1 Advertising Campaigns

- Advertising is any nonpersonal communication paid for by an identified sponsor. Advertising can influence a person's beliefs and attitudes about products; advertising can also help a consumer make purchase decisions.
- The steps for developing a successful advertising campaign are: set campaign goals, select the target audience, establish the budget, identify the media, create the message, measure the responses, and evaluate results.

Section 24.2 Creating Effective Ads

- Companies may use inside or outside resources to create advertising materials. The classic structure for an ad has four elements: headline, copy, graphics, and the signature.
- Advertising benefits society in many ways. Benefits include an increase in employment; competition among businesses resulting in better products at the lowest prices; a higher standard of living; an acceptance of new products; informed consumers and businesses; revenue to pay for broadcast programming and print vehicles; and an increased knowledge about health and social issues.

Review Your Knowledge

1. What is the main purpose of advertising?
2. What specific types of information does advertising usually provide to customers?
3. What is the best method of knowing whether an ad influenced sales?
4. Choose three forms of media and list one pro and con for each medium.
5. How do successful marketers determine the effectiveness of a campaign?
6. What are four ways a copywriter can use words to appeal to customers?
7. What are the two parts of an ad that grab attention?
8. Why is white space a useful tool for ad layout?
9. What is the main federal agency that regulates advertising?
10. List three benefits of advertising.

Evaluate

Assign the end-of-chapter activities.

Review Your Knowledge Answers

1. The main purpose is to persuade receivers to buy a product or accept an idea.
2. Advertising usually provides information about price, features, new items, store location, hours, and sales.
3. One way to know if an ad influences sales is to tie item purchases to a coupon.
4. Figure 24-3 lists the numerous correct answers available for each medium
5. They create metrics for each campaign to measure its success. They may also use posttesting to determine nonsales-related goals.
6. Four methods copywriters use to appeal to customers in ads are to create intrigue, appeal to the senses, sound newsworthy, and use action words.

7. The headline and graphics work together to attract the reader. Headlines usually appear in large type or have some other attention-getting graphic element. The graphics are often the first part of the ad a reader notices, especially when colorful or unusual.
8. White space acts as a frame for the message. It can also separate the parts of an ad so they stand out. Ads with little white space appear cluttered and are hard to read.
9. The main federal agency that regulates advertising is the Federal Trade Commission (FTC).
10. Answers may include increasing employment to keep up with demand for advertised products; stimulate competition among businesses so they offer the best products at the lowest prices; encourage consumers to seek a higher standard of living; speed up the acceptance of new products; inform consumers and businesses about product choices; provide revenue to pay for broadcast programming and print vehicles; and may help people learn about health and social issues.

Apply Your Knowledge

1. In an earlier chapter, you selected a company for which you are writing a marketing plan. Identify one product for which you will create an advertising campaign.
2. Identify the goals for your advertising campaign. What are you trying to accomplish with this element of the promotional mix?
3. Describe a segment of the target market for your product. Complete online research and write a profile that describes the demographics, interests, lifestyle, and typical daily activities and purchases of your market segment.
4. Make a list of the media you will include in this campaign. You may have already established a budget for your larger overall promotion campaign. If so, what amount did you allocate to advertising? If you did not allocate an amount, research how much you should consider.
5. Write a headline and copy for one print advertisement for your product. Make sure you use the AIDA model. The features and benefits of your product should be clear. The call to action will close the message. Contact information for your company should be obvious for customers to get samples, more information, or purchase.
6. Design and layout the advertisement. Include the headline, copy, graphics, and other necessary part of the ad. Ensure that your headline grabs attention, your copy gives compelling reasons to buy the product, your graphics and typography are visually appealing, and your signature includes all necessary elements. Compare and contrast two typefaces. Which typeface conveys the mood and message for your product and why?
7. Create metrics that you will use for your advertising campaign. Describe how you will use these to measure responses. How will you evaluate the results?
8. Describe your stand on social responsibility and advertising for your company.
9. Research an ethical controversy in advertising, such as the use of very young models in fashion ads. Describe the arguments made by both sides, and come to your own conclusion for a solution. How would you address ethics in your advertising?
10. Research local, state, and national advertising laws that will apply to your business. List and describe each. How will you take these in consideration for your campaign?

Apply Your Knowledge Answers

Student answers will vary for questions 1–10.

Apply Your Knowledge Teaching Tip

At the end of this unit, students will write the next phase of the marketing plan. Please note that the Apply Your Knowledge Questions prepare students for the next installment of the marketing plan that they are writing at the end of each unit. These questions help them assume the role of a marketing manager and begin applying concepts learned in the chapter.

If your class is not participating in the marketing plan activity at the end of the unit, Apply Your Knowledge questions can be used by directing students to select a business of their choice and answer each question about that business.

Marketing Plan

The marketing plan is almost complete. The promotion plan activities for this unit are the most time consuming part of the marketing plan. It is suggested that you assign the first part of the marketing plan as students finish this chapter.

Check Your Marketing IQ

Now that you have finished the chapter, see what you learned about marketing by taking the chapter posttest. If you do not have a smartphone, visit the G-W Learning companion website.

G-W Learning mobile site: www.m.g-wlearning.com

G-W Learning companion website: www.g-wlearning.com

Common Core

College and Career Readiness

CTE Career Ready Practices. Successful marketers model integrity in the workplace. Ethics is especially important in the promotion process. Research several popular ads that you see or hear often. Identify one ad in which the audience may have been misled. Name the product and how you think the presentation was misleading. Write bullet points for your findings and share with the class.

Listening. Informative listening is the process of listening to gain specific information from a speaker. Listen to several radio or television ads for your favorite products. Take notes. Evaluate the speaker's point of view. Did you listen closely enough to accurately record the important information?

Speaking. An oral presentation is a speech, address, or presentation given to an audience. Prepare an oral presentation on how to design an effective advertisement. Use digital media or visual displays to accompany your speech.

Teamwork

With a teammate, create a poster with collage of advertisements that you believe are excellent. Identify the headline, copy, logo, and signature on each ad. List all of the reasons you think these advertisements are effective.

G-W Learning Mobile Site

Visit the G-W Learning mobile site to complete the chapter pretest and posttest and to practice vocabulary using e-flash cards. If you do not have a smartphone, visit the G-W Learning companion website to access these features.

G-W Learning mobile site: www.m.g-wlearning.com

G-W Learning companion website: www.g-wlearning.com

Evaluate

Evaluate the students' understanding and knowledge. Assign the Chapter 24 posttest. The test may be accessed by using the QR code or by going to the companion website. What questions were students able to answer that they could not answer when they took the pretest?

25 Visual Merchandising

| Section 25.1 | Visual Merchandising and Display |
| Section 25.2 | Displays and Design |

"Visual merchandising is the art of implementing effective design ideas to increase store traffic and sales volume."

—Shari Waters, former About.com guide

College and Career Readiness

Reading Prep
As you read this chapter, stop at the Checkpoints and take time to answer the questions. Were you able to answer these without referring to the chapter content?

Check Your Marketing IQ

Before you begin the chapter, see what you already know about marketing by taking the chapter pretest. If you do not have a smartphone, visit the G-W Learning companion website.
G-W Learning mobile site: www.m.g-wlearning.com
G-W Learning companion website: www.g-wlearning.com

Explore
Assign the College and Career Readiness Reading Prep activity before students read the chapter. Reading Prep activities give students an opportunity to apply the Common Core State Standards.

Engage
Assign the Chapter 25 pretest. Discuss which questions students were unable to answer.

◆DECA Emerging Leaders

Business Operations Research Events, Part 2

Career Cluster and **Instructional Area** are not identified for this event.

Procedure, Part 2

1. In Chapter 24, you studied the skills assessed and procedures for this event.
2. This event will be presented to you as a written activity that will be created and submitted at the time of the event. For the presentation, the participants are to assume the role of management trainees in a single-unit or independent operation. The judge will evaluate the presentation, focusing on the effectiveness of public speaking and presentation skills and how well the participants respond to questions that the judge may ask following the presentation.
3. The oral presentation may be a maximum 15 minutes in length. The first 10 minutes will include an explanation and description of the project followed by 5 minutes for the judge's questions.
4. The participants will bring all visual aids to the event briefing. Only approved visual aids may be used during the presentation.

Research Topic

Although the research topic is the same for each career category, the topic for the Business Operations Research Events changes each year. The topic allows DECA members to conduct research in current areas of business operations, analyze the research study results, develop a strategic plan based on the research, and propose a solution or business practices to improve the business operations. Students enter an event based on the company/organization in which they conduct research.

Critical Thinking

1. Anticipating questions is a strategy presenters use to deliver effective presentations. Brainstorm questions your team may be asked during your presentation on the following:
    • participants' research methods;
    • details of the participants' findings and conclusions; and
    • participants' proposed plan.
2. Discuss your answers to the anticipated questions.

    Visit www.deca.org for more information.

Section 25.1 Visual Merchandising and Display

Objectives

After completing this section, you will be able to
- **describe** visual merchandising.
- **identify** the four elements of visual merchandising.

Key Terms

visual merchandising	store layout
display	fixture
store image	point-of-purchase
storefront	display (POP)
marquee	

Web Connect

Do an Internet search for *visual merchandising.* Write a definition and discuss the impact visual merchandising has on your shopping habits.

Critical Thinking

Think about the last time you went into a mall. Why did you walk into one store, but pass by another? Describe how visual merchandising entices you to enter the store.

Visual Merchandising

Visual merchandising is the process of creating floor plans and displays to attract customer attention and encourage purchases. It is often used as the sales promotion element of the promotional mix, especially in the B2C market. Visual merchandising attracts customers to examine the merchandise more closely. A **display** is a visual presentation of merchandise or ideas. Displays are designed to excite customers, motivate their interest in the merchandise, and entice them to buy.

Visual merchandising also helps to define the image of the store. **Store image** is created through the location, design, and décor of a business. Some words that describe store image are *trendy, sophisticated, discount, bargain, upscale, expensive, casual,* and *youthful.*

In an independent store, the store owner usually establishes the store image, or brand. In a chain store, the image is usually established at the headquarters by the marketing department based on company goals.

Visual merchandising is used primarily in retail situations and at trade shows. Retail stores arrange products in small and large displays to make them more appealing. Trade shows present products in displays on the exhibit floor—so customers can have a clear vision of what is being offered.

However, visual merchandising is also important for other types of businesses, such as service businesses, manufacturers, and wholesalers. Service businesses, such as hair salons, may also sell hair products to customers. They create displays to promote their products.

Many manufacturers of consumer products have showrooms to promote their prod-

Window displays, such as the traditional Macy's holiday-theme windows, are popular forms of visual merchandising.

littleny/Shutterstock.com

ucts to retailers. Other B2B manufacturers and wholesalers have showrooms with displays to show products to their buyers.

Visual Merchandising Elements

To accomplish the goal of visual merchandising, there are four components that must be considered: store exterior, store layout, store interior, and displays.

Store Exterior

The exterior is the first part of the store that a customer sees. The store exterior is often called the **storefront**, and it includes the store sign or logo, marquee, display windows, entrances, outdoor lighting, landscaping, and the building itself. All of these elements contribute to the store image.

The store sign is a major element of a store exterior. Many businesses develop a unique way of writing the company name, often with design elements. Businesses may also use the company logo. Often this is the way the name is displayed on the store sign.

Another use of exterior space is a marquee. A **marquee** is an overhanging structure containing a signboard located at the entrance to the store. The advantage to using a marquee is that it displays information that can be changed and provides a way to advertise store promotions and special events. Display windows are used to show a selection of merchandise available in the store.

The design of a business exterior is often part of the *place* decision. The location of the business often influences a store image. Stores located in a high-rent district create an image of upscale merchandise. Stores located in a mall may reflect family shopping and reasonable prices.

Best Buy uses its store-front to clearly promote the brand's promise: *get the best buys here.*

SeanPavonePhoto/Shutterstock.com

Store Layout

A **store layout** is a floor plan that shows how the space in a store will be used. A store layout is usually divided into four sections: the selling area, sales support area, storage, and customer comfort space.

The *selling area* is where the merchandise is presented to the customer. This area includes shelves or racks holding merchandise, displays of merchandise, and counters with cash registers for sales transactions.

The *sales support area* contains employee areas, such as offices, lockers, and a lunchroom. Sales support areas are clearly marked so that customers do not enter these areas mistakenly.

Storage space may be used to receive and store merchandise. Customers never see these areas. An additional area is referred to as *customer comfort space.* This area contains amenities for customers, such as restrooms, lounges, and cafes. Many stores have added luxury areas to appeal to customers.

Store Interior

The interior of the store must be appealing to customers. Its décor, including the colors, lighting, flooring, signage, and artwork, should reflect the preferences and taste of target market. The interior also includes the more permanent items, such as the floor and wall coverings, other furnishings, lighting fixtures, and display fixtures. A **fixture** is an item designed to hold something. Some fixtures are permanent, such as counters and display cases. Other fixtures are movable, such as tables, wall shelving, bins, and racks. Display fixtures are often customized to meet the needs of the particular product. For example, fixtures designed to display fishing rods will have a different shape from fixtures designed to display shoes.

Interior Displays

An *interior display* is located inside a store. Interior displays are strategically placed to draw the attention of visitors and move traffic through the store. Common

Display fixtures can be very creative and exciting, such as these in a clothing boutique.

Pavel L Photo and Video/Shutterstock.com

locations for interior displays include the store entrance, by elevators, at the ends of escalators, along major aisles, and near cash registers. Interior displays often provide information, such as how to wear new styles or coordinate accessories.

Displays are a critical part of visual merchandising. In fact, when people think of visual merchandising, they most often think of display creation. There are five types of merchandise presentation, or displays, that most retailers use: point-of-purchase, open, closed, and architectural displays, plus store decorations, as shown in Figure 25-1.

Point-of–Purchase Display (POP)

A **point-of-purchase display (POP)** is a special display usually found near a cash register where goods are purchased. A point-of-purchase display is designed to increase impulse purchases as customers are waiting to pay for their purchases. These displays may be developed and provided by

the manufacturer. They include the display itself as well as the merchandise. A POP may be temporary or permanent and is used to attract customers to new, special, or holiday products. An example of a POP is a gift card rack or candy display next to the sales register in a supermarket. An *interactive kiosk* where the customer can actually make a purchase is also a POP. Interactive kiosks are used for customer convenience.

Visual Displays
Point-of-Purchase Display (POP)
Open Display
Closed Display
Architectural Display
Store Decorations

Goodheart-Willcox Publisher

Figure 25-1 Most retailers use these five types of merchandise presentations.

Social Media

Pinterest

Pinterest was founded in 2010 as a new type of social networking called *visual networking* because it is primarily based on sharing images. By the end of 2012, it had over 20 million active users who avidly *pin* (the Pinterest word for posting) any images/products from websites they find interesting or want to share with others.

Users are encouraged to *re-pin* and *comment* on others' pins, which is how users are driven to companies' websites through hyperlinks on the images. If you are using Google Analytics, it can tell you how much money each customer from Pinterest is spending on your site. Businesses can set up a Pinterest account easily: simply click on "Request an Invite" on the Pinterest website that will allow you to sign in with your business e-mail. Create your business profile and the vision boards for other users to follow your pins. You also have the option to link your Pinterest account with your Twitter and Facebook accounts, which is highly recommended. Although Pinterest is a retail marketer's dream, other businesses can also take advantage of this growing form of social networking.

Open Display

In an open display, the merchandise is arranged so the shopper can view and handle the products. Most retail stores have open displays because customers want to know exactly what they are buying.

Closed Display

In a closed display, the merchandise is enclosed in a display case so that the shopper cannot touch it. Closed display cases may also be locked. Closed displays are often used for jewelry, china, and other expensive products, due to the risk of theft or breakage.

Redbox is a well-known interactive kiosk where customers can rent and return DVD movies and games.

Rob Wilson/Shutterstock.com

Architectural Display

An architectural display contains items that are arranged so that customers can get an idea how these products might look in their own homes. Examples of products used in architectural displays include cabinets and countertops. Architectural displays are found in home and furniture stores and at some trade shows.

Store Decorations

Store decorations are used for special products or occasions. Banners, signs, and other props may be used to decorate the store for holidays or special events. Decorative displays are usually seasonal, and they add to the atmosphere of the store.

Checkpoint 25.1

1. What is the difference between visual merchandising and displays?
2. Why is visual merchandising an important element of business-to-business (B2B) sales?
3. Explain interior displays and why they are important.
4. How is store image created?
5. Describe store decorations. What do they include?

Build Your Vocabulary

As you progress through this course, develop a personal glossary of marketing terms and add it to your portfolio. This will help you build your vocabulary and prepare you for a career. Write a definition for each of the following terms, and add it to your personal marketing glossary.

visual merchandising
display
store image
storefront
marquee
store layout
fixture
point-of-purchase display (POP)

Checkpoint Answers

1. Visual merchandising attracts customers into the store to examine the merchandise more closely. A display is a visual presentation of merchandise or ideas. Displays are designed to excite customers, get them interested in the merchandise, and entice them to buy.

2. Many manufacturers of consumer products have showrooms to promote their products to retailers. Other B2B manufacturers and wholesalers have showrooms with displays to show products to their buyers.

3. An *interior display* is located inside a store. Interior displays are strategically placed to draw the attention of visitors and move traffic through the store.

4. Store image is created by visual merchandisers through the design and de'cor of the store.

5. Store decorations are used for special products or occasions. Banners, signs, and other props may be used to decorate the store for holidays or special events.

Build Your Vocabulary Answers

Definitions for these terms can be found in the glossary of this text.

Section 25.2 Displays and Design

Objectives

After completing this section, you will be able to
- **list** the elements of design.
- **describe** the principles of design.
- **explain** how to develop a display.

Key Terms

design
color wheel
hue
value
intensity
color scheme
complementary
  color

analogous color
triadic color
texture
emphasis
movement
balance
proportion
prop

Web Connect

Do an online search for *retail display design ideas.* Find two display ideas for the business you chose to market. Sketch the ideas or make a collage showing how the displays would look in your business.

Critical Thinking

The next time you visit a shopping center or mall, list your favorite in-store and exterior displays. If possible, take a few pictures for reference. Why were those displays effective?

Elements of Design

Success in visual merchandising involves designing powerful and effective displays. Design is the purposeful arrangement of materials to produce a certain effect. Design is involved in many areas of human endeavor, including fine arts, advertising, fashion, and product development, as well as visual merchandising.

The *elements of design* include color, line, shape, texture, light, and motion. The elements of design are the building blocks that can be manipulated to create an effect. In both visual merchandising and advertising, the main goal is to grab the attention of the customer. Successful visual merchandisers and advertisers use their sense of design and their creativity to create displays and advertisements that work. Successful displays often use the elements of design in new and creative ways.

Color

Color is often the most dramatic and noticeable design element. Colors can grab attention, create a mood, or affect how someone feels. Psychologists have studied colors and the associations people have with them. Figure 25-2 shows common responses that Americans have to some colors. Notice that the same color can have both positive and negative reactions.

Colors have different meanings in different cultures. For example, brides in America wear white because white symbolizes purity and innocence. In China, brides

Engage

Ask students why they think the elements of design influence the consumer. Which element attracts their attention?

Color and Emotions in US Culture
Black. Elegant, sophisticated, strong, serious, wise, mysterious, tragic, sad, old, evil, gloomy
Gray. Modest, sad, old
White. Youthful, innocent, faithful, pure, peaceful
Violet. Royal, dignified, powerful, rich, dramatic, mysterious, passionate
Blue. Peaceful, calm, restful, tranquil, truthful, serious, cool, formal, spacious, sad, depressed
Green. Cool, fresh, natural, friendly, pleasant, calm, restful, lucky, envious, immature
Yellow. Bright, sunny, cheerful, warm, prosperous, hopeful, cowardly, deceitful
Orange. Lively, energetic, cheerful, joyous, warm, hospitable
Red. Exciting, vibrant, passionate, hot, aggressive, angry, dangerous

Goodheart-Willcox Publisher

Figure 25-2 The American culture tends to associate certain emotions with specific colors. However, the connection between color and emotion is not an exact science.

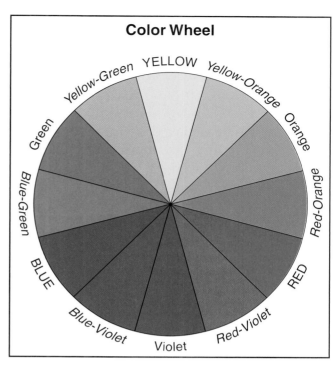

Goodheart-Willcox Publisher

Figure 25-3 Visual merchandisers use the color wheel as a tool to help them decide which colors to use in displays.

wear red because red symbolizes luck and joy. In China, white is the color of mourning. Colors can also have different meanings in different eras in the same culture. For example, the *in-fashion* colors change frequently. Visual merchandisers must use their artistic experience and their social awareness when using color.

Color Wheel

The perception of color is individual. Whether a person likes certain colors or color combinations is very subjective. However, many people tend to agree on which color combinations are pleasing. One tool that is used as a guide for developing color combinations is the color wheel. The **color wheel** is a standard arrangement of 12 colors in a wheel that shows the relationships among the colors. A color wheel is shown in Figure 25-3.

The *primary colors* are red, blue, and yellow. They are placed at equal distances on the color wheel. If equal amounts of two primary colors are mixed, the secondary colors are created. The *secondary colors* are green, violet, and orange. If equal amounts of a primary and secondary color are mixed, the intermediate colors are created. The *intermediate colors* are yellow-orange, yellow-green, blue-green, blue-violet, red-violet, and red-orange. Black, white, and gray are neutral colors.

A color has three distinct qualities: hue, value, and intensity. It is often helpful to visualize a tube of paint when trying to understand these concepts. **Hue** is the pure color itself, for example, red. Color is often used as a synonym for hue. **Value** refers to the lightness or darkness of the color, that is, how much white or black is mixed with the hue. Hues mixed with white are called tints.

For example, pink is a tint of red. Hues mixed with black are called shades. Burgundy is a shade of red. **Intensity** refers to the brightness or dullness of a color.

Color Schemes

A **color scheme** is a description of color combinations. There are many color schemes.

In fact, some industries, such as the fashion industry, try to come up with new color schemes every season. However, there are six basic color schemes, as shown in Figure 25-4.

In designing a display, it is important to understand the relationships among colors. Colors found opposite to one another on a color wheel are called **complementary colors.**

Six Basic Color Schemes			
Name	**Number**	**Location on Wheel**	**Examples**
Monochromatic	One color	Any color plus its tints or shades	
Accented Neutral	Two colors	One neutral plus one color from anywhere	
Complementary	Two colors	Opposite each other	
Split Complementary	Three colors	Choose one color; add the two colors on either side of the complementary color	
Triad	Three colors	Equal distances from each other	
Analogous	Three colors	Next to each other	

Figure 25-4 The six basic color schemes are based on the location of the colors on the color wheel. The tints and shades of each color can also be used for more variety.

Using complementary colors in a display, such as purple and yellow creates contrast. Analogous colors are adjacent to one another on the color wheel. Analogous colors go well together. Triadic colors are three colors that are equally spaced on the color wheel. Examples are orange-red, blue-purple, and yellow-green.

Line, Shape, Texture, and Light

Line refers to a one-dimensional mark that looks as if it were drawn by a pen. A line can be an actual line drawn by a pen. A line can also be a boundary, for example, where two walls meet or where a seam joins two pieces of fabric. Lines can be straight, curved, or jagged. A line also has direction. A line can be *vertical* (up and down), *horizontal* (side to side, like the horizon), or *diagonal* (at an angle). The direction of a line guides the eye from one point to another. The direction of lines gives movement to a design.

Shape refers to the shapes used in a design. The shapes can be two-dimensional, such as circles, triangles, and octagons; or three-dimensional, such as spheres, cubes, and cylinders. Shape also refers to the overall outline of an item or display, which is often called the *silhouette*.

Texture refers to the surface quality of materials. Aluminum foil has a shiny texture. A wool scarf has a dull texture. Some other words that describe texture include smooth, rough, fuzzy, shaggy, sheer, soft, hard, crisp, and furry.

So the viewer can see what is being shown, light is necessary in a window or display. Lighting can be from overhead lights, track lights, table lamps, and spotlights. Care must be taken that the lighting does not cast shadows that interfere with the design.

Motion

Motion may sometimes be an additional element of design. In merchandise displays, mechanical devices are often used to move the products in the display. The most common use of motion in displays is a rotating platform.

Motion can also refer to the interactivity of a display.

arindambanerjee/Shutterstock.com

Explain

Show the students a picture taken from a magazine or newspaper that has a color scheme and ask them to describe it and explain the effectiveness of color in the picture.

Engage

Use examples to demonstrate shape and texture. Encourage students to discuss how each element can enhance a specific design.

Graphic Designer

Products and service advertising can take many forms, including print, radio, online ads, and television. All of these except radio rely to some extent on graphic images to catch the eye of potential customers. The job of a graphic designer is to create graphics that present the products or services in an appealing manner for packaging, logos, brochures, and other items that represent the company. Other typical job titles for a graphic designer include *graphic artist, creative director, design director,* and *desktop publisher.*

Some examples of tasks that graphic designers perform include:

- consult the client or company executives to determine layout design;
- create designs and layouts for product packaging and company logos;
- use graphic design software to generate layouts;
- design the arrangement of illustrations and text; and
- prepare final layouts for printing or production.

Graphic designers need a solid knowledge of layout principles and design concepts, as well as artistic ability. They must also be familiar with design, illustration, photographic, and layout software. Good communication skills help them understand the client's requirements and produce designs that showcase products or services effectively. Many graphic design jobs require a bachelor degree, but talented and experienced designers may be hired without a four-year degree. For more information, access the *Occupational Outlook Handbook* online.

Sometimes, mechanical figures add motion, for example, in holiday displays.

Principles of Design

The principles of design are guidelines that can help to use the elements of design effectively. The principles of design include emphasis, movement, balance, and proportion.

Emphasis is drawing the attention of the viewer to the most important part of a display. Suppose a book is the most important part of a display. You can use lines that point toward the book to give it emphasis. You can use color by placing the book on a bright red cloth. You can use texture by surrounding the book with sparkling confetti. You can use light by pointing a spotlight on the book.

Movement refers to the way the design guides viewer eyes over an item or display. Readers of Western languages, such as English and Spanish, read from left to right. Therefore, people will tend to view windows and displays from left to right. A designer can use color, shape, line, texture, and light to direct the viewer's attention to move along a desired direction. Another way to direct the viewer's attention and focus is through use of mannequins or other items in a display. For example, the direction in which the mannequin looks can also direct the eyes of a viewer.

Balance refers to the way items are placed around an imaginary centerline. *Formal balance* means that you have an object on one side of the line, and another object of equal size the same distance from the line on the other side. *Informal balance* means that you have a large object on one side of the line. However, on the

Extend

Have students use items in the classroom to demonstrate each principle of design.

This colorful display of men's ties makes great use of both balance and proportion.

Rido/Shutterstock.com

other side, you have two smaller objects that together are about the same size as the larger object. Informal balance also occurs when you have a large pale object on one side and a smaller, but very bright object, on the other side. The small but bright object balances the larger but pale object.

Proportion refers to the size and space relationship of all items in a display to each other and to the whole display. Proportion can also be applied to a single item, for which you consider the size and space relationships

of all the parts of the item to the whole item. For example, imagine a very light colored, delicate dress; a wide, dark, heavy leather belt would be out of proportion. A narrow silver belt would look more in proportion.

Display Development

Before a display can be constructed, it must be planned. Obviously, when planning a display, the merchandise must be

Elaborate/Extend

Provide an opportunity for students to exhibit their understanding of concepts in context of the material as it is presented. As time permits, have students read and discuss the special features in the margins.

Explore

Select four or five objects in the classroom. Ask for a volunteer to arrange the items into a display using only objects available in the room. Have the class evaluate the creativity of the display.

Marketing Ethics

Truth-In-Advertising Laws

It is unethical to take part in deceptive advertising or marketing practices. Marketers must comply with truth-in-advertising laws and make sure that no product or service message is misleading. This is not only an ethical and legal consideration, but it is also considered a good business practice.

considered. However, socially responsible businesses also consider the culture of the customers who will be entering the store, as well as the impact the display may have on the environment. There are four steps in the development of a good display, as shown in Figure 25-5.

Select the Merchandise

The first step is to select the merchandise that will be featured. The merchandise should be eye-catching or notable in some way. For example, it may be a new product, a seasonal product, or one for a certain age group.

The next step is to determine the type of display. You might choose a one-item display that just shows one product. Instead, you might determine that a similar product display is more appropriate. For example, you may choose to display only purses and show multiple designer brands. Another approach is to show similar or complementing

products. If the merchandise relates to another product, such as coats and scarves, the two items may be displayed together. On the other hand, you may decide to show a variety of products and show an assortment of unrelated merchandise.

Choose a Theme

The theme for a display can be an artistic element, such as a color scheme. It can also be an idea, such as the beach or a carnival. Often, an entire store will have a theme, such as back-to-school. To complement the theme, you may decide to use props. **Props** are objects used in a display to support the theme or to physically support the merchandise. Props can be either decorative or functional. A beach ball for a swimsuit display is a decorative prop. Mannequins in beachwear are functional props.

Next, arrange the merchandise in a way that attracts customers and promotes the products. Place items at appropriate eye level for easy viewing. Develop signs for the display. Signs can be used to give information, such as the manufacturer or price of the items. Signs should be brief and easy to read.

Do not forget about lighting. There should be enough light to see the merchandise and read the signs. Spotlights can be used to focus on specific items in the display. The lighting design should minimize glare and shadows.

Display Development Steps
1.   Select the merchandise.
2.   Choose a theme.
3.   Set the display goals.
4.   Maintain the display.

Goodheart-Willcox Publisher

Figure 25-5 Utilize these four steps to help you develop a well-planned and effective display.

Elaborate/Extend

If students are using the optional *Marketing Dynamics* workbook, assign activities to engage active learning.

Extend

Ask students to describe a display that recently caught their attention. What one particular element stood out?

Set the Display Goals

The purpose of displays is to promote store image and sell products. Visual merchandisers usually evaluate each display to determine whether it is meeting these goals. These questions will help you determine the quality of the display:

- Does the display fit our store image?
- Does the display grab the attention of customers?
- Does the display focus attention on the merchandise?
- Are the signs clear and easy to read?
- Is there enough light, with minimal glare and shadows?
- Is the display clean and neat?
- Does the display accomplish your goal?

Get feedback from those with whom you work and see if you hit the mark.

Maintain the Display

Suppose you are looking at a clothing display. You notice that the mannequin has a broken hand, the shirts on the table are scattered about, and the bulb in the spotlight is out. What would you think? Dirty, messy displays can ruin the image of a store. To maintain a good image, a display must be kept clean and orderly. The following is a guide for good display maintenance:

- Check at least once a day to make sure the display looks as clean, crisp, and fresh as when it was first completed.
- Clean the floor, table, props, and merchandise regularly.
- Replace any merchandise that has been removed or damaged.
- If merchandise has been moved, put it back where it belongs.
- Check lights and replace as necessary.

Members of the American Marketing Association know that visual merchandising expands beyond eye-catching signs and colors. The organization recently shared a blog post from one of its partners that highlights the benefits of using instore technology to enhance sales. For example, strategically placed digital signs can improve the experience of a consumer waiting in line. Blog posts are available to AMA members and nonmembers. www.marketingpower.com

Apple

Many people have fond memories of holiday displays in windows of their favorite department stores. These displays are examples of visual merchandising. Visual merchandising plays an important role to attract customer attention and interaction.

Not just during holidays, but every day of the year, retailers are becoming more competitive and taking visual displays to all new levels. Take a look at the iconic Fifth Avenue Apple Store in New York City. The Apple cube store is a landmark as well as a tourist destination. The store was renovated in 2011 at a cost of over $6 million. The giant glass cube is a unique structure that creates a storefront demanding attention and reflecting the Apple image. Inside the store, customers find Apple products in tastefully designed displays. They also have the opportunity to demonstrate the latest in technology. The unmistakable Apple logo is visible throughout the store in displays and as decoration. Visual merchandising—where would we be without it?

Resource/Evaluate

Assign the optional Chapter 25 test for **EXAM**VIEW®
Assessment Suite as a formal assessment tool.

Checkpoint 25.2

1. What is the major purpose of displays?
2. What are some common locations for interior displays?
3. What is the difference between open displays and closed displays?
4. Name the two types of props and give one example of each.
5. What is the difference between formal balance and informal balance?

Build Your Vocabulary

As you progress through this course, develop a personal glossary of marketing terms and add it to your portfolio. This will help you build your vocabulary and prepare you for a career. Write a definition for each of the following terms, and add it to your personal marketing glossary.

design
color wheel
hue
value
intensity
color scheme
complementary color
analogous color
triadic color
texture
emphasis
movement
balance
proportion
prop

Evaluate

Assign the Checkpoint questions at the end of the section. Assess students' comprehension using the Checkpoint activity as a self-assessment tool. **Checkpoint Answers**

1. The major purpose of displays is to excite customer interest in the merchandise. Displays can also provide information about the products, show customers how to use or accessorize products, and add to the store image.
2. Common locations for interior displays include the store entrance, across from elevators, at the ends of escalators, along major aisles, and near cash registers.
3. In an open display, the merchandise is arranged so that the shopper can handle it. In a closed display, the merchandise is enclosed in a display case so that the shopper cannot touch

it. Closed display cases may also be locked.
4. Props can be either decorative or functional. A beach ball for a swimsuit display is a decorative prop. Mannequins in beachwear are functional props.
5. Formal balance means that you have an object on one side of the line, and another object of equal size the same distance from the line on the other side. Informal balance means that you have a large object on one side of the line, but on the other side, you have two smaller objects that together are about the same size as the larger object.

Build Your Vocabulary Answers

Definitions for these terms can be found in the glossary of this text.

Chapter Summary

Section 25.1 Visual Merchandising and Display

- Visual merchandising is the process of creating floor plans and displays to attract customer attention and encourage purchases. Visual merchandising attracts customers into the store to examine the merchandise more closely.
- To accomplish the goal of visual merchandising, there are four components that must be considered: store exterior, store layout, store interior, and displays.

Section 25.2 Displays and Design

- Design is the purposeful arrangement of materials to produce a certain effect. The elements of design include color, line, shape, texture, light, and motion. The elements of design are the building blocks that can be manipulated to create an effect.
- The principles of design are guidelines that can help you to use the elements of design effectively. The principles of design include emphasis, movement, balance, and proportion.
- The four steps of developing a display are: select the merchandise; choose a theme; set the display goals; and maintain the display.

Review Your Knowledge

1. What are the four sections in which a retail store is usually divided?
2. What is the advantage to having a marquee?
3. Describe the selling area in a store.
4. What is the purpose of a point-of-purchase display?
5. List the two types of props and give one example of each.
6. List the seven elements of design.
7. List the four principles of design.
8. Name the three distinct qualities of color.
9. What are the primary colors and the secondary colors?
10. As a principle of design, how is movement used in displays?

Evaluate

Assign the end-of-chapter activities.

Review Your Knowledge

1. A store interior is usually divided into four sections: the selling area, the sales support area, staff space, and customer comfort space.
2. The advantage to having a marquee is that it provides a way to advertise store promotions and special events.
3. The selling area is where the merchandise is presented to the customer. This area includes shelves or racks holding merchandise, displays of merchandise, and counters with cash registers for sales transactions.
4. A point-of-purchase display is designed to provoke impulse purchases as the customer is waiting to pay for his or her purchases.
5. Props can be either decorative or functional. A beach ball for a swimsuit display is a decorative prop. Mannequins in beachwear are functional props.
6. The elements of design include color, line, shape, texture, light, focal point, and motion.
7. The principles of design include emphasis, movement, balance, and proportion.
8. A color has three distinct qualities: hue, value, and intensity.
9. The primary colors are red, blue, and yellow; the secondary colors are green, violet, and orange.
10. People will tend to view windows and displays from left to right. A designer can use color, shape, line, texture, and light to direct the viewer attention to move along a desired direction. Another way to direct the viewer attention and focus is how mannequins are placed in a display. The direction in which the mannequin looks can also direct the eyes of a viewer.

Apply Your Knowledge

1. In your marketing plan, you will describe the image of your business. What image does your business project to customers?
2. Visit the website of the business for which you are writing your marketing plan. Find a picture of the business, and describe the store exterior for your business. How does it contribute to the store image?
3. If possible, find a layout for your store. If there is not a plan available, create a store layout using graph paper or another method that you think would work for your business.
4. Places of business have various fixtures to display merchandise. Make a list of both the permanent and temporary fixtures that are used in your business.
5. Management has requested you create new displays for the major product you market. There are five types of merchandise displays. Select two and describe why these displays work well for your business.
6. Describe two elements of design that will help you in creating a visual display.
7. Describe two principles of design that are needed to create display for your merchandise.
8. Make a list of the steps you will take to create your merchandise display.
9. Create a checklist to help you evaluate your display to see if you met your goals.
10. Create a checklist of how you will make sure that your merchandise is in good working order during the time of its display.

Check Your Marketing IQ

Now that you have finished the chapter, see what you learned about marketing by taking the chapter posttest. If you do not have a smartphone, visit the G-W Learning companion website.

G-W Learning mobile site: www.m.g-wlearning.com
G-W Learning companion website: www.g-wlearning.com

Apply Your Knowledge Answers

Student answers will vary for questions 1–10.

Apply Your Knowledge Teaching Tip

At the end of this unit, students will write the next phase of the marketing plan. Please note that the Apply Your Knowledge Questions prepare students for the next installment of the marketing plan that they are writing at the end of each unit. These questions help them assume the role of a marketing manager and begin applying concepts learned in the chapter. If your class is not participating in the marketing plan activity at the end of the unit, Apply Your Knowledge questions can be used by directing students to select a business of their choice and answer questions about that business. A good example to use for supply chain management information is Target. Visit their corporate website or do a search for Target distribution and supply chain.

Marketing Plan

The marketing plan is almost complete. The promotion plan activities for this unit are the most time-consuming part of the marketing plan. Build adequate time into your schedule for completing this activity.

College and Career Readiness

Common Core

CTE Career Ready Practices. It is important to use critical thinking skills to make sense of challenges that you will face as a marketing professional. Research point-of-purchase displays. Make a list of several options that are available in a retail location. Describe each option and its pros and cons.

Reading. Read a magazine, newspaper, or online article about a sales promotion for a small business that caused negative customer reaction. Determine the central ideas of the article and review the conclusions made by the author. Provide an accurate summary of your reading, making sure to incorporate the *who, what, when,* and *how* concepts.

Writing. Research the history of visual merchandising. Where did the concept originate? Write an informative report consisting of several paragraphs to describe your findings.

Teamwork

Working in teams, create a visual display for DECA products. Select a theme, write a plan, and actually create the display. Ask teachers in your school to judge the displays and select a winner.

G-W Learning Mobile Site

Visit the G-W Learning mobile site to complete the chapter pretest and posttest and to practice vocabulary using e-flash cards. If you do not have a smartphone, visit the G-W Learning companion website to access these features.

G-W Learning mobile site: www.m.g-wlearning.com

G-W Learning companion website: www.g-wlearning.com

Engage

Use the Teamwork exercise at the end of the chapter to engage students to solve a problem or make a group presentation.

Evaluate

Evaluate the students' understanding and knowledge. Assign the Chapter 25 posttest. The test may be accessed by using the QR code or by going to the companion website. What questions were students able to answer that they could not answer when they took the pretest?

26

Personal Selling

Section 26.1 | Role of Sales
Section 26.2 | Selling
Section 26.3 | After the Sale

"Internalize the Golden Rule of sales that says: All things being equal, people will do business with, and refer business to, those people they know, like, and trust."

—Bob Burg; best-selling author

Reading Prep
Think about what you already know about how marketing influences sales. What do you think marketers should know about selling products or services to consumers? As you read, evaluate how the ideas presented in the text compare to your own.

College and Career Readiness

Check Your Marketing IQ

Before you begin the chapter, see what you already know about marketing by taking the chapter pretest. If you do not have a smartphone, visit the G-W Learning companion website.
G-W Learning mobile site: www.m.g-wlearning.com
G-W Learning companion website: www.g-wlearning.com

G-W Mobile

Explore
Assign the College and Career Readiness Reading Prep activity before students read the chapter. Reading Prep activities give students opportunity to apply the Common Core State Standards.

Engage
Assign the Chapter 26 pretest. The test may be accessed by using the QR code or going to the companion website. Discuss which questions students were unable to answer.

◇DECA Emerging Leaders

Principles of Marketing Event

Career Cluster: Marketing
Instructional Area: Economics

Performance Indicators

- Describe marketing functions and related activities.
- Explain the role of business in society.
- Explain the concept of private enterprise.
- Describe types of business activities.

Purpose

Designed for first-year DECA members who are enrolled in introductory-level principles of marketing/business courses, this event measures the individual's ability to explain core business concepts in the format of a content interview in a role-play. This event consists of a 100-question, multiple-choice, business administration core exam and a content interview. Participants are not informed in advance of the performance indicators to be evaluated.

Procedure

1. The event will be presented to you through your reading of these instructions, including the performance indicators and interview task. You will have up to 10 minutes to review this information to determine how you will perform the task and demonstrate the performance indicators of this event. During the preparation period, you may make notes to use during the interview situation.
2. You will have up to 10 minutes with the judge, including five to seven minutes to accomplish the task and several minutes to respond to follow-up questions. (You may have more than one judge.)
3. You will be evaluated on how well you meet the performance indicators of this event. Turn in all your notes and event materials when you have completed the interview.

Interview Situation

You are to assume the role of candidate for a customer service representative position in the public relations department at Southwest Oil, a large energy company involved in the refining and distribution of gasoline and petroleum products. You have submitted your résumé and have been invited in for a personal interview with the **public information director (judge)**. This interview will be used to measure your knowledge and understanding of an aspect of the business. The public information director (judge) wants to make sure you understand the important role that business plays in society before offering you the customer service representative position.

The public relations department of Southwest Oil administers and communicates all civic and charitable contributions that the company makes. In the first part of the interview you will explain how the company's charitable contribution program benefits society and the role it plays in the overall marketing efforts of Southwest Oil. Your presentation must also include the additional performance indicators listed on the first page of this event. Following your explanation, the public information director (judge) will ask you to respond to additional questions.

The interview will take place in the public information director's (judge's) office. The public information director (judge) will begin the interview by greeting you and asking to hear your explanation on the role of business in society. After you have provided your explanation and have answered the director's (judge's) questions, the public information director (judge) will conclude the interview by thanking you for your presentation.

Critical Thinking

1. How does a company decide which civic or charitable causes deserve its financial support?
2. Do charitable donations produce higher sales for a business?
3. Is it better for a company to support one charity with one large contribution or to make smaller contributions to many charitable groups?

Visit www.deca.org for more information.

Section 26.1 Role of Sales

Objectives

After completing this section, you will be able to
- **explain** the value of personal selling.
- **describe** what it is like to have a career in sales.

Key Terms

business-to-business (B2B) selling
relationship selling
business-to-consumer (B2C) selling
telemarketing
call center

Web Connect

Sales careers are a very satisfying career choice for many people. Do an Internet search for sales positions in your area. Compare and contrast three classified advertisements. What do they have in common? Is this a career that might interest you?

Critical Thinking

Think about the two types of sales positions: B2B and B2C. Which type of position would fit your personality better? Make a list of your skills and talents that you think would lend themselves to one of these choices.

Value of Personal Selling

Selling is an important component of the promotional element of the marketing mix. Without the sales function, it would be difficult for a company to generate revenue. For that reason, companies have teams that perform personal selling.

Recall that *personal selling* is direct contact with a prospective customer with the objective of selling a product or service. As with other components of promotion, selling applies the marketing concept of customer satisfaction. By meeting customer needs with a product or service, a company can grow company sales.

A salesperson adds value to the promotional mix. Personal selling provides information that a marketing brochure or website cannot provide. A salesperson can persuade a customer to make a decision about how to meet a need or want. Customers can give feedback that helps product development meet customer

needs. People like personal contact when making a buying decision. While other parts of the promotional mix are important, personal contact is at the top of the customer list.

FYI

Salesperson, sales representative, and *sales rep* are terms that are used interchangeably.

Business-to-Business (B2B) Selling

Where does a store buy the products it sells to customers? Where does a school system buy desks for students? Where does a construction company buy a bulldozer? In most of these situations, the customer will not go to a sales location. Instead, a salesperson goes to the customer's place of business.

Explore

Review the vocabulary terms at the beginning of the section. Where have students encountered these terms before? Help students make educated guesses about the meanings of the terms with which they are least familiar.

Resource

Use the Chapter 26 presentation on the optional Instructor's Presentations for PowerPoint® CD as an outline for presenting the chapter.

Business-to-business selling (B2B) is a business selling to another business. B2B sales may also be called *field sales, industrial sales,* and *organizational sales.* Companies that sell equipment and raw materials to manufacturers are involved in B2B sales. Manufacturers that sell finished products to retailers are involved in B2B sales.

Often the term *B2B sales* also includes government and institutional sales. When a business sells to a government, it is often referred to as *government sales.* When a business sells to a nonprofit organization, such as a school or hospital, it is often called *institutional sales.*

There are typically two types of sales positions for B2B sales—inside salesperson and outside salesperson. An inside salesperson communicates with customers via phone or e-mail. An outside salesperson visits with the customer at his or her place of business. Some sales communication will be by phone or e-mail, but the primary contact is face-to-face and relationship selling. **Relationship selling** focuses on building long-term relationships with customers.

Business-to-Consumer (B2C) Selling

Business-to-consumer (B2C) selling is selling to consumers. Retail is a typical example of the B2C market. Most retail sales are made by a salesperson in the place of business. However, some retail businesses conduct the selling process by telephone. **Telemarketing** is personal selling done over the telephone.

Many larger retailers have call centers for the telemarketing function. A **call center** is an office that is set up for the purpose of receiving and making customer calls for an organization. Each telemarketer usually has a headphone, so that he or she can record orders on a computer. Some call centers specialize in *inbound* calls, or customers calling into the center. For example, Lands' End is a company that sells clothing, luggage, and home products. When customers want to order items from Lands' End, their call goes to an inbound call center.

Other call centers specialize in *outbound* calls, or salespeople making customer calls. For example, a local newspaper might have a telemarketer. This salesperson might call local businesses to ask them to advertise in the newspaper. Many nonprofit organizations use outbound call centers to raise money for their organizations. The people who make these calls are usually called *fund-raisers,* but their tasks are very similar to a telemarketer.

The Internet can be used for personal selling. The customer can visit a website, where a salesperson interacts with the customer in real time. If the customer visits a website and does not interact with a salesperson in real time, then it is not considered a personal-selling situation.

Green Marketing

Ecofriendly Marketing Premiums

Many businesses advertise through marketing premiums for customers, such as pens, recyclable tote bags, and other novelty items. When planning to purchase marketing premiums, consider the environment. The new ecofriendly bamboo USB drives are becoming a popular giveaway item with marketers. Bamboo is one of the fastest-growing wood plants on the planet. This renewable resource is a good choice for the case of a USB drive. USB drives are durable, reusable, and easy to carry and store. Your company name stands out on a useful item. Plus, potential customers appreciate sustainable products.

Career in Sales

Open any newspaper to the *Help Wanted* section and you will see a large number of ads for salespeople. Most businesses need someone to sell their products. Think of any good, service, or idea that interests you. You can probably find a job selling that product. Careers in sales provide great opportunities for financial and business success. Many corporations are headed by people who began their careers in sales.

Successful salespeople must have excellent work habits and are goal oriented. Personal traits include an eagerness to learn, initiative, and persistence. Most salaries include a commission or bonus for reaching sales goals, so hard work and determination is critical.

Strong ethics of honesty, integrity, responsibility, and confidentiality are required for establishing trust with customers. For successful long-term relationships that lead to repeat sales, ethics are important. Sales positions are generally independent and require minimal day-to-day supervision. A sales rep must be able to work a full day without clocking in.

Becoming a salesperson can be a rewarding career. Some people have a natural talent for sales. However, most people can learn the skills and develop the qualities of a successful salesperson. Community, technical, business, and four-year colleges provide courses in sales. Many businesses provide sales training for their employees. You can also learn about sales through experiences with student organizations, such as DECA.

AMA Tip

The American Marketing Association's dictionary offers definitions for a number of sales-related terms that can take your understanding of selling to the next level. For example, the AMA defines the salesperson career cycles as, "the sequence of stages that a salesperson passes through during the phases of his or her sales career." The dictionary is available to members and nonmembers. www.marketingpower.com

The job of a salesperson can be a rewarding career.

Yuri Arcurs/Shutterstock.com

Explore

Invite a panel of salespeople to talk with students about their careers. Ask them to talk about why they chose their career, what characteristics have made them successful; what challenges they face; and what they would tell a student interested in pursuing a career in sales.

Engage

Provide the DECA professional sales competitive event to students. Have students use the featured product to create their own professional sales presentation. Have a panel of salespeople to critique the presentations for a future DECA competition.

Marketing Ethics

Ethical Salespeople

In order to build trust with customers, a salesperson must be honest and responsible. An ethical salesperson does not oversell a product, promise more than the product or company can deliver, lie about the competition to make a sale, provide false product testimonials, or sell hazardous products.

Last, but not least, a salesperson needs a good attitude. Salespeople often encounter difficult situations. For example, customers can be unreasonable and rude. You might lose a sale to a competitor. A salesperson needs to be able to bounce back from disappointments, learn from mistakes, and move on to the next sale with a positive attitude.

Checkpoint 26.1

1. Why are salespeople important?
2. List three alternative names for business-to-business selling.
3. What are institutional sales?
4. What are the two types of call centers?
5. Why does a salesperson need a positive attitude?

Build Your Vocabulary

As you progress through this course, develop a personal glossary of marketing terms and add it to your portfolio. This will help you build your vocabulary and prepare you for a career. Write a definition for each of the following terms, and add it to your personal marketing glossary.

business-to-business (B2B) selling
relationship selling
business-to-consumer (B2C) selling
telemarketing
call center

Evaluate

Assign the Checkpoint questions at the end of the section. Assess students' comprehension using the Checkpoint activity as a self-assessment tool.

Checkpoint Answers

1. Personal selling provides information that a marketing brochure or website cannot. A salesperson can persuade a customer to make a decision about how to meet a need or want.
2. field sales, industrial sales, and organizational sales

3. These are sales from a business to a nonprofit organization.
4. Some call c enters specialize in *inbound* calls, or customers calling into the center. Other call centers specialize in *outbound* calls, or salespeople making customer calls.
5. A salesperson needs to be able to bounce back from disappointments, learn from mistakes, and move on to the next sale.

Build Your Vocabulary Answers

Definitions for these terms can be found in the glossary of this text.

Section **26.2** Selling

After completing this section, you will be able to
- **describe** ways to prepare to sell.
- **list** the steps in the sales process.
- **explain** ways to handle a lost sale.

preapproach
feature-benefit selling
lead
cold calling
approach
service approach
greeting approach
merchandise
  approach

substitute selling
objection
excuse
close
buying signal
overselling
suggestion selling

In order to be effective in a sales role, it is necessary to take steps to prepare for approaching customers correctly. Do an Internet search on *preparing to sell.* Outline the steps that will help you prepare for selling.

Selling is not a career that is appropriate for everyone. Do you think sales might be a good career choice for you? Write down your thoughts about why a career in sales would or would not be a suitable choice for you.

Preparing to Sell

A salesperson does not just go out and start selling. There are specific tasks that must be completed before making contact with the customer. The **preapproach** consists of tasks that are performed before contact is made with a customer. These tasks include product training and identifying potential customers.

Product Training

Product training is the first step in becoming a knowledgeable salesperson. It is important that the salesperson understands the product and can answer customer questions accurately. Sales training is generally a joint effort of the sales and marketing teams. The marketer or product trainer typically conducts training for new salespeople on how to use and sell the product. Ongoing training is usually provided throughout the year for the entire sales team. Many companies usually hold sales meetings on a regular basis. Sales meetings are a good place to introduce new products and for sales people to exchange selling tips.

The marketing team provides catalogs, brochures, and other materials presenting the features and benefits of the products. A competitive analysis helps the sales team to know how products compare with the competition. The **feature-benefit selling**

Many companies offer both formal and informal training for their sales reps.

Golden Pixels/Shutterstock.com

approach is the method of showing the major selling features of the product and how it benefits the customer. This is also known as *solution selling*. It is vital that the salesperson can convey how the product satisfies the needs of customers and makes their lives better or easier.

Product pricing is reviewed in depth so customer questions can be answered. Many companies have specific pricing levels that may vary depending on the customer, amount purchased, and other factors. Pricing is a very important part of the sale.

Products, such as financial investments, may require more formal training and certification. To gain this certification, accredited classes may be required at a local university. This training may take weeks or months to complete.

Other types of formal training may be provided by the company in a class or workshop format. A product expert may offer classes on a product, such as a piece of equipment, so that the salesperson understands how the product works. The marketer may follow this training with how to sell the feature and benefits of the product.

Informal training take places on an individual level. A salesperson will study and become familiar with the catalog, brochures, and information on the website about how to use the product. Most products are sold with printed information, such as care tags, content labels, and user manuals. Other print sources may include publications from manufacturers, consumer publications, and trade publications. Manufacturers often provide videos, booklets, and samples of their products.

The product itself can be the best source of information. If the product is consumable, such as food, the salesperson may do a taste test to understand the product. If the product is a piece of equipment, such as a lawn mower, it is helpful to use it before trying to sell it to a customer. A salesperson may be required to do a product demonstration, so the more that is known about the product, the better the demonstration will be.

Engage

Bring in a variety of items. Have students research the product and develop a chart listing the features and benefits.

Explain

Describe the differences between formal and informal training. Why are both necessary?

Identify Potential Customers

The next step in the approach stage of selling is identifying potential customers. Potential customers are often called **leads** or *prospects.* For a salesperson in a retail situation, the customers may walk in the store. However, for salespeople who need to call on customers, they must start with a list of contacts.

Identifying sales leads is used most often in B2B sales. Customer leads are generated in a variety of ways. Customers visiting a trade show may ask for someone to contact them about more information. People who visit a website or call customer support may ask for a salesperson to call them. A larger company may have a dedicated sales staff that generates leads. Some companies will purchase names of potential sales leads. Often, it will be a combination of one or more ways to acquire sales leads.

Once a sales lead is identified, it is important to gather additional information. The buyer or decision maker within that organization should be identified. Before making contact, the salesperson should know as much as possible about the company. Information about the company such as size, the current supplier the company is using, and the purchasing practices should be learned before making a call. Learning about the customer is called *qualifying the lead.* A customer's and salesperson's time is valuable. Calling on people who are not interested in buying a product may not be a productive use of time. It is important to know that the lead is qualified and may generate a sale.

However, cold calling is another way to prospect. **Cold calling** is the process of making contact with people who are not expecting a sales contact. Most sales forces use a customer-relationship management (CRM) system in which customer information is

Explain

Sales leads are an important topic of concern for salesperson. Ask a student volunteer to explain the need for leads and cold calling.

entered on a regular basis. The CRM system will have a list of potential customers for whom a rep may contact. Other cold calls may be based on phone directories, lists from a Chamber of Commerce, or other data sources.

In the context of selling, *prospecting* is the process of finding potential customers. Nearly every marketing activity is designed to generate prospects.

Sales Process

The *sales process* is a series of steps that a salesperson goes through to help the customer make a satisfying buying decision. There are generally six steps in the process as shown in Figure 26-1.

Sales Process
1. Approach the customer.
2. Determine the customer's needs.
3. Present the product or service.
4. Answer questions or objections.
5. Close the sale.
6. Provide follow-up after the sale.

Goodheart-Willcox Publisher

Figure 26-1 The six steps of the sales process should be followed in order to ensure customer satisfaction and a successful sale.

Approach the Customer

The **approach** is the step in which the salesperson makes the first in-person contact with a potential customer. That first contact is important to a successful sale. A salesperson should always lead with a handshake

College and Career Portfolio

Soft Skills

Employers and colleges review candidates for various positions. For example, the ability to communicate effectively, get along with customers or coworkers, and solve problems, are important skills for many jobs. These types of skills are often called *soft skills.* You should make an effort to learn about and develop soft skills you will need for your chosen career area.

1. Do research on the Internet to find articles about soft skills and their value in helping employees succeed.
2. Make a list of the soft skills that you possess that you think would be important for a job or career area. Select three of these soft skills. Write a paragraph about each one describing your abilities in this area. Give examples that illustrate your skills.
3. Save the document file in your e-portfolio. Place a printed copy in the container for your print portfolio.

and an introduction. It is customary to give the customer a business card. A salesperson should always

- be appropriately dressed;
- have good posture;
- smile;
- have pleasant tone of voice and clear speech;
- make direct eye contact; and
- focus on the customer.

Researchers say that strangers form an opinion of you within seven to 17 seconds. Many sales experts say that customers decide within four minutes whether they want to continue working with you. In those four minutes, you have to accomplish the following:

- get the customer's attention;
- project a positive, professional image of yourself and your products;
- show true concern and interest in the needs of the customer;
- show that you are trustworthy and honest; and
- make the customer feel comfortable.

Business-to-Business (B2B)

In business-to-business calls, the salesperson will typically make an appointment so the customer is expecting the visit. It is

important for the salesperson to be on time and prepared to present the product, leave brochures, and answer any questions the customer may have. B2B sales are often based on relationship selling, so it is acceptable to talk about current events or other conversation starters.

Business-to-Consumer (B2C)

B2C calls will typically be in a retail situation. Three types of approaches are often used in this setting: the service approach, the greeting approach, and the merchandise approach.

The **service approach** starts with the phrase "May I help you?" It is the most common sales approach and works well in many situations. Another wording for the service approach is "What can I help you with today?" This question might lead to a fuller response from the customer instead of "no thanks." However, the customer might still say "Nothing" or "I'm just browsing." A good response to a "no thanks" response is, "If you need anything, let me know."

The **greeting approach** consists of a friendly welcome to the store or department. Words, such as "hi," "hello," or "good afternoon" should be used. A genuine smile and

Explain

Teach students an easy approach using the acronym GNAP. G = Greeting (always formal – Hello, Good morning, Good afternoon, Good evening), N = Name (full name), A = Affiliation (company), and P = Purpose. This is a great way to present yourself to a customer. The rest of the conversation can flow from there. For example, "Hello, Mr. Jones, my name is Edwin Studebaker. I represent Steelcase, and I am here to meet with you about the new furniture line."

A good salesperson will provide helpful information and make the customer feel comfortable.

Alexander Raths/Shutterstock.com

eye contact helps make a positive impression. Calling customers by name when they enter the store is especially effective because it makes that person feel important.

The salesperson should customize what is said to each customer. If the salesperson knows the customer, that person can be approached with a personal greeting. If the salesperson does not personally know the customer, that person can be made to feel comfortable by making a comment on something that can be observed. For example, if the customer is wearing a sports team T-shirt, a remark can be made on the standing of the team. A comment on the weather or traffic is trite, but it often works. A compliment can also be a good way to make a connection.

In the **merchandise approach,** the conversation starts with a comment about the product. This approach works well when the salesperson takes notice which product the customer is considering. For example, a customer in a sporting goods store is holding a running shoe. The salesperson might walk up to the customer and say, "That shoe is on sale today for half price." The customer is provided with a money-saving tip, which can establish an immediate rapport. Product features are also used in a merchandise approach. Details such as availability, color, dependability, material content, newness, price, quality, size, special features, style, and warranty can be good conversation starters.

Often a combination approach works best. For example, a customer in a sporting goods store is holding a fishing rod. A comment such as, "Hi, Mr. Campos. Those fishing poles just arrived today and are selling like crazy." This approach combines the greeting and merchandise approaches. The salesperson made the customer feel welcome and provided information that might help sell the item.

Explore

Have students create a poster with each of the approaches. On the poster place a picture of a product and write one of each approach for the product along with the definition of the approach.

Determine the Customer Needs

The marketing concept of meeting customer needs is very important in the selling process. In a B2B selling situation, the needs may be defined during the qualifying process. In a B2C selling situation, the needs will probably be determined during the approach.

There are many reasons why customers buy a product. *Rational buying motives* are based on reason. For example, in a B2B sale, the customer knows that certain merchandise must be purchased for inventory—so the business can resell the products.

Emotional buying motives are based more on feelings than reason. For example, in a B2C sale, the customer may struggle over selecting a blue or red car. *Loyalty buying motives* are based on customer loyalty to a company with which they always do business. It is important that the salesperson understand the customer and the specific needs to be met.

There are three ways to determine customer needs and wants: observation, questioning, and listening. All three of these skills intersect as shown in Figure 26-2.

Observation is the first step in learning about the customer. Much can be learned through nonverbal communication. Recall from Chapter 22 that *nonverbal communication* is the expression or delivery of messages through actions, rather than words. This is often called *body language*. Behavior is also a part of nonverbal communication. Examples of nonverbal communication are facial expressions, raising an eyebrow, or the shrugging of shoulders.

The goal of questioning is to learn about the different needs and wants of different customers. The salesperson will use the answers to determine which products to offer to satisfy those needs and wants. Four types of questions are useful.

- Yes/no questions require a response of only yes or no.
- Choice questions offer the customer choices, and request the customer to select one.
- Clarifying questions request the customer to provide more details about the product he or she wants, for example, "What size do you need?"
- Open-ended questions request the customer to describe his or her wants and needs and often begin with one of the five *Ws*: *who, what, when, where,* and *why.*

After you have identified what the customer is looking for, your questions can be more refined. You can then learn more about the details of the product solution. However, it is important not to ask any embarrassing questions or too many questions.

Hearing is a physical process, while listening is an intellectual process. Listening combines hearing with evaluating. In addition, listening often leads to learning more information. Questioning is useless if the salesperson does not listen to the response. Listening is a skill that can be learned and improved with experience. A salesperson must carefully listen to what the customer does and does *not* say in order to improve sales and customer satisfaction.

Present the Product or Service

The product presentation stage is the heart of the sales process. This is where desire is created for the product. It is a chance

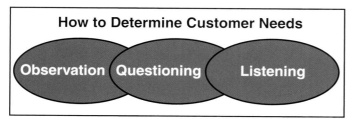

How to Determine Customer Needs

Observation   Questioning   Listening

Goodheart-Willcox Publisher

Figure 26-2 Good salespeople use all three techniques to learn how they can meet the needs of customers.

Engage

Have students choose a product. Then, ask students to write yes/no questions, multiple-choice questions, clarifying questions, and open-ended questions (two of each) that they might ask a customer about his or her product needs.

to tell the customer about the product, show how that product meets needs, and answer any questions or objections. It is the main opportunity for a salesperson to influence the customer to buy the product. Making a sales presentation is similar to an actor on a stage. The performance should be professional and polished. An unprofessional or unprepared presentation may lose a sale.

Select the Product

One of the keys to good selling is to select the appropriate products to show the customer. Knowing which products to show requires careful listening and extensive product knowledge on the part of the salesperson. Experience helps salespeople select appropriate products, as shown in Figure 26-3.

Substitute Sell

Sometimes, a customer may be looking for a specific brand that is not carried or is out of stock. Substitute selling is the technique of showing products that are different from the originally requested product. The goal is to get the customer to buy a different product that will still fit the need. It is important to not pressure the customer into buying something he or she does not really want. The customer must believe that the substitution is acceptable and that it will satisfy the original need.

Prepare the Presentation

In B2C sales, product presentations are usually informal. For example, in a retail store, the presentation may be showing an item off a rack and giving the price. Alternatively, for an automobile dealer, it might involve offering a test-drive and providing printed materials describing the features and benefits of the car.

In B2B sales, the salesperson often makes a formal presentation to a group of customers. Sales presentations are sometimes created by the marketing team. The salesperson can then take the presentation and customize it for his or her use.

Feature-benefit selling techniques that were learned in product training sessions are used. Many times a *script* is provided so that the presenter knows specifically what to say in each part of the presentation. A formal presentation may include an electronic slide show or short video focusing on the features and benefits of the product. Product samples may be given or marketing promotional items, such as coffee mugs, may be distributed. Marketing materials, such as a catalog, brochure, or sales sheet may be distributed.

A demonstration of the product or a website may also be appropriate. Demonstrations are most effective when the customer can actually try the product. While trying out

Figure 26-3
Successful salespeople are able to identify the best product to present to the customer.

Tips for Presenting Products to Customers
• If the customer requests a specific product, show that product first.
• If no specific request is made, show the product that seems most likely to fit the customer's needs.
• If it is not apparent which product will fit the customer's needs, show the most popular product or recently advertised product.
• If the product is available in a variety of price ranges, show a product in the middle price range.
• Show only two or three items at a time.
• Remove products that the customer has rejected as quickly as possible.

Goodheart-Willcox Publisher

Engage
In small groups, have students choose a product that a customer might want. They are then to brainstorm other products that could be sold to the customer as alternatives because their company no longer carries the initial product.

Substitute selling is the technique of showing the customer other product options when the original item requested is not available.

Monkey Business Images/Shutterstock.com

the product, customers often sell themselves on its benefits.

It is often effective to create a product display similar to, but smaller than, the one used for a trade show. Customers appreciate browsing the products the company offers. Having the opportunity to touch the product and get a firsthand look is beneficial to the sales process.

Answer Questions or Objections

During and after the presentation, the customer should be asked for comments and questions. Customers need to know why they should buy the product. It is important to reinforce the features and benefits of the product and how the purchase will make the individual's life easier or better.

Create Objections Grid

A salesperson should be prepared to overcome objections and excuses. **Objections** are concerns or other reasons a customer has for not making a purchase. **Excuses** are personal reasons not to buy.

One way to be prepared is to create a grid that shows common objections and excuses with responses to each. The marketing team may already have created this sales tool, so the salesperson should check to see if one is available. Remember, this grid is not for the customer to have, but to be used as reference for the salesperson.

Handle Objections

Objections give a salesperson insight into a customer's concerns. They also provide an opportunity to give information specific to that customer's needs.

It is important to listen, observe body language, and maintain eye contact. The customer should be allowed enough time to express the objection. Then, the salesperson should pause. A pause shows respect for the customer and the objection. It gives time to consider the objection and compose a response that meets this particular customer's needs.

The best way to show understanding of an objection is to empathize. To *empathize* means to show that you understand another person's feelings. The following statements work well:

- "I know how you feel."
- "I'm glad you asked that question."
- "I understand your concern."
- "You've made a good point."

Making these statements using a sincere tone of voice will encourage trust in the salesperson and help the customer communicate more freely.

Sales Objections or Excuses
• **Price:** "This price is more than I can afford."
• **Time:** "I was not planning to buy until the end of the season."
• **Need:** "Our store doesn't really need another product line to sell."
• **Product:** "I wanted blue pens instead of black pens."

Goodheart-Willcox Publisher

Figure 26-4 Some common objections and excuses may be based on these reasons.

Engage
Have students write objections and excuses for a product. Have them work with one or two other students to write responses to the objections and excuses.

Sometimes restating the customer's objection is helpful. Restating the objection shows that the customer's point of view is appreciated and understood. Specific product features or benefits can be restated that answer the objection. Then ask, "Have I answered your question?"

There is no right or wrong way to handle objections as long as courtesy and respect to the customer are given. Experience is the best teacher for deciding how to respond to a customer.

FYI

An effective sales person encourages trust and customer satisfaction.

Close the Sale

The goal of all sales activities is to close the sale. The **close** is the moment when a customer agrees to buy a product. It can occur at any point during the sales process. Some customers make decisions quickly and will decide to make a purchase soon after the approach or during a presentation. They might say, "I'll take it!" Giving the customer an opportunity to buy during the presentation is known as a *trial close.*

Other customers may be ready to buy, but they do not initiate the close. The salesperson's job is to determine when the customer is ready to buy and then close the sale. **Buying signals** are verbal or nonverbal signs that a customer is ready to purchase. Buying signals include comments, facial expressions, and actions. Buying signals often indicate mental ownership. Mental ownership has occurred when the customer acts and speaks as if the product is already his or hers. For example, the customer might say, "I have the perfect place for that in my living room." Evidence of mental ownership is an indication of readiness to buy.

Other customers require more time to make a decision. For those customers, there are different approaches to help them make the purchase, as shown in Figure 26-5.

The *assumption close* is used when it is assumed that he or she is going to purchase the product. "Mr. Wainwright, I will have the equipment delivered Thursday morning. Does that work into your schedule?"

The *bonus close* provides an additional *bonus*—either a free item or a second item at a reduced cost. Examples are buy one, get one free; or buy one, get one-half off. "Cynthia, if you purchase the mattress set today, the bed frame is included."

The *choice close* provides the customer with choices between two or three different products. The number of items to choose should be limited or the customer may become confused. "Mr. Lee, after using the one-stage and two-stage commercial coffee-maker, which do you prefer?"

The *satisfaction close* guaranteeing the customer will like the product. "Mr. Miller, you can try this worry-free for 60 days. If you aren't completely satisfied, you can return it for a full refund."

A *contingent close* is dependent on fulfilling a specific condition. "Ms. Stanis, if I can have the office furniture delivered and installed on Thursday, will that be soon enough for you?

The *direct close* is just that—asking the customer to buy. "Mrs. Clarkston, would you like me to finance the Ford Focus through Ford Credit?" is a direct close statement. This can sometimes be the best approach.

There are many ways to close a sale. However, salespersons should always avoid overselling, which is unethical. **Overselling** is promising more than the product or the business can deliver. The result might be a returned product, a customer who will never buy from the company again, or a lawsuit.

After the sale is closed, the salesperson may use suggestion selling. **Suggestion selling** is the technique of suggesting additional items to go with merchandise requested by a customer. Suggestion selling most often occurs after the customer has made a choice to purchase a specific item or items. For example, if a man buys a suit, the salesperson might recommend a shirt, tie, and belt that would go well with it. Often, the suggested item is something the customer needs but would have forgotten to buy. Customers are usually very appreciative when the salesperson knows enough to suggest appropriate merchandise.

FYI

Suggestion selling is also known as *up-selling*.

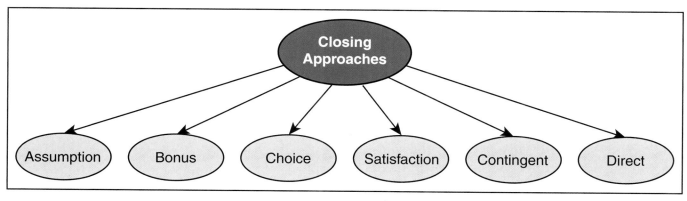

Goodheart-Willcox Publisher

Figure 26-5 While all of these closing approaches can be effective, the salesperson needs to allow the customer time to think about whether to make the purchase.

Engage

Ask students to discuss which closing approach they prefer from a salesperson. Students should support their answers with details and examples.

Case in Point

IBM

One important goal of most successful companies is to employ sales reps who are *solution providers* for the customer. Just making sales is not enough. Companies want the best and brightest sales representation that meets customer and business needs. To turn this goal into a reality, many companies provide their own training for sales reps to ensure selling excellence.

IBM is one example of a company that has a well-organized sales training program. The IBM program has multiple offerings to fit the needs of the individual sales employees, which also fulfills the needs of the company. Through live classroom instruction or virtual learning, participants can learn solution-based selling techniques. Classes are aimed at specific groups of employees to customize learning for the skills needed in their particular sales positions. These classes offer instruction not only on how to sell, but how to provide client satisfaction after the sale.

A company is only as successful as its sales team. As IBM has found, dedicating a large part of its resources for sales training is a win-win for everyone.

Provide Follow-Up after the Sale

After the transaction is complete, it is important for a salesperson to follow up with the customer. The purpose of following up after a sale is to ensure customer satisfaction. Customers have a large number of product choices and places to buy them. Research has shown that it is much more costly to find new customers than to keep current ones. One of the ways to keep customers is to follow up with them after a sale and make sure they are satisfied. Following up after the sale is part of relationship selling in marketing. Relationship marketing sees the customer relationship as starting at the approach, continuing indefinitely, and including many purchases.

Confirmation includes contacting the customer after the sale to make sure that the customer is satisfied. This call gives the salesperson the opportunity to solve any problems that might have occurred and thus increases customer satisfaction with the product and the company. For example, a customer bought a dress that needed alterations. The salesperson would check with the alterations department to make sure that the dress and alteration instructions were received. Next, the salesperson would check to see if the customer picked up the dress. Finally, the salesperson would call the customer to make sure the alterations were satisfactory.

Many salespeople send personal thank-you notes after the sale. This note not only thanks the customer but also invites him or her to purchase additional products. It is appropriate to include a business card and an update on new products or sales.

Sometimes, salespeople make a thank-you phone call and use it as an opportunity to determine customer satisfaction. If there are problems, the salesperson can then take steps to correct them.

Lost Sales

Not every sales opportunity actually closes. Even the experienced salesperson who executes the sales process perfectly may not be able to convince the customer to buy.

Engage

Ask: Have you or your parents had follow-up service after a sale? How would you rate the experience? Explain.

Elaborate/Extend

Assign the College and Career Readiness Portfolio activity at the end of the chapter.

For lost sales, it is necessary to evaluate exactly what happened and why. Customer feedback may provide reasons why the purchase was not made. It could be due to factors beyond the control of the salesperson, such as price, wrong product selection, delivery options, etc.

Feedback from coworkers or supervisors on the execution of the sales process may also be helpful. An impartial observer may be able to point out something that went wrong in the sales process. For example, perhaps the salesperson was not working with the proper decision maker in the company. Maybe the customer wanted accurate pricing information that the salesperson could not provide.

The most important thing to remember is that keeping a good attitude is important to do well in a sales career. Rejection is part of the process. Learning from experiences, both good and bad, will help close future sales.

Checkpoint 26.2

1. What are the steps in the preapproach stage of selling?
2. What are the six steps in the sales process?
3. What are the three types of approaches used in B2C selling?
4. Name three product features that can be used in the merchandise approach.
5. What are three types of motives that explain why a customer buys a product?

Build Your Vocabulary

As you progress through this course, develop a personal glossary of personal marketing terms and add it to your portfolio. This will help you build your vocabulary and prepare you for a career. Write a definition for each of the following terms, and add it to your personal marketing glossary.

preapproach
feature-benefit selling
lead
cold calling
approach
service approach
greeting approach
merchandise approach
substitute selling
objection
excuse
close
buying signal
overselling
suggestion selling

Section **26.3** After the Sale

Objectives

After completing this section, you will be able to
- **explain** the importance of customer service to the success of a business.
- **discuss** the importance of order processing to the success of a business.
- **describe** the functions of a customer support team.

Key Terms

customer service
quality service
customer-service
   mindset
customer support
   team

Web Connect

Customer service is an important asset for all businesses. Do an Internet search on *customer service*. Give examples of creative customer-service solutions that some companies have taken to win customers.

Critical Thinking

"The customer is always right." How many times have you heard this phrase? In your own words, interpret what you think this means.

Customer Service

You are no doubt familiar with the term *customer service*. **Customer service** is the way in which a business provides services before, during, and after a purchase. Successful businesses also provide good customer service. However, customer service means different things to each individual. For example, when you visited the website of a company, did it provide the information you were looking for? When you returned a purchase, was the salesperson courteous and helpful?

Good customer service should be provided by all employees in a company as a part of the marketing concept. *Company image* is often projected through employee performance. Whenever any employee has direct or indirect contact with a customer, customer service is provided in some form. It could be as simple as answering a question or saying *hello* when someone enters a store.

Obviously, the sales team is the first line of contact with a customer. The salesperson in a retail store or a restaurant probably has the first encounter with the customer. A successful business expects quality service from its sales team. **Quality service** meets customer needs as well as the standards for customer service set by the company. The difference between poor service and quality service is the difference between a sullen salesperson and a smiling salesperson. It is the difference between rushing customers to make a decision and giving them enough time and information to be comfortable and make a satisfying decision. It is the difference between a salesperson irritably saying, "No,

Customer service is important to any consumer who spends his or her hard earned money for a product or service.

dotshock/Shutterstock.com

we don't do that" and a salesperson cheerfully saying, "Let me see what I can do for you."

Exceptional customer service is service that meets and exceeds customer needs. The phrase *going above and beyond* is often used to refer to exceptional customer service. Every business can provide exceptional customer service. Businesses that are committed to the marketing concept focus their energies on the customer, including quality customer service. Businesses that succeed in providing exceptional customer service develop a customer-service mindset in all their employees. A **customer-service mindset** is the attitude that customer satisfaction always comes first.

Order Processing

An important part of customer service is efficient order processing. After the sale is complete, the product is transferred to the customer. In a retail situation, the customer typically leaves with the purchase. In a B2B sale, it will involve a purchase order and delivery arrangements.

Recall that a transaction is the exchange of payment and product. In retail sales, the transaction happens immediately. It is important that the merchandise is packed carefully. In a B2C sale, the customer will pay with cash, check, credit card, or debit card. For larger sales, such as an automobile, loans may be obtained by the customer. Good customer service is essential after the sale as well as during the sale.

For B2B sales, the customer will typically issue a purchase order and pay later with a check. Shipping will be arranged and any specific directions will be given.

In telemarketing or business sales, the transaction includes taking and processing the order plus arranging for shipment and payment. Courtesy and efficiency are important in this step. Paperwork must be handled quickly and accurately. An error made in a catalog number or price will create problems for the customer.

Extend
Ask students to describe order processing and the steps taken when ordering online from Amazon or some other e-tailer.

Companies that provide exceptional customer service usually ask for customer feedback, which is used to meet customers' needs in the future.

Customer Support Team

Even though customer service is provided by all employees, an organized customer support team is usually a part of the sales and marketing department. The **customer support team** consists of the employees who assist customers, take orders, or answer questions coming into the company via phone or website.

Marketing plays an important role in providing product information and training to the customer support team. Information about product features and benefits, pricing, and other vital information is usually provided by the marketer. Catalogs, brochures, and other marketing materials are sent to the customer support team so that they are aware of the information customers receive.

Receiving information from the customer is as equally important as giving information. Customer support training usually includes suggestions on how specific feedback can be gained from customers. For example, the customer may be asked how he or she learned about the product that is

being ordered. If it was from a brochure, the support person may ask for the number on the brochure. This information can then be sent to marketing to track metrics to evaluate the success of a marketing campaign.

A customer support person may also ask for feedback on a product that a customer ordered. Questions about likes and dislikes or what could be improved about the product can be asked of customers. This information can then be sent to the product development team to help create better product.

Online Support

Many organizations provide 24/7 customer support online. This support is usually through a website or social media. Online support can take several different forms and provide many types of information. Customers then have the option of using the support type for which they are most comfortable. Some company websites offer all forms of online customer support. Other

Elaborate/Extend

If students are using the optional *Marketing Dynamics* workbook, assign activities to engage active learning.

Elaborate/Extend

Provide an opportunity for students to exhibit their understanding of concepts in context of the material as it is presented. As time permits, have students read and discuss the special features in the margins.

organizations can only offer one or two. Online support is convenient for customers because they can find answers at the best times for them.

Frequently Asked Questions (FAQ) Pages

Frequently asked questions (FAQ) pages are the part of a website that gives detailed answers to questions or issues that show up the most often. FAQ pages are effective in answering customer questions quickly without taking the time of a support person. If new questions or issues are raised through e-mail or by phone, they can be added to the FAQ page.

E-mail Support

Many issues can be solved through e-mail, which is a fast and efficient online support option. However, when using e-mail support, the turnaround time to answer customer inquiries and issues is critical. A business must have sufficient personnel to respond to customer questions.

Product Tracking

Customers appreciate being able to track their orders. When orders are placed, the tracking information and link is sent to the customers by e-mail. The link provides a way to check the shipping progress at any time.

Online Chat

Perhaps the fastest-growing form of online customer support is the ability for customers to chat online with a support rep. Customers interact with staff dedicated to answering their questions and problem solving. One advantage to customer online chat support is the responses are immediate and problems can usually be solved quickly.

Social Media

Social media is a great way to address customer issues directly. Facebook and Twitter allow customers to post both positive and negative feedback. The person in charge of monitoring the company social media can

Customers appreciate the option of working through problems with customer service representatives in real time from the comfort of their own homes.

Andy Dean Photography/Shutterstock.com

Resource/Evaluate

Assign the optional Chapter 26 test for **EXAM**VIEW® Assessment Suite as a formal assessment tool.

Explain

Almost all e-tailers have FAQ pages. Print some examples to share with the class. Have students ever used this type of product support? Extend the discussion.

immediately address any questions or solve problems.

Discussion Boards

Discussion boards are public. Any customer or product user can answer the questions other customers might have. Discussion boards free the support staff to work with other customers. Discussion boards can also be used to post timely announcements, much like using social media.

Handling Customer Complaints

Customers bring all kinds of opportunities with them. Customers also create new opportunities when they disagree with store policies or make demands. The following are some common customer service problems:

- product is out of stock;
- store does not have the right size or color;
- salesperson does not speak the customer's language;
- customer becomes angry or upset over a store policy; for example, the store does not take his credit card or will not give a full cash refund; and
- not enough staff is available to efficiently help customers.

Customer service reps are trained to be polite and carefully handle unhappy customers. There will be company policies on how to address specific customer complaints. If the customer service rep is unable to resolve the issue, the call will probably be transferred to a supervisor.

Checkpoint 26.3

1. Which employees should provide customer service in a company?
2. What is the difference between quality service and exceptional service?
3. What is the difference between order processing in retail and B2B selling?
4. List two common customer service problems.
5. What are customer service reps trained to do?

Build Your Vocabulary

As you progress through this course, develop a personal glossary of personal marketing terms and add it to your portfolio. This will help you build your vocabulary and prepare you for a career. Write a definition for each of the following terms, and add it to your personal marketing glossary.
customer service
quality service
customer-service mindset
customer support team

Chapter Summary

Section 26.1 Role of Sales

- As with other components of promotion, personal selling applies the marketing concept of customer satisfaction. By meeting customer needs with a product or service, a company can grow company sales.
- Becoming a salesperson can be a rewarding career. While some people have a natural talent for sales, most people can learn the skills and develop the qualities of a successful salesperson.

Section 26.2 Selling

- There are specific tasks that must be done before selling to a customer. The preapproach consists of tasks that are performed before contact is made, such as product training and identifying potential customers.
- The six steps in the sales process are: approach the customer, determine the customer needs, present the product or service, answer questions or objections, close the sale, and provide follow-up after the sale.
- For lost sales, it is necessary to evaluate exactly what happened and why. Customer feedback may provide reasons why the purchase was not made.

Section 26.3 After the Sale

- Good customer service should be provided by all employees in a company as a part of the marketing concept.
- An important part of customer service is efficient order processing.
- The customer support team includes the employees who take orders or answer questions coming into the company via phone or website.
- Online support can take several different forms and provide different types of information. Frequently asked questions, e-mail support, product tracking, online chat, social media, and discussion boards are often provided through online support.

Review Your Knowledge

1. When is an Internet sale also considered a personal sale?
2. Why is it important for a salesperson to qualify the lead?
3. After a sales transaction is complete, what is the purpose of the follow-up?
4. Where can a salesperson gather contacts for cold calling?
5. What is the best way to show a customer you understand their objections?
6. What do buying signals usually indicate?
7. Why is following up after a sale important?
8. Name six forms of online customer support.
9. Identify an advantage to customer online chat support.
10. Explain how discussion boards are used to support customer service.

Apply Your Knowledge

1. As a marketing manager for the company for which you are writing a marketing plan, identify the role of the sales force in your company. Is the sales force operating in a B2B or B2C selling market?
2. Most businesses offer more than one product or service. List several ideas or suggestions for selling opportunities in your company.
3. The sales team will need product training for new products and ongoing training for the existing line of product. Make a list of the types of training you anticipate they will need.
4. Make a list of the features and benefits of the main product the sales team will be selling.
5. Research the Internet for companies that can provide customer leads for your industry. Make notes on the information that you find.
6. Draw a flowchart for the sales process for your sales team.
7. Give two ideas on how your company sales team could close a sale for your product.
8. What types of online customer service does your company offer? Which do you think customers use most often?
9. Write a one-page summary about what you believe is the difference between customer service and excellent customer service. Provide at least two examples.
10. Create an outline of this chapter. Be sure to include any major ideas and vocabulary. As you study, use the outline to help you recall important information from the chapter.

Check Your Marketing IQ

Now that you have finished the chapter, see what you learned about marketing by taking the chapter posttest. If you do not have a smartphone, visit the G-W Learning companion website.
G-W Learning mobile site: www.m.g-wlearning.com
G-W Learning companion website: www.g-wlearning.com

6. Buying signals often indicate mental ownership and let the salesperson know the customer is ready to buy.
7. Follow up after a sale to ensure customer satisfaction; to keep customers; and to build a relationship with customers.
8. Six forms of online customer support are FAQ pages, social media, e-mail, online chat, product tracking, and discussion boards.
9. An advantage to online chat support is the responses are immediate; problems can usually be solved quickly.
10. Any customer or product user can answer the questions other customers might have. Discussion boards can also be used to post timely announcements.

Apply Your Knowledge Answers

Student answers will vary for questions 1–10.

Apply Your Knowledge Teaching Tip

At the end of this unit, students will write the next phase of the marketing plan. Please note that the Apply Your Knowledge

Questions prepare students for the next installment of the marketing plan that they are writing at the end of each unit. These questions help them assume the role of a marketing manager and begin applying concepts learned in the chapter. If your class is not participating in the marketing plan activity at the end of the unit, Apply Your Knowledge questions can be used by directing students to select a business of their choice and answer each question about that business. A good example to use for supply chain management information is Target. Visit their corporate website or do a search for Target distribution and supply chain.

Evaluate

Evaluate the students' understanding and knowledge. Assign the Chapter 26 posttest. The test may be accessed by using the QR code or by going to the companion website. What questions were students able to answer that they could not answer when they took the pretest?

Common Core

College and Career Readiness

CTE Career Ready Practices. Sales and marketing people must apply appropriate technical skills to selling product. Make a list of ways that a salesperson would demonstrate technical skills when selling a computer to an adult consumer.

Writing. Create a sales script for selling a computer to an adult consumer. Write the script in a step-by-step format. The narrative should be clear and developed so that it is appropriate to the task of selling to the target audience.

Speaking. Select a member of your class to whom you will present the sales script from the last activity. Make use of displays or demonstrations to enhance the presentation.

Teamwork

Working with a teammate, select a DECA role-play activity that involves selling. Discuss and then write how you would role-play the situation. Have each teammate act as the salesperson and as a judge. Use the evaluation sheet provided to rate each individual. Write a plan for how you would improve the next time.

G-W Learning Mobile Site

Visit the G-W Learning mobile site to complete the chapter pretest and posttest and to practice vocabulary using e-flash cards. If you do not have a smartphone, visit the G-W Learning companion website to access these features.

G-W Learning mobile site: www.m.g-wlearning.com

G-W Learning companion website: www.g-wlearning.com

Marketing Plan

The marketing plan is almost complete. The promotion plan activities for this unit are the most time-consuming part of the marketing plan. Build adequate time into your schedule for completing this activity.

Unit 7 **Promotion Dynamics**
Building the Marketing Plan

Promotion may be one of the most important functions of marketing. It is the job of marketers to communicate with potential customers about what products are available and why people should buy those products. It is said that without products, there would be no businesses. However, without promotion, there would not be enough sales to keep the businesses profitable or open. The most effective form of promotion is through integrated marketing communications (IMC), or using elements of the promotional mix in a coordinated way.

Part 1 **Promotional Strategies**
Objectives

- Write promotional strategies for the elements of the promotional mix.

Directions

In this activity, you will complete the Marketing Strategies section of the marketing plan. The marketing strategies are the decisions made about product, price, place, and promotion. Access the *Marketing Dynamics* companion website at www.g-wlearning.com. Download the data files for the following activities.

1. **Unit Activity 7-1. Promotional Plan Objectives.** Each product or service may need its own individual promotion plan that will be included in the overall marketing plan. Write the objectives for your promotional plan.
2. **Unit Activity 7-2. Promotional Mix.** List and describe each part of the promotional mix for your campaign. Describe strategies for each part of the promotional mix: advertising, public relations, sales promotions, and personal selling. Include the job title of the team member responsible for managing or completing each activity. This information will be included in the final action plan.
3. **Unit Activity 7-3. Electronic Promotions.** You will incorporate electronic media in your plan. Create a grid of the electronic marketing activities you will be using for this promotion. Include the job title of the team member responsible for managing or completing each activity. This information will be included in the final action plan.
4. Open your saved marketing plan document. Locate the Marketing Strategies section of the plan. Write the Promotional Strategies subsection. Use the suggestions and questions listed to help you generate ideas. Delete the instructions and questions when you are finished recording your responses. Proofread your document and correct any errors in keyboarding, spelling, and grammar. Save your document.

Part 2 **Marketing Tactics**
Objective

- Create an action plan for your promotional plan.

Directions

In this activity, you will complete the Marketing Tactics section of the marketing plan. Marketing tactics are the specific activities used to carry out the promotional strategies. Access the *Marketing Dynamics* companion website at www.g-wlearning.com. Download the data file for the following activities.

1. **Unit Activity 7-4. Budget.** You have identified the campaign and promotional elements for your promotion plan. Now you will create the budget using electronic spreadsheet software.

2. **Unit Activity 7-5. Calendar.** Next, you will create the calendar for the promotional plan activities using electronic spreadsheet software. List each promotional activity in the order it will be performed. Next to each activity should be the job title of the person responsible, the start date to create the marketing piece, and the date each marketing piece must be finished or delivered. If it is a form of advertising, the start and end dates of the ad campaign must also be listed.

3. **Unit Activity 7-6 Action Plan.** Create an action plan for the promotional plan. The action plan includes a detailed timeline, budget, person responsible, and the metrics used to evaluate the effectiveness of the campaigns in the promotional plan. You will combine the necessary information from Unit Activities 7-2 through 7-5 to create the complete action plan using electronic spreadsheet software.

4. Open your saved marketing plan document. Locate the Marketing Tactics section of the plan. Reference the action plan here and place the final action plan in the Appendices section of the marketing plan. Use the suggestions and questions listed to help you generate ideas. Delete the instructions and questions when you are finished recording your responses. Proofread your document and correct any errors in keyboarding, spelling, and grammar. Save your document.

Dynamics of Marketing Management

Chapters

Eye-Catcher

Jeff Schultes/Shutterstock.com

Marketing Matters

Many products are created for use in the world of work. For those products, savvy marketers advertise where working people can see the product, hopefully use it, and experience its features and benefits. For example, Oracle exhibits at a technology conference in hopes of attracting new customers who may be looking for hardware or software for their business. Useful products reflect the marketing concept of customer satisfaction and lead to increased sales.

Marketing Core Functions Covered in This Unit

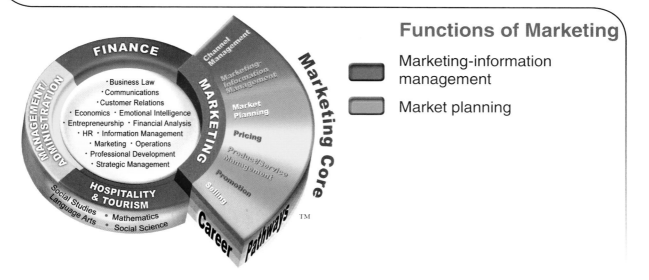

Functions of Marketing

- Marketing-information management
- Market planning

Developing a Vision

All employees are managers in some sense of the word. Management is the process of controlling and making decisions about a business. However, all managers do not manage people, but may manage projects instead.

Good management skills are not developed overnight. Like other skills, management skills take time and patience to develop. Determine how to be a team player and respect those with whom you work. Listen when fellow workers or customers talk to you. Learn from your experiences.

If you become a manager of people, there are many critical management functions and processes that must be mastered. Performing the management functions of planning, organizing, staffing, leading, and controlling helps managers reach their goals and the goals of the company.

CHAPTER

27 Management Skills

Section **27.1** | Achieving Success
Section **27.2** | Managing Teams
Section **27.3** | Advancing Your Career in Marketing

"Remarkable social media content and great sales copy are pretty much the same: plain spoken words designed to focus on the needs of the reader, listener, or viewer."

—Brian Clark, founder, Copyblogger

College and Career Readiness

Reading Prep
Before reading this chapter, read the opening pages for Unit 8 and review the chapter titles. What predictions can you make about the information you will be reading. List any questions you might have before reading. Search for answers to these questions as you read the chapter.

Check Your Marketing IQ

G-W Mobile

Before you begin the chapter, see what you already know about marketing by taking the chapter pretest. If you do not have a smartphone, visit the G-W Learning companion website.
G-W Learning mobile site: www.m.g-wlearning.com
G-W Learning companion website: www.g-wlearning.com

Explore

Provide an opportunity for students to explore by assigning a hands-on activity. Assign the College and Career Readiness Reading Prep activity before students read the chapter. Reading Prep activities give students opportunity to apply the Common Core State Standards.

Engage

Assign the Chapter 27 pretest. The test may be accessed by using the QR code or going to the *Marketing Dynamics* companion website. Discuss which questions students were unable to answer.

◇DECA Emerging Leaders

Marketing Communications Team Decision-Making Event, Part 1

Career Cluster: Marketing
Instructional Area: Selling

General Performance Indicators

- Communications skills—the ability to exchange information and ideas with others through writing, speaking, reading, or listening
- Analytical skills—the ability to derive facts from data, findings from facts, conclusions from findings, and recommendations from conclusions
- Production skills—the ability to take a concept from an idea and make it real
- Teamwork—the ability to be an effective member of a productive group
- Priorities/time management—the ability to determine priorities and manage time commitments
- Economic competencies

Specific Performance Indicators

- Explain the nature of effective verbal communications.
- Employ communication styles appropriate to target audience.
- Make oral presentations.
- Explain the nature and scope of the selling function.
- Discuss motivational theories that impact buying behavior.
- Explain the key factors in building a clientele.
- Explain the role of customer service as a component of selling relationships.

Purpose

Designed for a team of two DECA members, the events measure the team's ability to explain core business concepts in the format of a case study in a role-play. This event consists of a 100-question multiple-choice cluster exam for each team member and a decision-making case study situation. The Team Decision-Making Event provides an opportunity for participants to analyze one or a combination of elements essential to the effective operation of a business in the specific career area presented as a case study.

For the purposes of this text, you will be presented with the material for this event in two parts. Part 1 presents the knowledge and skills assessed and an overview of the event's purpose and procedure. Part 2 presents the remaining procedures and the event situation.

Procedure, Part 1

1. For Part 1 in this text, read both sets of performance indicators. Discuss these with your team members.
2. If there are any questions, ask your teacher to clarify.

Critical Thinking

1. Evaluate the marketing methods used to meet customer needs.
2. How is the marketing mix achieved?
   Visit www.deca.org for more information.

Section 27.1 Achieving Success

After completing this section, you will be able to
- **describe** ways to achieve workplace success as a manager.
- **explain** the importance of the workplace environment.

interpersonal skill   initiative
diversity   adaptability
stereotyping   procrastination
empathy   multitasking
attitude   work habit
optimism   ergonomics
self-motivation

Research the phrase *interpersonal skills* on-line. Make a list of those skills you think are important when working with others. Note the skills that you already possess and the ones that you need to improve.

There are many reasons why people are fired from a job. Not being qualified is generally the top cause. However, there are other reasons why individuals are not successful in the workplace. List three other reasons why a person might be fired.

Successful Managers

As you have learned in this text, marketing is an important function of business as shown in Figure 27-1. All of the functions of business work together to create an effective organization.

Marketing, like the other business functions, must have management to lead the team. A *manager* is the person responsible for carrying out the goals of the department.

There are a number of skills that successful managers possess. The list is endless, depending on the type of business. However, successful managers all have the following things in common. They possess
- good interpersonal skills;
- a positive attitude;
- efficient time management skills;
- productive work habits; and
- control of his or her personal well-being.

Interpersonal Skills

Interpersonal skills are the group of skills that enable a person to interact with others in a positive way. Good interpersonal skills enable you to get along with your coworkers. These skills also help you interact effectively with customers and vendors. Good interpersonal skills contribute to success in your personal relationships as well.

Communication skills are at the core of interpersonal skills. Sending clear messages and being an active listener are the basis of good interpersonal skills. In addition to good communication skills, good interpersonal skills involve the following qualities.

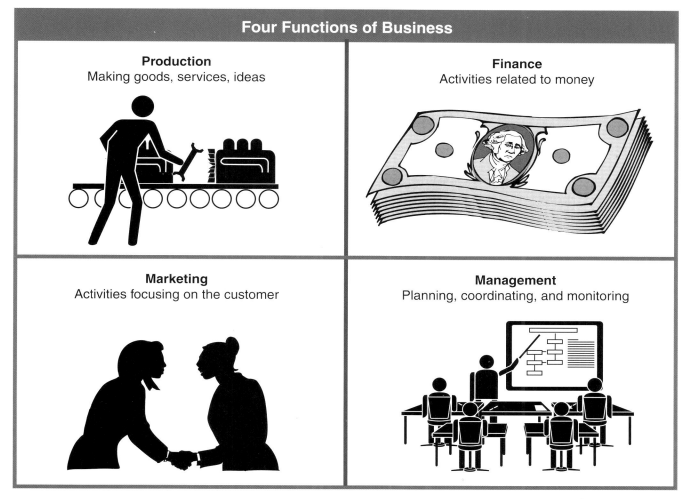

Goodheart-Willcox Publisher

Figure 27-1 Marketing managers play an important role in every business.

Respectfulness

Being respectful to those with whom you work is important to being a successful worker. As a member of a management team, you will come in contact with others in your organization as well as customers outside of the business. To show respect to those around you, always listen to what people are saying. Consider the point of view of others, and be polite and courteous.

Diversity means having people who are of different races or who have different cultures in a group or organization. The workforce is a diverse group of many different ages, ethnicities, physical and mental abilities, races, belief systems, and more. Successful workers overlook any differences to get along with everyone.

Classifying or making generalizations about a group of people with a given set of characteristics is known as **stereotyping.** It is not acceptable to stereotype. Stereotyping hinders business and communication efforts. These barriers can be overcome by focusing on issues and on the contributions of each person to the work at hand.

Extend
Review the four functions of business.

Engage
Discuss the importance of diversity in the workplace.

Showing respect and courtesy to others makes them feel important and valued. It also encourages them to show you respect and courtesy. Respect is especially important when you disagree with someone.

Empathy

Empathy is the ability to see things from the point of view of another person. As a result, you are better able to understand why people behave the way they do. With this better understanding, you can decide the best ways to respond to different employees. In addition, you will be able to respond better to peers and customers.

Open-Mindedness

Having an open mind means you are willing to consider a different point of view. It is impossible to be right all the time. Everyone makes mistakes. Learn how to accept criticism without taking offense. As a manager, learn how to give criticism in a tactful manner so that you do not hurt the other person's feelings.

Sense of Humor

A sense of humor is the ability to see the funny side of things. It is *not* making fun of others. People with a sense of humor are able to laugh together. Humor can be used to break tension and make communication easier.

Trustworthiness

Good interpersonal relations develop when people trust each other. Others see you as trustworthy when you keep your promises and deal fairly with them. Honesty and integrity are part of trustworthiness. Managers must be trustworthy to be effective.

Dependability

Dependable people are reliable. They follow through on their responsibilities. When they accept tasks, managers can depend on them to complete those tasks in a timely fashion.

Workers in the United States come from many types of families, educational backgrounds, and countries. An important interpersonal skill is learning how to get along with people whose ideas may be different from yours.

imaged.com /Shutterstock.com

Explain
Use humor with caution, as it can be risky, especially if dealing with people from different generations.

Engage
Ask students why a good attitude is important.

Attitude

Attitude is the way a person looks at the world and responds to events. Employers, customers, and coworkers want to be around people with a positive attitude. A positive and friendly attitude breeds optimism. **Optimism** is the expectation that things will turn out well.

Self-Motivation

Self-motivation is the inner urge to achieve set goals. Self-motivation includes a sense of enthusiasm about your work and your company. Self-motivated people have initiative. **Initiative** is the personal energy and desire that is needed to do something. People with initiative often come up with new ideas and ways to solve problems. Self-motivated people often volunteer for the challenging assignments.

Adaptability

Adaptability is the ability to make changes to be a better match, or fit, in new situations. The workplace is constantly changing. Every day brings new challenges and problems to solve. An adaptable person adjusts to changes and new conditions smoothly and with a positive attitude.

Time Management Skills

Time is limited. Managing that limited time is important in any job, especially for managers. Time management skills help you make the best use of time and help you get to places on time. For example, if your papers and tools are in order, you will not waste time trying to find them.

A major challenge to time management is handling paper, such as customer e-mails, coworker inquiries, and marketing files. One key to being organized is to handle each piece of paper only once. When a paper or message crosses your desk, do one of three things:

- act on it;
- file it; or
- toss or recycle it.

Create a system of file folders for paper documents so that papers relating to the same subject can be filed together. Label the folders so that you can easily find the papers on each subject. Take the same approach to

JohnKwan/Shutterstock.com

As you accomplish each activity, cross it off both your daily and master lists.

organizing your file folders on the computer. Do this for your e-mails as well as your electronic document files.

Tools for efficient time management include a calendar and a *to-do list.* Use your e-mail calendar on your computer, tablet, or phone. List all of your weekly, monthly, and annual appointments, meetings, and obligations. It is usually more efficient to keep personal and business items on the same calendar. It will help you to avoid conflicts between personal and business obligations.

Create to-do lists. A master to-do list is where you write down all the things you need to do in a week or other period of time. A daily to-do list is all the activities that you intend to accomplish that day.

Procrastination is the delay of doing something that should be done now. Procrastination can become a serious barrier to work success when it results in missed deadlines or substandard work. Start assigned tasks right away. The longer you put off a task, the more anxious and worried you are likely to become.

The term **multitasking** means performing several tasks at the same time. However, attempting to do more than one complex task at a time can cause workers to be less efficient and productive. For tasks that require quick action and decision making without complex thought, multitasking saves time and allows managers to accomplish more. For projects that require deep concentration and high accuracy, it is best to focus on only one task at a time.

Work Habits

Work habits are the basic, routine actions carried out every day at work. They provide the foundation for success at work. Good work habits, as shown in Figure 27-2, help you to be an efficient and productive employee and manager. Good work habits are similar to good study habits.

Good Work Habits
• Be on time.
• Be at work every day.
• Complete all work in a timely fashion.
• Keep your work area neat and organized.
• Check your work for accuracy.
• Report mistakes or problems immediately.
• Refrain from making personal calls from work.

Goodheart-Willcox Publisher

Figure 27-2 A successful businessperson practices good work habits.

Personal Well-Being

Personal well-being is also an important factor to being a successful manager. It starts with good health and appearance.

Good health is the foundation of everything you do in your life. However, good health is not automatic. Do not forget your health while you are trying to achieve career success. It is difficult to concentrate or do a good job when you are not feeling your best. Keep the following advice in mind to remain healthy.

- Get enough sleep. Most adults need seven to eight hours of sleep a night.
- Exercise regularly. Maintain fitness to keep your body in good condition.
- Eat a balanced diet. Include a variety of fruits and vegetables, and always eat a good breakfast.
- Avoid health risks. In America, obesity, tobacco use, and drug abuse are the biggest health risks.
- Manage stress. Prolonged periods of stress can contribute to a number of diseases, such as heart disease and high blood pressure.
- Balance work and home life. Do a good job at work, and then leave the office to enjoy your family.

Engage

Ask the students to think about a task that they decided to postpone doing until it was almost due. On a piece of paper, have them list the consequences of waiting to the last minute and then share those consequences either with a classmate or the entire class.

Explore

Show two pictures to the students, one with a person appropriately dressed for an interview contrasted with another showing a person with inappropriate interview attire. Ask students to name the items of apparel in each photo that will work for an interview as opposed to those that would not.

Dressing appropriately for the job will help you maintain a sense of confidence. Clothes that fit well, are clean, and are pressed reflect a professional image. If your workplace has a dress code, be certain to follow it. Be careful of "casual Fridays" and wear clothes that are respectable for your workplace. Project the image that you want people to remember about you.

Workplace Environment

The workplace environment is an important human resources issue. As a manager, you can do your part to make sure employees are in a comfortable, safe environment.

Ergonomics

Like other workers who spend long periods of time doing detailed work with a computer or tablet, marketers may be susceptible to eyestrain, back discomfort, and hand and wrist problems. Ergonomics is the science of adapting the workstation to fit the needs of the worker and lessen injury. Applying ergonomic principles results in a comfortable and efficient environment. There are many types of ergonomic accessories that may improve a computer workstation, including wrist rests, specially designed chairs, and back supports. Figure 27-3 identifies actions that can be done to create a comfortable environment and help prevent injury or strain to the operator's body.

Workplace Accidents

Falling hazards, lifting hazards, and material-storage hazards account for most of the workplace accidents that occur in offices. *Falling hazards* are sources of potential injuries from slipping or falling. Falls are the

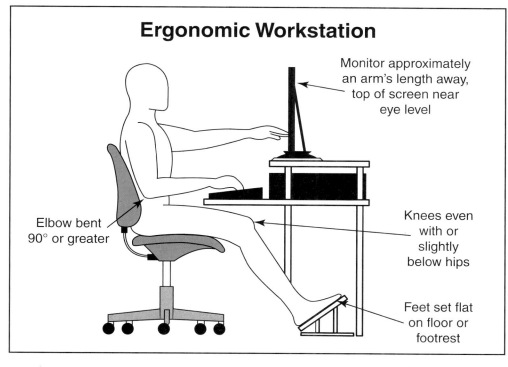

Ergonomic Workstation

Monitor approximately an arm's length away, top of screen near eye level

Elbow bent 90° or greater

Knees even with or slightly below hips

Feet set flat on floor or footrest

Goodheart-Willcox Publisher

Figure 27-3 Ergonomic workstations help prevent back and neck pain, eyestrain, and headaches caused by improper placement of monitors, chairs, and desks.

Explain

Use furniture, fixtures, and equipment in the classroom to illustrate ergonomic principles. Ask students to explain how specific features lessen the risk of injury.

Explore

Creating To-Do lists: www.studygs.net/todolist.htm/

Social Media

Targeting Posts on Facebook

Facebook has tools for businesses that allow only the most relevant people to see certain posts. There are two ways to target a post: limit the audience who can see it or add targeting filters. These tools make your page posts more efficient and are useful for special offers or for information only some people need. Even if people share your page's post with their friends, only those who are in the audience you choose for the post will be able to see it. Note: to limit *or* target your posts, first make sure your business page has *post privacy gating* turned on under *Manage Permissions.*

To limit a post's audience, select the dropdown *Public* menu after writing your post and select *Location/Language.* Type in the countries or languages of the people you want to see your post.

To add targeting filters, select the *target icon* in the sharing tool after writing your post. Select one or more filters: Gender, Relationship Status, Education, Interested In, Age, Location, or Language. As you add filters, the number of people your post is targeted to will update next to *Targeted to.* The more filters you add to a post, the fewer people will see it. The minimum number of people you can target your post to is 20.

---

most common workplace accident in an office setting. Falls can result in broken bones, head injuries, and muscle strains. Avoiding workplace falls is relatively simple:

- close drawers completely;
- do not stand on a chair or box to reach; and
- secure cords, rugs, and mats.

Lifting hazards are sources of potential injury from improperly lifting or carrying items. Most back injuries are caused by improper lifting. To avoid injuries resulting from lifting:

- make several small trips with items rather than one trip with an overly heavy load;
- use dollies or handcarts whenever possible;
- lift with the legs, not the back; and
- never carry an item that blocks vision.

Material-storage hazards are sources of potential injury that come from the improper storage of files, books, or office equipment. A cluttered workplace is an unsafe workplace. Material stacked too high can fall on employees. Paper and files that are stored

on the floor or hall are a fire risk. To prevent injuries:

- do not stack boxes or papers on top of tall cabinets;
- store heavier objects on lower shelves; and
- keep aisles and hallways clear.

Maintaining a safe workplace is the joint responsibility of the employer and employee. The employer makes sure the facility and working conditions are such that accidents are unlikely to occur. The employee uses common sense and care while at the office.

AMA Tip

The American Marketing Association provides valuable, relevant information to members and nonmembers through its Facebook and Twitter pages. Posts include links to articles and groundbreaking research, fun infographics, and updates from local AMA chapters. *Like* the AMA Facebook page and follow the AMA Twitter account for instant access. www.marketingpower.com

Explore
The CareerSafe Online Safety Awareness training course is designed to provide five hours of basic safety awareness training in either English or Spanish to youth who are currently or preparing to enter the workforce. Students who successfully complete the CareerSafe Online Safety Awareness training course receive a CareerSafe Online safety awareness training completion card.

Extend
With the Occupational Safety and Health Act of 1970, Congress created the Occupational Safety and Health Administration (OSHA) to assure safe and healthful working conditions for working men and women by setting and enforcing standards and by providing training, outreach, education and assistance.

Exploring Careers

Interactive Media Specialist

Everyone enjoys a good computer game, and in general, the better the graphics, the more enjoyable the game can be. An interactive media specialist creates the graphics, animations, 3D art, and special effects needed for computer games. They also provide graphics and animated sequences for music videos, films, commercials, and even full-length movies. Other typical job titles for an interactive media specialist are *animator, 3D artist, animation director,* and *creative director.*

Some examples of tasks that interactive media specialists perform include:

- create storyboards to show the intended animation of key scenes and characters;
- provide designs, drawings, and illustrations for multimedia presentations;
- create 2D and 3D images and animations using computer modeling and animation programs;
- write scripts for animated sequences; and
- create interactive sequences and animations for computer games and web pages.

Interactive media specialists need both artistic ability and creative vision. They must be skilled in using computer illustration, modeling, and animation software. Because they generally work under tight deadlines, interactive media specialists also need to be able to work well under pressure. A little more than half of the jobs in this field require a bachelor degree, usually in commercial arts or a related field. A well-developed portfolio to showcase graphics and animation skills is also helpful. For more information, access the *Occupational Outlook Handbook* online.

Checkpoint 27.1

1. List examples of interpersonal skills.
2. What should you do when a piece of mail crosses your desk?
3. List two tools for efficient time management.
4. What can you do to combat procrastination?
5. What are material-storage hazards?

Build Your Vocabulary

As you progress through this course, develop a personal glossary of personal marketing terms and add it to your portfolio. This will help you build your vocabulary and prepare you for a career. Write a definition for each of the following terms, and add it to your personal marketing glossary.

interpersonal skill
diversity
stereotyping
empathy
attitude
optimism
self-motivation

initiative
adaptability
procrastination
multitasking
work habit
ergonomics

Checkpoint Answers

1. They are empathy, respect, open-mindedness, humor, positive attitude, trustworthiness, and dependability.
2. You should act on it; file it; or toss or recycle it.
3. Two tools for efficient time management are a calendar and a to-do list.

4. Start assigned tasks right away. The longer you put off a task, the more anxious and worried you are likely to become.
5. Material-storage hazards are sources of potential injury that come from the improper storage of files, books, or office equipment.

Build Your Vocabulary Answers

Definitions for these terms can be found in the glossary of this text.

Section 27.2 Managing Teams

After completing this section, you will be able to
- **name** two types of basic teams.
- **list** the various skills that are essential for successful teams.
- **explain** how team leaders can conduct effective meetings.
- **describe** effective team members.

Key Terms

team
leadership
leader
collaboration
conflict
parliamentary
  procedure
motion
agenda

Web Connect

Effective teams use parliamentary procedure in their meetings. Do an Internet search on *parliamentary procedure.* Write a paragraph about the importance of following these guidelines when conducting a meeting.

Critical Thinking

Working in teams is important in the workplace. When individuals work together, a business can be more productive and employees can feel like they are making contributions. Write a paragraph on your opinion of the role of teams in business.

Types of Teams

Teams are an important aspect of the workplace. A **team** consists of two or more people who work together to achieve a common goal. Work teams have much in common with sports teams. In both situations, all members of the team must work together in order to achieve success.

Teams can be beneficial to business in the following ways.
- More people are involved in the decision making, and therefore the decisions are more likely to be implemented.
- Team members continually learn from each other.
- Discussions among team members often generate new ideas.

- A group of people in a team has more knowledge and resources than an individual.
- Teams are more likely to find and correct mistakes.
- Effective teams are usually more productive than individuals.

There are two basic types of teams: the functional team and the cross-functional team. In the *functional team,* each member has basically the same skills and qualifications. For example, sales teams are usually functional teams. All of the members of the team are salespeople.

In a *cross-functional team,* the members have different skills. For example, a product development team might be cross-functional. This team might be composed of a marketer, a design expert, an engineer, the production manager, and a salesperson.

Explore

Review the vocabulary terms at the beginning of the section. Where have students encountered these terms before? Help students make educated guesses about the meanings of the terms with which they are least familiar.

Engage

Use the Teamwork exercise at the end of the chapter to engage students to solve a problem or make a group presentation.

Team Skills

Team members need excellent communication and interpersonal skills. In addition, there are three other skill areas that are particularly valuable in a team: leadership, collaboration, and conflict resolution. Career and Technical Student Organizations (CTSO), such as DECA, which is the association for marketing students, Future Business Leaders of America (FBLA), Business Professionals of America (BPA), and SkillsUSA, provide many opportunities for working in teams and learning team skills.

Leadership

Leadership is the ability of a person to guide others to a goal. A person who guides others to a goal is called a **leader.** Leaders influence others and inspire excellence. Leadership skills are necessary for success in the workplace. Leadership skills are also valuable in other areas of life, such as in school, government, and civic organizations.

Some people are natural leaders, but most people can develop the traits that make a leader successful. The following traits are often identified with successful leaders: self-confidence, good communication skills, dependability, enthusiasm, flexibility, ability to set goals, ability to follow through, good problem-solving skills, and ability to inspire others.

Collaboration

Collaboration is working with others to achieve a common goal. Successful collaboration includes cooperation, sharing ideas and responsibilities, and compromising when necessary. When people compromise, each gives up a little of what he or she thinks is important, so the group can come to a decision or solve a problem.

Conflict Resolution

When people work together, there are likely to be some disagreements. Most people have different ideas of how to approach or

Working with others to prepare for a DECA group event can be both challenging and rewarding.

Konstantin Chagin/Shutterstock.com

Elaborate/Extend

Provide an opportunity for students to exhibit their understanding of concepts in context of the material as it is presented. As time permits, have students read and discuss the special features in the margins.

Extend

Ask for examples of conflicts and how they can be resolved.

handle situations. Successful teams, though, can manage disagreements to prevent them from becoming conflicts. A **conflict** is a situation in which disagreements lead to hostile behavior, such as shouting or fighting.

Disagreements can be useful. Disagreements about a solution to a problem often lead to a better solution. In these situations, all sides of the argument need to be presented and thoroughly discussed.

Disagreements can create problems when they develop into conflicts. The team leader, manager, or work supervisor has a special responsibility to manage disagreements and resolve conflicts. Sometimes conflicts are obvious. Other times, a team member will only tell the leader about a conflict. Figure 27-4 shows the steps in conflict resolution.

Effective Meetings

Meetings are a fact of life in the business world. Meetings are also important in government and civic organizations. If you are a member of student government, a club, or a CTSO, you have probably attended meetings. The general purpose of meetings is to make decisions or solve problems. A meeting is required

because more than one person is needed to make the decision or solve the problem.

Many meetings in the workplace are informal. A group of workers may get together to discuss a problem or coordinate their work. For example, some departments have weekly meetings. At these meetings, each person reports on the work that he or she has done during the preceding week. Any problems or projects that need input from other department members are discussed.

Sometimes, meetings are more formal. Formal meetings are usually run according to parliamentary procedure. **Parliamentary procedure** is a process for holding a meeting so that the meeting is orderly and democratic. Parliamentary procedure is based on the guidelines in *Robert's Rules of Order,* published in 1876. The central process of parliamentary procedure is proposing, discussing, and voting on motions. A **motion** is a recommendation for action to be taken by the group.

A key to accomplishing the goals of a meeting is to have a good leader of the meeting. The person running a formal meeting should be familiar with parliamentary procedure. A tool for keeping a meeting focused is an agenda. An **agenda** is the list of topics to be discussed, decisions to be made, or other goals for a meeting.

Figure 27-4 Most conflicts can be avoided by good leadership. However, when conflicts do arise, managers need to follow these proven steps to resolve the issue.

Steps to Resolve Conflict
1. Gather the facts: speak to people in private, and do not jump to conclusions.
2. Hold a meeting with everyone who is involved with the conflict. Make sure each person understands that he or she is responsible for the problem and its solution.
3 Brainstorm solutions. Make sure you get input from everyone involved.
4. Develop a workable solution. Focus on the behaviors that can be changed, rather than what a person says or thinks.
5. Gain agreement. When a solution has been agreed upon, make sure everyone understands and accepts it. This agreement may be either verbal or written or both.
6. Monitor the situation. Schedule a follow-up meeting to evaluate progress; if conflict continues, repeat the steps.

Goodheart-Willcox Publisher

Explore

Assign students to research parliamentary procedures. Have they ever used these in a meeting environment?

Extend

Use the Internet to find out the four steps to a motion, or the fixed order of business. www.robertsrules.org/rulesintro.htm/

In a meeting, a good leader is positive, supportive of all members, and knows how to keep the group focused.

Andrey_Popov/Shutterstock.com

A good meeting leader also knows how to move the discussion along without insulting anyone. For example, often there is one person at a meeting who wants to do all the talking. A skilled meeting leader will acknowledge that person, but also enable other people to talk.

Effective Team Members

An effective team is a team that accomplishes its goals. The first requirement of an effective team is to have effective team members. Effective team members participate fully in team meetings and complete team tasks. They contribute their ideas and feelings. Effective team members listen and are open to the ideas of other team members. They share information and provide help to other team members. They are reliable.

Effective team members have the ability to cooperate with each other. Cooperation is the willingness to do what it takes to get the job done. A cooperative worker follows

instructions and asks questions when he or she does not understand what to do.

Effective team members also have the ability to work well with a wide variety of people. Someone who has the ability to work with others is pleasant, agreeable, and does not create conflict or angry situations. Such a person understands and respects diversity. He or she can work with people from all kinds of backgrounds and points of view. He or she also knows how to resolve differences of opinion or conflicts in a positive way.

Effective team members are also committed to the success of the team and its goals. They feel an obligation to contribute. Teamwork on the job is much like being part of a basketball team or a drill team. The success of the whole team depends on the attendance, punctuality, good attitude, and skills of each person. If one team member does not perform well, the entire team will suffer. The same is true of teamwork on the job. Effective teams have the qualities shown in Figure 27-5.

Figure 27-5 Effective team members monitor the team processes and performance and work to improve them.

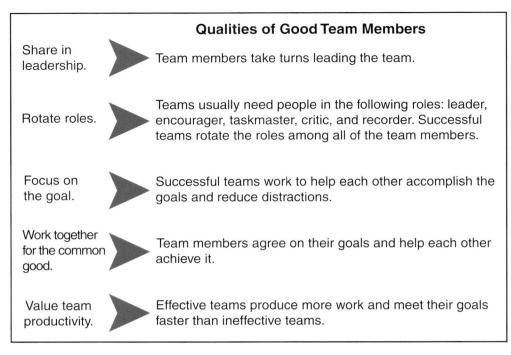

Qualities of Good Team Members

Share in leadership. ▶ Team members take turns leading the team.

Rotate roles. ▶ Teams usually need people in the following roles: leader, encourager, taskmaster, critic, and recorder. Successful teams rotate the roles among all of the team members.

Focus on the goal. ▶ Successful teams work to help each other accomplish the goals and reduce distractions.

Work together for the common good. ▶ Team members agree on their goals and help each other achieve it.

Value team productivity. ▶ Effective teams produce more work and meet their goals faster than ineffective teams.

Goodheart-Willcox Publisher

Checkpoint 27.2

1. Name two basic types of teams.
2. In addition to excellent communication and interpersonal skills, name three other skill areas that are particularly valuable on a team?
3. What happens when people compromise?
4. How can disagreements be useful?
5. What is the general purpose of meetings?

Build Your Vocabulary

As you progress through this course, develop a personal glossary of personal marketing terms and add it to your portfolio. This will help you build your vocabulary and prepare you for a career. Write a definition for each of the following terms, and add it to your personal marketing glossary.

team

leadership

leader

collaboration

conflict

parliamentary procedure

motion

agenda

Evaluate

Assign the Checkpoint questions at the end of the section. Assess students' comprehension using the Checkpoint activity as a self-assessment tool.

Checkpoint Answers

1. There are two basic types of teams: the functional team and the cross-functional team.
2. Three other skill areas particularly valuable in a team are leadership, collaboration, and conflict resolution.

3. When people compromise, each gives up a little of what he or she thinks is important so that the group can come to a decision or solve a problem.
4. Disagreements about a solution to a problem often lead to a better solution.
5. The general purpose of meetings is to make decisions or solve problems.

Build Your Vocabulary Answers

Definitions for these terms can be found in the glossary of this text.

Section 27.3 Advancing Your Career in Marketing

After completing this section, you will be able to
- **describe** ways an individual can advance a career.
- **explain** the adding of roles as an individual becomes an adult.

Key Terms

give notice
role

Web Connect

Do an Internet search on *continuing education*. What does the phrase mean to you? Write a paragraph on your findings.

Critical Thinking

Effective employees are always learning. This could include taking a class or completing self-study. List some ways that you think you could continue advancing your skills as you become part of the workforce.

Advancing Your Career

Some people are very happy with their jobs. They find their work to be challenging and rewarding. Some people want to advance because they have become bored with their jobs; they want to learn new skills and have new challenges. Others want to advance to make more money and take on different responsibilities. Active steps for advancement include continuing education, improving leadership skills, joining professional organizations, and, sometimes, changing jobs.

Continue Education

In order to advance, you must continually improve your job skills. Many employers offer classes and seminars for their employees. Take advantage of them. Some employers will pay for classes at a college or professional school if the classes are related to your job. Many professional organizations offer classes, workshops, and certification programs.

Explore

Review the vocabulary terms at the beginning of the section. Where have students encountered these terms before? Help students make educated guesses about the meanings of the terms with which they are least familiar.

Improve Leadership Skills

Leadership is a critical skill for people who want to get promoted to upper management or start their own businesses. You learned about the traits of a leader earlier in this chapter. You can gain valuable experience for a career by being in positions of leadership. People often develop leadership skills by volunteering to be team leaders at work.

People also develop leadership skills through involvement with social, community, civic, and professional organizations. As a student, involvement in Career and Technical Student Organizations (CTSOs), student government, clubs, and extracurricular activities can also provide leadership development opportunities. These groups are often willing to let someone with little experience but a lot of enthusiasm take leadership positions in their organizations. You can usually start small, for example, by chairing a committee. In addition, many of these groups offer leadership training.

Engage

Ask students why leadership skills are important to have even if you are not in a management position.

Leadership on high school sports teams is good preparation for leadership in the work-place.

Leadership skills learned in this way are directly transferable to the job.

Join Professional Associations

Involvement in professional associations is one of the main ways to keep up-to-date in your career. Professional associations usually have magazines, newsletters, and websites where they publish industry and career information. Many associations have monthly meetings and events. Here, you can learn about the latest trends and technology, meet others in your career, network, and learn about job opportunities. Many associations offer classes, seminars, and certificate programs. Professional associations and CTSOs also offer many opportunities to develop leadership skills.

Extend

Discuss the importance of student organizations in developing a career plan. Also, talk about organizations that people in the workplace might join.

Change Jobs

In order to move ahead, you may have to change jobs on occasion. If you like the company you are with, you can often move up the career ladder in the same company. You may get promoted to the next level. Or, you may still have to go through a formal process to apply for a different position in the same company. In other cases, you may want to change companies to get a higher-level position. Do not change companies too often, though, because it can seem like job hopping. New employers are looking for people who will commit to the company for some time.

Whenever you are looking for a new job while still in your old job, you must have integrity. Continue to fulfill all your obligations to your current employer. Avoid carrying

Case in Point

Walt Disney

Success is not always reached on the first attempt to meet your goal. As the old saying goes, "try, try, again." Walt Disney had that attitude. People think of Disney as a businessman who seemed to have been successful throughout his whole career. The truth is, he had many false starts as well as failures. At age 16, he was rejected by the Army, so he joined the Red Cross and went to Europe and drove an ambulance. After returning home at age 21, Disney tried to get work at the *Kansas City Star* newspaper as a cartoonist, clerk, and even a truck driver. But the newspaper turned him down for each position. However, drawing was his true calling, and with family encouragement, Disney pursued a career in animation and started his own company. At first, he was mildly successful but ran out of money and went bankrupt. Eventually, he moved to Hollywood and continued to have some failures as well as great successes. Disney went on to lead one of the best-known and loved corporations in the world. Determination and motivation can help you reach your goals.

out any job-hunting activities at your current place of work. If you need time to interview, take a personal day or vacation time.

Once you have obtained your new job, be professional about leaving your old job. Most businesses require that you give at least a two-week notice before leaving a job. To **give notice** means to notify a supervisor of the intention to leave a job. Usually, this is done by writing a letter of resignation. The *letter of resignation* should express appreciation for the time you have spent with the company, express regrets about leaving, and give the date of your last day on the job. This letter should be addressed to your supervisor. Then, take the letter with you when you tell your supervisor that you are leaving. Politely explain why you are leaving the company, express appropriate appreciation, and leave the letter with your supervisor.

The two-week notice gives the employer time to find someone to take your place. It also gives you time to finish up your projects and leave instructions for the next person.

Balancing Multiple Roles

One of the keys to success in life is balancing multiple roles. A **role** is the part that someone has in a family, society, or other group.

Elaborate/Extend

If students are using the optional *Marketing Dynamics* workbook, assign activities to engage active learning.

Roles come with responsibilities and expectations. Each person has many roles in life. For example, you currently have the role of student. In this role, you are expected to go to school, study your subjects, and do as well as you can. You also have a role as a family member. In your role as family member, you may have certain chores that you are expected to do. You are probably also expected to follow family rules, such as a curfew. You also have a role as friend. In your role as friend, you may be expected to join your friends at parties and other social activities.

One of the challenges in life is to balance different roles and the responsibilities that go with them. Often, the demands of different roles compete for your limited amount of time. For example, your role as a student requires time for homework. Your role as a friend requires time to develop friendships. Your role as a family member requires time for doing laundry. You must determine how to manage your time and your stress to meet these demands.

As you move through adulthood, you are likely to add many roles, such as the role of employee. The role of employee requires that you be at work at specific times and perform your job well. You will also add the role of citizen. Your role as citizen requires that you be informed about current issues and vote. You may also add the roles of spouse and

Extend

Ask students if they have ever quit a job. Did they quit in an appropriate manner?

Andresr/Shutterstock.com

For many people, the ability to balance work and family roles is an important factor when making choices about career opportunities.

parent. These roles add responsibilities for relating to and taking care of others.

You may also add the roles of community member and neighbor. In these roles, you may have responsibilities for organizing and participating in community activities. These roles may include volunteering your time to help others. You may also have other roles, related to your hobbies or special interests. For example, you may be a tennis player or a member of a choir. These roles will also take up time.

When you make your career decision, consider the other roles you want to have in your life. How will your career fit in with your other roles? Your time management skills will help you balance your many roles in life.

Checkpoint 27.3

1. List four steps an individual can take to advance in a job.
2. How can you gain leadership experience as a student?
3. What is one of the main ways to keep up-to-date in your career?
4. How should you notify your supervisor if you intend to leave your job?
5. Explain what it means to balance different roles in your life.

Build Your Vocabulary

As you progress through this course, develop a personal glossary of personal marketing terms and add it to your portfolio. This will help you build your vocabulary and prepare you for a career. Write a definition for each of the following terms, and add it to your personal marketing glossary.

give notice

role

Chapter Summary

Section 27.1 Achieving Success

- A manager is the person responsible for carrying out the goals of the department. Successful managers possess good interpersonal skills, positive attitudes, good time management skills, good work habits, and maintain their own personal well-being.
- The workplace environment is an important human resources issue. As a manager, you can do your part to make sure employees are in a comfortable, safe environment by paying attention to ergonomics and workplace safety.

Section 27.2 Managing Teams

- A team consists of two or more people who work together to achieve a common goal. Functional teams have members with the same skills and qualifications. Cross-functional teams have members with different skills.
- There are four skill areas that are particularly valuable for a team: good communication, leadership, collaboration, and conflict resolution.
- Meetings in the workplace may be formal or informal. Formal meetings are usually run according to parliamentary procedure.
- An effective team is a team that accomplishes its goals. Effective team members share ideas, share information, and are reliable.

Section 27.3 Advancing Your Career in Marketing

- Some people want to advance in their jobs for various reasons. Active steps for career advancement include continuing your education, developing leadership skills, being active in professional organizations, or changing jobs.
- As you move through adulthood, you are likely to add many roles. New roles may include that of an employee, citizen, spouse, or parent. These roles add responsibilities for relating to and taking care of others.

Review Your Knowledge

1. List some of the components of a positive attitude.
2. Why is it more efficient to keep personal and business items on the same calendar?
3. List six basic rules that will help you stay healthy.
4. What are the most common causes of accidents in office workplaces?
5. List four benefits of teams in the workplace.

Evaluate

Assign the end-of-chapter activities.

Review Your Knowledge Answers

1. Components of a positive attitude include the following: optimism, friendliness, self-motivation, teamwork, and adaptability.
2. Keeping personal and business items on the same calendar helps to avoid conflicts between personal and business obligations.
3. Six basic rules that will help you stay healthy are getting adequate sleep, exercising regularly, eating a balanced diet, avoiding health risks, managing stress, and balancing multiple roles.

4. Falling hazards, lifting hazards, and material-storage hazards account for most of the workplace accidents that occur in offices.
5. Students may list four of the following benefits: people are involved in the decision making, and therefore the decisions are more likely to be implemented; team members continually learn from each other; discussions among team members often generate new ideas; a group of people in a team has more knowledge and resources than an individual; teams are more likely to find and correct mistakes; and effective teams are usually more productive than individuals.
6. In the functional team, each member has basically the same skills and qualifications. In a cross-functional team, team members have different skills.

6. What is the difference between a functional team and a cross-functional team?
7. List five traits that are identified with successful leaders.
8. Name the six steps helpful in resolving conflicts.
9. What is the main difference between informal and formal meetings?
10. What information should you include in a letter of resignation?

Apply Your Knowledge

1. Write a report about multitasking, discussing both the positive and negative aspects of it. Refer to a time when multitasking helped you complete a project and a time when it might have hindered it.
2. Look at the list of interpersonal skills. Do you excel in any of these skills? List those skills you excel in and explain why you excel in them.
3. Look again at the list of interpersonal skills. Which one is the most important? Make your own list of skills in the order of their importance. Explain the reasoning for your order.
4. Evaluate several workstations around your home and in school. How might each one be improved?
5. As leaders, marketing managers need good speaking skills. Evaluate your speaking skills. Do you have any distracting habits? What could you do to improve your speaking skills?
6. How can disagreements in the workplace be useful?
7. Name someone who you think is a good leader. What are the qualities that make this person a good leader?
8. Do you consider yourself to be well organized? Why or why not? What can you do to improve your time-management skills?
9. Practice holding a formal meeting in the classroom using parliamentary procedure. First, determine the meeting topic, write the agenda, and elect a class leader to run the meeting.
10. Write a letter of resignation for a marketing position you have held for the past five years.

Check Your Marketing IQ

Now that you have finished the chapter, see what you learned about marketing by taking the chapter posttest. If you do not have a smartphone, visit the G-W Learning companion website.

G-W Learning mobile site: www.m.g-wlearning.com
G-W Learning companion website: www.g-wlearning.com

7. Students may list any of the following traits are often identified with successful leaders: self-confidence, good communication skills, dependability, enthusiasm, flexibility, ability to set goals, ability to follow through, good problem-solver, and ability to inspire others.
8. The following steps are helpful in resolving conflicts: gather the facts, hold a meeting, brainstorm solutions, develop a workable solution, gain agreement, and monitor the situation.
9. Informal meetings are when a group of workers get together to discuss a problem or to coordinate their work. Formal meetings are usually run according to parliamentary procedure.
10. The resignation letter should express appreciation for the time you have spent with the company, express regrets about leaving, and give the date of your last day on the job.

Apply Your Knowledge Answers

Student answers will vary for questions 1–10.

Evaluate

Evaluate the students' understanding and knowledge. Assign the Chapter 27 posttest. The test may be accessed by using the QR code or by going to the companion website. What questions were students able to answer that they could not answer when they took the pretest?

College and Career Readiness

Common Core

CTE Career Ready Practices. Successful managers model integrity and use effective management techniques. Research tips and advice from successful managers. Make a list of management techniques that would provide guidance for a new marketing manager. Rank the information according to your opinion of which one is most important.

Listening. Do an Internet search for speeches made on successful management techniques. After listening, analyze the effectiveness of the presentation. Was the presenter easy to follow and understand? Summarize the information you learned.

Speaking. Using your findings from the preceding listening activity, present the information to your class. Use a variety of strategies to improve the audience's comprehension of what you are sharing. This can be accomplished by using visuals, such as handouts or a media presentation. After the presentation, critique your approach. Were you successful in getting your message across to the audience?

Teamwork

Working with a teammate, create a process for managing conflict within a team. Use your class as the example of a team. Make a list of steps or procedures that individuals should follow when a conflict arises.

G-W Learning Mobile Site

Visit the G-W Learning mobile site to complete the chapter pretest and posttest and to practice vocabulary using e-flash cards. If you do not have a smartphone, visit the G-W Learning companion website to access these features.

G-W Learning mobile site: www.m.g-wlearning.com

G-W Learning companion website: www.g-wlearning.com

CHAPTER

28

Marketing Management

Section 28.1 Management Functions
Section 28.2 Marketing Finances

"To be successful and grow your business and revenues, you must match the way you market products with the way your prospects learn about and shop for your products."

—Brian Halligan, coauthor of *Inbound Marketing*, CEO of Hubspot

College and Career Readiness

Reading Prep
List four things you already know about management and four things you would like to know about management. As you read, think of how the material in the text compares or contrasts with your prior understanding of the topic. Make connections between what you know and what you learn throughout the chapter.

Check Your Marketing IQ

Before you begin the chapter, see what you already know about marketing by taking the chapter pretest. If you do not have a smartphone, visit the G-W Learning companion website.
G-W Learning mobile site: www.m.g-wlearning.com
G-W Learning companion website: www.g-wlearning.com

G-W Mobile

Explore
Provide an opportunity for students to explore by assigning a hands-on activity. Assign the College and Career Readiness Reading Prep activity before students read the chapter. Reading Prep activities give students opportunity to apply the Common Core State Standards.

Engage
Assign the Chapter 28 pretest. The test may be accessed by using the QR code or going to the companion website. Discuss which questions students were unable to answer.

◇DECA Emerging Leaders

Marketing Communications Team Decision-Making Event, Part 2

Career Cluster: Marketing
Instructional Area: Selling/Pricing

Procedure, Part 2

1. In the previous chapter, you studied the performance indicators for this event.
2. The event will be presented to you through your reading of the General Performance Indicators, Specific Performance Indicators, and Case Study Situation. You will have up to 30 minutes to review this information and prepare your presentation. You may make notes to use during your presentation.
3. You will have up to 10 minutes to make your presentation to the judge followed by up to five minutes to answer the judge's questions. You may have more than one judge. All members of the team must participate in the presentation, as well as answer the questions.
4. Turn in all of your notes and event materials when you have completed the event.

Case Study Situation

You are to assume the role of the marketing team for Dress to Impress, a large nonprofit organization that supports underprivileged teenagers. The **executive director (judge)** of Dress to Impress has called on your team to describe a sales and marketing strategy to overcome recent negative publicity.

The primary goal of Dress to Impress is to minimize the economic challenges encountered by teens. Each summer, Dress to Impress holds a month-long campaign in over 500 communities throughout the United States and Canada. The international campaign asks community members to donate new articles of clothing for teenage youth and bring them to the local drop-off location. At the end of the month-long campaign, Dress to Impress is able to award thousands of brand-new clothing to underprivileged teenagers in the community, just in time for fall. Dress to Impress is recognized as the best youth charity in North America. Dress to Impress has full-time staff located at the organization's headquarters and hires temporary workers in each Dress to Impress community to work during the

month-long campaign. Dress to Impress has several corporate partners that help promote the campaign and donate funds and clothing for the event.

Dress to Impress has recently encountered negative publicity. A Dress to Impress temporary worker in a mid-sized city was arrested on theft charges after being caught with stolen goods. The temporary worker had 20 brand-new clothing items, meant for donation, for sale on an Internet auction site. Upon further investigation, the temporary worker had already sold close to 50 articles of clothing meant for the charity. While this is a local occurrence, it has put the entire Dress to Impress organization in the spotlight. People across North America are now leery of donating clothing, for fear they will not end up with the intended recipients.

The executive director of Dress to Impress wants a marketing strategy to prevent negative publicity when conducting organizational campaigns. Your team must describe special procedures you will offer to prevent negative publicity when conducting organizational campaigns. Your team must describe the types of communication that will be the most effective for assuring donors their efforts are not in vain.

You will present your marketing strategy to the executive director of Dress to Impress in a meeting to take place in the executive director's office. The executive director of Dress to Impress will begin the meeting by greeting you and asking to hear your ideas. After you have presented your information about a marketing strategy to prevent negative publicity when conducting organizational campaigns, the executive director of Dress to Impress will conclude the meeting by thanking you for your work.

Critical Thinking

1. Which promotion activities are identified in the case study?
2. Which promotion activities focus on the company?
3. When is it appropriate to use items donated for charity as personal profit?
4. Provide recommendations with supportive rationale on how Dress to Impress should respond to this incident.

Visit www.deca.org for more information.

Section 28.1 Management Functions

Objectives

After completing this section, you will be able to
- **list** the five elements of the management function.
- **summarize** how marketing manages proprietary information.
- **describe** effective management styles.

Key Terms

strategic planning
tactical planning
operational planning
organizational chart
staffing
emotional
   intelligence
control
proprietary
   information

conflict of interest
insider trading
plagiarism
democratic style
autocratic style
consulting style
laissez-faire style

Web Connect

Research the term *strategic marketing*. Write a paragraph about why it is important for marketers to understand strategic marketing and how strategic marketing fits under the overall umbrella of marketing.

Critical Thinking

Compare and contrast the four different management styles. Which management style do you think you would adopt as a manager? Which style would you prefer to work under as an employee? Explain your answers.

Management Function

Among the many skills a marketer needs are good management skills. When a marketer adds employees to the team, he or she becomes a *manager. Management* is the process of controlling and making decisions about the business. *Marketing management* includes all of the activities required to plan, coordinate, and monitor the marketing function. There are five elements of the management function as shown in Figure 28-1. The five elements are plan, organize, staff, lead, and control.

The manager of a marketing team could be a person in a variety of positions. Examples of such positions are marketing

manager, communications manager, director of marketing, or vice president of marketing. Managers are responsible for making sure that all marketing tasks are completed. One task is to create and execute the marketing plan. Another task is to train individual team members to perform specific job duties. Still another task is to monitor the performance of individual team members.

Managers may also be responsible for working with customer service reps and providing product training. Providing excellent customer service is vitally important to maintaining customer satisfaction, or the marketing concept. The image of a company is positively reinforced through exceptional customer service.

Management Process	
Plan	Set goals and decide how to achieve them.
Organize	Arrange tasks, people, and resources to accomplish the work.
Staff	Hire the best and the most talented people.
Lead	Motivate and direct employees through clear instructions and by communicating policies and procedures.
Control	Monitor financial and personnel performance, compare actual performance with goals, and take corrective action when needed.

Figure 28-1 Marketing managers perform many tasks during the management process.

Goodheart-Willcox Publisher

Plan

Marketing managers are responsible for the success of the marketing team. During *marketing planning,* managers set goals and plans for the team.

Strategic planning is the process of setting the long-term marketing goals for the company. Long-term goals are usually those goals to be achieved over a period of three to five years. The senior management team sets the long-term goals for the company. Marketing then determines specific long- term marketing goals to help reach company goals.

Tactical planning is the process of setting the short-term goals for the company. Short-term goals are typically those set for the next 6 to 24 months. Marketing managers work with the sales team to set specific marketing goals and determine how to reach each goal.

Operational planning is the process of setting the day-to-day goals for the company. Marketing can refine those goals to reflect monthly, weekly, or daily tasks.

Organize

To *organize* is to coordinate the efforts of a team to reach its goals. A marketing manager organizes the marketing team by giving specific jobs or assignments to individuals.

The *chain of command* is the structure in a company from the highest to the lowest levels of authority. The chain of command is important so employees know to whom various positions report in the operation of the business. Most businesses create an organizational chart to show the chain of command. An **organizational chart** is a diagram of employee positions showing how the positions interact within the chain of command. An example of an organizational chart for a marketing team is shown in Figure 28-2.

Staff

Marketing managers must find the right employees to fill positions on the team. **Staffing** is the process of hiring people and matching them to the best position for their talents. Staffing is a challenging responsibility for all managers. *Human resources (HR)* are the employees who work for a

Elaborate/Extend

Assign the College and Career Readiness Portfolio activity at the end of the chapter.

Figure 28-2 Depending on the size of the organization, a marketing organizational chart may be small or large.

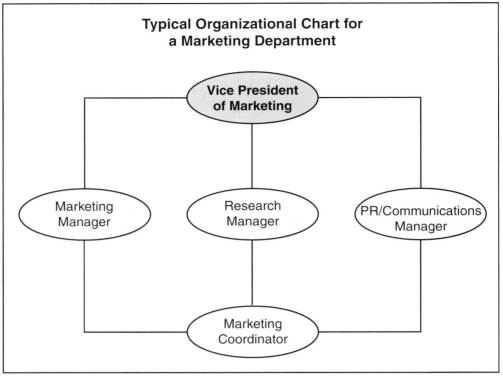

Typical Organizational Chart for a Marketing Department

Vice President of Marketing

Marketing Manager

Research Manager

PR/Communications Manager

Marketing Coordinator

Goodheart-Willcox Publisher

company. In larger companies, the *human resources department* helps to determine the human resources needs for a department or company. HR also helps find and hire the right employees for the open positions.

Lead

Successful marketing managers lead their teams by giving clear, concise directions. Managers must possess good interpersonal skills, business skills, and problem-solving skills. Time-management skills are also important. Leaders must be ethical and lead by positive example. Successful managers recognize the work of others and reward positive performance.

Sometimes, managers are faced with difficult situations that might be emotional in nature. Managers with high emotional intelligence are better able to control their own emotions and diffuse those of others. **Emotional intelligence** is the ability to recognize your emotions, realize how your emotions affect other people, and understand what those emotions mean. Marketing activities often involve identifying emotions that are attached to a product or brand to increase sales. Being able to both identify critical emotions and express them in advertising and other communications is key to success in marketing.

FYI

Emotional intelligence also involves empathy for those around you. Managers who understand how other people feel can manage relationships more effectively. People with high emotional intelligence are usually successful in most things they do.

Marketing Ethics

Sales Quotas

Sales and marketing teams have sales quotas that are expected to be met. Sometimes, because of the pressure to meet these goals, sales reps will put pressure on customers to purchase the product. High-pressure selling techniques are an unethical practice. Pressuring a customer to purchase what he or she does not want is not only unethical but could cost the company future business.

Control

Control is to monitor the progress of the team to meet its goals. Actual performance is compared to the stated goals. If the team is missing its goals, the manager must take corrective action and make adjustments. The employee evaluation process falls under this managerial function. Marketing managers are responsible for controlling marketing costs.

Manage Proprietary Information

By nature of the positions, marketers are exposed to important company information. New product development, competitive data, and other valuable information are handled by marketing. Managing a marketing team requires company information to be kept private. Proprietary information, sometimes referred to as *trade secrets*, is information a company wishes to keep private. It is not for public knowledge. Proprietary information can include many things, such as product formulas, customer lists, or manufacturing processes. All employees must understand the importance of keeping company information confidential. The code of conduct should explain that company information may only be shared with permission from human

resources. Employees who share proprietary information with outsiders are unethical and, possibly, breaking the law.

Before hiring an employee for the marketing team, your company may require the person sign a confidentiality agreement, as shown in Figure 28-3. A *confidentiality agreement* typically states that the employee will not share any company information with outsiders. A confidentiality agreement is especially important for the marketing department that might have product information that would benefit competitors if they had it. These agreements can also prevent former employees from working for a competitor for a certain period of time.

Conflict of Interest

A conflict of interest exists when an employee has competing interests or loyalties. For example, an employee tells you about a great opportunity to buy marketing promotional items at a low price. The employee convinces you that the items will be a big hit for the marketing team, and the cost of carrying the product will be low. What the employee did *not* tell you is that he or she gets a percentage of every sale made from the manufacturer. This is known as a kickback. A *kickback* is an amount of money given to someone in return for providing help in a business deal. This is clearly a conflict of interest.

Yours in Retro
Confidentiality Agreement

THIS AGREEMENT made on _____, 20_____, between Yours in Retro, a place of business at 101 Main Street, Anytown, IL, and _____, an employee of Yours in Retro.

As an employee of Yours in Retro, we require nondisclosure of any proprietary information about our products, employees, or business plans. This confidential information may include, but is not limited to, patents, trademarks, research, market analyses, or any other information concerning Yours in Retro.

All work contributed by the employee as part of the employee's paid position remains the property of Yours in Retro.

The obligations of this agreement shall continue two (2) years after employee leaves Yours in Retro.

Goodheart-Willcox Publisher

Figure 28-3 A confidentiality agreement helps to protect private company information that is often used in marketing.

Conflicts of interest can take many forms and harm a business. Some are illegal; others are unethical, yet legal. Be aware of how specific conflicts of interest could negatively affect your company. These situations should be addressed in the code of conduct.

Insider Trading

You have probably heard the term *insider trading*. Insider trading is when an employee uses private company information to purchase company stock or other securities for personal gain. Using company information for personal gain is both unethical and illegal. Sometimes, marketers help to develop new products or learn other information before it is made public that could affect the price of company stock. While it may be hard to control information, marketers and other employees should know the legal consequences of insider trading.

Internet

Marketers rely heavily on the Internet to perform many job duties including marketing research, monitoring the competition, and creating marketing materials. Recall that any information on the Internet belongs to the person who wrote and posted it. Even though there may not be a copyright notice, the material legally belongs to that person. Plagiarism is using the words of someone else without giving credit to the person who wrote them. Plagiarism is a form of copyright infringement. It is unethical and illegal. All documents, art, photos, and music are protected under copyright law. Therefore, marketers should never copy something from the Internet and use it without permission. It is also important that all employees understand that copyright infringement is a crime.

Explain

Students do not always understand copyright infringement. Discuss the implications of copying someone else's work.

Explore

Assign students to find a news story on insider trading. Ask for a

volunteer to discuss the findings.

Evaluate

Assign the Checkpoint questions at the end of the section. Assess students' comprehension using the Checkpoint activity as a self-assessment tool.

Marketing managers must manage many different types of people including outside vendors who help create marketing materials, such as this photographer.

Goodluz/Shutterstock.com

Company Equipment

Marketers use computers, printers, and other office equipment to complete their daily job duties and responsibilities. Company equipment is for performing business-related functions, such as sending electronic ad campaigns, updating social media, or managing time and resources. Using company equipment for personal tasks is unethical.

This may include sending personal e-mails, copying personal documents, and using the company telephone for personal calls. Some personal uses of company equipment add costs; others may take time away from job duties. The code of conduct should outline expected employee behavior while at work.

Many codes of conduct also have guidelines for visiting websites and rules for downloading to company computers. These

Explain

Ask: How might using company equipment for personal use take away from productivity?

rules protect the business' computer system and its private information. Some downloaded files and software contain computer viruses or other harmful *malware* designed to damage or disrupt a computer or network. Any person who purposefully introduces a virus to a computer or network has broken the law.

Management Styles

A *management style* is how a person leads a team. In general, there are four management styles. The four management styles are democratic, autocratic, consulting, and laissez-faire.

In the **democratic style** of management, the leader encourages team members to participate and share ideas equally. This style is often called the *participatory style*.

In the **autocratic style** of management, the leader makes all decisions without input from others. This is also known as *top-down management*.

The **consulting style** of management is a combination of the democratic and autocratic styles. The manager makes the final decision, but only after considering input from the employees.

A manager with a **laissez-faire style** allows employees to make their own decisions about how to complete tasks. There is little involvement from the manager.

Regardless of the style, effective managers are also good delegators, motivators, and are fair to all employees. They also learn from their mistakes and can manage stressful situations well. Good managers will never ask an employee to do something that they would not do. Managing by example is important for all people in leadership positions, especially marketers.

Checkpoint 28.1

1. List the elements of the management function.
2. Compare and contrast the three areas of planning.
3. What are human resources?
4. Why is high emotional intelligence important for marketing managers?
5. List the four styles of management.

Build Your Vocabulary

As you progress through this course, develop a personal glossary of marketing terms, and add it to your portfolio. This will help you build your vocabulary and prepare you for a career. Write a definition for each of the following terms, and add it to your personal marketing glossary.

strategic planning
tactical planning
operational planning
organizational chart
staffing
emotional intelligence
control
proprietary information

conflict of interest
insider trading
plagiarism
democratic style
autocratic style
consulting style
laissez-faire style

Section 28.2 Marketing Finances

Financial Planning

Financial planning is the process of setting financial goals and developing methods for reaching them. Most businesses set yearly goals and develop plans to achieve those goals. One of the most important goals is usually to earn a specific amount of revenue. **Revenue** is the money that a business makes for the products or services it sells. Revenue is also called *income* or *sales.*

The sales and marketing teams work with senior management to help define specific revenue goals for the company. The process begins with creating a sales forecast. A **sales forecast** is a prediction of future sales based on past sales and a market analysis for a specific time period. Historical sales figures are evaluated, marketing plan successes and failures are reviewed, and external and internal factors are considered. External factors are those things that are beyond company control, such as the economy or political events. Internal factors are events, such as changes in the distribution channel or labor problems.

By evaluating past performance, future performance can be predicted. A sales forecast helps define actions that the sales and marketing team will put into motion to meet those revenue goals.

Sales forecasts may be *quantitative,* or based on facts and figures. Quantitative data includes past sales history, market share, and the disposable income of the target market. One way to complete a sales forecast is to use the previous sales dollar amount and add a sales-increase factor. A **sales-increase factor** is the percentage of expected increase in sales. Many companies set sales goals based on a percentage of increase from the previous year. The formula for forecasted sales dollar increase is

previous-year sales dollars
    × sales-increase factor percentage
    = forecasted sales-increase dollars

For example, perhaps a company had a sales goal of a 20-percent increase in sales from year one to year two. If year-one sales were $80,000, then the expected amount of sales increase is $16,000.

$80,000 × 20% = $16,000

The formula for a sales forecast is

previous-year sales dollars
    + forecasted sales-increase dollars
    = forecasted sales-dollar goal

In the case of this company, the sales forecast for the year is $96,000 based on an expected 20 percent increase sales goal.

$80,000 + $16,000 = $96,000

Sales forecasts may also be *qualitative,* or based on judgment. Qualitative sales forecasts are most often used when a new business is opening or a new product is being introduced. In order to remain profitable, it is important for a company to constantly monitor its sales forecasts and make changes as necessary.

Budget

A **budget** is a financial plan that reflects anticipated revenue and shows how it will be allocated in the operation of the business. Budgets are often used during financial planning. Typically, each department in a company has a yearly budget, and the company has an overall budget. Budgets can be prepared for one month, one quarter, six months, or one year.

Accurate sales forecasts are based on actual-sales reporting.

Preparing a marketing budget may take input from the entire team.

For the marketing team, the marketing budget may be divided into two parts: operations and marketing activities. The operations budget includes payroll and other operating expenses for the team. The marketing activities budget includes amounts for advertising and other marketing activities.

Managers must determine which expenses and other costs are necessary to keep the business operating successfully and which ones are not necessary. **Cost control** means monitoring costs to stay within a planned budget. At year-end, managers compare the actual income, expenses, and other costs with the budgeted amounts. This comparison provides management with a tool for future planning.

Financial Reports

Financial reports are like student report cards. Financial reports reflect how a business is doing at a given time. It is important that all managers understand the financial statements for the business.

Two of the main financial reports are the balance sheet and the income statement.

Balance Sheet

A **balance sheet** is a financial report that shows the net worth of a company. The value of a company is called its **net worth** or *owners' equity.* A balance sheet is like a snapshot that shows the value of the business on a specific date.

A balance sheet lists the assets and liabilities of a company. *Assets* are property or items of value owned by a business. *Liabilities* are the debts of a business. A balance sheet is based on the following accounting equation:

$$\text{assets} = \text{liabilities} + \text{owners' equity}$$

A balance sheet is useful to marketing for several reasons. By reviewing inventory on the balance sheet, a marketing manager can evaluate how effectively he or she projected inventory needs. By reviewing accounts receivable,

Exploring Careers

Outside Sales Representative

To survive, wholesale companies and manufacturers need to sell their products, and to do that, they need people to present the products to potential buyers in a positive way. Outside sales representatives present, demonstrate, and sell the company's products to both businesses and individuals. Other typical job titles for an outside sales representative are *marketing associate, field representative, field marketing representative, account manager,* and *sales executive.*

Some examples of tasks that outside sales representatives perform include:

- Identify potential customers by following leads, attending trade shows and conferences, and using business directories;
- Monitor competitors' products, prices, and sales statistics;
- Determine which products to recommend, based on customer needs and interests;
- Demonstrate products and explain their features; and
- Provide price quotes, terms, warranties, and potential delivery dates.

Outside sales representatives are usually assigned specific territories, which may or may not require frequent traveling to maintain. They must have an excellent knowledge of their own products, as well as those of their competitors' products. They should understand the principles of promoting and selling products. Because nearly 100 percent of sale-rep job duties involves working with people, sales representatives should enjoy people and should have good communication skills. Most jobs in this field require on-the-job experience, training in a vocational school, or an associate degree. For more information, access the *Occupational Outlook Handbook* online.

a marketing manager can determine how much customers still owe to the business.

A marketing manager does not have to be an accountant. However, understanding basic accounting activities will help you become a more effective manager. Figure 28-4 shows an example of a balance sheet.

Income Statement

An **income statement** is a financial report that shows the revenue and expenses for a business during a specific period of time. An example of a company income statement is shown in Figure 28-5.

If income is larger than expenses, the result of this equation is a positive number. A positive result is referred to as *net income*

or a *profit.* If the expenses are larger than the income, the result of this equation is a negative number. A negative result is referred to as a *loss.* In accounting, a loss is indicated by placing the number in parentheses.

An income statement may be created for specific departments within the business. Each department can then evaluate its contribution to the overall profit for the company. This is especially useful for marketing, since its contribution to the bottom line is directly related to marketing activities.

An income statement may also be called *profit and loss statement, P&L,* or *statement of earnings.*

Sophia's Website Design Co.
Balance Sheet
December 31, 20--

Assets

Current Assets:
Cash	$ 36,000	
Accounts Receivable	22,000	
Total Current Assets		58,000

Fixed Assets:
Buildings	100,000	
Equipment	15,000	
Total Fixed Assets		115,000
Total Assets		$ 173,000

Liabilities

Current Liabilities:
Accounts Payable	$ 24,000	
Notes Payable	13,000	
Total Current Liabilities		$37,000

Long-Term Liabilities
Mortgage Payable	85,000	
Notes Payable	20,000	
Total Long-Term Liabilities		105,000
Total Liabilities		$ 142,000

Capital

Owners' Equity		131,000
Retained Earnings		42,000
Total Liabilities and Capital		$ 173,000

Figure 28-4 This is an example of a balance sheet.

Goodheart-Willcox Publisher

Green Marketing

Green Customers

When considering green alternatives for customers, do your homework. Green customers are not all the same. Some customers will only use 100-percent green products. Others will use items that are partially green. Consider the demographics of your customers and do the market research to determine their preferences.

Figure 28-5 This is
an example of an income
statement.

Foster's Service Business
Income Statement
Year Ended December 31, 20--

Revenue

Sales	$ 468,000	
Less Returns and Allowances	21,000	
Net Sales		447,000

Cost of Goods Sold

Beginning Inventory, January 1	$ 125,000	
Purchases	60,000	
Total Merchandise Available for Sale	185,000	
Less Ending Inventory, December 31	25,000	
Total Cost of Goods Sold		160,000
Gross Profit on Sales		287,000

Operating Expenses

Advertising Expense	$ 5,000	
Rent Expense	20,000	
Insurance Expense	6,000	
Supplies Expense	200	
Utilities Expense	1,800	
Total Operating Expenses		33,000

Net Income before Taxes **$254,000**

Goodheart-Willcox Publisher

Case in Point

Enterprise Rent-A-Car

Successful businesses realize the importance of the management function within the organization. They also understand the value of focused management training according to company standards. For example, Enterprise Rent-A-Car has a management-training program to teach managers-in-training to "build skills in every area of business from managing profit and loss statements to working with customers." Enterprise values performance and helps management trainees attain success, so they are able to manage their own stores. Management trainees are the future of their company. Just ask Andrew Taylor, CEO. He, too, started his career as a manager in training.

AMA Tip

Checkpoint 28.2

1. What is the most important data needed in a sales forecast?
2. What time periods can be used when preparing budgets?
3. What are the two basic types of business expenses?
4. Explain business assets and liabilities.
5. How do managers use an income statement when monitoring a budget?

Build Your Vocabulary

As you progress through this course, develop a personal glossary of marketing terms and add it to your portfolio. This will help you build your vocabulary and prepare you for a career. Write a definition for each of the following terms, and add it to your personal marketing glossary.

financial planning
revenue
sales forecast
sales-increase factor
budget
cost control
net worth
balance sheet
income statement

Checkpoint Answers

1. The most important data needed for a sales forecast are previous sales volumes.
2. Budgets can be prepared for one month, one quarter, six months, or one year. Many businesses prepare a yearly budget that is broken down by month.
3. Two basic expense types are cost of goods and operating expenses.

4. Assets are property or items of value owned by a business. Liabilities are the debts of a business.
5. Managers compare the estimates of revenue, expenses, and profit in the budget with the actual revenue, expenses, and profit on the income statement.

Build Your Vocabulary Answers

Definitions for these terms can be found in the glossary of this text.

Chapter Summary

Section 28.1 Management Functions

- The five elements of the management function are to plan, organize, staff, lead, and control. During marketing planning, managers set goals and plans for the team.
- Managing a marketing team requires that company information be kept private. Proprietary information, sometimes referred to as *trade secrets*, is information a company wishes to keep private.
- A management style is how a person leads a team. The four management styles are democratic, autocratic, consulting, and laissez-faire.

Section 28.2 Marketing Finances

- Financial planning is the process of setting financial goals and developing methods for reaching them. The sales and marketing teams work together to forecast sales. The most important data are previous sales volumes.
- A budget is a financial plan that reflects anticipated revenue and shows how it will be allocated in the operation of the business. Marketing management helps the company meet its sales goals while remaining within the marketing budget.
- Financial reports tell how a business is doing at a given time. Two of the main financial reports are the balance sheet and the income statement.

Review Your Knowledge

1. What are people in marketing management positions ultimately responsible for in their position?
2. Describe chain of command.
3. What stage of the management process involves setting goals?
4. How do marketing managers organize a team?
5. What is a confidentiality agreement, and why might it be important in a marketing department?
6. List and explain the two factors that influence sales forecasting.
7. Does a marketing manager need to know as much as an accountant? Why or why not?
8. List some typical marketing expenses.
9. On what equation is a balance sheet based?
10. Explain profit and loss in an income statement.

Evaluate

Assign the end-of-chapter activities.

Review Your Knowledge Answers

1. Marketing managers are responsible for making sure that all marketing tasks are completed, as well as the people who perform them.
2. The chain of command is the structure in a company from the highest to the lowest levels of authority. The chain of command is important so employees know to whom various positions report in the operation of the business.
3. Managers set goals in the planning stage.
4. Marketing managers organize the team by assigning specific job functions to individuals.
5. A confidentiality agreement typically states that the employee will not share any company information with outsiders. A confidentiality agreement is especially important for the marketing department that might have product information that would benefit competitors if they had it.
6. External and internal factors influence sales forecasting. External factors are those things that are beyond company control, such as the economy or political events. Internal events, such as changes in the distribution channel or labor problems, can affect sales forecasts.
7. A marketing manager does not have to be an accountant. However, understanding basic accounting activities will help you become a more effective manager.
8. Marketing expenses may include promotions, sales commissions, and advertising. Salaries, travel and entertainment, and office supplies are necessary to run the marketing department and sell products.
9. A balance sheet is based on the equation: Assets = Liabilities + Capital.
10. If income is larger than expenses, the result of this equation is a positive number. A positive result is referred to as net income or a profit. If the expenses are larger than the income, the result of this equation is a negative number. A negative result is referred to as a loss.

Apply Your Knowledge

1. As the marketing manager for your company, create an organizational plan for its marketing department.
2. Based on the business plan for your company, what proprietary information might the marketing department need to protect? Explain why that information should be private. What would be the consequences if that information became public?
3. Create a confidentiality agreement for employees in your company.
4. As a marketing manager, describe how you can protect your company and the marketing department in particular from the risk of plagiarism.
5. Which leadership style best motivates you to do your best work? Why?
6. List and describe the leadership skills you need to develop in order to be successful in a marketing-management position.
7. As the marketing manager for your company, write a short report about how you propose to control the marketing expenses for which you are responsible.
8. Based on the sales goals in your marketing plans, calculate the overall sales forecast for your business.
9. Examine the balance sheet in the business plan you are using to write the marketing plan for your company. Write a short explanation of what the balance sheet tells readers about the business.
10. Examine the income statement in the business plan you are using to write the marketing plan for your company. Write a short explanation of what the income statement tells readers about the business.

Check Your Marketing IQ

Now that you have finished the chapter, see what you learned about marketing by taking the chapter posttest. If you do not have a smartphone, visit the G-W Learning companion website.

G-W Learning mobile site: www.m.g-wlearning.com
G-W Learning companion website: www.g-wlearning.com

Common Core

College and Career Readiness

CTE Career Readiness Practices. It is important for an employee to apply both technical and academic skills in the workplace. Go online and search for desirable workplace skills. Then, conduct another search for top academic skills. Create a chart that shows your findings. Do any of these skills overlap? If so, describe the skills and the similarities.

Speaking. There are many instances when you will be required to persuade the listener. When you persuade, you convince a person to take a course of action that you propose. Prepare for a conversation with a classmate to persuade that person to approve your idea for a marketing-plan template.

Listening. Passive listening is casually listening to someone speak. Passive listening is appropriate when you do not have to interact with the speaker. Listen to a song on the radio. After it has played, evaluate what you heard and write down the lyrics that you remember.

Teamwork

Working with your team, create a one-page handout that lists each type of management style. Under each style, make a list of bullets that describe the characteristics of that type of manager. Duplicate enough of these handouts to distribute to your classmates. Ask if they will participate in an anonymous survey and select the characteristics that apply to him or her. Tally the votes. Which type of manager style was most dominant in your class?

G-W Learning Mobile Site

Visit the G-W Learning mobile site to complete the chapter pretest and posttest and to practice vocabulary using e-flash cards. If you do not have a smartphone, visit the G-W Learning companion website to access these features.

G-W Learning mobile site: www.m.g-wlearning.com

G-W Learning companion website: www.g-wlearning.com

Unit 8 **Dynamics of Marketing Management**

Building the Marketing Plan

Just like every function of business, marketing activities need to be managed properly to produce the desired results. Probably the biggest function of marketing management is to help the company increase sales, which will contribute to increased profits. Before a company can determine its sales goals though, previous actual sales must be analyzed along with the current economic environment. This exercise also helps marketers identify which marketing strategies and tactics are best to achieve those goals.

Objectives

- Create a sales forecast for your business.
- Create a best-opportunities list for the sales and marketing team.

Directions

In this activity, you will complete the Sales Analysis section of the marketing plan. This section involves analyzing the previous-year actual sales and applying the sales goals to create a sales forecast for the upcoming year. A best-opportunities list will help the sales and marketing teams focus on where to spend the marketing budget effectively. Access the *Marketing Dynamics* companion website at www.g-wlearning.com. Download the data file for the following activity.

1. **Unit Activity 8-1. Sales Forecast.** Study the business plan for your company. Locate the previous-year sales figures and the sales goals for the business. Based on that information, determine the forecasted sales by product for the upcoming year.

2. **Unit Activity 8-2. Best Opportunities.** Based on your knowledge of the target market, competition, and customer profile, determine the top-ten best sales opportunities for the company in the coming year.

3. Open your saved marketing plan document.

4. Locate the Sales Analysis section of the plan. Use the suggestions and questions listed to help you generate ideas. Delete the instructions and questions when you are finished recording your responses. Proofread your document and correct any errors in keyboarding, spelling, and grammar.

5. Save your document.

Unit 9

Professional Development Dynamics

Chapters

Eye-Catcher

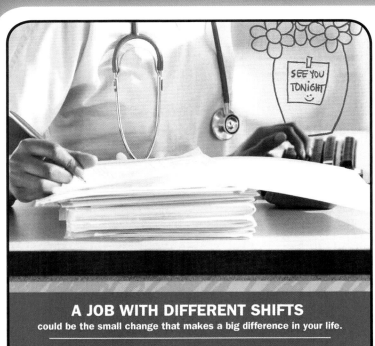

A JOB WITH DIFFERENT SHIFTS
could be the small change that makes a big difference in your life.

What does a better job mean to you? Is it 10-hour shifts? Getting home in time for date night? Whatever it is, Monster has the tools to find it. With thousands of nursing jobs and expert advice, we can easily find the job that's right for you. Visit www.nursinglink.monster.com and upload your resume today.

monster®
Find Better.™

monster.com

Marketing Matters

As you begin looking for your first job, you may choose to use an online job-search service. Monster.com is one service that uses integrated marketing communications to appeal to its customers, who are both job seekers and employers. One strategy it used in 2010 was the "Get a Monster Advantage" campaign. The multimedia campaign focused on Monster.com as a solutions provider to help employers and job seekers get an advantage they need for success.

Marketing Core Functions Covered in This Unit

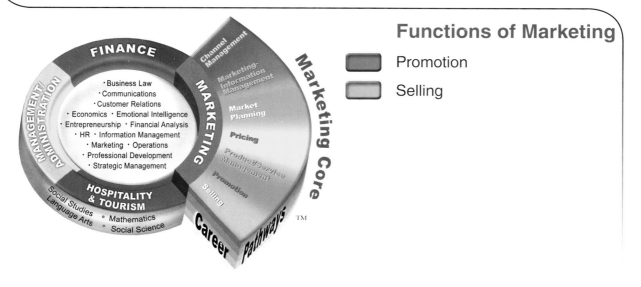

Functions of Marketing

- Promotion
- Selling

Developing a Vision

Marketing yourself is one of the most important challenges you will face in your career. Create the image you want to project and begin focusing on your talents and strengths. It is never too early to begin marketing your own brand.

To compete in today's fast-paced economy, it will be important to know who you are and the goals you want to pursue. Creating a plan for your future will help guide you through endless personal and professional decisions. You may want a career in marketing or prefer one in a completely different field. Regardless of the direction you choose, this unit will walk you through the basic steps of planning for success.

CHAPTER

29

Planning for Success

Section 29.1	Setting Goals
Section 29.2	Jobs and Careers

"Whatever you do, be different—that was the advice my mother gave me, and I can't think of better advice...if you're different, you will stand out."

—Anita Roddick, founder of The Body Shop

College and Career Readiness

Reading Prep
Before reading this chapter, flip through the pages and make notes of the major headings. Compare these headings to the objectives. What did you discover? How will this help you prepare to read new material?

Check Your Marketing IQ

Before you begin the chapter, see what you already know about marketing by taking the chapter pretest. If you do not have a smartphone, visit the G-W Learning companion website.
G-W Learning mobile site: www.m.g-wlearning.com
G-W Learning companion website: www.g-wlearning.com

Explore

Provide an opportunity for students to explore by assigning a hands-on activity. Assign the College and Career Readiness Reading Prep activity before students read the chapter. Reading Prep activities give students an opportunity to apply the Common Core State Standards.

Engage

Assign the Chapter 29 pretest. The test may be accessed by using the QR code or going to the companion website. Discuss which questions sutdents were unable to answer.

◇DECA Emerging Leaders

Business Services Marketing Series Event, Part 1

Career Cluster: Marketing
Career Pathway: Marketing Management
Instructional Area: Product/Service Management

General Performance Indicators

- Communications skills—the ability to exchange information and ideas with others through writing, speaking, reading, or listening
- Analytical skills—the ability to derive facts from data, findings from facts, conclusions from findings, and recommendations from conclusions
- Critical thinking/problem-solving knowledge and skills
- Production skills—the ability to take a concept from an idea and make it real
- Priorities/time management—the ability to determine priorities and manage time commitments

Specific Performance Indicators

- Describe factors used by businesses to position corporate brands.
- Explain the nature of marketing management.
- Explain the impact of product life cycles on marketing decisions.
- Describe the use of technology in the product/service management function.
- Describe word-of-mouth channels used to communicate with targeted audiences.

Purpose

Designed for an individual DECA member, the event measures the member's proficiency in the knowledge, skills, and attitudes in the business administration core and appropriate career cluster and pathway of a given career in a role-play. This event consists of a 100-question, multiple-choice, cluster exam and two role-play activities in a written scenario.

Participants are not informed in advance of the performance indicators to be evaluated. For the purpose of this textbook, sample performance indicators are given so that you may practice for the competition.

For the purposes of this text, you will be presented with the material for this event in two parts. Part 1 presents the knowledge and skills assessed and an overview of the event's purpose and procedure. Part 2 presents the remaining procedures and the event situation.

Procedure, Part 1

1. For Part 1 in this text, read both sets of performance indicators. Discuss these with your team members.
2. If there are any questions, ask your teacher to clarify.

Critical Thinking

1. Based on the performance indicators, what functions and tasks might be involved in the situation?
2. For each specific performance indicator, provide responses.
3. Explain the relationship between the General and Specific Performance Indicators.

Visit www.deca.org for more information.

Section 29.1 Setting Goals

Objectives

After completing this section, you will be able to
- **explain** how planning can help you achieve your career goals.
- **describe** how to learn about yourself through the process of self-assessment.

Key Terms

career plan
self-assessment
self-esteem
work values
Career and Technical
    Student Organization
    (CTSO)
activities-preference
    inventory
ability
aptitude

Web Connect

There are many potential marketing jobs that you may be interested in pursuing. Do an Internet search on a marketing career that interests you. Make notes on the educational requirements that are required and the specific job tasks for the position. After completing your research, determine if it would be a good future career for you. Why or why not?

Critical Thinking

Goal setting is an important activity for anything you do in life. Write three short-term goals and three long-term goals. These can be personal or professional. What did you learn from writing these goals on paper?

Why Plan for a Career?

Success and happiness usually do not happen by accident. Success is a lifelong journey. When you read about an *overnight success,* you usually discover that the person has been working hard for many years. Successful people often have a long-term goal, for example, to become a famous singer or president of a company. Successful people usually have a detailed plan for achieving that goal.

You may not have any goals or plans yet. However, now is the perfect time to start thinking and planning for your future. Learning how to plan can help you become successful in all areas of your life. Planning now for your future career can help assure your career success.

Planning actually has two steps. The first step is setting a goal. The second step is developing activities that will lead you to achieve your goal.

Goal Setting

As discussed in Chapter 1, a goal is something that you want to achieve in a specified time period. You can have a wide variety of goals. Areas in which people have goals include personal growth, finances, possessions, education, career, relationships, family, and community. For example, a personal-growth goal might be to successfully run a marathon. An educational goal might be to get a college degree.

The advantage of having goals is that they help you organize your activities to more efficiently achieve those goals. Having

Explore

Provide an opportunity for students to explore by assigning a hands-on activity. Review the vocabulary terms at the beginning of the section. Where have students encountered these terms before? Help students make educated guesses about the meanings of the terms with which they are least familiar.

Resource

Use the Chapter 29 presentation on the optional Instructor's Presentations for PowerPoint® CD as an outline for presenting the chapter.

a goal is like having a target market. Once you know your goal, you can make decisions to help you reach that goal. Not having a goal is like being in an airport and taking the first plane you see. You may or may not like your destination. Instead, if you know where you want to go before you get to the airport, you will buy the proper ticket and get there on time. These activities make sure that you will arrive at your chosen destination. You may have delays along the way, but you are more likely to get to the destination you chose.

There are two basic types of goals: short-term and long-term. A *short-term goal* is one that can be achieved in less than one year. A *long-term goal* is one that will take a longer time to achieve, usually longer than one year. *Goal setting* is a process of deciding what a person wants to achieve.

The goals you set for yourself have to make sense to you. Your goals must be based on who you are, your strengths, your interests, and what you want in life.

When setting career goals, it is important to make them SMART goals that are specific, measurable, attainable, realistic, and timely, as illustrated in Figure 29-1. SMART goals were discussed in Chapter 1.

The most helpful goals are specific. A specific goal points the way to achieving it. A general goal may be unclear or confusing. For example, a general goal might be to become a good runner. A specific goal would be to complete a marathon. A measurable goal enables you to tell when you have accomplished the goal. How can you tell when you are a good runner? That might be open to debate. However, you can tell when you have completed a marathon. A goal is usually more helpful when it includes an action that should be taken. "Being a good runner" is not an action statement. "Completing a marathon" is an action statement; it tells you the action required to accomplish the goal.

A goal should be realistic. In other words, the goal should make sense for who you are and what you want to achieve. A goal should fit with your interests, preferences, and values. For example, if you were not interested in sports, it would not make

Goodheart-Willcox Publisher

Figure 29-1 Creating SMART career goals will help you plan for your future.

sense to have a goal of working for a sports arena. Goals can be difficult to achieve and still be realistic. The key to accomplishing a difficult goal is to have a good plan.

Useful goals also have a time line. That is, a specific date is included for achieving the goal. If you do not specify a date for completion, you might never achieve the goal. The date can be modified as you work toward your goal.

Action Plans

A *plan* is a list of steps that lead to the accomplishment of a goal. These plans are often called *action plans* because you must take action in order for the plan to work. Action plans are especially helpful for long-term goals and for difficult goals. Recall that an action plan is also part of the promotional plan that lists every step needed to complete every marketing tactic.

An effective plan breaks a large or difficult goal into smaller steps. Each smaller step then becomes easier to accomplish. Accomplishing each step brings you closer to achieving a goal. For example, a person who wants to run a marathon will develop a detailed training plan. First goals will consist of running one to five miles. Subsequent goals will add more miles until the person reaches the goal of 26 miles. It is usually helpful to put your plan in writing and list the dates for each, completing the smaller steps.

In order to accomplish the goal, a person has to follow the plan. However, most people

encounter a variety of roadblocks. For example, a runner may get shin splints or the flu. Achievement of a goal may depend on your persistence. Your ability to keep going and to solve problems that arise will help you achieve your goal. A good motto to remember is "Winners never quit, and quitters never win."

One of the things that often helps motivate a person to achieve a goal is a clear vision of the goal. In this context, a vision is a vivid picture of accomplishing the goal. For example, the runner may have a picture in his or her mind of running across the finish line and being cheered by the crowd.

A career plan is a special type of action plan. A **career plan** is the list of steps that will enable you to achieve your career goal. However, before you can set a career goal and develop a career plan, you need to know more about yourself.

Growth and Change

Is career planning a one-time effort? Not usually. Career planning is a lifelong process. Think about how much you have changed in the past few years. Although your physical growth rate will slow down, you will continue to grow mentally, socially, and in your education and career throughout your lifetime.

You may ask, "If I am going to change anyway, what good is it to make a career plan now?" Making a career plan now points you in a direction that enables you to gain

If you want to pursue a career in scientific research, for example, you should take as many science classes as possible while still in high school to help you reach your goal.

experience and expertise in a particular area. Many people float along for years because they have not made any career decisions. They take whatever job comes along. They never assess their interests and abilities or try to match them to a career. These people are often very unhappy in their jobs.

As a teen, if you know yourself well and form a good plan, your future career will have a solid foundation. As you pursue a specific career goal through planning, you learn a great deal about yourself and the career. You might also discover that the career is not right for you. You will not have wasted your time pursuing the wrong career, though. You will have gathered important information about yourself and the world of work to develop your next career goal and plan.

During much of the 20th century, many people would find a job and stay with it their entire lives. By the end of the 20th century, it was rare for a person to stay in one job or career for a lifetime. Career counselors observe that the average person may have as many as five different careers over the course of a lifetime.

Part of the reason that people change careers so often is that the world of work keeps changing. New technology leads to changes in job requirements. Changes in the local and world economies also result in changes in jobs. During a recession, many businesses fail, and it may be hard to get the same kind of job you were doing. Changes in the worldwide economy may cause your industry to move overseas. People who are

Engage

Some students may have taken a career class in which career planning was covered. Discuss the importance of planning for a future career.

able to assess their skills and update their career plans are in the best situation to continually find good employment.

Learning About Yourself

Making decisions for yourself can be challenging. Which electives do you want to take? Which co-op job would be best for you? After high school, should you go straight to work or get more education? Which career should you choose? These decisions should be based on who you are and what you want.

However, sometimes it is hard to know yourself and what you want.

Self-assessment is the process of learning about yourself. There are many ways to assess yourself. One way is to reflect on your experiences. What do you do well? In which classes are you most alert and interested? How do you feel after you participate in a sport or committee meeting? How do you feel after babysitting or fixing your bike? Which activities make you feel good about yourself and others?

Examining the way you feel about your experiences impacts your self-esteem. **Self-esteem** is the confidence and satisfaction you

Sometimes, classes taken in school can become the means for exploring career possibilities, as seen with these students in an environmental studies class.

Goodluz/Shutterstock.com

Explore

Find a self-assessment test that students can take in class. Discuss the importance of assessing to help guide in career plans.

Extend

Ask the school counselor to come in to talk about self-assessment tools.

Exploring Careers

Telemarketer

Telemarketing is soliciting orders for products or services over the phone. It is a sales tool used by some companies as an alternative to more expensive marketing techniques. Charities also use telemarketing techniques to request donations. The two main types of telemarketers are those who place calls to potential customers and those who answer calls from customers responding to ads. Other typical job titles for telemarketers include *telephone sales representative (TSR), telesales specialist*, and *telemarketing sales representative.*

Some examples of tasks that telemarketers perform include:
- research names and telephone numbers of potential customers from directories, magazine reply cards, and lists purchased from other organizations;
- call businesses or individuals to solicit sales or to request donations for charitable causes;
- read prepared *sales talks* from scripts that describe the products or services they are selling;
- input customer information, including payment information, into computerized ordering systems; and
- answer telephone calls from potential customers who are responding to ads telling them to *call this number.*

Telemarketers need a good understanding of sales and marketing methods and strategies. They should have good speaking skills, including good diction and clear pronunciation, as well as a pleasing speaking voice. Because telemarketers sometimes encounter unpleasant responses, they should have an even temperament and be able to remain calm and pleasant at all times. Most telemarketing jobs require a high school diploma. For more information, access the *Occupational Outlook Handbook* online.

have in yourself. It is a way to measure your feelings of success. How important is self-esteem in the workplace? The importance is profound. People with positive self-esteem work well with others and tend to be encouraging. They want everyone to succeed. When facing difficult challenges or a lack of success, people with positive self-esteem keep moving forward and still strive for excellence. They value themselves and what they contribute in the workplace. The way you feel about yourself and others can influence your self-assessment. See Figure 29-2 for tips for building positive self-esteem.

When should you start the process of self-assessment? Right now is a good time. The following sections will help you explore your work values, interests, aptitudes, abilities, personal traits, and work focus.

Building Positive Self-Esteem
What can you do if you feel you have low self-esteem? Here are some helpful tips. • Focus on the positive by turning negative thoughts into positive ones. For example, turn "I always make mistakes" into "I do many things well." • Take good care of yourself by eating healthful foods, exercising, and taking the time to do things you enjoy. • Celebrate your achievements, no matter how big or small by making a list of them. • Help someone else—it is amazing how your self-esteem grows when you put the needs of others first. • Do an Internet search on *positive self-esteem*, and try some of the suggested activities.

Goodheart-Willcox Publisher

Figure 29-2 Everyone encounters self-doubt at some points in life. It is always good to know how to regain your self-esteem.

Extend
Ask students why values are important in personal life and at work.

It is very helpful to keep a journal recording what you learn about yourself. The process of writing down your interests, aptitudes, and so on will help you analyze them. Then, you can make decisions based on your interests, aptitudes, and so on. In addition, you will change and grow as you learn more about the world of work and yourself. You can use your journal to record and monitor these changes. This information can provide the basis for new career plans.

Work Values

What do you want from a job? The question is more complex than it may seem at first. Career counselors have discovered that people are often happiest at jobs that meet their values. For example, some people value working outside. Such people are not usually happy in office jobs. They would probably be happier in an outside sales job than an inside telemarketer job.

Work values are the aspects of work that are most important to a person. Work values are neither good nor bad. They represent what you want from a job or career. Some work values may not be discovered until you have experience in the workplace.

Work environment, activity level, control, and rewards are the main categories for work values, as shown in Figure 29-3.

The two basic categories of *work environment* are inside or outside. Inside work requires you to go to the same place of work every day. Outside work usually refers to outside sales. The sales representative goes to the location of the client. Consultants in various marketing specialties also go to the client.

Some jobs require a high *level of physical activity* and stamina. For example, most sales, warehouse, and teaching jobs involve a high level of movement, or physical activity. Jobs in telemarketing, graphic arts, writing, and marketing research usually involve less activity.

Control refers to how much you, as the worker, control what you do on the job. Some jobs require that you follow very strict and precise procedures. For example, a telemarketer may have a set script that must

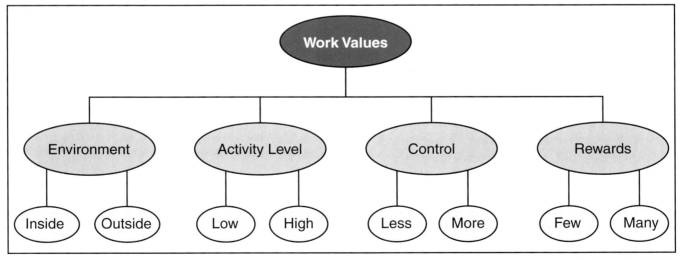

Goodheart-Willcox Publisher

Figure 29-3 Your work values play an important role in making the best career choices.

Social Media

Social Media Dashboards

One of the biggest challenges with using social media for marketing is managing the time it takes to monitor multiple sites. For example, you need to keep the business profiles current, interact with the followers of your business, and send relevant messages on a consistent basis. Social media dashboards, such as Hoot-Suite, TweetDeck, or SocialOomph, can help you effectively manage the time that needs to be spent on social media marketing. A social media dashboard is an interactive tool, much like a car dashboard, that organizes and presents information in an easy-to-read format. These tools allow you to schedule alerts and notifications, create groups, browse site activity, and send automatic updates or messages. While everything cannot, and should not, be automated, a social media dashboard can make the process of using social media for business easier and provide better results.

be read. Other jobs give the worker much more control of how the job gets done. For example, an outside sales representative can decide which clients to visit on which days and develop his or her own sales approach.

Rewards are related to the satisfaction you get from a job. Some jobs have higher salaries than others. However, higher salary jobs often require more education and harder work. They may also be more stressful. You need to consider many aspects of the job, however, not just salary. For example, you may want a career in a certain field where you know there is room for promotion and increased responsibilities. Or, you may simply enjoy performing some jobs more than others in a higher-paying field. Depending on the person, rewards come in many forms.

Interests

Interests are those things that capture your attention and that you are willing to spend time doing. What do you enjoy doing during your spare time? What hobbies do you have? Which classes do you enjoy most? What organizations do you belong to? School clubs, school government, scouting, social

clubs, sports clubs, religious clubs, and other youth organizations in which you participate indicate your interests. A Career and Technical Student Organization (CTSO) is an organization for high school students interested in a career area, such as DECA for marketing students. Participation in Career and Technical Student Organizations (CTSOs) help you learn about yourself and your interests.

Another way to become more aware of your interests is to take an activities-preference inventory. An activities-preference inventory is a test to determine which activities a person prefers when given a choice. Most high school guidance departments offer activities-preference inventory tests.

Abilities, Aptitudes, and Personal Traits

An ability is the skill to perform a task. Having an ability often involves learning a skill or a set of skills. For example, most jobs require that you know how to read, write, and do math. You have learned these skills in school.

An aptitude is a natural talent or natural ability to do something. If you have an

Many entry-level jobs can turn into long-term careers.

auremar/Shutterstock.com

aptitude for something, you can do it or learn it easily. For example, some people have an aptitude for working with numbers. They can easily learn the mathematics required for marketing research analysis. Someone who does *not* have this aptitude can learn the mathematics, but it would be harder. This person might not enjoy being a market research analyst, since that job requires using mathematics and statistics. People are usually happiest in jobs that use their aptitudes. A school counselor can give you an aptitude test to help you find out. This test will help you discover your natural strengths and weaknesses.

Most jobs have their own sets of specialized skills. You may need to learn these skills before you can get a job. Part of your career decision will be to decide whether you want to learn the required skills or obtain the education required for a certain career. For example, most advertising jobs require a college degree.

Your personal traits also affect your career decision. You have a variety of personal traits, including physical traits and

personality traits. Physical traits include how much energy and stamina you have. For example, many sales and sports coaching jobs require a great deal of physical stamina.

Personality traits include friendliness and creativity. For marketing jobs, such as sales associate, friendliness is more important. For marketing jobs such as copywriter or art director, creativity is more important.

FYI

The key to a successful career plan is to match your interests, abilities, aptitudes, personal traits, and work values, to a career that makes the best use of them.

Work Focus

There are many ways to analyze jobs. One of the most useful ways is to determine whether the job focuses more on people,

Case in Point

J.K. Rowling

Creating a plan for your success is important in everything you do. Successful people are in charge of their own futures. J.K. Rowling, author of the Harry Potter tales, is a good example of someone who took charge of her life after a divorce and a period of personal depression. She funneled her creative energies by putting her emotions and experiences in writing. Rowling had the story of Harry Potter in her head for several years before she finally began writing the first book. For this single mother living on Social Security, the road to publishing was long. However, through determination, she eventually found a publisher. The rest, as they say, is history. You, too, can take control of your life and create a plan for success.

objects, or data. Although many jobs require that you work with all three, most jobs focus on one.

A *people job* is one focused on working with people—usually helping them in some way. A sales job is a typical people job. Teaching is also a people job. An *objects job* is one focused on working with objects to build or create things. For example, visual merchandising is an objects job because visual merchandisers arrange items in space to create a display. A *data job* is one focused on working with data, such as numbers, words, and information. A data job can involve doing research, accounting, or writing. Marketing research analyst and

inventory management are data jobs. Figure 29-4 shows the general characteristics of people who have each type of focus.

People in supervisory or management roles usually have a people focus plus one of the others: objects or data. Their major responsibility is to work with people so that they are productive on the job. Supervisors also need to have strong data skills because they usually are responsible for planning and organizing.

General Characteristics of People for Each Type of Work Focus		
People Focus	**Objects Focus**	**Data Focus**
Enjoy being in groups	Enjoy working alone	Enjoy working alone
Belong to one or more organizations	Like to build, cook, sew, paint	Like to write or work with numbers and computers
Volunteer to help others	Good at building or repairing things	Enjoy research and learning
Outgoing and friendly	Collect things	Read many books

Goodheart-Willcox Publisher

Figure 29-4 An activities-preference inventory may also help you to discover your work-focus preference.

Evaluate

Assign the Checkpoint questions at the end of the section. Assess students' comprehension using the Checkpoint activity as a self-assessment tool.

Engage

Ask a student to present the information in Figure 29-4.

Checkpoint 29.1

1. Describe the difference between a short-term goal and a long-term goal.
2. What does the acronym SMART represent?
3. Self-assessment is the process of learning about yourself. Why is this important?
4. What is the difference between ability and aptitude?
5. Why is work focus important in your career?

Build Your Vocabulary

As you progress through this course, develop a personal glossary of personal marketing terms and add it to your portfolio. This will help you build your vocabulary and prepare you for a career. Write a definition for each of the following terms, and add it to your personal marketing glossary.

career plan
self-assessment
self-esteem
work values
Career and Technical Student Organization (CTSO)
activities-preference inventory
ability
aptitude

Checkpoint Answers

1 A short-term goal is a relatively small goal that is to be achieved within a year. A long-term goal is a large goal that will take more than a year to achieve.

2. SMART represents specific, measurable, action-oriented, realistic, and timely.

3. Looking at who you are and what you like helps you make good decisions for your career plan.

4. An ability is the skill to perform a task. Having an ability often involves learning a skill or a set of skills. An aptitude is a natural talent or natural ability to do something. If you have an aptitude for something, you can do it or learn it easily.

5. By focusing on things that you are good at or like, you will be more successful in your career choice.

Build Your Vocabulary Answers

Definitions for these terms can be found in the glossary of this text.

Section 29.2 Jobs and Careers

After completing this section, you will be able to
- **explain** the difference between a job and a career.
- **describe** ways to research a career in marketing.

occupation
career ladder
entry-level job
manager
information interview

job shadowing
internship
cooperative education program
employment trend

Do an Internet search on the term *career* and then a search on *job*. Compare and contrast the definitions you located. Write your opinion of the differences between a career and a job.

Look ten years into your future. Do you think you will have a marketing career? If so, what type of position do you think it will be? Why are you drawn to that type of work?

Job versus Career

In the world of work, the word job has two meanings. A *job* is a specific task done by a worker. A *job* is also the work a person does regularly in order to earn money. People work in jobs at businesses or in organizations. For example, a person can have a job as a retail sales associate for the local department store. On that job, the sales associate has the job, or task, of restocking the shelves as products are sold.

A *career*, on the other hand, is a series of related jobs in the same profession or industry. Occupation is the term used for a specific career area, such as advertising or sales. With each job, a worker usually gains greater knowledge and expertise. The series of jobs often leads to more responsibility and higher income. Getting a job is often a short-term goal. Having a career is a long-term goal. Many career counselors recommend that you think in terms of developing a career.

Often each job in a career requires more education and experience than the previous job. A series of jobs organized in order of education and experience requirements is called a **career ladder.**

The first job on a career ladder is called an **entry-level job.** Entry-level jobs require the least amount of education and experience. These first level jobs are called entry-level jobs because they are the jobs through which you enter the career. Some entry-level jobs have no education or experience requirements. Examples include cashiers, some sales jobs, and stock handler jobs. Other entry-level jobs require a four-year college degree. For example, most entry-level jobs in advertising,

Explain

Discuss the differences between a job and a career.

Engage

Use the Teamwork exercise at the end of the chapter to engage students to solve a problem or make a group presentation.

public relations, and marketing research require college degrees.

Not everyone wants to climb the career ladder. Many people are happy in their first-level jobs. These jobs suit their personalities, income requirements, and other needs. A person can turn an entry-level job into a career and perform the job with professionalism and great skill. For example, many retail sales associates make a career of retail sales.

Some people are interested in moving up the career ladder. An entry-level job can be considered a stepping-stone to a higher-level job. Each higher level on the career ladder requires more education or more experience or both. Each higher level on the career ladder usually involves more responsibility and more stress, but usually offers higher pay. Figure 29-5 shows a general career ladder in a corporation. Career ladders

vary with the specific career and in specific companies.

A **manager** is a worker who directs the work of others and makes decisions. There are three levels of management: upper, middle, and supervisory. Smaller companies may have only two levels: upper and supervisory. Large companies may have several levels of management in the middle.

Upper management is the top level of management. Upper management develops goals for the entire company and the strategies to meet those goals. The next level of managers reports to the upper management. *Middle management* consists of one or more levels of management between the top level and the supervisory level. They usually manage a group of supervisors in a particular region or area. *Supervisory management* is the level of managers closest to the workers.

A Generalized Career Ladder at a Corporation			
Career Level	**General Description**	**Minimum Education or Experience Requirements**	**Relative Wages or Salary**
Entry level	First job in the career area; worker must be trained and supervised	No experience or specific education required; high school diploma often preferred	$
Experienced Worker	Knows job well and can perform it with little supervision; number of levels and the titles for these positions vary	One year or more experience usually required; high school diploma preferred	$$
Supervisor	Responsible for training and supervising employees	Two or more years of experience, or a 2-year college degree and one or more years of experience	$$$
Manager	Responsible for running a department, including hiring and budgets	2-year college degree and 2 or more years of supervisory experience; a 4-year college degree often preferred	$$$$
Corporate manager	Responsible for a corporate division	4-year college degree and 10 or more years of management experience; graduate degree (MBA) often preferred	$$$$$

Goodheart-Willcox Publisher

Figure 29-5 Every career has a ladder of jobs with increasing pay and responsibilities.

Supervisors are usually responsible for a group of workers in a specific department.

FYI

Upper management may also be called *top management, executive management,* or *senior management.*

Researching a Marketing Career

Before you can match yourself to a career, learn about the careers you are considering. The field of marketing is very large, and you will need to narrow your choice to a career that really suits you.

As you work on your self-assessment and evaluate careers that relate to marketing, the career clusters become an important tool. In Chapter 1, you were introduced to the *career clusters,* which are 16 groups of occupational and career specialties that share common knowledge and skills. Each of the 16 career clusters includes several *career pathways.* Under these pathways, or career areas, you will find careers ranging from entry-level to those requiring advanced college degrees and years of experience. All of the careers within any given pathway share a foundation of common knowledge and skills. The career pathways that fall under the marketing career cluster include *Marketing Management, Professional Sales, Merchandising, Marketing Communications,* and *Marketing Research.* There are many careers in these pathways, and selected ones are listed in Figure 29-6.

Information Interviews

One of the ways to learn what it is like to have a marketing career is to talk to someone currently in a marketing position. Talking to someone to learn about his or her career is called an **information interview.** Suppose you are interested in being an advertising copywriter. You could enlist the help of your teacher or guidance counselor to help you find an advertising copywriter to meet. You could then arrange to have an information interview with the copywriter.

Before the interview, develop a list of questions. The questions should cover what

Careers Within the Marketing Career Pathways				
Marketing Management	**Professional Sales**	**Merchandising**	**Marketing Communications**	**Marketing Research**
• Chief Executive Officer • Entrepreneur • Inventory Clerk • Shipping/Receiving Manager • Small Business Owner	• Account Executive • Broker • Regional Sales Manager • Sales Executive • Technical Sales Specialist	• Store Manager • Department Manager • Merchandise Buyer • Retail Marketing Coordinator • Sales Associate	• Advertising Manager • Creative Director • Interactive Media Specialist • Public Relations Manager • Sales Representative	• Market Development Director • Brand Manager • Product Planner • Research Associate • Research Specialist

Goodheart-Willcox Publisher

Figure 29-6 These careers are just a few under the Marketing Career Pathways.

Engage

Ask students if they are considering marketing as a potential career. Bring in advertisements for marketing job openings and discuss what each one entails.

Extend

Invite a marketing or salesperson to class to talk about how they chose their career, what it involves, and related topics.

you most want to know about the career of copywriter. For example, you could ask the following questions. What do you like most about your job? How many hours do you work a day? What do you like least about your job? What was your first job in advertising? Which jobs and experiences were the most helpful in reaching your career goal? How much and what kind of education should I get? Do you have any advice for me?

Job Shadowing

Another way to learn about a job is to watch someone at his or her place of employment. Job shadowing is following a person while he or she does a job. Suppose you are interested in managing a hotel. You could call the manager of a nearby hotel. You could explain your interest in becoming a hotel manager. You could then ask if you could shadow him or her for a few hours.

On-the-Job Experience

An excellent way to learn about an industry is to actually work in the industry. As a student, you have several opportunities to work in marketing. You could get a part-time or a summer job at a retail business. In addition, your school may offer an internship or cooperative education program.

In an internship, students prepare for an occupation through a job that may be paid or unpaid. In a cooperative education program, students prepare for an occupation through a paid job while taking classes that are related in subject matter to the job. In these types of work programs, your school helps you find the part-time job. The job becomes a part of your educational experience and is usually considered equal to your classroom studies. Many schools also run school stores, where marketing students get a chance to learn a variety of marketing and business skills.

Internships can be found in every career. For example, if you have an interest in broadcasting or communications, you may want to consider an internship working as an announcer for a local radio station.

REDAV/Shutterstock.com

Review Employment Trends

An **employment trend** is the direction of change in the number of jobs in a particular career. Are the number of jobs increasing or decreasing in the career you are considering? It is always a good idea to look for a job in a career that is growing. For the near future, many occupations in marketing are growing. For example, the number of service-provider jobs, such as those in the wholesale and retail trades, are expected to increase by the year 2018.

There are two points to keep in mind about employment trends. First, employment trends can change quickly. There can be unexpected changes in the national economy. If the economy begins to contract again, jobs in many sectors may be lost. In addition, unexpected political events, such as war, can also affect employment. Secondly, when looking for a job, the economic environment in a city where you are looking is the most important factor.

In addition, many occupations that are *not* growing still need a large number of people each year. The reason is that a large number of people retire or change jobs on a yearly basis. There are many sources for information on careers and employment trends. Ask friends, family, and professionals you know for guidance.

US Department of Labor (DOL)

The US Department of Labor's Bureau of Labor Statistics compiles and publishes a great deal of information on occupations, industries, and jobs in the United States. One of the most useful documents is the *Occupational Outlook Handbook*. The *Occupational Outlook Handbook* is available in most libraries and online. The handbook provides information and statistics on a wide range of occupations and individual jobs. The information is revised every two years.

Another very useful publication is the *Occupational Outlook Quarterly*, also published by the DOL Bureau of Labor Statistics. It

covers a variety of topics in job search and career development, as well as ideas and information about specific careers. An online version is also available.

The DOL also developed O*NET, an online, interactive career resource at www.onetonline.org. This website enables you to research careers and their descriptions and match your skills to a career.

Another excellent resource is the CareerOneStop at www.careeronestop.org. It operates as a federal-state partnership and is a collection of online tools to help job seekers find jobs and employers find workers. It includes links to State Job Banks that list open jobs for each state. You can also access America's Career InfoNet, which includes information for making smart career decisions, such as how to find schools and scholarships.

AMA Tips

The AMA publishes a monthly career newsletter packed with career tips, job postings, and employer profiles. A recent newsletter, *Student Corner*, outlined what students can expect from a marketing career. First, marketing professionals assume a number of responsibilities throughout their careers. These job duties can include research, sales, brand management, and advertising. It is therefore important for marketers to remain flexible and knowledgeable about all aspects of marketing. Secondly, marketing is a results-oriented field. So, be prepared to demonstrate to management that your efforts are increasing sales or brand awareness. The *Occupational Outlook Handbook* from the Bureau of Labor Statistics has recent information about job duties and salaries for a variety of marketing careers. www.marketingpower.com

Professional Associations

Professional associations often provide continuing education, training seminars, and networking opportunities for people in different industries. They may also be called *trade associations.* Many also provide information about the industry and specific jobs within it. Many have a division or services specifically for students and others interested in the occupation. Many associations provide scholarships to students. Most have websites with more detailed information.

One of the largest associations for marketing professionals is the American Marketing Association (AMA). Many specific marketing occupations have their own professional associations. For example, in sales, there is the National Retail Federation and the National Automobile Dealers Association. In advertising, there is the American Association of Advertising Agencies. In the wholesale trade, there is the National Association of Wholesale-Distributors. The names of professional associations can be found in the *Occupational Outlook Handbook* or the *Directory of Associations.*

Professional Publications

There are many marketing-related newspapers, magazines, journals, and books. Many marketing associations have publications in their marketing area. Many are also available online. Some are available only to members, and others are more widely available. The *Wall Street Journal* is an excellent source for financial, business, and marketing news. The American Marketing Association publishes a variety of newspapers and journals, including *Marketing News.* Crain Communications, Inc., publishes a variety of newspapers and magazines, including *Advertising Age* and *B2B.* VNU Business Publications, USA, publishes *Adweek, Brandweek,* and *Sales and Marketing,* among others.

Checkpoint 29.2

1. What is the difference between a job and a career?
2. Name and describe the first step on a career ladder.
3. What are the three levels of management?
4. Name the five career pathways that fall under the marketing career cluster.
5. Name two sources of information on career and employment trends.

Build Your Vocabulary

As you progress through this course, develop a personal glossary of marketing terms and add it to your portfolio. This will help you build your vocabulary and prepare you for a career. Write a definition for each of the following terms, and add it to your personal marketing glossary.

occupation
career ladder
entry-level job
manager
information interview

job shadowing
internship
cooperative education program
employment trend

Checkpoint Answers

1. A job is the work a person does regularly in order to earn money. People work in jobs at businesses or in organizations. A career, on the other hand, is a series of related jobs in the same profession or industry.
2. The first job on a career ladder is called an entry-level job. Entry-level jobs require the least amount of education and experience. These first level jobs are called entry-level jobs because they are the jobs through which you enter the career.
3. The three levels of management are upper, middle, and supervisory.

4. The five career pathways are Marketing Management, Professional Sales, Merchandising, Marketing Communications, and Marketing Research.
5. Students may list any two of the following: the US Department of Labor (DOL), professional associations, and professional publications.

Build Your Vocabulary Answers

Definitions for these terms can be found in the glossary of this text.

Chapter Summary

Section 29.1 Setting Goals

- Planning now for your future career can help assure your career success. Planning actually has two steps. The first step is setting a goal. The second step is developing activities that will lead you to achieve your goal.
- Self-assessment is the process of learning about yourself to find a suitable career. It involves exploring your work values, interests, aptitudes, abilities, personal traits, and work focus.

Section 29.2 Jobs and Careers

- A job is also the work a person does regularly in order to earn money. A career, on the other hand, is a series of related jobs in the same profession or industry. Often each job in a career requires more education and experience than the previous job.
- There are three ways to research a possible career: conduct an information interview, job shadowing, and get into an internship or co-op program through your school.

Review Your Knowledge

1. Name the two steps of planning.
2. What is the advantage of having a goal?
3. Explain why a goal should be specific.
4. How can participating in a Career and Technical Student Organization (CTSO) help your career planning?
5. Explain why self-esteem is important.
6. Describe the importance of work values.
7. How much education is required for an entry-level job?
8. Explain the difference between job shadowing and on-the-job experience.
9. Name two points to keep in mind when looking at employment trends.
10. What is CareerOneStop?

Review Your Knowledge Answers

1. The first step of planning is setting a goal. The second step is developing activities that will lead you to achieve your goal.
2. The advantage of having goals is that they help you organize your activities to more efficiently achieve the goals.
3. The most helpful goals are specific. A specific goal points the way to achieving it. A general goal may be unclear or confusing.
4. Participation in Career and Technical Student Organizations (CTSOs), such as DECA, can help you learn about yourself and your interests.
5. When facing difficult challenges or a lack of success, people with positive self-esteem keep moving forward and still strive for excellence.
6. Work values are the aspects of work that are most important to you. Work values are neither good nor bad. They represent what you want from a job or career.
7. Entry-level jobs require the least amount of education and experience. The actual amount of education required depends on the position.
8. Job shadowing is following a person while he or she does a job, while actually working in an industry is getting on-the-job experience.
9. Employment trends can change quickly. When looking for a job, the economic environment in the city where you are looking is the most important factor.
10. CareerOneStop is a federal-state partnership and is a collection of online tools to help job seekers find jobs and employers find workers.

Apply Your Knowledge

1. Each individual has his or her idea of personal success. What is your definition of success?
2. Career planning is a lifelong process. Why?
3. Personal goals and preferences determine a future career choice. Why would your preference to work with people, objects, or data influence the type of job you would like to have?
4. Different types of education and training are appropriate at different times. What kind of education and experience can you get now as a high school student? What would be appropriate during the five years after high school? What might be appropriate in 15 years?
5. How might membership in a Career and Technical Student Organization (CTSO) help you learn about yourself, learn about careers, and prepare for a career? Which one would be most helpful to you right now?
6. Describe how a clear vision of a career goal can help motivate you as you make decisions about future educational options.
7. Suppose you found the perfect career, but the employment trends were down. Why might it make sense to pursue the career anyway?
8. Ask someone you know about a professional organization to which that person belongs. How has the organization helped this person with his or her career?
9. How can political events and the economy affect employment trends?
10. Why is the economy of the city in which you are looking for employment more important than the national economy?

Check Your Marketing IQ

Now that you have finished the chapter, see what you learned about marketing by taking the chapter posttest. If you do not have a smartphone, visit the G-W Learning companion website.

G-W Learning mobile site: www.m.g-wlearning.com
G-W Learning companion website: www.g-wlearning.com

Common Core

College and Career Readiness

CTE Career Ready Practices. As a student, you will be planning for your future career. Describe a plan on how to align career paths to your personal goals.

Reading. Do an Internet search for *personal branding.* Determine the central ideas the author explored about the importance of branding yourself when looking for a position. Summarize the key supporting details and ideas.

Writing. Using independent research, write a report in which you analyze and describe the use of aptitude tests, such as SAT, ACT, ACCUPLACER, and ASVAB. Why do these tests play such an important role in the post-high school plans of students? Cite specific evidence from the text and your research to support your understanding of this issue.

Teamwork

Working with a teammate, list ten marketing careers that interest you. Research the average salary for each. Record your information in a chart and distribute it to your classmates. Discuss your findings.

G-W Learning Mobile Site

Visit the G-W Learning mobile site to complete the chapter pretest and posttest and to practice vocabulary using e-flash cards. If you do not have a smartphone, visit the G-W Learning companion website to access these features.

G-W Learning mobile site: www.m.g-wlearning.com

G-W Learning companion website: www.g-wlearning.com

30 Preparing for Your Career

Section 30.1 Career Preparation
Section 30.2 Job Seeking

"Desire is the key to motivation, but it's determination and commitment to an unrelenting pursuit of the goal—a commitment to excellence—that will enable you to attain the success you seek."

—Mario Andretti, world champion racing driver

College and Career Readiness

Reading Prep
Before reading this chapter, review the highlighted terms and definitions to preview the new content. Building a business vocabulary is an important activity to broadening your understanding of new material.

Check Your Marketing IQ

Before you begin the chapter, see what you already know about marketing by taking the chapter pretest. If you do not have a smartphone, visit the G-W Learning companion website.
G-W Learning mobile site: www.m.g-wlearning.com
G-W Learning companion website: www.g-wlearning.com

G-W Mobile

Explore

Assign the College and Career Readiness Reading Prep activity before students read the chapter. Reading Prep activities give students opportunity to apply the Common Core State Standards.

Engage

Assign the Chapter 30 pretest. The test may be accessed by using the QR code or going to the companion website. Discuss which questions students were unable to answer.

◇DECA Emerging Leaders

Business Services Marketing Series Event, Part 2

Career Cluster: Marketing
Career Pathway: Marketing Management
Instructional Area: Product/Service Management

Procedure, Part 2

1. In the previous chapter, you studied the performance indicators for this event.
2. You will have up to 10 minutes to review this information to determine how you will handle the event situation. You may make notes to use during the role-play situation.
3. You will have up to 10 minutes to role-play your situation with a judge. You may have more than one judge.
4. Turn in all your notes and event materials when you have completed the role-play.

Event Situation

You are to assume the role of manager at JS SOLUTIONS, a software development company. The company owner (judge) has asked you to make recommendations, which will increase brand awareness and company revenue.

JS SOLUTIONS is a relatively new company that develops and markets business software. Begun just eight months ago, the company was founded on the strength of its four employees who possess years of practical business experience. When combined with the two-member software development team, business customers of JS SOLUTIONS have quickly discovered that the company's slogan, *Do It Better,* will do just that for them.

All company JS SOLUTIONS' operations exist only online at www.js_solutions.com. All prospecting, marketing, and selling are done through the company website. To date, JS SOLUTIONS has developed six different business-software programs. But, its most complex and expensive product is *Locate,* a warehouse management program. *Locate* is targeted to midsized warehouses looking to increase employee productivity, improve inventory accuracy, and reduce shipping errors.

As with any new business, having customers find you and accept your products as legitimate is a challenge—especially when selling computer software online. The company's software sales have not met initial forecast levels, but it is believed that the program with the greatest potential is *Locate.* According to the company, *Locate* is at the forefront of the next generation of warehouse management software. Competitor's software clearly lags behind *Locate* when considering function and overall benefit for the customer. For now, the owner would like to see most of the company's marketing efforts directed to *Locate.*

The owner of JS SOLUTIONS has requested a meeting with you to obtain your analysis and recommendations to increase brand awareness and to increase revenue. Specifically:

- List and explain strategies that would increase the customer confidence level in new products being developed and marketed by JS SOLUTIONS.
- Identify and explain strategies that will help to increase the sales revenue for *Locate* as well as for other JS SOLUTIONS software.
- State one strategy that could be implemented immediately that would address a company need yet be cost effective at the same time.

You will present your analysis to the company owner in a role-play to take place in the owner's office. The owner will begin the role-play by greeting you and asking to hear your ideas. After you have presented your analysis and have answered the owner's questions, the owner will conclude the role-play by thanking you for your work.

Critical Thinking

1. What are the advantages for the company not having an actual brick-and-mortar location?
2. In addition to selling online, identify another possible distribution channel for JS SOLUTIONS.

Visit www.deca.org for more information about this event.

Section 30.1 Career Preparation

Objectives

After completing this section, you will be able to
- **explain** the roles of education and training in career preparation.
- **describe** why an ongoing career plan is important.

Key Terms

tech prep
postsecondary
certificate programs
continuing professional
  education

Web Connect

Before you begin your career exploration, consider completing a self-assessment. Do an Internet search for *self-assessment tools for students.* Select one that appeals to you and complete it. What did you find out about yourself?

Critical Thinking

You are in the process of making plans for your career. What type of education or training are you planning to pursue? What factors influenced your decision?

Education and Training

After you have decided on a career goal, it will be necessary to create a plan of action to achieve that goal. Depending on your choice of careers, you will probably need some formal education and training.

Education

Education is the general process of acquiring knowledge and skills. Education can occur anywhere and continues throughout your life. However, *formal education* refers to the education you get from a school, college, or university. The level of formal education attained is usually confirmed by awarding the student a diploma, degree, or other document that verifies the level of education attained. Figure 30-1 shows the general order of degrees.

High School

For most jobs, the minimum educational requirement is a high school diploma. Very few jobs are available for people without a high school diploma. To an employer, a diploma indicates that you have basic reading, writing, and math skills. It also indicates that you were able to follow a course of study to its completion.

FYI

Hundreds of high schools in the United States offer marketing education programs. Marketing education programs combine general marketing courses that provide an overview of the industry, work experience, and DECA.

Explore

Review the vocabulary terms at the beginning of the section. Where have students encountered these terms before? Help students make educated guesses about the meanings of the terms with which they are least familiar.

Resource

Use the Chapter 30 presentation on the optional Instructor's Presentations for PowerPoint® CD as an outline for presenting the chapter.

Degrees Obtained Through Formal Education			
Degree	**Description**	**Example of Degree**	**Careers That Usually Require or Prefer the Degree**
High School Diploma	Obtained after completing four years of high school.		• Retail Supervisor
Certificates	Obtained from a career center, vocational-technical school, professional career school, community college, or a professional organization. Focuses on a specific vocational skill or set of skills. Usually takes a year or less. Can be taken at any point in a person's career.	• E-Commerce • Protective Services • Web Designer • National Professional Certification in Customer Service • Real Estate Certification	• Real Estate Broker • Security Officer • Web Designer
Associate Degree	Obtained from a community college, vocational-technical school, or professional career school. Focuses on career training. Usually takes two years.	• Business • Computer Graphics • Marketing • Small Business Management • Technical Sales	• Retail Management Trainee • Technical Sales Representative
Bachelor Degree	Obtained from a four-year college or university. Usually requires core courses such as English, math, and social sciences, followed by courses in a major subject or vocational area. Usually takes four years.	• Business • Communications • Entrepreneurship • Industrial Distribution Management • International Business • Marketing • Production and Management Science • Public Relations	• Advertising Account Representative • Advertising Copywriter • Public Relations Specialist • Teaching • Warehouse Manager
Master Degree	Obtained from a college or university, after the bachelor degree has been obtained. Usually intensive, advanced study in a specific area. Length of time varies, depending on whether student is going to school full-time or part-time.	• Entrepreneurship • International Business • Marketing • Operations • Real Estate	• Middle Management • Upper Management
Doctorate Degree	Obtained from a college or university, after the bachelor's degree has been obtained. Requires more courses and a doctoral dissertation. Usually takes four or more years beyond the bachelor degree. Often required for careers in research or college teaching.	• Econometrics and Statistics • Marketing • Organizations and Markets	• Director of Research • Executive Management • University Professor

Goodheart-Willcox Publisher

Figure 30-1 Different careers require different levels of formal education.

Engage

Talk with the students about the number and type of degree(s) you have attained along with the number and kinds of courses you needed to take to obtain your degree.

Explain

Compare and contrast degrees. Ask students what their future goal is? Discuss other options in addition to college, including the military and certificate programs.

Case in Point

Spencer Bryan and TaskRabbit

Marketing yourself as the right person for an employer takes *not* only planning but creativity also. Spencer Bryan from TaskRabbit can attest to this. TaskRabbit is a website that connects individuals with people in their neighborhoods who can run errands and complete other tasks for a fee. Spencer Bryan, then a Tuck Business School student at Dartmouth, liked the concept and became interested in working at TaskRabbit. However, writing a résumé and completing an application, was not in Spencer's approach to getting an interview. Instead, just like any other person wanting to use the site, Spencer created a task on TaskRabbit. It was not for someone to mow the lawn or pick up groceries, though. Spencer's task requested that someone at TaskRabbit meet him in person. Brian Rothenberg, the director of TaskRabbit, saw the posted task and accepted it. He thought Spencer was very creative, met him for an interview, and within a week, offered him a job. Remember, marketing yourself may take more than just a well-written résumé. It may require some creative ideas to get the job you really want.

Students can gain valuable work experience while still in high school in multiple ways. A paid *cooperative education (co-op) program* is for students enrolled in a Career and Technical Education course of study. Co-op programs allow students to gain work experience in positions such as a sales clerk or office assistant. The school's teacher-coordinator arranges for a local employer to provide job training. The student takes regular classes for half a day and is dismissed from school early in order to go to work. A co-op student generally works between 15 and 20 hours a week.

Paid or unpaid *internships* do not require a related class in school. Internships are for students who may or may not be enrolled in a Career and Technical Education program. Internships allow a high school student to gain work experience in positions for which they would not typically be employed without additional training, such as nursing, accounting, or human resources.

Another type of career preparation program for students is called tech prep. **Tech prep** is a career preparation program that combines the last two years of high

school with two years of postsecondary education. It does not include the on-the-job component. **Postsecondary** means after high school. Tech prep programs are also called 2+2 programs because they include two years of high school coursework plus two years of postsecondary classes. The postsecondary classes are often taken at a community college or a professional career school. At the end of the program, the student has a high school diploma and an associate degree or a technical certificate. The student is prepared to enter the workforce or continue his or her education at a four-year college.

Many high schools offer students the opportunity to join a Career and Technical Student Organization (CTSO), such as DECA. CTSOs provide a variety of activities that enable students to learn more about the career; meet professionals in the field; and develop interpersonal, leadership, career, and technical skills. In addition, many career and technical student organizations offer scholarships.

A CTSO will usually have a chapter in a school. Students join the school chapter. Through the school chapter, students participate in chapter meetings and civic, service,

Explain

Discuss the importance of student organizations. DECA has been emphasized throughout the text. However, there are other organizations with which your students may be familiar.

Explore

Have students identify a minimum of one professional organization in a field they are interested in pursuing.

social, and fund-raising activities. In addition, many CTSOs have competitive events. These competitive events provide the opportunity for students to develop career and technical skills. Students can compete at the school, state, national, and international levels. Participating in competitive events can be a motivating experience.

Four CTSOs have specific marketing activities: DECA (an Association of Marketing Students), Future Business Leaders of America (FBLA), Business Professionals of America (BPA), and SkillsUSA.

Part of a career plan is researching what post-secondary education you might need to reach your career goal. There are many public and private options to consider.

Steve Pepple/Shutterstock.com

Engage

Discuss the advantages of involvement in CTSOs. Poll the students to see if they or anyone they know is a member of DECA. Encourage students to describe their experiences if they are members.

Explore

Have students meet with their counselor or co-op director to discuss internships or co-op programs.

Postsecondary Schools

Postsecondary education is available at professional career schools, vocational-technical schools, community colleges, and business and career colleges. These educational institutions offer education for specific careers. These programs can last from six months through two years, depending on the program. The programs usually include a combination of classroom learning and hands-on experience. These schools offer certificates, diplomas, and associate degrees in a variety of careers.

Professional career schools focus on preparing students for a specific career. In the marketing area, a common professional school is the real estate academy. These schools prepare students for careers in real estate and to pass the real estate licensing examinations.

Vocational-technical schools are accredited high schools that combine academic course work with vocational training. Many offer post high school vocational training in a number of occupations, such as marketing, nursing and graphic arts.

Community colleges provide education in a variety of subjects including marketing. Community colleges offer certificates, diplomas, and associate of science degrees. Examples of programs include business administration, marketing, management, computer graphics, technical sales, and protective services.

Many *business and career colleges* and *four-year universities* offer diplomas, certificates, and associate degrees, as well as bachelor degrees in business and marketing. Some may also offer master degrees in business. For example, Robert Morris College offers associate and bachelor degrees in business. Majors offered include advertising, corporate communications, public relations, and real estate.

Colleges and Universities

Many marketing jobs and most management-level positions require a bachelor degree or higher. Bachelor degrees can be obtained at four-year colleges and universities, as well as technical and career colleges. A four-year college program usually requires English, math, and social science courses in addition to courses in your major.

College can be expensive. However, in 2011, the US Census Bureau reported that wage earners with a master degree could expect to earn an average of $1.3 million more during their lifetimes than people with only a high school diploma. There are many sources for money to help pay for college, such as government-subsidized student loans. Many professional organizations offer scholarships. Career and technical student organizations also provide many scholarship opportunities. For example, the DECA Scholarship Program provides over $300,000 in scholarships each year. Money for DECA scholarships is provided by more than 50 corporations.

AMA Tips

As you complete your education and begin to pursue your future career, it is critical that you access as many resources as possible to secure your first internships or career positions. The AMA has a Career Management section dedicated to employers and job seekers. It features many resources to assist you in finding that perfect job. The site allows job seekers to post their résumés and research career and internship postings. There is also a link to ask an expert about your career questions. The Careers Management section is open to both members and nonmembers.
www.marketingpower.com

Graduate School

Graduate school is a college or university education taken after a bachelor degree has been earned. The degrees offered are master and doctorate degrees. Many marketing professionals who want to be top-level managers find that a master of business administration (MBA) is necessary. Many universities offer these programs on a part-time, evening basis. This helps students to continue working while studying for the graduate degree.

Training

Training is usually instruction on a specific skill or task needed for a job. Training often takes place on the job. However, some training programs are offered through colleges, universities, professional associations, and private companies.

On-the-Job Training

Most entry-level jobs provide on-the-job training. Higher-level jobs expect applicants to

The job as a chef is one that requires specific skills that must be learned through training and hands-on experience.

wavebreakmedia/Shutterstock.com

Explore

Have students log on to a CTSO state and national website and answer questions developed by the instructor.

Explore

Have students research two postsecondary programs to see what would best fit their career plans.

Green Marketing

Customer Incentives

Marketing can help shape customer behavior when done well. Give your customers some incentives to use green behaviors and help your business *go green*. Offer coupons or other benefits if customers provide evidence of green actions. For example, you could offer 20 percent off coupons to customers who participate in the town *clean up the parks event*. If your business has a parking lot, set aside the two or three closest parking places for hybrid cars or those getting over 50 mpg. Give customers a small discount for bringing in their own reusable bags. There are many ways businesses can reward their customers for green activities. As a marketer, think about some customer incentives that might work well for your company.

---

have some knowledge gained in school and from previous job experience. However, higher-level jobs usually provide some on-the-job training. Every business has its own way of doing things. Every new employee will need some job training.

In addition, companies sometimes get new equipment or develop new procedures. Therefore, the company will usually provide on-the-job training for all employees using the new equipment or procedures.

Certificate Programs

Universities and colleges have also developed many nondegree-training programs in business and marketing. Some of these are intended for individuals entering the field, while others are designed for experienced executives. These nondegree-training programs are called **certificate programs.** Certificate programs are perfect for the worker who needs advanced training but who has little time to spend going to school. These classes are also offered as online courses for student convenience. Certificate programs usually range from 15 to 24 credit hours of course work or approximately five to eight courses. Most certification programs require students to pass a test. Once the certification course is completed and the test is passed, the student receives a certificate that

states that he or she has mastered that knowledge or skill.

Continuing Professional Education

For a professional, learning never stops. In business and marketing, new technology, new products, and new procedures require new learning. Knowledge of trends and changes in customer wants and needs also require new learning. **Continuing professional education** is education for people who have already completed their formal schooling and training. It is also called *professional development*.

Continuing professional education helps managers and workers stay up-to-date on new trends and issues. Some continuing professional education is sponsored by the employer and takes place on the job. Some employers will provide tuition money for professional education that takes place outside of the job. Other professionals seek continuing education based on their own interests and job commitment.

Many community colleges, business and career colleges, four-year colleges, and universities offer continuing professional education classes. In addition, many professional associations provide continuing professional education. Continuing professional education is often offered in the format of short courses and brief workshops and

Engage
Ask the students to describe training they have received when starting a part time job.

Explore
Have students identify two in-state and two out-of-state institutions that offer the major they may be interested in pursuing.

seminars. Once the course or workshop is completed, the student usually receives a certificate that states that he or she has completed the course.

Your Career Plan

You should now have a better understanding about yourself, possible careers in marketing, and educational requirements. The challenge is to choose a career that matches your work values, interests, aptitudes, abilities, personal traits, and work focus. The career choice you make now is not necessarily permanent. People often change careers over the course of their working lives. However, making a career choice and setting a career goal in high school can be very beneficial. By making a commitment to a career, you will learn a great deal about that career and yourself. You will also have a solid way to earn a living. Once you have a career, you can always make changes along the way.

Once your career goal is chosen, you can develop your career plan based on what you have learned about the required education and skills. A career plan is like a map used to guide you to your career goal. Many people can have the same career goal, but each one will develop a unique career plan. In addition, a career plan is never final. It may change as you develop and gain experience in your career. Figure 30-2 shows a career plan for a student who wants to be a marketing director for a nonprofit company.

Possible Career Plan for a Marketing Director for a Nonprofit Organization			
	Education and Training	**Job Experience**	**Extracurricular and Volunteer Activities**
During Middle School	Career exploration course	Summer camp counselor-in-training	Volunteer at animal shelter
During High School	Take college preparatory program and marketing courses	Co-op job, summer job as camp counselor, summer job as cashier	Join DECA, run for DECA officer, volunteer at animal shelter
During College	Obtain college degree in marketing	Internship in public relations at local hospital	Volunteer to do marketing for a nonprofit
After College	Take seminar in grant writing	Find a job in the marketing or fund-raising department of a nonprofit	Join the Association of Fund-raising Professionals

Goodheart-Willcox Publisher

Figure 30-2 A career plan is a guide. A person can make changes as he or she learns more and has more work experiences.

Evaluate

Assign the Checkpoint questions at the end of the section. Assess students' comprehension using the Checkpoint activity as a self-assessment tool.

Explore

Some students may have already completed a career plan in another class. Give students Internet time to explore how to create a career plan.

Checkpoint 30.1

1. What is the minimum educational requirement for most jobs?
2. What is the advantage of enrolling in a tech prep program?
3. List some of the activities provided by a CTSO.
4. What type of degree do most management-level jobs require?
5. Why is a career plan never final?

Build Your Vocabulary

As you progress through this course, develop a personal glossary of marketing terms and add it to your portfolio. This will help you build your vocabulary and prepare you for a career. Write a definition for each of the following terms, and add it to your personal marketing glossary.

tech prep
postsecondary
certificate program
continuing professional education

Checkpoint Answers

1. For most jobs, the minimum educational requirement is a high school diploma.

2. At the end of the program, you have a high school diploma and an associate degree or a technical certificate. You are prepared to enter the workforce or continue your education at a four-year college.

3. CTSOs provide a variety of activities that enable students to learn more about the career; meet professionals in the field; and develop interpersonal, leadership, career, and technical skills. In addition, many career and technical student organizations offer scholarships.

4. Most management-level positions require a bachelor degree or higher.

5. A career plan is never final. It may change as you develop and gain experience in your career.

Build Your Vocabulary Answers

Definitions for these terms can be found in the glossary of this text.

Section 30.2 Job Seeking

Objectives

After completing this section, you will be able to
- **discuss** what it means to market yourself.
- **explain** how to find job leads.
- **list** the steps to take when tracking job leads.
- **describe** the documents needed to prepare for applying for jobs.
- **explain** the job application process.
- **describe** the interview process.

Key Terms

job lead   job application
want ad
networking
letter of inquiry
reference
résumé
scannable résumé
cover message
portfolio

Web Connect

You have learned about marketing a product. Now it is time to market yourself as a potential employee. Do an online search for the phrase *marketing yourself*. Make notes on ideas that the article provided to help you learn how to present yourself as a potential employee.

Critical Thinking

Companies receive many résumés from potential employees. Your résumé should look professional. Do not use flashy fonts or colorful paper. Keeping this in mind, how can you make your résumé impressive enough that the employer will read it? Write down your ideas.

Market Yourself

In Chapter 29, you were introduced to the many careers in marketing. In addition, you have learned many marketing strategies throughout this text. Many of the same marketing strategies used for products can be applied to your job search. You are the product and the brand. The employer is the target market. You want the employer to buy your services by hiring you for a job and paying you wages.

First, make sure that you are the right product. Conduct marketing research on the jobs and employers. You also have to analyze yourself and make sure that you have the right stuff for the positions you seek. Match your skills and qualities with the needs of the right employer.

Next, think about the marketing concept. One of the major aspects of the marketing concept is meeting the needs of the customer. When you apply for a job, think in terms of what you can do for the employer. What specific needs does the employer advertise? How can you meet those needs? How can you contribute to making the business successful?

Finally, actively market yourself to the employer. Make sure that you are appropriately packaged. You have to launch an organized promotional campaign.

You are now ready to market yourself. After brushing up your communication skills, you are ready to find that first job on your career plan. Keep the marketing attitude toward your job search as you follow

Explore

Provide an opportunity for students to explore by assigning a hands-on activity. Review the vocabulary terms at the beginning of the section. Where have students encountered these terms before? Help students make educated guesses about the meanings of the terms with which they are least familiar.

Engage

Use the Teamwork exercise at the end of the chapter to engage students to solve a problem or make a group presentation.

Explain

Ask the students to describe the types of clothing both appropriate and inappropriate for a job interview.

these four steps: finding job leads, applying for jobs, interviewing, and following up.

Find Job Leads

A *job lead* is information that leads you to a job opening. Job leads are all around, if you know where to look. The most common ways of finding job leads are newspapers, social media, networking, and direct employer contact. Other potential places include friends and relatives, school placement services, direct employer contact, trade and professional journals, and government and private employment agencies. A *want ad* is a written advertisement for a job, placed by the company that needs the worker. Want ads appear in a variety of places.

Many people do find jobs through newspapers. It is a good idea to check this source in addition to online newspapers.

Elena Elisseeva/Shutterstock.com

Newspapers

The traditional place to start looking for a job is in the newspaper want ads. Reading the want ads can give you a good idea of the types of jobs available and which companies are hiring. Some print newspapers are also available online. However, research has shown that only about 15 percent of available jobs are advertised in the newspaper.

Social Media

Social media networking sites can be very effective in finding job leads. Twitter and Facebook are several examples of free social media tools that businesses use for recruiting purposes. Social media sites for professionals, such as LinkedIn, also have many job listings that sometimes are found nowhere else.

Company Websites

If there is a company you are interested in working for, check out its website. It may be possible to find openings in the company and even complete a job application on the website.

Online Employment Sites

Numerous online sites exist for applicants to search job listings at no cost to them. Many sites also give job seekers the ability to upload their résumés for employers to view. Employment websites like Monster, Indeed, CareerBuilder, and SimplyHired are well-known job boards for finding open positions.

Career and College Placement Offices

Career and technical centers, colleges, and universities operate career placement offices as a student service. The placement offices encourage businesses to post job listings that will fit the skills of enrolled students. It is a free service for students to search for open jobs.

Job Fairs

Job fairs are a great way to meet potential employees in person. Various organizations sell booth space for employers to present information about their businesses. Job seekers visit the booths to discuss job opportunities, submit résumés, and complete applications.

Networking

There is a tremendous amount of competition for each job that is posted online or in print. So what else can the job hunter do? Most career counselors will suggest networking with others. **Networking** is the process of making connections with people in the work world. The idea behind networking is to meet people who are as enthusiastic about your career area as you are. Through networking, you get to know these people and can share your enthusiasm with them. You also express your interest in finding a job in the career area. People who are in the position to hire may have a hard time finding the right person. They are often happy to consider someone they know who has shown interest and commitment to their career area.

A good place for students to network is through Career and Technical Student Organizations (CTSOs). One purpose of CTSOs is to put students in contact with professionals in their career and technical interest areas.

College and Career Portfolio

Hard Skills

Employers review candidates for various positions and colleges are always looking for qualified applicants. When listing your qualifications, you may discuss software programs you know or machines you can operate. These abilities are often called *hard skills.* Make an effort to learn about and develop the hard skills you will need for your chosen career.

1. Do research on the Internet to find articles about different types of hard skills and their value in helping employees succeed.
2. Make a list of the hard skills you possess that you think would be important for a job or career area. Select three of these hard skills. Write a paragraph about each one that describes your abilities in this area. Give specific examples that illustrate your skills.
3. Save the document file in your e-portfolio. Place a printed copy in the container for your print portfolio.

Where do you meet such people? Your school guidance or career counselor may be able to put you in touch with people. You can also network with family, neighbors, and friends. They may not be in your career area, but they may know people who are.

Networking should go on throughout your career, not just when you are job hunting. Networking keeps you up-to-date on changes in the field. Networking can also provide resources when you have problems to solve at work. Once you are in the work world, membership in a professional organization can be a good way to network.

Direct Employer Contact

Many people are successful in finding jobs by directly contacting the employers for whom they would like to work. Direct contact is most successful when you have researched the company and know a great deal about it. Before contacting an employer, make sure you have a clear idea of what you can offer the company as an employee.

The first step is to send a letter of inquiry.

A **letter of inquiry** expresses your interest in working for that company, highlights your job qualifications, and asks about any job openings. The letter should be addressed to the person most likely to hire you. If you do not have that name, do more research to find the company human resources department information. Determine which area or department you would like to work in and the name of the head of that department. Address the letter to the head of that department. Your résumé may accompany the letter of inquiry.

Keep the letter to one page. Also, ask for an appointment to visit the person and discuss job possibilities. Follow up with a phone call. You might have to make several phone calls. Some companies have a policy of not responding to unsolicited résumés and letters. It is generally not advisable to just show up at a business and ask to speak with someone about a job. However, for some entry-level jobs, such as sales associate or fast-food server, you may stop by the place of business and fill out an application.

Explain
Discuss the importance of letter writing and how it will impact a job opportunity.

Track Job Leads

One of the most important things to do while job hunting is to keep track of your job leads. Set up a filing system, either on note cards or on a spreadsheet. For each lead, you should record the following information:

- name, address, phone number, and e-mail address of the company;
- job title of the position you are seeking;
- name and title of the person with whom you should speak; and
- source of the lead.

There should be space for noting all contacts with the company. For example, if you send a résumé, you should note the date that you sent it. If you call the company and speak with someone, you should record the date and time of the call, the name and title of the person you spoke with, and the content of the discussion. In addition, if you have a print ad or other information from the Internet, that information should also be filed in an orderly way.

Prepare to Apply

Before you apply for a job, you need to prepare several documents. These documents include a personal fact sheet, references list, application form, résumé, and cover message. It is often valuable to prepare a portfolio.

Be sure to proofread all written documents. Whenever possible, have another person proofread them. It is very easy to make keying, spelling, and grammar errors and not notice them yourself.

Personal Fact Sheet

During the process of applying for a job, you will be asked to provide a great deal of information about yourself. Most jobs require applicants to fill out a job application form. You will also be writing letters and developing a résumé. To make these tasks easier, it is useful to compile a personal fact sheet.

Your personal fact sheet should contain any information that an employer may want.

Adults in your life who know your work ethic, positive qualities, and skills make good references.

bikeriderlondon/Shutterstock.com

It is especially helpful for information that you might forget or do not currently know. Examples of such information include names and addresses of all schools attended and dates of attendance, skills, honors, activities, hobbies, and interests. It should also include detailed information about your work or volunteer experience, such as name and address of employers, dates of employment, supervisor's name, salary, and job duties.

References

Many job applications ask for several references. A **reference** is a person who is willing to talk with employers about your job qualifications and personal qualities. You might also be asked for a list of references during an interview. When an employer is interested in hiring you, he or she will contact your references. The employer will ask your references questions about your job qualifications and work attitudes. The employer might ask your references whether they think you would be a good fit in the job for which you have applied.

It is advisable to have at least three people on your reference list. It is also important that you choose the right people. In general, the following people are *not* recommended as references: parents, other relatives, and friends. Choose people who are over 21 and not related to you. Teachers, employers, clergy, coaches, and club advisors are good choices.

You should always call each reference before giving his or her name to an employer. Ask your potential references if they are willing to be a reference for you. If they say *yes*, ask them for an address and phone number that you can write on an application. Also, ask for their job titles and places of work. Then, tell them about the kind of work you are trying to get and discuss your strengths and qualifications.

Once you have the information and consent from your references, add the information to your references list. Be sure to include your name and contact information at the top of the page. Make several copies. Bring your references list and your personal information sheet to an interview. Many career counselors recommend that you include the following phrase at the end of your résumé: "References available upon request."

Résumés

A **résumé** (pronounced rez-uh-may) is a written document that lists your qualifications for a job, including education and work experience. Many want ads request that you e-mail, fax, or mail a résumé, as shown in Figure 30-3.

Your name, address, telephone number, and e-mail address go at the top of the page. The order of the headings in a résumé depends on the person. Someone with little experience might place the education heading after job objective. Someone with a great deal of experience might place the experience heading after objective. Others list their skills and abilities right after the job objective. In general, a résumé has the following headings.

Name and Personal Information

Include your name, address, telephone number, and e-mail address at the top of the résumé. When applying for a job, be sure to use an e-mail address that is your real name or at least a portion of it. E-mails with nicknames or screen names do not make a professional impression.

Objective

A job objective should only be used if applying for a specific type of position. This is an optional heading.

ROBERT R. JEFFRIES
518 Burnett Road
Randallstown, MD 21123
Home: 301-555-1234
Mobile: 301-555-4321
E-mail: rjeffries@e-mail.com

OBJECTIVE
To obtain an administrative position as assistant to a senior-level executive in an institution of higher education, private industry, or large government agency.

EXPERIENCE
August, 2009–present
Administrative Assistant to the Director of Education, College of San Mateo, Redwood City, CA
Develop Correspondence
- Screen the director's correspondence and assist with preparation of responses
- Prepare e-mails, memorandums, and letters to ensure accuracy and timely response
- Assist with research, editing, and final preparation of reports
Assist with Staff Management
- Manage the calendars of five staff members and the director
- Write meeting notifications, agendas, and minutes
- Schedule meetings and make special arrangements, such as catering and A/V equipment
- Maintain up-to-date personnel data for staff members
- Supervise two student clerks

June, 2008–August, 2009
Receptionist and Administrative Assistant, Principal's Office, Jefferson High School
- Scheduled appointments for student, faculty, and parents
- Answered telephones, screened, and directed calls
- Greeted visitors, faculty, and students and provided assistance as needed
- Prepared letters and documents
- Scheduled appointments and maintained the calendars of the principal and vice principals

EDUCATION
Associate   Degree, June, 2008, Essex Community College, Baltimore, MD
Major: Office Administration

SPECIAL SKILLS
Computer: Microsoft Office Suite, Adobe InDesign, HTML
General: Excellent speaking and written-communication skills, highly organized, and able to prioritize organizing and planning of multiple projects.

Figure 30-3 A résumé gives the employer a quick way to learn about your qualifications.

Skills and Abilities

This section can be used to highlight your most important skills and abilities. It is especially useful if you have little experience or if your experience is in a different field.

Education

List the schools you attended with the most recently attended school first. Include the name of the school, the degree or diploma you earned, and the time of attendance. List courses that are relevant to your job objective. This list usually begins with the high school attended. Do *not* include elementary and middle schools.

Experience

List your work experiences with the most recent job first. Include the name of the company, your job title, and the time that you worked there. Briefly describe your duties. Include any volunteer jobs, and indicate that you were a volunteer.

Awards and Honors

List any awards or honors you have received and when you earned them. Include a brief description of why you got the award or honor.

Activities

List activities that indicate job-related skills. Examples may include school government, clubs, career and technical student organizations, sports teams, and youth organizations such as Boy or Girl Scouts. Indicate any leadership positions or relevant projects. If you are not involved in these types of activities, you can use the heading *Hobbies* or *Interests* to list any career-relevant hobbies or interests.

References

Under the References head, use the phrase, "References available upon request." Make sure that you have a typed list of references available to send or bring with you to interviews.

Electronic and Scannable Résumés

The process of applying for a job is often completed online, through either a company website or an online job-search site. You may need to send your résumé as an e-mail attachment or upload it as a file. In these cases, your résumé should be formatted in the file just as if it were printed. However, be aware that the reader may not have any unusual fonts you have used. So, just use common fonts, such as Arial or Times New Roman. If you use a font that the reader does not have, a font substitution is made when the file is opened by the receiver. This substitution may drastically change your formatting.

In some cases, you will need to cut and paste your résumé into an online application form. This process usually strips out formatting such as bold, tabs, and indentations. You may need to adjust the layout of your résumé after it is pasted into the online application.

You may choose to create your own website and post your résumé as a web page on it. To do so, set up the résumé using HTML or other programming language, so you may upload the page to your website. Refer to books on programming websites for more information. After your résumé web page is live, you can then provide the URL to employers when you apply for a job.

Some employers also scan résumés that they receive in printed form to enter the data into a database. A **scannable résumé** is formatted to eliminate typographical elements, such as bold, bullets, italics, and indents. Some guidelines to follow for scannable résumés include

- use a one-column format;
- avoid horizontal lines, boxes, or shading to set off sections;
- avoid asterisks, dashes, parentheses, and brackets;

- use all capital letters for headings;
- do not use italics, underlining, or graphics; and
- double space between items in each section.

Cover Message

A **cover message** is a letter or e-mail that accompanies your résumé and expresses your interest in a job, as shown in Figure 30-4. A cover message and résumé are usually sent in response to a specific advertised job opening. They can also be sent in response to a job opening that you learn about through networking.

The purpose of the cover message is to request an interview. Three paragraphs are usually enough. The first paragraph describes how you learned about the job opening and why you are interested. The second paragraph gives a brief description of your qualifications for the job. This paragraph should refer the reader to your résumé for more details. In the third paragraph, request an interview. Provide information on how to reach you to arrange for the interview. If you send an electronic résumé, the cover message without the personal information should appear at the beginning of the e-mail that contains the résumé.

When possible, address the letter to the person who is responsible for hiring that position. This information may be included in the want ad. If it is not, call the company and request the name and title of the person hiring for that job.

Portfolio

A **portfolio** is a selection of materials that you collect and organize to show your qualifications, skills, and talents. When you apply for a job, community service, or college, you will need a portfolio to showcase your qualifications for it. The portfolio is usually shown during an interview, not sent in before the meeting.

There are two types of portfolios: a print, or paper, portfolio and an electronic portfolio, called an e-portfolio. An e-portfolio is also known as a *digital portfolio.*

The interview is an opportunity for a job applicant and the employer to get to know each other.

Goodluz/Shutterstock.com

Jennifer S. Fitzpatrick
204 West Pickford Road
Jefferson City, MO 65001
(Home) 573-555-1234
(Cell) 573-555-4321

June 5, 20--

Ms. Cheryl Lynn Sebastian
Director of Administration
Jefferson City Convention & Visitors Bureau, Inc.
100 E. High Street
Jefferson City, MO 65101

Dear Ms. Sebastian:

Introduction → The position you advertised in the *Network Journal* on March 14 for a customer service trainee is exactly the kind of job I am seeking. According to your ad, this position requires good business communication skills. As you can see by my résumé, my educational background and experience working at a travel agency prepare me for this position.

Body → For the past two years, I worked as a part-time receptionist at the Barcelona Travel Agency. While working there, I gained experience dealing with customers on the telephone, as well as greeting walk-in customers and handling their requests for information. I also had the opportunity to observe the full-time staff at work and attend department meetings. At these meetings, I learned the importance of satisfying customer needs and meeting the challenges of working with the general public.

As the enclosed résumé shows, I will graduate from Southeast High School in early June. I took several business courses, including a business communication class. These classes helped me develop good English and verbal communication skills. In addition to my education and work experience, I can offer your organization a strong work ethic and the ability to fluently speak Spanish.

Conclusion → I would like very much to meet you and hope that you will contact me by phone or e-mail to schedule an interview for the position. If I do not hear from you within the next couple of weeks, I hope you will not mind if I follow up with a phone call.

Sincerely yours,

Jennifer S. Fitzpatrick

Enclosure

Figure 30-4 A cover message should be no longer than one page.

Choose items that show the skills and abilities that are valuable for the job you want. Choose only your best and most impressive work. Figure 30-5 lists some ideas of what you might include, but the list is endless. For a print portfolio, put each item in a plastic sleeve, and then place the items in a ring binder. Each item should have a caption or a brief paragraph that explains why it is in the portfolio and what it shows about your abilities. For a digital portfolio, you may create a web site or a digital binder. Follow the same guidelines for identifying each item that you are displaying.

Examples of Portfolio Components
• Copy of diplomas, certificates, and degrees
• Final school transcripts
• Awards
• Job evaluations
• Samples of original written, artistic, or photographic work
• List of volunteer work
• List of organizations to which you belong

Goodheart-Willcox Publisher

Figure 30-5 Not every portfolio will have all of these items. Make sure the portfolio you show is relevant to the position you want.

Apply for Jobs

Once you have prepared your personal fact sheet, reference list, résumé, and portfolio, you are ready to apply for jobs. Sort through the job leads you have. Discard information for the jobs you do not want or for which you are not qualified. Then, put the leads in order from most interesting to least interesting.

Most companies require job seekers to complete a form called a **job application** when applying for an open position This

form has spaces for information about you, your education, and your work experience. Most of the information you need to fill out a job application is on your personal fact sheet.

Job application forms may sometimes be completed and submitted online. If asked to fill out a printed form, print the answers clearly and neatly as possible. For some sales associate jobs, you can pick up a job application at the place of work. You then can take the application home, fill it out, and return it. For many jobs, you are given a job application to fill out when you go for an interview. Be sure to bring a pen for this purpose. Many businesses provide online application forms on their websites.

Once you have applied for a job, you must wait for a response. If you do not hear back within a week or two, call the company to find out if the job was filled. If the job is not yet filled, express your interest in it and your desire for an interview. Ask if there is any additional information you could send the hiring manager. To some extent, getting a job is a numbers game. The more jobs for which you apply, the greater the chance of getting at least one job offer.

Interview

It is rare for someone to get a job without an interview. An *interview* is a formal meeting between two or more people, during which questions are asked of one person. Being invited to a company for an interview is an important accomplishment. It means that the employer is impressed by your résumé or application and wants to learn more about you. Many companies conduct phone interviews before inviting job candidates in for a personal interview.

In an interview, the job applicant wants to impress the employer and learn about the job. The employer wants to learn about the job applicant and decide whether to offer the applicant the position. Usually, the employer interviews several candidates for the same job. The purpose of the interview for the employer is to decide which candidate will be the best for the job.

First Impressions Count

How quickly do people form an opinion of a new person they meet? Studies show that an opinion is often formed in 90 seconds or less. Once that opinion is formed, it is often difficult to change. Therefore, when interviewing, you want to make the best first impression.

It is only human nature to be influenced by appearances. If you want employers to look further into your qualifications, you

must impress them at your first meeting. Appropriate appearance and behavior are very important when interviewing.

Your grooming and dress for an interview should be clean, neat, and professional. A business suit always makes a good impression, even if you will be wearing a uniform on the job. If you know the business well, you can dress for the interview in the same style as the employees do. However, if you are not sure, conservative dress is better. Figure 30-6 provides general guidelines for dressing for an interview.

The way in which you greet the interviewer makes a strong impression. Stand tall. Smile, maintain eye contact, and give the interviewer a firm handshake. Use the interviewer's name in the greeting. For example, "Hello, Ms. Reed. My name is Arif Iqbal. I am here to interview for the management trainee position."

Appropriate Attire for a Job Interview

Women
- Wear a suit or dress with a conservative length.
- Choose solid colors over prints or flowers.
- Wear pumps with a moderate heel or flats.
- Keep any jewelry small.
- Have a well-groomed hairstyle.
- Use little makeup.
- Avoid perfume or apply it very lightly.
- Nails should be manicured and of moderate length without decals.

Men
- Wear a conservative suit of a solid color.
- Wear a long-sleeved shirt, either white or a light color.
- Tie should be a solid color or a conservative print.
- Wear loafers or lace-up shoes with dark socks.
- Avoid wearing jewelry.
- Have a well-groomed haircut.
- Avoid cologne.
- Nails should be neatly trimmed.

Goodheart-Willcox Publisher

Figure 30-6 Keep in mind that you are dressing to fit the job that you want.

Prepare for the Interview

If you are well prepared for the interview, it is likely to go smoothly and you will make a good impression. Before the personal interview, prepare yourself in the following areas.

Place of Interview

Make sure you know where the interview will take place and exactly how to get there. Find out how long it will take to get there. If you are unfamiliar with the location, make a trial run before the interview. Know the name and title of the person who will interview you. Call the day before to confirm the time and place.

Introduction

Prepare a few sentences of introduction. Practice speaking slowly and clearly. Practice your handshake. Use your right hand to grasp the other person's hand firmly. End the handshake after three seconds.

Questions to Ask Interviewers

The interview is also a time for you to learn about the job by asking relevant questions. You need to learn enough about the job and the work environment to determine whether you would be happy working there. In addition, asking questions shows that you are seriously interested in the company and have thought about the job. Prepare some questions ahead of time, as shown in Figure 30-7.

Questions Interviewers May Ask

The interviewer will ask questions to learn about you and your qualifications for the job. There may be more than one person in the interview who is determining if you are the right person for the job. The interviewers will also be deciding if you will fit in with the team that is already in place. Figure 30-8 presents some typical questions that interviews may ask. Practice your answers ahead of time.

Questions to Ask During an Interview

- What is the policy regarding overtime work?
- May I expect to have a written job description, so that I will know exactly what is expected of me?
- When will I be eligible for a vacation, and how much vacation time will I receive each year?
- Will I be required to join a union or professional association as a condition of employment?
- What is the salary range for the job, and how often could I expect to receive a raise?
- What is the company's policy regarding sick days, personal leave days, and holidays?
- What health benefits will I receive; medical, dental, and vision insurance?
- Does the company have a retirement plan?
- Does the company have a deferred compensation plan, such as 401(k)?
- Does the company have an employee credit union?
- Does the company have a stock purchase or profit-sharing plan?
- Does the company pay bonuses, and how does an employee earn a bonus?
- Will the company pay tuition for employees who take job-related courses and are any in-service training or seminars offered?
- Does the company provide free parking for employees?

Goodheart-Willcox Publisher

Figure 30-7 Asking thoughtful and informed questions during an interview makes a good impression on the interviewers.

Resource/Evaluate

Assign the optional Chapter 30 test for **EXAM**VIEW®
Assessment Suite as a formal assessment tool.

Questions You May Be Asked at an Interview

- Tell me about yourself.
- Why are you interested in working for this company?
- Tell me about your education.
- Why have you chosen this particular field?
- Describe your best/worst boss.
- In a job, what interests you most/least?
- What is your major weakness?
- Give an example of how you solved a problem in the past.
- What are your strengths?
- How do others describe you?
- Where do you see yourself in three years?
- How do you think you will fit into this department/company?
- If you were hired, what ideas/talents would you bring to the position and our company?
- Do you have any questions for me?

Goodheart-Willcox Publisher

Figure 30-8 It is wise for job applicants to have prepared responses to all of these questions before going to any interview.

Also, practice showing your portfolio as part of your answers.

Questions Interviewers Should Not Ask

When applying for a job, you have certain legal rights that are protected by federal law. These laws protect you from discrimination during the hiring process. To protect your rights, there are certain questions that interviewers may *not* ask during an interview or on a job application. Figure 30-9 provides examples of illegal questions.

Some interviewers do not know the law very well and do not realize that certain questions are illegal. Your response to such questions might be as follows: "Please explain how that relates to the job," or "I would rather not answer personal questions."

Engage

Pick several questions and ask the student why they think these questions are illegal.

Illegal Interview Questions

- What is the name of your spouse?
- What is the occupation of your spouse?
- Have you ever filed a workers' compensation claim or been injured on the job?
- Do you have any physical impairments?
- Have you ever been arrested?
- What is your height or weight?
- Have you ever been hospitalized? If so, for what condition?
- Have you ever been treated by a psychiatrist or psychologist?
- How many days were you absent from work last year due to illness?
- Are you taking any prescribed drugs?
- Have you ever been treated for drug addiction or alcoholism?

Goodheart-Willcox Publisher

Figure 30-9 It is illegal for an employer to discriminate based on race, color, religion, national origin, sex, age, and disability. Therefore, they may not legally ask certain questions that apply to these subjects.

Successful Interviews

The following guidelines will contribute to successful interviews.

- Arrive a few minutes early; allow enough time for travel and parking.
- Do not bring anyone with you to the interview. If someone drove you, have him or her wait for you in the car or at a nearby shop.
- Do not chew gum or smoke.
- Speak clearly, avoid mumbling, and use standard English.
- Bring your information. Bring your personal fact sheet, two copies of your résumé, two copies of your references, paper, pen (blue or black ink), and your portfolio.
- Bring any other papers the interviewer may have requested, such as a work permit. You should have something in which to carry your loose papers. You do not have to buy an expensive business case. A nice folder with a closure from an office supply store is fine.

Engage

Set up mock interviews. Have students take turns being the interviewer.

Follow Up

When the interview is over, the interviewer will give you some cues. For example, the interviewer might get up and say, "Thank you for coming in. We plan to make a decision by the end of the week." At that point, thank the interviewer for his or her time and interest. Smile, shake hands, and then leave.

After an interview, you should always write a thank-you letter or e-mail. The letter can be brief. Thank the interviewer for his or her time and interest. If you are interested in the job, say a few words expressing your interest and your strongest qualifications for the job. Sending a thank-you letter shows you are sincerely interested in the position and helps you to stand out from the candidates who did not send thank-you letters.

Make notes about the interview in your job-leads file. Analyze your performance honestly. What did you do well? What might need improvement? Also, note the result of the interview. When the interviewer contacts you, make a note of what he or she says, and if you got the job.

It will probably take from a few days to a few weeks before the interviewer makes a hiring decision. The interviewer must interview all applicants. The employer will probably also check your references. The hiring manager may also call your schools to ensure that you graduated and verify your grades.

If you do not have an answer after a week or two, call the employer. Ask for the person who interviewed you. Give your name and the date of your interview. Ask if a decision has been made regarding the job. If a decision has not been made, express your interest in the job. Ask if the interviewer needs any more information from you. Ask when the decision will be made or when you may call again. Respond to any request immediately.

Checkpoint 30.2

1. How can the marketing concept be applied in a job search?
2. List the steps of the job search process.
3. What are some potential ways to find a job lead?
4. How can networking help you find a job?
5. Why is it important to follow up after an interview?

Build Your Vocabulary

As you progress through this course, develop a personal glossary of personal marketing terms and add it to your portfolio. This will help you build your vocabulary and prepare you for a career. Write a definition for each of the following terms, and add it to your personal marketing glossary.

job lead
want ad
networking
letter of inquiry
reference

résumé
scannable résumé
cover message
portfolio
job application

Chapter Summary

Section **30.1** Career Preparation

- Education and preparation for a career can be organized into three categories: education, training, and continuing education.
- Once your career goal is chosen, you can develop your career plan based on what you have learned about the required education and skills. A career plan is like a map that you used to guide you to your career goal.

Section **30.2** Job Seeking

- The job search process is like a marketing campaign. Many of the same strategies marketers use for products can be applied to your job search, allowing you to show potential employers your skills and abilities.
- The most common ways of finding job leads are want ads, the Internet, networking, and direct employer contact.
- The important information needed for tracking leads includes the company contact information, the job title, the name and title of the person with whom you should contact, and the source of the lead.
- The documents used in the job search process include a personal fact sheet, references list, application form, résumé, and cover message. It is often valuable to prepare a portfolio.
- The application process often starts by sorting through job leads you have, discarding information for the jobs you do not want or for which you are not qualified, and then putting the leads in order from most interesting to least interesting.
- An interview is a formal meeting between two or more people, during which questions are asked of one person. Prior to the interview, an applicant should know the place of the interview, prepare an appropriate introduction, have questions to ask, and be prepared to answer likely questions.

Evaluate

Assign the end-of-chapter activities.

Review Your Knowledge

1. What is formal education?
2. List four types of schools for postsecondary education.
3. Explain how a career plan is like a map.
4. Name three free social media networking sites for finding job leads.
5. When is direct employer contact most successful?
6. How long does it usually take to make a first impression?
7. Whom should you choose as references?
8. What information is at the top of a résumé?
9. What is the purpose of a cover message and how long should it be?
10. What should you do after an interview?

Apply Your Knowledge

1. Describe your college and career readiness plans after high school graduation.
2. What does it mean to market yourself to a potential employer?
3. Personal branding is important to your career. What is the personal brand that you want employers to recognize?
4. Explain the importance of ongoing networking for professionals.
5. List some potential networking opportunities that you might have with professionals. This could be at a community meeting, sports event, or other location where you may talk to people who are in careers. How might these people help you with ideas for college or career?
6. How would you respond to an employer who says you did not get the job for which you applied?
7. Prepare a résumé. Use the examples in this chapter as a guide.
8. Select an advertisement for a job from a print or online source. Write a letter of application for the position. Use the example in this chapter as a guide.
9. Completing job applications takes practice. Do an Internet search for *job applications* and print three that are appropriate for your age group. Use a pen to practice completing an application as neatly as possible without making mistakes.
10. Imagine you just went through a successful interview process. Write a thank-you letter to the interviewer. Use the guidelines described in this chapter.

Review Your Knowledge Answers

1. Formal education refers to the education you get from a school, college, or university.
2. Postsecondary education can be received at professional career schools, vocational-technical schools, community colleges, and business and career colleges or universities.
3. A career plan is like a map used to guide you to your career goal.
4. Social media sites that are good for networking include Twitter, Facebook, and LinkedIn.
5. Direct contact is most successful when you have researched the company, know a great deal about it, and have a clear idea of what you can offer the company as an employee.
6. Studies show that a first impression is often formed in 90 seconds or less.

7. Choose people who are over 21 and not related to you. Teachers, employers, clergy, coaches, and club advisors are good choices. Do not choose parents, other relatives, and friends.
8. Your name, address, telephone number, and e-mail address go at the top of the page.
9. The purpose of the message is to request an interview. It should be three paragraphs long.
10. After an interview, you should always write a thank-you letter or e-mail.

Apply Your Knowledge Answers

Student answers will vary for questions 1–10.

Check Your Marketing IQ

Now that you have finished the chapter, see what you learned about marketing by taking the chapter posttest. If you do not have a smartphone, visit the G-W Learning companion website.

G-W Learning mobile site: www.m.g-wlearning.com
G-W Learning companion website: www.g-wlearning.com

Common Core

College and Career Readiness

CTE Career Ready Practices. The Internet can provide opportunities to enhance the career search process and increase your productivity. There is much information available about how to make the job application process efficient. List five things you can do to improve your skills in completing a job application.

Reading. Using the Internet, research information on the use of social networks to find career opportunities. Delineate and evaluate the specific claims of pros and cons of using social networking.

Speaking. Using the information you found about social networking, present your findings to the class. Your information should be presented in a way that the listeners can follow your line of reasoning. Use an approach that is appropriate to the audience.

Teamwork

Working with a teammate, conduct a mock job interview. One team member should be the employer and the other team member the person being interviewed. The person being interviewed should have a completed application form, letter of application, and résumé. Practice interviewing techniques and rotate roles of employer and interviewee. Working together, create a thank-you letter for the interview.

G-W Learning Mobile Site

Visit the G-W Learning mobile site to complete the chapter pretest and posttest and to practice vocabulary using e-flash cards. If you do not have a smartphone, visit the G-W Learning companion website to access these features.

G-W Learning mobile site: www.m.g-wlearning.com
G-W Learning companion website: www.g-wlearning.com

Evaluate

Evaluate the students' understanding and knowledge. Assign the Chapter 30 posttest. The test may be accessed by using the QR code or by going to the companion website. What questions were students able to answer that they could not answer when they took the pretest?

Unit 9 **Professional Development Dynamics**

Building the Marketing Plan

At this point in your career research, you will have completed a career plan. You should have already decided what activities are needed to move the plan forward and reach your unique career goal. A marketing plan is similar to a career plan in that marketing goals are identified, and the ways to achieve them are listed. Because a marketing plan is much longer, though, it is important to give the reader a way to quickly learn about what the plan contains and where to find what they are looking for. This takes place in the Executive Summary and the Table of Contents.

Executive Summary

Objective

- Write the Executive Summary and the Table of Contents.

Directions

In this activity, you will write the Executive Summary and the Table of Contents sections for your marketing plan. An executive summary provides the overview of the marketing plan by highlighting the critical points of the plan. A table of contents shows the major sections of a plan in the order they appear. These two sections of a plan should be written last because they reflect the entire plan you have spent so much time researching and writing. Access the *Marketing Dynamics* companion website at www.g-wlearning.com. Download the data file as indicated for the following activity.

1. **Unit Activity 9-1.** Executive Summary. Download the file for Activity 9-1. Start the Executive Summary with an introductory paragraph designed to entice the reader to review the entire document. Finally, give an overview of the topics the marketing plan addresses. This section should be no longer than two pages.

2. Open your saved marketing plan document.

3. Locate the Executive Summary section of the marketing plan and write the Executive Summary. Use the suggestions and questions listed to help you generate ideas. Delete the instructions and questions when you are finished recording your responses.

4. Locate the Table of Contents page in your plan document. Make sure what is listed in red from the marketing plan template reflects the actual sections of your plan in the correct order. If not, rearrange the sections to match your plan. Make sure your Table of Contents appears in black type. Include page numbers. Proofread your document and correct any errors in keyboarding, spelling, and grammar.

5. Save your document.

Engage

Provide the students will several examples of action plans and timelines using your school system's strategic plan.

Dynamics of Entrepreneurship

Chapters

Eye-Catcher

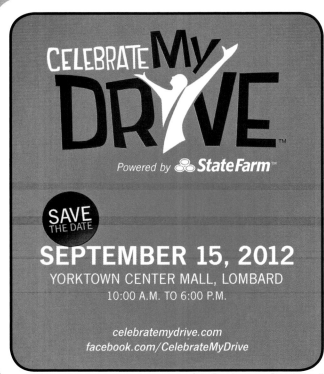

CELEBRATE **My** DR**I**VE™

Powered by **State Farm**™

SAVE THE DATE

SEPTEMBER 15, 2012
YORKTOWN CENTER MALL, LOMBARD
10:00 A.M. TO 6:00 P.M.

celebratemydrive.com
facebook.com/CelebrateMyDrive

State Farm Insurance, Bloomington, IL

Marketing Matters

Successful marketing is not just measured by how much money a business makes. Other metrics can be used, one of which is degree of social responsibility. A socially responsible business shows concern for the community, the country, and the world. State Farm Insurance is an example of a corporation supporting the community. The State Farm® Teen Driver Safety website provides support for teens as they learn to drive safely. By providing a comprehensive website, teens and parents can obtain valuable information for staying safe through the learning-to-drive process. Marketing does matter.

Marketing Core Functions Covered in This Unit

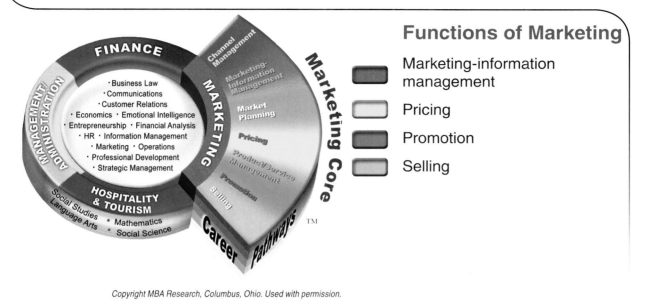

Functions of Marketing

- Marketing-information management
- Pricing
- Promotion
- Selling

Copyright MBA Research, Columbus, Ohio. Used with permission.

Developing a Vision

You may already know that you want to start your own business someday. Your career plan may be to gain marketing and business experience first, then pursue your own dreams of starting a business. Real-world experience is a teacher that can prepare you to become an entrepreneur.

Entrepreneurs are people who have ideas, are creative, and figure out how to finance their ideas. They are risk takers who learn how to manage risks. They are persistent and will not take no for an answer. Studying this unit may help you decide if becoming an entrepreneur is in your future.

31 Entrepreneurship

| Section 31.1 | Entrepreneurs |
| Section 31.2 | Business Ideas |

"To any entrepreneur: If you want to do it, do it now. If you don't, you're going to regret it."

—Catherine Cook, youth entrepreneur and cofounder of myYearbook.com, a social networking digital yearbook

Reading Prep
Before you begin reading this chapter, preview the section heads and vocabulary lists. Make a list of questions that you have before reading. Search for answers to your questions as you continue reading the chapter.

College and Career Readiness

Check Your Marketing IQ

Before you begin the chapter, see what you already know about marketing by taking the chapter pretest. If you do not have a smartphone, visit the G-W Learning companion website.
G-W Learning mobile site: www.m.g-wlearning.com
G-W Learning companion website: www.g-wlearning.com

G-W Mobile

Explore

Provide an opportunity for students to explore by assigning a hands-on activity. Assign the College and Career Readiness Reading Prep activity before students read the chapter. Reading Prep activities give students opportunity to apply the Common Core State Standards.

Engage

Engage the students by providing an activity or question that will connect students to what they already know. Assign the Chapter 31 pretest. The test may be accessed by using the QR code or going to the *Marketing Dynamics* companion website. Discuss which questions students were unable to answer.

◇DECA Emerging Leaders

Food Marketing Series Event, Part 1

Career Cluster: Marketing
Career Pathway: Marketing Management
Instructional Area: Pricing

General Performance Indicators

- Communications skills—the ability to exchange information and ideas with others through writing, speaking, reading, or listening
- Analytical skills—the ability to derive facts from data, findings from facts, conclusions from findings, and recommendations from conclusions
- Production skills—the ability to take a concept from an idea and make it real
- Teamwork—the ability to be an effective member of a productive group
- Priorities/time management—the ability to determine priorities and manage time commitments
- Economic competencies

Performance Indicators

- Explain the nature and scope of the pricing function.
- Describe the role of business ethics in pricing.
- Explain the use of technology in the pricing function.
- Describe factors used by marketers to position products/businesses.
- Explain factors affecting pricing decisions.

Purpose

Designed for an individual DECA member, the event measures the member's proficiency in the knowledge, skills, and attitudes in the business administration core and appropriate career cluster and pathway of a given career in a role-play. This event consists of a 100-question, multiple-choice, cluster exam and two role-play activities in a written scenario.

Participants are not informed in advance of the performance indicators to be evaluated. For the purpose of this textbook, sample performance indicators are given so that you may practice for the competition.

For the purposes of this text, you will be presented with the material for this event in two parts. Part 1 presents the knowledge and skills assessed and an overview of the event's purpose and procedure. Part 2 presents the remaining procedures and the event situation.

Procedure, Part 1

1. For Part 1 in this text, read both sets of performance indicators. Discuss these with your team members.
2. If there are any questions, ask your teacher to clarify.

Critical Thinking

1. List responses to each performance indicator. In what areas do your need additional information?
2. Anticipate the role you might assume in food marketing based on the performance indicators. What questions might be asked about pricing?
3. How will you respond to the questions?

   Visit www.deca.org for more information.

Section 31.1 Entrepreneurs

Objectives

After completing this section, you will be able to
- **describe** the traits and skills necessary to become an entrepreneur.
- **discuss** reasons why a person might choose to be an entrepreneur.
- **list** and **explain** the ownership options for starting a business.

Key Terms

entrepreneur
entrepreneurship
self-assessment
sole proprietor
DBA license
unlimited liability
partner
general partnership

limited partnership (LP)
limited liability
partnership agreement
stock
stockholder
corporate formality

Web Connect

Do an Internet search for your local chamber of commerce. How does the chamber of commerce help entrepreneurs in your community? How would you use the chamber of commerce if you were starting a local business?

Critical Thinking

There are several ways for entrepreneurs to start a business. If you were starting a new business, what form would that business take? Explain your reasoning.

Becoming an Entrepreneur

Have you ever had the goal of owning your own business and being your own boss? Are you creative and have an idea about a product or service that could make money. An **entrepreneur** is a person who starts a new business. **Entrepreneurship** is taking on both the risks and responsibilities of starting a new business.

While entrepreneurs have always been the backbone of the US economy, they are even more important since the recession of 2008. Carl Schramm, president and chief executive officer of the Kauffman Foundation said, "Americans in big numbers are looking

to entrepreneurs to rally the economy. More than 70 percent of voters say the health of the economy depends on the success of entrepreneurs. And a full 80 percent want to see the government use its resources to actively encourage entrepreneurship in America."

Traits of Successful Entrepreneurs

Many marketing professionals become entrepreneurs. Being a marketer exposes you to business activities that other employees may never see. Marketers participate in business and market planning, interact with customers, and work with sales teams. These experiences, and others, mean that marketing professionals are also involved in the

Explain

Discuss examples of young entrepreneurs. Are any of your students aiming for such a career?

Resource

Use the Chapter 31 presentation on the optional Instructor's Presentations for PowerPoint® CD as an outline for presenting the chapter.

fundamental practices of business. Many marketers enjoy these activities and take those experiences to create their own businesses. Your marketing studies and experiences may lead you to becoming a business owner sometime in your future.

Do you have what it takes to start a business? There are many traits that entrepreneurs have in common. *Traits* are behavioral and emotional characteristics that make each person unique. Have you thought about what your unique traits might be? Personality traits include the five Ps for entrepreneurs—passion, perseverance, persistence, planning, and problem solving, as shown in Figure 31-1.

You do not need to be at work 24 hours a day, 7 days a week to be a business owner. However, you do need to enjoy the work and have the ability to sell your products, ideas, or services. It is important that you evaluate your aptitudes, attitudes, traits, and skills as you consider starting your own business.

One way to evaluate yourself is by completing a **self-assessment,** which is a tool that helps a person understand and identify personal preferences, strengths, and weaknesses. The goal is to use that personal information when making your career decisions. There are many self-assessment tools available from your counselors and on the Internet.

Skills of Successful Entrepreneurs

There are more traits and skills commonly associated with successful entrepreneurs.

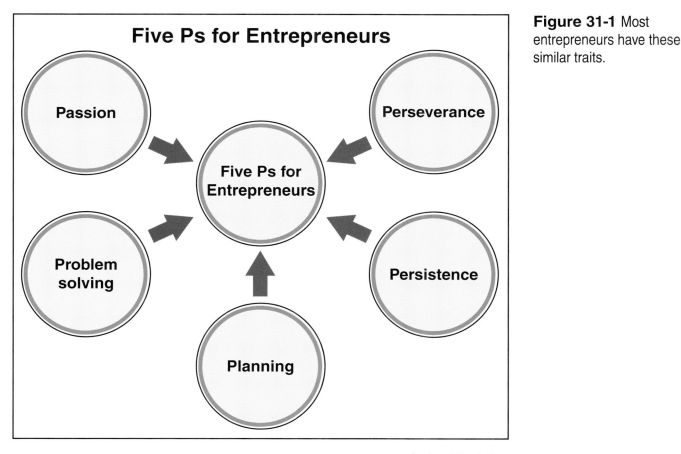

Figure 31-1 Most entrepreneurs have these similar traits.

Elaborate/Extend

Assign the College and Career Readiness Portfolio activity at the end of the chapter.

Engage

Ask a student to present Figure 31-1 and explain why the five Ps are important.

Case in Point

Girlpez

Many teenage entrepreneurs are starting businesses on the Internet because both funding and prior experience are not always necessary for success. For example, Savannah Britt is considered to be the youngest magazine publisher in the world. She began her business venture by creating a website for teen girls called Girlpez.com at the age of 14. Her goal was to use her influence to strengthen girls and their communities. Girlpez also became a hard copy magazine called *Girlpez Fashion Magazine* with features, such as concert event coverage and interviews. When asked about the driving force behind her willingness to publish a magazine at such a young age, she states, "I like a challenge. I think what drove me to start my magazine was the fact that I was so young, and I was doing something that nobody around me was doing. That pushed me, honestly, to start my magazine." Britt's magazine eventually made the transformation to an online-only format. Becoming an entrepreneur can be as easy as having a product or idea that people will buy along with a willingness to succeed. As Britt states, "There is no reason to be hesitant… becoming an entrepreneur is a learning experience."

Skills are the things that you do well. Many entrepreneurial skills can be learned at school. Others are learned through life experiences. These skills include communication, math, business, computers, problem solving, decision making, and human relations.

Entrepreneurs need excellent communication skills. They will need to explain their businesses to banks to get loans. All entrepreneurs should write business plans, promote their products to customers, work with suppliers, and organize their businesses. Reading, writing, listening, and speaking are essential skills.

Math skills are needed to calculate start-up costs, monitor sales and profits, and prepare financial statements and tax returns. Inventory management also requires good math skills. Math skills are also needed for pricing.

Some entrepreneurs start their businesses without much business knowledge or experience. However, they quickly learn that they need to know about the economy, accounting, financing, marketing, and business management. Both high school and college courses, continuing education courses, and books help entrepreneurs gain those skills. A mentor or business consultant can also provide business knowledge and expertise.

Problem solving and decision making are two skills that work together. Entrepreneurs confront many new situations and problems when starting a business. Entrepreneurs need to be able to analyze a problem, brainstorm and research solutions, and then decide on the best course of action.

Being successful in business requires good human relations skills. Entrepreneurs need to be able to get along with other people, encourage cooperation, and persuade people to understand their point of view. Entrepreneurs also need to know how to negotiate fairly and honestly.

Figure 31-2 lists effective entrepreneurship traits and skills, although there are many more. How many of the traits and skills on the list describe you?

Elaborate/Extend

If students are using the optional *Marketing Dynamics* workbook, assign activities to engage active learning.

Extend

Invite an entrepreneur from your community to talk with the class about the experience of starting a business.

Entrepreneurial Traits and Skills		
• Achievement-oriented	• Good with money	• Perseverance
• Adaptable	• Honest	• Plans ahead
• Competitive	• Independent	• Positive attitude
• Creative	• Intuitive	• Resourceful
• Disciplined	• Learns quickly	• Risk-tolerant
• Empathetic	• Motivated	• Self-confident
• Energetic	• Nonjudgmental	• Self-starter
• Goal-oriented	• Organized	• Visionary

Figure 31-2 Many successful entrepreneurs have these skills and traits in common.

Goodheart-Willcox Publisher

Why Become an Entrepreneur?

Why would a person want to be an entrepreneur? Many people would respond, "Because you can make a lot of money!" Money is not the only reason to start a business, though. The reasons for starting a business are countless. Controlling your destiny is an exciting reason to be an entrepreneur. Other rewards include

- **being your own boss.** You can determine your own work schedule, set your own prices, and see the hard work pay off.
- **taking advantage of your earning potential.** With high unemployment and global issues, an entrepreneur can continue working and not depend on someone else for an income.
- **enjoying your career.** As an entrepreneur, you can do something you truly like, are good at, and believe in; you can apply your creativity with no limits.
- **making a difference in the world.** Most entrepreneurs do not start a business solely for the potential profit. They start a business because they are passionate about what they are doing.

Every new venture comes with risks. In general, the higher the risk, the greater

potential for both reward and loss. Being aware of the risks makes you better prepared for a career as an entrepreneur. For example, a profit may not be realized for many months, so you will not collect a regular paycheck. It is important to be financially prepared as an uncertain income may be a hardship for an owner. Other risks can include

- taking responsibility for the good and bad decisions you might make;
- working long hours; as an owner of a new businesses, you will probably work long days that can put stress on personal health and emotions as well as affect the family; and
- risking personal finances: start-up costs and expenses may need to come from your personal funds; new businesses often do not make a profit for several months to several years.

There are other risks that are associated with creating a new business. Creating a thorough business plan will identify the risks so you can overcome them.

Ownership

If you start your own business, you will also decide on the form of business ownership. In Chapter 3, you learned about the three

Explore

Ask for additional reasons to start a business.

basic forms of ownership: sole proprietorship, partnership, and corporation as shown in Figure 31-3. There are advantages and disadvantages to each type of ownership structure. It is wise to seek professional advice before signing any ownership documents.

Sole Proprietorship

A **sole proprietor** is the one person who owns the business and is personally responsible for all its debts. A sole proprietor has total responsibility for the business and receives all the profits. Recall that *liability* means legal responsibility. In business, owners may or may not be held personally liable for the losses a business may have.

Many counties and states require sole proprietors to apply for a DBA license before starting a new business. A **DBA license,** or a *doing business as* license, is needed to register a business. Some types of businesses also require a specific license or permit for a service business, such as a hair stylist or dentist.

FYI

In some states, a DBA license is known as a *fictitious name registration.*

Many home-based businesses are sole proprietorships. Examples include dog walking, website development, and marketing consulting. Sole proprietorships are the easiest to start. And, if they are home- or Internet-based businesses, they may not involve a large amount of money to open and operate.

However, operating as a sole proprietorship has its drawbacks. As a sole proprietor, you must raise all of the money to start the business. You personally bear all of the risk involved in the business. A sole proprietor has *unlimited liability* in the business. **Unlimited liability** means you alone are responsible for all risks. If you are sued and lose, you alone must pay the damages. Figure 31-4 shows some of the advantages and disadvantages of a sole proprietorship.

Partnership

A *partnership* is the relationship between two or more people who join to create a business. Each person involved in owning a partnership is called a **partner.** The partners share the legal and financial responsibilities as well as the profits.

The main advantage of a partnership is that two or more people are giving ideas, sharing the work, and sharing the responsibility. Two or more people can generate more excitement and

Figure 31-3 Entrepreneurs have several business ownership choices. The best choice often depends on the type of business and the number of investors.

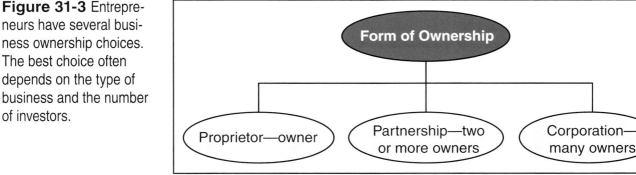

Explain

Compare and contrast the types of ownership.

| Advantages and Disadvantages of Sole Proprietorship ||
Advantages	Disadvantages
Complete control of business	Unlimited liability
Keep 100 percent of the profits	Assume 100 percent of the losses
Easy to create	Sole responsibility
Possible tax benefits	May need other professional expertise

Goodheart-Willcox Publisher

Figure 31-4 A sole proprietorship may be a good way for a young entrepreneur to get started.

motivation. Partners can keep each other going during the rough times. A partnership can often be more creative in problem solving and decision making. Partnerships can often gather more money to start the business.

However, this advantage of shared control and responsibility is often the main disadvantage of the partnership. Partners often disagree about how the business should be run and how much of the profits each partner should receive. Each partner in the business is responsible for the decisions made by the other partners. Suppose one partner decides to sign a contract to buy a building for the business. All the other partners are bound by that contract. Figure 31-5 shows some of the advantages and disadvantages of a partnerhip.

There are two types of partnerships. The most common is a *general partnership*. A **general partnership** is a business structure in which all partners have unlimited liability. The personal assets of each partner, including savings, investments, and homes, can be used to pay off the debts of the business.

The second type is a limited partnership (LP). In a **limited partnership (LP),** there is one managing partner and at least one limited partner. Limited partners have limited liability. **Limited liability** means that a partner or owner cannot lose more than the amount originally invested by that person. They are not personally liable for the debts of the business.

If you are going to form a partnership, hire a lawyer to draw up the partnership agreement. Look for a lawyer who has experience in this area. The **partnership agreement** details how much each partner will invest, each partner's responsibilities, and how profits

| Advantages and Disadvantages of Partnership ||
Advantages	Disadvantages
Individual strengths	Personality conflicts
Shared risk; limited liability for limited partners	Unlimited liability for general partners
Ease of setup	Share profits and losses
More financial resources	Obtaining loans more difficult
Tax benefits	Bound by the agreement

Goodheart-Willcox Publisher

Figure 31-5 Before entering into a partnership, consider both the pros and cons of this form of business ownership.

Explore

Assign students to use the Internet to find a partnership agreement. Ask for a volunteer to explain an agreement that he or she found.

Social Media

When to Pay for Social Media

Companies are turning more and more to social media to reach their customers. Social media is viewed as a free way to engage with both current and potential customers. Technically, social media does cost companies some money. Sure, it is free to create a Facebook page, Twitter account, Pinterest, and Yammer, but companies still need to bring customers to those pages. In order to do that, they must invest employee time, possibly pay for social endorsements on their customer feeds, and even pay for additional display ads on the social media sites. Even though it is not free, paying for display ads is a popular way to communicate because it is easy to start and popular with most target customers. A Pew Research Center survey showed that 65 percent of adult Internet users in the United States used social networking sites in 2011, which is up 31 percent from 2008.

---

are to be shared. All partners must agree to the terms of the agreement because it is a legal document.

Corporation

A corporation is the most complicated form of ownership. Recall that the US Supreme Court defines a *corporation* as "an artificial being, invisible, intangible, and existing only in contemplation of the law." A corporation is considered to be a legal entity and is, in the eyes of the law, a person. As a legal entity, a corporation can perform all business activities. A corporation can buy property, run a business, manufacture products, earn money, pay taxes, sue, and be sued. A corporation can even buy businesses and other corporations.

Owners of a corporation buy stock, or a percentage of ownership in the corporation. They receive one or more certificates stating the number of shares they own based on how much they invested in the corporation. Owners are also called stockholders because they hold stock in the corporation. The stockholders then get the profits from the business, based on the number of shares they own.

In order for a corporation to be established, a *charter* or *certificate of incorporation* is needed. The people who want to start the corporation apply for this legal document from a state government. There are both advantages and disadvantages to incorporating as illustrated in Figure 31-6.

Because a corporation is considered a legal entity, if a shareholder sells stock, the company continues to exist, which is called *perpetual life*. In addition, stockholders, as owners, have limited liability for the corporation. Corporations sell stock to raise investment funds. Having the notation *Inc.,* which stands for incorporated, at the end of a company name adds credibility for many potential customers. However, forming a corporation is also the most expensive and complicated form of business ownership. In some types of corporations, both the individual stockholders and the corporation's profits are taxed. This is called *double taxation* and is seen as a disadvantage to many business founders.

Corporate formalities are the records and procedures that corporations are required by law to complete. If the corporation fails to meet any of the formalities, the business may lose the limited liability protection of being a corporation.

Advantages and Disadvantages of Corporations	
Advantages	**Disadvantages**
• Perpetual life	• Double taxation
• Investors raise capital	• Cost of entry
• Credibility	• Corporate formalities
• Limited liability for owners	

Goodheart-Willcox Publisher

Figure 31-6 Due to the advantage of limited liability, some small business owners choose to incorporate. However, also consider the disadvantages of incorporation.

FYI

Stock is also known as *shares of ownership.* People who buy shares of stock in a company are called its stockholders or *shareholders.*

Alternative Forms of Ownership

There are two alternative forms of ownership that resemble both a partnership and a corporation: *limited liability company (LLC)* and *limited liability partnership (LLP).* Both of these forms limit the personal liability of the owners and can provide tax benefits.

The owners of an LLC are called *members.* LLCs can choose any organizational structure agreed upon by the members. One disadvantage of the LLC is that it has a limited life—the business ends on the retirement or death of one member. It also ends if a member decides to leave the business. LLCs are more expensive to form than sole proprietorships and partnerships. They are also subject to more state and federal regulations.

The owners of an LLP are called *partners.* The LLP has a similar business structure to a limited partnership (LP) but has no managing partner. All of the partners have limited personal liability. Professionals often prefer to organize as an LLP because no partner wants to be liable for another's mistakes.

Profits from LLCs and LLPs are reported on personal tax returns. There is limited liability, less paperwork, and owners can share the profits however they choose. In addition, there is no limit to how many stockholders can be a part of the business.

LLPs and LLCs are not permitted in all states. Each state allowing LLPs determines the amount of limited liability for the partners, which can make it less desirable. Most states require LLPs to carry liability insurance and register with the state.

AMA Tip

If you have an interest in entrepreneurship, you can test out your planning and leadership skills by starting a collegiate chapter of the American Marketing Association once you enter college. As the founding member of a chapter, you will learn to write a constitution, promote the chapter to new members, interact with a faculty advisor, and create a budget. For more information about starting a collegiate chapter, e-mail collegiate@ama.org. www.marketingpower.com

Evaluate
Assign the Checkpoint questions at the end of the section. Assess students' comprehension using the Checkpoint activity as a self-assessment tool.

Checkpoint 31.1

1. Why would a person want to be an entrepreneur?
2. Give examples of skills entrepreneurs need to be successful.
3. Name the three common types of business ownership.
4. What are the two main types of partnerships?
5. What is a charter or certificate of incorporation?

Build Your Vocabulary

As you progress through this course, develop a personal glossary of marketing terms and add it to your portfolio. This will help you build your vocabulary and prepare you for a career. Write a definition for each of the following terms, and add it to your personal marketing glossary.

entrepreneur
entrepreneurship
self-assessment
sole proprietor
DBA license
unlimited liability
partner
general partnership
limited partnership (LP)
limited liability
partnership agreement
stock
stockholder
corporate formality

Checkpoint Answers

1. A person would want to be an entrepreneur for many reasons: to determine your own work schedule, be your own boss, take advantage of your earning potential, enjoy your career, and make a difference in the world are some examples.
2. Examples of entrepreneurial skills are communication, math, business, computers, problem solving, decision making, and human relations skills.
3. Three common types of business ownership are sole proprietorship, partnership, and corporation.

4. Two types of partnerships are general partnership and limited partnerships.
5. In order for a corporation to be established, a charter or certificate of incorporation is needed. The people who want to start the corporation apply for this legal document from a state government.

Build Your Vocabulary Answers

Definitions for these terms can be found in the glossary of this text.

Section 31.2 Business Ideas

Objectives

After completing this section, you will be able to
- **discuss** the process of creating a business.
- **explain** three options for creating a business.
- **describe** the importance of a business plan.

Key Terms

entrepreneurial discovery process
feasible
business operations
franchise
franchisor
franchisee
franchise agreement
franchise fee
business plan

Web Connect

The Small Business Administration (SBA) has a special website for teens interested in entrepreneurship. Visit the site and select *Meet Successful Young Entrepreneurs* and read about one of the featured teens. What qualities helped this young entrepreneur become successful? How could this website help you start a business?

Critical Thinking

Think about the activities that you enjoy most. You are probably good at them as well. Take time to observe needs in the community that also tie into your favorite activities. This could lead to a potential entrepreneurial idea. List four of your favorite activities and how they might become business ideas.

Creating a Business

You know you want to start your own business some day. Your personality and career goals are a perfect match for becoming an entrepreneur. But how do you come up with an idea that will work? Entrepreneurs are always thinking. They are thinking about new and innovative uses for existing products and brand new products or services.

Business opportunities are those ideas that have potential to become successful commercial ventures. Many people have good ideas, but most do not turn into businesses. Finding business opportunities requires that you actively engage with other people and organizations. Before starting the new business, entrepreneurs must go through a discovery process and then determine if the new business will work.

Explore

Provide an opportunity for students to explore by assigning a hands-on activity. Review the vocabulary terms at the beginning of the section. Where have students encountered these terms before? Help students make educated guesses about the meanings of the terms with which they are least familiar.

Discovery Process

In its simplest form, the **entrepreneurial discovery process** is about finding a need for a product or service. The entrepreneurial discovery process actually consists of two parts:
- the recognition of a need or want that is not being met and
- the willingness to take the risk to exploit the opportunity.

Recall that a *need* is something necessary for survival, such as food, clothing, and shelter. A need can also be defined as something necessary to function in society, such as schoolbooks, transportation, and electricity. A *want* is something that a person desires, but could function without, such as a new cell phone or a vacation.

Engage

Use the Teamwork exercise at the end of the chapter to engage students to solve a problem or make a group presentation.

Is My Idea Feasible?

One of the biggest challenges an entrepreneur will face is determining the feasibility of a business idea. **Feasible** means that something can be done successfully. Successful entrepreneurs and businesses conduct some form of feasibility analysis, often called a *feasibility study*, before starting a new business. The analysis helps them determine if their new product or service idea is worth pursuing. This requires some research to determine if customers will buy the product or service and if investors would be likely to fund the business. Feasibility studies must be based on reality, not theory.

There is a wealth of research on the Internet. Look at chambers of commerce, industry organizations, and government resources, such as the Small Business Administration (SBA). Through SBA you can reach the Service Corps of Retired Executives (SCORE). The members of SCORE are retired executives who volunteer their time to help new entrepreneurs develop their business plans and run new businesses. Other government sources of information include Small Business Investment Companies (SBIC), Minority Enterprise Small Business Investment Companies, the Economic Development Administration, and state and local governments. Local and large-market newspapers can also be useful sources of information. Find statistics about the industry, good business locations, and who the customers are. Will the time, effort, and money that would go into starting a venture be worthwhile? What type of business will you open?

- A *manufacturer* turns raw materials from natural resources into new products for sale.
- A *wholesaler* purchases large amounts of goods directly from the manufacturer. The wholesaler then sells those products to retailers.
- The *retailer* buys product and resells to the consumer.
- A *service business* earns money by providing services and expertise to businesses or consumers.

There are many different types of businesses for young entrepreneurs, such as this fashion designer, that can be started from home to save on start-up costs.

Diego Cervo/Shutterstock.com

- A *nonprofit* is an organization that exists to serve some public purpose. Any profit it makes goes to support the nonprofit goal.

Only a small percentage of business ideas and new products achieve long-term success. Business failure rates are high for new businesses. Some of those failures could have been prevented if the owners had studied the feasibility of their businesses *before* starting them.

Business Options

Once you have decided on the business idea, you will decide how to create it. You may opt for a brand new business that you start from the ground up. Or, you may decide to buy an existing business. Another option is to buy into a franchise. The choice is yours.

Start a New Business

Many entrepreneurs decide to start their businesses totally on their own. Starting totally on your own gives you the opportunity to develop the business the way you want it. You can take your own ideas and turn them into reality. A new business could be a storefront for providing existing products or services to consumers. Examples of this type of business include a day spa, car repair garage, or restaurant. Another alternative is to create a new product or service that does not exist yet. Research the ideas, get a patent to protect the ownership, manufacture, and sell it.

Buy an Existing Business

From time to time, a business is offered for sale. Businesses for sale may be listed in the newspaper in the classifieds section under the heading *Business Opportunities.* There are also websites that specialize in listing businesses for sale. These sites often list advertising agencies and other marketing businesses for sale, as well as many consumer businesses.

There are many advantages to buying an existing business. The business already has customers, employees, a location, business equipment, and working business operations. **Business operations** are the day-to-day activities necessary to keep a business up and running. An existing business also has records that describe its financial history. In addition, the person selling the business may be willing to act as a consultant to help you get started in the business.

The main disadvantage of buying an existing business is that you might be buying problems. The most important question to ask when buying an existing business is, "Why is this business being sold?" Many businesses are sold because they are not

Marketing Ethics

Social Media
Social media is commonly used by organizations to reach customers and find new ones. Because it is so available and easy to use, those who are writing communications for the organization must be careful when using sites, such as Facebook or Twitter, for business purposes. Makes sure that any information posted is accurate and verifiable. Do not violate any copyrights. Keep your messages honest and return messages from those who have taken time to respond to your communications. Use good judgment and represent the organization in a professional manner.

Elaborate/Extend

Provide an opportunity for students to exhibit their understanding of concepts in context of the material as it is presented. As time permits, have students read and discuss the special features throughout the chapter.

Explore

Have students look on the Internet for businesses for sale. Ask for a volunteer to describe what types of businesses can be purchased.

Business operations depend on the type of business. For example, this young computer engineer started his own IT service business to help other companies.

zhu difeng/Shutterstock.com

making a profit. However, some businesses are sold because the owner is ready to retire. Such a business might be an excellent choice.

Buy a Franchise

A franchise is the right to do business using the brand and products of another business. Many franchises have well-known names, such as H&R Block or Subway. The company or person who owns the business and the brand is called the franchisor. The person who buys the right to sell the brand products is the franchisee.

The legal document that sets up a franchise is called a franchise agreement. The franchise agreement includes the rules and standards that the buyer, or franchisee, must follow in running the franchised business. The franchisee owns the franchise business, but is legally connected to the franchisor by the franchise agreement. A franchise agreement also states the franchise fee. The franchise fee is the money that the franchisee pays the franchisor for the right

to use the business brand name and sell its products.

There are many advantages to buying a franchise. One advantage is that you have an established product or service with a known reputation. In addition, the franchisor provides assistance for new franchisees with many aspects of starting and running the business.

However, there are some disadvantages to owning a franchise. The franchisor makes many of the product and marketing decisions. The franchisee must follow the rules and requirements set by the franchisor. From the beginning, the franchisor will set certain requirements that must be met in order to be considered for buying a franchise.

In addition, the initial cost to buy the franchise can be large. Initial franchise fees vary, but fees for well-known and successful franchises are often in the $20,000 to $75,000 range, or more. In addition, you usually have to pay an ongoing monthly franchise fee, often called a royalty fee. Typically, the franchisor

Explore

Ask students to pick their favorite retailer or restaurant and research what it takes to buy into the franchise.

can terminate the franchise agreement for any number of reasons. If this happens, the franchisee may lose all of his or her investment.

FYI

According to the SBA, 69 percent of all new business will survive the first two years of operation. On average, a business has a 50 percent chance of surviving after the first five years of operation. Only 34 percent survive 10 years or more.

Write the Business Plan

A **business plan** is a written document that describes a new business, how it will operate, and make a profit. A business plan is a required part of a business loan application. Writing a business plan is also a valuable planning tool. Researching and writing a business plan will help you figure out how to start and run your business successfully.

There are many ways to lay out a business plan. A well-written business plan will have the sections shown in Figure 31-7. Once a

Sections of a Business Plan
• Title Page
• Table of Contents
• Executive Summary
• Business Description
• Market Evaluation
• Operations
• Financial Plans
• Conclusion
• Bibliography
• Appendices

Goodheart-Willcox Publisher

Figure 31-7 It is worth the time and effort to carefully and thoroughly research your business plan.

Resource/Evaluate

Assign the optional Chapter 31 test for **EXAM**VIEW® Assessment Suite as a formal assessment tool.

business plan is written and the loan is obtained, the business plan can be used as an operating guide. Business plans should be reviewed and updated regularly to take advantage of new business opportunities and any economic changes.

Title Page

All formal reports include a title page that shows the name of the company, owner, and date the plan is presented. The title page makes the first impression of what will follow in the business plan.

Table of Contents

A table of contents is necessary so that the reader knows what will be included in the business plan and where each section is located. Prepare the table of contents after the business plan is completed.

Executive Summary

The executive summary is the first part of a business plan, but it is usually the last part written. In it, you should present the key points in a way that makes the reader excited about your business and its potential for success. The executive summary is the first thing that the lenders will read. If they are not impressed with the summary, they might not bother to read the rest of the business plan.

Description of Business

The description of the business should include the business concept, goals, products, and ownership structure. Emphasize what is unique about the business and what will make it successful.

Market Evaluation

This section describes the current state of the industry and economy in the area where

Exploring Careers

Regional Sales Manager

For companies that do business nationally or internationally, coordination of sales efforts is important to keep sales running smoothly and efficiently. These companies often divide their sales territories into regions and employ a regional sales manager to direct the sales activities in each region. The regional managers then work together under a national or international sales manager to coordinate the sales activities with the rest of the organization. Other typical job titles for a regional sales manager include *sales supervisor, general manager,* and *district sales manager.*

Some examples of tasks that regional sales managers perform include

- oversee the activities of local sales managers in their region;
- direct the hiring and training of staff, including local sales managers in their region;
- control sales and service programs in their region;
- project sales and monitor profitability; and
- resolve customer complaints as needed.

Regional sales managers may need to travel often, depending on the size of their region. They must be able to manage employees and offer them advice on both selling techniques and product demonstrations. This requires not only knowledge of sales principles but also an excellent knowledge of the products being sold. The ability to think critically to solve problems is also helpful. In addition, regional sales managers should have a background in economics and understand accounting principles. Most jobs in this field require a bachelor degree and considerable previous sales experience or on-the-job training. For more information, access the *Occupational Outlook Handbook* online.

you want to start your business. Include a description of the competitors and an analysis of the need for the business. Describe the competitive edge the business will have over its competitors. Customers will be crucial to the success of your business. In this section, describe the target market. Estimate how many customers you expect to have and how much they might spend at your business.

Operations

This section covers the proposed organizational chart and operations procedures. It also includes the necessary material resources, technology, human resources, and the staffing plan. In this section, detail how you will tell your customers about your business and convince them to buy your products and services. Describe what kind of

advertising you plan and whether you will have a sales force. You will also need to estimate your marketing budget and plan a timetable for the initial marketing program.

Financial Plan

The financial plan describes how you plan to fund the business and expect to make a profit. First, present the start-up costs. Next, describe how you will get the money to cover the start-up costs. Include how much of your own money you plan to use and the amount and sources of any loans. When discussing the loans, explain how you will pay them back. Also, present anticipated sales and profits. This section will include many financial documents, such as budgets, cash flow analysis, profit and loss statement, and balance sheet.

Conclusion

The conclusion summarizes why your business will be successful and ends with a specific request for financing. Write your conclusion so it is easy to read and highlights all the points important to potential investors and lenders.

Bibliography

The bibliography lists all of the resources used to develop the business plan. This might include interviews you conducted; books, periodicals, and websites cited; or other information you gathered while researching your business plan. The bibliography is an important record of the sources used to write the business plan.

Appendices

This may include résumés, financial statements, promotional plans, and other documents that support your plan.

Writing a business plan helps entrepreneurs think through many issues involved in starting a new business.

Steven Coburn/Shutterstock.com

Checkpoint 31.2

1. What purpose does a feasibility analysis serve?
2. What are some resources available for researching business ideas?
3. List two advantages of buying an existing business.
4. Explain why the franchise agreement is so important to both the franchisor and the franchisee.
5. What are the two main functions of a business plan?

Build Your Vocabulary

     As you progress through this course, develop a personal glossary of marketing terms and add it to your portfolio. This will help you build your vocabulary and prepare you for a career. Write a definition for each of the following terms, and add it to your personal marketing glossary.

entrepreneurial discovery process   franchisee
feasible   franchise agreement
business operations   franchise fee
franchise   business plan
franchisor

Chapter Summary

Section 31.1 Entrepreneurs

- Entrepreneurship is taking on both the risks and responsibilities of starting a new business. Successful entrepreneurs have traits and skills that help them start a business.
- There are many reasons why individuals decide to start a business. Money is one of the reasons but not the only reason. Controlling your destiny is an exciting reason to be an entrepreneur.
- If you start your own business, you will decide on the form of business ownership. There are three basic forms of ownership: sole proprietorship, partnership, and corporation.

Section 31.2 Business Ideas

- The discovery process helps entrepreneurs identify wants and needs that could be met by a new business. There are five types of businesses to consider: manufacturer, wholesaler, retailer, service business, or a nonprofit.
- Once you decide what type of business to open, analyze the best form for it. You may start a new business, buy an existing business, or buy into a franchise.
- A business plan is a written document that describes a new business, how it will operate, and make a profit. The business plan should include a title page, table of contents, executive summary, business description, market evaluation, business operations, financial plans, and a conclusion.

Review Your Knowledge

1. What are the five Ps for entrepreneurs?
2. Name one way a person can evaluate their traits, and skills.
3. Describe two advantages of being part of a partnership.
4. Explain double taxation.
5. What is the difference between an LLP and LLC?
6. Name the two parts of the entrepreneurial discovery process.
7. What are the five types of businesses an entrepreneur might start?
8. List three ways to start a business.
9. Why should a business plan be reviewed and updated on a regular basis?
10. What is the Market Evaluation section of a business plan?

Review Your Knowledge Answers

1. The five Ps for entrepreneurs are passion, perseverance, persistence, planning, and problem solving.
2. One way to evaluate yourself is by completing a self-assessment, which is a tool that helps a person understand personal preferences and identify strengths and weaknesses.
3. Students may list any two of the following: there are two or more people giving ideas, sharing the work, and sharing the responsibility. Two or more people can generate more excitement and motivation. Partners can keep each other going during the rough times. A partnership can often be more creative in problem solving and decision making. Partnerships can often gather more money to start the business.
4. In some types of corporations, both the individual stockholders and the corporation's profits are taxed.
5. The owners of an LLC are called members. LLCs can choose any organizational structure the members agree to. One disadvantage of the LLC is that it has a limited life—the business ends on the retirement or death of one member. It also ends if a member decides to leave the business. LLCs are more expensive to form than sole proprietorships and partnerships. They are also subject to more state and federal regulations. The owners of an LLP are called partners. The LLP has a similar business structure to a limited partnership (LP) but has no managing partner. All of the partners have limited personal liability. Professionals often prefer to organize as an LLP because no partner wants to be liable for another's mistakes.
6. The two steps in the discovery process are the recognition of a need or want that is not being met and the willingness to take the risk to exploit the opportunity.
7. An entrepreneur might start a manufacturing, wholesaling, retailing, service business, or a nonprofit.

Apply Your Knowledge

1. How could the classes you have taken or plan to take help if you decided to become an entrepreneur? Explain your answer.
2. Could you be an entrepreneur? Which entrepreneurial traits and skills do you possess? What traits and skills do you think are most important for an entrepreneur to be successful?
3. Research *self-assessment tools* online. Take two different ones and compare the results. What did you learn about yourself? Do you have the personality and drive to become an entrepreneur?
4. Write several paragraphs about one or two business ideas that you would consider creating. Is it a new business, established business you would purchase, a franchise, or is there a product you want to invent?
5. Franchises are one way to become an entrepreneur. Make a list of franchise businesses in your community. Would any of these franchises be opportunities that you would like to consider? Why or why not?
6. In this chapter, ownership was discussed. Which form of ownership would you prefer—proprietorship, partnership, or corporation? Defend your decision.
7. If you create a business, what are some of the risks you might face as an entrepreneur? Brainstorm ways you could overcome each risk.
8. Failure to do research is one of the reasons some businesses fail. What kind of research would you do to make sure your idea for a business is feasible? How could you ensure that your business will not fail?
9. If you were to start a business tomorrow, make a list of experts or people that you would want to have help you and explain exactly why you would need them.
10. Research business plans online. Pick three and list their similarities and differences. Which one do you think is best? Explain why.

Check Your Marketing IQ

Now that you have finished the chapter, see what you learned about marketing by taking the chapter posttest. If you do not have a smartphone, visit the G-W Learning companion website.

G-W Learning mobile site: www.m.g-wlearning.com
G-W Learning companion website: www.g-wlearning.com

Common Core

College and Career Readiness

CTE Career Ready Practices. Becoming an entrepreneur in your community would require that you model integrity, ethical leadership, and effective management. Make a list of actions that you could take to meet these requirements.

Listening. Research the positives and negatives of opening a new business. Using the Internet, find video footage of at least three speeches or news broadcasts that discuss the opportunities for opening a business. Compare and contrast the speakers' information, points of view, and opinions. How are they similar and different? Using the information presented, create a list of positives and negatives that you might encounter when starting a business.

Speaking. A presentation is usually a speech given to a group. For example, a presentation may be a demonstration for a few people, a report to a committee, or a speech to a large group of people. This chapter talked about different ways to start a business. Research the process involved in buying a franchise. Present your findings and evidence in a speech that you organize and develop in a style appropriate for your classmates. After you make your presentation, ask for feedback from the audience.

Teamwork

Working with a teammate, make a list of personality traits that you observe in that person. Then, have your teammate make a list of your personality traits. Discuss your opinions with each other. What did you learn from this experience?

G-W Learning Mobile Site

Visit the G-W Learning mobile site to complete the chapter pretest and posttest and to practice vocabulary using e-flash cards. If you do not have a smartphone, visit the G-W Learning companion website to access these features.

G-W Learning mobile site: www.m.g-wlearning.com

G-W Learning companion website: www.g-wlearning.com

32 Risk Management

Section 32.1 Identify Risk
Section 32.2 Manage Risk

"We all have to decide how we are going to fail…

by not going far enough or by going too far."

—Sumner Redstone, executive chairman of Viacom and CBS

College and Career Readiness

Reading Prep
Recall all the things you already know about risk management. As you read, think of how the new information presented in the text matches or challenges your prior understanding of the topic. Think of direct connections you can make between what you knew and what you learned.

Check Your Marketing IQ

Before you begin the chapter, see what you already know about marketing by taking the chapter pretest. If you do not have a smartphone, visit the G-W Learning companion website.
G-W Learning mobile site: www.m.g-wlearning.com
G-W Learning companion website: www.g-wlearning.com

Explore

Provide an opportunity for students to explore by assigning a hands-on activity. Assign the College and Career Readiness Reading Prep activity before students read the chapter. Reading Prep activities give students opportunity to apply the Common Core State Standards.

Engage

Engage the students by providing an activity or question that will connect students to what they already know. Assign the Chapter 32 pretest. The test may be accessed by using the QR code or by going to the *Marketing Dynamics* companion website. Discuss the questions students were unable to answer.

◇DECA Emerging Leaders

Food Marketing Series Event, Part 2

Career Cluster: Marketing
Career Pathway: Marketing Management
Instructional Area: Pricing

Procedure Part 2

1. In Chapter 31, you studied the performance indicators for this event.
2. The event will be presented to you through your reading of these instructions, including the Performance Indicators and Event Situation. You will have up to 10 minutes to review this information to determine how you will handle the role-play situation and demonstrate the performance indicators of this event. During the preparation period, you may make notes to use during the role-play situation.
3. You will have up to 10 minutes to role-play your situation with a judge. You may have more than one judge.
4. You will be evaluated on how well you meet the performance indicators of this event.
5. Turn in all your notes and event materials when you have completed the role-play.

Event Situation

You are to assume the position of owner/manager of a small gourmet food shop, The Brown Bag. One of your **sales associates (judge)** has asked you to discuss the shop's pricing decisions.

The Brown Bag is a specialty gourmet food shop located in a small historic town. The Brown Bag carries many gourmet and unique foods that cannot be found in the local grocery stores. The town is about 25 miles from a larger metropolitan area. The population of the area is diverse. However, there are a growing number of young professionals in the community who entertain quite a bit for work and pleasure. The Brown Bag remains a favorite store for many of the residents and weekend visitors.

The shop has been open for three years and has recently undergone extensive renovations. The exterior and interior of the store have been redesigned to match the historical era of the town. A gourmet dine-in deli and coffee shop have been added. Customer service operations have also been added, including carryout and delivery service, on-line ordering, and reward cards. A new computer system provides customer information and makes on-line and specialty ordering easier.

A recently hired sales associate has only been working at The Brown Bag for six weeks but has become a favorite with customers. The sales associate has commented that customers have asked about the high prices of some of the products. The sales associate has asked you to explain pricing so that he/she may better understand and answer customer questions.

You have asked the sales associate to meet with you in the store's office. The sales associate will begin the role-play by thanking you for taking the time to explain pricing. Once you have completed your presentation and have answered the sales associate's questions, he or she will end the role-play by thanking you for explaining the pricing.

Critical Thinking

1. In a small town like this, do we even have to consider competition when pricing?
2. Is competitive pricing more important than other marketing functions such as customer service, promotion, and product selection?
3. Will the purchase of the new computer system affect pricing?

Visit www.deca.org for more information.

Section 32.1 Identify Risk

Objectives

After completing this section, you will be able to
- **explain** the nature of risk.
- **describe** the four types of risk.

Key Terms

risk
controllable risk
insurance
uncontrollable risk
natural risk
economic risk
market risk
product obsolescence

planned obsolescence
human risk
shoplifter
burglary
robbery
embezzlement
fraud

Web Connect

Research the topic of *risk management* on the Internet. Summarize your findings and make recommendations on how a marketing manager can create a plan for risk management in a business.

Critical Thinking

All individuals face some type of risk. Identify the various risks an individual might encounter. Make a list of the top ten risks you could face at some point in your personal life.

Nature of Risk

A **risk** is the possibility of loss, damage, or injury. *Business risk* is the possibility of loss or injury that might occur in a business. Businesses must plan for the unexpected and identify possible risks. They must also assess the seriousness of the risks and the likelihood of loss.

A **controllable risk** is one that cannot be avoided, but can be minimized by purchasing insurance or implementing a risk management plan. For example, the risk of fire is controllable because it is covered by insurance. **Insurance** is a financial service used to protect individuals and businesses against financial loss.

Uncontrollable risk is a situation that cannot be predicted or covered by purchasing insurance. For example, a price war started by competitors is an example of an uncontrollable risk. There are no insurance plans to cover this type of financial loss.

Risk can also be identified as a speculative risk or pure risk. A *speculative risk* carries with it the chance of a profit or loss. For example, starting a business is a speculative risk because the business may or may not be successful. A *pure risk* is the threat of loss with no chance for profit. For example, if a natural disaster happens, there is no possibility of gain from this event. Some pure-risk events can also be considered liability risks. A *liability risk* is one that has the possibility of losing money or other property as a result of legal proceedings.

Explore

Provide an opportunity for students to explore by assigning a hands-on activity. Review the vocabulary terms at the beginning of the section. Where have students encountered these terms before? Help students make educated guesses about the meanings of the terms with which they are least familiar.

Explain

Discuss the word *risk* and how it affects both personal and business life. Compare and contrast *controllable risk* and *uncontrollable risk*.

Types of Risk

There are four basic types of business risk: natural, economic and political, market, and human. Each will cost a business money should one of these risks happen. These risks are shown in Figure 32-1.

Natural Risks

Natural risk is a situation caused by acts of nature. Tornadoes, hurricanes, floods, and earthquakes are examples. Natural risks are considered controllable risks. Insurance can help recover the losses from damage from a controllable risk.

Economic and Political Risks

Economic risk is a situation that occurs when the economy suffers due to negative business conditions in the United States or the world. Local, national, and world economic conditions can affect the success of a business. Economic risk is hard to predict and is uncontrollable. For example, during times of recession, many people lose their jobs. As a result, people stop spending on luxuries, putting businesses at risk. Political conditions can create risks for companies doing business globally.

Market Risks

Market risk is the potential that the target market for new products or services is much less than originally thought. The market for many goods, services, and ideas is very unpredictable. Introducing a new product is especially risky. Will customers be willing to buy it? Will they be happy with it? Research shows that most new products fail in their first year on the market.

Another market risk is competition. Just because your product is currently successful does not mean that it will always be successful. Competitors might enter your market with an improved product or a new, better product. Customers might prefer products from the competition. As a result, your business might lose sales and earn less revenue.

A related market risk is product obsolescence. In the event of product obsolescence, a product becomes out-of-date over time. Product obsolescence is a major problem in fashion and technology businesses. Many types of clothing go out of style very quickly. People often do not want to buy last year's fashions. In technology, faster products with newer features make the older ones obsolete. This obsolescence is particularly obvious in products, such as cell phones and computers. Some products have short life

Four Types of Business Risk	
Natural Risks	Situations caused by nature
Economic and Political Risks	Situations caused by economic or political conditions
Market Risks	Situations caused by product or competition
Human Risks	Situations caused by employees and customers

Figure 32-1 Every business faces some form of risk.

Goodheart-Willcox Publisher

Elaborate/Extend

Assign the College and Career Readiness Portfolio activity at the end of the chapter.

Explain

Ask students to explain how human risks affect marketing.

cycles. **Planned obsolescence** is evaluating and updating current products or adding new ones to replace older ones.

Human Risks

Human risk is a negative situation caused by human actions. Employees and customers pose potential human risks of accidental injury, theft, or fraud as shown in Figure 32-2.

Accidents

Accidents can happen easily in the workplace. Employees and customers run the risk of falling or becoming involved in situations that lead to injury. For example, a customer may break a leg by tripping over a bucket left in an aisle. An employee may be injured

while using heavy equipment. In such cases, the business is responsible for all associated costs of injuries that occur on the premises. The business may even face a negligence lawsuit.

Theft

There are two types of theft: customer theft and employee theft. Examples of customer theft are:
- **Shoplifting.** A **shoplifter** is a person, posing as a customer, who takes goods from the store without paying for them.
- **Burglary.** A **burglary** occurs when a person breaks into a business to steal merchandise, money, valuable equipment or take confidential information.
- **Robbery.** A **robbery** is a theft involving another person, often by using force or with the threat of violence.

Employee theft costs businesses thousands of dollars each year. *Employee theft* occurs when employees steal from the business. **Embezzlement** occurs when an employee steals either money or goods entrusted to him or her. Employees who handle money have many opportunities to take cash from a business. They can overcharge customers, steal gift cards, and commit a variety of other activities to take cash from the business.

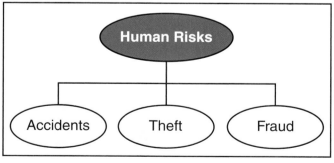

Goodheart-Willcox Publisher

Figure 32-2 Human risks include accidental injury, theft, or fraud.

FYI

Shrinkage is the term that identifies inventory losses due to shoplifting, employee theft, paperwork errors, and vendor fraud.

Fraud

Fraud is cheating or deceiving a business out of money or property. Employees, vendors, and customers can commit fraud. Examples of fraud include vendor theft, writing bad checks, using expired or stolen credit cards, using counterfeit money, and hacking data, as shown in Figure 32-3.

Types of Business Fraud
• **Vendor theft.** Vendor theft is when dishonest vendors deliver less than what was ordered but charge for the full order.
• **Bad checks.** Dishonest customers may try to make purchases with checks that are fake or stolen. They may also write checks that have no money in the bank to cover the purchase.
• **Expired credit cards.** Expired or stolen credit cards that have no value may be used by dishonest customers.
• **Counterfeit money.** Counterfeit money is fake and not legal tender.
• **Data security.** Businesses that use e-commerce are vulnerable to hackers who may steal sensitive customer and credit card information.

Goodheart-Willcox Publisher

Figure 32-3 Fraud is one of the hardest forms of business risk to detect.

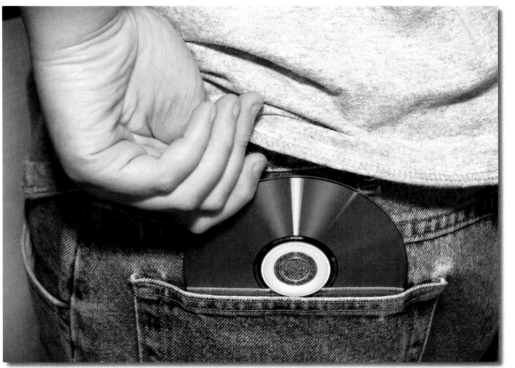

Customer and employee theft are human risks that can cause a business to suffer a loss in profit.

Anita Patterson Peppers/Shutterstock.com

Evaluate

Assign the Checkpoint questions at the end of the section.
Assess students' comprehension using the Checkpoint activity as a self-assessment tool.

Checkpoint 32.1

1. What is a business risk?
2. Name the four types of business risk.
3. What types of risks are posed by employees and customers?
4. What are the two forms of theft in a business?
5. Name three types of fraud that can happen in a business.

Build Your Vocabulary

As you progress through this text, develop a personal glossary of marketing terms that will help you build your vocabulary and prepare you for a career in marketing. Write out a definition for each of the following terms, and add it to your personal marketing glossary.

risk
controllable risk
insurance
uncontrollable risk
natural risk
economic risk
market risk
product obsolescence

planned obsolescence
human risk
shoplifter
burglary
robbery
embezzlement
fraud

Section 32.2 Manage Risk

After completing this section, you will be able to
- **summarize** the importance of risk management.
- **explain** how market and human risks can be avoided or reduced.
- **describe** how to transfer risk.
- **explain** what it means to assume risk.

lawsuit
risk assessment
security
surveillance
hazard
emergency
emergency action
  plan
insurance premium
uninsurable risk

Do a search for employee theft on the Internet. Identify the financial impact that employee theft has on businesses in your industry. What is the dollar amount?

Which types of risks do you think a marketing professional might encounter? How would these risks differ from the risks that the business would face?

Risk-Management Techniques

Businesses and individuals are liable for their risks. Recall that the word *liable* means responsible. In the context of damages and responsibility, *liability* means legal responsibility for actions and costs. A **lawsuit** is the process of bringing a complaint to a court for resolution. The purpose of a lawsuit is to have an impartial party (a judge and/or jury) determine who is liable for the costs of the damage or injury.

How do individuals and businesses handle liability? First, they assess the risks.

Risk assessment is the process of analyzing a situation for possible risks. Risk assessments should be done on a regular basis as risks may change over time. Through proper risk management, risks may be avoided, reduced, transferred, or assumed as shown in Figure 32-4.

A person, business, or organization that has been harmed has the right to sue the person, business, or organization that may be liable for the harm.

Figure 32-4 Careful planning helps a business decide which method of risk management works best for different types of risk.

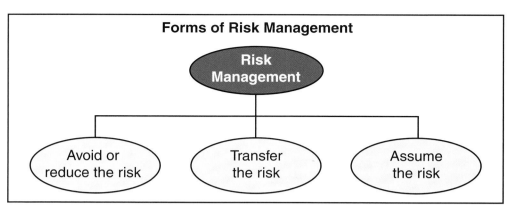

Goodheart-Willcox Publisher

Avoid or Reduce the Risk

One of the first steps in risk management is to assess those risks that can be avoided or reduced. Market risks and human risks are examples of risks in this category.

Market Risk

Business success depends on selling products. Which products will sell well? If a product is selling well now, will it continue to sell well? Businesses use marketing research to answer these questions. One of the purposes of marketing research is to prevent losses from marketing mistakes. Market research will help avoid risk.

Human Risks

By putting safeguards in place, some human risks can be avoided. Many business losses are caused by people who steal, damage property, or harm employees and customers. Security consists of actions taken to prevent crime and protect the safety of people and property.

External Theft

To avoid theft, security precautions are needed. Security activities can be classified as structural security, surveillance, and security policies.

Structural security consists of security features in a building, such as lights, alarms, locks, and computerized security systems. Valuable merchandise is often displayed in locked display cases. Retailers may attach security tags to their merchandise. Security tag detectors are then placed at the exits of the store. When a customer buys an item, the security tag is removed. If a person tries to walk out of the store without paying, the security tag on the item will set off the security tag detector and alarms.

Surveillance is the process of closely observing what is going on in order to prevent crimes. Many businesses hire security guards to provide surveillance. Video and closed-circuit TV cameras are also used for observation.

Security policies are the rules that employees must follow to ensure security. There may be security policies for handling money, locking the building, and obtaining supplies. Keeping careful inventory records is also a security measure. Inventory records can show if items are missing. If items are missing, someone may have stolen them. Sales associates learn what to do during a robbery and how to recognize shoplifters. Cashiers receive training on how to identify

College and Career Portfolio

Portfolio Organization

You have collected various items for your portfolio in earlier activities. Now you will organize the materials in your print portfolio. Your instructor may have examples of portfolios that you can review for ideas. You can also search the Internet for articles about how to organize a print portfolio. You should provide a table of contents for the items. This will allow the person reviewing the portfolio to find items easily. Keep separate the sections of the portfolio that are for your use only, such as your contacts database and sample interview answers. You should continue to add and remove documents as you complete assignments or gain new skills. Update the table of contents when you make changes to the portfolio.

1. Review the documents you have collected. Select the ones you want to include in your career portfolio. Make copies of certificates, diplomas, and other important documents. Keep the originals in a safe place.
2. Create the table of contents. You also may want to create a title page for each section.
3. Place the items in a binder, notebook, or other professional-looking container.
4. Conduct the same exercise for organizing your electronic documents in your e-portfolio.

---

counterfeit money. Cashiers also learn the proper techniques for accepting checks and credit cards.

Employee Theft

Retailers and other businesses also have problems with employee theft. Theft is usually grounds for immediate dismissal and possibly prosecution. In order to reduce employee theft, employers use a variety of methods of prevention including

- hire honest, reliable employees;
- place video or closed-circuit TV cameras at cash registers;
- use a computerized accounting system to keep close track of cash register transactions; and
- use computerized inventory systems to keep track of inventory.

Accidents

Health and safety procedures are the actions taken to prevent illness and injury. Businesses are responsible for the health and safety of

customers while they are on company property. For example, at a restaurant, customers could become ill from improperly prepared food. Local government regulations require every foodservice business to meet specific health and sanitation standards. Most businesses have procedures to try to prevent hazards. A **hazard** is a situation that could result in injury or damage. For example, water on the floor is a hazard that might cause a customer to slip and fall. If floors become wet, signs are posted to warn that floors may be slippery.

Businesses are also responsible for the health and safety of their employees. Most businesses have rules for office, warehouse, and store accident prevention. In an office, file drawers must be closed when not in use, and electric cords must be kept out of the way. In a warehouse, workers must wear protective clothing. In a retail store, merchandise must be displayed in a safe way.

To encourage employers to make the workplace safe, the Occupational Safety and Health Act was passed in 1970. This act

Many businesses, especially retailers, use security cameras to reduce the risk of theft.

requires employers to make the workplace free of hazards that might cause injury or death to employees. The act also established the Occupational Safety and Health Administration (OSHA). OSHA develops job safety and health standards; it then enforces those standards through inspections.

Many businesses provide safety training for employees. Safety training should cover three areas: general safety rules, specific job-related safety rules, and safety attitude.

General safety rules apply to everyone in the business. Sample topics include hazards, safe lifting, and emergency procedures. Specific job-related safety training should be tailored to each specific job. For example, warehouse workers need special training in the equipment they use to move heavy loads. *Safety attitude* is an important area. A positive attitude toward safety must be promoted. Employees should be made aware of how important safety is to their well-being and continued employment.

Emergencies can occur at any time and in any place. An **emergency** is an unforeseen event that can cause harm to people and property. One of the goals of training is to help employees keep minor emergencies from becoming major emergencies.

Employees must also know when and how to call for help. In many companies, employees must report any accident, large or small, to their supervisors. An **emergency action plan** is a detailed plan that describes what to do in case of an emergency. The plans describe what to do in case of fires and other disasters. A major part of an emergency action plan is an evacuation plan.

FYI

Emergency action plans are also called *emergency response plans.*

Transfer the Risk

Many risks can be transferred by purchasing insurance to cover different risk events. The cost of an insurance policy is a payment called an **insurance premium**. In exchange for the premium, the insurance company agrees to pay the costs in case of a specific list of damages. The cost of insurance depends on how likely the buyer is

Resource/Evaluate

Assign the optional Chapter 32 test for **EXAM**VIEW®
Assessment Suite as a formal assessment tool.

Case in Point

Ocean Publishing

Good business is not all about making money; it also involves being prepared in case of a disaster. On August 22, 1992, Florida and much of the Gulf coast experienced the devastation of a Category 5 hurricane named *Andrew*. Hurricane Andrew claimed 65 lives and caused $26.5 billion in home and business losses. Fortunately, Frank Gromling, the owner of Ocean Publishing in Dade County took steps to prepare his business for emergencies. Gromling's plan included: 1. creating a disaster plan; 2. training employees on how to use the plan; 3. storing important business documents off-site; 4. having insurance coverage for business interruptions; and 5. planning to provide for employees after a disaster. Since Gromling was prepared, he was able to rebuild his business. Having a risk-management plan may mean the difference between saving your business and closing its doors.

to use the insurance. When the possibility of using insurance is high, the premium is usually more expensive. For a business, there are three basic types of insurance: property, liability, and crime.

Property insurance pays for loss or damage of property owned by the business. Property insurance usually covers losses due to fires, tornadoes, hail, accidents, burglary, and arson.

Liability insurance provides payment if the business is sued and the court determines that the business is liable. Customers and employees might sue if they are injured at the business. Customers might sue if an item they purchase causes injury. If the court determines that the business is liable, then it usually requires the business to pay money to the victim. Liability insurance will cover the cost to pay the victim. *Professional liability insurance* protects against losses caused by negligent acts of a professional, such as an attorney.

Crime insurance pays for losses due to crimes, such as theft, arson, forgery, and embezzlement. This form of insurance is very important for any type of business.

A *surety bond* is a document signed by a contractor to fulfill a service agreed upon by the parties. A surety bond company issues the bond. If the contractor fails to perform,

monetary compensation is made to the person to which the services are owed.

Risk management: Your passion for entrepreneurship could provide a boost to your résumé—according to a recent career tip from the AMA, young entrepreneurs make great employees for small businesses. If you have entrepreneurial experience of any kind, be sure to include this experience on résumés and cover letters and during interviews. Show your potential employer that your entrepreneurial experience means that you are innovative and open to new ideas and that you understand the hard work required of a small business owner. www.marketingpower.com

Assume the Risk

Unfortunately, insurance may not be available for all of the risks that need to be covered. An **uninsurable risk** is one that an insurance company will not cover. All businesses must assume the full risk and be responsible for losses associated with those risks that cannot be avoided or insured. For example, no insurance will cover economic or market risks.

Elaborate/Extend

If students are using the optional *Marketing Dynamics* workbook, assign activities to engage active learning.

A tornado is an example of a natural disaster that can strike at any time.

Alexey Stiop/Shutterstock.com

A business may choose to self-insure by saving money to cover some risks should they happen. One way to self-insure is by setting up a bank account for that purpose. This could be a designated account where money is deposited each month to cover a future loss. Setting up a special account is similar to paying a premium to an insurance company. The difference is that the premium is paid to the business, and the business assumes 100 percent of the risk. That way, if something happens, self-insurance money is available to draw on to cover losses. State regulations may require a business to prove it can finance self-insurance before allowing it.

Checkpoint 32.2

1. What are three ways that risks can be managed?
2. What precautions can be taken to manage external theft?
3. What is OSHA?
4. What is the most common way to transfer risk?
5. Why would a business or individual assume risk and not buy insurance?

Build Your Vocabulary

As you progress through this text, develop a personal glossary of marketing terms, which will help you build your vocabulary and prepare you for a career in marketing. Write a definition for each of the following terms, and add it to your personal marketing glossary.

lawsuit
risk assessment
security
surveillance
hazard

emergency
emergency action plan
insurance premium
uninsurable risk

Chapter Summary

Section 32.1 Identify Risk

- A risk is the possibility of loss, damage, or injury. Controllable risk is one that cannot be avoided, but can be minimized by purchasing insurance or implementing a risk plan. Uncontrollable risk is a situation that cannot be predicted or covered by purchasing insurance.
- There are several types of risks with which an individual or business needs to be concerned. These include natural risk, economic and political risk, market risks, and human risk.

Section 32.2 Manage Risk

- Businesses and individuals are liable for their risks. Risk assessment is the process of analyzing a situation for possible risks. Through proper risk management, risks may be avoided, reduced, transferred, or assumed.
- One of the first steps in risk management is to assess those risks that can be avoided or reduced. One of the purposes of marketing research is to prevent losses from marketing mistakes. By putting safeguards in place, some human risks can be avoided. Security consists of actions taken to prevent crime and protect the safety of people and property.
- Many risks can be transferred by purchasing insurance. In exchange for the premium, the insurance company agrees to pay the costs in case of a specific list of damages. For a business, there are three basic types of insurance: property, liability, and crime.
- An uninsurable risk is one that an insurance company will not cover. All businesses must assume the full risk and be responsible for losses associated with those risks that cannot be avoided or insured.

Review Your Knowledge

1. How can a business plan for risks?
2. Name and describe the two classifications of risks.
3. What is a liability risk?
4. Describe the four types of risks.
5. How might employees steal from a business?
6. What types of risk can be avoided or reduced?
7. Describe four ways to reduce employee theft.
8. What is the importance of an emergency action plan?
9. Explain how insurance is priced.
10. Explain how a business may choose to self-insure.

Evaluate

Assign the end-of-chapter activities.

Review Your Knowledge Answers

1. Businesses must plan for the unexpected and identify possible risks. They must also assess the seriousness of the risks and the likelihood of loss. It is important to plan for both controllable and uncontrollable risks.
2. A speculative risk is a risk that carries with it the chance of a profit or loss. Pure risk is the threat of loss with no chance for profit.
3. A liability risk is one that has the possibility of losing money or other property as a result of legal proceedings.
4. Natural risks caused by acts of nature. Economic risk is a situation that occurs when the economy suffers due to negative business conditions in the United States or the world. Local market risk is the potential that the target market for new products or services is much less than originally thought. Human risks are negative situations caused by humans.
5. Employees who handle money have many opportunities to take cash from a business. They can overcharge customers, steal gift cards, and commit a variety of other activities to take cash from the business.
6. Market risks and human risks are examples of risks that can be reduced or avoided.

Apply Your Knowledge

1. Identify each specific risk the business for which you are writing your marketing plan might encounter and label each as controllable or uncontrollable.
2. List examples of the natural risks your business might face.
3. List examples of human risks your business might face.
4. Considering the current economy, which specific economic and political risks might be challenging for your business?
5. Considering the current economy, describe specific market risks your business might face. As a marketer, how can you help your company reduce those risks?
6. Risks may be speculative risks or pure risks. Give examples of each that your business might face.
7. Describe a plan for reducing risks that pertains to the employees in your business.
8. Describe a plan for reducing risks from burglary or robbery in your company.
9. How will you protect your company's technology assets from risks?
10. Describe a plan for transferring risks in your business. Describe the types of insurance your company should have and why they are necessary.

Check Your Marketing IQ

Now that you have finished the chapter, see what you learned about marketing by taking the chapter posttest. If you do not have a smartphone, visit the G-W Learning companion website.

G-W Learning mobile site: www.m.g-wlearning.com
G-W Learning companion website: www.g-wlearning.com

7. Employee theft can be reduced by hiring honest, reliable employees; placing video or closed-circuit TV cameras at cash registers; using a computerized accounting system to keep close track of cash register transactions; and using computerized inventory systems to keep track of inventory.
8. An emergency response plan describes what to do in case of emergencies, such as fires and disasters. A major part of an emergency action plan is an evacuation plan.
9. The cost of insurance depends on how likely the buyer is to use the insurance. When the possibility of using insurance is high, the premium is usually more expensive.
10. A business may choose to self-insure by saving money to cover some risks should they happen. One way to self-insure is to set up a special account that is similar to paying a premium to an insurance company. The difference is that the premium is paid to the business, and the business assumes 100 percent of the risk. That way, if something happens, self-insurance money is available to draw on to cover losses.

Apply Your Knowledge Answers

Student answers will vary for questions 1–10.

Evaluate

Evaluate the students' understanding and knowledge. Assign the Chapter 32 posttest. The test may be accessed by using the QR code or by going to the companion website. What questions were students able to answer that they could not answer when they took the pretest?

Common Core

College and Career Readiness

CTE Career Ready Practices. Read the Marketing Ethics features presented throughout this book. What role do you think that ethics and integrity have in risk management? Think of a time when you used your ideals and principles to make a decision that involved some type of risk. What process did you use to make the decision? In retrospect, do you think you made the correct decision? Did your decision have any consequences?

Listening. When others are directing you, help them out by actively listening to what they are saying. Ask someone to give you directions on how to file an insurance claim. As you listen to the directions, anticipate what specific information you will need. When possible, give feedback to the speaker to show you understand what is being presented. Actively listen to what that person is sharing. What did you learn from the information that was given to you?

Speaking. Make an impromptu speech on risk management. Applying what you learned in this chapter, give your opinion as to which method of risk management is the most effective for a business. Then give your opinion for the method of risk management you think is most effective for individuals.

Teamwork

Working in teams, research the most common natural risks for your area. Find out how often these risks usually occur, what they cost both individuals and businesses, and what recommendations are made by government and insurance companies to deal with these risks. Present your findings to the class.

G-W Learning Mobile Site

Visit the G-W Learning mobile site to complete the chapter pretest and posttest and to practice vocabulary using e-flash cards. If you do not have a smartphone, visit the G-W Learning companion website to access these features.

G-W Learning mobile site: www.m.g-wlearning.com
G-W Learning companion website: www.g-wlearning.com

CHAPTER

33

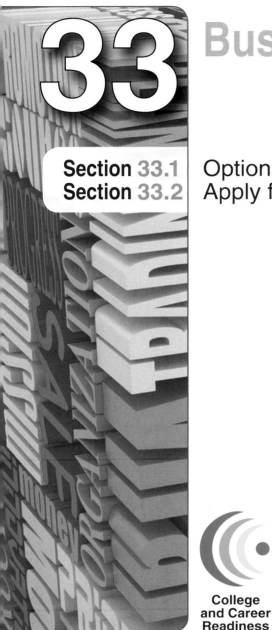

Business Funding

| Section 33.1 | Options for Funding |
| Section 33.2 | Apply for Financing |

"In all realms of life, it takes courage to stretch your limits, express your power, and fulfill your potential. It's no different in the financial realm."

—Suze Orman, financial consultant and author

Reading Prep
In preparation for reading the chapter, read a newspaper or magazine article on business funding. As you read, keep in mind the author's main points and conclusions.

College and Career Readiness

Check Your Marketing IQ

Before you begin the chapter, see what you already know about marketing by taking the chapter pretest. If you do not have a smartphone, visit the G-W Learning companion website.
G-W Learning mobile site: www.m.g-wlearning.com
G-W Learning companion website: www.g-wlearning.com

G-W Mobile

Explore

Provide an opportunity for students to explore by assigning a hands-on activity. Assign the College and Career Readiness Reading Prep activity before students read the chapter. Reading Prep activities give students opportunity to apply the Common Core State Standards.

Engage

Engage the students by providing an activity or question that will connect students to what they already know. Assign the Chapter 33 pretest. The test may be accessed by using the QR code or by going to the *Marketing Dynamics* companion website. Discuss the questions students were unable to answer.

◇DECA Emerging Leaders

Entrepreneurship—Growing Your Business Event

Career Cluster and **Instructional Area** are not identified for this event.

Knowledge and Skills Assessed

The participants will demonstrate knowledge and skills needed to address the components of the project as described in the content outline and evaluation forms as well as learn/understand the importance of

- communications knowledge and skills—the ability to exchange information and ideas with others through writing, speaking, reading, or listening;
- analytical knowledge and skills—the ability to derive facts from data, findings, from facts, conclusions from findings, and recommendations from conclusions;
- critical thinking/problem-solving knowledge and skills;
- production knowledge and skills—the ability to take a concept from an idea and make it real;
- teamwork—the ability to plan, organize, and conduct a group project;
- priorities/time management—the ability to determine priorities and manage time commitments and deadlines;
- identification of competitive conditions within market areas;
- the basic steps involved in starting a small business; and
- the ability to self-evaluate personal skills, knowledge, abilities, and willingness to take risks.

Purpose

Designed for one to three chapter members, the plan involves the idea generation and strategy development needed to grow an existing business. Participants will analyze their current business operations and identify opportunities to grow and expand the business. At least one team member must currently own and operate an existing business. The Entrepreneurship—Growing Your Own Business Event consists of two major parts: the written document and the oral presentation by the participants.

Procedure

1. The written document will account for 60 points, and the oral presentation will account for the remaining 40 of the total 100 points. The body of the written entry must be limited to 30 numbered pages, including the appendix (if an appendix is attached), but excluding the title page and the table of contents. Prior to the presentation, the judge will evaluate the written portion of the entry. The major emphasis of the written entry is on the content. Drawings, illustrations, and graphic presentations (where allowed) will be judged for clarity.

2. The oral presentation may be a maximum 15 minutes in length worth 40 points. The presentation begins immediately after the introduction of participants to the judge by the adult assistant. Each participant must take part in the presentation. At the beginning of the presentation, you will spend no more than 10 minutes describing the proposal and making the request for financing. Each participant may bring a copy of the written entry or note cards pertaining to the written entry and use these as a reference during the presentation. The judge will spend the remaining five minutes questioning the participants. Each participant must respond to at least one question posed by the judge. Review Written Entry Format Guidelines and Checklist Standards in the DECA Guide. Visit www.deca.org/_docs/conferences-competitions/DECA_Guide.pdf.

Project

The business expansion may include franchising, expanding into new markets, opening a second location, licensing agreements, merging with or acquiring another business, diversifying product lines, forming strategic alliances with other businesses, expanding to the internet, etc.

Critical Thinking

1. What existing business will you expand?
2. How will you expand the business?
3. What is the rationale for selecting this growth and expansion?

Visit www.deca.org for more information.

Section 33.1 Options for Funding

Objectives

After completing this section, you will be able to
- **list** the ways to fund a start-up business.
- **discuss** different sources for start-up capital.
- **explain** considerations owners have when starting a new business.

Key Terms

bootstrapping
start-up capital
equity
equity financing
angel investor
venture capitalist
debt financing
collateral

line of credit
peer-to-peer lending
trade credit
start-up cost
operating expense
fixed expense
variable expense

Web Connect

There are many ways to obtain business financing. Conduct an Internet search for *small business financing*. Make a list of the different financing options available for entrepreneurs.

Critical Thinking

Financing a business is a big step in anyone's career. What challenges might you as as an entrepreneur face when looking for ways to finance a new business?

Funding Strategies

Entrepreneurs need to create strategies for funding their new businesses. However, before seeking funds from outside sources, they often evaluate alternative strategies for getting the business off the ground.

When starting a new business, most entrepreneurs practice the art of bootstrapping. **Bootstrapping** is cutting all unnecessary expenses and operating on as little cash as possible. In your personal life, you may have used bootstrapping practices without realizing it. Perhaps you reduced extra spending to save for a vacation, buy a car, or get a new phone. There are many ways to practice bootstrapping when starting a business, as shown in Figure 33-1.

Explore

Provide an opportunity for students to explore by assigning a hands-on activity. Review the vocabulary terms at the beginning of the section. Where have students encountered these terms before? Help students make educated guesses about the meanings of the terms with which they are least familiar.

Use Free Resources

There will be many times when you need professional advice on starting a business. Before hiring someone to advise you, look for free services. There are many professional resources and services available at no cost to business owners. SCORE, the SBA, and state websites offer advice and other resources at no charge. Social media is also a free resource to use as a marketing tool.

Use Personal Assets

Many entrepreneurs start businesses from home to save on start-up and operating costs. They use their own equipment, such as a computer, fax, and printer. If additional equipment is needed, leasing instead of buying will help to save the up-front costs.

Resource

Use the Chapter 33 presentation on the optional Instructor's Presentations for PowerPoint® CD as an outline for presenting the chapter.

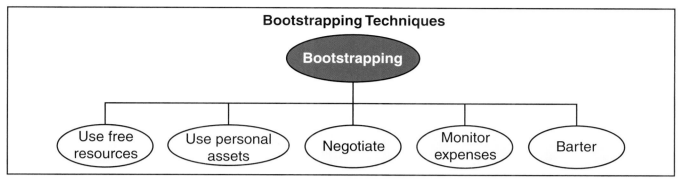

Goodheart-Willcox Publisher

Figure 33-1 Bootstrapping techniques can reduce the amount of money that would otherwise need to be borrowed.

Negotiate

Many vendors are willing to offer better terms than what they advertise. Some of them began as small business owners and are willing to help new entrepreneurs. They may not negotiate on price, but might be willing to negotiate terms. Instead of a payment due in 30 days, ask if the vendor will give you a 45- or 60-day payment window.

Monitor Expenses

Create a budget and monitor your personal expenses. Cut back on utilities, reduce your phone or subscription TV plan, and postpone a vacation. There are many more ways to conserve cash.

Barter

Bartering is the exchange of products or services for other products or services. No money changes hands. Rather than pay for professional services, try bartering. For example, perhaps you are opening a catering business. You are in need of an accountant who needs a catering service for a client meeting. You exchange catering services for accounting services. No money was exchanged, but both parties provided a service needed for their businesses.

Elaborate/Extend

Assign the College and Career Readiness Portfolio activity at the end of the chapter.

Start-Up Capital

As an entrepreneur, you will need cash to get a business up and running. **Start-up capital** is the cash used to start the business. Very few people have enough cash on hand to completely fund a business. Therefore, many entrepreneurs must look for other sources of start-up capital. Two common sources of financing are equity financing and debt financing, as shown in Figure 33-2.

Equity Financing

Equity is the amount of ownership a person has in a business. If you start a business by using only your own funds, you have 100 percent equity in that business. This is called *self-funding.*

Equity financing is raising money for a business in exchange for a percentage of the ownership. For example, selling stock to raise money is really selling a percentage of ownership in your company. Many entrepreneurs use a combination of self-funding and equity financing.

Personal Savings

Many entrepreneurs use their own money as equity capital. This can include money from savings accounts, selling stock, cash in a retirement fund, or use other personal resources.

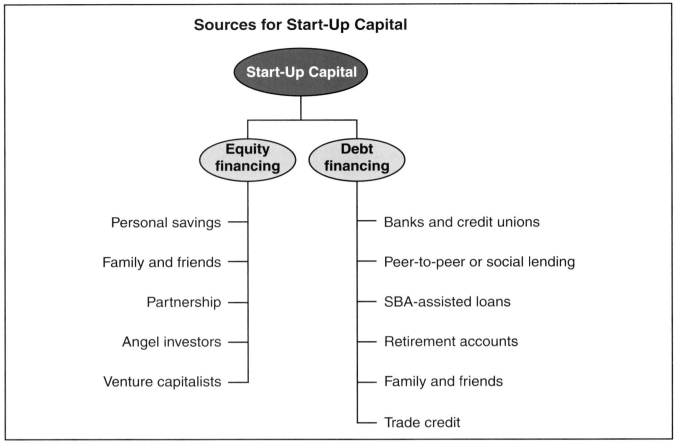

Figure 33-2 There are many sources of start-up capital to fund new business. Both debt and equity financing can be used.

Family and Friends

Sometimes entrepreneurs ask people they know to help fund a business. However, before asking family and friends to invest in your company, think about what could happen to the relationships should something go wrong with the business. There may be other alternatives that are better suited to your situation.

Partnership

Another option for raising equity capital is to take on partners in the business. Partners can contribute to the start-up funding and share in responsibility and operations of the business. Like other equity options, a formal partnership agreement is necessary.

Angel Investors

Angel investors, or *angels,* are private investors who are interested in funding promising start-up businesses. An angel investor often has business experience that will help the new company. He or she is interested in adding value as well as making a return on the investment.

FYI

Angel investors can be a good source for new-business funding because they will often take on more risk than a bank.

Sometimes family members make great business partners like this father and daughter who own a bookstore.

Some angel investors actively participate in the business to protect their investment. They may charge a monthly management fee. Other angels do not choose active participation in the operation. However, they are part owners in the company and expect a good return on the money invested.

Venture Capitalists

Venture capitalists, or *VCs*, are professional investors or investing groups that fund new start-ups or expansions of existing companies. *Venture capital* is the money invested in businesses by venture capitalists. VCs manage large investment funds and are always looking for suitable investment opportunities. They are willing to invest more money than angels in riskier start-ups to earn a high rate of return on the investment. Most venture capitalists require 25 percent or more equity in the company.

Venture capitalists usually prefer investing in start-ups run by experienced entrepreneurs. They often fund new or expanding high-tech or other successful companies. Less than 1 percent of all businesses are funded by VCs.

Unlike angel investors, venture capitalists rarely have personal experience in the industries in which they invest. Many, however, do have general management experience and want to remain involved in the business to protect the investment. Like some angel investors, there are also some VCs who leave the daily business operations to the experts.

Debt Financing

Debt financing is borrowing money for business purposes. Debt financing is one way to start or expand a business. One advantage of debt financing is that the entrepreneur remains the business owner. One disadvantage is that, just like credit card debt, the loan must be repaid plus the interest. For those with poor credit, the interest rates can be higher.

To obtain debt financing, an application process is required. Like other types of loans, it is important to have a good credit rating. Some larger loans require collateral. Collateral

Exploring Careers

Forecasting Manager

One of the many tasks contributing to a company's success is managing product flow. Not having enough of a product carries the risk of running out of stock. On the other hand, having too much of the product increases the need for warehousing, which in turn increases the company's costs. Forecasting managers are responsible for managing the flow of products through a company. They analyze purchasing patterns to forecast the need for specific products. Forecasting managers coordinate the activities of the production, purchasing, warehousing, and distribution departments to ensure that products flow smoothly from production or purchase through final sales and distribution. Other typical job titles for a forecasting manager are *supply chain manager, supply chain director,* and *supply chain coordinator.*

Some examples of tasks that forecasting managers perform include

- analyze inventories to determine how quickly products are turned over;
- create demand and supply plans to ensure the timely availability of materials or products;
- monitor industry forecasts to identify trends that may affect the supply chain; and
- coordinate purchasing, manufacturing, sales, marketing, warehousing, and distribution of products.

Forecasting managers need a sound knowledge of production processes and should be able to maximize the efficient manufacture or purchase and distribution of products. They should understand transportation and distribution. In addition, they must have excellent math skills and an ability to analyze data to find purchasing trends. Most jobs in this field require a bachelor or master degree in accounting or a related field, as well as several years of experience. For more information, access the *Occupational Outlook Handbook* online.

---

is an asset pledged that will be claimed by the lender if the loan is not repaid. Loans that require collateral are known as *secured loans.* Examples of collateral for a loan can include a home, vehicle, or IRA.

Loans that do not require collateral, like credit card transactions, are known as *unsecured loans.* For bank loans less than $100,000, collateral may not be required and might be based primarily on credit history. Sources for debt financing include banks and credit unions, peer-to-peer loans, SBA-assisted loans, retirement accounts, family and friends, or trade credit.

Banks and Credit Unions

The traditional way to obtain start-up capital is to obtain a loan through a bank or credit union. After a business is established and has a good credit history, though, a bank

or credit union may extend a line of credit. A **line of credit** is a specific dollar amount that a business can draw against as needed. The business accesses money from the line of credit and pays it back on a regular basis, usually monthly.

Banks and credit unions might also extend credit to an established company through an overdraft agreement. An *overdraft agreement* allows a business to write checks for more than what is in the checking account. The institution pays the check through a line of credit and charges the company a fee for the overdraft protection.

Peer-to-Peer or Social Lending

Peer-to-peer lending is borrowing money from investors via a website and is gaining in popularity for loans under $25,000. Applicants

Banks and other lending institutions are the most common places that entrepreneurs go to for business loans.

Goodluz/Shutterstock.com

create and post a loan listing that explains the purpose of the loan and the amount needed. Potential investors review the loan listings and choose to fund loans that meet their criteria. Like banks and credit unions, the loans go through an approval process. Good credit scores ensure better interest rates.

FYI

Peer-to-peer lending is also known as *social lending.*

In this process, there is no lending institution. It is more like borrowing money from family or friends, except in most cases, the borrowers and lenders do not know each other. The advantages of peer-to-peer loans are potentially lower interest rates and short repayment time frames. The disadvantages are up-front fees, personal information is on a public site, and low loan amounts.

SBA-Assisted Loans

The SBA does not directly lend money, but it works closely with banks to provide small business loans. Instead, the SBA operates its Small Loan Advantage program. Under this program, the SBA guarantees 85 percent of a bank loan up to $150,000. For loans greater than $150,000, the SBA guarantees 75 percent of the loan amount. To qualify, a business owner must personally guarantee the loan by showing sufficient cash available for repayment. There are a number of different types of SBA-assisted lending programs for small business funding.

Retirement Accounts

Many people do not realize they can borrow from their IRA or 401(k). However, caution should be used when borrowing from retirement accounts. There are very strict IRS laws about how loans from retirement accounts can be used and repaid. There may also be tax consequences for borrowing from an IRA.

Money can be borrowed from an IRA interest free for 60 days, which might be helpful to get through a short-term cash flow problem. Some 401(k) plans permit borrowing for any reason, but most allow loans only for specifically defined reasons outlined in the plan. A person may borrow up to $50,000 from savings in a 401(k), but must pay interest along with the repayment of the loan.

Family and Friends

You may decide to ask for a loan from a relative or friend to help fund the business. One advantage to getting a loan from someone you know is the possibility of negotiating a lower interest rate. A family member or friend may also give you a better repayment schedule than a bank or credit union might. It is important to sign a formal agreement with *any* lender so there are no misunderstandings and there is legal protection for both sides.

Trade Credit

Trade credit is when one business grants a line of credit to another business for the purchase of goods and services. The line of credit is most often 30 or 60 days. This means that it is possible to make an interest-free purchase for 30 or 60 days. Payment is due in full at the end of the time period. The real benefit of trade credit is that you are getting products interest free for 30 or 60 days. Trade credit is most often used by established businesses. While most new businesses may have difficulty getting trade credit initially, it never hurts to ask.

Starting the Business

New business owners must plan for a number of things before actually opening the doors. It is important for owners to project the start-up costs and operating expenses, budget for owner cash withdrawal, and price their products or services correctly.

Project Start-Up Costs and Operating Expenses

Start-up costs are the initial expenses necessary to open the doors of a business. Some expenses will be one-time costs, such as equipment, filing DBA license, utility deposits, and the initial inventory.

While identifying the exact start-up costs for a business, determine whether each expense is essential. For example, if your current computer is adequate, do not include a new one as equipment in the start-up budget. Typical one-time start-up costs are similar to those in Figure 33-3. There are start-up cost calculators on the Internet to help estimate these costs.

Other start-up costs, such as rent and utilities, are also reoccurring operating expenses. **Operating expenses** are the ongoing expenses that help keep a company functioning.

Operating expenses are classified as fixed and variable expenses. **Fixed expenses** are those expenses that remain the same every

Figure 33-3
Entrepreneurs think of ways to save money on one-time start-up costs.

One-Time Start-Up Costs	
• Rent deposit	• DBA license
• Tenant improvements	• Utility deposits
• Furniture	• Initial inventory
• Computer, printer, and other office equipment	

Goodheart-Willcox Publisher

month. They include items such as mortgage payments and insurance. **Variable expenses** are expenses that can change on a monthly basis. They include the cost of advertising, insurance, and utilities, as shown in Figure 33-4.

According to Hiscox USA research, 20 percent of small business owners underestimated their start-up costs. The same study shows that over one-third of small business owners underestimate their operating expenses. For many business owners, underestimating start-up costs and operating expenses can mean the end of the business.

Follow the *rule of two:* expect everything to cost twice as much and take twice as long as you think it will. Project exactly what the business can afford before incurring expenses. Review financial reports from other companies in your industry to learn their types of operating expenses.

Ask area business owners who are not direct competitors about their typical operating expenses. Use a start-up cost calculator on the Internet to help estimate start-up costs. A SCORE mentor may also be able to help set realistic amounts for start-up and operating expenses. Consider working with an accounting professional to help guide you through this process.

Budget for Owner Cash Withdrawal

A business owner does *not* receive a salary from the business. Salaries are compensation for employees, not the owner. However, an owner may withdraw cash or assets from the business for personal use. It is very common for owners to make a cash withdrawal, called a *draw,* from the business to cover his or her personal expenses.

Price Products and Services Correctly

Accurate pricing of products and services is crucial to business success. Before pricing products, do research and seek professional advice to help set pricing. Pricing must be competitive and allow the business to make a profit. *Profit margin* is the amount by which product sales exceed the cost to the business of producing them. Profit margin is typically shown as a percentage.

Each industry has acceptable profit margin guidelines for pricing purposes. Some businesses calculate the cost of creating the product and then double that amount to set the price. Other businesses add a percentage of desired profit to the cost of creating the product. Your industry and the competition will dictate what is acceptable.

Monthly Operating Expenses	
Fixed Expenses	**Variable Expenses**
• Insurance	• Advertising
• Mortgage	• Fees
• Phone	• Office supplies
• Rent	• Utilities
• Salary	• Miscellaneous

Goodheart-Willcox Publisher

Figure 33-4 Be realistic when estimating ongoing operating expenses.

Forecast Sales Accurately

Sales forecasting is a complicated part of the business plan. The goal of the sales forecast is to not only project revenue but to make sure the business has enough products to sell. Accurate sales forecasts are necessary to predict revenue and profits. Follow the *rule of two* by cutting your best sales estimate in half. It is better to underestimate potential revenue than to overestimate it and come up short on revenue. Sales forecasting should be done in dollars as well as number of units that are projected to be sold.

There are multiple methods used to forecast sales. Use a sales-forecasting worksheet for your projections. You can find samples at the SCORE or SBA websites. Sales forecasts are usually done for monthly, quarterly, and yearly time periods.

Calculate the Break-Even Point

Recall from Chapter 19 that the *break-even point* is the amount of revenue a business must generate in order to equal its expenses. It is only after the break-even point is reached that profits are earned. Do not assume that by selling more products or services profits will increase. This may happen over time. However, variable expenses may also initially increase and actually reduce the profit margin. Many entrepreneurs do not know their break-even points and end up running out of cash before making a profit.

First, estimate total costs by adding the fixed and variable expenses. Then, project sales for a year. Plot the sales and expenses on a graph, as shown in Figure 33-5. The break-even point is where the two lines intersect.

After reaching the break-even point, evaluate the marginal benefit and cost to producing various quantities of additional

Figure 33-5 After finding the break-even point, assume it will take more sales than you project to reach that point.

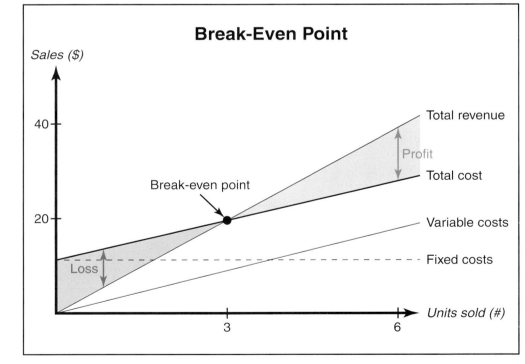

Resource/Evaluate

Assign the optional Chapter 33 test for **EXAM**VIEW®
Assessment Suite as a formal assessment tool.

products. *Marginal benefit* measures the potential gains of producing more products that sell because the profit margin is higher. *Marginal cost* measures the potential losses from producing more products that might not sell. While the products may cost less to make, there is also the risk they will not sell and will decrease profits.

AMA Tip

Consider taking advantage of the benefits of AMA membership by joining as a student member or forming a collegiate chapter. The American Marketing Association website contains more information on the features and resources that are highlighted in each chapter of this book. Visit the association website for access to journal and magazine articles, event information, and membership details. www.marketingpower.com

Checkpoint 33.1

1. List five common bootstrapping practices.
2. Why do some entrepreneurs use bootstrapping?
3. What is a risk of equity financing?
4. Give examples of financial institutions where you can obtain debt financing.
5. List some of the typical start-up costs a new owner may encounter.

Build Your Vocabulary

As you progress through this course, develop a personal glossary of marketing terms and add it to your portfolio. This will help you build your vocabulary and prepare you for a career. Write a definition for each of the following terms, and add it to your personal marketing glossary.

bootstrapping
start-up capital
equity
equity financing
angel investor
venture capitalist
debt financing
collateral
line of credit
peer-to-peer lending
trade credit
start-up cost
operating expense
fixed expense
variable expense

Section 33.2 Apply for Financing

Objectives

After completing this section, you will be able to
- **explain** the business loan application process.
- **describe** three pro forma statements that accompany a business loan application.

Key Terms

cosigner
pro forma financial statement
pro forma cash flow statement
pro forma income statement
pro forma balance sheet
asset
fixed asset
liquid asset
accounts receivable
liabilities
accounts payable
owner's equity

Web Connect

Visit the Small Business Administration (SBA) website at www.sba.gov. This website lists multiple small business tools and loan programs to help entrepreneurs. Select one of these tools or programs and describe how it can help you get your business started.

Critical Thinking

When applying for a loan, lenders want information about your personal finances as well as your business projections. Make a list of items you think a financial institution will want from entrepreneurs seeking a loan.

Business Loan Application Process

Applying for a business loan is a complex process. A bank or credit union may be more likely to lend to existing customers with other accounts. However, there is no guarantee you will be granted a loan. It may be necessary to apply for a loan multiple times until you are successful.

What Lenders Require

All lenders have a loan application that must be completed. The application will ask for many details, so it is important to take your time and complete it fully and accurately. Education, experience, past jobs, current debt, and the business projections all help the lender evaluate your application.

When applying for debt or equity financing, applicants are asked to provide documentation proving they are good credit risks. Items that are typically required for any small business loan application are shown in Figure 33-6.

Explore

Provide an opportunity for students to explore by assigning a hands-on activity. Review the vocabulary terms at the beginning of the section. Where have students encountered these terms before? Help students make educated guesses about the meanings of the terms with which they are least familiar.

Documents Required for Loan Applications
• Résumés
• Personal financial statement
• Business plan with pro forma financial statements
• Income tax returns
• Bank statements
• Collateral documentation, if necessary

Goodheart-Willcox Publisher

Figure 33-6 The quality of these documents may be the deciding factor in getting a business off the ground.

It is important to provide résumés for all owners. Most lenders require that the applicants have some management or business experience, especially for start-up loans. Many loan programs require owners with more than a 20 percent ownership in a business to submit signed personal financial statements. This is true for sole proprietorships, partnerships, and corporations.

All business loan programs require a sound business plan be submitted with the loan application. The financial plans section of the business plan includes details about raising capital and future plans for the business. It also contains the pro forma income, cash flow, and balance sheet financial statements. In addition, the following items may be requested, which are included in the business plan appendices:

- DBA, licenses, and registrations required to conduct business;
- partnership agreement or Articles of Incorporation;
- copies of supplier contracts;
- franchise agreement; or
- commercial leases.

Most business loan programs require applicants to submit personal and, if possible, business income tax returns for the previous three years. Many loan programs also require one year of personal and business bank statements.

Collateral requirements vary greatly, often by the requested loan amount and degree of risk. It is a good idea to prepare a document describing the cost and value of any collateral used to secure a loan.

How Lenders Evaluate Applicants

Lenders making personal loans evaluate applicants on character, capacity, and capital, which are known as the *three Cs of credit*. However, when applying for a business loan, the criteria are somewhat different. This criteria is known as the *five Cs of banking*. The five Cs of banking include character, cash flow, capital, collateral, and conditions.

Character

All lenders run a credit report to learn an applicant's history of creating and paying debt. The report will come from a credit bureau that tracks individuals and their debt. Each consumer is rated according to the types of debt they have, on-time payments, and how quickly debt is repaid. The higher a credit score, the better the rating. Credit scores play a part in the ability to get a loan. Also, having very good credit may also qualify you for a lower interest rate.

Social Media

Follow the Competition

Perhaps one of the most important things to consider when using social media marketing is that your competition is using it, too. Just as you monitor your competitors' print and broadcast advertising efforts, you should know exactly how they are using social media. The first step is to *like* them on Facebook. Then, monitor their LinkedIn postings, follow them on Twitter and/or Pinterest, and subscribe to their blogs. Once you know exactly how your competitors are using each social media platform, you can tailor your own efforts to meet or beat theirs.

Some business loan applicants may use their homes as collateral for a large loan.

Cash Flow

Lenders want to know that a business can generate enough cash flow to repay the loan on time. Sometimes, lenders ask for a cosigner on the loan. A cosigner is a person who signs a loan with the applicant and takes on equal responsibility for repaying it. The cosigner usually has a better-established financial history than the primary applicant.

Capital

Applicants are asked about the amount of personal resources invested in the business and how it was obtained. It is important that there are enough assets in the business to keep things running.

Collateral

If the loan is large enough, lenders require collateral to secure it. Collateral comes in many forms and is valued by lenders in different ways. For example, an entrepreneur may use the equity in his or her house as collateral for a loan.

Conditions

Lenders assess the economic conditions of the business' industry, the potential for the business to grow, and the form of ownership. They also consider the business location, competition, and applicant's insurance coverage. Given the conditions they find, the lender defines the terms under which a loan would be given. These terms may be as simple as the owner buying insurance for the business, or they may be more complex.

Pro Forma Financial Statements

Each component of the loan application process is important. One of the major parts is the pro forma financial statements that support the business plan. Pro forma financial statements are financial statements based on the best estimate of future revenue and expenses for a new business. Lenders need to see evidence that the new business will make enough money to repay the loan in a timely manner. The pro forma cash flow statement, pro forma income statement, and pro forma balance sheet will be completed as part of the application. They are also included in the Appendices of the business plan.

Sophia's Web Design Co.
Pro Forma Cash Flow Statement
Year Ended December, 20--

	Jan.	Feb.	Mar.	Apr.	May	June	July	Aug .	Sept.	Oct.	Nov.	Dec.
Cash Receipts	$2,000	$3,500	$4,000	$4,200	$5,600	$8,200	$8,500	$8,600	$9,000	$9,100	$9,200	$9,600
Cash Disbursements												
Advertising Expense	200	200	200	200	200	300	200	200	200	200	200	200
Rent Expense	400	400	400	400	400	400	400	400	400	400	400	400
Insurance Expense	50	50	50	50	50	50	50	50	50	50	50	50
Supplies Expense	100	100	50	50	50	75	25	25	200	25	25	25
Utilities Expense	150	150	150	150	150	150	150	150	150	150	150	150
Total Disbursements	900	900	850	850	850	975	825	825	1,000	825	825	825
Net Cash Flow	$1,100	$2,600	$3,150	$3,350	$4,750	$7,225	$7,675	$7,775	$8,000	$8,275	$8,375	$8,775

Figure 33-7 Use a pro forma cash flow statement to predict the best and worst outcomes.

Pro Forma Cash Flow Statement

A **pro forma cash flow statement** reports the anticipated flow of cash into and out of the business. An example of projected cash flow for a service business is shown in Figure 33-7.

To prepare a pro forma cash flow statement, project the amount of sales, or cash in, expected for the first twelve months. Next, project the expenses, or cash out, for the same time period. If you project receiving more cash from sales than is spent on expenses, the cash flow is positive. If you project spending more than the amount of cash taken in, the cash flow is negative. It is a good idea to project several levels of sales to understand the best- and worst-case scenarios.

FYI

The pro forma income statement is also known as a *pro forma profit and loss statement (P & L).*

Pro Forma Income Statement

A **pro forma income statement** projects the financial progress of the business. The two main sections of a pro forma income statement are projected revenue and expenses. A lender or investor may require a forecast for one year or multiple years. An example of a pro forma income statement for a three-year period is shown in Figure 33-8.

Pro Forma Balance Sheet

The **pro forma balance sheet** reports the assets, liabilities, and owner's equity for a proposed business. An example of a pro forma balance sheet is shown in Figure 33-9.

Assets are the property or items of value owned by a business. Assets may be fixed or liquid. **Fixed assets** are the items of value that may take time to sell. A building or heavy equipment is a fixed asset. **Liquid assets** are cash and the items a business owns that can be easily turned into cash. A checking account and accounts

Figure 33-8 The pro forma income statement is used to project net income over a period of time.

Sophia's Web Design Co.			
Pro Forma Income Statement			
Year Ended December, 20--			
	Year 1	Year 2	Year 3
Revenue			
Sales	$76,500	$81,500	$92,000
Expenses			
Advertising Expense	15,000	16,000	18,000
Rent Expense	48,000	48,000	48,000
Insurance Expense	600	700	800
Supplies Expense	750	900	1,200
Utilities Expense	1,800	2,000	2,100
Total Expenses	66,150	66,150	70,100
Net Income	$10,350	$15,350	$21,900

receivables are considered liquid assets. **Accounts receivable** is money owed to a business by customers for goods or services delivered. In accounting, accounts receivable are considered an asset.

Liabilities are what the business owes to others. Liabilities may be short-term or long-term debt. *Short-term liabilities* are those expected to be paid within the current year. This includes salaries and accounts payable. **Accounts payable** is the money a business owes to its suppliers for goods or services received. In accounting, accounts payable are considered a liability. *Long-term liabilities* are debts that extend beyond the current year.

Long-term liabilities can include repayment of a bank loan and rent.

The difference between a business' assets and its liabilities is called **owner's equity.** Owner's equity is also known as the owner's *net worth.* This information on a balance sheet is expressed as the *accounting equation:*

$$\text{assets} = \text{liabilities} + \text{owner's equity}$$

A lender may also ask for personal financial statements showing assets and liabilities unrelated to the business. Personal financial status will be reviewed along with the financial status of the business.

Case in Point

Warby Parker

As consumers, friends Neil Blumenthal, David Gilboa, Andrew Hunt, and Jeffrey Raider were frustrated by the high cost of designer eyeglasses, which can cost as much as $500 a pair. These friends knew glasses are often marked up two to three times. They decided to start their own business, Warby Parker, to sell designer-style prescription glasses for under $100. For each pair the company sells, it helps a person in need to buy one pair of glasses. In order to fund the business idea, the group turned to some famous angel investors, including the former CEO of Tommy Hilfiger, Ashton Kutcher, and Lady Gaga manager Troy Carter. Most recently, a venture capital firm helped Warby Parker raise $12 million from Tiger Global, Menlo Talent Fund, and existing investors. This is an example of entrepreneurs creating a successful business as well as demonstrating social responsibility.

Sophia's Web Design Co.
Pro Forma Balance Sheet
Year Ended December, 20--

Assets

Cash	$5,000	
Accounts Receivable	9,600	
Equipment	32,000	
Total Assets		46,600

Liabilities

Accounts Payable	$12,000	
Notes Payable	10,000	
Total Liabilities		22,000

Owner's Equity

Sophia Nguyen, Capital		24,600
Total Liabilities and Owner's Equity		$46,600

Figure 33-9 This pro forma balance sheet provides a snapshot of a business' financial position at the time of the loan application.

Goodheart-Willcox Publisher

Checkpoint 33.2

1. Why do banks use the three Cs of Credit to evaluate applicants for loans?
2. What purpose do pro forma statements serve?
3. Name three pro forma statements required in the loan application process.
4. What is the difference between a fixed asset and a liquid asset?
5. What is the difference between short-term and long-term liabilities?

Build Your Vocabulary

As you progress through this course, develop a personal glossary of marketing terms and add it to your portfolio. This will help you build your vocabulary and prepare you for a career. Write a definition for each of the following terms, and add it to your personal marketing glossary.

cosigner
pro forma financial statement
pro forma cash flow statement
pro forma income statement
pro forma balance sheet
asset

fixed asset
liquid asset
accounts receivable
liabilities
accounts payable
owner's equity

Chapter Summary

Section 33.1 Options for Funding

- Before seeking funds from outside sources, most entrepreneurs often evaluate alternative strategies for getting the business off the ground. This practice is known as *bootstrapping*.
- For entrepreneurs without enough cash on hand to completely fund a business, sources for start-up capital include equity financing and debt financing.
- New business owners must plan for a number of things before actually opening the doors. It is important for owners to project the start-up costs and operating expenses, budget for owner cash withdrawal, and price their products or services correctly.

Section 33.2 Apply for Financing

- As part of the process of obtaining a business loan, the applicant must provide certain documentation to help determine whether the business is creditworthy. The applicants are reviewed on character, cash flow, capital, collateral, and conditions.
- A pro forma cash flow statement, income statement, and balance sheet are required as part of the business loan application process.

Review Your Knowledge

1. What percentage of equity does a self-funding entrepreneur have in his or her business?
2. Why are angel investors a particularly good source of funding for a new business?
3. Describe the loan application process.
4. What are the five Cs of banking?
5. Why does the lender require an applicant to produce pro forma financial statements?
6. What purpose does providing a pro forma cash flow statement serve?
7. Why does the lender want a pro forma income statement?
8. What is a pro forma income statement also known as?
9. What does a pro forma balance sheet represent?
10. State the accounting equation.

Review Your Knowledge Answers

1. A self-funding entrepreneur has 100 percent equity in his or her business.

2. Angel investors often will take on more risk than a bank.

3. The loan application process includes providing résumés, a personal financial statement, a business plan, income tax returns, bank statements, and collateral documentation, if necessary.

4. The five Cs of banking are character, cash flow, capital, collateral, and conditions.

5. Lenders need to see evidence that the new business will make enough money to repay the loan in a timely manner.

6. A pro forma cash flow statement reports the anticipated flow of cash into and out of the business. It helps to show the business' ability to repay the loan.

7. A lender or investor may require a forecast of revenue and expenses for one year or multiple years. It helps to show the business' ability to repay the loan.

8. The pro forma income statement is also known as a pro forma profit and loss statement (P & L).

9. The pro forma balance sheet provides a snapshot of a business' financial position at the time of the loan application. It includes the assets, liabilities, and owner's equity of the business.

10. The accounting equation is assets = liabilities + owner's equity (net worth).

Apply Your Knowledge

1. Create a chart for ways to bootstrap your business. For each method suggested in the chapter, write a description for how you would apply this to your business. For example, for personal assets, write down each personal asset you are willing to use for your business.
2. Create a chart for equity financing options for your business. For each method suggested in the chapter, write a description for how you would apply this to your business. For example, for personal savings, write down each account you have and the amount of money you are willing to use for your business.
3. Create a chart for debt financing options for your business. For each debt financing method suggested in the chapter, write a description of how you would apply this to your business. For example, for banks and credit unions, list potential places you would contact for a loan.
4. Research *applying for a small business loan* online and report your findings. Did your research uncover any challenges that you did not anticipate?
5. When you are ready to apply for a loan, you will have to complete an application. Research small business loan applications on the Internet. Select an application form and complete it. How long did it take you to complete the form? What did you learn from this exercise?
6. When you apply for a loan, you will have to show collateral. Make a list of items you could use as collateral for a loan.
7. Research the loan application process for one equity financing option and for one debt financing option. Report what you learned.
8. You will have many start-up costs for your business. Research start-up costs for your type of business. Report your findings. Were there any surprises as to the investment required?
9. Find a start-up cost calculator on the Internet and calculate what your start-up costs will be for your business. Were the costs affordable?
10. Create a personal balance sheet of your assets, liabilities, and owner's equity.

Check Your Marketing IQ

Now that you have finished the chapter, see what you learned about marketing by taking the chapter posttest. If you do not have a smartphone, visit the G-W Learning companion website.

G-W Learning mobile site: www.m.g-wlearning.com
G-W Learning companion website: www.g-wlearning.com

College and Career Readiness

Common Core

CTE Career Ready Practices. The ability to read and interpret information is an important workplace skill. Presume you are starting a business. You will need to locate three reliable sources for financing. Research financing options that may be available to you at a local financial institution. Read and interpret the information you locate. Then, write a report summarizing your findings in an organized manner.

Reading. Read a magazine, newspaper, or online article about a current ethical or unethical situation that has occurred involving an entrepreneur. Determine the central ideas and conclusions of the article. Provide an accurate summary of your reading, making sure to incorporate the *who, what, when,* and *how* of this ethical or unethical situation.

Writing. Research the history of borrowing money. Where did the concept of loans originate? Write an informative report, consisting of several paragraphs to describe your findings.

Teamwork

This chapter discusses the process for funding a start-up business. Working with your team, evaluate the ways to obtain debt financing. Rank these alternatives in the order that your team thinks is the most desirable financing choice for a new business owner and why. Present your opinions to the class.

G-W Learning Mobile Site

Visit the G-W Learning mobile site to complete the chapter pretest and posttest and to practice vocabulary using e-flash cards. If you do not have a smartphone, visit the G-W Learning companion website to access these features.

G-W Learning mobile site: www.m.g-wlearning.com

G-W Learning companion website: www.g-wlearning.com

Unit 10 Dynamics of Entrepreneurship

Building the Marketing Plan

Entrepreneurs are also marketers. After coming up with an idea for new business, they must also *sell* the idea to a great many people before actually opening the doors. Most entrepreneurs need some form of start-up capital from lenders or investors. In order to obtain the necessary funding, the customers (or people who can grant that funding) must want (or believe in) the product (the new business) and want to buy it (invest in it or lend money to the owner). The features and benefits of the business must be clear in a business plan. There are some parts of a business plan that are just like a marketing plan, such as the Bibliography and the Appendices. Both are important so that all of the resources, research, financials, and other information is shown to be accurate and reasonable.

Bibliography and Appendices

Objectives

- Create the Bibliography.
- Collect documents for the Appendices.

Directions

In this activity, you will create the remaining parts of your marketing plan, the Bibliography and the Appendices. A bibliography is necessary to list of the sources for all of the primary and secondary research you used in the plan. The appendices are all of the documents that are referenced in the plan and are included as attachments to the plan. Access the *Marketing Dynamics* companion website at www.g-wlearning.com. Download the data files as indicated for the following activities.

1. **Unit Activity 10-1. Bibliography.** Make sure you know the style your instructor wants you to use when listing sources. The Bibliography might include interviews, books, periodicals, and websites cited; or other information you gathered while researching your marketing plan.
2. **Unit Activity 10-2. Appendices.** List every document that you refer to in the plan in a logical order. These documents create the Appendices, or the attachments necessary to back up the information presented in the plan.
3. Open your saved marketing plan document.
4. Locate the Bibliography section of the marketing plan and list every source. Use the suggestions and questions listed to help you generate ideas. Delete the instructions and questions when you are finished recording your responses.
5. Locate the Appendices page in your plan document. Locate all of the documents listed in the Appendices, proof them for any errors, and make any corrections. Print the documents. Make sure to include them in the Table of Contents under Appendices.
6. Locate the Table of Contents. Insert the final page numbers for the Bibliography and Appendices.
7. Proofread your entire marketing plan document. Make any final additions or corrections.
8. Save your document.
9. Print the document and gather the printed attachments. Assemble and bind it in a professional manner.

Congratulations. You have finished your marketing plan.

Math Skills Handbook

Table of Contents

Getting Started

Math skills are needed in everyday life. You will need to be able to estimate your purchases at a grocery store, calculate sales tax, or divide a recipe in half. This section is designed to help develop your math proficiency for better understanding of the concepts presented in the textbook. Using the information presented in the Math Skills Handbook will help you understand basic math concepts and their application to the real world.

Using a Calculator

There are many different types of calculators. Some are simple and only perform basic math operations. Become familiar with the keys and operating instructions of your calculator so calculations can be made quickly and correctly.

Shown below is a scientific calculator that comes standard with the Windows 8 operating system. To display this version, select the **View** pull-down menu and click **Scientific** in the menu.

Click to change the type of calculator shown

Positive or negative

Division (÷)

Multiplication (×)

Parentheses

Display

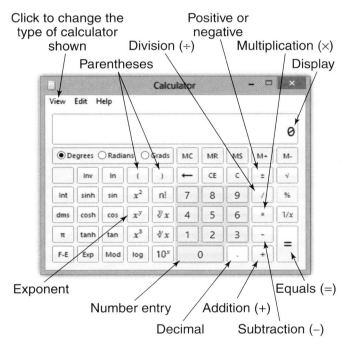

Exponent

Number entry

Addition (+)

Equals (=)

Decimal

Subtraction (−)

Solving Word Problems

Word problems are exercises in which the problem is set up in text, rather than presented in mathematical notation. Many word problems tell a story. You must identify the elements of the math problem and solve it.

There are many strategies for solving word problems. Some common strategies include making a list or table; working backward; guessing, checking, and revising; and substituting simpler numbers to solve the problem.

Strategy	How to Apply
List or table	Identify information in the problem and organize it into a table to identify patterns.
Work backward	When an end result is provided, work backward from that to find the requested information.
Guess, check, revise	Start with a reasonable guess at the answer, check to see if it is correct, and revise the guess as needed until the solution is found.
Substitute simpler information	Use different numbers to simplify the problem and solve it, then solve the problem using the provided numbers.

Number Sense

Number sense is an ability to use and understand numbers to make judgments and solve problems. Someone with good number sense also understands when his or her computations are reasonable in the context of a problem.

Example
Suppose you want to add three basketball scores: 35, 21, and 18.
- First, add $30 + 20 + 10 = 60$.
- Then, add $5 + 1 + 8 = 14$.
- Finally, combine these two sums to find the answer: $60 + 14 = 74$.

Example
Suppose your brother is 72 inches tall and you want to convert this measurement from inches to feet. Suppose you use a calculator to divide 72 by 12 (number of inches in a foot) and the answer is displayed as 864. You recognize immediately that your brother cannot be 864 feet tall and realize you must have miscalculated. In this case, you incorrectly entered a multiplication operation instead of a division operation. The correct answer is 6.

Numbers and Quantity

Numbers are more than just items in a series. Each number has a distinct value relative to all other numbers. They are used to perform mathematical operations from the simplest addition to finding square roots. There are whole numbers, fractions, decimals, exponents, and square roots.

Whole Numbers

A whole number, or integer, is any positive number or zero that has no fractional part. It can be a single digit from 0 to 9, or may contain multiple digits, such as 38.

Place Value

A digit's position in a number determines its *place value.* The digit, or numeral, in the place farthest to the right before the decimal point is in the *ones position.* The next digit to the left is in the *tens position,* followed by next digit in the *hundreds position.* As you continue to move left, the place values increase to thousands, ten thousands, and so forth.

Example

Suppose you win the lottery and receive a check for $23,152,679. Your total prize would be *twenty-three million, one hundred fifty-two thousand, six hundred seventy-nine dollars.*

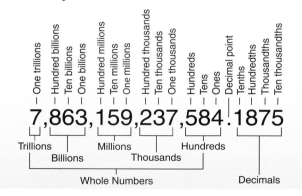

Addition

Addition is the process of combining two or more numbers. The result is called the *sum.*

Example

A plumber installs six faucets on his first job and three faucets on his second job. How many faucets does he install in total?

$$6 + 3 = 9$$

Subtraction

Subtraction is the process of finding the *difference* between two numbers.

Example

A plumber installs six faucets on her first job and three faucets on her second job. How many more faucets did she install on the first job than the second? Subtract 3 from 6 to find the answer.

$$6 - 3 = 3$$

Multiplication

Multiplication is a method of adding a number to itself a given number of times. The multiplied numbers are called *factors,* and the result is called the *product.*

Example

Suppose you are installing computers and need to purchase four adaptors. If the adaptors are $6 each, what is the total cost of the adaptors? The answer can be found by adding $6 four times:

$$\$6 + \$6 + \$6 + \$6 = \$24$$

However, the same answer is found more quickly by multiplying $6 times 4.

$$\$6 \times 4 = \$24$$

Division

Division is the process of determining how many times one number, called the *divisor,* goes into another number, called the *dividend.* The result is called the *quotient.*

Example

Suppose you are installing computers and buy a box of adaptors for $24. There are four adaptors in the box. What is the cost of each adaptor? The answer is found by dividing $24 by 4:

$$\$24 \div 4 = \$6$$

Decimals

A decimal is a kind of fraction with a denominator that is either ten, one hundred, one thousand, or some power of ten. Every decimal has three parts: a whole number (sometimes zero), followed by a decimal point, and one or more whole numbers.

Place Value

The numbers to the right of the decimal point indicate the amount of the fraction. The first place to the right of a decimal point is the tenths place. The second place to the right of the decimal point is the hundredths place. As you continue to the right, the place values move to the thousandths place, the ten thousandths place, and so on.

Example

A machinist is required to produce an airplane part to a very precise measurement of 36.876 inches. This measurement is *thirty-six and eight-hundred seventy six thousandths* inches.

$$36.876$$

Addition

To add decimals, place each number in a vertical list and align the decimal points. Then add the numbers in each column starting with the column on the right and working to the left. The decimal point in the answer drops down into the same location.

Example

A landscaper spreads 4.3 pounds of fertilizer in the front yard of a house and 1.2 pounds in the backyard. How many pounds of fertilizer did the landscaper spread in total?

$$\begin{array}{r} 4.3 \\ + \ 1.2 \\ \hline 5.5 \end{array}$$

Subtraction

To subtract decimals, place each number in a vertical list and align the decimal points. Then subtract the numbers in each column, starting with the column on the right and working to the left. The decimal point in the answer drops down into the same location.

Example

A landscaper spreads 4.3 pounds of fertilizer in the front yard of a house and 1.2 pounds in the backyard. How many more pounds were spread in the front yard than in the backyard?

$$\begin{array}{r} 4.3 \\ - \ 1.2 \\ \hline 3.1 \end{array}$$

Multiplication

To multiply decimals, place the numbers in a vertical list. Then multiply each digit of the top number by the right-hand bottom number. Multiply each digit of the top number by the bottom number in the tens position. Place the result on a second line and add a zero to the end of the number. Add the total number of decimal places in both numbers you are multiplying. This will be the number of decimal places in your answer.

Example

An artist orders 13 brushes priced at $3.20 each. What is the total cost of the order? The answer can be found by multiplying $3.20 by 13.

$$\begin{array}{r} \$3.20 \\ \times \qquad 13 \\ \hline 960 \\ + \ 3200 \\ \hline 41.60 \end{array}$$

Division

To divide decimals, the dividend is placed under the division symbol, the divisor is placed to the left of the division symbol, and the quotient is placed above the division symbol. Start from the *left* of the dividend and determine how many times the divisor goes into the first number. Continue this until the quotient is found. Add the dollar sign to the final answer.

$$
\begin{array}{r}
3.20 \\
3\overline{)9.60} \\
9 \quad \text{Product of } 3 \times 3 \\
06 \quad \text{Bring down the 6} \\
6 \quad \text{Product of } 2 \times 3 \\
0 \quad \text{No remainder}
\end{array}
$$

Example

An artist buys a package of three brushes for $9.60. What is the cost of each brush? The quotient is found by dividing $9.60 by 3.

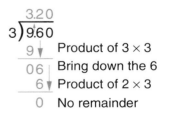

Rounding

When a number is rounded, some of the digits are changed, removed, or changed to zero so the number is easier to work with. Rounding is often used when precise calculations or measurements are not needed. For example, if you are calculating millions of dollars, it might not be important to know the amount down to the dollar or cent. Instead, you might *round* the amount to the nearest ten thousand or even hundred thousand dollars. Also, when working with decimals, the final answer might have several more decimal places than needed.

To round a number, follow these steps. First, underline the digit in the place to which you are rounding. Second, if the digit to the *right* of this place is 5 or greater, add 1 to the underlined digit. If the digit to the right is less than 5, do not change the underlined digit. Third, change all the digits to right of the underlined digit to zero. In the case of decimals, the digits to the right of the underlined digit are removed.

Example

A company's utility expense last year was $32,678.53. The owner of the company is preparing a budget for next year and wants to round this amount to the nearest 1,000.

Step 1: Underline the digit in the 10,000 place.

$$\$3\underline{2},678$$

Step 2: The digit to the right of 2 is greater than 5, so add 1.

$$2 + 1 = 3$$

Step 3: Change the digits to the right of the underlined digit to zero.

$$\$33,000$$

Fractions

A fraction is a part of a whole. It is made up by a numerator that is divided by a denominator.

$$\frac{numerator}{denominator}$$

The *numerator* specifies the number of these equal parts that are in the fraction. The *denominator* shows how many equal parts make up the whole.

Proper

In a *proper fraction,* the numerator is less than the denominator.

Example

A lumber yard worker cuts a sheet of plywood into four equal pieces and sells three of them to a carpenter. The carpenter now has 3/4 of the original sheet. The lumber yard has 1/4 of the sheet remaining.

Improper

An *improper fraction* is a fraction where the numerator is equal to or greater than the denominator.

Example

A chef uses a chili recipe which calls for 1/2 cup of chili sauce. However, the chef makes an extra-large batch that will serve three times as many people and uses three of the 1/2 cup measures. The improper fraction in this example is 3/2 cups of chili sauce.

Mixed

A mixed number contains a whole number and a fraction. It is another way of writing an improper fraction.

Example

A chef uses a chili recipe that calls for 1/2 cup of chili sauce. However, the chef makes an extra-large batch that will serve three times as many people and uses three of the 1/2 cup measures. The improper fraction in this example is 3/2 cups of chili sauce. This can be converted to a mixed number by dividing the numerator by the denominator:

The remainder is 1, which is 1 over 2. So, the mixed number is 1 1/2 cups.

Reducing

Fractions are reduced to make them easier to work with. Reducing a fraction means writing it with smaller numbers, in *lowest terms.* Reducing a fraction does not change its value.

To find the lowest terms, determine the largest number that *evenly* divides both the numerator and denominator so there is no remainder. Then use this number to divide both the numerator and denominator.

Example

The owner of hair salon asks ten customers if they were satisfied with the service they recently received. Eight customers said they were satisfied, so the fraction of satisfied customers is 8/10. The largest number that evenly divides both the numerator and denominator is 2. The fraction is reduced to its lowest terms as follows.

$$\frac{8}{10} = \frac{8 \div 2}{10 \div 2} = \frac{4}{5}$$

Addition

To add fractions, the numerators are combined and the denominator stays the same. However, fractions can only be added when they have a *common denominator.* The *least common denominator* is the smallest number to which each denominator can be converted.

Example

A snack food company makes a bag of trail mix by combining 3/8 pound of nuts with 1/8 pound of dried fruit. What is the total weight of each bag? The fractions have common denominators, so the total weight is determined by adding the fractions.

$$\frac{3}{8} + \frac{1}{8} = \frac{4}{8}$$

This answer can be reduced from 4/8 to 1/2.

Example

Suppose the company combines 1/4 pound of nuts with 1/8 cup of dried fruit. To add these fractions, the denominators must be made equal. In this case, the least common denominator is 8 because

$4 \times 2 = 8$. Convert 1/4 to its equivalent of 2/8 by multiplying both numerator and denominator by 2. Then the fractions can be added as follows.

$$\frac{2}{8} + \frac{1}{8} = \frac{3}{8}$$

This answer cannot be reduced because 3 and 8 have no common factors.

Subtraction

To subtract fractions, the second numerator is subtracted from the first numerator. The denominators stay the same. However, fractions can only be subtracted when they have a *common denominator.*

Example

A snack food company makes a bag of trail mix by combining 3/8 pound of nuts with 1/8 pound of dried fruit. How much more do the nuts weigh than the dried fruit? The fractions have common denominators, so the difference can be determined by subtracting the fractions.

$$\frac{3}{8} - \frac{1}{8} = \frac{2}{8}$$

This answer can be reduced from 2/8 to 1/4.

Example

Suppose the company combines 1/4 pound of nuts with 1/8 cup of dried fruit. How much more do the nuts weigh than the dried fruit? To subtract these fractions, the denominators must be made equal. The least common denominator is 8, so convert 1/4 to its equivalent of 2/8. Then the fractions can be subtracted as follows.

$$\frac{2}{8} - \frac{1}{8} = \frac{1}{8}$$

This answer cannot be reduced.

Multiplication

Common denominators are not necessary to multiply fractions. Multiply all of the numerators and multiply all of the denominators. Reduce the resulting fraction as needed.

Example

A lab technician makes a saline solution by mixing 3/4 cup of salt with one gallon of water. How much salt should the technician mix if only 1/2 gallon of water is used? Multiply 3/4 by 1/2:

$$\frac{3}{4} \times \frac{1}{2} = \frac{3}{8}$$

Division

To divide one fraction by a second fraction, multiply the first fraction by the reciprocal of the second fraction. The *reciprocal* of a fraction is created by switching the numerator and denominator.

Example

A cabinet maker has 3/4 gallon of wood stain. Each cabinet requires 1/8 gallon of stain to finish. How many cabinets can be finished? To find the answer, divide 3/4 by 1/8, which means multiplying 3/4 by the reciprocal of 1/8.

$$\frac{3}{4} \div \frac{1}{8} = \frac{3}{4} \times \frac{8}{1} = \frac{24}{4} = 6$$

Negative Numbers

Negative numbers are those less than zero. They are written with a minus sign in front of the number.

Example

The number −34,687,295 is read as *negative thirty-four million, six hundred eighty-seven thousand, two hundred ninety-five.*

Addition

Adding a negative number is the same as subtracting a positive number.

Example

A football player gains nine yards on his first running play (+9) and loses four yards (−4) on his second play. The two plays combined result in a five yard gain.

$$9 + (-4) = 9 - 4 = 5$$

Suppose this player loses five yards on his first running play (−5) and loses four yards (−4) on his second play. The two plays combined result in a nine yard loss.

$$-5 + (-4) = -5 - 4 = -9$$

Subtraction

Subtracting a negative number is the same as adding a positive number.

Example

Suppose you receive a $100 traffic ticket. This will result in a −$100 change to your cash balance. However, you explain the circumstance to a traffic court judge, and she reduces the fine by $60. The effect is to subtract −$60 from −$100 change to your cash balance. The final result is a −$40 change.

$$-\$100 - (-\$60) = -\$100 + \$60 = -\$40$$

Multiplication

Multiplication of an odd number of negative numbers results in a *negative* product. Multiplication of an even number of negative numbers results in a *positive* product.

Example

If you lose two pounds per week, this will result in a −2 pound weekly change in your weight. After five weeks, there will be a −10 pound change to your weight.

$$5 \times (-2) = -10$$

Suppose you have been losing two pounds per week. Five weeks ago (−5) your weight was 10 pounds higher.

$$(-5) \times (-2) = 10$$

Division

Division of an odd number of negative numbers results in a *negative* quotient. Division of an even number of negative numbers results in a *positive* quotient.

Example

Suppose you lost 10 pounds, which is a −10 pound change in your weight. How many pounds on average did you lose each week if it took five weeks to lose the weight? Divide −10 by 5 to find the answer.

$$-10 \div 5 = -2$$

Suppose you lost 10 pounds. How many weeks did this take if you lost two pounds each week? Divide −10 by −2 to find the answer.

$$-10 \div -2 = 5$$

Percentages

A percentage (%) means a part of 100. It is the same as a fraction or decimal.

Representing Percentages as Decimals

To change a percentage to a decimal, move the decimal point two places to the left. For example, 1% is the same as 1/100 or 0.01; 10% is the same as 10/100 or 0.10; and 100% is the same as 100/100 or 1.0.

Example
A high school cafeteria estimates that 30% of the students prefer sesame seeds on hamburger buns. To convert this percentage to a decimal, move the decimal point two places to the left.

$$30\% = 0.30$$

Representing Fractions as Percentages

To change a fraction to a percentage, first convert the fraction to a decimal by dividing the numerator by the denominator. Then convert the decimal to a percentage by moving the decimal point two places to the right.

Example
A high school cafeteria conducts a survey and finds that three of every ten students prefer sesame seeds on hamburger buns. To change this fraction to a percentage, divide 3 by 10, and move the decimal two places to the right.

$$3 \div 10 = 0.30 = 30\%$$

Calculating a Percentage

To calculate the percentage of a number, change the percentage to a decimal and multiply by the number.

Example
A car dealer sold ten cars last week, of which 70% were sold to women. How many cars did women buy? Change 70% to a decimal by dividing 70 by 100, which equals 0.70. Then multiply by the total number (10).

$$0.70 \times 10 = 7$$

To determine what percentage one number is of another, divide the first number by the second. Then convert the quotient into a percentage by moving the decimal point two places to the right.

Example
A car dealer sold 10 cars last week, of which seven were sold to women. What percentage of the cars were purchased by women? Divide 7 by 10 and then convert to a percentage.

$$7 \div 10 = 0.70$$
$$0.70 = 70\%$$

Ratio

A ratio compares two numbers through division. Ratios are often expressed as a fraction, but can also be written with a colon (:) or the word *to*.

Example
A drugstore's cost for a bottle of vitamins is $2.00, which it sells for $3.00. The ratio of the selling price to the cost can be expressed as follows.

$$\frac{\$3.00}{\$2.00} = \frac{3}{2}$$

$$\$3.00{:}\$2.00 = 3{:}2$$

$$\$3.00 \text{ to } \$2.00 = 3 \text{ to } 2$$

Measurement

The official system of measurement in the United States for length, volume, and weight is the US Customary system of measurement. The metric system of measurement is used by most other countries.

US Customary Measurement

The following are the most commonly used units of length in the US Customary system of measurement.

- 1 inch
- 1 foot = 12 inches
- 1 yard = 3 feet
- 1 mile = 5,280 feet

Example

An interior designer measurers the length and width of a room when ordering new floor tiles. The length is measured at 12 feet 4 inches (12′ 4″). The width is measured at 8 feet 7 inches (8′ 7″).

Example

Taxi cab fares are usually determined by measuring distance in miles. A recent cab rate in Chicago was $3.25 for the first 1/9 mile or less, and $0.20 for each additional 1/9 mile.

Metric Conversion

The metric system of measurement is convenient to use because units can be converted by multiplying or dividing by multiples of 10. The following are the commonly used units of length in the metric system of measurement.

- 1 millimeter
- 1 centimeter = 10 millimeters
- 1 meter = 100 centimeters
- 1 kilometer = 1,000 meters

The following are conversions from the US Customary system to the metric system.

- 1 inch = 25.4 millimeters = 2.54 centimeters
- 1 foot = 30.48 centimeters = 0.3048 meters
- 1 yard = 0.9144 meters
- 1 mile = 1.6093 kilometers

Example

A salesperson from the United States is traveling abroad and needs to drive 100 kilometers to meet a customer. How many miles is this trip? Divide 100 kilometers by 1.6093 and round to the hundredth place.

```
                    62.138
    1.6093.) 100.0000.000
           –96558
            34420
           –32186
            22340
           –16093
            62470
           –48279
           141910
          –128744
            13169
```

Estimating

Estimating is finding an *approximate* answer and often involves using rounded numbers. It is often quicker to add rounded numbers, for example, than it is to add the precise numbers.

Example

Estimate the total miles a delivery truck will travel along the following three segments of a route.

- Detroit to Chicago: 278 miles
- Chicago to St. Louis: 297 miles
- St. Louis to Wichita: 436 miles

The mileage can be estimated by rounding each segment to the nearest 100 miles.

- Detroit to Chicago: 300 miles
- Chicago to St. Louis: 300 miles
- St. Louis to Wichita: 400 miles

Add the rounded segments to estimate the total miles.

$$300 + 300 + 400 = 1,000 \text{ miles}$$

Accuracy and Precision

Accuracy and precision mean slightly different things. *Accuracy* is the closeness of a measured value to its actual or true value. *Precision* is how close measured values are to each other.

Example

A machine is designed to fill jars with 16 ounces of peanut butter. The machine is considered accurate if the actual amount of peanut butter in a jar is within 0.05 ounces of the target, which is a range of 15.95 to 16.05 ounces. A machine operator tests a jar and measures the weight to be 16.01 ounces. The machine is accurate.

Suppose a machine operator tests 10 jars of peanut butter and finds the weight of each jar to be 15.4 ounces. The machine is considered precise because it fills every jar with exactly the same amount. However, it is not accurate because the amount differs too much from the target.

Algebra

An *equation* is a mathematical statement that has an equal sign (=). An *algebraic* equation is an equation that includes at least one variable. A *variable* is an unknown quantity.

Solving Equations with Variables

Solving an algebraic equation means finding the value of the variable that will make the equation a true statement. To solve a simple equation, perform inverse operations on both sides and isolate the variable.

Example
A computer consultant has sales of $1,000. After deducting $600 in expenses, her profit equals $400. This is expressed with the following equation.

$$sales - expenses = profit$$
$$\$1,000 - \$600 = \$400$$

Example
A computer consultant has expenses of $600 and $400 in profit. What are her sales? An equation can be written in which sales are the unknown quantity, or variable.

$$sales - expenses = profit$$
$$sales - \$600 = \$400$$

Example
To find the value for sales, perform inverse operations on both sides and isolate the variable.

$$
\begin{array}{rcr}
sales & - \ \$600 \ = & \$400 \\
& + \ \$600 \ + & 600 \\
\hline
sales & = & \$1,000
\end{array}
$$

Order of Operations

The order of operations is a set of rules stating which operations in an equation are performed first. The order of operations is often stated using the acronym *PEMDAS*. PEMDAS stands for parentheses, exponents, multiplication and division, and addition and subtraction. This means anything inside parentheses is computed first. Exponents are computed next. Then, any multiplication and division operations are computed. Finally, any addition and subtraction operations are computed to find the final answer to the problem. The equation is solved from left to right by applying PEMDAS.

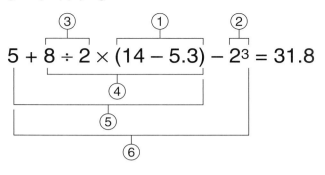

$$5 + 8 \div 2 \times (14 - 5.3) - 2^3 = 31.8$$

Recursive Formulas

A *recursive formula* is used to determine the next term of a sequence, using one or more of the preceding terms. The terms of a sequence are often expressed with a variable and subscript. For example, a sequence might be written as a_1, a_2, a_3, a_4, a_5, and so on. The subscript is essentially the place in line for each term. A recursive formula has two parts. The first is a starting point or seed value (a_1). The second is an equation for another number in the sequence (a_n). The second part of the formula is a function of the prior term (a_{n-1}).

Example
Suppose you buy a car for $10,000. Assume the car declines in value 10% each year. In the second year, the car will be worth 90% of $10,000, which is $9,000. The following year it will be worth 90% of $9,000, which is $8,100. What will the car be worth in the fifth year? Use the following recursive equation to find the answer.

$$a_n = a_{n-1} \times 0.90$$

$$\text{where } a_1 = \$10,000$$

$$a_n = \text{value of car in the } n^{th} \text{ year}$$

Year	Value of Car
$n = 1$	$a_1 = \$10,000$
$n = 2$	$a_2 = a_{2-1} \times 0.90 = a_1 \times 0.90 = \$10,000 \times 0.90 = \$9,000$
$n = 3$	$a_3 = a_{3-1} \times 0.90 = a_2 \times 0.90 = \$9,000 \times 0.90 = \$8,100$
$n = 4$	$a_4 = a_{4-1} \times 0.90 = a_3 \times 0.90 = \$8,100 \times 0.90 = \$7,290$
$n = 5$	$a_5 = a_{5-1} \times 0.90 = a_4 \times 0.90 = \$7,290 \times 0.90 = \$6,561$

Geometry

Geometry is a field of mathematics that deals with shapes, such as circles and polygons. A *polygon* is any shape whose sides are straight. Every polygon has three or more sides.

Parallelograms

A *parallelogram* is a four-sided figure with two pairs of parallel sides. A *rectangle* is a type of parallelogram with four right angles. A *square* is a special type of parallelogram with four right angles (90 degrees) and four equal sides.

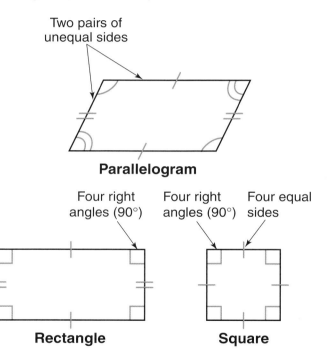

Parallelogram

Rectangle   **Square**

Example
Real-life examples of squares include ceramic floor and wall tiles, and each side of a die. Real-life examples of a rectangle include a football field, pool table, and most doors.

Triangles

A three-sided polygon is called a *triangle.* The following are four types of triangles, which are classified according to their sides and angles.

- *Equilateral:* Three equal sides and three equal angles.
- *Isosceles:* Two equal sides and two equal angles.

- *Scalene:* Three unequal sides and three unequal angles.
- *Right:* One right angle; may be isosceles or scalene.

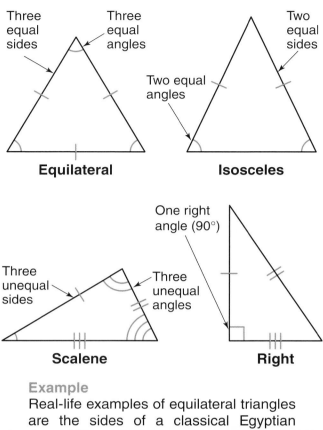

Equilateral   **Isosceles**

Scalene   **Right**

Example
Real-life examples of equilateral triangles are the sides of a classical Egyptian pyramid.

Circles and Half Circles

A *circle* is a figure in which every point is the same distance from the center. The distance from the center to a point on the circle is called the *radius.* The distance across the circle through the center is the *diameter.* A half circle is formed by dividing a whole circle along the diameter.

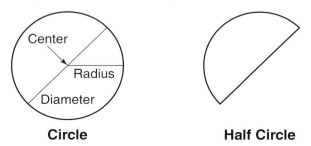

Circle   **Half Circle**

Example
Real life examples of circles include wheels of all sizes.

Perimeter

A *perimeter* is a measure of length around a figure. Add the length of each side to measure the perimeter of any figure whose sides are all line segments, such as a parallelogram or triangle. The perimeter of a circle is called the *circumference.* To measure the perimeter, multiply the diameter by pi (π). Pi is approximately equal to 3.14. The following formulas can be used to calculate the perimeters of various figures.

Figure	Perimeter
parallelogram	2 × width + 2 × length
square	4 × side
rectangle	2 × width + 2 × length
triangle	side + side + side
circle	π × diameter

Example

A professional basketball court is a rectangle 94 feet long and 50 feet wide. The perimeter of the court is calculated as follows.

2 × 94 feet + 2 × 50 feet = 288 feet

Example

A tractor tire has a 43 inch diameter. The circumference of the tire is calculated as follows.

43 inches × 3.14 = 135 inches

Area

Area is a measure of the amount of surface within the perimeter of a flat figure. Area is measured in square units, such as square inches, square feet, or square miles. The areas of the following figures are calculated using the corresponding formulas.

Figure	Area
parallelogram	base × height
square	side × side
rectangle	length × width
triangle	1/2 × base × height
circle	$\pi \times radius^2 = \pi \times radius \times radius$

Example

An interior designer needs to order decorative tiles to fill the following spaces. Measure the area of each space in square feet.

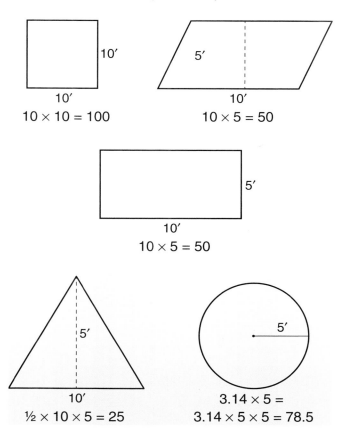

10 × 10 = 100   10 × 5 = 50

10 × 5 = 50

½ × 10 × 5 = 25   3.14 × 5 = 3.14 × 5 × 5 = 78.5

Surface Area

Surface area is the total area of the surface of a figure occupying three-dimensional space, such as a cube or prism. A *cube* is a solid figure that has six identical squares faces. A *prism* has bases or ends which have the same size and shape and are parallel to each other, and each of whose sides is a parallelogram. The following are the formulas to find the surface area of a cube and a prism.

Object	Surface Area
cube	6 × side × side
prism	2 × [(length × width) + (width × height) + (length × height)]

Example
A manufacturer of cardboard boxes wants to determine how much cardboard is needed to make the following size boxes. Calculate the surface area of each in square inches.

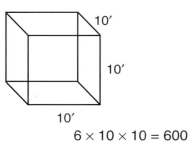

$$6 \times 10 \times 10 = 600$$

Cube

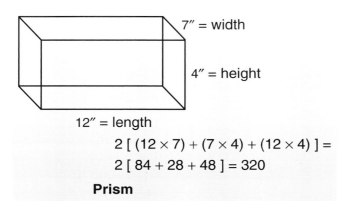

$$2\,[\,(12 \times 7) + (7 \times 4) + (12 \times 4)\,] =$$
$$2\,[\,84 + 28 + 48\,] = 320$$

Prism

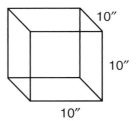

$$10 \times 10 \times 10 = 1000$$

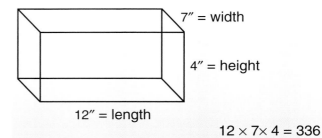

$$12 \times 7 \times 4 = 336$$

Volume

Volume is the three-dimensional space occupied by a figure and is measured in cubic units, such as cubic inches or cubic feet. The volumes of the following figures are calculated using the corresponding formulas.

Solid Figure	Volume
cube	side³ = side × side × side
prism	length × width × height
cylinder	π × radius² × height = π × radius × radius × height
sphere	4/3 × π × radius³ = 4/3 × π × radius × radius × radius

Example
Find the volume of packing material needed to fill the following boxes. Measure the volume of each in cubic inches.

Example
Find the volume of grain that will fill the following cylindrical silo. Measure the volume in cubic feet.

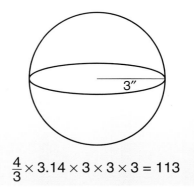

$$3.14 \times 5 \times 5 \times 10 = 785$$

Example
A manufacturer of pool toys wants to stuff soft material into a ball with a 3 inch radius. Find the cubic inches of material that will fit into the ball.

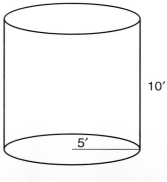

$$\frac{4}{3} \times 3.14 \times 3 \times 3 \times 3 = 113$$

Data Analysis and Statistics

Graphs are used to illustrate data in a picture-like format. It is often easier to understand data when they are shown in a graphical form instead of a numerical form in a table. Common types of graphs are bar graphs, line graphs, and circle graphs.

A *bar graph* organizes information along a vertical axis and horizontal axis. The vertical axis runs up and down one side; the horizontal axis runs along the bottom.

A *line graph* also organizes information on vertical and horizontal axes; however, data are graphed as a continuous line rather than a set of bars. Line graphs are often used to show trends over a period of time.

A *circle graph* looks like a divided circle and shows how a whole object is cut up into parts. Circle graphs are also called *pie charts* and are often used to illustrate percentages.

Example

A business shows the following balances in its cash account for the months of March through July. These data are illustrated below in bar and line graphs.

Month	Account Balance	Month	Account Balance
March	$450	June	$800
April	$625	July	$900
May	$550		

Example

A business lists the percentage of its expenses in the following categories. These data are displayed in the following circle graph.

Expenses	Percentage
Cost of goods	25
Salaries	25
Rent	21
Utilities	17
Advertising	12

Monthly Expenses

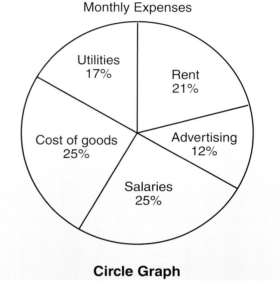

Circle Graph

Account Balance

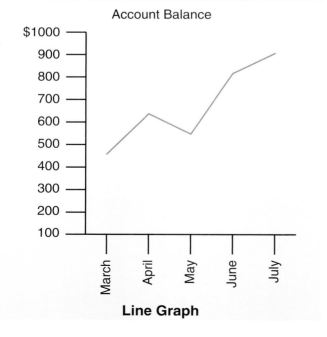

Line Graph

Math Models for Business and Retail

Math skills used in business and retail are the same math skills required in everyday life. The ability to add, subtract, multiply, and divide different types of numbers is very important. However, this type of math is often focused on prices, taxes, profits, and losses.

Markup

Markup is a retailing term for the amount by which price exceeds the cost. One way to express markup is in dollars. Another way to express markup is percentage. The *markup percentage* is the amount of the markup as a percentage of the cost.

Example
A retailer pays $4 for a pair of athletic socks and prices them for sale at $7. The dollar markup is $3.

selling price − cost = dollar markup

$$\$7 - \$4 = \$3$$

Example
A pair of athletic socks, which cost $4, is priced at $7. The dollar markup is $3. To find the markup percentage, divide $3 by $4. The markup percentage is 75%.

markup dollars ÷ cost = markup percentage

$$\$3 \div \$4 = 0.75 = 75\%$$

Percentage Markup to Determine Selling Price

The selling price of an item can be determined if you know the markup percentage and the cost. First, convert the markup percentage to a decimal. Next multiply the cost by the decimal. Then, add the markup dollars to the cost to determine the selling price. Another way to find the selling price is to convert the markup percentage to a decimal and add 1.0. Then multiply this amount by the cost.

Example
A pair of athletic socks costs $4, which the retailer marks up by 75%. Find the selling price.

1. Convert the markup percentage to a decimal.

$$75\% = 0.75$$

2. Multiply the cost by the markup.

cost × markup = dollar markup

$$\$4 \times 0.75 = \$3$$

3. Add the $3 markup to the $4 cost to find the selling price. The selling price is $7.

$$\$4 + \$3 = \$7$$

Example
A pair of athletic socks costs $4, which the retailer marks up by 75%. Find the selling price.

1. Convert the 75% markup percentage to 0.75 and add 1.0.

$$0.75 + 1.0 = 1.75.$$

2. Multiply 1.75 by the $4 cost to find the selling price.

$$\$4 \times 1.75 = \$7$$

Markdown

A *markdown* is the amount by which the selling price of an item is reduced. Sometimes a markdown is also called a *discount.* To find the amount of a markdown, subtract the new or discounted price from the original price. A markdown can also be expressed as a percentage of the original price. Sometimes this is called a *percentage discount.*

Example
A package of meat at a supermarket is originally priced at $10. However, the meat has not sold and is nearing its expiration date. The supermarket wants to sell it quickly, so it reduces the price to $6. This is a markdown of $4.

selling price − discounted price = dollar markdown

$$\$10 - \$6 = \$4$$

Example

A package of meat at a supermarket is originally priced at $10. However, the meat has not sold and is nearing its expiration date. The supermarket wants to sell it quickly, so it marks down the price by $4. The markdown percentage is determined by dividing the $4 markdown by the original $10 price.

markdown ÷ selling price = markdown percentage

$$\$4 \div \$10 = 40\%$$

Gross Profit

Gross profit is a company's net sales minus the cost of goods sold. *Gross margin* is often expressed as a percentage of revenue.

Example

A wristband manufacturer generated net sales of $100,000 last year. The cost of goods sold for the wristbands was $30,000. The net sales of $100,000 minus the $30,000 cost of goods sold leaves a gross profit $70,000.

net sales − cost of goods sold = gross profit

$$\$100,000 - \$30,000 = \$70,000$$

Example

The gross profit of $70,000 divided by the net sales of $100,000 is 0.70, or 70%.

gross profit ÷ net sales = gross margin percentage

$$\$70,000 \div \$100,000 = 0.70 = 70\%$$

Net Income or Loss

Net income or loss is a company's revenue after total expenses are deducted from gross profit. Total expenses include marketing, administration, interest, and taxes. A company earns a *net income* when gross profit exceeds expenses. A *net loss* is incurred when expenses exceed gross profit.

Example

A wristband manufacturer had a gross profit of $70,000. In addition, expenses for marketing, administration, interest, and taxes were $50,000. Net profit is calculated by subtracting the total expenses of $50,000 from the gross profit of $70,000. The net profit was $20,000.

gross profit on sales − total expenses = net income or loss

$$\$70,000 - \$50,000 = \$20,000$$

Break-Even Point

A *break-even point* is the number of units a company must sell to cover its costs and expenses and earn a zero profit. Use the following formula to find a company's break-even point.

total costs ÷ selling price = break-even point

Sales Tax

Sales tax is a tax collected on the selling price of a good or service. The sales tax rate is usually expressed as a percentage of the selling price. Sales tax is calculated by multiplying the sale price by the tax rate.

Example

Suppose you buy a T-shirt for $10.00. How much is the sales tax if the tax rate is 5%? Convert 5% to a decimal (.05) and multiply it by the sale price.

sale price × sales tax rate percentage = sales tax

$$\$10 \times 0.05 = \$0.50$$

Return on Investment

Return on investment (ROI) is a calculation of a company's net profit as a percentage of the owner's investment. One way to determine ROI is to divide net profit by the owner's investment.

Example

Suppose you start a dry-cleaning business with a $100,000 investment, and you earn a $20,000 net profit during the first year. Divide $20,000 by $100,000, which equals a 20% return on your investment.

net income ÷ owner's investment = return on investment (ROI)

$$\$20,000 \div \$100,000 = 0.20 = 20\%$$

Glossary

80/20 inventory rule. The rule that states that 80 percent of the sales for a business come from 20 percent of its inventory. (21)

A

ability. The skill to perform a task. (29)

accounts payable. Money a business owes to its suppliers for goods or services received. In accounting, accounts payable are considered a liability. (33)

accounts receivable. Money owed to a business by customers for goods or services delivered. In accounting, accounts receivable are considered an asset. (33)

accounts receivable aging report. Document that shows when accounts receivables are due as well as the length of time accounts has been outstanding. (19)

action plan. Detailed time line, the budget, and the metrics to evaluate the effectiveness of a campaign. (4)

action word. A verb telling the readers what to do. (24)

active listening. When the listener is focused on what is being said. (22)

active reading. When the reader is thinking about what he or she is reading. (22)

activities-preference inventory. Assessment to determine which activities a person prefers when given a choice. (29)

adaptability. The ability to make changes to be a better match, or fit, in new situations. (27)

adding value. Enhancing a feature or service to inspire a customer to purchase. (3)

advertising agency. A firm that creates ads, commercials, and other parts of promotional campaigns for its clients. (24)

advertising campaign. A coordinated series of linked ads with a single idea or theme. (24)

Advertising Self-Regulatory Council (ASRC). Organization that establishes the policies and procedures for advertising self regulation. (24)

agenda. The list of topics to be discussed, decisions to be made, or other goals for a meeting. (27)

agent. Someone working on the behalf of another party. (20)

agent/broker channel. Path of selling in which the producer hires an agent to sell to the wholesaler. (20)

AIDA. Acronym for customer attention, interest, desire, and action. (23)

analogous colors. Colors that are adjacent to one another on the color wheel. (25)

angel investor. Private investors who want to fund promising start-up businesses. (33)

antitrust. A term created by the government in an effort to fight the big corporate trusts that operate as monopolies. (11)

approach. Step in which the salesperson makes the first in-person contact with a potential customer. (26)

aptitude. Natural talent or natural ability to do something. (29)

art. All of the elements that illustrate the message of an ad. (24)

assets. Property or items of value owned by a business. (33)

attitude. How a person feels about something or the way a person looks at the world and responds to events. (12, 27)

autocratic style. A style of management in which the leader makes all decisions without input from others. (28)

B

bait and switch. Practice of advertising one product with the intent of persuading a customer to buy a more expensive item when they arrive in the store. (18)

balance. The way items are placed around an imaginary centerline. (25)

balance of trade. Difference between the exports and imports of a nation. (9)

balance sheet. Financial report that shows the net worth of a company. (28)

barriers. Anything that prevents clear, effective communication. (22)

barter. Exchange of one good or service for another good or service. (3)

base price. General price at which the company expects to sell the product. (19)

behavioral segmentation. Dividing a market by the relationships between customers and the product or service. (12)

benefit. Attribute of a product that will be an advantage for the customer. (11)

bid. Formal written proposal that lists all the goods and services that will be provided, their prices, and time line. (14)

blog. A website in a journal format created by a person or organization. (23)

body language. Communication through facial expressions, gestures, body movements, and body position. (22)

bootstrapping. Cutting all unnecessary expenses and operating on as little cash as possible. (33)

brand. Name, term, or design that sets a product or business apart from its competition. (16)

brand equity. Value of having a well-known brand name. (17)

brand loyalty. Situation in which the customer will only buy a certain brand of product. (17)

brand name. The name given to the product consisting of words, numbers, or letters that can be read and spoken. (17)

break-even point. The point at which revenue from sales equals the costs. (19)

brick-and-mortar. The term for a physical store. (20)

budget. Financial plan that reflects anticipated revenue and shows how it will be allocated in the operation of the business. (28)

buffer stock. Additional stock kept above the minimum amount required to meet forecasted sales. (21)

bulk-breaking. Process of separating a large quantity of goods into smaller quantities for resale. (20)

burglary. An event that occurs when a person breaks into a business to steal merchandise, money, valuable equipment, or take confidential information. (32)

business. All of the activities involved in developing and exchanging products and services. (1)

business cycle. Cycle that consists of alternating periods of expansion and contraction in the economy. (8)

business market. Customers who buy products for use in a business. (3)

business operations. Day-to-day activities necessary to keep a business up and running. (31)

business plan. Written document that describes a new business, how it will operate, and make a profit. (31)

business product. An item sold to businesses to keep them operating, as in B2B. (15)

business purchasing. Acquiring goods or services to accomplish the goals of an organization. (14)

business-to-business (B2B). Business market of businesses selling primarily to other businesses. (3)

business-to-business (B2B) selling. Process of selling from one business to another business. (26)

business-to-consumer (B2C). Consumer market of businesses selling primarily to individual consumers. (3)

business-to-consumer (B2C) selling. Process of selling to consumers. (26)

buyer. The person responsible for planning and ordering inventory. (14)

buying motive. The reason a consumer seeks and buys a product or service. (13)

buying signal. Verbal or nonverbal sign that a customer is ready to purchase. (26)

buying status. When a customer will buy a product or service. (12)

C

call center. Office that is set up for the purpose of receiving and making customer calls for an organization. (26)

capital. All of the tools and machinery used to produce goods or provide services. (6)

capital good. Product businesses use to produce other goods, rather than being bought by consumers. (6)

career. Series of related jobs in the same profession. (1)

Career and Technical Student Organization (CTSO). An organization for high school students interested in a career area, such as DECA for marketing students. (29)

career clusters. Sixteen groups of occupational and career specialties that share common knowledge and skills. (1)

career ladder. Series of jobs organized in order of education and experience requirements. (29)

career pathways. Career areas included in the career clusters that consist of careers ranging from entry-level to those requiring advanced college degrees and years of experience. (1)

career plan. List of steps that will enable you to achieve your career goal. (29)

category manager. Manager who performs the same functions as a product manager but is responsible for an entire category of products. (15)

certificate program. Nondegree training programs. (30)

chamber of commerce. Group of businesses whose main purpose is to encourage local business development. (10)

channel. Different routes products take from the producers to the customers. (2) How a message is transmitted, such as face-to-face conversation, telephone, e-mail, text, or any other appropriate vehicle. (22)

channel management. Handling activities involved in getting products through the different routes from the producers to the customers. (2)

channel of distribution. Path that goods take through the supply chain. (20)

circulation. Number of copies distributed to subscribers and stores for sale. (23)

close. The moment when a customer agrees to buy a product. (26)

code of conduct. Statements that list specific behaviors expected from employees representing the company in business situations. (5)

code of ethics. Statements that provide general principles or values, often social or moral, that guide the organization. (5)

coincident indicator. Indicator that changes at the same time as changes in economic activity. (8)

cold calling. Process of making contact with people who are not expecting a sales contact. (26)

collaboration. Working with others to achieve a common goal. (27)

collateral. An asset pledged that would be claimed by the lender if the loan were not repaid. (33)

collection agency. A company that collects past-due bills for a fee. (19)

collusion. A situation that occurs when business leaders work together to eliminate their competition, set prices, and control distribution. (11)

color scheme. A description of color combinations. (25)

color wheel. Standard arrangement of 12 colors in a wheel that shows the relationships among the colors. (25)

command economy. Economy is one in which the government makes all of the economic decisions. (6)

commercial. Buying and selling on a large scale. (3)

commercialization. Introduction stage of the product life cycle. (16)

common carrier. An independent trucking company. (20)

communication process. Series of actions on the part of the sender and the receiver of the message. (22)

competition-based pricing. Strategy based primarily on what the competitors charge. (19)

competitive advantage. Offering better value, features, or service than the competition. (11)

complementary colors. Colors found opposite to one another on a color wheel. (25)

conflict. A situation in which disagreements lead to hostile behavior, such as shouting or fighting. (27)

conflict of interest. When an employee has competing interests or loyalties. (28)

consulting style. A style of management that combines the democratic and autocratic styles. The manager makes the final decision, but only after considering input from the employees. (28)

consumer. Person who buys products or services and also uses them. (1)

consumer behavior. Actions taken by people to satisfy their needs and wants including what they buy. (13)

consumer credit. Credit given to an individual by a retail business. (19)

consumer market. Customers who buy products for their own use. (3)

consumer price index (CPI). Measure of the average change in the prices paid by urban consumers for typical consumer goods and services over time. (7)

consumer product. Products sold to consumers for their personal use, as in B2C. (15)

continuing professional education. Education for people who have already completed their formal schooling and training. It is also called professional development. (30)

contract. Legally-binding agreement. (3)

control. Monitor the progress of the team to meet its goals. (28)

controllable risk. A risk that cannot be avoided, but can be minimized by purchasing insurance or implementing a risk management plan. (32)

convenience good. A good that is usually bought often with little effort and for immediate use. (15)

cooperative education program. A program that prepares students for an occupation through a paid job and classes at school. (29)

copy. Text that provides information and sells the product. (24)

copyright. Exclusive right to copy, license, sell, or distribute material. (5)

corporate culture. How the owners and employees of a company think, feel, and act as a business. (5)

corporate formalities. Records and procedures that corporations are required by law to complete. (31)

corporate social responsibility. Actions a business takes to further social good. (5, 17)

corporation. As defined by the US Supreme Court, is "an artificial being, invisible, intangible, and existing only in contemplation of the law." (3)

cosigner. A person who signs a loan with the applicant and takes on equal responsibility for repaying it. (33)

cost control. Practice of monitoring costs to stay within a planned budget. (28)

cost of credit. Variable expense that influences the pricing decisions for products. (19)

cost-based pricing. Method that uses the cost of the product to set the product selling price. (19)

cost-push inflation. Inflation that occurs when increasing business costs push up production costs and consumer prices. (7)

cover message. Letter or e-mail that accompanies your résumé and expresses your interest in a job. (30)

creative plan. Outline of the goals, primary message, budget, and target market for different ad campaigns. (24)

creativity. The ability to make new things or think of new ideas. (16)

credit bureau. Private firm that maintains consumer credit data and provides credit information to business for a fee. (19)

credit report. A record of a business or person's credit history and financial behavior. (19)

credit risk. Potential of credit not being repaid. (19)

creditor. Individual or business to whom money is owed for goods or services provided. (19)

currency. Money that a country uses. (9)

customer. Individual or group who buys products. (2)

customer loyalty. Continued and regular patronage of a business when there are other places to purchase the same or similar products. (19)

customer profile. Detailed description of the typical consumer in a market segment. (12)

customer relationship management (CRM). System to track contact and other information for current and potential customers. (5)

customer satisfaction. Degree to which customers are pleased with a company's goods or services. (2)

customer service. The way in which a business provides services before, during, and after a purchase. (26)

customer support team. The employees who assist customers, take orders, or answer questions coming into the company via phone or website. (26)

customer-service mindset. The attitude that customer satisfaction always comes first. (26)

cyber bullying. Using the Internet to harass or threaten an individual. (5)

D

data. Pieces of information gained through research. (10)

data mining. Searching through large amounts of digital data to find useful patterns or trends. (10)

database. Organized collection of data most often in digital form. (10)

database marketing. Gathering, storing, and using customer data for marketing directly to them based on their histories. (10)

DBA license. Also known as a *doing business as license*, is needed to register a business. (31)

debt financing. Borrowing money for business purposes, such as to start or expand a business. (33)

debtor. Individual or business who owes money for goods or services received. (19, 27)

debtor-creditor relationship. Legal relationship existing between a debtor and a creditor based on good faith that both parties will uphold their end of the agreement. (19)

deceptive pricing. Pricing products in a way to intentionally mislead a customer. (18)

decline stage. Stage of the product life cycle during which product sales begin to decrease. (15)

decline stage. Stage of the product life cycle during which product sales begin to decrease. (15)

decoding. Translating a message into terms that the receiver can understand. (22)

demand-based pricing. Pricing strategy based on what customers are willing to pay. (19)

demand-pull inflation. Inflation that occurs when increasing demand pulls up prices. (7)

democratic style. A style of management in which the leader encourages team members to participate and share ideas equally. (28)

demographic segmentation. Dividing the market of potential customers by their personal statistics. (12)

demographic trend. Changes in the size of different segments of the population. (10)

demographics. Qualities, such as age, gender, and income, of a specific group of people. (10)

depression. Economic contraction that is very severe and long lasting. (8)

design. Purposeful arrangement of materials to produce a certain effect. (25)

developed country. A country with a strong base of industrial production, good infrastructure, and a high standard of living. (9)

developing country. A country that has a lower standard of living, weaker infrastructure, and less industry than a developed country. (9)

diary. Written record of the thoughts, activities, or plans of the writer during a given period of time. (10)

direct channel. Path of selling goods or services directly from the manufacturer to the end user without using intermediaries. (20)

direct competitors. Companies that sell products or services identical or very similar to the ones another company sells. (11)

direct mail. Advertising message sent through the US Postal Service to current or potential customers. (23)

directions. The steps that must be carried out in a specific order to complete a task successfully. (15)

discretionary income. Remaining take-home pay after life necessities are paid for. (12)

display. Visual presentation of merchandise or ideas. (25)

disposable income. Take-home pay a person has available to dispose of, meaning spend. (12)

diversity. Having people who are different races or who have different cultures in a group or organization. (22, 27)

dynamic. Something that is constantly changing, such as the needs and wants of customers. (2)

E

economics. Science that deals with examining how goods and services are produced, sold, and used. (6)

economic growth rate. General direction of growth for the overall economy. (7)

economic input. Resources used to make products. (6)

economic output. All the goods and services produced by an economic system during a specific time. (6)

economic recovery. Period of expansion after a trough. (8)

economic risk. Situation that occurs when the economy suffers due to negative business conditions in the United States or the world. (32)

economic system. Organized way in which a state or nation allocates its resources to create goods and services. (6)

economy of scale. Decrease in unit cost of a product resulting from large scale manufacturing operations. (21)

elastic demand. Product demand in which the percent change in demand is greater than the percent change in price. (18)

electronic data interchange (EDI). Standard transfer of electronic data for business transactions between organizations. (21)

electronic promotion. Any promotion that uses the Internet or other technology like smartphones. (23)

embargo. Government order that prohibits trade with a foreign country. (9)

embezzlement. A situation in which an employee is stealing either money or goods entrusted to him or her. (32)

emergency. An unforeseen event that can cause harm to people and property. (32)

emergency action plan. Detailed plan that describes what to do in case of an emergency. (32)

emotional intelligence. Ability to recognize your emotions, realize how your emotions affect other people, and understand what those emotions mean. (28)

empathy. The ability to see things from the point of view of another person. (22, 27)

emphasis. Drawing the attention of the viewer to the most important part of a display. (25)

employment trend. Direction of change in the number of jobs in a particular career. (29)

encoding. Process of turning the idea for a message into symbols that are communicated to others. (22)

entrepreneur. A person who starts a new business. (31)

entrepreneurial discovery process. The process of finding a need for a product or service. (31)

entrepreneurship. Willingness and ability take on the risks and responsibilities of starting a new business. (6, 31)

entry-level job. The first job on a career ladder that requires the least amount of education and experience. (29)

Environmental Protection Agency (EPA). Federal agency that provides information about environmental-compliance rules and regulations. (5)

equilibrium. Point at which the supply equals the demand for a product. (7)

equity. Amount of ownership a person has in a business. (33)

equity financing. Raising money for a business in exchange for a percentage of the ownership. (33)

ergonomics. The science of adapting the workstation to fit the needs of the worker and lessen injury. (27)

e-tailer. A retailer that sells through the Internet. (20)

ethics. Set of rules of behavior based on ideas about what is right and wrong. (5)

event marketing. Promotional activity that encourages customers to participate rather than just observe. (23)

excuse. A personal reason not to buy. (26)

expansion. Period when GDP is rising. (8)

expense. Money that goes out of a business to pay for the items or services it buys. (28)

exclusive distribution. Placement that occurs when there is only one channel member, or distributor of products, in a market area. (20)

export. Good that is sold to another country. (9)

export management company. Independent company that provides support services, such as warehousing, shipping, insuring, and billing on behalf of the business. (20)

extensive decision-making process. Decision-making process that involves a great deal of research and planning. (13)

external influence. Motivator or change factor from outside the business. (14)

external theft. Theft that is stealing by people who are not employed or otherwise associated with the retailer. (21)

externality. Something that affects people not directly connected to an economic activity. (8)

F

factor of production. Economic resource nations use to make products and supply services for their citizens. (6)

fad. Something that is very popular for a short time and dies out quickly. (10)

false advertising. Overstating the features and benefits of products or services or making false claims about them. (5)

feasible. A term that means that something can be done successfully. (31)

feature. Fact about a product or service. (11, 15)

feature-benefit selling. Method of showing the major selling features of the product and how it benefits the customer. (26)

Federal Trade Commission (FTC). Main federal agency that enforces advertising laws and regulations. (5)

feedback. Response of the receiver to a message, and it concludes the communication cycle. (22)

finance. All activities involving money. (3)

financial planning. Process of setting financial goals and developing methods for reaching them. (28)

fiscal policy. Tax and spending decisions made by the President and Congress. (8)

fixed assets. Items of value that may take time to sell. (33)

fixed expense. An expense that does not change and is not affected by the number of products produced or sold. (18)

fixed expenses. Expenses that remain the same every month. (33)

fixture. Item designed to hold something. (25)

floating currency. State that occurs when the exchange rate is set by the supply and demand in the foreign exchange market. (9)

focus group. Group of 6 to 9 people with whom an interview is conducted. (10)

foreign exchange rate. Cost to convert one currency into another. (9)

form utility. Value that is added when a business changes the form of something to make it more useful. (3)

four Cs of writing. Elements of clear, concise, courteous, and correct communication. (22)

four Ps of marketing. Element of product, price, place, and promotion. (2)

franchise. The right to do business using the brand and products of another business. (31)

franchise agreement. Legal document that sets up a franchise. (31)

franchise fee. Money that a franchisee pays the franchisor for the right to use the business brand name and sell its products. (31)

franchisee. The person who buys the right to sell the brand products is the franchisee. (31)

franchisor. Company or person who owns the business and the brand. (31)

fraud. Cheating or deceiving a business out of money or property. (32)

free-trade-zone. Group of countries that have reduced or eliminated trade barriers among themselves. (9)

freeware. Fully functional software that can be used forever without purchasing it. (5)

freight forwarder. A company that organizes shipments. (20)

frequency. Number of times the ad appears before the customer. (24)

full employment. When every person who is willing and able to work has a job. (7)

function. General word for a category of activities. (1)

functions of business. Elements of production, finance, marketing, and management. (1)

G

general partnership. Form of ownership in which all partners have unlimited liability. (31)

generation. Group of people born during a certain time in history. (12)

generic brand. Product that lacks a widely recognized name or logo is a generic brand. (17)

geographic segmentation. Segmenting a market based on where customers live. (12)

give notice. To notify a supervisor of the intention to leave a job. (27)

global economy. Economic activity of every nation in the world. (9)

globalization. State that occurs when nations become connected through freely moving goods, labor, and capital across borders. (9)

goal. Something a person wants to achieve in a specified time period. (1)

goal setting. Process of deciding what a person wants to achieve. (1)

good. Physical item that can be touched. (2)

goodwill. Advantage a business has due to its good reputation. (5)

government market. A market that includes national, state, and local government offices and agencies. (14)

greeting approach. An approach to selling that consists of a friendly welcome to the store or department. (26)

gross domestic product (GDP). Market value of all final products produced in a country during a specific time period. (7)

growth stage. Stage of the product life cycle during which product sales increase rapidly. (15)

gross profit. Amount of profit before subtracting the costs of doing business. (19)

growth stage. Stage of the product life cycle during which product sales increase rapidly. (15)

guarantee. A promise that a product has a certain quality or will perform in a specific way. (15)

H

hazard. Situation that could result in injury or damage. (32)

headline. Words designed to grab attention so viewers will read the rest of the ad. (24)

hierarchy of needs. Belief that some needs must be satisfied before others. (13)

hook. Aspect of an ad that grabs attention is often called the hook. (24)

hue. Pure color itself, for example, red. (25)

human risk. A negative situation caused by human actions. (32)

hypothesis. Statement that can be tested and proved either true or false. (10)

I

idea. Concept, cause, issue, image, or philosophy that can be marketed. (2)

image. The idea that people have about someone or something. (16)

import. Good that is purchased from another country. (9)

impulse buying decision. Purchase made with no planning or research. (13)

income statement. Financial report that shows the revenue and expenses for a business during a specific period of time. (28)

indicator. Sign that shows the condition or existence of something. (7)

indirect channel. A channel that uses intermediaries to get the product from the manufacturer to the end users. (20)

indirect competitors. Companies that offer different, but similar, products or services that could also meet customer needs. (11)

industrial good. Good used in the production of other goods or consumed by a business. (20)

industry. Group of businesses that produce similar goods or services. (3)

inelastic demand. Demand for a product that is not affected by price. (18)

inflation. Term for a general rise in prices throughout the economy. (7)

inflation rate. Rate of change of prices calculated on a monthly or yearly basis. (7)

information interview. Talking to someone to learn about his or her career. (29)

information utility. Value that is added when marketing provides information about a product to a customer. (3)

infrastructure. Transportation systems and utilities necessary for a modern economy. (6)

initiative. The personal energy and desire that is needed to do something. (27)

inseparability. When the creation of the service cannot be separated from its use. (15)

insider trading. When an employee uses private company information to purchase company stock or other securities for personal gain. (28)

installation. The act or process of making a good ready for use in a certain place. (15)

installment loan. A loan paid in regular payments, known as installments, with interest until the loan is paid in full. (19)

institution. Public and private nonprofit organization, such as a school, hospital, or museum. (14)

institutional promotion. Promoting a company, rather than a specific product. (23)

insurance. A financial service used to protect individuals and businesses against financial loss. (32)

insurance premium. The payment cost of an insurance policy. (32)

intangible. Something that cannot be touched, tried out before purchase, or returned. (15)

integrated marketing communications (IMC). Combining the use of all forms of marketing communication in a coordinated way. (23)

intellectual property. Something that comes from a person's mind, such as an idea, invention, or process. (17)

intensity. Brightness or dullness of a color. (25)

intensive distribution. Placement of a product in every potential sales situation possible. (20)

intermediary. Person or business in between the manufacturers or producers and the end users. (20)

internal influence. Motivator or change factor that come from within the business itself. (14)

internal theft. Theft that is committed by employees of a store, a supplier, or a delivery company. (21)

international trade. State that occurs when the economies of nations become interconnected through free movement of goods, labor, and capital across borders. This is also called globalization. (9)

internship. A program that allows students to leave school to work in a career for a set amount of time each day and receive classroom credit. Internships may be paid or unpaid. (29)

interpersonal skills. Group of skills that enable a person to interact with others in a positive way. (27)

interview. Formal meeting between two or more people to obtain certain information. (10)

introduction stage. Stage of the product life cycle during which a new product is first brought to the market. (15)

inventory. Assortment or selection of items that a business has in stock to sell to a customer. (14, 21)

inventory management. Process of buying and storing inventory while keeping the costs associated with the inventory low. (21)

inventory shrinkage. Difference between the perpetual inventory and the actual physical inventory is called inventory shrinkage. (21)

invoice. Vendor bill requesting payment for goods shipped or services provided. (21)

J

jingle. A tagline or slogan set to music. (17)

job. Work a person does regularly in order to earn money. (1)

job application. Form with spaces for information about you, your education, and your work experience. (30)

job lead. Information that leads to a job opening. (30)

job shadowing. Following a person while he or she does a job. (29)

just-in-time (JIT) inventory-control system. A system that keeps a minimal amount of production materials or sales inventory on hand at all times. (21)

K

keystone pricing. Doubling the total cost of a product to determine its base price. (19)

L

labor. Work performed by people in businesses. (6)

labor force. All people who are capable of working and who want to work. (7)

lagging indicator. Indicator that changes after a change in economic activity. (8)

laissez-faire. Economic policy allowing businesses to operate with very little interference from the government. (8)

laissez-faire style. A style of management in which the leader allows employees to make their own decisions about how to complete tasks. (28)

land. All of a nation's natural resources. (6)

law of diminishing marginal utility. Idea that consuming more units of the same product decreases the marginal utility from each unit. (18)

law of supply and demand. Law that says that the greater the demand for a given supply of a product, the price will be higher. (7)

lawsuit. Process of bringing a complaint to a court for resolution. (32)

layout. Arrangement of the headline, copy, and art on a page. (24)

lead. A potential customer. (26)

lead time. The time between reserving the ad space and when it actually runs. (24)

leader. A person who guides others to a goal. (27)

leadership. The ability of a person to guide others to a goal. (27)

leading indicator. Indicator that changes before a change in economic activity. (8)

letter of inquiry. A letter that highlights job qualifications, and asks about any job openings, and expresses interest in working for a company. (30)

liability. Legal responsibility. (3) A debt of the business, or what it owes to others. (33)

limited decision-making process. Decision-making process that requires some amount of research and planning. (13)

limited liability. Form of ownership in which a partner or owner is not personally liable for the debts of the business. (31)

limited partnership (LP). Form of partnership where there is one managing partner and at least one limited partner. (31)

line of credit. Specific dollar amount that a business can draw against as needed. (33)

liquid assets. Cash and the items a business owns that can be easily turned into cash. (33)

list price. Established price of a product printed in a catalog, on a price tag, or in a price list. (18)

logo. Picture, design, or graphic image that represents a brand. (17)

long-term goal. Goal that will take a longer time to achieve, usually longer than one year. (1)

loss leader. Pricing an item much lower than the current market price or the cost of acquiring the product. (18)

M

management. Process of controlling and making decisions about a business. (3)

manager. Worker who directs the work of others and makes decisions. (29)

manual-tag system. A system that tracks sales by removing price tags when the products are sold. (21)

manufacturer's suggested retail price (MSRP). Price recommended by the manufacturer. (18)

marginal utility. Additional satisfaction gained by using one additional unit of the same product. (18)

market. Anywhere a buyer and a seller convene to buy and sell goods. (1) People who might buy something. (12)

market demand. Total demand of every individual willing and able to buy a specific product. (7)

market economy. Economy in which individuals are free to make their own economic decisions. (6)

market planning. Creating an actionable marketing plan designed to achieve business goals. (2)

market risk. Potential that the target market for new products or services is much less than originally thought. (32)

market segmentation. Process of dividing a large market into smaller groups. (4)

market share. Percentage of total sales in a market that is held by one business. (4, 11)

market size. The total sales per year for a specific product. (11)

market structure. How a market is organized based on the number of businesses competing for sales in an industry. (11)

market supply. Total supply of every seller willing and able to sell a specific product. (7)

marketing. Dynamic activities that identify, anticipate, and satisfy customer demand while making a profit. (1)

marketing concept. Approach to business that focuses on satisfying customers as the means of achieving profit goals. (2)

marketing mix. Plan of action for marketing a product; it consists of the decisions made about each of the four Ps for that product. (2)

marketing objective. Goals a business wants to achieve during a given time, usually one year, by implementing the marketing plan. (4)

marketing plan. Document describing business and marketing objectives and the strategies and tactics to achieve them. (4)

marketing professional. Person who helps determine the marketing needs of a company, develops and implements marketing plans, and focuses on customer satisfaction. (1)

marketing research. Gathering and analyzing information to help make good marketing decisions. (10)

marketing strategy. Decision made about product, price, place, and promotion. (4)

marketing tactic. Specific activity to carry out the marketing strategies. (4)

marketing trend. Pattern of change in consumer behavior that leads to changes in the marketing mix. (10)

market-share leader. The company with the largest combined market share. (11)

marketing-information management (MIM). Gathering and analyzing information about markets, customers, industry trends, new technology, and the competing businesses. (2)

marketing-information system (MkIS). Organized system of gathering, sorting, analyzing, evaluating, and distributing information for marketing purposes. (10)

markup. Amount added to the cost of a product to determine the base price. (19)

marquee. Overhanging structure containing a signboard located at the entrance to the store. It displays information that can be changed. (25)

mass market. Overall market or group of people who might buy a product or service. (12)

mass marketing. Using one marketing mix of product, price, place, and promotion for a product. (12)

maturity stage. Stage of the product life cycle during which product sales are stable. (15)

medium of exchange. Concept that money is used in exchange for goods and services. (3)

memo. Brief message sent to someone within an organization. (22)

merchandise approach. An approach to selling that consists of a conversation that starts with a comment about the product. (26)

metaphor. Word or phrase for one thing used in reference to a very different thing in order to suggest a similarity. (17)

metric. Standard of measurement. (4)

mission statement. Company message to customers about why the business exists. (4)

mixed economy. Economy in which both the government and individuals are involved in making economic resource decisions. (6)

mobile app. Software application developed for use by mobile devices. (23)

monetary policy. Policy that regulates the money supply and interest rates by a central bank. (8)

money. Anything of value that is accepted in return for goods or services. (3)

monopolistic competition. A large number of small businesses selling similar, but not identical, products at different prices. (11)

monopoly. A market structure with one business that has complete control of a market's entire supply of goods or services. (11)

motion. A recommendation for action to be taken by the group. (27)

motivate. To provide the internal push that results in action. (13)

motive. Internal push that causes a person to act. (13)

movement. The way the design guides the viewers' eyes over an item or display. (25)

multicultural society. Society consisting of people from many cultures. (22)

multigenerational. Idea that people of different generations are in the same place, such as living in the same home or working together in the same office. (22)

multinational corporation. Corporation that produces and sells products in foreign countries as well as inside its borders. (9)

multitasking. Performing several tasks at the same time. (27)

N

national brand. A brand created by a manufacturer for its own products. (17)

natural resources. Raw materials found in nature, such as soil, water, minerals, plants, and animals. (6)

natural risk. Situation caused by an act of nature. (32)

need. Something necessary for survival, such as food, clothing, and shelter. (1)

net profit. What is left after all company expenses are subtracted from total revenue. (19)

net worth. Value of a company. (28)

netiquette. Accepted social and professional guidelines for communicating using the Internet. (5)

networking. Process of making connections with people in the work world. (30)

new product. A product that is different in some way from existing products. (16)

niche market. Piece of the target market that is very narrow and specific. (12)

nominal GDP. The GDP in current dollars, calculated without adjusting for inflation. (7)

nonprice competition. Competitive advantage based on factors other than price. (11)

nonprice competition. Way other than price to win business. (7)

nonprofit organization. Organization that is an entity that exists to serve some public purpose. (3)

nonverbal communication. Actions, as opposed to words, that send messages. (20)

North American Industry Classification System (NAICS). Numerical system used to classify businesses and collect economic statistics. (14)

O

objection. A concern or other reason a customer has for not making a purchase. (26)

occupation. Term used for a specific career area, such as advertising or sales. (29)

oligopoly. A market structure with a small number of large companies selling the same or similar products. (11)

operating expenses. Ongoing expenses that help keep a company functioning. (33)

operational planning. Process of determining the day-to-day goals for the company. (28)

opportunity cost. Value of the best option you did not choose. (6)

optimism. The expectation that things will turn out well. (27)

option. A feature that can be added to a product by customer request. (15)

order bias. Skewing of results caused by the order in which questions are placed in a survey. (10)

organizational buyer. A person who buys products for a business. (14)

organizational chart. A diagram of employee positions showing how the positions interact within the chain of command. (28)

overselling. Promising more than the product or the business can deliver. (26)

owner's equity. Difference between a business' assets and its liabilities. (33)

P

packaging. Something that protects products until customers are ready to use them. (15)

packing slip. Document that lists the contents of the box or container. (21)

parliamentary procedure. A process for holding a meeting so that the meeting is orderly and democratic. Parliamentary procedure is based on the guidelines in Robert's Rules of Order. (27)

partner. Form of ownership in which two or more people own the business. (31)

partnership. Relationship between two or more people who join to create a business. (3)

partnership agreement. Agreement that details how much each partner will invest, each partner's responsibilities, and how profits are to be shared. (31)

passive listening. When the listener hears the message, but does not pay attention to what is being said. (22)

peak. Highest point in a business cycle. (8)

peer pressure. Social influence exerted on individuals by their peers. (13)

peer-to-peer lending. Borrowing money from investors via a website. (33)

per capita GDP. The GDP of a nation divided by its population. (7)

perception. Mental image a person has about something. (17)

perfect competition. Competition that is characterized by a large number of small businesses selling the same products at the same prices. (11)

periodic inventory-control system. A system that involves taking a physical count of merchandise at regular periods, such as weekly or monthly. (21)

perishability. The idea that services are intangible and cannot be stored for later use. (15)

perpetual inventory-control system. Method of counting inventory that shows the quantity on hand at all times. (21)

personal brand. The sum of the differences between you and than those around you. (17)

personal selling. Any direct contact between a salesperson and a customer. (23)

persuasion. Logic to change a belief or get people to take a certain action. (23)

philanthropy. Promoting the welfare of others—usually through volunteering, protecting resources, or donating money or products. (5)

phishing. Use of fraudulent e-mails and copies of legitimate websites to trick people into providing personal, financial, and other data. (3)

physical inventory. Actual count of all items in inventory at that time. (21)

pipeline. Line of connected pipes that are used for carrying liquids and gases over a long distance. (20)

place strategy. Decision about how and where the products will be produced, acquired, shipped, and sold to customers. (4)

place. Activities involved in getting a product or service to the end users, and is also known as distribution. (2)

place utility. Value that is added when products are available at convenient places. (3)

plagiarism. Using the words of someone else without giving credit to the person who wrote them. (28)

planned obsolescence. Evaluating and updating current products or adding new ones to replace older ones. (32)

point-of-purchase display (POP). Special display usually found near a cash register where goods are purchased. (25)

point-of-sale (POS) software. Software that electronically records each sale when it happens by scanning product bar codes. (21)

portfolio. Selection of materials that you collect and organize to show your qualifications, skills, and talents. (30)

possession utility. Value added when it becomes easier for a customer to acquire a product. (3)

postsecondary. A term that means *after high school*. (30)

posttesting. Measuring the changes in brand awareness or attitudes toward the brand after a campaign. (24)

preapproach. Tasks performed before contact is made with a customer. (26)

predatory pricing. Setting very low prices to remove competition, such as foreign companies that price their products below the same domestic ones to drive the domestic companies out of business. (18)

prejudice. Feeling of like or dislike for someone, especially when it is not reasonable or logical. (22)

preselling. Creating interest and demand for a product before it is available for sale. (23)

press conference. Meeting set by a business or organization in which the media is invited to attend. (23)

press kit. Packet of information distributed to the media about a new business opening or other major business events. (23)

press release. A story featuring useful company information written by the company PR contact. (23)

pretesting. Measuring the effectiveness of an ad before it is seen by the general public. (24)

price. Amount of money requested or exchanged for a product. (2)

price ceilings. When the government sets maximum prices for certain goods and services it thinks are being priced too high. (18)

price competition. When a lower price is the main reason for customers to buy from one business over another. (11)

price discrimination. When a company sells the same product to different customers at different prices based on personal characteristics. (18)

price floors. When the government sets minimum prices for certain goods and services that it thinks are being priced too low. (18)

price gouging. Raising prices on certain kinds of goods to an excessively high level during an emergency. (18)

price strategy. Business decision about pricing and how prices are set to make a profit. (4)

price-fixing. When a group of competitors come together and set a high price for a specific product. (18)

pricing objectives. Goals defined in the business and marketing plans for the overall pricing policies of the company. (19)

primary data. Pieces of information collected by you or your organization. (10)

private carrier. A company that transports its own goods. (20)

private warehouse. A warehouse owned by a company for storage of their own goods. (20)

private-label brand. Products owned by and created specifically for large retailers. (17)

pro forma balance sheet. A statement that reports the assets, liabilities, and owner's equity for a proposed business. (33)

pro forma cash flow statement. A statement that reports the anticipated flow of cash into and out of the business. (33)

pro forma financial statement. Financial statements based on the best estimate of future revenue and expenses for a new business. (33)

pro forma income statement. A statement that projects the financial progress of the business. (33)

procrastination. The delay of doing something that should be done now. (27)

producers. Business that buy raw materials and equipment, which they use to make products and product components. (14)

product. Anything that can be bought or sold. (2)

product depth. Number of product items within a product line. (15)

product item. Specific model, color, or size of products in a line. (15)

product line. Group of closely related products within the product mix. (15)

product life cycle. Stages a product or a product category goes through from its beginning to end. (15)

product manager. Marketing professional who guides the selection of products and oversees the marketing and sales of those products. (15)

product mix. All of the products and services that a business sells. (15)

product obsolescence. A product that, over time, becomes out-of-date. (32)

product planning. Process of deciding which product elements to include that will appeal to the target market. (15)

product promotion. Promoting specific products or services offered by the business. (23)

product specification sheet. A sheet that provides product facts including sizes, colors, materials, and weights. (21)

product strategy. Decision marketers use to help make about what products a business should sell. (4)

product trend. Change in current product features or a new product being developed. (10)

product width. Number of product lines a company offers. (15)

product/service management. Determining which products a business should offer to meet customer needs. (2) Organizational structure that manages the development, marketing, and sale of a product or products. (15)

production. Any activity related to making a product. (3)

productivity. Amount of work a person can do in a specific amount of time. (6)

profession. Term used for jobs in a business field requiring similar education, training, or skills. (1)

profit. Money that a business has left after all the expenses and costs of running the business are paid. (2)

profit motive. When business owners earn profits and are motivated to start and expand businesses. (7)

promotion. Process of communicating with potential customers in an effort to influence their buying behavior. (2)

promotion strategy. Decision about which selling, advertising, sales promotions, and public relations activities to pursue in the promotional mix. (4)

promotional campaign. Coordination of marketing communications to achieve a specific goal. (23)

promotional mix. Combination of the elements used in a promotional campaign. (4)

proportion. Size and space relationship of all items in a display to each other and to the whole display. (25)

proprietary information. Information a company wishes to keep private. (28)

props. Objects used in a display to support the theme or to physically support the merchandise. (25)

prototype. Working model of a new product for testing purposes. (16)

psychographic segmentation. Dividing the market by certain preferences or lifestyle choices. (12)

psychographics. Data about the preferences or choices of a group of people. (12)

psychological influences. Influences that come from within a person or why a person has specific needs and wants. (13)

psychological pricing. Pricing techniques that create an image of a product to entice customers to buy (19_.

public relations. Type of promotion that focuses on creating a positive image of a company rather than the product. (2)

public warehouse. A warehouse that offers storage space to any company. (20)

pull promotional concept. Using promotions to make customers actively seek out the product. (23)

purchase incentive. Item that helps persuade a customer to make a purchase, such as rewarding loyal customers with discounts or free products. (2)

purchase order (PO). The form a buyer sends to the vendor to officially place an order. (21)

purchasing agent. A person who buys goods and services that the company needs internally to operate its business. (14)

push promotional concept. Taking the product directly to the customer. (23)

Q

qualitative data. Data that provide insight into what people think about a topic. (10)

quality. The degree of a product's excellence usage. (15)

quality control. Activity of checking goods as they are produced or received to ensure the quality meets expectations. (21)

quality service. Providing service that meets customer needs as well as the standards for customer service set by the company. (26)

quantitative data. Data from which conclusions can be drawn. (10)

quick response (QR) codes. Bar codes that, when scanned with a smartphone, connect the user to a website or other digital information. (23)

quota. Amount of a product imported into a country during a specific period of time. (9)

R

radio frequency identification (RFID). A system that uses computer chips attached to inventory items and radio frequency receivers to track inventory. (21)

reach. Number of viewers expected to see an ad. (24)

reading for detail. Reading all of the words and phrases and considering their meanings. (22)

real GDP. The GDP in constant dollars, calculated with an inflation adjustment. (7)

receiver. Person who gets the message. (22)

receiving barriers. Events that occur when the receiver says or does something that causes a message to not be received as intended. (22)

receiving record. The form on which all merchandise received is listed as it comes into the place of business. (21)

recession. Period of great decline in total output, employment, trade, and income. (8)

reference. One who is willing to talk with employers about your job qualifications and personal qualities. (30)

reference group. A group of people who influence buying decisions. (13)

relationship selling. The focus on building long-term relationships with customers. (26)

release date. The date a new product is available for sale. (16)

reorder point. A control that triggers the time to place an order before the inventory gets too low. (21)

repackaging. Using new packaging on the same product, is another common way to create a new product. (16)

report. A longer discussion of a topic presented in a structured format. Reports often include references to research. (22)

repositioning. Marketing an existing product in a new way to create a new position in the minds of customers to increase sales. (16)

research sample. Group of people or target market on which the research is done. (10)

resellers. Businesses that buy finished products to resell them to consumers. (14)

résumé. Written document that lists your qualifications for a job, including education and work experience. (30)

retailer channel. Path of selling goods from the producer to the retailer, then the retailer to the consumer. (20)

return on investment (ROI). Ratio that shows the efficiency of an investment by comparing the gains from the investment to its cost. (4) Common measure of profitability based on the amount earned from the investment made in the business. (19)

return on marketing investment (ROMI. A measurement showing the overall effectiveness of a marketing campaign or yearly budget. (19)

revenue. Money that a business takes in for the products or services it sells. (28)

reverse engineering. Taking apart an object to see how it was made—usually in order to produce something similar. (16)

risk. Possibility of loss, damage, or injury. (32)

risk assessment. Process of analyzing a business for possible risks. (32)

robbery. Theft involving another person, often by using force or with the threat of violence. (32)

role. The part that someone has in a family, society, or other group. Roles come with responsibilities and expectations. (27)

routine buying decision. Purchase made quickly and with little thought. (13)

S

sales forecast. Prediction of future sales based on past sales and a market analysis for a specific time period. (28)

sales-increase factor. Percentage of expected increase in sales, which is usually a sales goal. (28)

Sarbanes-Oxley Act. Law that requires companies to be open and honest in their accounting and reporting practices. (5)

saturated market. Occurs when most of the potential customers who need, want, and can afford a product have bought it. (15)

scannable résumé. Résumé that is formatted to eliminate typographical elements, such as bold, bullets, italics, and indents. (30)

scanning. Moving the eyes quickly down the page to find specific words and phrases. (22)

scarcity. Event that occurs when demand is higher than the available resources. (6)

search engine optimization (SEO). Process of indexing a website to rank it higher on the list when a search is conducted. (23)

secondary data. Data that already exists and can be found in a variety of sources. (10)

security. Series of actions taken to prevent crime and protect the safety of people and property. (32)

selective distribution. Placement of a product based on selecting specific places where the manufacturer or wholesaler wants the product to be sold. (20)

self-actualization. The need to express a person's true self through reaching personal goals and helping others. (13)

self-assessment. A tool that helps a person learn about his- or herself, understand personal preferences, and identify strengths and weaknesses. (29, 31)

self-esteem. Personal confidence and satisfaction and a way to measure your feelings of success. (29)

self-motivation. The inner urge to achieve set goals. (27)

selling. All personal communications with customers. (2)

selling price. Actual price paid for a product, after any discounts or coupons are deducted. (18)

sender. Person who has a message to communicate is the sender. (22)

sending barriers. Events that occur when the sender says or does something that causes the receiver to tune out the message. (22)

service. Action that is done for you, usually for a fee. (2)

service approach. An approach to selling that begins with the phrase "May I help you?" (26)

service business. Businesses that provide services to consumers or other businesses. (14)

service mark. A mark that identifies a service rather than a product. (17)

shareware. Copyrighted software that is available free of charge on a trial basis, then must be purchased for continued use. (5)

shoplifter. A person, posing as a customer, who takes goods from the store without paying for them. (32)

shopping good. A good that is usually purchased after making the effort to compare price, quality, and style in more than one store. (15)

short-term goal. Goal that can be achieved in less than one year. (1)

signature. Identification of the person or company paying for the ad. (24)

situation analysis. Snapshot of the environment in which a business has been operating over a given time, usually the last 12 to 16 months. (4)

situational influence. Influencers from the environment in which the business exists. (14)

situational influences. Influences that come from the environment. (13)

skimming. Quickly glancing over the entire document to identify the main ideas. (22)

SMART goals. Goals that are Specific, Measurable, Attainable, Realistic, and Timely. (1)

social democracy. Socialist system of government achieved by democratic means. (6)

social influences. Influencers from the society in which a person lives. (13)

social responsibility. Behaving with sensitivity to social, environmental, and economic issues. (5)

social trend. Pattern of change in society. (10)

software piracy. Illegal copying or downloading of software. (5)

sole proprietor. The one person who owns a business and is personally responsible for all its debts. (31)

sole proprietorship. Business owned by one person. (3)

spam. Electronic messages sent in bulk to people who did not give a company permission to e-mail them. (5)

specialization. Worker or group of workers who perform a specific task for increased efficiency. (7)

specialty good. Unique item that consumer are willing to spend considerable time, effort, and money to buy. (15)

staffing. Process of hiring people and matching them to the best position for their talents. (28)

standard of living. Financial well being of the average person in a country. (7)

start-up capital. Cash used to start the business. (33)

start-up costs. Initial expenses necessary to open the doors of a business. (33)

stereotyping. Classifying or generalizing about a group of people with a given set of characteristics. (27)

stock. Right of ownership in a corporation. (7) Percentage of ownership in a corporation. (31)

stock market. System for buying and selling stocks or a place where stocks are bought and sold. (7)

stock market index. Index that tracks the performance of a specific group of stocks. (7)

stockholder. A person who buys shares of stock in a corporation and is an owner. (31)

stockout. When stock is running out. (21)

store image. Image for the business created through the location, design, and décor of a business. (25)

store layout. Floor plan that shows how the space in a store will be used. (25)

store of value. Item that can be saved, or stored, and used at a later date while holding its value. (3)

storefront. Store exterior that includes the store sign or logo, marquee, display windows, entrances, outdoor lighting, landscaping, and the building itself. (25)

strategic planning. Process of determining the long-term goals for the company. (28)

substitute selling. Technique of showing products that are different from the originally requested product. (26)

suggestion selling. The technique of suggesting additional items to go with merchandise requested by a customer. (26)

supplier. A business that sells to organizational buyers. Also known as a vender. (14)

supply and demand. Economic principle relating the quantity of products available to meet consumer demand. (6)

supply chain. Businesses, people, and activities involved in turning raw materials into products and delivering them to end users. (20)

supply chain management. Coordinating the events happening throughout the supply chain. (20)

supply chain manager. The person who coordinates and monitors all the activities from the building of the product to delivery to the end user. (20)

surveillance. Process of observing everything going on at the business to detect and prevent crimes. (32)

survey. Organized study in which people are asked the same questions. (10)

SWOT analysis. Strengths, weaknesses, opportunities, and threats the business faces. (4)

T

tactical planning. Process of determining the short-term goals for the company. (28)

tagline. Phrase or sentence that summarizes some essential part of the product or business. (17)

target market. Specific group of customers whose needs a company will focus on satisfying with its products and services. (2, 12)

target marketing. Using unique marketing mixes for different target markets. (12)

tariff. Government tax on imported goods. (9)

team. Two or more people who work together to achieve a common goal. (27)

tech prep. Career preparation program that combines the last two years of high school with two years of postsecondary education. (30)

technology. Use of science to invent useful things or to solve problems. (6)

telemarketing. Personal selling done over the telephone. (26)

telephone etiquette. Using good manners on the telephone. (22)

template. Document that already has a basic format that can be used many times. (4)

test marketing. Introducing a new product to a small portion of the target market, one city for example, to learn how it will sell. (16)

texture. The surface quality of materials. (25)

time utility. Value that is added when products are made available at the times that customers need and want them. (3)

time value of money. Idea that money is worth more today than it would be in the future. (3)

total assets. Cash value of everything a company owns. (19)

trade agreement. Document listing the conditions and terms under which goods are imported and exported between countries. (9)

trade association. Organization of people in a specific type of business or industry. (10)

trade character. Animal, real or fictional person, or object used to advertise a good or service. (17)

trade credit. Granting a line of credit to another business for a short period of time to purchase its goods and services. (19) When one business grants a line of credit to another business for the purchase of goods and services. (33)

trade deficit. State that occurs when a nation has more imports than exports, which results in a negative balance. (9)

trade sanction. Embargo affecting only one or several goods. (9)

trade show. Large gathering of businesses for the purpose of displaying products for sale. (16)

trade surplus. When a nation has more exports than imports, which results in a positive balance. (9)

trademark. Identifier that protects taglines, names, graphics, symbols, or any unique method to identify a product or company. (17)

trading bloc. Group of countries that join together to trade as if they were one country. (9)

traditional economy. Economy is one in which most citizens have just enough to survive. (6)

transmission. Act of sending a message. (22)

transportation. The physical movement of products through the channel of distribution. (20)

trend. Emerging pattern of change. (10)

triadic colors. Three colors that are equally spaced on the color wheel. (25)

trial run. Testing the service on a few select customers to make sure that everything runs smoothly. (16)

trough. Lowest stage of a business cycle that marks the end of a recession. (8)

turnover rate. Number of times inventory has been sold during a time period, usually one year. (21)

typeface. A particular style for the printed letters of the alphabet, punctuation, and numbers. (24)

typography. Visual aspect of the words printed on a page. (24)

U

uncontrollable risk. Situation that cannot be predicted or covered by purchasing insurance. (32)

unemployment rate. Percentage of the civilian labor force that is unemployed. (7)

uniform resource locator (URL). The unique address of a document, web page, or website on the Internet. (23)

uninsurable risk. A risk that an insurance company will not cover. (32)

unique selling proposition (USP). Statement summarizing the features and benefits of a company, how it is different from the competition, or how its products are better than the competition. (4, 11)

unit of value. Common measure of what something is worth or what something costs. (3)

unit pricing. A price that allows customers to compare the prices based on a standard unit of measure, such as an ounce or a pound. (18)

unit-control system. A system that uses a visual determination to decide when more stock is needed. (21)

unlimited liability. When an individual is responsible for all the debts and actions of the business. (31)

usage rate. How often a customer buys or uses a product or service. (12)

usage. The way something is used. (15)

utility. Characteristics of a product that satisfies human wants and needs. (3)

V

value. What a person believes in. (12) Relative worth of something. (13) Lightness or darkness of a color and how much white or black is mixed with the hue. (25)

value proposition. Idea that the value of the product over others that are similar. (18)

variability. The idea that each service is nearly always unique. (15)

variable. Something that changes or can be changed. (10)

variable expense. An expense that changes based on the activities of the business. (18)

variable expenses. Expenses that can change on a monthly basis. (33)

venture capitalist. Professional investors or investing groups looking to fund new start-ups or expansions of existing companies. (33)

verbal communication. Communication through the spoken word. (22)

viral marketing. Information about products that customers or viewers are compelled to pass along to others. (23)

virtual test market. Computer simulations of consumers, companies, and market environments. (16)

vision statement. Overall goal for the future of the company. (4)

visual merchandising. Process of creating floor plans and displays to attract customer attention and encourage purchases. (25)

volume pricing. Lowering the list price based on the higher number of units purchased at the same time. (19)

W

wages. Money earned for working. (3)

want. Something that a person desires, but could live without, such as a new cell phone or a vacation. (1)

want ad. Written advertisement for a job, placed by the company that needs the worker. (30)

warranty. A written document stating the quality of a product and promising to correct specific problems that might occur. (15)

web-based pricing software. Technology that helps businesses to maximize profit by pricing products correctly. (19)

weight. Thickness and slant of the letters. (24)

white space. Blank areas on a page where there are no art or copy. (24)

wholesaler channel. Path the product takes from the producer, to a wholesaler, and the retailer before reaching the end user. (20)

word-of-mouth publicity. Informal conversation people have about their experiences with a business and its products. (13)

work habits. The basic, routine actions carried out every day at work. (27)

work values. Aspects of work that are most important to a person. (29)

writing process. Set of sequential stages for each writing task. The process includes prewriting, writing, post writing, and publishing. (22)

written communication. Recording of written words. (22)

Index

W